People of the Prophet's House

People of the Prophet's House
Artistic and Ritual Expressions of Shiʿi Islam

Edited by
Fahmida Suleman

Azimuth Editions
in association with
The Institute of Ismaili Studies
in collaboration with the
British Museum's Department
of the Middle East

In Memoriam
Oleg Grabar 1929–2011
Melanie Michailidis 1966–2013

Azimuth Editions
in association with
The Institute of Ismaili Studies
in collaboration with the
British Museum's Department
of the Middle East

The Institute of Ismaili Studies
210 Euston Road, London NW1 2DA
www.iis.ac.uk

Azimuth Editions
7 Egerton Gardens, London SW3 2BP, UK

Distributed by
Oxbow Books in the United Kingdom and Europe
Casemate Academic in North America

First published 2015

British Library Cataloguing-in-Publication Data
A Catalogue record of this book is available from the British Library

ISBN 978-1-898592-32-7

Printed in Italy

Cover: Blue doors with door knockers in the form of female hands (*khamsas*). Believed to protect the home and sometimes identified with the five members of the Prophet's household. Sidi Bou Said, Tunisia

Frontispiece: The Prophet, ʿAli, Fatima, al-Hasan and al-Husayn, with the Christians at Najran. Painting from al-Biruni's *Āthār al-bāqiya,* Cairo, *circa* 1560, Bibliothèque Nationale de France, Paris MSO ARABE 1489

The Institute of Ismaili Studies was established in 1977 with the object of promoting scholarship and learning on Islam, in the historical as well as contemporary contexts, and a better understanding of its relationship with other societies and faiths.

The Institute's programmes encourage a perspective which is not confined to the theological and religious heritage of Islam, but seeks to explore the relationship of religious ideas to broader dimensions of society and culture. The programmes thus encourage an interdisciplinary approach to the materials of Islamic history and thought. Particular attention is also given to issues of modernity that arise as Muslims seek to relate their heritage to the contemporary situation.

Within the Islamic tradition, the Institute's programmes promote research on those areas which have, to date, received relatively little attention from scholars. These include the intellectual and literary expressions of Shiʿism in general, and Ismailism in particular.

In the context of Islamic societies, the Institute's programmes are informed by the full range and diversity of cultures in which Islam is practised today, from the Middle East, South and Central Asia, and Africa to the industrialized societies of the West, thus taking into consideration the variety of contexts which shape the ideals, beliefs and practices of the faith.

These objectives are realised through concrete programmes and activities organized and implemented by various departments of the Institute. The Institute also collaborates periodically, on a programme-specific basis, with other institutions of learning in the United Kingdom and abroad.

The Institute's academic publications fall into a number of interrelated categories:

1. Occasional papers or essays addressing broad themes of the relationship between religion and society, with special reference to Islam.
2. Monographs exploring specific aspects of Islamic faith and culture, or the contributions of individual Muslim thinkers or writers.
3. Editions or translations of significant primary or secondary texts.
4. Translations of poetic or literary texts which illustrate the rich heritage of spiritual, devotional and symbolic expressions in Muslim history.
5. Works on Ismaili history and thought, and the relationship of the Ismailis to other traditions, communities and schools of thought in Islam.
6. Proceedings of conferences and seminars sponsored by the Institute.
7. Bibliographical works and catalogues which document manuscripts, printed texts and other source materials.

This book falls into category six listed above.

In facilitating these and other publications, the Institute's sole aim is to encourage original research and analysis of relevant issues. While every effort is made to ensure that the publications are of a high academic standard, there is naturally bound to be a diversity of views, ideas and interpretations. As such, the opinions expressed in these publications must be understood as belonging to their authors alone.

Contents

Part 5: Ritual expressions

Map 1: North America, Africa, Europe and the Middle East
Map of sites mentioned in the book. Modern political boundaries are for reference only. The width of the Atlantic Ocean is not shown to scale on this map

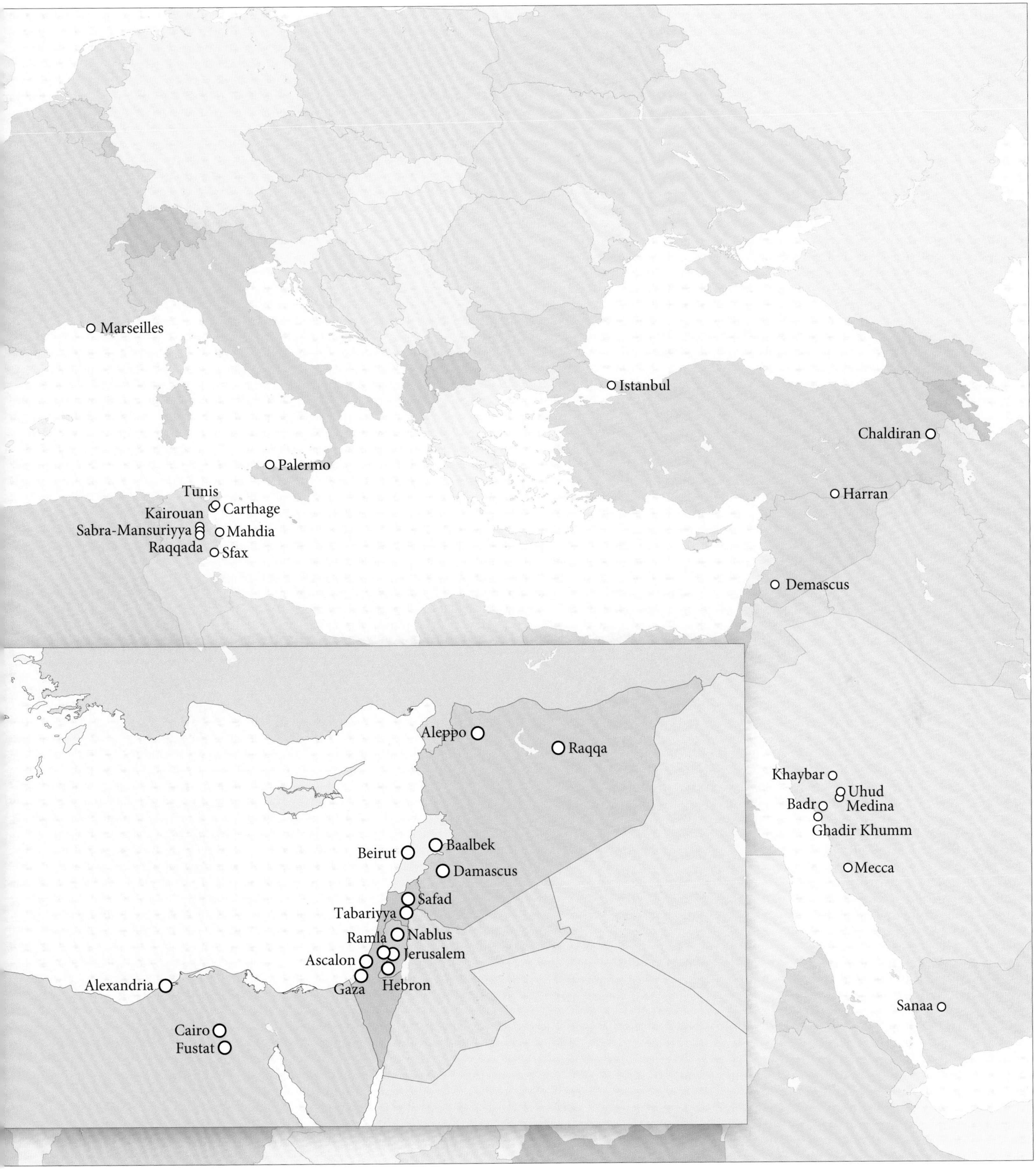
Marseilles
Istanbul
Chaldiran
Palermo
Tunis
Carthage
Kairouan
Sabra-Mansuriyya
Mahdia
Raqqada
Sfax
Harran
Demascus
Aleppo
Raqqa
Khaybar
Uhud
Badr
Medina
Ghadir Khumm
Baalbek
Beirut
Damascus
Mecca
Safad
Tabariyya
Nablus
Ramla
Jerusalem
Ascalon
Alexandria
Gaza
Hebron
Sanaa
Cairo
Fustat

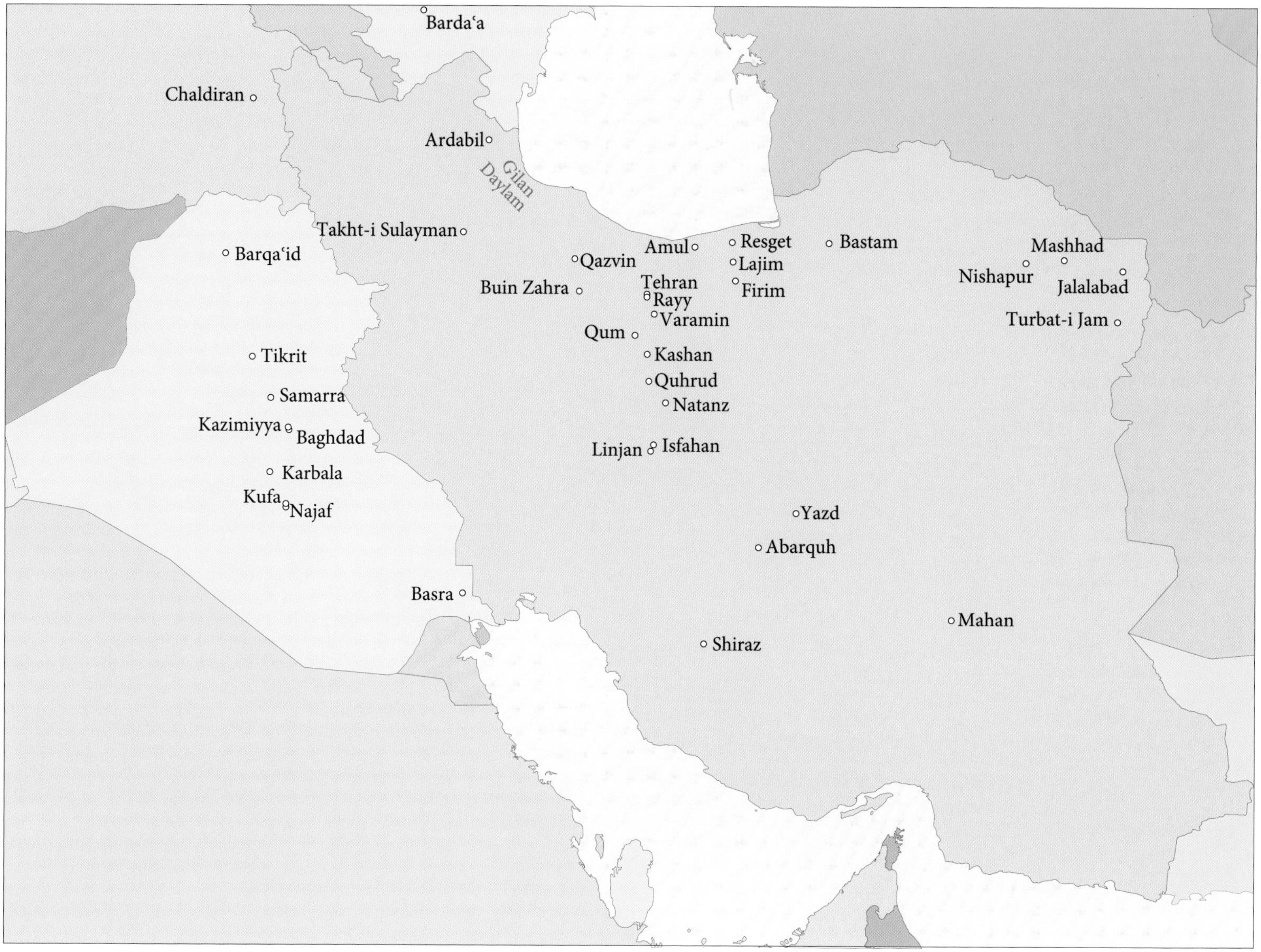

Map 2: Iraq and Iran
Map of sites mentioned in the book.
Modern political boundaries are for reference only

Map 3: Central and South Asia and Western China
Map of sites mentioned in the book.
Modern political boundaries are for reference only

historical moments that gradually shaped central Shiʿi beliefs and practices. Paramount among these beliefs is the notion of *imāma* (the Imamate), the Shiʿi model of authority that espouses temporal and spiritual leadership of the *umma* (community) as vested in the descendants of the Prophet Muhammad. The introduction also highlights the themes that emerge from the volume and provides an overview of the essays. This chapter will also examine the evolving understanding of who constituted the *Ahl al-bayt* and consider their status and role, which came to transcend the Sunni-Shiʿa divide in many contexts and offered opportunities of fostering attitudes of rapprochement in the Muslim world.

There are four main themes that have emerged from the volume. These include: the use of specific Qur'anic verses and hadiths as proof texts; rituals and material culture connected to the tragedy at Karbala; art and architecture related specifically to the Imams and their family; and love for the *Ahl al-bayt* beyond Sunni and Shiʿi demarcations.

The introductory essay is complemented by the second chapter in the volume by Oleg Grabar, who presented the opening lecture at the conference in which he posed the question: 'Are there Shiʿi forms in art?' First, Grabar distinguishes objects and monuments that are formally proclaimed, or 'labelled' as Shiʿi, from those that are 'innately Shiʿi' from the contexts in which they were created and used. In the second part of his essay, he attempts to apply his theories by interpreting a group of religious objects from a patently Shiʿi context – Fatimid Egypt.[4]

Who are the Shiʿa?

Who are the Shiʿa and what is Shiʿism?[5] Who constitute the *Ahl al-bayt* and what makes their role and impact in Muslim societies an enduring feature such that it provides a platform for transcending Shiʿa–Sunni demarcations? Inherent to these questions are a series of other related questions: Who are the Sunnis and what is Sunni Islam? Who are the Kharijites and what is Khariji Islam? For Shiʿi Islam took root and evolved in tandem with and in response to these and other significant movements in Islamic history. For the purpose of this essay, however, we shall restrict our discussions to the genesis of Shiʿi Islam.[6]

Our understanding and articulation of what constitutes Shiʿi Islam has been influenced by a number of factors. The diverse religious, social and political milieu of seventh-century Arabia had a formative influence on the origins and development of Islam of which Shiʿism is an interpretation, just as it did on the genesis of other branches of Islam. In many instances, the Shiʿi perspective was represented as a dissident voice or heterodoxy, both in traditional Sunni Muslim sources as well as by early Western scholarship, impacting later perceptions of Shiʿism. Although recent scholarship has presented a more balanced view, what we today understand Shiʿi Islam to be is also shaped by contemporary interpretations, including its portrayal through the media's focus on specific political regimes and radical movements. Thus, by rejecting the view that there is an 'orthodox Islam' from which Shiʿism is a departure, we are able to approach Islam as a multivalent phenomenon that continues to have a plurality of expressions.

Proximity to the Prophet: definitions and articulations

The Prophet Muhammad's advent in sixth-century Arabia introduced a prophetic model of authority and leadership guided by a singular all-powerful and all-knowing deity – Allah. The Prophet was a charismatic figure who brought and expounded the divine revelation, the Qur'an, which emphasised the lofty purpose and destiny of mankind, and he paved the pathway for its realisation through the establishment of a Muslim community and polity in Medina. The Prophet's demise in 632 brought to the fore the challenges of the need for a successor to his authority to continue to provide direction and guidance for the nascent Muslim community. How could prophetic authority and his model of leadership be replicated if Muhammad's appointment had been divinely ordained? Who was to be this leader? What credentials was he to have? What relationship, if any, was he to have with the Prophet? What was the nature and scope of his authority? A number of existing precedents and models of leadership were drawn upon as Muslims evolved responses to these perennial concerns, which, over the course of time, led to a range of doctrinal formulations and established positions.[7]

Proximity to the Prophet became a defining feature in the succession to the Prophet. How this proximity was defined, understood and

Fig.1
Brass standard engraved with the names of the Shiʿi Imams, India or Iran, 18th–19th century. British Museum, OA+.7432

Fig.2
Carnelian in a gold ring inscribed with the names of the Twelve Imams as a horseman representing Imam ʿAli holding *Dhu'l-faqār*, Iran, 18th–19th century. British Museum, 1866,1229.99

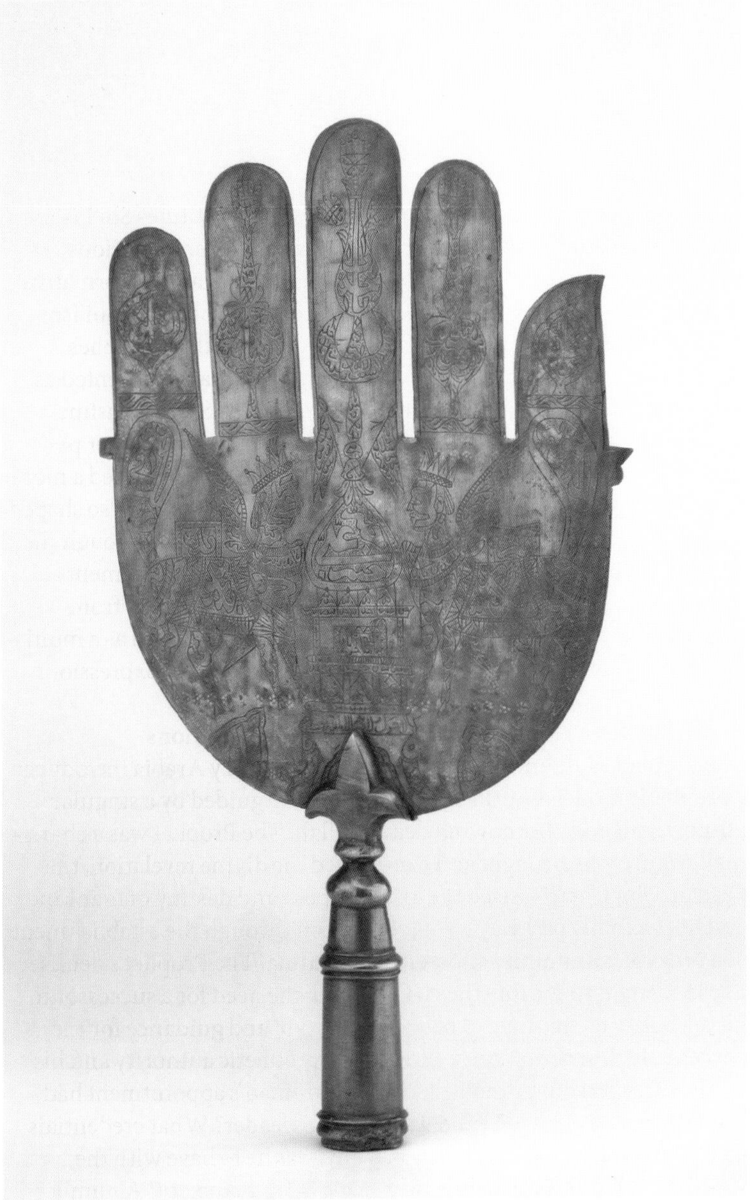

Fig.1

Fig.2

exercised, however, was not unanimously agreed within the nascent *umma*. For some, the yardstick to measure this proximity meant privileging a genealogical closeness to the Prophet, whereas others championed those individuals who were perceived as the most committed to the Prophet's cause regardless of their lineal blood ties. The Shiʿi approach to authority and leadership emerged as one response to these debates, according to which God instructed the Prophet to designate a figure of authority to continue the social, moral and spiritual guidance of the community, and that successor was to be from his household, the *Ahl al-bayt*.

Accordingly, the Shiʿa held that the Prophet designated his cousin and son-in-law, ʿAli b. Abi Talib, and pronounced his public appointment on 18 Dhu'l-Hijja 10/16 March 632 on the way back to Medina following his final pilgrimage to Mecca, at the pool of Ghadir Khumm.[8] The Shiʿi position maintains that as the Imam (Arabic *imām*, lit. 'leader'), the leader designate, ʿAli was entrusted with the temporal guidance and spiritual salvation of the Muslim community (fig.2).[9] The historical accounts of the event at Ghadir Khumm are summarised as follows by Laura Veccia Vaglieri:

> As he [the Prophet] wanted to make an announcement to the pilgrims who accompanied him before they dispersed, and as it was very hot, they constructed for him a dais shaded with branches. Taking ʿAli by the hand, he asked of his faithful followers whether he, Muhammad, was not closer (*awlā*) to the Believers than they were to themselves; the crowd cried out: 'It is so, O Apostle of God!'; he then declared: 'He of whom I am the *mawlā* (the patron/master), of him ʿAli is also the *mawlā* (*man kuntu mawlāhu fa-ʿAlī mawlāhu*).'[10]

For the Shiʿa this explicit designation is further encapsulated in the section of the Prophet's final sermon, later referred to as the *ḥadīth al-thaqalayn* (hadith of the two weighty things), where he bequeathed the Holy Qur'an (*kitāb Allāh*) and his progeny (*Ahl al-bayt*) as beacons of guidance for his community.[11] Notably, some amidst the group that coalesced into the Sunni branch of Islam, the *Ahl al-sunna wa'l-jamāʿa* (lit. People of the Example of the Prophet and the Community), interpreted the term *Ahl al-bayt* in this hadith as the 'People of the House of

Allah (i.e. the Kaʿba)', in effect, the entire community of Muslim believers. In a variant version of this hadith it was reported that the second 'weighty thing' entrusted by the Prophet to his community was his *sunna* (his example).[12] This illustrates how the same text was interpreted differently by the early Muslim community, reflecting viewpoints that developed over the course of time into two broad streams, with the Shiʿi model of authority predicated on leadership designated from the Prophet's family and the Sunni model privileging the consensus of the community.[13]

Who constituted the *Ahl al-bayt*?

While reverence for the Prophet and respect for his family is a hallmark of Muslim belief and practice, the question of who constituted the *Ahl al-bayt* and the nature and scope of their authority remained debated issues among Muslims.[14] For the Sunnis, esteem is accorded to the *Ahl al-bayt* as they are part of the Prophet's family and in honouring them they express their love for the Prophet. This is qualitatively different from the Shiʿi notion that temporal, moral and spiritual authority is inherently and exclusively vested in the *Ahl al-bayt*. Distinctions were also made regarding the composition of the *Ahl al-bayt* as, for the Sunnis, the Prophet's wives were included, whereas the Shiʿa came to define the *Ahl al-bayt* as the descendants of the Prophet Muhammad through ʿAli b. Abi Talib and Fatima, the Prophet's daughter and only surviving child, and through their sons, al-Hasan and al-Husayn and their progeny.[15]

Qur'anic verses and particular hadiths extolling love for the Prophet and his family were drawn upon as proof texts of this Shiʿi viewpoint.[16] One significant Qur'anic verse interpreted by Shiʿi exegetes included 33:33 from sura *al-Aḥzāb* (The Coalition):

> God only wishes to remove from you all impurities, O People of the House (*Ahl al-bayt*) and purify you with a complete purification (*innamā yurīdu llāhu li-yudhhiba ʿankumu'l-rijsa ahla'l-bayti wa-yuṭahhirakum taṭhīrā*).[17]

As part of the interpretation of this particular verse, Shiʿi scholars invoked the well-known tradition of the *ḥadīth al-kisā'* (hadith of the Cloak or Mantle [of the Prophet]), quoted by Sunni and Shiʿi scholars alike. On the basis of this hadith, the notion of the 'holy pentad' – comprising the Prophet, ʿAli, Fatima, al-Hasan and al-Husayn – was established. The hadith is summarised and translated as follows:

> The Prophet is reported to have said: 'This *āya* [33:33] was revealed for me and for ʿAli, Fatima, Hasan and Husayn.' When the verse was revealed, the tradition goes on to say, the Prophet took a 'cloak' or 'cape' (*kisā'*, meaning his robe or garment), wrapped it around his son-in-law, his daughter and his two grandchildren and said: 'O God, these are my family (*ahl baytī*) whom I have chosen; take the pollution from them and purify them thoroughly.'[18]

The essays in this volume by Hillenbrand, Blair, Tabbaa and Keshani all examine the significance of the Qur'anic and hadith inscriptions as Shiʿi proof texts on architecture from Iran, Syria and India. Robert Hillenbrand's careful reading of a group of relatively unknown 14th-century tomb towers in the city of Qum, attests to their unmistakeable Shiʿi messaging from the choice of Qur'anic verses to the multiple references to Imam ʿAli and his legitimacy as the rightful heir to the Prophet. Sheila Blair examines inscriptions on buildings and objects from Ithna ʿashari Shiʿi contexts spanning the 10th to early 16th centuries. One such inscription on a lustre mihrab made for the shrine of Imam Reza (ʿAli al-Rida) at Mashhad in 1215 boldly states: 'a visit to Mashhad is equivalent to a thousand visits to the Kaʿba'. This confirms that the practice of pilgrimage (*ziyāra*) to the tombs of the Imams was not only well established at this time, but was elevated, perhaps to alleviate the pressure on Shiʿi pilgrims who, under persecution, were unable to travel safely to Mecca.

Yasser Tabbaa's innovative study of the Shiʿi shrines in Syria also investigates the Qur'anic and hadith inscriptions in these buildings, which, along with the architectural plan and the glittering surface decoration are meant to 'amplify the *walāya* (devotion) of the worshippers' and bring them closer to the *nūr* (divine light) of the Imam and his family. Hussein Keshani examines the dramatic use of Arabic epigraphs on the facade of the Hussainabad Imambara at Lucknow. Constructed under the patronage of the ruler of Awadh in 1837, Keshani argues that its extensive inscription programme 'underpins Awadhi Twelver Shiʿism'.[19]

Charismatic figures and epochal events

Historical sources relate that during his lifetime, ʿAli b. Abi Talib was sought for his knowledge by a number of prominent Companions of the Prophet, tribal chiefs, esteemed Qur'an readers, and others, their numbers growing over the course of time.[20] In the Shiʿi tradition his role came to epitomise a charismatic teacher and an exemplary guide.[21] ʿAli took part in almost all military expeditions during the Prophet's lifetime, often as his standard-bearer (fig.3). Accounts of ʿAli's displays of courage on the battlefield became legendary, particularly at the pivotal battles of Badr (624), Uhud (625) and Khaybar (628). It is reported that the Prophet gave Imam ʿAli the legendary sword, *Dhu'l-faqār*, at Badr or Uhud and that Muhammad then uttered the well-known phrase: *lā fatā illā ʿAlī, lā sayfa illā Dhu'l-faqār* (There is no hero except ʿAli and no [mighty] sword except *Dhu'l-faqār*).[22] In chronicles depicting the Muslim capture of Khaybar, ʿAli's physical strength and heroics astounded the people, particularly when he ripped a heavy fortress door off its hinges to use as a shield. It took eight men to put the door back into its place.[23]

The essay by Zeynep Yürekli traces the iconography of Imam ʿAli's legendary sword *Dhu'l-faqār* not within a Shiʿi context, but rather within the setting of the 16th-century Sunni Ottoman world. As an emblem and an amulet of the Ottoman *ghazā'* warriors, the symbol of the *Dhu'l-faqār* was transformed into a shared religious iconography for both Shiʿa and Sunnis, since the Ottoman clergy were 'resolved not to allow the Safavids to monopolise the legacy of the *Ahl al-bayt*'. The figure of Imam ʿAli is also of central importance to the contemporary Iranian artist, Khosrow Hassanzadeh (b. 1963), whose works are discussed by Venetia Porter. Hassanzadeh's artistic homage to the traditional wrestlers (*jahān pahlavān*) of Iran is based on his deep admiration for these champions who 'always bowed before heroes such as Imam ʿAli'. As part of their routine exercises, the *pahlavān*s lift large wooden door-shaped shields, seeking to mirror ʿAli's courageous actions at Khaybar.

Despite the expectation of ʿAli and those in Medina who saw the succession as his prerogative, upon the Prophet's death, leadership of the community was passed on successively to three prominent members of the community, the first three caliphs of Islam: Abu Bakr (*r.* 632–634), ʿUmar (*r.* 634–644) and ʿUthman (*r.* 644–656).[24] During the politically volatile latter half of Caliph ʿUthman's reign, which led to the first civil war in Islam, the *Shīʿat ʿAlī* or 'partisans of ʿAli', as they came to be called, centred in Kufa in southern Iraq, referred to themselves as *Shīʿat Ahl al-bayt* and *Shīʿat Āl-Muḥammad* (partisans of Muhammad's family).[25] Following the murder of ʿUthman, ʿAli was made the fourth caliph (*r.* 656–661). Yet his main opponents, Muʿawiya, ʿUthman's kinsman and governor of Damascus, and ʿAisha', the daughter of Abu Bakr and wife of the Prophet, withheld their allegiance. A lengthy civil war ensued. ʿAli's acceptance of arbitration with Muʿawiya fostered opposition in the ranks of his army, leading to the genesis of the Kharijites who then murdered ʿAli in Ramadan 40/January 661.[26]

The early Shiʿa survived the tragic death of Imam ʿAli and turned to his eldest son, al-Hasan (d. 669) for continued leadership of the community. He however chose to abdicate from public life.[27] Meanwhile, Muʿawiya asserted himself as caliph and in securing his own son's succession, initiated the Umayyad dynasty. Muʿawiya's son, Yazid (*r.* 680–683), lacked his father's sagacity and statesmanship and was abhorred by a significant cross section of the Muslim community. Consequently, the Shiʿa invested their aspirations in al-Husayn (d. 680), who chose to rise against the oppressive rule of the Umayyads and to restore the leadership of the *umma* in the *Ahl al-bayt*.

Imam Husayn's refusal to give allegiance to Yazid, even at the cost of sacrificing his life and that of his immediate family members at Karbala on 10 Muharram 61/10 October 680, became a marker of principled resistance to tyrannical rule.[28] Muslims of all persuasions have traditionally accepted that the brutal killing of Imam Husayn and his family at Karbala marks one of the greatest calamities of early Muslim history. Among the Shiʿa, the martyrdom of the only surviving grandson of the Prophet 'infused a new fervour to the Shiʿi cause and contributed significantly to the consolidation of Shiʿi ethos and identity'.[29] The annual remembrance of this event during the first ten days of Muharram, culminating on the Day of ʿAshura' (lit. the tenth [day]), enables believers to commemorate the ultimate sacrifice of the Imam and the other Shiʿi martyrs for the cause of the *Ahl al-bayt*.[30]

The continued importance and diversity of this ritual commemoration by Shiʿa across the globe is demonstrated in the essays by

حمزه ایدوربن ایر شنجه عتبه یه قلیج اوربجه کوردم که علی
عتبه اولدوردي قريش غريو قلب حمزه نك عليك اوستنه
دیدلر ابو جهل قریش اولولر له چاغرشدلر ایتدلر انصاف ایلمدوکز
دیدلر اوچ کیشی بر کیشی یه اوشدوکوز آچ ارسلانلر کبی بر قیونك

Fig.3

Fig.4

Chelkowski, Flaskerud, Porter, Pak-Shiraz, Leichtman and Lyons. In his essay, Peter J. Chelkowski, the pre-eminent expert on the study of Twelver Shiʿi Muharram rituals, presents aspects of his decades of primary research on the arts, architecture and rituals in Iran, India and Trinidad that centre on the collective commemoration of the tragedy at Karbala. His chapter includes an exploration of the rituals and ritual spaces of *rowzeh-khānī*, *taʿziya*, Muharram processions and the *pardah* painting tradition, and how these have been adapted and translated by Shiʿi Muslims in varied contexts (fig.4).

Ingvild Flaskerud's study focuses on a lesser-known Muharram tradition in Iran, the theatrical performance of *ʿArūze Qāsem* (lit. the wedding of Qasim) directed, performed and participated by women in Shiraz over the ten days of Muharram. Centred on the account of a wedding ritual arranged by Imam Husayn for his nephew and daughter, prior to Qasim's martyrdom on the battlefield, this ceremony introduces additional Shiʿi religious iconography, such as the *ḥijla* (nuptial chamber), which continues to be taken up as an artistic motif by contemporary Iranian artists today as discussed in Porter's essay. While focusing on Iran, Nacim Pak-Shiraz's essay investigates how Iranian film provides a new medium of expression for the narrative of Karbala. Her analysis of the films of the notable director, Bahram Beyzaie (b. 1938), brings to the fore the innovation exercised by Iranian filmmakers to reinterpret and reintroduce this pivotal narrative to general Iranian audiences, within the backdrop of more recent objections levied by some religious clergy towards popular Muharram practices.

The last two essays that fall firmly within the theme of rituals and material culture connected to the tragedy at Karbala explore Shiʿi communities outside Iran. Mara Leichtman's chapter on the Shiʿa of Senegal, West Africa, reveals the peoples' multi-layered identities within that region, drawn from their indigenous African, Sufi and Shiʿi histories and allegiances. Their low-key ritual commemorations of ʿAshuraʾ ʿaim to educate Senegalese about the history of the Battle of Karbala and emphasise the closeness that African Sufis also feel towards the *Ahl al-bayt*ʾ. This restraint is certainly not shared in the

Fig.3
Page from Darir's *Siyer-i Nebī* (Life of the Prophet) depicting the Prophet blessing Imam ʿAli and Hamza at the Battle of Badr (624); Turkey, *circa* 1594.
British Museum, 1985,0513,0.1

Fig.4
A Muharram procession in southern India, with men bearing a magnificent *taʿziya*, *ʿalam*s, flywhisks and swords, with musicians, fakirs and riders on an elephant and camel, Tiruchirapalli, Tamil Nadu, 1820–1830.
British Museum, 2005,0716,0.1.7

Fig.5

port city of Multan, Pakistan, as evidenced by Tryna Lyons' ethnographic study of the spectacular Multani *ta'ziyas* (Muharram shrines) and their processions through the city. As in Chelkowski's study of *Hosay* rituals in Trinidad, Muharram observances in Multan are inclusive – commemorated by Sunnis and Shi'a alike. Lyons maintains that sectarian divisions are difficult to demarcate, and may even be irrelevant, as one of her informants said, 'there is not much to distinguish a Shi'a who poses as a Sunni from a Sunni whose heart is touched by the Karbala tragedy.'

Visits to Karbala for public lamentations at Imam Husayn's burial site are recorded from as early as 684.[31] However, a number of locations have been identified as the interment sites of the Imam's severed head. These include the Iraqi cities of Najaf, Kufa and Karbala; at Medina in the Baqi' cemetery; the Syrian cities of Damascus and Raqqa; and finally, in Cairo, where it was allegedly transferred by the Fatimid caliphs and remains to this day under the famous mosque of al-Husayn.[32] From the 12th century till today, millions of predominantly Sunni Egyptians together with Shi'i Muslims from across the world visit the mosque of Sayyidna al-Husayn, especially during Ramadan and other festive occasions. There they seek his intercession (*shafā'a*) for the alleviation of their worldly cares and aspire for the *baraka* of the beloved grandson of the Prophet (fig.5).[33]

The crystallisation of Shi'i doctrine

Following the tragic massacre of his family at Karbala, 'Ali Zayn al-'Abidin (d. 714), the sole surviving son of Imam Husayn and next designated Imam, adopted a politically quiescent position while continuing to contribute to the vibrant intellectual milieu of his time.[34] His son, Imam Muhammad al-Baqir (d. *circa* 732), maintained a similar stance, and articulated Shi'i doctrines to an increasing circle of disciples. Amongst the scholars of his generation he gained distinction as an authentic reporter of hadith and a teacher of law.[35] He introduced the principle of *taqiyya*, the precautionary dissimulation of one's true belief and practice, so as to protect the Imam and his followers under adverse circumstances. His son and subsequent Imam, Ja'far al-Sadiq (d. 765), continued his father's doctrinal teaching, articulating the Shi'i doctrine of the Imamate to his followers.[36] He acquired a steadfast reputation as a teacher, scholar and jurist and some of the most eminent Sunni and Shi'i hadith scholars and theologians of the time affiliated themselves as his students.[37] Such was his influence that he was retrospectively cast as the eponymous founding figure of the Imami Shi'a Ja'fari *madhhab* (religious school of law) (fig.6).

During Imam Ja'far's lifetime, he witnessed two pro-'Alid revolts – that of Zayd b. 'Ali in 740 and Muhammad al-Nafs al-Zakiyya in 762 – as well as the (initially) Shi'i-based Abbasid revolution in 750. The Abbasid definition of the *Ahl al-bayt* included the Banu Hashim, the Prophet's extended family, which therefore included the descendants of the Prophet's uncles, Abu Talib and 'Abbas, the progenitor of the Abbasids themselves.[38] All along, Ja'far al-Sadiq refused to align with any of these Shi'i contenders and 'served as symbol for those Shi'a who refused to rise…[adhering to the] principle of *qu'ūd*, that the true *imām* need not attempt to seize power unless the time be ripe, and can

Fig.5
Husayn the martyr par excellence, abstract painting of the head of Imam Husayn covered by a prayer scroll, by Aneh Muhammad Tatari (b. 1957), Iran, 1998. British Museum, 2000,0724,0.1

Fig.6
Du'ā' of Imam Ja'far al-Sadiq (d. 765), copied after the handwriting of Mawlana Muhammad Baqir Majlisi (d. 1698), Iran, Safavid period. British Museum, 1938,1210,0.3

be content to teach.'[39] He was also the last Imam recognised by both Twelver and Ismaili Shi'a.

According to the doctrine of *imāma* first outlined by Imam Ja'far, there was a permanent need for an Imam, who was a divinely guided, infallible (*ma'ṣūm*) and authoritative leader on material and spiritual matters for the community.[40] He was entitled to political leadership as well as religious authority, but his Imamate was not dependent on the former at any time. The main difference, therefore, between the role of the Messenger of God (*rasūl Allāh*) and the Imam was that the latter did not receive divine scripture. However, the Imam was the authoritative interpreter of the Qur'an, in both its exoteric (*ẓāhir*) and esoteric (*bāṭin*) meanings, due to his *'ilm* (divine knowledge), which was transferred to him from the Prophet through *naṣṣ* (explicit designation). Consequently, each successive Imam receives the perfect knowledge of his predecessor through *naṣṣ*.[41]

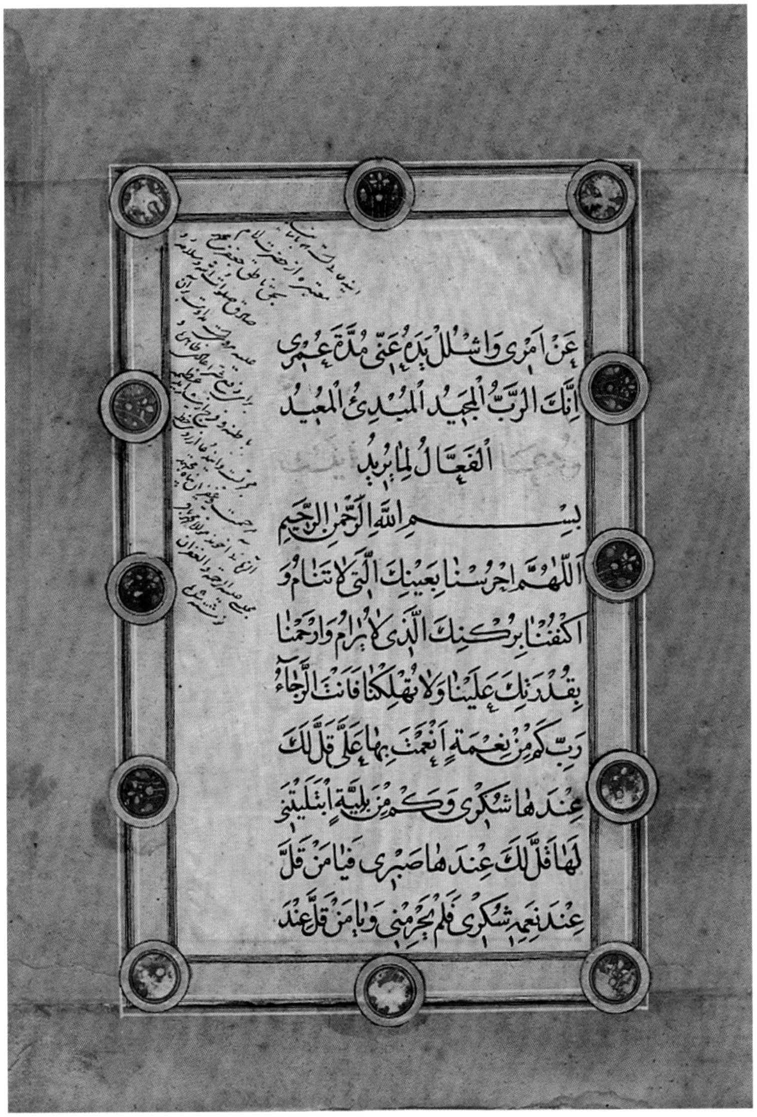

Fig.6

The Imams are invested by God with *wilāya* (spiritual authority) and are due the *walā'* (allegiance) and *walāya* (devotion) of the believers.[42] This devotion and absolute obedience to the Imam is such an essential element in Shi'i doctrine, that the Shi'i invocation of the extended *shahāda* (Muslim creed), that is, *ashhadu an lā ilāha illā llāha, lā sharīka lahu, wa-ashhadu anna Muḥammadan rasūlu llāh* (I bear witness that there is no god except Allah, there is none beside Him, and Muhammad is the messenger of Allah), also includes for many Shi'a the third phrase, *wa ashhadu anna 'Aliyyan Amīr al-Mu'minīn walī ullāh'* (I bear witness that 'Ali, Commander of the Faithful, is God's *walī* (trustee/friend) [on earth]).[43] Shi'i rulers from the late tenth century onwards used this tripartite *shahāda* and other phrases on their official coinage to publicly express their allegiance to Imam 'Ali and his descendants and exhibit their love for the *Ahl al-bayt*. Luke Treadwell analyses these types of inscriptions on the coins of several Shi'i dynasties from the 10th to 12th centuries with some unexpected conclusions, as some rulers, such as the Buyids, did not wish to declare their Shi'i allegiances on their coinage.

The Zaydiyya, the Isma'iliyya and the Ithna 'ashariyya

While the Imamate is quintessential to the Shi'i worldview, questions regarding the identity of the Imam and the factors that legitimise his authority were matters of vigorous debate among the early Shi'a. As a result, variations of viewpoints eventually led to the formation of distinct Shi'i groups such as the Zaydis and the Imamis, and the latter subsequently bifurcated into Ismailis and Ithna 'asharis (fig.7). During the Imamate of Ja'far al-Sadiq, the branch of the Shi'a known as the Zaydiyya (i.e. the Zaydis) arose out of the unsuccessful revolt in Kufa of Zayd b. 'Ali b. al-Husayn (d. 740), the son of Imam Zayn al-'Abidin. Zayd, unlike his brother, Imam Muhammad al-Baqir, or his nephew, Imam Ja'far al-Sadiq, espoused armed action against what he considered to be the illegitimate Sunni regime as a religious duty of a legitimate Imam.[44] According to early Zaydi doctrine, the Imam could be any adult male descendant of the *Ahl al-bayt* (although later Zaydi doctrine required descent from al-Hasan or al-Husayn). While knowledge of the religious sciences was a requisite for the Zaydi Imam, inherent authority – through hereditary succession and explicit designation (*naṣṣ*) – was not deemed part of the Zaydi doctrine. Neither was the

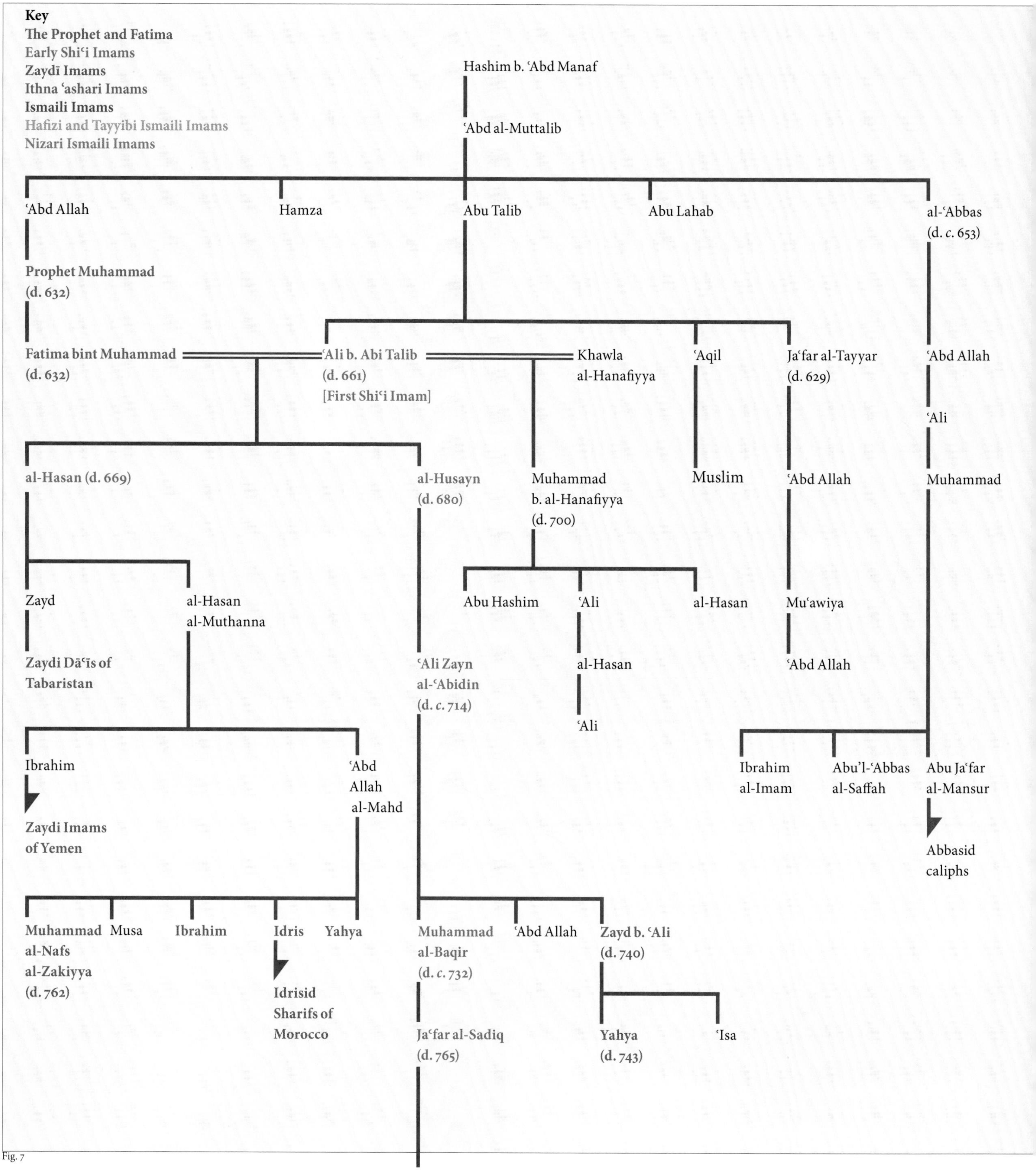
Key
The Prophet and Fatima
Early Shiʿi Imams
Zaydī Imams
Ithna ʿashari Imams
Ismaili Imams
Hafizi and Tayyibi Ismaili Imams
Nizari Ismaili Imams
Hashim b. ʿAbd Manaf
ʿAbd al-Muttalib
ʿAbd Allah
Hamza
Abu Talib
Abu Lahab
al-ʿAbbas (d. c. 653)
Prophet Muhammad (d. 632)
Fatima bint Muhammad (d. 632)
ʿAli b. Abi Talib (d. 661) [First Shiʿi Imam]
Khawla al-Hanafiyya
ʿAqil
Jaʿfar al-Tayyar (d. 629)
ʿAbd Allah
ʿAli
al-Hasan (d. 669)
al-Husayn (d. 680)
Muhammad b. al-Hanafiyya (d. 700)
Muslim
ʿAbd Allah
Muhammad
Zayd
al-Hasan al-Muthanna
Abu Hashim
ʿAli
al-Hasan
Muʿawiya
Zaydi Dāʿīs of Tabaristan
ʿAli Zayn al-ʿAbidin (d. c. 714)
al-Hasan
ʿAbd Allah
ʿAli
Ibrahim
ʿAbd Allah al-Mahd
Ibrahim al-Imam
Abu'l-ʿAbbas al-Saffah
Abu Jaʿfar al-Mansur
Zaydi Imams of Yemen
Abbasid caliphs
Muhammad al-Nafs al-Zakiyya (d. 762)
Musa
Ibrahim
Idris
Yahya
Muhammad al-Baqir (d. c. 732)
ʿAbd Allah
Zayd b. ʿAli (d. 740)
Idrisid Sharifs of Morocco
Jaʿfar al-Sadiq (d. 765)
Yahya (d. 743)
ʿIsa

Fig. 7

Continues on the next page

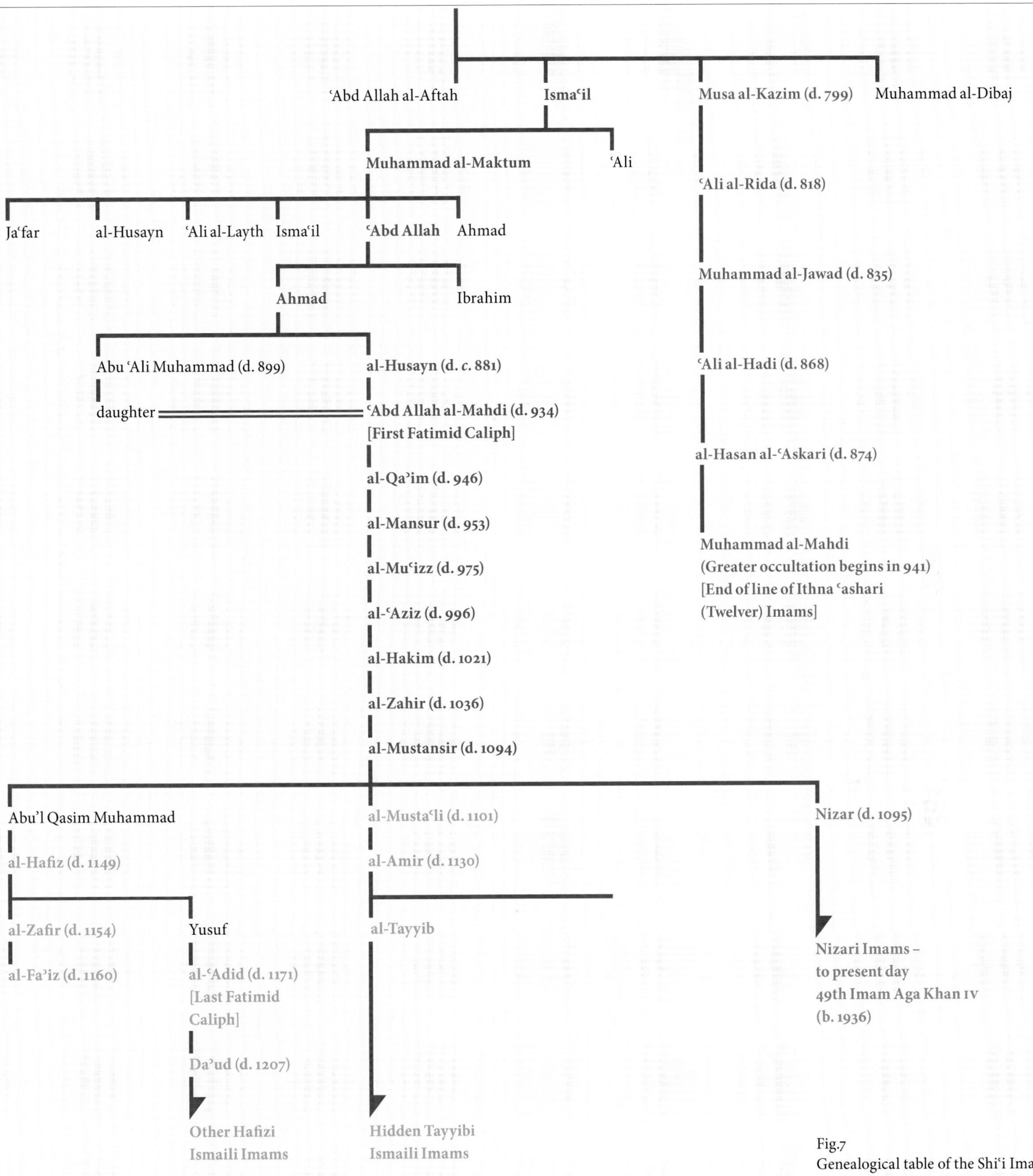

Fig.7
Genealogical table of the Shiʿi Imams and the divisions of the Zaydiyya, Ismaʿiliyya and Ithna ʿashariyya branches of Shiʿi Islam.

principle of *taqiyya* of relevance to them since the establishment of the just state by the Zaydi Imam through armed action was incumbent in the here and now.

Following a series of abortive revolts supported by the Kufan Zaydis, the group's activities shifted to remote mountainous regions south of the Caspian Sea and in Yemen, far from the reach of the Abbasids in Baghdad. The essay by Melanie Michailidis briefly discusses the architectural patronage of the Zaydis in order to provide the context for a more focussed assessment of their rivals, the Shiʿa Bavandids who, unlike the Zaydis, did not claim descent from the Prophet, but rather, traced their lineage to the pre-Islamic Sasanian dynasty. Her study demonstrates that the funerary monuments of the Bavandids were not built for the customary focus of Shiʿi *ziyāra*, but were modelled on Sasanian rituals and practices.

Following the death of Imam Jaʿfar, another major schism occurred over the succession to the Shiʿi Imamate.[45] At this time, Abbasid persecution of the Shiʿi was at its peak and the caliph al-Mansur (*r.* 754–775) reportedly sent spies to Medina to have the appointed successor killed.[46] Within this politically hazardous milieu, the ensuing events of the Imam's succession remain contested in the sources. The majority of Jaʿfar al-Sadiq's followers traced the succession to three of his sons, Ismaʿil, ʿAbd Allah and Musa. Those who followed Ismaʿil came to be known as the Ismaʿiliyya (i.e. the Ismailis).[47] ʿAbd Allah died shortly after his father and left no male offspring.[48] Those who had accepted ʿAbd Allah, turned to his younger half-brother Musa (d. 799, later called al-Kazim) and developed into the Ithna ʿashariyya (i.e. Twelver) Shiʿa.[49]

The historical development of Ithna ʿashari and Ismaili Shiʿism, their evolving doctrines and beliefs, and the various communities and religious traditions that resulted from these branches over time, are well documented and too lengthy to discuss in this essay.[50] The significant doctrinal development of *ghayba* (lit. 'absence [of the Imam]'), was formulated following the occultation of the twelfth Ithna ʿashari Imam, Muhammad b. al-Hasan al-Mahdi in 874, whose emergence (*ẓuhūr*) is still being awaited. Twelver Shiʿism, thus, developed eschatological and messianic notions of the *Mahdī* (the rightly-guided one), who was expected to return, restore religion and institute a reign of justice before the end of time (fig.8).[51]

By comparison, the aspirations of the Ismaili Shiʿi communities continued to be bolstered through a line of successive Imams. The line of the Mustaʿli Ismaili Imams lasted into the 12th century, after which time Imam al-Tayyib went into concealment (*satr*) in 1130. Guidance of the Mustaʿlian Ismaili community was transferred to the office of a succession of *dāʿī muṭlaq*s (supreme authorities), whose function continues to this day.[52] In contrast, the line of Imamate for the Nizari Ismaili communities has continued and, at present, they pay their allegiances to their 49th hereditary Imam, Prince Karim Aga Khan IV (b. 1936), who traces his lineage to Imam ʿAli and the *Ahl al-bayt*.[53]

Nizari Ismaili communities are scattered across 25 countries and, as a result, they represent a vast spectrum of ethnic and cultural diversity, which is reflected in their religious practices. Amier Saidula shares his ethnographic research on a religious rite among the Ismailis of Xinjiang, China. The *Chirogh rawshan* (lit. luminous lamp) ceremony is a quintessential Central Asian/Chinese Ismaili funerary ritual that has been maintained for centuries in virtual isolation and has allowed the communities in these regions to maintain their sense of identity in the face of adversity and political uncertainty.

Shiʿi dynasties: from persecution to polity

The fortunes of the Shiʿa on the political stage reached unprecedented heights around the mid-tenth century. Shiʿi polities had already been established in the Zaydi states of Yemen and the Caspian region and in Morocco under the Idrisid dynasty. However, the establishment of the Ithna ʿashari Shiʿi Buyid dynasty as the overlords to the now-weakened Abbasids in 945 facilitated the permeation of Shiʿism across Abbasid lands. Furthermore, after over a century of covert Ismaili Shiʿi *daʿwa* (missionary) activity, the Ismaili Imam publicly proclaimed the establishment of the Fatimid state in North Africa in 909, which following the founding of the capital in Cairo in 969, resulted in the flourishing of a cosmopolitan Shiʿi dynasty that lasted over two-and-a-half centuries (*r.* 909–1171).

The Fatimids, Buyids and the Shiʿi Hamdanid dynasty in Mesopotamia and northern Syria sponsored Shiʿi scholarship, the religious sciences and the arts and encouraged the public celebration of Shiʿi rituals and commemorations such as the ʿId al-Ghadir and ʿAshura'. Notwithstanding

Fig.8

their own political rivalries, the cultivation and advancement of the intellectual, cultural and religious activities under these Shiʿi dynasties, with the support of a state apparatus, cumulatively contributed to the further crystallisation of their respective Shiʿi traditions.

The Fatimids, named after the Prophet's daughter, Fatima, drew upon their *Ahl al-bayt* genealogy to assert their claim as the legitimate Imam-caliphs of the Muslim world.[54] When the new capital city of al-Qahira (the victorious, i.e. Cairo) was established, the Imam-caliph brought along the coffins of his predecessors and had them reinterred in the precincts of the palace.[55] Little remains of the Fatimid palaces or their dynastic cemetery, but several mosques built during the dynasty's reign have survived and continue to function, including the mosques of al-Azhar, al-Hakim (al-Anwar) and al-Aqmar. Jonathan Bloom surveys these and other Fatimid monuments from North Africa and Egypt to ascertain the influence of Ismaili Shiʿi beliefs in their plans, decoration and inscriptions. Both Grabar and Bloom have researched Fatimid art and architecture for several decades and their contrary positions on the 'Ismaili Shiʿi nature' of these monuments have effectively inverted over time. Thus, Bloom is deeply sceptical of finding Ismaili meanings in Fatimid architectural forms and suggests that an examination of the use of these buildings may bring to light possible Shiʿi meanings.

Despite a hiatus during the establishment of these Shiʿi polities, a period at its peak often referred to as the 'Shiʿi Century', the threat of imminent persecution and murder remained recurring topoi in the history of the Imams and their followers of the Shiʿi branches of Islam.[56] As a result, distinctive ceremonies and traditions have evolved that centre on and pay homage to important Shiʿi personages who often lived in very hazardous circumstances under oppressive regimes. For Ithna ʿashari Shiʿa, visiting (*ziyāra*) the tombs of the Imams and their descendants, known in Persian as *imāmzādas*, is given eminent importance, with rewards for such *ziyāras* often equated with the pilgrimage to Mecca and Medina (fig.9). Among these tombs, the most important are at Najaf (Imam ʿAli), Karbala and Cairo (Imam Husayn), al-Kazimayn in Baghdad (fifth and ninth Imams), Mashhad (Imam Reza), and Samarra (tenth and eleventh Imams), which is also where

Fig.8
Poster depicting (from the right) Imam ʿAli, Hazrat ʿAbbas (half-brother of Imam Husayn), and Imam Husayn, with the words 'There is no hero but ʿAli and no sword but *Dhu'l-faqār*'; 'Abu'l-Fazl, the standard-bearer of Karbala!'; 'Husayn b. ʿAli, the master of martyrs, peace be upon him!', Tehran, 2005. British Museum, 2005,0511,0.7

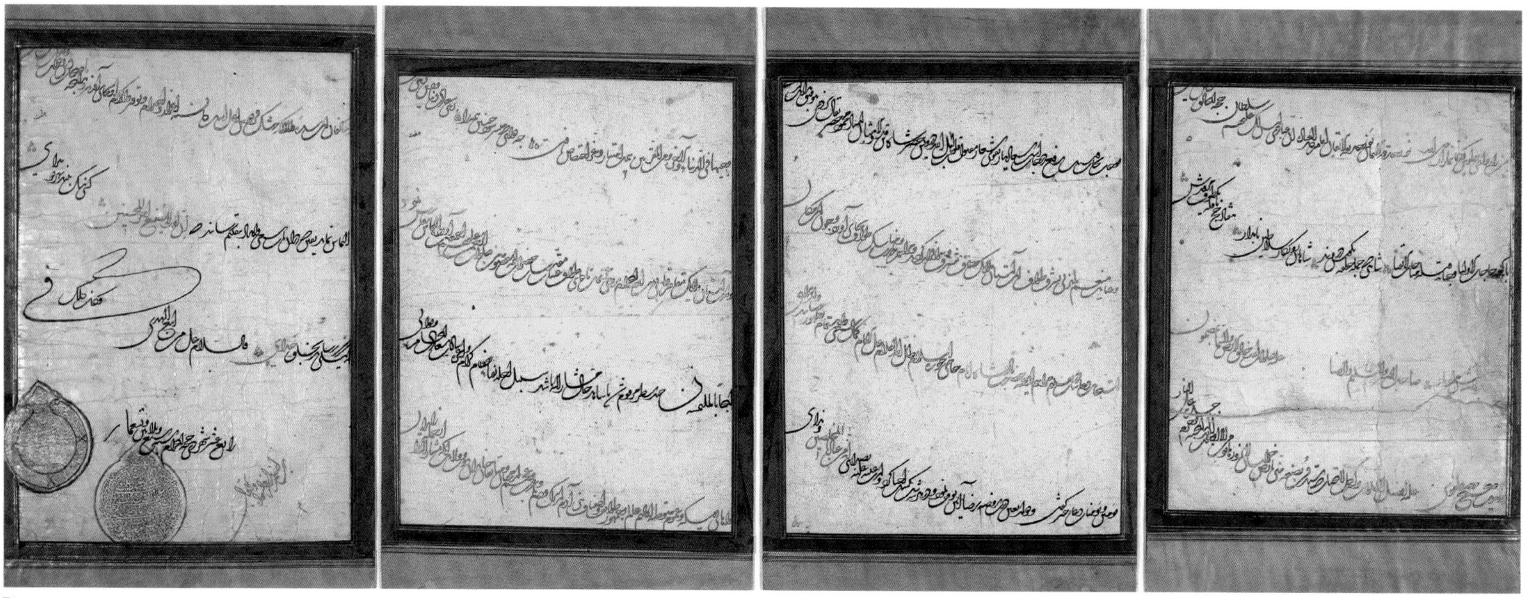

Fig.9

the twelfth Imam went into occultation. Other sites of pilgrimage include Qum, in Iran, where Fatima, the sister of the eighth Imam ʿAli Reza, is buried; and Damascus, in Syria, which is associated with Zaynab, the sister of Imam Husayn.

The significance of architecture and artefacts directly connected with the Imams and their descendants forms the third theme of the volume and is borne out in the essays by Allan, Canby, Farhad, Ekhtiar, Yürekli, Suleman and Bloom (discussed above). The theme is also covered by the chapters already discussed by Blair, who examines some of the inscriptions of the shrine of Imam Reza at Mashhad and on other *imāmzāda*s in Iran, and by Tabbaa, who concentrates on the Damascus shrines of Sayyida Zaynab (daughter of Imam ʿAli and sister of Imam Husayn) and Sayyida Ruqayya (daughter of Imam Husayn). James Allan provides a valuable study of the Ithna ʿashari Imams' shrines at Najaf, Karbala, Kazimayn and Samarra, focussing on their architectural elements and treasuries of artefacts. Usually inaccessible to Western visitors and even for Muslims in recent times, Allan's historical survey of the patronage of these shrines, by Sunnis and Shiʿa alike, underscores the transcending of sectarian motivations of the patrons.

The Safavid rulers, whose founder, Shah Ismaʿil (*r.* 1501–1524) proclaimed Twelver Shiʿism as the state religion of Iran in 1501, were great patrons of both religious and secular arts and donated many objects to the holy shrines of the Imams. Sheila Canby examines a group of Qur'an manuscripts that were given by the Safavid Shah ʿAbbas (*r.* 1587–1629) to the shrine of Imam Reza at Mashhad. It has been purported that specific Imams penned these Qur'ans and included their 'signatures' as proof but, in reality, they are stylistically dated to at least one, if not two centuries after their death. Canby, therefore, investigates the regime's motivations behind these false attributions. Similarly, *fālnāma*s (books of omens) were prognostication manuals, sometimes elaborately illuminated with large-scale paintings, which were falsely ascribed to key Shiʿi figures, such as Imam ʿAli and Imam Jaʿfar al-Sadiq. Massumeh Farhad investigates the religious iconography and significance of a group of *fālnāma* manuscripts from the 16th to early 17th centuries from the Safavid and Ottoman worlds and makes a case for shared religious practices during that time that transcended Sunni–Shiʿa demarcations.

Finally, the essays by Ekhtiar, Yürekli and Suleman focus on religious iconography connected to the *Ahl al-bayt*. Maryam Ekhtiar explores a later Shiʿi Iranian dynasty, the Qajars (*r.* 1785–1925), who were the inheritors of the Safavid public devotion for the *Ahl al-bayt*, and their use of religious imagery (*shamā'il*) as talismans and for divinatory practices. The Qajars, moreover, 'elevated religious imagery to an art form and popularised it', making the production and exchange of images of the *Ahl al-bayt* a lucrative trade. Yürekli's treatment of the subject of Imam ʿAli's legendary sword, *Dhu'l-faqār*, has already been discussed in the context of a shared iconography claimed by Sunni and Shiʿi communities alike. In her chapter on the so-called Hand of Fatima, Fahmida

Fig.9
Four sections of a *ziyārat-nāma* from the shrine of Imam Reza, dated 14 Dhu'l-Hijja 944/5 July 1533, Mashhad, Iran, 1533. British Museum, 1996,0521,0.1.a-d

Fig.10
Sufi hat embroidered with the *Nād-i ʿAlī* prayer seeking the help and intercession of Imam ʿAli; Iran or Turkey, *circa* 1900. Aga Khan Museum, AKM678

Suleman attempts to trace the origins and significance of this ubiquitous talismanic motif and investigates possible connections with the historical figure of the daughter of the Prophet, Hazrat Fatima (d. 632).

Sufism and Shiʿism in the post-Mongol era

The Shiʿi Buyids were displaced by the newly-converted Sunni Saljuq Turks (*r.* 1038–1194). As both Turkic chieftains and Abbasid *amīrs*, they patronised the state-sponsored Nizamiyya network of madrasas that promoted Sunni Shafiʿi Islam as mainstream Islam across the territorially vast and religiously and ethnically diverse Abbasid Empire. Saljuq-sponsored scholars, such as Abu Hamid Muhammad Ghazali (d. 1111), were influential in ostracizing Shiʿi Islam, particularly the intellecually potent Nizari Ismailis, which contributed to the segregation between Sunni and Shiʿi Islam. Conversely, Ghazali's writings in favour of Sufi Islam assured the inclusion of the hitherto marginalised Sufi *ṭarīqa*s (orders) into so-called mainstream Islam.[57] This had significant ramifications for Shiʿi Islam in the post-Mongol milieu.

Indifferent to the Sunni–Shiʿa polemics and partialities, the catastrophic Mongol devastation of the Muslim world swept asunder a number of Muslim polities such as the Nizari Ismaili state in 1256

Fig.10

and the Sunni Abbasid Caliphate in 1258. Following this levelling of politically and ideologically defined infrastructures, a number of Sufi-oriented movements emerged across the Muslim world to restore the spiritual, social and moral fibre of the Muslims. Their notion of a righteous guide, who is imbued with *ʿilm* (knowledge) and *ḥikma* (wisdom) of the *ḥaqāʾiq* (essential truths), who is a *wasīla* (intercessor) charged with charting and mentoring the believer's path to spiritual enlightenment, had shared familial resemblances to Shiʿi Islam. Likewise, the Sufi principle of a *silsila*, a chain of spiritual succession from one master to the next, has a sociological affinity to the Shiʿi notions of succession as does the Sufi reverence for the *Ahl al-bayt*, evident in the tracing of the spiritual ancestry of their *murshid*s (masters) through Imam Jaʿfar al-Sadiq to Imam ʿAli (fig.10).[58]

The Sufi reverence for Imam ʿAli and his descendants was also reflected in a more general attitude within Sunni Islam, referred to as *tashayyuʿ ḥasan* (praiseworthy Shiʿism). This term denotes a positive orientation towards the veneration of the Prophet's family, and ʿAli in particular, which is a religious obligation that does not imply any formal affiliation to the schools of Shiʿi law and theology.[59] Hence, although the establishment of the Safavids (*r.* 1501–1722) in Iran led to Ithna ʿashari Shiʿism becoming fully embedded in Iranian soil, and Ottoman-Safavid rivalries further deepened the differences between Sunni and Shiʿi Islam, the notion of the *Ahl al-bayt* continued to transcend the ideological moorings of sectarian interpretations.[60]

The pan-Islamic reverence and love for the People of the Prophet's Household, the fourth and final theme that has emerged from the essays, recurs time and again in this volume. The supreme status of the *Ahl al-bayt* and their pre-eminence in Muslim thought has remained paramount through the course of the centuries. In the contemporary period, this is evident in a variety of Muslim practices and expressions of piety including the supplication by Muslims –Sunni and Shiʿa – at the shrines of the members of the Prophet's progeny. The majority of Muslims continue to venerate the *Ahl al-bayt* as beacons of the Prophet, and therefore recipients of his light – *nūr Muḥammadī*. Thus the Household of the Prophet continues to be honoured by Muslims as the archetypal family and as sources of *baraka* and *shafāʿa* (intercession) during times of hardship and need.

1 The authors wish to thank Hasan Al-Khoee for his comments on an earlier draft of this chapter.
2 Seyed Hossein Mousavian, 'Sectarian War, the Major Threat to the Middle East', *Asharq al-Awsat* online (10 August 2013), http://www.aawsat.net/2013/08/article55313070. See also the article by Shireen T. Hunter, 'Politics Fuels a Rising Sectarian Fire', *Asia Times Online* (7 August 2013), http://www.atimes.com/atimes/Middle_East/MID-02-070813.html; and her in-depth analysis of the roots of the sectarian tensions and intensity in her, *The Regional and International Politics of Rising Sectarian Tensions in the Middle East & South Asia*. Prince Alwaleed Bin Talal Center for Muslim-Christian Understanding (ACMCU), Occasional Papers Series (Washington, DC, July 2013), published online: http://issuu.com/georgetownsfs/docs/shireen_hunter_the_regional_and_int.
3 Most recent monographs and edited volumes include, James W. Allan, *The Art and Architecture of Twelver Shiʿism: Iraq, Iran and the Indian Subcontinent* (London, 2012); Nacim Pak-Shiraz, *Shiʿi Islam in Iranian Cinema: Religion and Spirituality in Film* (London and New York, 2011); Ingvild Flaskerud, *Visualizing Belief and Piety in Iranian Shiism* (London and New York, 2010); Pedram Khosronejad, ed., *The Art and Material Culture of Iranian Shiʿism: Iconography and Religious Devotion in Shiʿi Islam* (London, 2012); Peter J. Chelkowski, ed., *Eternal Performance: Taʿziyeh and Other Shiite Rituals* (Calcutta, 2010); Kamran Scot Aghaie, ed., *The Women of Karbala: Ritual Performance and Symbolic Discourses in Modern Shiʿi Islam* (Austin, TX, 2005); and Patricia L. Baker, *Islam and the Religious Arts* (London and New York, 2004). See their extensive bibliographies for earlier works, focussed studies on religious art and architecture under specific Shiʿi dynasties and key articles on the subject.
4 Previous studies of this nature include: Irene A. Bierman, *Writing Signs: the Fatimid Public Text* (Berkeley, CA, 1998); Paula A. Sanders, *Ritual, Politics, and the City in Fatimid Cairo* (Albany, NY, 1994); and Caroline Williams, 'The Cult of ʿAlid Saints in the Fatimid Monuments of Cairo. Part I: The Mosque of al-Aqmar', *Muqarnas*, 1 (1983), pp.37–52.
5 Key works to consult on the topic include: Wilferd Madelung, 'Shiʿa', *EI2*, vol.9, pp.420–424; Wilferd Madelung, 'Zaydiyya', *EI2*, vol.11, pp.477–481; Farhad Daftary, *A History Of Shiʿi Islam* (London, 2013); Hamid Mavani, *Religious Authority and Political Thought in Twelver Shiʿism: From Ali to Post-Khomeini* (London, 2013); Etan Kohlberg, ed., *Shiʿism* (Aldershot, Hants; Burlington, VT, 2003); Farhad Daftary, *The Ismāʿīlīs: Their History and Doctrines* (2nd ed., Cambridge and New York, 2007); Azim Nanji and Farhad Daftary, 'What is Shiʿi Islam?' in Vincent J. Cornell, ed., *Voices of Islam, Volume 1: Voices of Tradition* (Santa Barbara, CA, 2006), pp.217–244. Published online at http://www.iis.ac.uk/view_article.asp?ContentID=108482; Heinz Halm, *Shiʿism*, trans. J. Watson and M. Hill (2nd ed. Edinburgh, 2001); Andrew J. Newman, *The Formative Period of Twelver Shīʿism: Ḥadīth as a Discourse Between Qum and Baghdad* (Richmond, Surrey, 2000); Mohammad ʿAli Amir-Moezzi, *The Divine Guide in Early Shiʿism: The Sources of Esotericism in Islam*, trans. D. Streight (Albany, NY, 1994); Etan Kohlberg, *Belief and Law in Imāmī Shīʿism* (Aldershot, Hants; Burlington, VT, 1991).
6 For the formative period of Islamic history, the general reader is referred to Patricia Crone, *Medieval Islamic Political Thought* (Edinburgh, 2004).
7 For an in-depth and original study of the problem of succession to the Prophet see, Wilferd Madelung, *The Succession to Muḥammad: A Study of the Early Caliphate* (Cambridge, 1997. repr. 2004).
8 Laura Veccia Vaglieri, 'Ghadīr Khumm', *EI2*, vol.2, pp.993–994.
9 See Wilferd Madelung, 'Imāma', *EI2*, vol.3, pp.1164–1169.
10 Vaglieri, 'Ghadīr Khumm', p.993. She suggests the multi-layered term *mawlā* is translated as 'patron?' [with a question mark]. Significantly, Vaglieri explains that most of the sources which form the basis of our knowledge of the life of the Prophet, the earliest of which are compiled in the Abbasid era, do not mention the sermon at Ghadir Khumm as they feared the hostility of the reigning Sunni regime for providing evidence for the Shiʿa claim to ʿAli's right to the caliphate. As a result, Western biographers of Muhammad equally make no reference to the events at Ghadir Khumm.
11 M. M. Bar-Asher, *Scripture and Exegesis in Early Imami Shiism* (Leiden, 1999), esp.pp.94–97 for discussion on the *ḥadīth al-thaqalayn* and Shiʿi exegesis of (Q.55:31).
12 See G. H. A. Juynboll, 'Sunna', *EI2*, vol.9, pp.878–881; and M. Sharon, 'People of the House', *EQ*, vol.4, pp.49–53. Only one version of this tradition refers to the two things as the book of God (*kitāb Allāh*) and the Prophet's practice (*sunnat nabiyyihi*). Other versions of this tradition, recorded in both Sunni and Shiʿi works, refer to them as the Qur'an and the *Ahl al-bayt*. See Meir M. Bar-Asher, 'Shīʿism and the Qur'ān', *EQ*, vol.4, pp.596–597.
13 See C. van Arendonk and W. A. Graham, 'Sharīf', *EI2*, vol.9, pp.330–337.
14 Ali S. A. Asani, 'Family of the Prophet', *EQ*, vol.2, p.177; Sharon, 'People of the House', pp.49–53.
15 I. Goldziher, C. van Arendonk, and A. S. Tritton, 'Ahl al-Bayt', *EI2*, vol.1, p.258.
16 Many of these hadith and Qur'anic verses are translated in Yadollah Gholami and Matthew Melvin-Koushki, "Alī b. Abī Ṭālib', *EIS*, vol.3, pp.477–583.
17 Other significant verses for Shiʿi exegesis on this matter include (Q.3:33–34, 6:84–89, 28:5, 32:24 and 55:31). See the article and bibliography in Bar-Asher, 'Shīʿism and the Qur'ān', pp.596–597; Bar-Asher, *Scripture and Exegesis*, esp.pp.125ff; and Azim Nanji, 'Towards a Hermeneutics of Qur'ānic and Other Narratives in Ismaʿili Thought', in R. C. Martin, ed., *Approaches to Islam in Religious Studies* (Tucson, AZ, 1985), pp.164–173.
18 Sharon, 'People of the House', pp.49–50. Also see his, '*Ahl al-Bayt* – People of the House', *Jerusalem Studies in Arabic and Islam*, 8 (1986), pp.169–184; For Sunni reports on the 'Hadith of the Cloak' see, M. Ayoub 'The Excellences of Imām Ḥusayn in Sunnī Ḥadīth Tradition', in *Alserāt*, 12 (1986), esp.pp.60–62.
19 The first Muslim rulers in southern India to adopt Twelver Shiʿism as their state religion were the ʿAdil-Shahis of Bijapur (*r.* 1490–1686), followed by Sultan Quli (*r.* 1496–1543), the founder of the Qutb-Shahi dynasty of Golconda. Despite some persecution of the Shiʿa within the Sunni Mughal Empire, Shiʿi communities flourished, especially in the region of Hyderabad in the south and at the north Indian kingdom of Awadh (*r.* 1722– 1856) with its capital at Lucknow. See Deborah S. Hutton, "Ādil Shāhīs', *EI3*, vol.2010–2, pp.23–25. R. M. Eaton, 'Ḳuṭb Shāhī', *EI3*, vol.5, pp.549–550; Sadiq Naqvi, *The ʿĀshūr khānas of Hyderābād City* (Hyderabad, 2006).
20 On ʿAli's life see, Robert M. Gleave, "Alī b. Abī Ṭālib', *EI3*, vol.2008–2, pp.62–71; and Laura Veccia Vaglieri, "Alī b. Abī Ṭālib', *EI2*, vol.1, pp.381–386.
21 Reza Shah-Kazemi, *Justice and Remembrance: Introducing the Spirituality of Imam ʿAli* (London, 2005); ʿAlī b. Abī Ṭālib, *Nahjul Balāgha (Peak of Eloquence): Sermons, Letters*

and Sayings of Imam ʿAlī ibn Abī Ṭālib (Tehran, 1980), translated by Sayed Ali Raza.

22 Francesca Bellino, 'Dhū l-Faqār', *EI3*, vol.2012–4, pp.77–79. Quoted from Ibn Hisham's edition of Ibn Ishaq's *Sīra*. We have rendered the phrase in the usual order it appears inscribed on objects, most commonly swords. However, Bellino has quoted it from Ibn Hisham with the mention of the sword first, followed by ʿAli's praise.

23 Laura Veccia Vaglieri, 'Khaybar', *EI2*, vol.4, pp.1137–1143.

24 See W. Montgomery Watt, 'Abū Bakr', *EI2*, vol.1, pp.110–111; Wilferd Madelung and Farhad Daftary, eds., 'Abū Bakr', *EIS*, vol.1, pp.563–593 G. Levi Della Vida and M. Bonner, ''Umar (1) b. al-Khaṭṭāb', *EI2*, vol.10, pp.818–821; and G. Levi Della Vida and R. G. Khoury, ''Uthmān b. ʿAffān', *EI2*, vol.10, pp.946–949.

25 Arzina R Lalani, 'Shīʿa', *EQ*, vol.4, p.592; on Caliph ʿUthman's reign see, G. Levi Della Vida and R. G. Khoury, ''Uthmān b. ʿAffān', *EI2*, vol.10, pp.946–949.

26 For the full account see Gleave, ''Alī b. Abī Ṭālib'.

27 Laura Veccia Vaglieri, '(al-)Ḥasan b. ʿAlī b. Abī Ṭālib', *EI2*, vol.3, pp.240–243.

28 For the full account see, Laura Veccia Vaglieri, '(al-)Ḥusayn b. ʿAlī b. Abī Ṭālib', *EI2*, vol.3, pp.607–616.

29 Nanji and Daftary, 'Shiʿi Islam', Online reference, p.12; Mahmoud Ayoub, ''ĀŠŪRĀ', *EIR*, vol.2, Fasc. 8, pp.874–876.

30 Mahmoud Ayoub, *Redemptive Suffering in Islam: A Study of the Devotional Aspects of* ʿAshura' *in Twelver Shiʿism* (The Hague, 1978).

31 F. M. Denny, 'Tawwābūn', *EI2*, vol.10, p.398.

32 Vaglieri, '(al-)Ḥusayn', p.611.

33 Ibn Jubayr, a tourist in Cairo in 1187, recorded the experiences of the visitors to the mosque: 'We observed men kissing the blessed tomb, surrounding it, throwing themselves on it... calling out invocations...and offering up humble supplications such as would melt the heart and split the hardest flint.' Caroline Williams, *Islamic Monuments in Cairo: The Practical Guide* (Cairo, 2002), pp.193–194.

34 Etan Kohlberg, 'Zayn al-ʿĀbidīn', *EI2*, vol.11, pp.481–483; Imam Zayn al-ʿĀbidīn, *The Psalms of Islam: al-Ṣaḥīfat al-kāmilat al-sajjādiyya*, trans. W. C. Chittick (London, 1988).

35 Arzina Lalani, *Early Shīʿī Thought: the Teachings of Imam Muḥammad al-Bāqir* (London, 2004); Etan Kohlberg, 'Muḥammad b. ʿAlī Zayn al-ʿĀbidīn, Abū Djaʿfar, called al-Bāḳir', *EI2*, vol.7, pp.397–400.

36 For the doctrine of the Imamate expounded by the various Sunni *madhhabs*, see Madelung, 'Imāma', *EI2*, vol.3, pp.1163–1165.

37 Among his students was Abu Hanifa (d. 765), the eponymous founder of the Sunni Hanafi School of law. M. G. S. Hodgson, 'Djaʿfar al-Ṣādiḳ', *EI2*, vol.2, pp.374–37.

38 See Goldziher, et al., 'Ahl al-Bayt', p.258; and also, M. Sharon, 'People of the House', *EQ*, vol.4, pp.49–53.

39 Hodgson, 'Djaʿfar al-Ṣādiḳ', p.374.

40 Daftary, *Ismāʿīlīs*, pp.83–84. Undoubtedly, the Ithna ʿashari and Ismaili doctrines of *Imāma* continued to evolve over the centuries.

41 Nanji and Daftary, 'Shiʿa Islam', Online reference, p.5.

42 For an explanation of the terms *wilāya* and *walāya* in Sunni and Shiʿi contexts see, Mawil Y. Izzi Dien and Paul E. Walker, 'Wilāya', *EI2*, vol.11, pp.208–209; and Maria Massi Dakake, *The Charismatic Community: Shiʿite Identity in Early Islam* (Albany, NY, 2007). On the institution of *walāʾ* see, Patricia Crone and Arent Jan Wensinck, 'Mawlā', *EI2*, vol.6, pp.874–882.

43 Matthias Radscheit, 'Witnessing and Testifying', *EQ*, vol.5, esp.pp.498–499; Sadeq Sajjadi and Muhammad Isa Waley, 'Amīr al-Mu'minīn', *EIS* vol.3, pp.702–706.

44 For the full history see, Madelung, 'Zaydiyya', pp.477–481.

45 According to Twelver tradition, Imam Jaʿfar was poisoned on the orders of the Abbasid caliph al-Mansur. He was buried in the Baqiʿ cemetery in Medina, which became a pilgrimage site for both Shiʿi and Sunni Muslims before it was destroyed by the Wahhabis. See Hodgson, 'Djaʿfar al-Ṣādiḳ', pp.374–375. For a full account of the dispute over the succession to Imam Jaʿfar see Daftary, *Ismāʿīlīs*, pp.88–91.

46 According to Kohlberg, al-Sadiq, in anticipation of the Caliph's actions, is said to have spread news shortly before his death that he had appointed five legatees, in order to thwart Abbasid plans. Etan Kohlberg, 'Mūsā al-Kāẓim', *EI2*, vol.7, p.645.

47 Most sources report that Imam Jaʿfar had designated (through *naṣṣ*) his eldest son, Ismaʿil, but according to some, he predeceased his father. The group that formed the nucleus of the later Ismaʿiliyya (i.e. the Ismailis) accepted that the Imamate passed to Ismaʿil's son, Muhammad b. Ismaʿil (d. *circa* 179/796). The mother of Ismaʿil and his full brother, ʿAbd Allah, was the granddaughter of al-Hasan, thus an ʿAlid. See Daftary, *Ismāʿīlīs*, pp.89, 97.

48 Ibid., p.89.

49 See Kohlberg, 'Mūsā al-Kāẓim', pp.645–648.

50 For detailed accounts, see the bibliography mentioned earlier.

51 The period of the 'lesser occultation' (*al-ghayba al-sughra*) covered the years 874–941 and was followed by the 'greater occultation' (*al-ghayba al-kubra*), which started in 941 and continues to this day. See Wilferd Madelung, 'al-Mahdī', *EI2*, vol.5, esp.pp.1235–1237.

52 Also, based on a hereditary succession designated through *naṣṣ*. Farhad Daftary, 'al-Ṭayyibiyya', *EI2*, vol.10, pp.403–404.

53 For the Aga Khan see http://iis.ac.uk/view_article.asp?ContentID=103467.

54 Daftary, *Ismāʿīlīs*, p.128.

55 Ibid., p.162.

56 The phrase 'Shiʿi Century' is used to describe the period from the mid-10th to the mid-11th centuries when the Buyids, Fatimids and other Shiʿi dynasties controlled much of the Middle East.

57 W. Montgomery Watt, 'al-Ghazālī', *EI2*, vol.2, pp.1038–1041.

58 On Sufism see the multi-authored article, 'Taṣawwuf', *EI2*, vol.10, pp.313–340.

59 Gholami and Melvin-Koushki, ''Alī b. Abī Ṭālib'.

60 For example, the Sunni Hanbali scholar and harsh Shiʿi critic, Ibn Taymiyya (d. 1328), advocated the distinguished rank of the founding figures of Shiʿi Islam, whom he considered among the *Ahl al-bayt*, including the Imams ʿAli Zayn al-ʿAbidin, Muhammad al-Baqir and Jaʿfar al-Sadiq.

2

Are there Shiʿi forms of art?

Oleg Grabar[1]

By asking me to give one of the introductory papers at this conference, the organisers did not, I trust, expect a scholarly discussion of the question or questions they raised, but rather an introduction to the learned presentations that follow.[2] I shall begin with a few general observations to set the issues to be discussed within the broader context of the history and criticism of visual forms in general and within the Islamic world in particular. I will then propose four broad principles, hypotheses, or premises for the conference to accept, reject, or modify.

First, then, some general thoughts. When, quite some time ago, I agreed to participate in this conference, I remember feeling that the topic 'Islamic art and Shiʿism' was an invitation to explore a major issue in our understanding of the arts from Muslim lands and in fact a major issue in visual culture and art criticism, even in a field little prone to innovations like the history of art or too young to develop procedures and theories of its own like the study of the arts of the Islamic world. The issue is whether there are specific forms or restricted subjects which are inspired by discrete and easily identifiable features of religious movements or which became, when first created or throughout their use, associated, for whatever reason, with followers of a religious movement or with practices associated with that movement. Such forms and subjects allow then or even compel the identification of whatever one sees with that particular group.It becomes possible to locate a form in its appropriate social or cultural setting without needing to know the circumstances and purposes of its manufacture. From the standpoint of a theoretical analysis of the arts, the issue is fundamental, as it deals with the ways in which we interpret (or should interpret) what we see.

An appropriate parallel is that of language, as we can (or could) identify the age, education, social or territorial origins of individuals, and even a great deal about their character or abilities, from hearing them speak, as accent, intonation in speech, vocabulary, and grammar do reflect one's own history or that of the family or tribe to which one belongs. Clothes and jewellery are another category of implements that can lead to similar results, identifying a person or a thing with a restricted religious, social, or cultural entity. The problem with clothes or jewellery, however, is that they lend themselves much more easily than language to borrowing and to reuse, as well as to make others believe that one is something one is not. The making of works of art or of material culture also lends itself to such masquerading uses and thus complicates the practice of judging objects or monuments of architecture exclusively from the forms they were given. Once a Fatimid princely rock crystal becomes a Christian liturgical vessel, is it a Christian object or still a courtly item from a Muslim ruler? Furthermore, in contrast with the physical or natural sciences, the evidence is only statistically valid; there are always exceptions to whatever generality one proposes, but this is a point I will not discuss in the context of this conference.

An issue like Shiʿism and art is not only important for theories of art and the consequences of visual perception. It is also important for our knowledge and understanding of the Islamic world. Once again, clothing offers an interesting parallel. Until the 20th century, it was possible to identify almost everywhere the social, tribal and cultural affiliations of any one person by reading his or her clothes, as was still very clear nearly 60 years ago when I first visited the suq in Damascus, or, a couple of decades later, the shrine of Imam Reza (ʿAli al-Rida) in Mashhad or the bazaars of old Kabul. The incursion of globalisation everywhere has probably changed this state of affairs. I was assured, however, during a recent trip to Qatar, that such distinctions are not visible (or is it no longer visible?) for religious differentiations, for instance to distinguish Shiʿa from Sunnis, although my informant, a significant figure in the Saudi establishment, thought that he might be able to recognise Sufi tendencies through the attire of some individuals. He also thought that he could recognise Arab tribal or national associations and belonging from the type of robe worn and from the ways in which a *kūfiyya* (men's headdress) was set whenever traditional clothes were worn, but not from a suit or from a hat which established distinctions of taste rather than of ethnic and religious belonging.

And it is true that in the modern world a globalisation of taste and of vestimentary customs limits the social or cultural value of one's observations and judgments. But it was not so in the past and, in theory at least, it should be possible to recognise forms that identified different religious groups like Muslim, Christian, Jewish, Buddhist, Hindu, or Zoroastrian, each one of these broad categories being presumably visually distinguishable from the other through the mediation of the clothes that are worn, the architectural shapes or decoration provided to one's surroundings, or the objects acquired and owned. This possible conclusion is never absolute or exclusive. In general, a Christian was not likely to carry a restricted Islamic sign, but he was not limited to Christian signs only. In the early medieval period, the quality of being a vizier or a military commander was probably more important to make visible than religious affiliation as a Muslim, a Jew or a Christian. Necessity of formal identification only appears when other factors, social or political, are involved; it must always be set in a historical – what some of us call chronotopic – context.

And then internal divisions within any one of these entities can or should also be visually identified. A recent trip through the Baltic states made quite clear to me the visual differences in interiors, not necessarily exteriors, between Lutheran and Catholic churches, whilst Jesuit churches in Lithuania were not quite like other Catholic churches, and the western Christian churches were clearly different from Orthodox ones. I did not during this trip notice significant differences in attire, although I clearly remember from my youth before the Second World War, the common but not compulsory differences between the clothes worn by Catholics and Protestants, especially on Sundays, and more so in a provincial town like Strasbourg than in cosmopolitan Paris.

Both a theoretical investigation of forms that would have become restricted in their associations and any attempt to list ways developed within the Islamic world to illustrate religious, cultural, or social differences require investigative techniques developed in many different fields, especially ethnography and anthropology, rather than those of art history and criticism. Both theoretical investigations and any attempt to identify specific associations within the Islamic world also require awareness of procedures from other areas, especially Christianity with its wealth of visual creativity and with the existence of institutions like the Church which could and did command or reject forms of any sort and which served over the centuries as an arbiter of taste, a preserver of traditions, and a sponsor of liturgical or other continuous uses of the same symbolic forms. Comparable ways existed in the practices associated with Buddhism and with Hindu beliefs.

The point of these first remarks is that the question of 'Shiʿi art' belongs, on the one hand, to a broad enquiry on the associations made with visual forms and, on the other, with the complex of 'things' used, owned, and created by various communities within the Muslim world. This is probably true of the traditional world, since the contemporary one has introduced too many new practices and techniques to allow for the same sort of general conclusions and hypotheses.

Let me turn to the second aspect of my remarks, an attempt to provide examples of the kinds of research needed to answer the more fundamental queries I have raised within the more specific context of Shiʿism and art. I will also propose a few methodological principles and historical premises for us to consider, accept, or reject. I limited myself to suggestions rather than conclusions based on documents, because I no longer have easy access to available information, nor the physical energy needed to scan such information as exists or to seek new information in texts. But also, as is demonstrated by James W. Allan's book on Shiʿi art and architecture, the evidence is immense and far richer for the era that begins with the Safavids in 1505 than for the earlier period with which I am more familiar.[3]

I will restrict myself to four points.

My first principle or idea is a relatively obvious one and should not lead to many objections. The principle is that there is a clear distinction between two categories of Shiʿi identifications. One can be called a form of *labelling*, as objects or monuments are formally proclaimed to be Shiʿi, whether they were meant to be such or not. The most common and most obvious means to label is through inscriptions, but other ways existed as well of proclaiming the Shiʿi sponsorship or possession of a monument or of an object. But, while such labelling makes a specific thing Shiʿi, it does not mean that such objects or monuments are always recognisable as Shiʿi without the adjunction of writing or of other signs and without the observer's awareness of their meaning and capacity to read these texts. Labelling can and should, therefore, be seen from two points of view: the desire of a sponsor and maker and the perception and understanding of a user or onlooker.

The second category of possible Shiʿi modes of identification can be called *innate*. It lies in forms and in subjects that are always recognisable as Shiʿi, the way in which most 'Madonna and Child' images are Catholic or Orthodox, not Protestant, with stylistic rather than iconographic differences separating Catholic from Orthodox examples. *Innate* features could be self-generated like the cross so clearly identified with Christianity and military signs of rank, or they are imposed by some, friendly or not, external authority, like the colour of clothes forced on Jews in the Middle Ages and on prisoners today. Whether self-generated or imposed from the outside, such features only work when there is a stable institution – the Church, the state, the army, or, in our own times, a large hospital – to require and enforce their presence. It becomes, therefore, important not simply to propose an 'innate' Shiʿi form of identification, but to identify the process by which it was created and authenticated.

The more difficult question is the practical one of how to discover these Shiʿi features, innate or labels, and to gauge their impact. For the 16th and later centuries, the *taʿziya* (Passion play) and all sorts of semi-liturgical and semi-theatrical performances of behaviour expected around the commemoration of the martyrdom of Imam Husayn created objects and symbols which are clearly restricted to Shiʿi communities in Iran and in India; but is it true wherever there are Shiʿis, as in Yemen or Syria? Most of these objects are found in ethnographic collections and whether they should be considered as works of art is perhaps questionable. But the standards, masks, heads of devils, and so on, which belong to these liturgical or theatrical activities and which were specifically created for them, are clearly examples of a restricted Shiʿi patronage and use.

For an earlier period, there are, for instance, in the Museum of Islamic Art in Cairo and elsewhere, a number of very strange wooden

Fig.1

tablets known as 'portable mihrabs', which they are not (fig.1). Most of them are empty in the centre and the empty space is surrounded by an arch on columns. On the edges we have the names of the Twelve Imams and at times even a mention of the hidden Imam to come.[4] All this is clearly Shiʿi and the technique makes them all early Fatimid, as no such objects are known to me in Safavid Iran. They may, however, be related to the contemporary *turba*s (prayer stones) of Shiʿi Lebanon and Iraq which are made from Karbala soil or clay and are used for prayer in commemorative feasts. But what were the early wooden examples used for? Hardly likely to be equivalents of prayer rugs, they were interpreted as objects set in front of the praying man to rest his head during prayer. Some were found in tombs and may have an eschatological meaning. In a general way they are perhaps comparable to icons in being at the same time reminders of key features of one's belief which accompany the owner wherever he or she is and useful for some pious practice.

A static equivalent with commemorative implications would be the often-illustrated stucco plaque in the early 14th-century Sufi shrine in Linjan near Isfahan where a written sequence of descendants of the Prophet was transformed into a carefully composed calligraphic image that must have been created by or for a Shiʿi patron (fig.2). But are such compositions necessarily Shiʿi? Or is it only once the words are read that the form becomes Shiʿi? This is an instance where careful research using both anthropological evidence and pious sources, as well as an investigation of parallel types of objects in other religions, could resolve the problem.

To my knowledge, no such movable plaques or equivalent types of objects exist outside of Fatimid Egypt during the first six centuries of Islam's existence. Is it because of the unique nature of preservation of objects in the dry climate of Egypt and therefore without broad historical value? In as much as small movable objects will become quite common in late Shiʿi Iran and in India, their existence in Shiʿi Egypt may indeed associate them with Shiʿism, but it is also possible that the early phenomenon should be connected horizontally with Christianity rather than vertically with a closed Islamic system.

However one will answer this question, my second principle is connected to it. It is that the two obvious periods of major Shiʿi power and association with a strong state, general wealth, and missionary purpose – the 10th to 12th centuries in central Islamic lands dominated by the Fatimids in Cairo and then the 16th and later centuries dominated by Iran and extending most particularly into southern India – do not seem to share forms, iconography, or functions that would distinguish them from the rest of the Muslim world, with one possible exception to which I shall return in a moment. At some point, especially whenever a formal practice began, the patronage of the state was essential in the development of sanctuaries and occasionally in harnessing –*labelling* in my terminology – for pious or religious purposes, forms, and techniques developed within the secular world, ceramics, glass, or textiles, and of course architecture. But, at some point, most obviously in the Indian subcontinent, popular forces and practices took over and imposed their taste and their ways.

And it is at this level that I want to present my third idea-principle. A large percentage of the chapters deal with it and I already suggested it some forty years ago, although not understanding then the theoretical implications of my reasoning. The principle now would be that, whatever other features contributed to its appearance, growth, and distribution all over the Muslim world, the commemoration through building and inscriptions (I am not sure about objects and am curious about textiles and whether we can distinguish between cloth made for Sunni or Shiʿi believers) as well as through pious behaviour and perhaps even liturgies, the commemoration of the dead, religious or secular, was first developed by and because of Shiʿism. And here a distinction should be made in our thinking. It may be argued that the growth of the mausoleum of al-Shafiʿi in Cairo and other examples in Syria or Iraq were the result of a direct impact of Shiʿi practice, but this does not make these monuments or the forms they use Shiʿi. The importance taken by the dome in these ensembles is easy to explain for all funerary architecture between India and the Atlantic, but it is difficult, I think, to argue for a Shiʿi meaning of the dome in general or even for specific domes in Shiʿi sanctuaries from Iran, Central Asia, or Iraq (and now Syria) of Safavid and later times. Should one make a distinction between Safavid motifs and Shiʿi motifs? And are they, or were they, basically different from the 10th to 12th-century domes in the Levant? Or should one argue that the form of a dome has no ethnic or religious

Fig.1
Carved wooden tablets in the form of mihrabs on columns, 10th–11th centuries, Egypt. Museum of Islamic Art, Cairo, inv. no. 15552

Fig.2

association, only a social or liturgical one, but the colour and decoration put on it is what identifies it as Shiʿi art? The implications of whatever answer we provide for a general appreciation of Islamic art is enormous, for they may lead to the conclusion that, in architecture as well as in the art of objects, surface decoration is far more important than the construction of the object.

And this then brings me to my fourth and last example. It is a more complex one and requires an understanding of how I came to it and to the hypothesis it brings up.Following my own temporary conclusion that it is unlikely that there were forms and subjects shared by the Safavid and Fatimid ways of expressing their religious beliefs, I decided that I simply did not know enough about religious culture in Safavid times to argue anything worthwhile (I will make an exception to this wise conclusion in a few minutes). But the Fatimids are old acquaintances and 30 or 40 years ago I wrote several articles dealing, directly or indirectly, with their art.[5] I reread some of them and discovered that, when dealing with the success or impact of Shiʿi art I, and for that matter most of those who wrote in those days, almost never talked about Shiʿism, largely because in these days of scholarship, we rarely talked about religious matters, our own beliefs, if any, or those of others. What made the Fatimids interesting was their apparent rediscovery of representational arts, an alleged 'realism' in images, the connections with Baghdad, Antiquity, and Sicily, the accumulation of treasures known now through the *Kitāb al-Dhakhā'ir* (Book of Gifts and Rarities)[6] but already apparent through al-Maqrizi's *Khiṭaṭ*, and the transformation of Cairo into a world capital.[7] Religious matters appeared only in the interpretation of a few details in the Hakim mosque and in the facade of the much later Aqmar mosque.[8] The important point in these examples is that they occurred on the outside of buildings and seemed to serve as a sort of official publicity for the Shiʿi vision of Islam. In other words, for the perception and understanding of non-Shiʿa rather than for strengthening Shiʿi beliefs or compelling Shiʿi practice. In their effectiveness, they were meant to be connected to the royal ceremonies described by al-Maqrizi which transformed the Fatimid caliph progressing through the mosques of the capital into someone akin to the semi-divine emperors of Late Antiquity or to the more or less hidden Imam.[9] These creations and ceremonies were meant to affect and to be understood by a wide public that was not necessarily Shiʿi. Their language, therefore, had to be part of some other visual language than that of Shiʿism. While they showed a language of power, they did not necessarily show a language of beliefs.

All of this was fairly well known and I saw no point in rehashing it. But then I discovered that a great deal of new information has accumulated on the doctrine and beliefs of Ismailis in Fatimid times. And I began to go over this new material. I used primarily three sources, the *Kitāb al-Munāẓarāt* (Book of Discussions) with fascinating information about the objects surrounding medieval Ismaili missionaries' personages, Hamid al-Din al-Kirmani's *al-Daʿwa* (The Call), and Nasir Khusraw's *Ghushāyish wa rahāyish* (Knowledge and Liberation), from the late 10th and 11th centuries.[10]

My objective was not to further my understanding of the political and military ambitions and successes of the early Fatimids, but to try to feel something of what made them different, of what they understood the world around them to be, the purposes of life as they saw it, and the practical side of their idiosyncratic beliefs.[11] As I went on reading these books and perusing a few of the recent studies on these early centuries, a vision began to emerge of a system of beliefs that may well have been a coherent philosophical and theological construction. And this construction could lend itself to translation into visual forms. I am not prepared either to present that system nor to compare it to other systems of the same time, but some elements in it began to explain to me one very strange development of Fatimid religious art in the 12th century. I will first outline the ideology I thought I detected and then the works which seemed to me to reflect them. I am not suggesting that I am right, simply that, if further elaborated, my explanation is a possibility and that the direction it has taken is worth pursuing.

The broad argument is suggested by a passage in Nasir Khusraw: 'He who knows [the power of the] creation of the world knows the power of his own creation, and he can fashion the form of his soul with the same balance according to which the form of the body has been fashioned.'[12] The nature of creation, whether divine or human, is a permanent concern of these texts and consists always of two components, one clear and visible (*ẓāhir*), the other hidden and invisible

Fig.2
Carved stucco panel with the names of the Fourteen Infallibles in kufic script, shrine of Pir-i Bakran, late 13th or early 14th centuries, Linjan, Iran; *height* 192 cm, *width* 92.5 cm, *depth* 29.5 cm. Museum of Islamic Art, Cairo, inv. no. 421

(*bāṭin*). Here are a few fixtures that seemed to me to be particularly striking for their possible visual parallels:

1. The contrast between *tawḥīd*, the One and ultimate unity of all creation (*waḥdat al-wujūd*), and *ta'wīl* (interpretation), the return to that unity through *tanzīl* or revelation, in a sense through a mystery; the visual idea could be that what you see reveals a truth you cannot see;

2. The visible is like a veil *(sitr)* or a secret (*kashf*) which leads to the truth without being the truth; this idea may involve the complex of associations involved in the symbolism of forms;

3. The importance of numbers, a set of prime numbers like three sides to reality, five primary angels, first five holy Shiʿi men and women, special holy months, seven planets, and then walls of the city of God with seven pathways through the walls and seven gates; also four and twelve occur in various lists; numbers translate into geometry, a constant of Islamic art;

4. The contrast between body and soul or between form and matter, meaning that what we see always corresponds to something real, but not necessarily whatever is seen;

5. The summarising of creation through the activities of craftsmen, jewellers or tailors.

And there are many more such written themes, just as these particular ones can be refined and set within broader currents of medieval and Late Antique thought. But, as I was reading these texts and creating my own vision of a religious thought that was both describing the universe and reflecting on the mystery of seeing it, it occurred to me that they can explain a specific phenomenon of Fatimid art which has been known for quite some time, but for which no Fatimid and religious explanation has to my knowledge been proposed, although one recent writer has come close to suggesting one.

The phenomenon consists in the mihrabs made for the mosques of Sayyida Nafisa (figs 3–4) and Sayyida Ruqayya in Cairo, the *minbar* (pulpit) made for the shrine of Imam Husayn now in Hebron, and a commemorative cenotaph for Imam Husayn in the Museum of Islamic Art, Cairo (fig.5).[13] I am sure that there are other items to be put in this group characterised by two features which appear to reflect specifically Shiʿi religious thought: the coexistence of concrete material

Fig.3

Fig.4

Fig.5

details like fairly naturalistic plants of all sorts with a rigid geometric structure whose specifics can only be understood by extending what is shown much beyond the object on which it appears. On an interesting wood panel (fig.6), the geometry has been weakened in intensity and living beings appear; is this an extension of a Shiʿi form to a simply aesthetic aim?[14] Less spectacular uses of numbers and geometry appear in printed amulets and on a lustre plate with a geometric design based on the number five and a series of letters which may have a magical significance (fig.7).[15]

I would like to argue that these examples which seem peculiar to the art of Fatimid times in the 12th century use segments of what would have been complete geometric panels in the later art of the Mediterranean and western Islam, as though it was important to suggest that the visible form is only a section of a much larger geometric figure framing the real world. What is now an important task for research is to compare this Fatimid use of geometry to what was happening at the same time in northern and northeastern Iran and Central Asia. There, too, geometry transformed the look of buildings, but it is not the same geometry as in the Mediterranean Islamic world and Shiʿism did not at this time play a major role there, at least not in official architecture, although there are exceptions.[16] One may recall here the suggestion made recently by a group of physicists about the elaborate principles underlying the decoration of some 12th-century mausoleums in northwestern Iran.[17]

I am not arguing that my explanation is correct, only that it seems to me to be possible and that a thorough investigation of the geometry involved in Egyptian woodwork could explain it as an attempt to make visible aspects of Ismaili doctrine and beliefs, that there is a basic mysterious (not fully visible) geometric structure to the universe and to whatever man creates and that this structure has mathematical principles we do not perceive immediately. Nor do we fully understand them, but they are necessary to introduce a visible world comprised of discrete vegetal designs.

Further work with these and all comparable texts are more than likely to bring additional suggestions for the interpretation of works made in Fatimid times, once we understand that such analyses do not explain all of that art. They only highlight the more restricted themes found there, the ones that identify the needs of a religious facet of the culture, not the social or political sides which have by now been much explored. It is perhaps not an accident that these Shiʿi themes appear so prominently late during Fatimid rule, when a different psychological attitude existed from the triumphal one of the late 10th and early 11th centuries. And, I suspect, although I have not pursued the matter, that a similar study of unusually rich religious Shiʿi texts of the Safavid period may bring similar results. For example, the theories of colours and of their meanings developed in Ismaili tracts of that time may have had an impact on some pious compositions like the celebrated ʿAli page in Istanbul (fig.8) and perhaps could even have affected the painters of the courts with their primarily secular subjects.

I would like to conclude my introductory remarks with two final observations, again more methodological and theoretical. One is that our field

Fig.3
Mihrab of carved and inlaid wood for the mosque of Sayyida Nafisa with geometric and vegetal patterns, 1138–1145, Cairo; *height* 192 cm, *width* 92.5 cm, *depth* 29.5 cm. Museum of Islamic Art, Cairo, inv. no. 421

Fig.4
Detail of fig.3

Fig.5
ʿCenotaph of Imam Husaynʾ of carved teak with geometric and floral designs and Qurʾanic inscriptions, 12th century, Egypt; *width* 35 cm, *length* 1.8 m, *height* 35 cm. Museum of Islamic Art, Cairo

Fig.6

Fig.7

has not always known how to distinguish works of art from those of material culture, especially in the Middle Ages. The ways to identify piety and belief in visual matters implies or requires other ways of organising the material we possess, by categories of use – social, ethnic, religious, daily – rather than by styles, techniques, or quality, which are so typical of art historical research. As is happening in the study of Christian art, and perhaps of Buddhist and Hindu art as well, we must learn to separate 'things' connected with piety and religious behaviour from those which reflect beliefs and represent or intimate the divine. And the second observation is that, in dealing with religious or pious identification of forms, we should think more about the receiver rather than the maker of the objects involved. The two are often different from each other and require different manners of description and identification. But we are far less well-equipped to deal with the former than with the latter.

Fig.6
Carved door panel with geometric, vegetal and figural motifs, 12th century, Egypt; *height* 61 cm, *width* 29 cm. Museum of Islamic Art, Cairo, inv. no. 441

Fig.7
Lustre dish with five-pointed star and inscriptions, 11th century, Egypt; *diameter* 21 cm, *height* 6.5 cm. Museum of Islamic Art, Cairo, inv. no. 15966

Fig.8
Calligraphic fourfold on the name of ʿAli, 15th century, Istanbul, Topkapı Palace Museum, Istanbul, H 2152, folio 9v

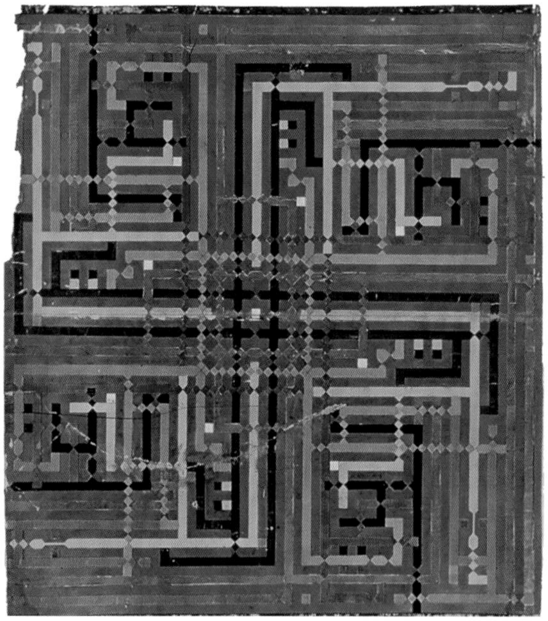

Fig.8

1 Editor's note: Professor Grabar passed away on 8 January 2011 before this volume was published. Sincere thanks to Sheila Blair for supplying the image and caption for fig.2.

2 This paper combines the introductory talk I gave at the conference in 2009 with some of the conclusions I developed at the end of the meeting and some thoughts that occurred to me afterwards. The paper reflects the spoken mode of the presentation. The notes are only to direct and immediate pertinence to the topic discussed. I should add that I learned a lot from reading, after the conference, a manuscript of Professor James W. Allan's richly documented book on the subject of Shi'i art (see note 3 below). I am very grateful to him for his generosity and kindness. We do not always agree, but our differences result from different approaches to the topic rather than to disagreements on interpretations.

3 James W. Allan, *The Art and Architecture of Twelver Shi'ism: Iraq, Iran and the Indian Sub-Continent* (London, 2012).

4 Bernard O'Kane, ed., *The Treasures of Islamic Art in the Museums of Cairo* (Cairo, 2006), p.62; Jean David-Weill, *Catalogue général du Musée arabe du Caire: les bois à épigraphes* (Cairo, 1931), pp.55ff and pl.x; Elise Anglade, *Catalogue des boiseries de la section islamique: Musée du Louvre* (Paris, 1988), p.53; and Wilfried Seipel, ed., *Schätze der Kalifen: Islamische Kunst zur Fatimidenzeit* (Vienna, 1998), cat. no.115, p.152.

5 Most of these articles are found in Oleg Grabar, *Early Islamic Art, 650–1100*, vol.1 of *Constructing the Study of Islamic Art* (Ashgate, 2005).

6 Ibn al-Zubayr, *Book of Gifts and Rarities. Kitāb al-Hadāyā wa al-tuḥaf: Selections Compiled in the Fifteenth Century from an Eleventh-Century Manuscript on Gifts and Treasures,* tr. Ghada al-Hijjawi al-Qaddumi (Cambridge, 1996).

7 Jonathan M. Bloom, *Arts of the City Victorious: Islamic Art and Architecture in Fatimid North Africa and Egypt* (London, 2007). For the works of Mamluk historian al-Maqrīzī (d. 1442) see, F. Rosenthal, 'al-Maḳrīzī', *EI2*, vol.6, pp.193–194.

8 Caroline Williams, 'The Cult of 'Alid Saints in the Fatimid Monuments of Cairo. Part I: The Mosque of al-Aqmar', *Muqarnas*, 1 (1983), pp.37–52; and ibid, 'The Cult of 'Alid Saints in the Fatimid Monuments of Cairo. Part II: The Mausolea', *Muqarnas*, 3 (1985), pp.39–60; for a different view, see Christopher S. Taylor, 'Reevaluating the Shi'i Role in the Development of Monumental Islamic Funerary Architecture: The Case of Egypt', *Muqarnas*, 9 (1992), pp.1–10.

9 Among other places, see Irene A. Bierman, *Writing Signs: The Fatimid Public Text* (Berkeley, CA, 1998).

10 Ibn al-Haytham, *The Advent of the Fatimids: A Contemporary Shi'i Witness. An edition and English translation of Ibn al-Haytham's Kitāb al-Munāẓarāt*, ed. and tr. Wilferd Madelung and Paul E. Walker (London, 2000); Paul E. Walker, *Ḥamīd al-Dīn al-Kirmānī: Ismaili Thought in the Age of al-Ḥākim* (London, 1999); Nāṣir Khusraw, *Knowledge and Liberation: A Treatise on Philosophical Theology A new edition and English translation of Gushāyish wa Rahāyish of Nāṣir-i Khusraw*, ed. and tr. Faquir M. Hunzai (London, 1998).

11 Farhad Daftary, *The Ismā'īlīs: Their History and Doctrines* (2nd ed. Cambridge, 2007); Paul E. Walker, *Fatimid History and Ismaili Doctrine* (Ashgate, 2008).

12 Nāṣir Khusraw, *Knowledge and Liberation*, p.40.

13 Seipel, *Schätze der Kalifen*, cat. no.113, p.151; O'Kane, *Treasures of Islamic Art*, no.81; for the texts of the inscriptions, see David-Weill, *les bois à épigraphes*, for items 446 and 421.

14 Edmond Pauty, *Catalogue général du Musée arabe du Caire: les bois sculptés jusqu'a l'époque ayyoubide* (Cairo, 1931), plates. XXXIX and XLIV; Seipel, *Schätze der Kalifen*, cat. no.7, pp.79–80.

15 Ibid., cat. no.136, p.183.

16 Raya Shani, *A Monumental Manifestation of the Shī'ite Faith in late Twelfth-Century Iran: the Case of the Gunbad-i 'Alawyān, Hamadān* (Oxford, 1996). For a general survey, see the slightly antiquated book by Mitkhat Sagadatdinovich Bulatov, *Geometricheskaia Garmonizatsiia v Arkhitekture Sredneĭ Azii, IX–XV vv: Istoriko-Teoreticheskoe Issledovanie* (Moscow, 1988).

17 Peter J. Lu and Paul J. Steinhardt, 'Decagonal and Quasi-Crystalline Tilings in Medieval Islamic Architecture', *Science*, 315 (2007), pp.1106–1110.

Part 2: Pilgrimage and patronage

3

The Shiʿi shrines of Iraq

James W. Allan

The Shiʿi shrines of Iraq are rivalled only by the shrine of Imam Reza (ʿAli al-Rida) in Mashhad for their religious importance to the Shiʿi community.[1] Yet they are continually omitted from books on Islamic architecture, and it is virtually impossible to read about them in any Western language. In part, this is due to the long-standing harsh restrictions on and at times, hostility towards, Westerners visiting the shrines. But it is also due to the fact that the only books and articles that deal with them in detail by Suʿad Mahir, Muhammad Hasan Al Yasin, and Ibrahim al-Samarraʾi, are all in Arabic and are unavailable in most Western libraries.[2] The result is that few scholars or students are aware of the architectural development of the individual shrines, or their architectural importance. The initial objective of this essay is therefore to rectify this situation.

First, however, we must identify the Iraqi shrines. The shrine of the first Imam, ʿAli b. Abi Talib (d. 661), is at Najaf, south of Baghdad; that of the third Imam, al-Husayn (d. 680), at Karbala, south-west of Baghdad; those of the seventh and ninth Twelver Imams, Musa al-Kazim (d. 799) and Muhammad al-Jawad (d. 834), are at Kazimiyya in Baghdad itself (this shrine is also known as Kazimayn, 'the two Kazims'); and those of the tenth and eleventh Imams, ʿAli al-Hadi (d. 868; also known as ʿAli al-Naqi) and al-Hasan al-ʿAskari (d. 874), are at Samarra, to the north.[3]

Historic illustrations of the Iraqi shrines are few and far between. Not many travellers bothered to go near them, let alone draw what they saw. The German traveller, Carsten Niebuhr (d. 1815), ever enterprising, was one of the few, and in 1765 he made small drawings of Kazimayn and the shrine of Imam ʿAli at Najaf, together with that of the shrine of Imam Husayn at Karbala, which were subsequently included in his book. Unfortunately he does not seem to have gone inside the buildings.[4] Another source of information consists of the paintings of Matrakçi Nasuh, a historian, soldier, calligrapher and painter, who travelled with the army of Süleyman the Magnificent on his campaign against the Safavids in 1533–1536. He witnessed the conquest of Iraq by the Ottoman army and recorded what he saw of the monuments in pictorial form. His pictures provide a unique view of the shrines at Najaf and Karbala in the 16th century (fig.1), though sadly he does not seem to have visited Kazimayn, for his painting of that shrine is too sketchy to suggest he had actually seen it himself. The focus of this essay will be first on the architectural importance of the shrines, and then, following a brief excursus on shrine treasuries, it will turn to the patronage of the shrines.

Fig.1

Fig.1
Painting of the shrine of Imam Husayn at Karbala, by Matrakçi Nasuh, Istanbul, 1533–1536, Istanbul University Library, T.5964

Architectural elements

There are a number of distinct architectural elements in the buildings as they survive today: domed chambers, *īwāns* (barrel-vaulted halls), surrounding walls, minarets, porticos, halls and porches.[5] A domed chamber is at the heart of every shrine of a Shi'i Imam. In Arabic the dome is denoted by the word *qubba*. The earliest record of such a structure seems to be for the shrine of 'Ali at Najaf, which by the year 900 is known to have had a *qubba* (fig.2). Early in the 10th century we know that another magnificent *qubba* (dome) was constructed there, and this is described as having four doors – one presumably on each side. Perhaps we should imagine something along the lines of the well-known mausoleum of Isma'il the Samanid in Bukhara – a large cubical structure with four entryways and a central dome, dated to the 920s.[6] By the mid-10th century, the shrine at Samarra was also covered by a dome (fig.3). *Qubba*s were probably standard from around the year 1000 onwards.

The architectural term *īwān* refers to a barrel-vaulted space that is open at one end, often onto a courtyard. The earliest record of an *īwān* at a shrine comes from Kazimayn, in 1237–1238. The *īwān*s which survive today at the great Iraqi shrines, however, are all much later additions, like the Iwan al-'Ulama' at Najaf (fig.2) which is 16th-century Safavid.

Fig.3

In contrast, the earliest record of a minaret associated with an Imam's shrine comes from Mashhad, dated around the year 1000, which was built by Mahmud of Ghazna's governor of Khurasan, Abu'l-Fadl Suri. A mosque was built at much the same time, and the two may have been connected in purpose, but the Ghaznavid taste for commemorative minarets and towers makes the precise role of this particular example unclear. Just how confusing the relationship of minarets to shrines can be, is demonstrated by those at Kazimayn (fig.4). In 1058, a minaret as well as a mosque was included in a rebuilding, suggesting that the role of the minaret was defined by the presence of the mosque. However, in 1097 the Saljuq vizier, Majd al-Mulk, reconstructed Kazimayn with two minarets. Nearly a century later, in 1180, Kazimayn was rebuilt with several minarets. But in the Jalayirid rebuild of 1367–1368 it returned to two minarets. Subsequently, in 1508 the first Safavid ruler, Shah Isma'il I (*r.* 1501–1524), increased the number to four. And of course there were not only four large minarets but also four small ones rising from the corners of the roof.

Another important architectural element in the shrines is the *bahw*, the covered gallery, and a series of these might completely or partially surround a shrine's domed tomb chamber. A large *bahw* was included in the 1052–1053 rebuilding of Kazimayn, and in 1349–1350 there is record of the strengthening of the *bahw* in front of the shrine at

Fig.2

Fig.2
The shrine of Imam ʿAli at Najaf, showing the *qubba* in the centre and the Iwan al-ʿUlama' to its left

Fig.3
Gilded dome and minarets of the shrine of Imams ʿAli al-Hadi and al-Hasan al-ʿAskari, Samarra (before the 2006 bombing)

Samarra, so these halls have a long history. By the end of the Safavid period, all shrines probably had them. The lack of information about covered galleries in these buildings is tantalising, and good photographs are urgently needed. The importance of such covered galleries is clear from the 15th-century Dar al-Huffaz in the shrine at Mashhad (today overlaid with mirror-work), and in the magnificent covered galleries of the shrine of the Sufi master, Shah Ni'matullah Wali, in Mahan, Iran, built by Shah 'Abbas in the 17th century. Seen from inside, those in Mahan are some of the greatest examples of vaulted halls in the central Islamic lands, and give some idea of the beauty of the Safavid galleries that may once have surrounded some of the great Iraqi shrines.

Today the great shrines of Shi'ism all stand within walled enclosures (fig.5). Such enclosures go back to the 10th and 11th centuries, including: Samarra (944–945), Kazimayn (*circa* 950), and Karbala and Najaf (*circa* 1020). The purpose of such walls is rarely specified, but they would have had a number of important functions. First, they would have defined the sacred territory. Secondly, they would have provided protection against unwanted intruders or sectarian attacks – a point to which I shall return. Thirdly, they would have provided some defence, at least against flooding which was an annual problem in lower Iraq. It was a particular problem for Kazimayn, which was badly damaged or destroyed by floods at least five times in the space of 175 years between the years 1073 and 1249.[7]

Another architectural feature of the shrines of the Imams was the *riwāq*, an arcade or portico, which was probably introduced to act as a covered walkway around the inside of the enclosure walls, providing shade and shelter. Porticos, like the *bahws*, were probably added between the 10th and 12th centuries. Certainly, those at Samarra were built in 978–979, those at Karbala in the 10th century, and at Kazimayn in around the year 1180. A parallel may be provided by the porticos of the Friday Mosque in Na'in in Iran, which date from the 10th century. Today, the shrines are surrounded not by *riwāqs*, but by niches facing onto a courtyard with doorways at the back leading to rooms, called in Persian a *kunj*, which was very popular in the Safavid period. Such niches and rooms surround the sacred areas at Kazimayn, Karbala and Najaf.

The evidence cited suggests that, although shrines developed in a fairly haphazard way, by the time of the Mongol invasions in the mid-13th century, a form had indeed evolved. This consisted of a *qubba*, with perhaps porticos, covered galleries, minarets and *īwāns* – some or all of them, and in varying numbers, and the whole was set within a walled enclosure. However, this was by no means the end of the story, for four particular architectural or decorative features had not yet been developed. First, the gilding of domes, *īwāns* and minarets, which are outstanding features of most of the great Shi'i shrines today. The earliest example of architectural gilding appears to have been at Mashhad under the Safavid ruler, Shah Tahmasp (*r.* 1524–1576), in the 1530s. This

Fig.4

Fig.5

followed his successful third campaign against the Uzbeks in 1533. The immediate catalyst for the gilding of the dome appears to have been a dream in which Tahmasp saw Imam ʿAli, who asked him to build a dome like the one in Najaf. The significance of the golden dome, however, was greatly increased by Tahmasp's act of repentance the same year. This followed another dream, in which Mir Sayyid Muhammad, the preacher of Medina, ordered Tahmasp to repent for all his sins so that victories would be attained in his wars against the Uzbeks. After Tahmasp had made this act of repentance, and had come out of the war with the Uzbeks victorious, the golden dome probably became a symbol of the covenant between the Safavid dynasty and the Shiʿi Imams.[8]

The reference to Imam ʿAli asking Shah Tahmasp to build a dome like the one in Najaf is fascinating, because so far no other evidence has come to light to suggest that the dome at Najaf was already covered with gold by 1533. The only Islamic dome to have been gilded which would have still been standing at that period was that of the Dome of the Rock in Jerusalem, but even that, by the 16th century, had been changed, and was almost certainly leaded,[9] so the origin of the idea for gilding the dome at Mashhad is uncertain. The golden dome at Mashhad had a chequered history, due to looting and earthquakes, but it must have been the fashion setter. In 1743–1744 the Afsharid ruler, Nadir Shah (*r.* 1736–1747), replaced the tilework of the dome, *īwān* and minarets at Najaf with gilded copper plaques, and reconstructed and gilded Shah Tahmasp's minaret at Mashhad.

From then onwards gold became increasingly important in the Iraqi shrines. Karbala attracted the attention of the founder of the Qajar dynasty, Agha Muhammad Khan Qajar (*r.* 1786–1797), who had the dome and minarets covered in gold. On his death in 1797, his work was continued by his nephew and successor, Fath ʿAli Shah Qajar (*r.* 1797–1834), who used gold left over from Karbala to gild the two domes and the four small minarets at Kazimayn, a project completed in 1814, and he also regilded Karbala's dome after the Wahhabi looting of 1801. In 1868–1869, Nasir al-Din Shah was responsible for the gilding of the dome of the shrine of Imam al-ʿAskari at Samarra, which used some 72,000 tiles, and the minarets were also gilded. The gold left over from that work was used by his representative, Shaykh ʿAbd al-Husayn

Fig.4
Kazimayn, the shrine of Imams Musa al-Kazim and Muhammad al-Jawad, showing the two domes, the four minarets and one of the clock towers

Fig.5
Aerial view of Kazimayn showing the walled enclosure

Fig.6

al-Tehrani, to gild the large *īwān* at Kazimayn, a project which was finished in 1869. Hence the gilding of parts of the shrines was an ongoing process over a period of some three hundred years.

Another item which should be mentioned briefly is the clock tower. For example, Kazimayn has two (fig.4). In 1870–1871, the Persian vizier Dust Muhammad Khan visited the shrine and gave a clock, for which a tower above the east entrance was then built, completed in 1883–1884. In 1885–1886, however, a larger clock was donated by one Haj Muhammad Mahdi Abushahri, which was then set up over the south gate. Clock-towers were built all over the Middle East and the Indian sub-continent in the 19th and early 20th centuries, especially in the Ottoman Empire, where they were championed by Sultan Abdulhamid II (*r.* 1876–1909). At least 50 were built during this period in Anatolia. An early example is the Nusretiye clock tower in Istanbul, which dates from the reign of Sultan Abdulmecid I (*r.* 1823–1861) in the 1850s, but perhaps the most famous is the Dolmabahçe clock tower built between 1890–1895.[10]

More important, however, because they were not part of such an obvious fashion, were the platforms and porches. The platforms (*dikka*) are used as approaches to the mausoleums, and provide the base on which the second item, the porch (*ṭārima*) sits, and this combination of features is, like the gilding, one of the most striking elements in today's shrines. Both these items, however, are very late. At Kazimayn, the two platforms were not built until 1864–1865. In that year the first porch was constructed, the second followed in 1867–1869, and the third in 1903–1914. At Karbala, the porches are also to be dated to the second half of the 19th century. At Samarra the porches were not constructed until 1948–1949 and 1960–1961. The origin of these platforms and porches is uncertain. In Safavid and Qajar Iran we find the *tālār*, an external area featuring a flat roof supported by tall wooden columns that is open to the environs, often in a palatial setting (such as at the Chihil Sutun or the ʿAli Qapu palaces in Isfahan). This is also a tradition widespread in Central Asia, as for example in the 19th-century Hazrat Khyzr Mosque in Samarqand.[11]

Although today we have an image of what a Shiʿi shrine looks like, it is clear that in many ways the growth of the shrines as architectural complexes was haphazard. It was subject both to the prevailing style of contemporary architecture, and to the whims of individual patrons.

Shrine treasuries

The second topic to be introduced in this essay is the use of shrines as repositories of treasures, and as exhibition galleries where they could be displayed. The picture of the bier of Iskandar (Alexander the Great) from the Great Mongol Shahnama provides the best image from medieval Islamic times of the riches of a royal mausoleum, showing in particular the textiles, lamps and candlesticks that would have adorned such buildings (fig.6). The great Shiʿi shrines of Iraq would have been similarly adorned, and would almost certainly have shown off some or all of the following items. In woodwork there would have been cenotaphs, shutters and doors, either of carved wood or of marquetry (*khātam-kārī*). We know that fine examples were placed in Kazimayn by the first Safavid ruler, Shah Ismaʿil I, in 1519 and in Samarra by the last Safavid ruler Shah Sultan Husayn (*r.* 1694–1722) in 1687, who probably also installed new cenotaphs in Karbala.[12] Woodwork at the shrine of ʿAli in Najaf was apparently ordered by Jaʿfar Khan Zand who was the brother of the Persian dynastic ruler, Karim Khan Zand (*r.* 1750–1779).[13] The cenotaph which stands today in the mausoleum of Shah Ismaʿil I at Ardabil, dated 1524, uses ebony, jujube, citron and teak woods, ivory, camel and horse bone, shells, and moulded pieces of bronze and coloured metals, some gilded and some silvered, and gives a good idea of the amazing richness and intricacy of the carving and inlaying on such objects (fig.7).[14]

Textiles were major elements in the internal decoration of the shrines. First they would have been included as grave covers for the cenotaph. The shrine treasury of Imam ʿAli at Najaf contains a large number of superb complete or partial pieces: five velvet panels and five silk tomb covers of the Safavid period, an 18th-century silk panel and silk tomb cover, and six silk covers dating from the 17th and 18th centuries.[15] How precisely the panels were used remains unclear; of particular importance is one of the velvet panels, which dates from the

Fig.6
Iskandar's bier from the Great Mongol *Shāhnāma*, Iran, 1328–1336, Freer Gallery of Art, Smithsonian Institution, F1938.3

Fig.7
Cenotaph of Shah Ismaʿil I, Ardabil, 1524, showing wood-carving and inlay in a variety of wood, bone, shell and precious metals

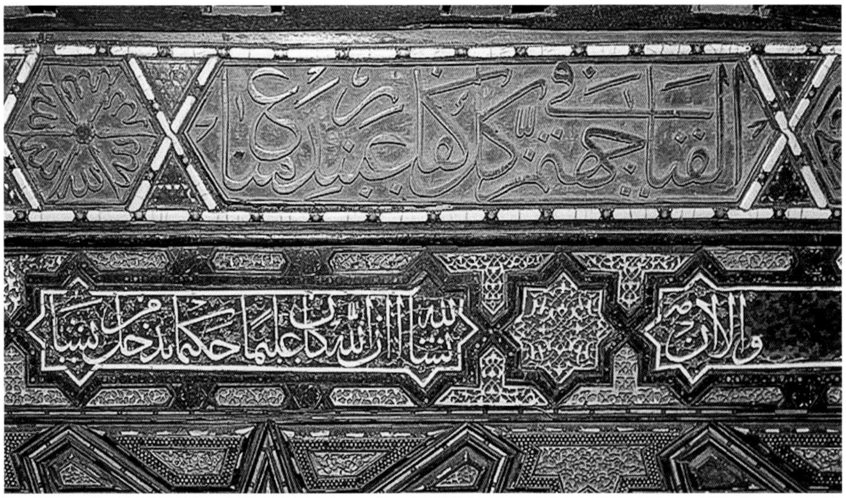

Fig.7

16th century.[16] It has a dark red ground and is decorated with gold and polychrome silk embroidery. Its central medallion, field medallions and border medallions contain a variety of figural designs, including a battle between a dragon and a phoenix, *peri*s (angels), horsemen, fantastical kylins, youths, musicians and foxes. Another panel of the late 16th or early 17th century is in fact one of a set of five, so there are considerably more than the catalogue suggests.[17]

Textiles were also used as hangings in the interiors. For example, the Hamdanid Nasir al-Dawla (d. 969) adorned the tomb of Imam Hasan al-ʿAskari in Samarra with curtains, while later in the century the Buyid ruler ʿAdud al-Dawla (d. 983) curtained the tomb with brocade.[18] So too, another Hamdanid, ʿAbdallah Abu'l-Hayja' (d. 929), decorated the shrine at Karbala with wonderful curtains.[19] In 1302, Ghazan, the Mongol Ilkhanid ruler (*r.* 1295–1304), visited Imam ʿAli's tomb at Najaf and hung with his own hands the curtains he had ordered for the shrine.[20] The shrine treasury in Najaf also contains two splendid Safavid hangings, both of which are dated.[21] One is inscribed with the name of the weaver, Ibn Qutb al-Din, and the date 1036 (i.e. 1626), and was donated 'by the slave of the Shah-e Velayat's Shrine, Muhammad ʿAli'. It is decorated with a landscape design within a niche, with trees and flowers, herons, clouds, water, fish and ducks (fig.8).[22] The second is dated 1129/1716–1717 and, according to Mehmet Aga-Oglu, contains a 'well-known saying referring to Imam ʿAli and his heroic deed at the "Battle of Khandaq" which was fought during the siege of al-Madinah in the year 627'.[23] The outstanding quality and sheer quantity of precious metal thread used point to a royal source of patronage for such pieces.

The shrine of ʿAli at Najaf also contains textile garments, in particular two talismanic jackets, both of which bear appropriate inscriptions – sections of the Qur'an, prayers, and/or the names of the Twelve Imams.[24] The reason for donating a garment to a shrine was presumably the original owner's gratitude for its effectiveness in warding off enemy arrows in battle. Another textile treasure from Najaf is a *ziyārat-nāma* (pilgrimage prayer plaque) dated 1870, which is adorned with a prayer to be said by a pilgrim by the cenotaph of Imam ʿAli.[25] It is decorated with pearls and a gold border.

Precious carpets would have once enriched the floors of all the shrines although the majority remain unpublished (and many were looted) apart from the carpets of the Najaf shrine treasury.[26] Among them is an enormous silk carpet, now in two parts, which must have been commissioned by Shah ʿAbbas the Great in the early 17th century:

Fig.8

Fig.9

Fig.8
Silk brocade hanging from the shrine of Imam ʿAli, Najaf, signed and dated 1036/1626 by the weaver

Fig.9
Gold tomb finial set with precious stones, 1531, from the Najaf shrine treasury

Fig.10
Painting of Imam ʿAli's shrine at Najaf, by Matrakçi Nasuh, Istanbul 1533–1536

its original size was 14.03 × 9.56 metres.[27] It is of silk, brocaded with silver and silver gilt thread, and has a crimson ground. An extremely close parallel is provided by the so-called Aberconway carpet fragment in the Victoria and Albert Museum.[28]

In metalwork, as we know from many historical texts, and as the image from the Great Mongol Shahnama shows (fig.6), silver and gold lamps would have been suspended from the ceiling, and candlesticks or torch stands would have stood on the floor. In the shrine of Imam ʿAli at Najaf there is, for example, a gold lamp which was presented in 945/1538–1539, and a gold lampstand which was a gift of ʿAli Murad Zand in 1197/1782–1783, and a gold lamp presented by a lady by the name of Najm al-Sultana in 1301/1883–1884.[29] In addition, tombs often seem to have been decorated at their four corners with precious metal tomb finials – a gold finial (fig.9), set with precious stones, dating from 1531, in the Najaf shrine treasury is almost certainly one of those to be seen in the painting of the shrine of Imam ʿAli by Matrakçi Nasuh (fig.10).[30] The quality of the Najaf tomb finial may be judged by comparing it to a silver and zinc bowl with gold filigree and precious stones, from the early 16th century, now in Topkapı Saray Museum.[31]

*Ziyārat-nāma*s (pilgrimage prayer plaques) were made to be hung beside the tomb, to help pilgrims recite a prayer for the peace upon the Imam and the *Ahl al-bayt*.[32] We have already mentioned a textile example, and the Najaf shrine also includes a gold *ziyārat-nāma* dated 1162 (i.e. 1749),[33] while a steel example from Karbala is in the Tanavoli collection.[34] Steel was also used for the *ʿalam*s (religious standards) that would be standing nearby for use in the annual Muharram processions, while the cenotaph itself would usually be surrounded by a steel *zarīḥ* or cage. A superb example of a pair of doors for such a cage dates from 1698–1699 and is signed by an Isfahani steelworker, Kamal al-Din Nazuk. It could well have been made for one of the Iraqi Shiʿi shrines, as we shall see below.[35]

All of these objects would have been seen, noted and admired by craftsmen and other pilgrims, and the fame of such objects in these shrines is indicated by the 13th-century geographer, Yaqut al-Rumi (d. 1229), who, in his *Dictionary of Learned Men*, records that the scholar Abu Hasan ʿAli b. ʿAbdallah b. Wasif al-Nashiʾi (d. 975–976), a poet of the family of the Prophet (*Ahl al-bayt*), was a master craftsman who worked in brass openwork, and that he had made a magnificent square lamp for the shrine at Kazimayn.[36] The fact that Yaqut knew about the lamp shows that it must have been well known and widely appreciated by pilgrims.

The ceremonies that accompanied the donation and installation of objects would have further heightened their fame. A rare record survives of the installation of new steel *zarīḥ*s at Kazimayn.[37] In around 1630, Shah ʿAbbas I apparently ordered one or more huge steel *zarīḥ*s to be made, presumably in the Safavid capital, Isfahan, and to be installed over the two wooden cenotaphs. This was in order to protect them against theft and plunder. Following the interrupting of diplomatic relations between the Safavids and Ottomans, transport of the *zarīḥ*s was delayed a long time and they finally arrived some 70 years later, in November 1703. They were accompanied by an Iranian delegation that included a large number of people of high religious rank, ministers and others, preceded by the Shaykh of Islam, Shaykh Jaʿfar al-Kamraʾi. After the installation of these steel *zarīḥ*s over the two graves there was a big celebration, which included thousands of Iranians and Iraqis.

The shrines of the Imams attracted gifts of the highest possible artistic quality and workmanship, and must have acted as public galleries

Fig.10

for them to be admired by visitors. Craftsmen who visited the shrines would have been challenged by seeing the quality of the objects shown in them, and inspired to excel themselves in producing even greater works of art. Hence, I believe that the shrines must have had a significant impact on the continuing production of the highest quality of works of art in Iraq and Iran.

Patronage

Now let us return to the patronage of the Iraqi shrines. That there were Shiʿi patrons of the shrines is to be expected, and we can easily cite a few of them. Most notable were the Hamdanids, the Buyids and the Safavids. Thus, for example, the Hamdanid, ʿAbdallah Abu'l-Hayja' (*r.* 905–929), constructed a magnificent *qubba* (dome) over Imam ʿAli's tomb,[38] while his Hamdanid successor, Nasir al-Dawla (*r.* 929–969), built a wall around the Samarra shrine.[39] Among the Buyids, Muʿizz al-Dawla (*r.* 945–967), rebuilt Kazimayn,[40] and built a dome over the shrine of Imam al-ʿAskari at Samarra in 948–949.[41] He, himself, was buried next to the tombs of the Imams Musa al-Kazim and Muhammad al-Jawad at Kazimayn, as were Jalal al-Dawla (d. 1044), Buyid viziers and other leading men of the period. The great Buyid ruler, ʿAdud al-Dawla (*r.* 978–983), was a patron of the tomb of Imam al-ʿAskari, and he chose to be buried at the mausoleum of Imam ʿAli at Najaf, as did other Buyid rulers.[42]

The Safavids are well known as patrons of the shrine of Imam Reza at Mashhad, but Shah Ismaʿil I (d. 1524) – and this fact seems rarely to be mentioned in Western literature – was also an important patron of the Iraqi shrines. In 1508 he made a pilgrimage to the holy sites of Iraq, where, to the shrine of ʿAli at Najaf, he gave 'excellent presents, and marvellous rarities, and on the residents of the town he bestowed honours and wondrous gifts'.[43] In the same year, he ordered new wooden cenotaphs for the shrines at Samarra and completed the tile mosaic there, which had been installed by the Jalayirids.[44] Most importantly, he completely rebuilt Kazimayn. This included the expansion of the *rawḍa* (the sacred precinct around the shrine), marble paving for the porticos, two new cenotaphs, the embellishing of the *mashhad* (the shrine itself) and its exterior with Qur'anic tiles and historical texts, four minarets to replace the two already there, a new large mosque on the south side of the *ḥaram* (sanctuary), the removal of the stables in the courtyard (presumably to provide uncluttered circulation space), and a suitable donation of furniture and lamps to furnish the shrine. The remains today include: a Qur'anic frieze around the inside of the *rawḍa*, finished in the year 1524, during Tahmasp's reign; a frieze on the outside of the eastern portico, finished in the year 1520; two wooden cenotaphs dated 1520; and three wooden *ḥaram* doors, now in the Museum.[45] It is clear from the work which Shah Ismaʿil initiated in Iraq that he saw the great shrines of the Imams there as a propaganda key to his politico-religious ambitions. The loss of them to the Ottomans was therefore a major blow, and explains the radical redirection of later Safavid architectural energy to the shrine of the eighth Imam, ʿAli al-Rida, in Mashhad.

Shiʿi patronage continued under the Qajars, but that has already been discussed in connection with the gilding of domes and minarets, and the building of platforms and porches, so now let us turn to Sunni rulers who patronised the shrines. Of course many Sunnis revered the Prophet's family, but such patronage is surprising when one considers the way in which sectarian strife could engulf the Sunni and Shiʿi communities in Iraq. Ibn al-Athir (d. 1233) provided a vivid description of such an event from Kazimayn in his grand annalistic history entitled *al-Kāmil*:

> In Safar of this year [443/beginning of July 1051] there was renewed trouble in Baghdad between the Sunnis and the Shiites, which was many times worse than it had been before...The reason for this rioting was that the men of Karkh had started to repair the Fishmongers' Gate and those in the Qalla'in to repair what remained of the Gate of Masʿud. When the inhabitants of Karkh had finished, they built some towers on which they inscribed in gold 'Muhammad and ʿAli are the best of men'. The Sunnis objected to this and claimed that the inscription [should be] 'Muhammad and ʿAli are the best of men. Whoever 'accepts' is a grateful believer, and whoever 'denies' is an unbelieving ingrate.'[46] The men of Karkh objected to the addition and said, 'We have not gone beyond our normal practice when we put an inscription on our mosques.'...so the fighting went on until the 3 Rabiʿ I [15 July 1051]. A Hashemite on the Sunni side was killed.

His family carried him on a bier around the Harbiyya and the Basra Gate and all the other Sunni quarters, and roused the people to take revenge. Later they buried him near Ahmad ibn Hanbal after a great crowd had gathered, many time larger than ever before.

Returning from the burial they made for the Shrine of the Straw Gate [i.e. Kazimayn]. Its gate was closed, but they dug holes in the wall and threatened the doorkeeper, who, in fright, opened the gate and in they came. They plundered the lamps, the gold and the silver prayer niches, the hangings etc., and stole what was in the tombs and chambers. Night fell and they went away. When morning came they gathered in numbers and marched on the Shrine. They set fire to all the tombs and vaults. Fire destroyed the tomb of Musa and that of his grandson, Muhammad ibn ʿAli, and the neighbourhood, and the two teak domes that covered the two shrines. The facing and adjacent tombs of the Buyid rulers, Muʿizz al-Dawla and Jalal al-Dawla, and of the viziers and leading men were burnt, as were the tombs of Jaʿfar, son of Jaʿfar al-Mansur, and the Emir Muhammad, son of al-Rashid, and of his mother, Zubayda. Nothing like this dreadful affair had ever been seen before.[47]

How was it, then, that Sunnis were among the major patrons of the shrines? Let us look briefly at two examples, first that of the later Abbasid caliphs, who, just before the Mongol invasions, emerge as patrons on a grand scale. Various rebuildings and repairs took place under Abbasid patronage, and it is striking to realise how much time and money was involved in this. The reason for the Abbasid involvement in the shrines lies in the policies of the caliph al-Nasir li-Din Allah (*r.* 1180–1225).[48] Al-Nasir, unlike his contemporaries Nur al-Din (*r.* 1146–1174) in Syria, and Salah al-Din (*r.* 1169–1193) in Syria and Egypt, was not concerned to unite Sunnism against Shiʿism: on the contrary, his aim was to bring these two major parts of Islam together, and to unite them under Abbasid caliphal authority. Indeed, in the words of one authority, 'al-Nasir's policy aimed at orienting and obligating all Muslims towards the caliphate as the sole spiritual and secular centre of this [post-Buyid and post-Saljuq] world.'[49] For this purpose, amongst other things, he enlisted the support of the influential Shafiʿi Sufi shaykh, Abu Hafs ʿUmar al-Suhrawardi (d. 1234), who advocated union between Sunnis and moderate Shiʿis. He also built close contact with Shiʿi *naqībs* (local leaders), and appointed Shiʿa as viziers and other high officials. His successors continued this policy, and his grandson al-Mustansir's madrasa in Baghdad was the first universal Sunni madrasa, serving the needs of all four *madhhabs* (schools of law).[50]

As a second example of Sunni patronage, let us turn to the Afsharid ruler of Iran, Nadir Shah (*r.* 1736–1747). In 1740–1741 Nadir Shah sent gifts to the shrine at Kazimayn, and his favourite wife, Radiyya Sultan Begum, daughter of the Safavid ruler Sultan Husayn, presented the shrine at Karbala with 20,000 *nādirī*s for building improvements on the occasion of her pilgrimage.[51] And then came all the gold which we have already mentioned: at Najaf, the replacement of the tilework of the dome, *īwān* and minarets with gilded copper plaques, and the reconstruction and gilding of Shah Tahmasp's minaret at Mashhad. So why was he, as a Sunni ruler, so determined to support the shrines? Nadir Shah's relationship with the Shiʿi shrines of Iraq seems to have gone hand in hand with his proposals for the religious reform of Iranian Shiʿism.[52] On taking the throne in 1736, he ordered the abandonment by the Shiʿa of two of the practices traditionally most offensive to Sunni sentiment – the ceremonial vilification of the caliphs Abu Bakr and ʿUmar, as well as other Companions of the Prophet, and the rejection of the legitimacy of the first three *al-Rāshidūn* caliphs ('rightly-guided caliphs', i.e. Abu Bakr, ʿUmar and ʿUthman). Shiʿism was to be reabsorbed into the main body of Islam as the fifth *madhhab*, or legal school, the Jaʿfari *madhhab*, named after the sixth Imam Jaʿfar al-Sadiq. In 1743 during his Iraqi campaign, Nadir Shah convened a meeting of Sunni and Shiʿi *ʿulamāʾ* (theologians) at Najaf to try and reconcile the two groups. Although this proved inconclusive, it was during this year that he had Najaf's tilework replaced with gold – an attempt, one assumes, to further his aims on the ground, as well as in his meetings with the rival theologians.

The last Abbasid caliphs and Nadir Shah had a common interest in trying to unite Islam, and therefore needed to draw in the Shiʿi community by patronising the Shiʿi shrines. The unification of Islam today seems a long way off – indeed there is little evidence that it is on the agenda of anyone in a position of power within the contemporary Islamic world. Is there hope for the future of the shrines in a multicultural

Iraq, an Iraq deeply divided between Sunnis and Shiʿis, an Iraq in which Samarra has already been dealt the sort of blow which, as we have already recounted, decided the fate of Kazimayn 950 years before?[53] If we can learn from the past, then perhaps it is the model of Sultan Süleyman the Magnificent (*r.* 1520–1566), and the Ottoman rulers of Iraq, to which we need to turn. For the Sunni Ottomans were also concerned for the well-being of the shrines, but Ottoman motives were essentially pragmatic. Süleyman the Magnificent, on capturing Baghdad in 1534, patronised the Sunni population by building a dome over the tomb of the great Sunni theologian and lawyer, Abu Hanifa (d. 767). In a similar vein, he patronised the Sufis by restoring the tomb of the founder of the Qadiriyya order, Shaykh ʿAbd al-Qadir al-Gilani (d. 1166). Finally, and most important from our perspective, he patronised the Shiʿa by ordering the completion of the shrine and mosque of Kazimayn, started by the Safavid Shah Ismaʿil I. Sultan Süleyman also made pilgrimages to the tombs of Imams ʿAli and Husayn, and in 1554 ordered the completion of the repairs at Najaf begun by Shah Ismaʿil, which had been left unfinished by the Ottoman defeat of the Safavids.[54] These activities suggest a desire to bring all the different Baghdadi communities on side, rather than a desire to impose any specific beliefs of the Ottoman Sultan. Perhaps it is here that the future lies: with rulers who are pragmatic and wise enough to see that power is best served by bringing on board the different communities through the patronage of their most precious monuments. May we live to see that day in Iraq.

1 This article is a greatly reduced version of sections of my book, *The Art and Architecture of Twelver Shiʿism: Iraq, Iran and the Indian Sub-Continent* (London, 2012). The reader is referred to this work for the full details.

2 Suʿad Mahir, *Mashhad al-Imām ʿAlī fī al-Najaf wa-mā bihi min al-hadāyā wa-al-tuḥaf*, 3 vols. (Cairo, 1969); Yunus Ibrahim al-Samarra'i, *Ta'rīkh madīnat Sāmarrā'*, vol.2 (Baghdad, 1971); Muhammad Hasan Al Yasin, *Tārīkh al-Mashhad al-Kaẓimī* (Baghdad, 1967); Muhammad Hasan Al Yasin, 'al-Mashhad al-kāẓimī fi'l-ʿaṣr al-ʿAbbāsī', *Sumer*, 18 (1962), pp.119–128; Muhammad Hasan Al Yasin, 'al-Mashhad al-kāẓimī min badīʿ iḥtilāl al-mughulī ilā nihāyat al-iḥtilāl al-ʿuthmānī', *Sumer*, 19 (1963), pp.155–170.

3 The eighth Imam, ʿAli al-Rida (d. 818), is buried in Mashhad; the twelfth Imam went into the major occultation in the year 940; the remaining Imams were buried in Medina, but their mausoleums were destroyed by the Wahhabis in 1806. See, Heinz Halm, *Shiism* (Edinburgh, 1991), p.145, n. 2.

4 Carsten Niebuhr, *Voyages en Arabie & en d'autres pays circonvoisins*, trans. F. L. Mourier, (Amsterdam and Utrecht, 1776–1780), vol.2, plate XLII.

5 References will not be given for every detail in the architectural section of this article. The reader is referred to Mahir, *Mashhad al-Imām ʿAlī*, for details of the history of the buildings in the shrine of ʿAli at Najaf and the article by Ernest Honigmann and Clifford E. Bosworth, 'al-Nadjaf', *EI2*, vol.7, pp.859–861; to the three publications by Al Yasin listed in note 2 for those at Kazimayn; to Arnold Nöldeke, *Das Heiligtum al-Husains zu Kerbelā* (Berlin, 1909); and to al-Samarra'i, *Ta'rīkh madīnat Sāmarrā'*, for those at Samarra. The history of the shrine at Mashhad is to be found in May Farhat, *Islamic Piety and Dynastic Legitimacy: the Case of the Shrine of ʿAli b. Musa al-Rida in Mashhad (10th–17th century)*, (Ph.D. dissertation, Harvard University, 2002).

6 Colour illustration on p.86 of this volume.

7 Flooding occurred in 1073–1074, 1159, 1163–1164, 1217, and 1248–1249.

8 Farhat, *Islamic Piety*, pp.123, 143–148.

9 Keppel Archibald Cameron Creswell, *Early Muslim Architecture: Umayyads, A.D. 622–750*, vol.1, part 1 (Oxford, 1969), pp.92–96.

10 Klaus Kreiser, 'Public monuments in Turkey and Egypt. 1840–1916', *Muqarnas*, 14 (1997), p.110; Kemal Özdemir, *Ottoman Clocks and Watches* (Istanbul, 1993), pp.200, 205.

11 Alexandre Papadopoulo, *Islam and Muslim Art* (London, 1980), plate 874; Galina Anatol'evna Pugachenkova, *A Museum in the Open* (Tashkent, 1981), plates 19, 78, 137.
12 For Shah Isma'il see Bashir Fransis and N. Naqshbandi, 'al-Āthār al-khashb fī dār al-āthār al-'arabiyya', *Sumer*, 5 (1949), pp.62–64. For Sultan Husayn see N. al-Naqshbandi, 'Ṣanādīq marāqid al-a'imma fī 'Irāq', *Sumer*, 6 (1950), pp.195–199.
13 al-Naqshbandi, 'Ṣanādīq marāqid', p.199.
14 James W. Allan, 'Early Safavid Metalwork', in Jon Thompson and Sheila R. Canby, ed., *Hunt for Paradise: Court Arts of Safavid Iran*, 1501–1576 (Milan and London, 2003), p.234 and plates 8, 26–27; Robert Hillenbrand, 'The Tomb of Shah Isma'il I at Ardabil', in Sheila R. Canby, ed., *Safavid Art and Architecture* (London, 2002), pp.3–8; and Robert Hillenbrand, 'The Sarcophagus of Shah Isma'il at Ardabil', in Andrew J. Newman, ed., *Society and Culture in the Early Modern Middle East: Studies on Iran in the Safavid Period* (Leiden and Boston, 2003), pp.165–190.
15 Mehmet Aga-Oglu, *Ṣafawid Rugs and Textiles: The Collection of the Shrine of Imām 'Alī at al-Najaf* (New York, 1941), nos XII–XVII, and XXI; and pp.33–41, plates vii–xxviii.
16 Ibid., plate vii and p.33.
17 Ibid., plate x and p.34.
18 al-Samarra'i, *Ta'rīkh madīnat Sāmarrā'*, vol.2, pp.117–118.
19 Nöldeke, *Das Heiligtum*, p.38.
20 Joseph F. von Hammer-Purgstall, *Geschichte der Ilchane, das ist der Mongolen in Persien* (Darmstadt, 1842–1843), vol.2, p.119.
21 Aga-Oglu, *Ṣafawid Rugs*, nos XVIII–XIX.
22 Ibid., plate XVIII and pp.36–37.
23 Ibid., plate XIX and p.38.
24 Mahir, *Mashhad al-Imām 'Alī*, plates 58–60.
25 Ibid., plate 89.
26 Aga-Oglu, *Ṣafawid Rugs*, nos I–VI.
27 Ibid., plate I.
28 Inv. no. T.36–1954. Aga-Oglu, *Ṣafawid Rugs*, fig.4; Ian Bennett, 'Isfahan "Strapwork" Carpets', *Hali*, 41 (1988), p.43; Sheila R. Canby, *Shah 'Abbas: The Remaking of Iran* (London, 2009), cat. no.121.
29 Mahir, *Mashhad al-Imām 'Alī*, plates 73–75.
30 Ibid., plates 84–85; Nasuh, Matrakçı. *Beyan-ı* menazil-*i sefer-i Irakeyn-i Sultan Süleyman Han. Nasuhü's-Silahi (Matrakçı); tıpkı basımı yayına haz.* Yurdaydın, H. G., ed., (Ankara, 1976), plates 58b, 64b.
31 Allan, 'Early Safavid Metalwork', p.204, plate 8.2.
32 For a steel *ziyārat-nāma* see James W. Allan and Brian Gilmour, *Persian Steel: The Tanavoli Collection* (Oxford, 2000), p.306; for a gold one and for a textile example see Mahir, *Mashhad al-Imām 'Alī*, plates 88–89.
33 Mahir, *Mashhad al-Imām 'Alī*, plate 88.
34 Allan and Gilmour, *Persian Steel*, pp.306.
35 Ibid., pp.290–292.
36 Yāqūt al-Rūmī, *The Irshād al-arīb ilā ma'rifat al-adīb, or Dictionary of Learned Men of Yāqūt*, David S. Margoliouth, ed., (London and Leiden, 1907–1927), vol.6, p.237.
37 Al Yasin, '*al-Mashhad al-kāẓimī*, 1963', pp.164–165.
38 Muḥammad b. Ḥawqal, *Configuration de la Terre. (Kitāb Ṣūrat al-Arḍ). Introduction et traduction, avec index, par J. H. Kramers et G. Wiet. Configuration de la Terre (Kitāb Ṣūrat al-Arḍ)*, trans. Johannes H. Kramers and Gaston Wiet (Beirut and Paris, 1964), p.232; text p.240.
39 al-Samarra'i, *Ta'rīkh madīnat Sāmarrā'*, vol.2, p.117.
40 Ibid., vol.2, p.117; Al Yasin, '*al-Mashhad al-kāẓimī*, 1962', p.122.
41 al-Samarra'i, *Ta'rīkh madīnat Sāmarrā'*, vol.2, p.117.
42 Ibid., vol.2, p.118.
43 Mahir, *Mashhad al-Imām 'Alī*, p.137.
44 al-Samarra'i, *Ta'rīkh madīnat Sāmarrā'*, vol.2, p.121.
45 Al Yasin, '*al-Mashhad al-kāẓimī*, 1963', pp.158–163.
46 Professor Wilferd Madelung has suggested to me that 'accepts' (*raḍiya*) is probably here being used in an absolute sense as the opposite of *rāfiḍa* (to reject), and that what is at issue is the historic order of the first four caliphs. It is nevertheless odd that the Sunnis accepted, if only for a while, the first part of the statement as it stands. In 1089 the Shi'a of Karkh district were obliged to accept a much less ambiguous Sunni inscription on their mosques. In the first half of the 14th century Ibn Baṭṭūṭa found Bedouin at al-Qutayf, who, as declared Rafidis, pronounced after the last *takbīr* of their prayer 'Muhammad and 'Ali are the best of men. Whoever disobeys them is an unbeliever'. Quoted by D. S. Richards in his translation and edition of, 'Izz al-Dīn b. al-Athīr, *The Annals of the Saljuq Turks: Selections from al-Kāmil fi'l-Ta'rīkh of 'Izz al-Dīn Ibn al-Athīr* (London, 2002), p.79, n. 38.
47 Ibn al-Athīr, *The Annals of the Saljuq Turks*, pp.79–81.
48 For his policies see Angelika Hartmann, 'al-Nāṣir Li-Dīn Allāh', *EI2*, vol.7, pp.996–1003.
49 Hartmann, 'al-Nāṣir', p.997.
50 Carole Hillenbrand, 'al-Mustanṣir'. *EI2*, vol.7, pp.727–729.
51 Ernest Honigmann, 'Karbalā'', *EI2*, vol.4, p.638.
52 Hamid Algar, 'Religious forces in Eighteenth- and Nineteenth-Century Iran', in *The Cambridge History of Iran*, vol.7, *From Nadir Shah to the Islamic Republic*, ed. Peter Avery, Gavin Hambly and Charles Melville (Cambridge, 1991), pp.706–710.
53 The Samarra shrine was bombed most recently in February 2006.
54 Gilles Veinstein, 'Süleymān', *EI2*, vol.9, p.834; Al Yasin, '*al-Mashhad al-kāẓimī*, 1963', p.164; see also 'Adnan 'A. Duri, 'Baghdād', *EI2*, vol.1, esp.pp.903–904.

4

Glorifying the Imamate: architecture and ritual in the Shiʿi shrines of Syria

Yasser Tabbaa

The past three decades have witnessed a substantial increase in the number of Shiʿi shrines in Syria coupled with an unprecedented surge in the number of visitors to these shrines (fig.1). In addition to their number, these shrines stand out for their flamboyant architectural style, which sharply contrasts with the overall drabness of their surroundings and even transgresses the rules and statutes that mandate a measure of conformity in buildings created within historical contexts. If anything, the showy presence of these shrines seems to have contributed to their huge popularity among Shiʿi pilgrims, Sunni visitors and non-Muslim tourists. This has turned the shrine of Sayyida Ruqayya into the second most visited religious structure in the walled city of Damascus, after the venerable Umayyad Mosque, and the shrine of Sayyida Zaynab, a few kilometres south, into a veritable pilgrimage city visited by hundreds of thousands every year.[1]

Just in the past 15 years or so, scholars have begun to recognise the unique opportunities and interesting problems presented by the study of Shiʿi shrines and the rituals of visitation in Syria. At a time when Iraq is all but closed to Western scholarship and Iran nearly so, the Syrian shrines were, until quite recently, completely open to non-Muslim visitors and quite accessible for study.[2] Their recent expansion or complete rebuilding, if not outright invention, often with Iranian funding, presents interesting problems in architecture, sectarian relations and even politics.[3] Their popularity among women pilgrims, including some Sunni women, also raises interesting sociological and gender issues, which have been discussed by historians and anthropologists (fig.2).[4] Their unprecedented expansion in Syria and Lebanon has also raised some acclaiming voices but many more voices of disapprobation. Finally, their use as arenas of Shiʿi rituals, from simple prayers and evocations to complex *taʿziya*s and ʿAshuraʾ celebrations, have equally attracted the attention of historians of religion.[5]

The problems and paradoxes raised by Shiʿi monuments in Syria require a different approach than has generally been deployed for Islamic architecture. Neither their rejection as garish intrusions upon the traditional urban fabric, nor their normalisation within a pan-Islamic discourse have contributed to a deeper understanding of their place within contemporary Islamic architecture and culture. In response to this pan-Islamist essentialist dogma, some scholars have recently called for questioning the value of interpretation in Islamic architecture unless supported by contemporary and specific textual

Fig.1

Fig.1
Shrine of Sayyida Zaynab, south of Damascus

Fig.2
Women touching the grille of the cenotaph at Sayyida Zaynab's shrine

Fig.3
Chart of the main tenets of Ithna ʿashari Shiʿism

Fig.2

evidence that directly refers to the monument at hand. Disavowing meaning and intentionality in Islamic architecture – Shiʿi architecture in particular – has led some scholars to conclude that there is nothing Shiʿi about Shiʿi architecture.[6]

But this unwarranted conclusion seems to be an answer to the wrong question, a question that is asked from a strictly formalist perspective rather than one that takes into account the culture of Shiʿism. In other words, what should be queried is not so much whether there are essential Shiʿi descriptors in Shiʿi architecture but if Shiʿi architecture, especially of shrines, responds or corresponds to the fundamental tenets of Shiʿism that are rooted in past practice but also alive in the present. It follows then that by viewing the uncommon forms, images and practices presented by these shrines as manifestations of their own system of representation we should be able, I believe, to gain a deeper understanding of their place within the cultural history of Shiʿism, generally and in Syria.

To that end, this essay attempts a phenomenological approach in which the Shiʿi shrines, particularly those in Syria, are examined against normative and widely accepted Shiʿi core beliefs and ritual practices. Of the core beliefs of Twelver Shiʿism, none is more central and foundational than the Imamate of the *Ahl al-bayt*, that is the belief in the secular and religious leadership of the successors of ʿAli and his male descendants through Fatima, the daughter of the Prophet Muhammad. These Imams, who are infallible (*maʿṣūm*) by definition, have been invested by God with *wilāya* (spiritual authority) and are due the *walā*ʾ (allegiance) and *walāya* (devotion) of the believers.[7] *Walāya*, in turn, is activated in real time by *ziyāra*, the ritual of visitation of the shrines of the Imams and their male and females descendants. The *ziyāra* both honours the Imams and achieves the purpose of *shafāʿa* and *tawassul* (intercession of the *Ahl al-bayt*). This *shafāʿa* is achieved, both physically and metaphorically, through the *nūr* or blissful radiance of the Imams, to which physical proximity is especially meritorious (fig.3).[8]

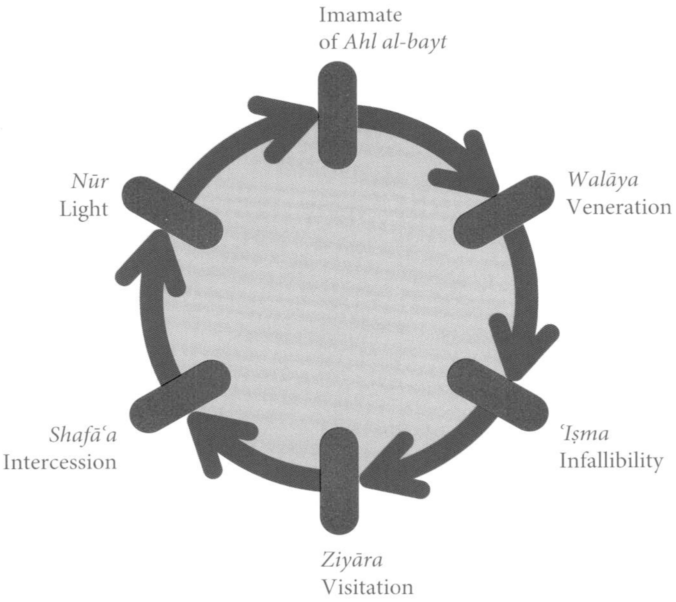

Fig.3

These central tenets of Shiʿism converge upon the shrine, the nexus of Shiʿi beliefs and the focus of most Shiʿi ritual practices, whether daily, weekly, or on high holidays. By viewing the architectural features of Shiʿi shrines in the light of these central tenets, I hope to demonstrate the various levels of interaction and integration between the two realms – religious and architectural – and even the mutually enriching process that links them together. Avoiding the potential cyclicality of this methodology, which could result from an overly stringent selection of evidence, I have aimed for a less selective and more comprehensive approach that aims toward a deeper appreciation of the meaning and intentionality of these shrines and a keener understanding of their differences and distinctions.[9]

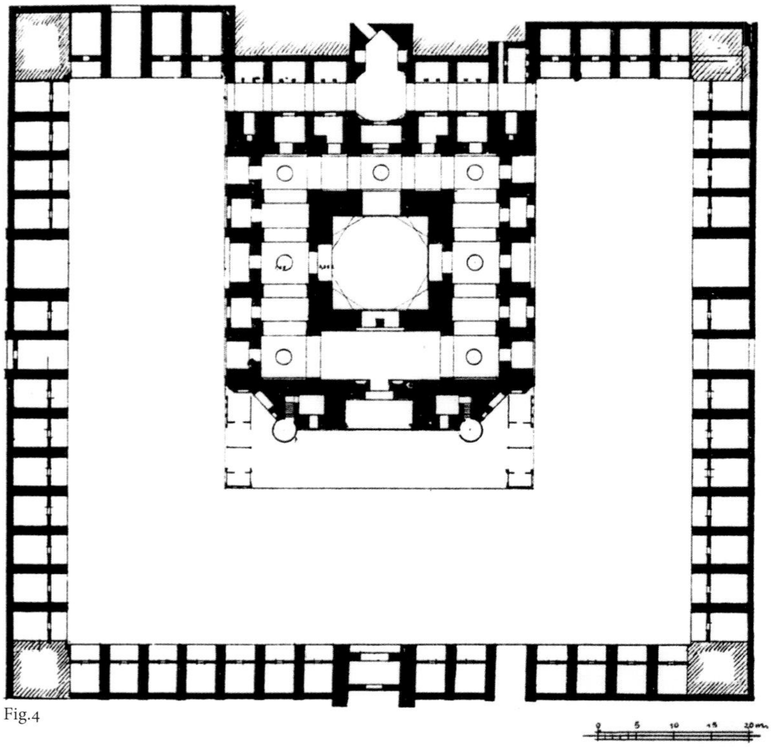
Fig.4

1. Commemoration of the Imamate of the *Ahl al-bayt*

Perhaps the most basic concept that underlies Shiʿi shrines is that they are not mosques but shrines, whose primary function is to commemorate an Imam or one of his descendants. Variably referred to in Arabic and Persian as *maqām, mashhad, marqad, mazār* or more rarely *ʿatabāt-i muqaddasa*, these shrines should be distinguished from mosques proper, whether a *masjid* (daily mosque) or *masjid jāmiʿ* (Friday mosque).[10] Although most Shiʿi shrines are used for prayer, and communal prayer is often held in them, their primary function is commemoration not prayer.

This rather obvious difference is actually quite significant for the architecture of these shrines, for communal prayer requires direction, whereas visitation calls for circumambulation. Thus, whereas mosques must be directed towards Mecca and are generally arrayed to allow for parallel rows of congregants, a shrine is primarily centred on the cenotaph, *dharīḥ* (Persian, *zarīḥ*), or spot of commemoration. This is not to say that the worshippers prostrate in the direction of the cenotaph – prayers must always be performed in the direction of Mecca – but rather that the predominantly commemorative function of these shrines has been accommodated within a centrifugal architectural design, focused on the *dharīḥ*.

In smaller and simpler shrines, which typically consist of a domed square, this directional tension is partly resolved by placing the cenotaph in the centre and including a mihrab (prayer niche) in the *qibla* wall, in such a manner that the *duʿā'* (supplications) pronounced for the 'saint' would not be confused with the prayer (*ṣalāt*) which is only due to God.[11] But in the larger and grander Shiʿi shrines that must accommodate thousands of visitors, this simple solution does not easily present itself. As a result, the plan for nearly all larger Shiʿi shrines abandons the directionality of mosques for a plan with multiple enclosed squares or rectangles that focus on the *dharīḥ* itself (fig.4). We find this plan in all the Iraqi shrines – Najaf, Karbala, Samarra, and Kazimayn in Baghdad – and, in a somewhat more additive form, in the great Iranian shrines of Qum and Mashhad.[12] The plan is also used in Syria for the shrine of Sayyida Zaynab, daughter of Imam ʿAli and sister of Imam Husayn, where the *dharīḥ* rests within a domed square sanctuary, which is surrounded by a spacious courtyard, itself enclosed by a ring of chambers pierced by axial entrances. At the more modest shrine of Sayyida Ruqayya, daughter of Imam Husayn, the plan is adapted to the restrictions of the triangular plot. But, even here, the architect has made an attempt to establish the precedence of the cenotaph by having it domed, surrounded by an ambulatory, and preceded by a spacious courtyard.[13]

Fig.4
Ground-plan of shrine of Imam ʿAli, Najaf

Fig.5
Men at the cenotaph of the shrine of Sayyida Zaynab

The centrality of the domed cenotaph in all Shiʿi shrines quite likely reflects the centrality of the Imam in Shiʿi theology and ritual practice. Expanding centripetally in a series of squares from the inner sanctum, the plan reflects and confirms the centrality of the Imam to Shiʿi belief and his blissful presence in the lives of the believers. In fact, the radiating sense of the design of the shrine seems to allude to the luminous essence of the Imams, the blissful light emitted by them till the end of time. We shall return to this point below.

2. *Wilāya/walāya* (authority/veneration) and *ziyāra* (visitation)

Veneration and visitation are spatially congruent as they take place at the shrine, often as near to the cenotaph as possible. The two concepts are also mutually consequent, for the ultimate objective of the *ziyāra* is the veneration or devotion (*walāya*) of the spiritual authority of the Imam, while the *wilāya* (authority) of the Imams mediates between humans and the transcendent God of Islam. A hadith attributed to the sixth Imam, Jaʿfar al-Sadiq, affirms, 'The sigh of the sorrowful for the wrong done to us is an act of praise of God, his sorrow for us is an act of worship, and his keeping of our secret is a struggle in the way of God.'[14] By visiting the shrines of the Imams, the faithful in effect 'share in the pains of the Imams, weep with them, and together with them wage a symbolic battle against the forces of evil.'[15] As a faith that rests on the remembrance and commemoration of the death and martyrdom of Shiʿi Imams and their various male and female descendants, Shiʿism has long sanctioned and recommended the visitation of the tombs of these holy figures.

Although this essay does not focus on Shiʿi ritual – which has been discussed in numerous publications – it unreservedly acknowledges the centrality and pivotal significance of ritual practices for understanding Shiʿi shrines. Indeed, a visit to any shrine on any day of the week will vividly illustrate the role of Shiʿi ritual in animating the spaces and surfaces of the shrine and in linking the worshipper to the living memory of the Imam. Alone or led by a guide, the visitors engage in physical and verbal rituals – including touching, rubbing, grabbing or even circumambulating the cenotaph; or reciting prescribed prayers and supplications (*duʿāʾ*) – that serve to enhance the *wilāya* of the Imam and to amplify the *walāya* of the worshipper to his presence (fig.5). All parts of the ritual are in fact fully described in little booklets, written in Arabic or Persian, at the entrance to the shrines, which also give a hagiography of the saint, the significance of the shrine, and the merits derived from the *ziyāra*.[16]

3. *Shafāʿa* and *tawassul* (intercession)

In addition to venerating the Imam and mourning his martyrdom, visitors to Shiʿi shrines also hope to derive spiritual or worldly benefit from the *shafāʿa* of the Imam or his descendant. Although intercession is often discussed in theological or sociological terms and quite correctly linked with the palliative and integrative function of ritual, this concept can also be examined through the shrines themselves, whose architecture, ornament and inscriptions can in fact highlight and deepen the experience of the visitors. By coming

Fig.5

Fig.6

into direct contact with the images and words in the shrines, the visitor is brought closer to the foundations of Shiʿism and to the memory of the venerated personage.

One of the main ways that Islamic architecture makes itself legible is of course through inscriptions, which are especially important in Shiʿi architecture. In fact, there is an embarrassment of epigraphic riches in all Shiʿi shrines, especially those of relatively recent construction or rebuilding, exceeding any comparable Sunni monument in the number, size and variety of their inscriptions. For example, in the relatively small shrine of Sayyida Ruqayya, inscriptional friezes crown all exterior walls and completely surround the courtyard; encircle the dome's exterior drum and its internal springing zone; highlight the portals and the cenotaph; and ornament the inner walls with numerous inscribed cartouches and medallions (fig.6).

Islamic architecture, particularly of earlier periods, has thrived on the study of inscriptions, seeking to find in them an epigraphic programme comparable in significance and intent to the iconographic programmes of Christian architecture.[17] This approach has yet to be applied to the study of Shiʿi shrines, including those of Syria, and this brief account is only a preliminary attempt in that direction. In terms of content, the inscriptions at the shrines of Sayyida Ruqayya and Sayyida Zaynab are of four types: (1) Qur'anic verses, (2) foundation and *waqf* (endowment) inscriptions, (3) hadith (4) and various invocations (*duʿā'*), of which a few are in Persian. The Qur'anic verses include some common verses, including the Throne Verse (2:255, *Āyat al-kursī*) and the Light Verse (24:35, *Āyat al-nūr*), found respectively on the outer drum and inner springing of the dome at Sayyida Ruqayya; and other somewhat less common short verses, including sura *al-Kawthar* (108, A River in Paradise), above the shrine's main entrance.

Despite their normative presence in many Islamic monuments, Shiʿi and Sunni alike, these verses are interpreted quite differently by Shiʿi theologians, most commonly by interceding the Imam between God and the worshipper. Twelver Shiʿism, which was strongly influenced by Ishraqi Sufism, generally interpreted the Light Verse as God's bestowing light upon Muhammad, Fatima and the Twelve Imams, who would guide humanity thereafter. Thus, the phrase '*nūrun ʿalā nūr*' or 'light upon light' was understood to mean 'Imam succeeding Imam', an interpretation that affirms the continuing role of the Imams in spreading God's wisdom and grace for future generations.[18]

Furthermore, these inscriptions also include Qur'anic verses that have historically been used predominantly in Shiʿi buildings. These verses, including 33:33 (from sura *al-Aḥzāb*) and 32:24 (from sura *al-Sajda*), refer to the *Ahl al-bayt*, emphasising their purity (*ṭahāra*) and their Imamate, or God-given right to lead the Muslim community.

Fig.6
Inscriptions on the shrine of Sayyida Ruqayya, Damascus

Fig.7
Qur'anic verse 28:5 from sura *al-Qaṣaṣ* inscribed in a frieze on the shrine of Sayyida Zaynab

Fig.8
Detail of a hadith referring to Imam ʿAli, inscribed on courtyard tiles at the shrine of Sayyida Ruqayya

One of the most frequent and evocative of these inscriptions is 28:5 (from sura *al-Qaṣaṣ*), which speaks of the reward of legitimate rule that God will bequeath upon those who have been oppressed in the world, an allusion that the Shiʿa have long believed refers to their own community (fig.7).[19]

Whereas the Qurʾanic verses have both a pan-Islamic sense and a specifically Shiʿi intent, the hadith selection in these shrines is exclusively Shiʿi in content and recension. At the Sayyida Ruqayya, these hadiths are generally presented within roundels or cartouches placed around the inner walls of the shrine and the arches and spandrels below the dome, surrounding the shrine like icons in an Orthodox church. Placed at eye-level and written in a reasonably legible calligraphic style, these inscriptions were meant to be read, or at least to reinforce the similar verbal exhortations repeatedly made by the various *khaṭībs* (who recite sermons or *khuṭbas*) in the shrine. Relatively rare in Sunni mosques and religious institutions, the abundance of hadith inscriptions in Shiʿi shrines not only identified the Shiʿi nature of the shrine but also contributed pietistic, theological and even polemical dimensions to its significance.

In terms of content, these hadith inscriptions emphatically reiterate the basic tenets of Twelver Shiʿism, including the *wilāya* (spiritual authority) of the Twelve Imams (fig.8); their rightful succession (fig.9); their *ʿiṣma* (infallibility) and *ṭahāra* (purity); and their *shafāʿa* (intercession) for the worshipper with God. Two examples of these hadiths, out of several dozens from the shrine of Sayyida Ruqayya, will hopefully illustrate their overall significance. As with all hadiths, both of these begin with 'the Prophet said' or 'the Messenger of God said', and some of the hadith inscribed in the shrine end by citing the reference of the hadith, such as Sulayman al-Qunduzi's (d. 1877) *Yanābīʿ al-mawadda* or Muhammad Baqir al-Majlisi's (d. 1699) *Biḥār al-anwār*. In the first example (fig.8) the hadith says: 'The Prophet said: He who has accepted ʿAli's authority (*walāʾ*) has accepted my authority and the authority of God'. The second hadith (fig.9) says: 'The Messenger of God said: My trustees after me are twelve, the first of whom is ʿAli and the last is al-Qaʾim, and he [the Prophet] said al-Mahdi, of the descendants of Fatima'. Here, the latter inscription also includes the source of the hadith as *Yanābīʿ al-mawadda*.

In addition to their specific intent and purposeful location within the monument, these inscriptions, by their sheer number and length, may also suggest a more generalised intention. In other words, this overabundance of inscriptions – amounting in the shrine of Sayyida Zaynab and all the main Iraqi and Iranian shrines to hundreds of metres in length – may not have been used for its specific significance but rather to beautify and sanctify every portion of the shrine while also immersing the worshipper in the divine presence. Being surrounded by Qurʾan and hadith inscriptions also emphasises the active presence of God in the world through the mediation of His words and the example of the Imams.

4. *Nūr* (radiance of the Imams)

All Shiʿi Imams are said to be possessed with a divine light, a blissful illumination that has been imbued within them since eternity by God and that continues to radiate from their shrines. In a well-known hadith, Imam Husayn describes the Imams as 'silhouettes of light revolving around the throne of the All Merciful', attesting to the firmly held belief in the blissful light (*nūr*) that emanates from the Fourteen

Fig.7

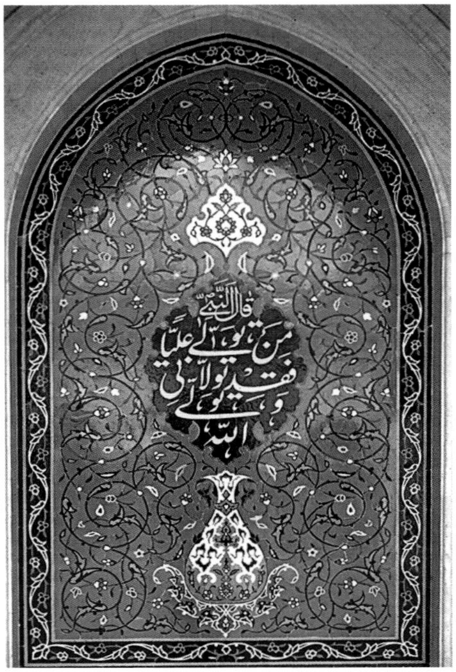

Fig.8

Fig.9

Infallibles: Prophet Muhammad, Fatima and the Twelve Imams.[20] Although there are some tantalising examples of a visual iconography of light in some medieval Islamic monuments,[21] it is only in the Safavid and Qajar periods that a consistent cosmology and iconography of light is developed, creating comprehensive and saturating luminescent interiors, largely dominated by domes.[22]

Since complete Safavid domes with radiant patterns are quite rare and non-existent outside Iran, the following will focus exclusively on the most typical and striking ornamental techniques in all Shiʿi shrines, namely mirror-glass mosaic or *āʾīna-kārī*. Briefly, this showy ornamental technique was first used as early as the late 17th century in some Safavid palaces, where mirror-glass fragments were inserted among the geometric and *muqarnas* (honeycomb) wall decoration.[23] But it is only in the 19th century that this technique was applied quite densely and comprehensively to the interior of the domes of Shiʿi shrines, becoming so popular that even earlier tiled domes were apparently torn down and resurfaced with mirror-glass mosaic.

The Syrian shrines of Sayyida Ruqayya and Sayyida Zaynab – and even some of the smaller ones in Darayya, Raqqa and Baalbek – are no different. Polychrome tiles, gilt and enamelled doors, and faceted mirror-work cover every surface of these buildings (fig.10). A peak of excess is reached in the massive cenotaph, invariably made as a silver grille, crowned by a lavishly decorated baldachin, and sheltered by a stupendous *muqarnas* dome inlaid with mirror-glass mosaic. More than reflecting or even fracturing images or forms, the mirror mosaic seems to radiate with an inner glow, even in the dimly lit interiors, quite likely a metaphor of the eternal radiance of the Imam (fig.11).

The combined effect of the constant prayers, forceful inscriptions, and brilliant ornament create an immersive atmosphere of luxury and directness, of sacred texts made accessible through the mediation of

Fig.9
Detail of a hadith referring to the succession of the Twelve Imams, inscribed on tiles near the cenotaph inside the shrine of Sayyida Ruqayya

Fig.10
Mirror-glass mosaic work (*āʾīna-kārī*) in the dome of the shrine of Sayyida Ruqayya

Fig.11
Dome with mirror-glass mosaic at the shrine of Sukaina bint al-Husayn, Darayya, Syria

Fig.10

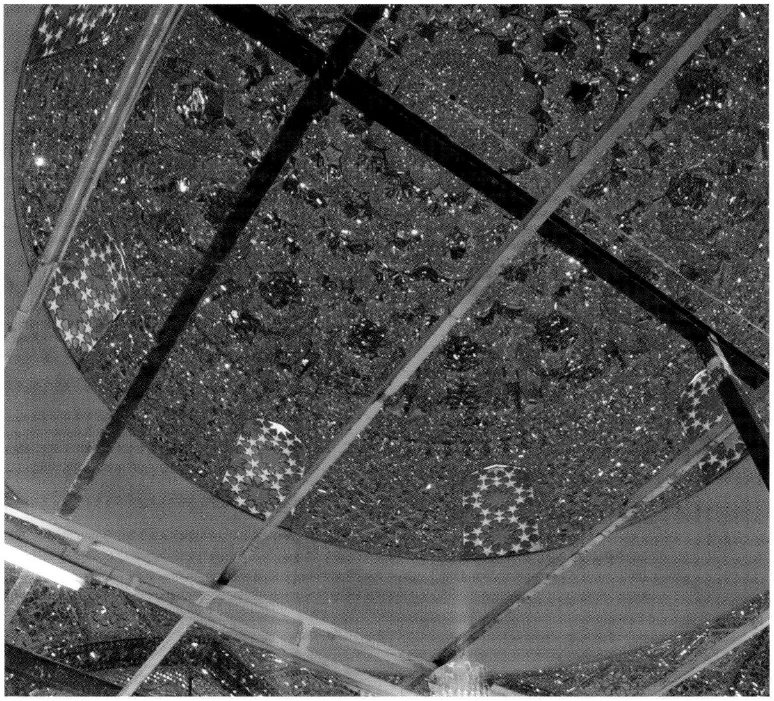

Fig.11

ornament. It is a specifically Shiʿi sense of decorum, in which the Word of God and the traditions of the Imams are infused with colourful and sparkling patterns, much like the cenotaphs of the Imams during the ʿAshura' processions are covered in brilliant silks and satins.[24] The ultimate objective of these multiple visual and aural stimuli is not quite transcendence, as it would be for Sufism, but rather total immersion in the presence of the Imams; proximity to their radiant essence; and the glorification of their memory.

Conclusion

This essay has attempted to discuss Shiʿi shrines – mainly in Syria but in other regions as well – from a phenomenological perspective, exploring the various ways that the central tenets of the faith were reflected, affirmed and even amplified by the most salient and significant feature of these shrines. Viewing the architecture of Shiʿi shrines through the lens of Shiʿi core beliefs and ritual practices, the essay has highlighted the dynamic interplay between these religious concepts and architectural and ornamental forms. Rather than insisting on essential Shiʿi features in the architecture of Shiʿism, or dismissing them thereof, this paper has sought to envisage Shiʿi shrines – in their plan, design, ornament and inscriptions – within a discursive relationship with Shiʿi concepts and principles. As such, the architecture of Shiʿism emerges, in Syria and elsewhere, not as an aggregate of imported Iranian features, but one whose significant features reflect and amplify the main tenets of Shiʿism.

If there is a single overriding theme that would bring together the architectural, ornamental, epigraphic, and ritualistic aspects of Shiʿi shrines, it is perhaps immersion and saturation. From the moment worshippers enter the shrine, they are engulfed by images, words, sounds, and even scents and textures, that transform their sense of place and time and deepen their sense of belonging. Their journey is neither personal nor transcendent but communal and immersive, leading to the presence of the Imam.

1 This is not based on a scientific survey but on direct observation over several years of the huge number of pilgrims visiting this shrine. It is also based on the presence of the Sayyida Ruqayya shrine on all online tourist itineraries to Syria, whether for religious tourism or otherwise.

2 Unfortunately, the current state of insurgency and civic unrest in Syria makes it all but impossible to conduct research in it for some time to come.

3 See Yasser Tabbaa, 'Invented Pieties: The Revival and Rebuilding of Shi'ite Shrines in Contemporary Syria', in Linda Komaroff, ed., *Artibus Asiae* (special issue, *Festschrift for Priscilla Soucek*), 66 (2006), pp.142–171, for an assessment of the overall phenomenon and a more in-depth discussion of the shrine of Sayyida Ruqayya. This article also proposes that the earlier political rhetoric of the Iranian Revolution, which contributed to the creation and expansion of this shrine, has now given way to a more generalised Shi'i piety that has found wide pan-sectarian appeal.

4 These include Sabrina Mervin, 'Sayyida Zaynab: banlieue de Damas ou nouvelle ville sainte chiite?', *Cahiers d'Etudes sur la Méditerranée Orientale et le monde Turco-Iranien*, 22 (1996), pp.149–162; and Irène Calzoni, 'Shiite Mausoleums in Syria with Particular Reference to Sayyida Zaynab Mausoleum', in Biancamaria Scarcia Amoretti, ed., *La Shi'a nell'impero Ottomano. Roma 15 April 1991* (Rome, 1993), pp.193–201.

5 Khalid Sindawi, 'The Zaynabiyya *Hawza* in Damascus and its Role in Shi'i Religious Instruction', *Middle Eastern Studies*, 45, 6 (2009), pp.859–879; and Khalid Sindawi, 'The Shiite Turn in Syria', *Current Trends in Islamist Ideology*, 8 (2009), pp.82–107.

6 See, for example, Jonathan Bloom, *Arts of the City Victorious: Islamic Art and Architecture in Fatimid North Africa and Egypt* (New Haven, CT, and London, 2007), whose interpretive reticence counters the author's earlier explorations of meaning in Fatimid architecture, including his article, 'The Mosque of al-Hakim in Cairo', *Muqarnas*, 1 (1983), pp.15–36.

7 For an explanation of the terms *wilāya* and *walāya* in Sunni and Shi'i contexts see, Mawil Y. Izzi Dien and Paul E. Walker, 'Wilāya', *EI2*, vol.11, pp.208–209; and Maria Massi Dakake, *The Charismatic Community: Shi'ite Identity in Early Islam* (Albany, NY, 2007). On the institution of *walā'* see, Patricia Crone and Arent Jan Wensinck, 'Mawlā', *EI2*, vol.6, pp.874–882.

8 Entire books have been written on any one of these Shi'i tenets and ritual practices. Nearly all are discussed in Mohammad Ali Amir-Moezzi, *The Spirituality of Shi'i Islam: Beliefs and Practices* (London, 2011). For light, see Mullā Ṣadrā Shīrāzī, *On the Hermeneutics of the Light Verse in the Qur'ān: Tafsīr āyat al-nūr*, ed. Latimah-Parvin Peerwani (London, 2004).

9 The author intends to apply the basic methodology used in this paper to a book-length study of Shi'i shrines in the Arab world and Iran.

10 Robert Hillenbrand suggests that the multiplicity of terms for the mausoleum might be due to the fact that 'the role of the mausoleum in Islamic society was not defined with any precision.' Robert Hillenbrand, *Islamic Architecture: Form, Function and* Meaning (Edinburgh and New York, 1994), pp.255–257.

11 This commonplace design can be found in numerous small shrines, including many published in Hillenbrand, *Islamic Architecture*, pp.256–297. In fact, it seems that the elaboration of the mausoleum into a veritable shrine, with preceding courtyards and ancillary chambers, does not begin before the Mongol or even Timurid periods.

12 For plans of these shrines, see most recently James W. Allan, *The Art and Architecture of Twelver Shi'ism: Iraq, Iran and the Indian Subcontinent* (London, 2012). Allan has also argued that the courtyard surrounding the dome, which he calls the *bahw*, is known from perhaps as early as the 12th century.

13 Prayer halls (*muṣallās*) do exist in all these shrines, but the space dedicated for communal prayer tends to be either the courtyard around the shrine or a sequestered space, as in the Sayyida Ruqayya. This could in fact be related to the contested views on the Friday congregational prayer in Shi'ism, with Usuli and Akhbari legal schools taking different positions on it. For example, Juan Cole proposes that 'many Shi'i ulama held Friday congregational prayer invalid in the absence of the Twelfth Imam.' See, Juan R. Cole, *Roots of North Indian Shi'ism in Iran and Iraq: Religion and State in Awadh, 1722–1859* (Berkeley, CA, 1988), p.20.

14 Mahmoud M. Ayoub, *Redemptive Suffering in Islam: A Study of Devotional Aspects of 'Āshūrā in Twlever Shī'ism* (Berlin, 1978), p.142.

15 Yann Richard, *Shi'ite Islam: Polity, Ideology, and Creed*, trans. Antonia Nevill (Oxford, 1995), p.11.

16 Much of the information in these booklets appears to be derived from various ritual compendiums, of which the most popular is Shaykh 'Abbās al-Qummī (d. 1941), *Mafātīḥ al-jinān: wa yalīhi kitāb al-bāqīyāt al-ṣāliḥāt* (Beirut, 2011), long known in Persian, but recently translated into Arabic.

17 The paradigm for this methodology is quite likely Oleg Grabar's, 'The Umayyad Dome of the Rock in Jerusalem', *Ars Orientalis*, 3 (1959), pp.65–85.

18 See below, note 19.

19 See, for example, Jonathan Bloom, 'The Mosque of al-Hakim in Cairo', pp.15–36.

20 Much has been written on the integration of Ishraqi Neoplatonist philosophy with Imami Shi'ism, particularly in the Safavid period. See, for example, William C. Chittick, ed., *The Essential Seyyed Hossein Nasr* (Bloomington, IN, 2007), pp.111–119; and Amir-Moezzi, *Spirituality of Shi'i Islam*, pp.133–168.

21 These include the facade of al-Aqmar Mosque in Cairo (built in 1125); the portal with a frieze of lamps at the Mashhad al-Husayn in Aleppo (late 12th century); and even the star-and-cross lustre tiles in various Iranian shrines, which at least one prominent scholar has linked with Shi'i shrines. See, Oliver Watson, 'The Masjid-i 'Alī, Quhrūd: An Architectural and Epigraphic Survey', *British Institute of Persian Studies*, 13 (1975), pp.59–74.

22 The iconography of light in Shi'i architecture, the subject of a current study by the present author, has not been adequately studied nor distinguished from more general studies of the iconography of light in Islamic architecture. See, for example, Doris Behrens-Abouseif, *Beauty in Arabic Culture* (Princeton, NJ, 1999), pp.197–200, where the author largely dismisses any meaning or symbolism in Islamic art, including light.

23 Little work has been done on Iranian mirror-glass mosaic. Eleanor G. Sims, 'Ā'īna-kārī', *EIR*, vol.7, pp.692–694.

24 See, for example, Kamran S. Aghaie, *The Martyrs of Karbala: Shi'i Symbols and Rituals in Modern Iran* (Seattle, WA, and London, 2004).

5

Evanescent meaning: the place of Shiʿism in Fatimid mosques

Jonathan Bloom

The Fatimids, who claimed direct descent from the Prophet Muhammad through his daughter Fatima, were the most successful Shiʿi dynasty of the Islamic middle ages. In 909 the Fatimid leader wrested power from the Aghlabids, who had governed North Africa for the Abbasids, and established his rule in Kairouan. He and his successors established new capitals at Mahdia on the coast and at Sabra-Mansuriyya near Kairouan, but in 973 the caliphs moved to a new capital city in Egypt, whence they quickly but temporarily gained control of Syria and the Hijaz. The two centuries of Fatimid rule in Egypt played out against a series of succession crises and an ever-diminishing realm, so that when Saladin extinguished the dynasty in 1171, the Imam-caliph was barely recognised beyond Cairo and the surrounding region.[1]

An unusually large number of large and small Fatimid mosques survive in whole or in part from North Africa, Egypt and Syria, while still others are known from the chronicles, histories, geographies, and topographies that enrich our knowledge of Fatimid history.[2] Over the past few decades, many authors have endeavoured to see particular Shiʿi messages encoded in the stones from which Fatimid mosques were built, but after several decades of studying Fatimid architecture and art, I am less convinced of a specifically Fatimid iconography than I once was. Furthermore, some scholars have been led by their relative unfamiliarity with the broad range of Islamic architecture and its decoration outside Fatimid Egypt to conclude erroneously that certain features of Fatimid architecture are unique.

Fatimid history – and architecture – spanned two and a half centuries in North Africa and Egypt, so it is simplistic to think that an early Fatimid mosque in North Africa responded to the same needs as did a late Fatimid mosque in Cairo. Furthermore virtually all Fatimid mosques – in North Africa and in Egypt – have been extensively restored or rebuilt in the 20th century with varying degrees of fidelity to the original Fatimid structures.

Upon the proclamation of the Imamate-Caliphate in 909, the new Fatimid rulers of North Africa continued to use the congregational mosque of Kairouan, which the Aghlabid rulers had built on the typical Abbasid model in several stages over the course of the ninth century. In 921, al-Mahdi, the first Fatimid ruler, moved to his new capital city, Mahdia, which he had ordered built on a peninsula jutting into the Mediterranean sea halfway between the cities of Sousse and Sfax. The mosque at Mahdia is one of two Fatimid structures to remain at the site, although it was largely dismantled and rebuilt in the 1960s according to the excavators' best interpretations of the original Fatimid remains.[3] Measuring approximately 55 × 75 metres, the mosque is a stone building comprising a roughly square courtyard preceding a rectangular prayer hall. The Fatimid prayer hall, which had already collapsed and been rebuilt in the medieval period, had a central aisle supported on doubled columns leading to a dome in front of the mihrab (prayer niche); the dome was supported on fluted piers. All of these features – the doubled supports along the axial aisle, the dome over the mihrab, and the arcades perpendicular to the *qibla* (direction of prayer) – are directly modelled on the congregational mosque at Kairouan, but the most notable feature of the Kairouan mosque, the massive minaret opposite the *qibla*, was replaced by a massive projecting portal modelled on the design of a Roman triumphal arch, of a type that still stands in the Tunisian countryside (fig.1).[4] Considering the long tradition of Aghlabid monumental inscriptions in North Africa and the Fatimids' demonstrated interest in monumental inscriptions,[5] it is indeed surprising that this structure was nowhere inscribed, although the repeated destruction of the prayer hall and complete reconstruction in the 1960s may have obliterated any traces of inscriptions on the interior.

Nothing at all remains of the second Fatimid mosque, which the third Imam-caliph, al-Mansur, is known to have erected at his capital

Fig.1

Fig.2

known as Sabra or al-Mansuriyya, which he built outside of Kairouan in 946. A unique report states that the mosque there was called *al-Azhar*, 'luminous' or 'radiant,' which would be the name by which the first Fatimid mosque in Egypt would eventually come to be known.[6] The Egyptian al-Azhar mosque (fig.2) was begun in 970, nine months after the Fatimid general Jawhar began constructing the new Fatimid settlement in Egypt, for the Fatimid troops had used the city's pre-existing congregational mosques – the mosque of ʿAmr and the mosque of Ibn Tulun – in the interim, although some friction developed between the largely Sunni Egyptians and the Shiʿi immigrants over such matters as the formulas used in the call to prayer. In size, proportions, materials of construction, and decoration, al-Azhar fits nicely into Egyptian building traditions going back to the mosque of ʿAmr, suggesting that foreign workers were not involved in its construction. Reused antique columns, capitals and bases retrieved from some antique buildings supported arcades parallel to the *qibla* wall, which in turn supported the roof.[7] The original Fatimid mosque has been encased both inside and out in later constructions, so the Fatimid core is visible in only a very few places. Several of the interior walls, particularly those along the central aisle and along the left-hand side, as well as the mihrab hood, preserve Fatimid-era carved stucco-work bearing vegetal designs outlined with bands of Qurʾanic inscriptions. Al-Maqrizi wrote of a royal balcony (*manẓara*) in the east corner of the prayer hall from which the Imam-caliph could watch what was happening in the

Fig.1
Portal of the mosque of al-Mahdi,
Mahdia, Tunisia, 921

Fig.2.
Interior of the mosque of al-Azhar,
Cairo, 970 and later

Fig.3
Courtyard (after 1980s restoration),
mosque of al-Hakim, Cairo, 990–1013

mosque.[8] Some 150 years later, the Imam-caliph al-Hafiz ordered the court of the mosque lined with an arcade culminating in a domed pavilion, called a *maqṣūra* in the sources, at the entrance to the prayer hall. The interior of the dome is decorated with Qur'anic inscriptions, but its function remains unclear.[9]

A few years after al-Azhar, Durzan, a consort of the Imam-caliph al-Mu'izz and mother of the future Imam-caliph al-'Aziz, ordered the construction of a mosque 'in the style of' al-Azhar. Located in the Qarafa district to the south of Fatimid Cairo and to the east of Fustat, the mosque is known only from an extensive description preserved by al-Maqrizi.[10] The mosque had extraordinary carved and painted decoration on the interior, which prompted al-Maqrizi to compose a famous excursus about a contest between painters.[11] In the absence of any monumental evidence, the debates about the mosque's form now seem rather pointless, but the larger question remains why was this mosque built there?

The largest Fatimid mosque (fig.3) was completed in 1013 by the Imam-caliph al-Hakim, after whom it is known.[12] Begun by his father al-'Aziz in 990 just outside the northern city wall, it measures approximately 120 × 113 metres, or nearly two and a half times larger than al-Azhar. The outer walls, which were largely built of rough-cut stone, were completed in 1002–1003, according to the inscriptions on the facade, while the interior, of brick covered with plaster, was finished later. The facade comprises a monumental projecting portal covered with bands of epigraphic, vegetal and geometric decoration, as well as towers at either end. There are domes at the lateral corners of the prayer hall along the *qibla* wall, a feature unique to this mosque. Al-Hakim's son, al-Zahir (*r.* 1020-1035) added an extension (*ziyāda*) for ablutions to the south of the mosque,[13] and in later years the mosque was incorporated within Badr al-Jamali's walls protecting the city.[14]

Some early Fatimid mosques, however, were very small. For example, in 1015-1016, the Imam-caliph al-Hakim ordered the restoration of the Lu'lu'a (pearl) mosque in the Qarafa district. Each room once contained a mihrab flanked by small windows, but in later centuries the ground around the building was quarried for its stone. According to Ibn al-Zayyat's medieval pilgrimage guide, the mosque was celebrated for the granting of prayers said there.[15] While most Fatimid architectural patronage was focused in the capital city of Cairo, the Fatimids are also known to have restored the al-Aqsa mosque in Jerusalem during the first half of the 11th century, but it has been very difficult to determine exactly what they did, for all Fatimid-era constructions were substantially transformed after the Crusaders took the city in 1099. Following the 1034–1035 earthquake, the Imam-caliph al-Zahir ordered the Aqsa mosque reconfigured and reduced in size from its earlier state.[16]

During and following the long reign of al-Zahir's son al-Mustansir (*r.* 1036–1094), a series of famines, civil disturbances, and succession crises led to the transformation of Fatimid rule, as the once-powerful Imam-caliphs lost authority to increasingly dominant viziers. Patrons did not

Fig.3

have (or chose not to spend) the money to build big congregational mosques, particularly since there were several large ones – whether Fatimid or pre-Fatimid – already in Cairo and Fustat, and the famines and disturbances would have reduced the population using them. Nevertheless, several viziers and at least one Imam-caliph are known to have constructed relatively modest mosques in the capital or in provincial cities.[17] Al-Mustansir's vizier, Badr al-Jamali, ordered a celebrated *minbar* (pulpit) for the shrine of Imam Husayn at Ascalon, which was subsequently moved to Hebron, and Badr's son al-Afdal ordered a stucco mihrab for the mosque of Ibn Tulun. In 1081–1082, a high Fatimid official, Fakhr al-Mulk Sa'd al-Dawla Sartakin, erected a tower next to the mosque at Isna, a town further up the Nile.[18]

Badr al-Jamali is perhaps best known for constructing an intriguing yet remarkably inaccessible structure on top of the Muqattam hills overlooking Cairo and its cemeteries in 1085, two years before he began work on the city's defences. The entrance is surmounted by a tower and flanked by a room containing a cistern and another containing a stair; a small courtyard follows flanked by vaulted rooms and leads to a sanctuary of six vaulted bays, of which the one over the mihrab is covered by a high dome. The interior is quite plain, except for an exquisite stucco mihrab (fig.4), a beautiful inscribed band of stucco around the base of the dome, and a carved stucco medallion in its centre. Scholars have struggled to explain why such a building would have been erected in such an inaccessible location, and it has been explained as everything from a commemorative structure to a fortified watchtower to a mosque plain and simple.[19]

Al-Ma'mun al-Bata'ihi, chief of staff for the former vizier al-Afdal, Badr al-Jamali's son, is said to have built many congregational and smaller mosques in several localities in Upper and Lower Egypt.[20] The exquisite al-Aqmar mosque (fig.5) is the only other extant structure commissioned by al-Ma'mun. Built on a small plot north of the Great Eastern Palace facing the main north-south street of al-Qahira, the building was begun in 1122 and completed in 1125. The slightly projecting entrance leads to a small courtyard surrounded by arcades of three arches on each side. On the *qibla* side of the court, the arcades create a small prayer hall three bays deep, elsewhere they are but one bay deep. The court arcades are outlined with inscriptions carved in the plaster; only fragments of them remained before the building's recent – and drastic – restoration. While the interior arrangement of the mosque is exactly what one might expect for a small Fatimid hypostyle mosque, the exterior of the building is unusual and innovative: instead of being oriented to the interior of the mosque, the facades are oriented to the adjacent streets, creating spaces between the lines of the outer and inner walls that have been filled with small rooms and a staircase to the roof. The mosque's main facade, perhaps the most beautiful ensemble of Fatimid stonework to survive, was originally a symmetrical composition arranged around a salient entrance about 7 metres wide and set forward about 70 cm from the line of the facade. Two magnificent foundation inscriptions cross the facade. Each side now contains a slightly recessed panel capped by a ribbed arch, with the arched panel flanked by small panels of fine stonework.

Apart from the Fakahani mosque – a remnant of the Afkhar mosque constructed by al-Zafir – of which only fragments of Fatimid-era woodwork on two sets of doors remain, and Tala'i''s mosque at Qus of 1156,[21] the last Fatimid mosque was constructed by the vizier al-Salih Tala'i' b. Ruzzik directly outside Bab Zuwayla in 1160 during the death-throes of

Fig.4

Fig.5

the Fatimid state.[22] It is a hypostyle structure with a prayer hall three bays deep preceded by a courtyard surrounded by arcades, but it is somewhat larger than the Aqmar mosque and largely free-standing (fig.6). The mosque's principal facade is also unusual because it consists of an open loggia of five arches flanked by two suites of three rooms, one of which projects from either corner of the mosque, but most of the mosque, apart from the prayer hall, was rebuilt by the Comité de Conservation in the early 20th century. Little if anything in this building suggests that it was the last gasp of Fatimid architecture, since many of its decorative features reappear in subsequent Ayyubid and Mamluk architecture.

This quick survey of Fatimid religious architecture reveals several aspects of their plans, architectural forms and decoration. Little, if anything, would serve to distinguish the plan of a 'Fatimid' congregational mosque, whether large or small, from a contemporary mosque elsewhere in the Muslim world. Likewise, Fatimid Ismailis would have been largely comfortable in the spaces of Sunni mosques. That the first Fatimid mosque in Mahdia was closely modelled on that of Kairouan,

Fig.6

Fig.4
mihrab (before restoration) of the *mashhad* al-Juyushi, Cairo, 1085

Fig.5
Facade of the mosque of al-Aqmar, Cairo, 1125

Fig.6.
General view of the mosque of al-Salih Tala'i', Cairo, 1160

Fig.7

a hotbed of Maliki conservatism, should put that issue to rest. The function of the unique domes in the rear corners of al-Hakim's prayer hall remains unexplained, as does the purpose of al-Hafiz's domed *maqṣūra* on the courtyard for al-Azhar, which has several parallels in mosques in Kairouan, Tunis and Sfax.

The small three-bay mosque, exemplified by such buildings as the Hadra Sharifa, the Mashhad al-Juyushi, or the tomb of Sayyida Ruqayya (fig.7), with three domed or vaulted chambers with mihrabs preceded by a portico or courtyard, appears to be a specifically funerary type, but whether it is specifically Fatimid or Shiʿi or more generally associated with Egyptian funerary practices remains to be determined.[23] One could say the same for the nine-bay mosque, one example of which is known from Fatimid times.[24]

The most obvious 'Fatimid' innovation in mosque design is the projecting portal, which first appeared at Mahdia and remained a regular feature of Fatimid mosques for another two centuries. Portals had never been an important feature of early mosques, but a few ninth-century mosques had fancy entrances. Many years ago, I suggested that the Fatimids, like most Shiʿa, preferred to give the call to prayer from the doorway of the mosque rather than a tower, for they followed the tradition that the call to prayer should be given from no place higher than the mosque's roof.[25] In building the portal, the architect of the first Fatimid mosque at Mahdia certainly adapted the form – but surely not the meaning – of a Roman triumphal arch, and the persistence of this form during the Fatimid centuries in Egypt suggests that it continued to have some resonance among patrons and builders.[26] Virtually nobody – whether Sunni or Shiʿi – could object to a mosque having a fancy portal, and indeed fancy portals begin to appear on mosques from Spain to Iran around this time.[27]

Medieval authors – whether Fatimid or otherwise – are usually silent about how individuals viewed and interpreted the buildings they saw, so we are forced to imagine that Fatimid patrons were initially reluctant to embellish their mosques with towers, which they appear to have viewed as innovations particularly associated with their Abbasid rivals. Fatimid patrons' growing acceptance of towers can be interpreted as evidence for a process that was taking place during the Fatimid centuries, the transformation of the tower's meaning from a specifically sectarian symbol to a universal marker of an Islamic place of worship.At the beginning of the Fatimid period, towers had to be avoided; by the end of the Fatimid period, however, a tower on a mosque would have provoked little comment, particularly since some, if not many, of the actual patrons did not share the sectarian beliefs of their rulers.

In his monumental study of Egyptian Islamic architecture, K. A. C. Creswell assembled a sequence of extant Fatimid mihrabs to show the evolution of their form.[28] Nevertheless, many Fatimid mihrabs are lost, heavily damaged, missing their inscriptions or recently restored. Surely the Fatimid mihrabs that have survived, such as in the Mashhad

Fig.7.
General view of the shrine of
Sayyida Ruqayya, Cairo, 1133

al-Juyushi (fig.4), would not have been 'objectionable' to later Sunnis, although their sectarian messages are not always as explicit to us today as the mihrab the Ilkhanid sultan Uljaytu added to Isfahan's congregational mosque.[29]

The decorative vocabulary of Fatimid mosques consists of a fairly limited use of vegetal and geometric motifs combined with an extensive use of inscriptions. In only exceptional cases were Fatimid inscriptions deliberately defaced, presumably because a later reader found the sectarian expressions offensive.[30] That surviving Fatimid inscriptions were not further disfigured suggests that most later readers either didn't read the inscriptions or didn't care what they said.

Al-Azhar is the first Fatimid mosque to preserve epigraphic and vegetal decoration. The reluctance to repeat the vegetal decoration in the Fatimids' next major project, the mosque of al-Hakim, suggests that if the vegetal decoration had had meaning at al-Azhar, within a few decades this meaning had been lost or ignored. Decoration on the mosque of al-Hakim was concentrated on the facade and above the interior arcades; otherwise the building was quite plain. The portal and towers of the main facade were decorated with bands of vegetal and geometric ornament and inscriptions, although the two towers were quickly encased within massive bastions decorated with a single elegant band of kufic script. Apart from some window grilles, long quotations from the Qur'an form the major decoration on the interior of the mosque, where a continuous band runs around the interior, above the arcades and just below the ceiling. Just as the plan of the mosque of al-Hakim was modelled on the earlier mosque of Ibn Tulun, the extensive use of inscriptions in the Fatimid mosque was similarly modelled on the Tulunid example, where the inscription bands – but now carved plaster rather than carved wood – are in exactly the same location.[31] In any event, later Fatimid mosques would no longer have inscription bands all over their interiors. The inscriptions of later buildings, whether Qur'anic or foundation, are focused on street and court facades, around mihrabs, and on and around the interior of domes.

Many of these different aspects come together in the interpretation of the elaborate decoration of the Aqmar mosque facade (fig.5). At the simplest level, the facade has been explained as a projection of the mosque's interior on to the street, a gigantic *qibla* wall articulated by the blind arcades that suggest the multiple mihrabs found in several shrines of the Fatimid period, such as the undated mausoleum of Ikhwat Yusuf in the Qarafa cemetery (*circa* 1145).[32] There is no evidence, however, that the Aqmar mosque ever had more than one mihrab inside, and the significance of multiple mihrabs in Fatimid shrines remains to be explained. The facade has also been interpreted as a highly charged image in the context of Fatimid Ismailism, where each element – niche, radiating rib, *muqarnas* (honeycomb design), lamp and door – would have had a specific esoteric meaning in Ismaili thought. Thus the arrangement of three main niches could represent the Imams ʿAli, al-Hasan and al-Husayn, while the entire composition of seven recesses would recall the seven Imams of the Ismaili line.[33] Another interpretation places the facade in the context of the elaboration of Fatimid ceremonial under the Imam-caliph al-Amir, in which the building was meant to celebrate the return of the city and its palace to splendour.[34]

If we are to accept the premise that this building – and by extension any other Fatimid building – was meant to have such a symbolic meaning, then we must first establish either that Fatimid builders and patrons had long been familiar with the practice of giving their buildings such meanings, a principle not supported by the earlier evidence, or that the patron or designer of this particular building came up with the idea himself. Whatever the specific meanings the patron and builders may have assigned to the mosque, there was no social mechanism – whether in Fatimid Egypt or in the Islamic lands in general – for maintaining such meanings over any substantial period, and succeeding generations – particularly of Sunnis – appear to have seen nothing particularly Ismaili or sectarian about this facade. Like much Islamic religious art from other times and places, therefore, the facade of the Aqmar mosque is ambiguous.

This is not to say, however, that Fatimid mosques were devoid of content. Rather than looking for Shiʿi meaning in architectural forms, we should look for meanings in the ways in which these forms were used.[35] As the evidence for Fatimid ceremonial and liturgical practice is even more fragmentary than the buildings themselves, perhaps the discovery of new documents will allow further exploration of that question in the future.

1 For an overview of Fatimid history and art, see Jonathan M. Bloom, *Arts of the City Victorious: Islamic Art and Architecture in Fatimid North Africa and Egypt* (New Haven, CT, and London, 2007). For Fatimid Cairo, see Ayman Fu'ad Sayyid, *La Capitale de l'Égypte jusqu'à l'époque Fatimide: al-Qāhira et al-Fusṭāṭ, essai de reconstitution topographique* (Beirut, 1998).

2 The primary and secondary sources are discussed by Paul E. Walker, *Exploring an Islamic Empire: Fatimid History and its Sources* (London and New York, 2002). The basic work on Fatimid architecture is K. A. C. Creswell, *The Muslim Architecture of Egypt* (2 vols, Oxford, 1952–1959).

3 Alexandre Lézine, *Mahdiya: recherches d'archéologie islamique* (Paris, 1965).

4 Earlier scholars had proposed that this portal would have been erected as a symbol of al-Mahdi's triumphalist intent in his new capital. See, for example, Alexandre Lézine, 'Notes d'archéologie ifriqiyenne IV: Mahdiya: quelques precisions sur la "ville" des premiers fatimides', *Revue des études Islamiques*, 35 (1967), pp.82–101. I suggested in Jonathan M. Bloom, 'The Origins of Fatimid Art', *Muqarnas*, 3 (1985), pp.20–38 that this structure was erected by the first Fatimids to replace the tower minaret with a structure more in line with their beliefs and practices.

5 In addition to the Fatimids' well-known use of monumental inscriptions later in Egypt, the first Fatimid ruler is said to have immediately ordered the erasure of the Aghlabids' names from all public inscriptions. See Bloom, 'Origins', p.21. Several fragmentary inscriptions from the Fatimid period survive in North Africa as well, for which see Bloom, *Arts of the City Victorious*, chapter 2.

6 Bloom, *Arts of the City Victorious*, p.40.

7 The basic discussion of al-Azhar is in Creswell, *Architecture of Egypt*, vol.1, pp.36–64. See also Nasser Rabbat, 'Al-Azhar Mosque: An Architectural Chronicle of Cairo's History', *Muqarnas*, 13 (1996), pp.45–67; and Marianne Barrucand, 'Les chapiteaux de remploi de la mosquée al-Azhar et l'émergence d'un type de chapiteau médiévale en Égypte', *Annales islamologiques*, 36 (2002), pp.37–75.

8 Rabbat, 'Al-Azhar', p.50. This 'royal box' is roughly equivalent to the *maqṣūra*, typically a screened area near to or in front of the mihrab where the ruler could participate in worship without interference. Oddly enough, we know of no Fatimid examples of the royal enclosure type of *maqṣūra*, although a domed structure of that name was added to the courtyard of al-Azhar. For the *maqṣūra*, see Robert Hillenbrand, *Islamic Architecture: Form, Function and Meaning* (Edinburgh, 1994), pp.48–53.

9 The domed pavilion is in the same position as domed pavilions in the mosques of Kairouan, Tunis and Sfax that seem to have been added to the buildings in the late 10th century, but the function of these domed structures also remains a mystery. For these structures, see Georges Marçais, *Architecture musulmane d'occident* (Paris, 1954).

10 Bloom, *Arts of the City Victorious*, p.70 with reference to my article, 'The Mosque of the Qarafa in Cairo', *Muqarnas*, 4 (1987), pp.7–20. My interpretation was disputed by Yusuf Ragib, 'La Mosquée d'al-Qarāfa et Jonathan M. Bloom', *Arabica*, 41 (1994), pp.419–421 and more reasonably by Rabbat, 'Al-Azhar'. The recent interpretation by Delia Cortese, 'The political and economic contexts of Fātimid female patronage during the reign of al-ʿAzīz (365/975–386/996)', *I Fatimidi e il Mediterraneo: Il systema di relazioni nel mondo dell'Islam e nell'area del Mediterraneo nel periodo della daʿwa fatimide (sec. X-XI): instituzioni, società, cultura, Atti del Convegno, Palermo 3–6 Dicembre 2008, Alifbâ: Studi arabo-islamici e mediterranei*, 22 (2008), pp.81–94, sees the building as part of a royal land-development scheme.

11 The actual text is not by al-Maqrīzī, as many have believed, but from the lost work of al-Qudaʿi, a Shafiʿi jurist who had served as deputy *qāḍī* (judge) under the Fatimids before his own death in 1062. See Bloom, *Arts of the City Victorious*, pp.113–114, with reference to T. W. Arnold, *Painting in Islam* (Oxford, 1928), p.22 and Maqrīzī, *al-Mawāʿiẓ wa-al-iʿtibār fī dhikr al-khiṭaṭ wa-al-āthār li-Taqī al-Dīn Aḥmad ibn ʿAlī ibn ʿAbd al-Qādir al-Maqrīzī*, ed. Ayman Fu'ad Sayyid, vol.4, part 1, (London, 2002–2004), pp.288ff.

12 Creswell, *Architecture of Egypt*, vol.1, pp.65–106; Jonathan M. Bloom, 'The Mosque of al-Hakim in Cairo', *Muqarnas*, 1 (1983), pp.15–36.

13 Bernard O'Kane, 'The Ziyada of the Mosque of al-Hakim and the Development of the Ziyada in Islamic Architecture', in Marianne Barrucand, ed., *L'Égypte Fatimide: son art et son histoire. Actes du colloque organisé à Paris les 28, 29 et 30 mai 1998* (Paris, 1999), pp.141–158.

14 In the 12th century, Frankish Crusaders were imprisoned there, and the Ayyubids made it the congregational mosque of al-Qahira. Although the mosque was restored in the Mamluk period, when the 'pepper-pot' minaret finials were added, the building was eventually abandoned. In 1798 the French invaders transformed it into a fortress, and in the 19th century it was used for workshops before becoming the home of the Arab Museum. A school was erected in the courtyard during the Nasser period.

15 Creswell, *Architecture of Egypt*, vol.1, pp.113–115.

16 Oleg Grabar, *The Shape of the Holy: Early Islamic Jerusalem* (Princeton, 1996), p.149.

17 Badr al-Jamali ordered a mosque constructed on Roda Island adjacent to the Nilometer, the plan of which was recorded during the French expedition of 1798, as were the three inscriptions of Badr al-Jamali embedded in its walls. See Creswell, *Architecture of Egypt*, vol.1, pp.217–219 and Etienne Combe et al, *Répertoire chronologique d'épigraphie arabe*, vol.7 (Cairo, 1931–1982), pp.265–269.

18 The base is a square brick prism supporting a tapering cylindrical shaft crowned by a three-storey lantern. A marble plaque is inscribed with a long text specifying the patron's titles, who is identified as the sword (*ḥusām*) of the Commander of the Believers, but the ruling Imam-caliph is otherwise neither mentioned nor named, perhaps indicating his tenuous authority in this region so far from the capital. The inscription is also remarkable because it is the first surviving example of the use of the word *miʾdhana* (place from which the call to prayer is given) in Egyptian epigraphy, and it thereby makes the intended function of this tower perfectly clear. Gaston Wiet, 'Nouvelles inscriptions fatimides', *Bulletin de l'Institut de Egypte*, 24 (1941–1942), pp.145–155; Etienne Combe et al., *Répertoire chronologique d'épigraphie arabe*, vol.11 (Cairo, 1931–1982), p.263, no.2733a.

19 The various explanations are summarised in Bloom, *Arts of the City Victorious*, pp.131–134.

20 Sayyid, *Capitale*, pp.507–537.

21 For the Fakahani mosque, see Sayyid, *Capitale*, pp.544–547; and Jonathan M. Bloom, 'The "Fatimid" Doors of the Fakahani Mosque in Cairo', *Muqarnas*, 25 (2008), pp.231–242. For the mosque at Qus, see Jean-Claude Garcin, 'Remarques sur un plan topographique de la grande mosquée du Qûs', *Annales Islamologiques*, 9 (1970), pp.97–108; and Jean-Claude Garcin, *Un Centre musulman de la haute-Égypte médiévale: Qūṣ* (Cairo, 1976).

22 Creswell, *Architecture of Egypt*, vol.1, pp.275–288; Doris Behrens-Abouseif, *Islamic Architecture in Cairo: An Introduction* (Leiden, 1989), pp.76–77.

23 Bloom, *Arts of the City Victorious*, p.71; Creswell, *Architecture of Egypt*, vol.1.

24 The Mosque of the Elephants (*jāmiʿ al-fiyala*) got its name from the rounded shape of its nine domes, which supposedly resembled the backs of elephants (Arabic *fīl*, *fiyala*). See Bloom, *Arts of the City Victorious*, p.136; and Sayyid, *Capitale*, pp.469–482.

25 Jonathan M. Bloom, *Minaret: Symbol of Islam.* Oxford Studies in Islamic Art VII (Oxford, 1989), pp.99–103.

26 Bloom, *Arts of the City Victorious*, p.26.

27 For Spain, see most recently Pedro Marfil Ruiz, *La Puerta de los visires de la mezquita omeya de Córdoba* (Cordoba, 2009); for Iran, see Sheila S. Blair, *The Monumental Inscriptions from Early Islamic Iran and Transoxiana* (Leiden, 1992), pp.52–53 (Jurjir mosque).

28 Creswell, *Architecture of Egypt*, vol.1, plates. 114–121.

29 For varying interpretations of the inscriptions on the Juyushi mihrab, see Max van Berchem, 'Une mosquée de temps des fatimites au Caire: Notice sur le Gâmiʿ el Goyûshi', *Mémoires de l'Institut Égyptien*, 2 (1889), pp.605–619; Oleg Grabar, 'The Earliest Islamic Commemorative Structures', *Ars Orientalis*, 6 (1966), pp.7–46; Caroline Williams, 'The Cult of ʿAlid Saints in the Fatimid Monuments of Cairo. Part I: The Mosque of al-Aqmar', *Muqarnas*, 1 (1983), pp.37–52; and Yusuf Ragib, 'Un Oratoire fatimide au sommet du Muqaṭṭam', *Studia Islamica*, 65 (1987), pp.51–67. For the Isfahan mihrab, see Sheila S. Blair and Jonathan M. Bloom, *The Art and Architecture of Islam:* 1250-1800 (New Haven, CT, and London, 1994), pp.10–11 with reference to Max van Berchem, 'Une inscription du sultan mongol Uldjaitu', *Mélanges Hartwig Derenbourg* (Paris, 1909), pp.367–378.

30 Bloom, *Arts of the City Victorious*, fig.7; and Georges Marçais and Lucien Golvin, *La Grande Mosquée de Sfax* (Tunis, 1960). Caroline Williams hinted that the empty roundel on the facade of the Aqmar mosque might have contained an inscription later deemed offensive. See, Williams, 'Cult', Part I, p.47.

31 For the inscriptions in the Mosque of Ibn Tulun, see K. A. C. Creswell, *Early Muslim Architecture* (Oxford, 1932–1940), vol.2, p.345.

32 Robert Hillenbrand, *Islamic Art and Architecture* (London, 1999), pp.77–78. For the mausoleum of Ikhwat Yusuf, see Caroline Williams, 'The Cult of ʿAlid Saints in the Fatimid Monuments of Cairo, Part II: The Mausolea', *Muqarnas*, 3 (1985), pp.48–49.

33 Williams, 'Cult', Part I; Jaʿfar us Sadiq M. Saifuddin, *Al Aqmar: A Living Testimony to the Fatemiyeen* (London, 2000).

34 Doris Behrens-Abouseif, 'The Facade of the Aqmar Mosque in the Context of Fatimid Ceremonial', *Muqarnas*, 9 (1992), pp.29–38.

35 Perhaps the first to attempt this was Konstantin Aleksandrovich Inostrantsev in his *La Sortie solennelle des califes Fatimides* (St Petersburg, 1905). Marius Canard followed with two articles, 'Le Cérémonial Fatimide et le cérémonial Byzantin: essai de comparaison', *Byzantion*, 21 (1951), pp.355–420 and 'La Procession du nouvel an chez les Fatimides', *Annales de l'Institut d'Etudes Orientales*, 10 (1952), pp.364–395. Most recently Paula Sanders dealt with some aspects of this topic in *Ritual, Politics, and the City in Fatimid Cairo* (New York, 1994).

6

A Shiʿi building boom in 14th-century Qum: the case of the Bagh-i Sabz towers

Robert Hillenbrand

It is well known that the Mongol invasion of the Iranian world from 1220 onwards caused a virtual hiatus of some 70 years in the building industry – clear proof of the sheer scale of the trauma suffered by the people of Iran as a result of these cataclysmic events.[1] It is equally common knowledge that the turning point came with the conversion to Islam of Ghazan Khan (*r.* 1295–1304), and, in his wake, much of the Mongol élite, in 1295.[2] Very soon afterwards, Ghazan embarked on an ambitious and ostentatious programme of public works in which religious buildings figured prominently.[3] He caused houses for *sayyid*s (*dār al-siyāda*) to be built all over the empire;[4] he diligently visited many shrines,[5] including those of Imams ʿAli at Najaf[6] and Musa al-Kazim in Baghdad;[7] he gave massive curtains to the shrine of Imam Husayn at Karbala[8] and ensured that it was well provided with water;[9] he gave generous alms to the residents of shrines,[10] and improved the agricultural base on which they depended; [11] and he honoured holy men.[12] It is not inconceivable that at some level this sustained, practical demonstration of high-profile piety was tacit reparation for the damage inflicted on the Iranian psyche by successive Mongol invasions in previous generations. And the emphasis on Shiʿism could be related to its many rituals involving mourning. At all events, these building activities helped to trigger a construction boom throughout the country which lasted until the end of the Ilkhanid dynasty in 1336, and indeed kept up a certain momentum for at least a generation thereafter.[13]

Locally important shrines throughout the land were particular beneficiaries of these building campaigns[14] – Bastam,[15] Ardabil,[16] Natanz,[17] Linjan[18] and Turbat-i Jam[19] in Iran proper, to say nothing of examples in the wider Iranian world such as the Shah-i Zinda in Samarqand[20] and the shrine of Najm al-Din Kubra in Kunya Urgench (in north-western Turkmenistan).[21] Such shrine complexes typically developed around the burial places of prominent Sufi holy men. Qum offers the major example in medieval Iranian architecture of the clustering of mausoleums around a major shrine,[22] and it is significant that the major spurt in a building campaign that extended over several centuries on that site occurred precisely in the early 14th century.

The purpose of this essay is to present a trio of tomb towers in Qum which are part of a remarkable group of at least 15 funerary monuments erected in that staunchly Shiʿi city in the 14th century, a phenomenon which has not attracted the attention it deserves. Their sheer number distinguishes them from the groups of mausoleums found around the same time in other Iranian cities such as Yazd[23] and Abarquh.[24] They cannot be linked directly to the shrine complexes or 'little cities of God' discussed so penetratingly by Golombek, but are a collateral development, since they flourished within the ambit of a major centre of Shiʿi pilgrimage, namely the shrine of Fatima (d. 816, sister of Imam Reza), which itself received a major makeover in Ilkhanid times, which in the fashion of the time – a fashion also found in some of the local mausoleums[25] – included a rich selection of lustre tilework.[26] Other key Shiʿi shrines, such as Mashhad, Najaf and Karbala, however, offer no parallel for this clustering of individual tombs of descendants of the Imams (*imāmzāda*s) over an extensive surface area within a holy city. For it is also important to note that the location of these tombs does not reflect another preoccupation of funerary architecture in the medieval Islamic world, namely the desire to be buried as close as possible to the resting place of a holy person, as shown, for example, by the competition to be buried as close as possible to the tomb of Ibn Hanbal in Baghdad.[27] The tombs of the Bagh-i Sabz considered in this essay, for example, are located near the old Kashan Gate, a few hundred metres west of the modern Qum–Kashan road.

An Iranian example of the effects of this desire to be buried in maximum proximity to the holy person can be seen at Ardabil, where even rulers had to be content with gap sites for their tombs,[28] so highly prized was the *baraka* exuded by Shaykh Safi, whose cylindrical tomb tower was the heart of the dynastic shrine that grew up there over the centuries.[29] Clearly something rather different was going on at Qum in the 14th century, with *imāmzādas* – as distinct from secular mausoleums – scattered over various parts of the city. Moreover, it is likely enough that what remains today is only a fraction of what was built at this time. The sheer quantity of these buildings, and their unmistakably religious character, would have sacralised the cityscape of Qum (not a large city at the time) to a most unusual degree. But over and above the variations in form, scale and ornament contingent on their differences in chronology, function and location, all the buildings mentioned so far attest in their different ways to the veneration of saints in medieval Islam and to the ever-expanding network of pilgrimage sites that were the natural outgrowth of that veneration.[30]

Quite apart from this general trend, Qum itself enjoyed a particular reputation in medieval times as a centre of Twelver Shiʿism;[31] indeed, Hamdallah Mustawfi (d. after 1339), writing in the early 14th century, refers to its Twelver Shiʿi inhabitants as extremely bigoted.[32] In the Saljuq period it provided the sultans with a stream of *rāfiḍī* (i.e. proto-Twelver Shiʿi) viziers, *mustawfīs* (accountant-generals) and other administrators, many of them generous patrons,[33] and was renowned for its nine madrasas and its two Friday mosques, as well as its sanctuaries, lofty minarets and libraries.[34] The Sunni élite also visited the shrine of Fatima.[35]

It is likely enough, then, that the surviving early-14th-century tombs of Qum, numerous as they are, represent only a fraction of those that were built. Over a century ago, when Friedrich Sarre visited the city, it was very much smaller than it has since become, and its medieval monuments enjoyed a correspondingly higher profile. Farajollah Bazl and Donald Wilber carried out the first detailed architectural survey of these buildings under the auspices of Arthur Upham Pope's *Architectural Survey* in successive campaigns that began in 1935.[36] This fieldwork established that there was no overall pattern to their location. Some were relatively isolated; others, such as those associated with the complex of Musa Mubarqʿ (son of the ninth Imam, Muhammad Jawad al-Taqiyy), clustered together.[37]

The outstanding example of the latter type remains the trio of tomb towers in the Bagh-i Sabz (fig.1).[38] All of them seem to have belonged originally to the same architectural type, a very unusual design, in which the exterior has a pronounced pyramidal shape extending smoothly[39] from the apex of the building down to the base of the zone of transition. One of them has lost much of this superstructure, and the other two have been so violently restored as to remove the architectural articulation of the upper half of the building, leaving an extensive smooth surface in its place. So all three of them are now mere shells of what they originally were, though they bear unusually rich stucco ornamentation which is preserved in a condition that varies from good to pristine. It will be convenient to examine these structures in turn and in detail.[40] The essay will end by assessing their importance within the wider framework of 14th-century architecture in Iran.

1. The Imamzada ʿAli b. Abi'l-Maʿali b. ʿAli Safi

The Imamzada ʿAli b. Abi'l-Maʿali b. ʿAli Safi (fig.2), popularly known as the tomb of Khwaja Asil al-Din, is located at the southern end of the Bagh-i Sabz (an enclosed orchard). It is locally known as that of Saʿd (or Sayyid) Maʿsum, and is in all probability identical with the 'Imamzada Saʿd Sayyid Masʿud' mentioned by Wilber.[41] That said, Tabatabaʾi in his book on the buildings of Qum lists this monument under the title 'Asil al-Din'.[42] It has lost its original roof, which was probably

Fig.1

Fig.1
The Bagh-i Sabz towers, left: Imamzada ʿImad al-Din/Khwaja ʿAli Safi; centre: Gunbad-i Sabz; right: Mausoleum of ʿAli b. Abi'l-Maʿali b. ʿAli Safi

pyramidal,[43] but is otherwise sound, though there is much modern restoration – not just the present dome,[44] but also the outer face of the west-south-west side and the intrados of the internal arch on the south-south-east side. Modern plaster covers the lower parts of the interior arches and the places where the lower inscription has gone. The angles where the sides of the building meet become more complex *circa* 1.5 metres above ground level, which suggests that the area below this point is restored. So is the doorway, since it breaks a band of decoration, while another doorway photographed by Wilber has been blocked up, and the line of failure visible then has been filled. The tower rests on a 12-sided foundation, which extends to 2.95 metres beyond the building and suggests that the dodecagonal exterior plan is indeed the original one. The present ground level is 63 cm above the original floor of the tower. There are shallow recessed rectangular panels on ten sides, each containing a blank arch, with deep niches for the doorway on the north-west side and for the east-north-east side, where the recessed blank arch is a little more than half the height of the others. Above it is a smaller recessed arch; this contains the outer archway leading to an intramural staircase not accessible at ground level. The external transition zone has four windows facing north-north-west, south-south-east, west-south-west and east-north-east. The exterior is plain but for the name "*Alī*" rendered in brick on the south side below the outer arch.

The interior (fig.3) presents a total contrast to this severity in its luxuriant and technicolour stucco ornament. The lower part of the interior is octagonal. Each side contains a rectangular recessed panel framed by inscribed bands and enclosing a blank arch. There was formerly a mihrab which reached to the springing of the arch.[45] The side with the entrance has an additional smaller arch. Above these panels is an inscription band on which rest the 16 rectangular panels of the hexadecagonal zone of transition, each in turn containing an arch – four of them windows, the remainder blank. These are crowned by a second inscription band, badly damaged in places, which serves as the collar of the dome. This dome is of modern construction and is undecorated.

The only colours now visible in the high-quality carved stucco are white and brownish red, but Sarre, who visited the site between 1895 and 1900, also noted blue and green in the inscription bands and medallions.[46] The surface of the blank arches in the octagon is coated in plaster with incised false joints and carved brick-end plugs. The tympana of these arches contain roundels of geometric and floral design within a decorative geometric or epigraphic band. No two of these are identical. Together they constitute a *tour de force* of highly original stucco decoration, distinguished by a bold and brilliant use of colour and an ability to use void space as a positive factor both within the composition and in the background. The inner frames of both the lower and the upper zone of blank arches carry various geometric and vegetal designs also found in Ilkhanid book painting. The spandrels of the lower zone contain inscribed roundels, while those of the hexadecagon display only geometric patterns, perhaps as a deliberate contrast to the riotous foliate growth in the inscription bands above and below. The lower cursive inscription has thin decorative bands above and below it. The soffits of the arches in the lower zone have borders with various geometrical motifs – cable mouldings, undulating motifs and a thrice-repeated Greek key design. But the overwhelming message of one soffit after another, easily visible, is the endless repetition of one name – "*Alī*" – in a chequerboard pattern, totalling about a hundred times per arch in some cases. So the entire building is visually dedicated to Imam ʿAli. What is striking about this whole decorative scheme is the way it covers all the available space, and yet is easily controlled and made legible by the articulating framework of arches, panels and epigraphic bands.

This epigrasphic material is indeed rich; it is all in Arabic. There are three main inscription bands – two in cursive script above and below the zone of transition, and one in kufic set against a mechanically hatched ground and framing the panels of the lower octagon. This is incomplete on every side. The now-vanished mihrab was framed by

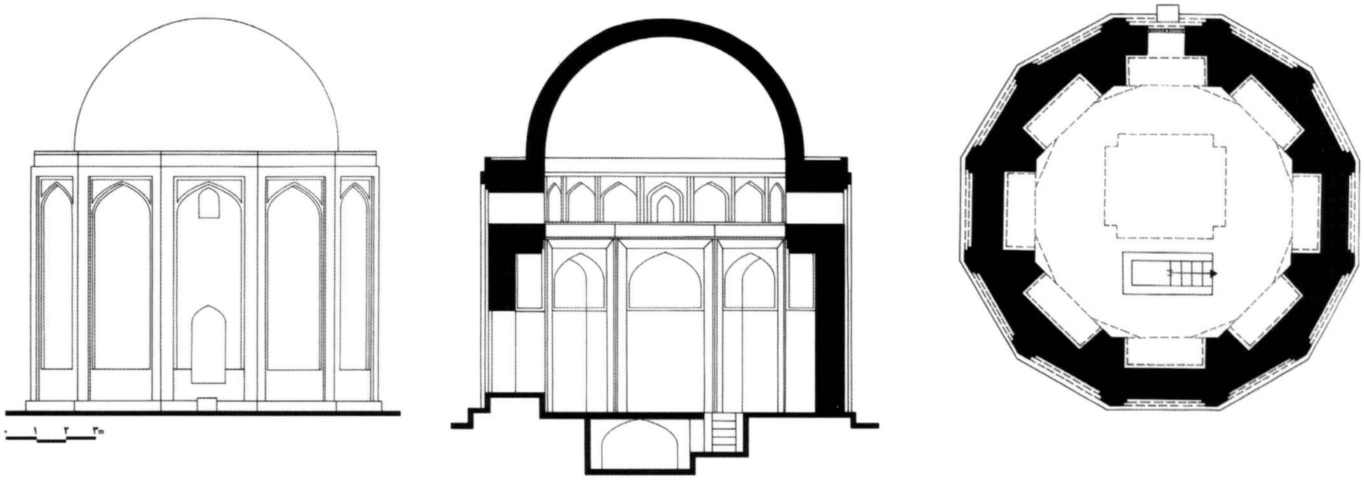

Fig.2

a very fragmentary cursive Qur'anic inscription – 17:80 (sura *al-Isrā'*, Night Journey).[47] There are also 16 inscribed roundels in the spandrels of this octagon. They give the names of the Twelve Imams,[48] among them a novel *chahār ʿAlī*, and the names of Muhammad and al-Husayn are repeated several times. In addition, one is encircled by a kufic band reading 'Power belongs to God', while another yields the name of the architect and the date: '…*hādhihi'l-ʿimārat bi ʿamal Ḥasan b. ʿAlī Kh.l.w. Abi'l-Bannā'*[49] *wa kutiba fī Rajab* 761' (i.e. May 1360; this date is given in figures). Above the entrance, in each spandrel of the larger arch, is a panel with a *naskhī* inscription. Together they read: 'ʿAli b. Muhammad b. (A)bi Shujaʿ made it'. It is conceivable that one of these two historical inscriptions refers to the architect and the other to one of the craftsmen working on the building.

The upper cursive inscription contains the first four verses of Qur'an 48 (sura *al-Fatḥ*, Victory).[50] The kufic inscriptions are Qur'anic and include the beginning of sura 76 (*al-Insān*, The Human),[51] plus part of sura 97 (*al-Qadr*, Power).[52] Their style is mannered and lifeless; the shafts are too spindly to give the text the necessary volume and monumentality. The heads of the shafts are bi-lobed with a hole bored through the middle. The first metre or so of the much-mutilated lower cursive inscription is missing; it probably contained the *basmala*. It then reads, initially in rhyming prose: 'The mention of the Eternal One is most lofty and is most worthy of memorial (*dhikru'l-qadīm aʿlā wa bi-taqdīmi ʿūlā*).[53] There ordered the establishment of this lofty tomb (*al-buqʿa al-rafīʿa*) and this mighty seat (*al-sudda al-manīʿa*) the client, the most exalted, just Lord of the Arabs and non-Arabs…*al-Dunya wa'l-Dīn Ṣafī al-Islām wa'l-Muslimīn ʿAlī*,[54] may God honour his companions and redouble his capacities. He designed (*rasama*) the resting place (*marqad*) of his uncle the lord…*Aṣīl al-Dawla wa'l-Dīn, Jamāl al-Islām wa'l-Muslimīn* and his son, and the apple of his eye [lit. 'part of his liver', *fildha kabdihi*[55]], the martyred, pardoned lord (*al-ṣāhib al-shahīd al-maghfūr*) *Jamāl al-Dawla wa'l-Dīn, Aṣīl [al-Islām wa'l-Muslimīn]*[56] *ʿAlī b. Abi'l-Maʿālī b. ʿAlī Ṣafī*. May God make the resting place for the two of them cool and make Paradise the place to which the two of them return.[57] In the months of the year 761' (i.e. 1360).

This complex inscription is rendered doubly difficult by its lacunae and by the surfeit of 'ʿ*Ali*s' mentioned in it. The clearest way through the thicket of similar-sounding titles and repetitions of the name ʿAli

Fig.3

Fig.2
Mausoleum of ʿAli b. Abi'l-Maʿali b. ʿAli Safi: elevation, section and plan

Fig.3
Mausoleum of ʿAli b. Abi'l-Maʿali b. ʿAli Safi: interior

is to emphasise that the inscription identifies the person who ordered the tomb as a certain Safi al-Islam wa'l-Muslimin ʿAli. He built it for two people. One of these was certainly his own uncle, whose personal name is not given. But the exact identity of the second person buried here, whose personal name was ʿAli, is uncertain. The phrase rendered above as 'the apple of his eye', though perhaps intended to avoid such a confusion of identity, does not seem to fix conclusively the relationship that he bears to either Safi al-Islam wa'l-Muslimin ʿAli or to the latter's uncle. He is termed 'his son' (*waladhi*), and the person mentioned immediately beforehand is the uncle of the patron. In that case, 'his son' (ʿAli) would be the cousin of the patron. But the addition of the word *wa* (and) before 'the apple of his eye' could mean that the latter phrase is not necessarily in apposition to 'his son' and would therefore make this much-loved ʿAli the son of the patron rather than the son of the patron's uncle. And the love so vividly expressed in the phrase 'the apple of his eye' would fit a son better than a cousin. What is not possible is that a third person is being mentioned here, because the dual is used. Unfortunately, the inscription refers to the father of this much-loved ʿAli only by his *kunya* (Abu'l-Maʿali), and omits both his *ism* (his personal name) and his *laqab* (title). The latter omission is all the more curious in an inscription so stuffed with titles as this one is. To make confusion worse confounded, the father of Abu'l-Maʿali is another ʿAli Safi. It seems unlikely that this ʿAli Safi is identical with the builder of the mausoleum, in the sense of the person who ordered it. Indeed, his status as the grandfather of the grandson who was one of the two tenants of this mausoleum makes it likely that he was long since dead.

One may, in short, conclude tentatively that the tomb houses two people: a certain ʿAli b. Abi'l-Maʿali, and the unnamed uncle of the Safi al-Islam wa'l-Muslimin ʿAli who ordered *and designed* this mausoleum. It remains unclear from this inscription whether ʿAli b. Abi'l-Maʿali was the son or the cousin of Safi al-Islam wa'l-Muslimin ʿAli. It is worth remembering that it was common Muslim practice for a grandson to bear, as here, the *ism* of his grandfather. Tabataba'i states at the outset of his entry on this building that the tomb houses Khwaja Asil al-Din and his son Khwaja ʿAli Asil, the first *amīr* of the dynasty of ʿAli Safi.[58] Neither of these names corresponds exactly to the nomenclature of the inscription, so Tabataba'i may be using other sources to which he does not refer here. In any event, it was precisely the ʿAli Safi family that controlled Qum during much of the 14th century, enjoying virtual independence, to the extent that Mahmud b. Safi (d. 1390 at the latest) even issued his own coins.[59] The Arabic history of Qum, the principal source for the Islamic history of the city up to the end of the 10th century, was translated into Persian as *Tārīkh-i Qum* for his son, Ibrahim b. Mahmud b. Muhammad b. ʿAli al-Safi, in 1402–1404.[60] And while both Zakariya al-Qazwini[61] and Hamdallah Mustawfi[62] agree that Qum lay mostly in ruins after the Mongol invasion, during which much of the population had been massacred, a report by Abu'l-Fida', writing before 1329, describes Qum as one of the large and important (*muʿtabar*) cities of ʿIraq al-ʿAjam,[63] and the Mongols invested heavily in dams in this area.[64]

2. Gunbad-i Sabz

The Gunbad-i Sabz is the northernmost tower of the group (figs 4–5).[65] It is also known locally as the Gunbad-i Saʿd va Saʿid (Sayyid?) va Masʿud.[66] The condition of the exterior is good, but over-restored; the roof has been retiled and the entire zone of transition blocked up, so that it now presents a smooth 16-sided facade. Since good photographs of its earlier state exist (fig.4), the description which follows ignores this restoration.[67] The lower storey is octagonal inside and out. On the exterior, each side has one deep double-stepped niche flanked by two much smaller ones of identical plan. The deep shadow lines thus created emphasise the monumentality of the exterior, with its strongly marked alternation of projecting and recessed forms. The external intermediate zone, set well back from the octagon below, and with a distinct batter, sets up a different but complementary rhythm, with its 16 recessed blank arches, half of which enclose small arched openings on the chord of the eight much larger niches directly below them. These regularly spaced dark accents are the principal articulating device of the entire elevation. The interior, of course, cannot use natural light in this way. Its lower part is dominated by the single deep niche on each side. The upper part of this octagonal zone has axial windows, while the hexadecagon above has windows on the main axes and diagonals, making eight windows in total.[68] The inner dome is crowned by an outer 16-sided tent roof. On the exterior, the tower rests on a newly restored

Fig.4
Imamzada ʿImad al-Din/Khwaja ʿAli Safi (left) and Gunbad-i Sabz (right), 1897

Fig.5
Gunbad-i Sabz: elevation, section and plan

Fig.4

brick platform. The walls of its lower zone and zone of transition both display, as already noted, a perceptible batter. The lower zone has a deep arched niche on each side, flanked by shallow rectangular panels set one above the other, each containing a blank pointed arch. The 16-sided zone is set well back from the cornice of the zone below. Its articulation features inset rectangular panels which enclose in alter-nation blank pointed arches and arched windows.

On the interior (fig.6), the floor is 88 cm below the entrance. The eight sides each have a thin plain rectangular brick moulding. This encloses an inscription (1) which in turn frames a rectangular panel with a deeply recessed pointed arch. This extends dramatically from the floor to the base of the hexadecagon, creating successive deep wells of space, carved as it were out of the perimeter wall. The tympana of the four axial arches are open; those of the other four arches are blank, and slightly offset at the springing. The lower part of each panel contains a second arch which (as the difference in brick sizes shows) was once open but was blocked at a later date. Nevertheless, it is likely that the tower as originally designed had no such arches, for the carved plaster surface of the lower part of the niches is broken by the lower arches. At least three building campaigns can thus be distinguished – the last perhaps quite recent. Above the rectangular niches is an inscription band (2) surmounted by the usual zone of 16 rectangular panels with windows (now – as noted above – blocked on the exterior) above each of the main eight sides. The panels over the angles of the octagon have blank arches. Above this zone is another inscription band (3) on which the dome rests.

The quantity of windows, arched openings, blank arches and reveals make this one of the most complicated and spatially sophisticated of Iranian tomb towers in plan and section. Load-bearing walls are

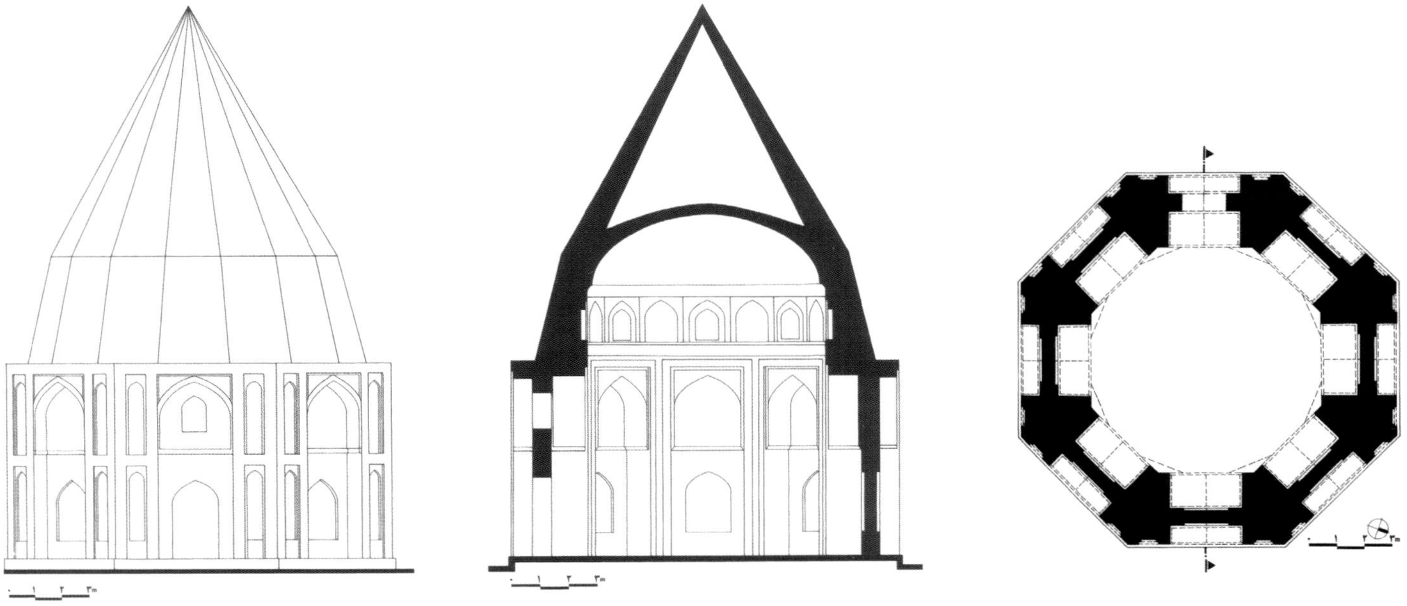

Fig.5

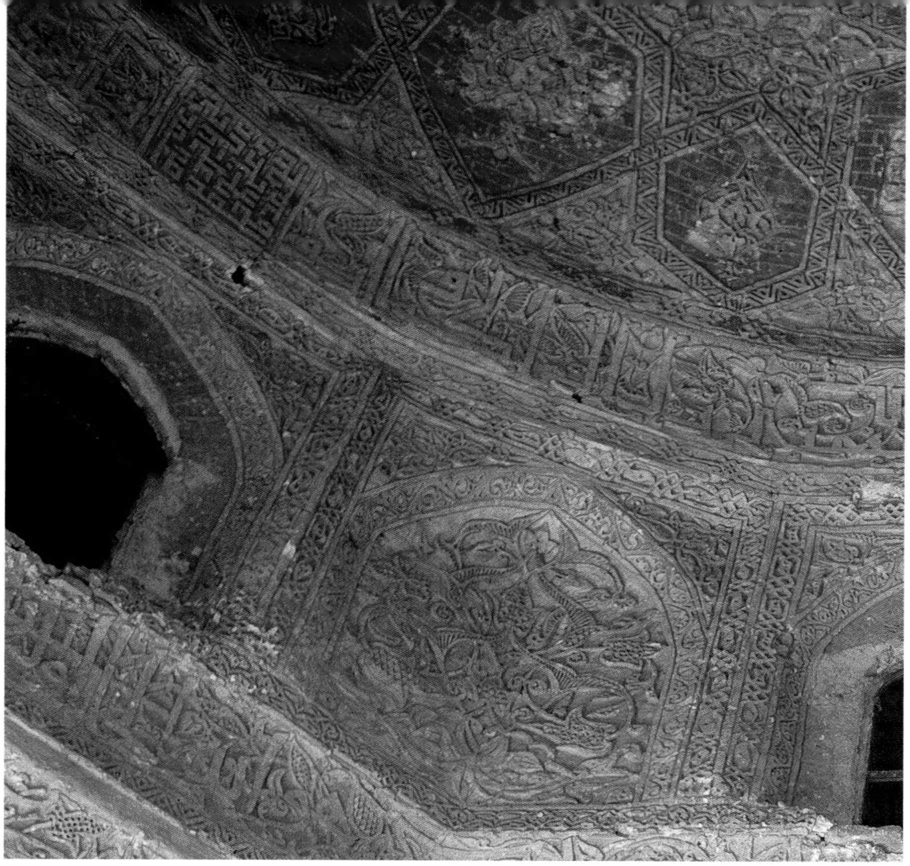

Fig.6

reduced to a minimum and the elevation keeps a fine balance between open and closed areas. This alternation marks each tier of the elevation, though it avoids direct vertical correspondences – which would be too obvious. The building thus displays a carefully calculated reciprocity of parts which acts as a powerful unifying factor. The decoration of the dome, as explained below, follows the same syncopated rhythm. One can only admire the ingenuity of the architect in applying a basically simple idea in so many different ways.

The architect's motive in breaking up the wall surface as much as possible, thereby letting in the light, may have been to connect the building with its setting. If this was originally a garden, as it is now and has been for at least 150 years, a link with open-plan garden pavilions is a strong possibility. This type of open plan became increasingly popular for mausoleums in the post-Mongol period, as a series of buildings in north-east Khurasan attest.[69]

The decoration is exclusively of raised stucco or incised plaster. Given that the 14th century was a golden age for glazed tilework, this unremitting focus on plaster as the sole means of decoration is remarkable. False joints, with joint plugs spelling out sacred names, and combining to spell "*'Alī*"[70] or to form larger geometric patterns, cover the lower walls of the chamber. Some of the joint plugs bear rather unusual designs.[71] The heads of the arches of the octagon were once filled with moulded plaster *muqarnasāt* with carved and painted decoration; of all this, very little remains. Important architectural features, particularly the mouldings of arches and panels, are marked by narrow friezes bearing inscriptions in square (or 'Chinese seal') kufic – usually repeated mottoes – geometric patterns and arabesques or floral scrollwork. The soffits of the main arches are divided into compartments by such friezes. Floral designs fill the blank arches of the hexadecagon. A net pattern creating diminishing hexagons and eight-pointed stars covers the dome, its ribs formed of narrow friezes with geometrical motifs. This decoration follows Saljuq models,[72] but significantly enough the ribs are not highly raised as in Saljuq domes, but virtually flush. So the ornament is no longer plastic but applied. This feature is symptomatic of the changes which marked the transition from the Saljuq to the Mongol style. Another innovation is the circular central

Fig.6
Gunbad-i Sabz: interior

Fig.7
Imamzada 'Imad al-Din/Khwaja 'Ali Safi: elevation, section and plan

medallion which interrupts the net design. The ground of the pattern is of deep red plaster painted with false joints; superimposed on it, and standing proud of it, are carved and painted medallions or vegetal escutcheons. The arrangement of the motifs within the polygonal voids created by the net pattern displays a deliberate alternation between the crowded and the comparatively open field. This alternation varies from one tier to the next. It can be seen as the equivalent in decoration to the articulation of the building itself. Colour further emphasises these contrasts. Thus the master has ensured that the eye is never still for long.

There are three major inscriptions, labelled (1), (2) and (3) above, apart from those already noted in the narrow frieze, joint plugs and patterns made of such plugs. They are in kufic, cursive and *thuluth* respectively. The first (1), is written in an ugly hybrid style, more kufic than cursive but still an uneasy combination. It contains all of Qur'an 97, *al-Qadr*, the sura of Power,[73] together with a brief fragment of another text. The next (2), is very damaged in places, but the decipherable parts include sections of Qur'an 59:22–24 (sura *al-Ḥashr*, Banishment). These verses extol Allah; there is no funerary connotation. The last (3), contains parts of Qur'an 55 (sura *al-Raḥmān*, The Beneficent).[74] No dated inscription survives. It is clear that the building dates from the 14th century, and its close similarities to the neighbouring pair of buildings suggests that it dates from the second half of that century.

3. Imamzada ʿImad al-Din/Khwaja ʿAli Safi

The Imamzada ʿImad al-Din is the central tomb in the Bagh-i Sabz (figs 4 and 7).[75] Tabataba'i calls it the tomb of Khwaja ʿAli Safi,[76] while Wilber calls it the tomb of ʿImad al-Din.[77] In a sense both are right. The exterior has been restored at least twice in modern times, leaving the upper part looking just like the Gunbad-i Sabz. But its lower exterior has twelve rather than eight sides, with a doubly stepped niche on each side. A precious photograph showing the entire building on the entrance side as it was before restoration has been published by Mechkati.[78] Happily the interior is in mint condition, with an arched niche on each of the eight sides, a 16-sided zone of transition with windows on its axes, and an inner dome. Externally it has a 16-sided tent roof, and the windows are set in the upper tympana of the 12-sided zone – in other words, the external hexadecagon does not correspond with the internal one, but is well over a metre above it. The modern restorations have not affected this relationship. It follows that the space between the two domes is considerably more than appears from the exterior. Old photographs show that the present opening at the base of the tent roof is an original feature. This was perhaps the top of an internal staircase.

The exterior of the tower rests on a recently constructed (or reconstructed) brick platform. As with the other towers in the Bagh-i Sabz, stairs lead down to the entrance. Apart from the entrance (see below) each side has a recessed rectangular panel with a blank pointed arch. The 16-sided drum, which is set back from the cornice of the duodecagon, repeats this scheme on a smaller scale. The walls of both the lower zones have a slight batter. The outer angles of the entrance side each have a hollowed-out niche containing a round engaged column, *circa* three metres high. Between them is the customary rectangular panel, comprising two blank arches with three arched openings inside them. The decoration seen in the 19th century by Jane Dieulafoy has all gone.[79]

In its essential lineaments the interior is identical to that of the Gunbad-i Sabz but for a few details. These include the absence of a window in the octagon; the presence of blocked arches in the lower part of the octagon on only three of the four axes rather than on all eight sides;[80] use of windows only on the main axes of the hexadecagon; and an intramural winding staircase on the south side. The interior is much better preserved than that of the Gunbad-i Sabz, and this allows it to make a much more powerful impression. A great deal of spatial variety is crammed into a relatively limited space and this expands the interior

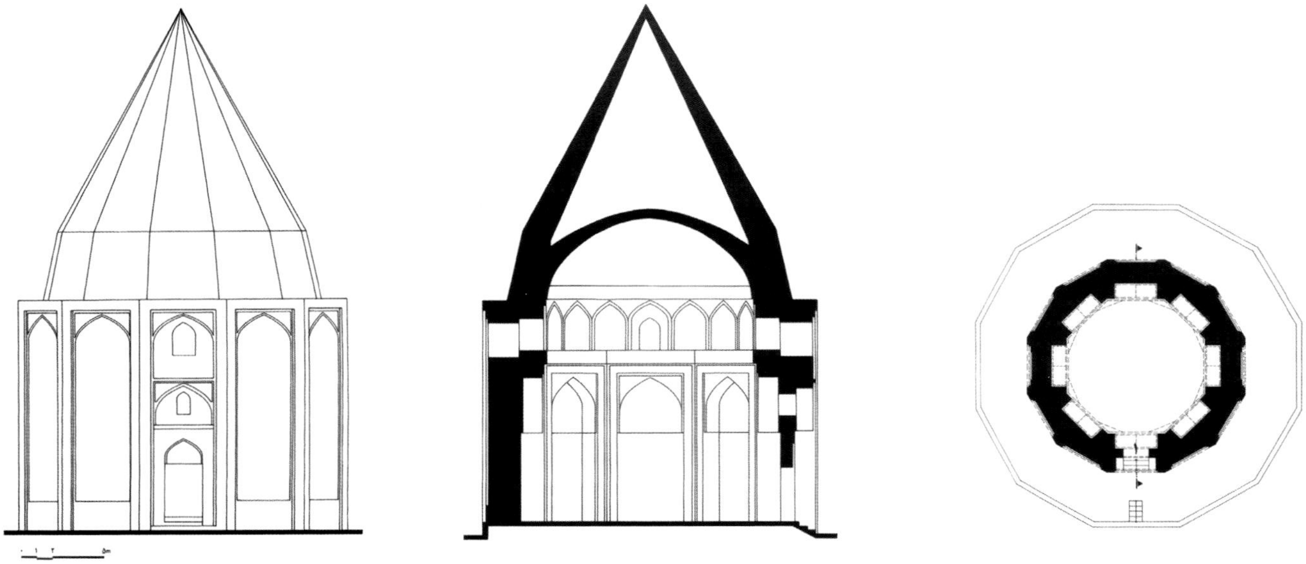

Fig.7

illustionistically. There is no square chamber at ground level (figs 8–9). Instead, the lofty, deeply recessed arches of the octagon shoot up from the floor to the base of the hexadecagon in a single grand sweep. The billowing volumes of these niches keep space in constant motion.

The composition of the hexadecagon, which also differs from that of the Gunbad-i Sabz, takes up this same theme but in a new visual language. The reason is not far to seek: the architect constantly rings the changes in the 16 arches of this zone. The axial arches enclose arched windows, and these four brightly lit openings determine the rhythm of the entire zone. Thus the hexadecagon is carefully articulated to ensure maximum variety, with a regular alternation of arches on the axes enclosing recessed open windows, arches on the diagonals enclosing recessed blank arches, and splayed blank arches over the corners of the octagon. The repeated alternation of these three different accents gives this zone the illusion of constant movement. The arches bridging the corners of the octagon bear painted patterns mimicking decorative brickwork (a common 14th-century device) and forming lozenge designs with a central cross.[81] Similarly executed zigzag designs outline the windows and smaller blank arches in this zone. Incidentally, the lack of a dado rising from the floor in all three towers would be explicable if they had formerly been decorated with lustre tiles that were later removed. The soffits of all arches in the hexadecagon bear mouldings packed with delicately carved stucco. And tiny inscription panels bearing sacred names fill the spandrels of the hexadecagon. So delicacy complements strength.

Yet the overall impact of this interior is not of decorated surface but rather of concentrated power. As such it belongs with the other masterpieces of spatial experiment in the 14th century, namely the tomb of Uljaytu in Sultaniya[82] and that of Turabek Khatun in Konya Urgench.[83] Its monumentality, especially in the disposition of its internal spaces, exceeds that of any 14th-century tomb tower and here, too, it is firmly abreast of the fashion of the time.[84] And this monumentality depends not on brute size – this tower cannot compare with either of these mausoleums on that score – but on the adroit massing of volumes so as to suggest that it is bigger than it really is.

But that is not all. This is probably the best-preserved example of an entirely polychromed medieval interior in all of Iran, and its quality

Fig.8

Fig.9

is superb.[85] Perhaps its outstanding feature is the lavish use of colour. The whole interior is drenched in a rich honey tone; important details stand out in a luminous light blue. Joint plugs acquire extra prominence because the pl ain surrounding plaster is coloured red, blue and green. Patterns created out of identical joint plugs are made to seem different simply by varying their colours. These colours also appear on the spandrels and soffits of the main arches in the octagon; the inscriptions have a blue ground. Some of the patterns in the blank arches of the octagon – e.g. on the northeast and southwest sides – are reminiscent of Saljuq decorative brick bonding. The northeast side has a lower dado of white reversed swastikas alternating with hatched rings – an unusual and attractive motif. On the south-east side yellow and white plaster alternate. Perhaps as a result of this preoccupation with colour and its effects, the joint plugs are not very varied – the three usual sacred names and a four-leaved flower are the commonest designs. Each tympanum in the octagon has a decorative medallion of carved stucco surrounded by a carved frieze; all the designs except one are floral. The exception is one with the name '*'Alī*' repeated three times to form a circular pattern. The decorative friezes in this tower are more abundant than in the Gunbad-i Sabz. Thus an outer moulding of plain brick and an inner one of carved stucco enclose the arch soffits in the octagon, while the spandrels have their own separate moulding.

This tomb has the most complex of the dome designs which were popular in Qum during this period,[86] of which net patterns such as this were the most ambitious. It is executed principally in yellow plaster, embellished with a range of other colours creating a host of subsidiary accents wherever one looks. But while it is lavishly prinked out, the abiding impression is of a vast enclosed space whose components seem to be funnelled upwards, rushing steeply inwards to lose themselves in the central oculus. The whole interior works on several levels, from the overall design of the net pattern to its interstitial spaces, packed with densely carved medallions, of both circular and oval form, picked out in light blue, green and white. Its circular outer band carries a square kufic frieze, while its ribs display undulating and zigzag motifs, and the ground between them bears painted squares and saltire crosses that serve to frame the medallions. The plaster skin meticulously imitates actual brickwork.

There was once a mihrab, as the decoration above the modern re-walling shows; the *qibla* arch is the only one where continuous stucco ornament fills the entire tympanum. The decoration of the *qibla* wall consists mostly of joint plugs spelling out sacred names. That of 'Ali predominates, and is usually the centrepiece.[87]

The ensemble has a quiet splendour far removed from the bolder brilliance of glazed tilework, but its colours blend more smoothly and the stucco worker took advantage of his medium to draw on a far richer palette. It is fitting that this masterpiece should consummate the long tradition of polychrome stucco in Iran, a tradition still full of sap in the 14th century[88] and, while largely eclipsed in the next century by the popularity of tile mosaic, by no means entirely forgotten.[89]

The inscriptions are arranged like those in the Gunbad-i Sabz, with the addition of medallions in the central part of the inner dome; according to the *Rahnāma-yi Qum,* these bear the names of the Shi'i Imams,[90] but this is mistaken. The actual texts given by Tabataba'i[91] reveal something rather different. Their general message – and it has to be remembered that this is conveyed by means of words written in widely separated medallions, so that, visually speaking, there is little sense of a single continuous text – is a proclamation of the truth of Islam through the Prophet Muhammad and Imam 'Ali. In true Shi'i fashion, they confirm 'Ali as the heir of Muhammad. The text as given by Tabataba'i reads: 'There is no god but God, the King, the Clear Truth. Muhammad is the Messenger of God, he who keeps his promises. 'Ali is the Friend of God, the Commander of the Faithful, the Heir of the Messenger, Lord of the Worlds, [the Confirmer of] the truth of Almighty God, and [the Confirmer of] His noble Messenger, and we are amongst the witnesses to that'.[92] This lofty, ringing assertion of basic Shi'i beliefs is rendered more solemn still by the insistent rhyme in *–īn* which runs right through the entire text: *al-mubīn...al-amīn... al-mu'minīn...al-'ālimīn...al-shāhidīn*. There is also a Qur'anic inscription in *thuluth* in the central circular band: 3:17–18 (sura *Āl-'Imrān*, Family of 'Imran), whose content, with its reference to angels, is visually appropriate to its location.[93] The inscription at the base of the dome, whose upper border consists of a continuous but uneven repetition in square kufic of the names '*'Alī*', '*Muḥammad*' and '*Allāh*', is in a mechanical plaited kufic; the plaits are sometimes applied to unusual

Fig.8
Imamzada 'Imad al-Din/Khwaja 'Ali Safi: upper interior

Fig.9
Imamzada 'Imad al-Din/Khwaja 'Ali Safi: inner dome

letters like *nūn*, and where a series of letters without shafts occurs, a redundant pair of plaited shafts is added above as a make-weight to fit the predetermined regular rhythm of the inscription. The text is Qur'an 76:1–6 (sura *al-Insān*, The Human), finishing at the penultimate word of verse six. The content of this text, with its references to the rewards awaiting the righteous after death, is eminently suitable for a mausoleum. The cursive inscription[94] framing the arches of the octagon features decorative plaiting at the corners and is written on a ground of intertwined tendrils with lobed leaves projecting from them at intervals. The text is Qur'an 36:1–45 (sura *Yā-sīn*),[95] a text recited on the approach of death.[96] The lower main inscription band of the hexadecagon has a much more prominent background of fleshy, lobed vegetal elements.[97] Its cursive text (in *thuluth*) is the most important one in the building.[98] It begins with Qur'an 23:1–8 (sura *al-Mu'minūn*, Believers), a passage which is very rare in Qur'anic epigraphy and whose other two recorded occurrences are also to be found in Iran,[99] and which defines believers who will attain a happy state as those who humble themselves in prayer, turn away from all that is frivolous and are intent on inner purity, unlike the licentious,[100] and who keep their promises.

The inscription then invokes the mercy of God on the occupants of this 'pleasant tomb' (*al-marqad al-laṭīf*). These are *al-ṣāḥib al-aʿẓam al-dastūr al-aʿlim al-mushraf qāṭiba al-alqāb*[101] *Khwāja Jamāl al-Ḥaqq wa'l-Dīn ʿAlī* and his son (*wa ibnahu*) *al-amīr Jalāl al-Dīn* and his brother (*wa akhāhu*) *Khwāja ʿImād al-Dīn Maḥmūd*, the two sons of (*ibnā*[102]) *al-Khwāja Ṣafī al-Dīn*. The inscription continues with the words *wa-udkhulhum fī raḥmatika wa-anta arḥamu al-rāḥimīn* (and You are the most merciful of those who dispense mercy) and it then ends 'in the year 792' (1390) – the year is given in figures. Three people, all related to each other, were thus buried here; and indeed Mechkati notes that the building is known as the tomb of the three brothers.[103] Tabataba'i gives the additional information that the first of the people mentioned in the inscription was known as Khwaja ʿAli Safi and that he was the second of the rulers of the ʿAli Safi dynasty.[104] Given the role of this family as the ruling élite of Qum,[105] it seems permissible to regard this as a dynastic mausoleum – although the days of that dynasty were numbered, for Iskandar b. ʿUmar Shaykh killed the last of the line in 1412–1413.[106]

Conclusion

These three buildings are important on several counts. First, to some extent they – along with the other dozen or so 14th-century mausoleums that survive in the city – give the lie to the image of immediately post-Saljuq Qum found in the medieval sources, which paint a sombre picture of a town in ruins. Secondly, they may all – or, at the very least, the two that are better preserved – be the work of the same master. Supporting evidence includes their location in the same patch of ground, that they are all dated or datable to the period 1360–1390, the fact that all three were built to the same kind of design (though two are octagonal and one duodecagonal, with two of them attesting a most unusual upper elevation), and that in their decoration, too, they all followed the same basic template – which, nevertheless, left ample scope for the exercise of individuality by members of the team of craftsmen. Incontrovertible proof of the master's identity in the form of several inscriptions identifying this person is lacking, though the likelihood is that he was one of the two craftsmen mentioned in the inscriptions of the tomb of ʿAli b. Abi'l-Maʿali b. ʿAli Safi, either Safi al-Islam wa'l-Muslimin ʿAli, who, given his title with its reference to the city's ruling family, is unlikely to have been a craftsman, despite the telling use of the word *rasama* (he designed) or – more likely, in view of his sobriquet – Hasan b. ʿAli Kh.l.w. Abi'l-Banna'. If the latter was indeed the architect, as his professional title strongly indicates (i.e. *al-bannā'*, architect), there is indeed incontrovertible evidence of his work on two buildings, namely the tomb of 1361 in the Bagh-i Sabz and that of Khadija Khatun at Khaljistan near Qum.[107]

Here, then, is at least one other instance of an excessively rare phenomenon in the medieval Iranian architecture that survives – a man responsible for more than one building, like al-Zanjani who built the two Kharraqan towers[108] or Muhammad b. al-Husayn b. Abi Talib al-Damghani, who inscribed his name in various places on buildings at Bastam.[109] And it is plausible that the architect responsible for the great south dome of the Isfahan Friday mosque also built the north dome very shortly afterwards. In this latter case, as in that of al-Zanjani, it seems that he was a man who devised his own distinctive version of a given building type and who in his later work improved on his own earlier performance.

Thirdly, two of these mausoleums, as already noted, are architecturally unusual. The distinctive upper elevation found in the two better-preserved tomb towers is otherwise unparalleled in medieval Iranian architecture. It combines a loftiness not found elsewhere in the funerary architecture of Qum with a massive solidity accentuated by the marked batter of the lower walls. Yet the agile articulation, with its constantly changing rhythms of open and closed, solid and void, its discreet mouldings, its razor-sharp planes, adds a touch of lightness and grace that admirably sets off their monumentality. Fourthly, the interior decoration is quite outstanding. It is characterised by the dovetailing of intricate carved stucco and a multi-tiered elevation composed with transparent logic, by the complex net pattern of the inner dome, culminating in the suggestion of a great oculus at the apex, and by its joyous celebration of colour, which makes visitors catch their breath on entering. Finally, its pronounced Shiʿi character, expressed in its multiple references to Imam ʿAli himself and in the way it highlights the key principles of Shiʿism in cartouches that orbit the solar disc of the dome like stars in the firmament, brings to a dramatic and fitting conclusion the building boom of Shiʿi monuments in 14th-century Qum.[110]

1 For the evidence, see Donald N. Wilber, *The Architecture of Islamic Iran. The Il Khānid Period* (Princeton, NJ, 1955), pp.4, 105–118.
2 Charles Melville, '*Pādshāh-i Islām*: the Conversion of Sultan Maḥmūd Ghāzān Khān', in Charles Melville, ed., *Pembroke Papers* 1. *Persian and Islamic Studies In Honour of P.W. Avery* (Cambridge, 1990), pp.159–177.
3 Rashīd al-Dīn, *Rashiduddin Fazlullah's Jamiʿu't-tawarikh – Compendium of Chronicles: A History of the Mongols*, trans. Wheeler M. Thackston (Cambridge, MA, 1998), p.663.
4 Ibid., p.663.
5 Ibid., p.622 (shrine of Abu Hanifa); and p.641 (shrine of Abu'l-Wafa').
6 Ibid., p.672.
7 Ibid., p.622.
8 Ibid., p.641.
9 Ibid., p.669.
10 Ibid., pp.641, 663 and 670.
11 Ibid., pp.669–670.
12 Ibid., p.618.
13 Wilber, *Architecture*, pp.182–186 (14 buildings dated or datable between 738/1337–1338 and 768/1366–1367 as distinct from 67 dated or datable between 700/1300–1301 and 736/1335–1336). This almost five-fold contrast in building activity between these two generations tells its own story of the political and social disintegration that followed the fall of the Ilkhanids. See note 54 below.
14 For a general discussion of this phenomenon, see Lisa Golombek, 'The Cult of Saints and Shrine Architecture in the Fourteenth Century', in Dickran K. Kouymjian, ed., *Near Eastern Numismatics, Iconography, Epigraphy and History. Studies in Honor of George C. Miles* (Beirut, 1974), pp.419–430.
15 June H. Taboroff, *Bistam, Iran: The Architecture, Setting and Patronage of an Islamic Shrine* (Ph.D. dissertation, New York University, 1982).
16 Alexander H. Morton, 'The Ardabīl Shrine in the Reign of Shāh Ṭahmāsp I', *Iran*, 12 (1974), p.25.
17 Sheila S. Blair, *The Ilkhanid Shrine Complex at Natanz, Iran* (Cambridge, MA, 1986).
18 Wilber, *Architecture*, pp.121–124; Claire Hardy-Guilbert, *Le mausolée de Pir-i-Bakran et le décor Il-Khanide* (thèse de doctorat, Université de Paris IV: Paris-Sorbonne, 1992).
19 Lisa Golombek, 'A Thirteenth Century Funerary Mosque at Turbat-i Shaykh Jām', *Bulletin of the Asia Institute*, 1 (1969), pp.13–26; Lisa Golombek, 'The Chronology of Turbat-i Shaikh Jām', *Iran*, 9 (1971), pp.27–44.
20 Nina B. Nemtseva, translated, with additions, by J. Michael Rogers and ʿAdil Yasin, 'Istoki Kompozitsii i Etapy Formirovaniya Ansamblya

Shakhi-Zinda (The Origins and Architectural Development of the Shāh-i Zinda)', *Iran*, 15 (1977), pp.51–73.

21 Mukhammed Mamedov and Ruslan Muradov, *Gurgandzh. Arkhitekturnii Putevoditel* (Istanbul, 2000), pp.33–39.

22 Though it should be noted that the *waqf* revenues of the shrine of Fatima have been 'decidedly less important' than those of the Mashhad shrine (Jean Calmard, 'Ḳum', *EI2*, vol.5, p.369).

23 Wilber, *Architecture*, pp.160–161, 186 and plates 139–143, 205–207; Yuka Kadoi, 'Aspects of Frescoes in Fourteenth-Century Iranian Architecture: the Case of Yazd', *Iran*, 43 (2005), pp.217–240; some lesser monuments with wall paintings are published by Iraj Afshar, *Yādgārhā-yi Yazd*, vol.2, (Tehran, 1347 Sh./1969), pp.1155 and 1295.

24 Wilber, *Architecture*, pp.154–155, 176 and plates 80, 121 and 123; André Godard, 'Abarḳūh (Province de Yazd)', *Athār-e Irān*, 1/1 (1936), pp.60–66, 68 and 70; Afshar, *Yādgārhā*, vol.1, plates 205–206.

25 For example, the tomb of 'Ali b. Ja'far; see Yedda Godard, 'Pièces datées de céramique de Kāshān à décor lustré', *Athār-e Īrān*, 2, 2 (1937), pp.309–312 and 314–327; Mudarrissi Tabataba'i, *Turbat-i pākān. Āthār va bināhā-yi qadīm makhdūdat kanūnī Dār al-Mu'minīn Qum*, vol.2, (Qum, [25]35/1976), pp.47–50 and plates 32–42. Oliver Watson also notes four other tombs at Qum, apart from the shrine itself, with examples of lustre tilework. See Oliver Watson, *Persian Lustre Ware* (London, 1985), pp.184–185 and plates 120–121.

26 Tabataba'i, *Turbat-i pākān*, vol.1, pp.46–50 and plates 2–12; Watson, *Lustre Ware*, pp.124, 184 and plate 103.

27 Heribert Busse, *Chalif und Grosskönig. Die Bujiden in Irak. Politik, Religion, Kultur und Wissenschaft.* 945–1055 (Beirut, 1969), p.201; Thomas Leisten, *Architektur für Tote: Bestattung in architektonischem Kontext in den Kernländern der islamischen Welt zwischen 3./9. und 6./12. Jahrhundert* (Berlin 1998), p.128, no.87.

28 Robert Hillenbrand, 'The Tomb of Shah Isma'il, Ardabil', in Sheila R. Canby, ed., *Safavid Art and Architecture* (London, 2002), pp.3–8.

29 See Kishwar Rizwi, *The Safavid Dynastic Shrine. Architecture, Religion and Power in Early Modern Iran* (London and New York, 2010), especially pp.57–69.

30 Leisten, *Architektur*; Christopher S. Taylor, *In the Vicinity of the Righteous: Ziyāra and the Veneration of Muslim saints in late Medieval Egypt* (Leiden, 1999); Joseph Meri, *The Cult of Saints among Muslims and Jews in Medieval Syria* (Oxford, 2002); and Daniella Talmon Heller, *Islamic Piety in Medieval Syria: Mosques, Cemeteries and Sermons under the Zangids and Ayyūbids* (Leiden, 2007).

31 Lambton notes that the histories of Qum have a sectarian emphasis and are dominated by interest in Ithna 'ashari Shi'ism; see Ann K. S. Lambton, 'Persian Local Histories: the Tradition Behind Them and the Assumptions of their Auhors', in Biancamaria Scarcia Amoretti and Lucia Rastagno, eds., *Yādnāma in memoria di Alessandro Bausani. Volume I. Islamistica* (Rome, 1991), p.233.

32 Ḥamdallāh Mustawfī, *The Geographical Part of the Nuzhat-al-Qulūb composed by Ḥamd-allāh Mustawfī of Qazwīn in 740 (1340)*, trans. Guy Le Strange (Leiden and London, 1919), p.71.

33 The term *al-Rāfiḍa* refers to the proto-Imamiyya and, subsequently, the Twelver Shi'a. Jean Calmard, 'Le chiisme Imamite en Iran à l'époque seldjoukide, d'après le *Kitāb al-Naqd*', *Le Monde Iranien et l'Islam*, 1 (1971), p.58.

34 Ibid., p.60.

35 Ibid., p.64, quoting the *Kitāb al-Naqd* of Shaykh 'Abd al-Jalil Qazwini Razi.

36 Arthur U. Pope, 'Research Program of the Institute. The Institute Survey of Persian Architecture. Preliminary Report of the Sixth Season of the Survey. Part II. Preliminary Report on the Tombs of the Saints at Qum', *Bulletin of the American Institute for Persian Art and Archaeology*, 4, 1 (1935), pp.36–38.

37 Wilber, *Architecture*, p.115.

38 Two further tombs, those of Shahzada Ibrahim and 'Ali b. Ja'far, are also located near the old Kashan gate (Arthur U. Pope, 'Islamic architecture. *H.* Fourteenth Century', in Arthur U. Pope and Phyllis Ackerman, ed., *A Survey of Persian Art from Prehistoric Times to the Present* [London and New York, 1939], p.1098).

39 There is only a slight kink at the top of the transition zone.

40 The basic fieldwork upon which this paper is based was carried out in 1970 and 1973. The text therefore takes no account of any subsequent changes to which these buildings have been subjected. See Robert Hillenbrand, *The Tomb Towers of Iran to 1550* (unpublished D.Phil. thesis, University of Oxford, 1974), vol.2, nos, 77, 80 and 82, pp.288–293, 302–307 and 313–318; vol.4, plates 249b–255, 261b–267b and 273–280.

41 Wilber, *Architecture*, p.116.

42 Tabataba'i, *Turbat-i pākān*, vol.2, pp.56–58 and plates 53–64.

43 See the drawing in Pascal Coste, *Les Monuments modernes de la Perse* (Paris, 1867), p.39. The earliest Western note of the tombs in the Bagh-i Sabz is to be found in Eugène Flandin, *Voyage en Perse par E. Flandin et Pascal Coste, pendant les années* 1840 *et* 1841 (Paris, 1843–1847), plate XXXVI.

44 See André Godard, 'Les Coupoles', *Āthār-é Īrān*, 4/2 (1949), pp.274–275 and fig.231 for a photograph of this building without a dome.

45 Friedrich Sarre, *Denkmäler Persischer Baukunst* (Berlin, 1901–1910).

46 Sarre, *Denkmäler*, p.72.

47 Ibid., plate LX (Lieferung 2).

48 For the later development of this theme, see Mehr Ali Newid, *Der schiitische Islam in Bildern. Rituale und Heilige* (Munich, 2006), pp.130–159; Mahnaz Shayesteh Far, *Shī'ah Artistic Elements in the Tîmûrid and the Early Safavid Periods: Book Illustrations and Inscriptions* (London, 1999), pp.271–289. Ghazan's 100-*mithqāl* gold coins, weighing 453.2 grams, with the names of the Twelve Imams on them, were so valued, says Rashīd al-Dīn disingenuously, 'that no one who gets one ever wants to part with it' (Rashīd al-Dīn, *Compendium of Chronicles*, p.710).

49 This same person is named in an inscription in the mausoleum of Khadija Khatun at Khaljistan near Qum (Tabataba'i, *Turbat-i pākān*, vol.2, p.205).

50 Anon., *Rahnāma-yi Qum* (Tehran, 1317/1938), pp.132–133; Tabataba'i, *Turbat-i pākān*, vol.2, p.53.

51 Sarre, *Denkmäler*, p.72, citing the readings of van Berchem and Hartmann.

52 Tabataba'i, *Turbat-i pākān*, vol.2, p.54 and note 5.

53 This same formula, with its elaborate puns, introduces the major historical inscription in the mausoleum of Khadija Khatun (ibid., p.204). It can be seen as invoking the blessings of Allah on the tenants of these mausoleums.

54 Ernst Herzfeld, 'Die Gunbadh-i 'Alawiyyân und die Baukunst der Ilkhane in Iran', in Thomas W. Arnold and Reynald A. Nicholson, ed., *A Volume of Oriental Studies Presented to E. G. Browne on His 60th Birthday (7 February 1922)* (Cambridge, 1922), p.195, note 3 very tentatively suggests, instead of the reading '...'Ali...', the rather different reading 'Shah Shuja'...Ghiyyath' and argues that this could be the Muzaffarid Jalal al-Din Shah Shuja', 1357–1384; but this would not accord with the evidence from the other towers at Qum in favour of local and comparatively modest patronage for these towers. Moreover, in his 'Reisebericht', *Zeitschrift der Deutschen Morgenländischen Gesellschaft*, Neue Folge 5, 3 (1926), p.235, published slightly later, Herzfeld notes that neither of the dated tombs in the Bagh-i Sabz name an overlord, 'der Anarchie dieser dunklen Zeit der persischen Geschichte entsprechend'.

55 For evidence supporting this reading, see Edward W. Lane, *An Arabic-English Lexicon* (London, 1877, repr. Beirut, 1980), Part 6, p.2439. The phrase could also be read less figuratively as 'his own blood' or 'his own child'. I gratefully acknowledge the help of my wife Carole in interpreting the inscriptions discussed in this paper.
56 This is the emendation suggested by Tabataba'i, *Turbat-i pākān*, vol.2, p.54, even though earlier in this very inscription the title was given as Asil al-Dawla wa'l-Din. But since a similar change has overtaken the title Jamal al-Islam wa'l-Muslimin, which is shortly followed by the title Jamal al-Dawla wa'l-Din (and neither title is an emendation), one must consider the possibility that father and son bore closely related, but not identical, titles in which the same elements were shuffled around in slightly different combinations, and thereby asserted their close relationship.
57 There is an echo here of the familiar Qur'anic phrase 'Lo! We are Allah's and lo! Unto Him we are returning' (sura *al-Baqara*, 2:156; see Marmaduke Pickthall, *The Meaning of the Glorious Koran: An Explanatory Translation* [London, 1930], p.43).
58 Tabataba'i, *Turbat-i pākān*, vol.2, p.53.
59 Ann K. S. Lambton, 'Qum: the Evolution of a Medieval City', *Journal of the Royal Asiatic Society of Great Britain & Ireland (New Series)*, 122, 2 (1990), p.329.
60 Ann K. S. Lambton, 'An Account of the *Tārīkhi Qumm*', BSOAS, 12, 3–4 (1948), p.586.
61 Lambton, 'Qum', p.328.
62 See Ibid., p.329; he adds, however, that part of its wall was still standing at the time that he was writing (probably the first two decades of the 14th century).
63 Ibid.
64 Calmard, 'Ḳum', p.371.
65 Tabataba'i, *Turbat-i pākān*, vol.2, pp.59–60 and plates 81–92.
66 Wilber, *Architecture*, p.116; there may be confusion here with his no.77.
67 To be supplemented by Wilber, *Architecture*, plate 182.
68 These are now all blocked; the savage 'restoration' of the two larger towers in the Bagh-i Sabz has made them a travesty of what they were.
69 William M. Clevenger, 'Some Minor Monuments in Khurāsān', *Iran*, 6 (1968), pp.59–64.
70 This occurs on four of the eight sides. On the south-west and south sides the plugs which combine to spell "Alī' are darker than the other plugs on those sides, thus giving his name special prominence.
71 E.g. the name '*Muḥammad*' spelt backwards; the word *al-mulk* with "*Alī*' adjoining it above and below; and the names '*Muḥammad*', '*Allāh*' and "*Alī*' in groups of three. In the case of 'Ali, this triple repetition is a common invocation; see Shayesteh Far, *Artistic Elements*, pp.261–264. The north-west and west sides have especially noteworthy designs.
72 For examples, see the Friday Mosques of Qurva, Sujas and Isfahan.
73 The same text is found on the minaret of Nigar.
74 Tabataba'i, *Turbat-i pākān*, vol.2, p.60.
75 Ibid., vol.2, pp.56–59 and plates 53–80.
76 Ibid., p.56, where he calls him 'Ali Safi the second.
77 Wilber, *Architecture*, p.188 and plates 208–210.
78 Nosratollah Mechkati, *Fihrist-i bināhā-yi tārīkhī va amākin-i bāstānī-yi Īrān* (Tehran, n.d.; *circa* 1968), p.182. This is missing from the French translation.
79 Jane Dieulafoy, *Le Tour du Monde. La Perse, la Chaldée et la Susiane* (Paris, 1887), p.96.
80 On the south side there was probably a mihrab.
81 Cf. the walls of the domed Friday mosque at Sujas: Robert Hillenbrand, 'Salǧūq Monuments in Iran: III The domed Masǧid-i Ǧāmi' at Suǧās', *Kunst des Orients*, 10, 1–2 (1976), pp.57–58, figs 11–12.
82 S. P.Seherr-Thoss, *Design and Color in Islamic Architecture. Afghanistan, Iran, Turkey* (Washington, DC, 1968), colour plate 44.
83 Mamedov and Muradov, *Gurgandzh*, pp.51–58 and plates 58–65 and colour plate 66.
84 Bernard O'Kane, 'Monumentality in Mamluk and Mongol Art and Architecture', *Art History*, 19, 4 (December 1996), pp.499–522.
85 See the penetrating analyses of Wilber, *Architecture*, p.188, and Bernard O'Kane, 'Timurid Stucco Decoration', *Annales Islamologiques*, 20 (1984), p.63.
86 For other examples see Tabataba'i, *Turbat-i pākān*, vol.2, plates 2 (Shah Ja'far), 17–18 ('Ali b. Ja'far), 85 (Gunbad-i Sabz), 95 (Sayyid Sar Bakhsh), 102 (Shah Ahmad-i Qasim), 121 (Shah Ibrahim), 150 (Imamzada Sayyid Abu Ahmad) and 254–255 (Khadija Khatun).
87 This fact helps to explain the otherwise puzzling juxtaposition of *al-mulk* and "*Alī*'.
88 Bernard O'Kane, 'Naṭanz and Turbat-i Jām: New Light on Fourteenth Century Iranian Stucco', *Studia Iranica*, 21 (1992), pp.85–92.
89 O'Kane, 'Timurid Stucco', pp.61–84.
90 Anon., *Rahnāma-yi Qum*, p.132.
91 Tabataba'i, *Turbat-i pākān*, vol.2, p.57.
92 The translation does not pick up on the grammatical mistakes in the text.
93 Tabataba'i, *Turbat-i pākān*, vol.2, p.56.
94 Identified as *riq'a* by Nosratollah Mechkati, trans. Issa Sepahbodi and Issa Behnam, *Monuments et Sites Historiques de l'Iran* (Tehran, n.d.; *circa* 1969), p.223.
95 Anon., *Rahnāma-yi Qum*, p.132; Tabataba'i, *Turbat-i pākān*, vol.2, p.58.
96 Pickthall, *Glorious Koran*, p.450.
97 These show a decided decline from the level of similar Saljuq decoration, e.g. that of the Qazwin Jami'; see Arthur U. Pope, 'Notes on the Stucco Ornament in the Sanctuary of the Masjid-i-Jami', Qazvin', *Bulletin of the American Institute for Persian Art and Archaeology*, 4 (1936), pp.209–216; and Jean Bergeret and Ludvik Kalus, 'Analyse de décors épigraphiques et floraux à Qazwin au début du VI/XII siècle', *Revue des Études Islamiques*, 45, 1 (1977), pp.89–130.
98 Tabataba'i, *Turbat-i pākān*, vol.2, p.58.
99 On the outer northern face of the Friday mosque of Isfahan (Oleg Grabar, *The Great Mosque of Isfahan* [New York, 1990], pp.32–33 and 50;) and in the Mashhad *ḥaram*, dated 612/1215 (Erica C. Dodd and Shereen Khairallah, *The Image of the Word* [Beirut, 1980], vol.2, p.83). The same passage is embedded in a longer quotation (verses 1–14) on the screen arch of the Quwwat al-Islam mosque in Delhi, dated 587/1191 (ibid.).
100 In the case of the Friday mosque of Isfahan, Grabar tentatively suggests that this choice of Qur'anic text may have been driven by a particular set of circumstances and was intended to make a topical point (Grabar, *Great Mosque*, pp.32–33).
101 These five words obstinately refuse to yield connected sense. They are ungrammatical, but appear to contain the notion that these deceased notables have accumulated honorific titles and were knowledgeable rulers.
102 This word should be *ibnay*; a few lapses in the grammar of this inscription obscure the actual relationships between the people mentioned in it.
103 Mechkati, *Monuments*, p.223.
104 Tabataba'i, *Turbat-i pākān*, vol.2, p.56.
105 One of the many obscure ruling groups of medieval Iranian history: see Mudarrisi Tabataba'i, 'Khāndān-i 'Alī Ṣafī, Shahriyārānī-yi gumnān II', *Barrasīhā-yi Tārīkhī*, 8, 4 (1352 Sh./1974), pp.55–59; and his 'The Family of 'Ali-Safi, a Little Known Dynasty', *Historical Studies of Iran*, 4 (1974), pp.46–55 and 69–70.
106 Lambton, 'Qum', p.329.
107 See n. 49 above.
108 Samuel M. Stern, 'The Inscriptions of the Kharraqān Mausoleums', *Iran*, 4 (1966), pp.21, 23–25.
109 Wilber, *Architecture*, pp.45, 47 and 127.
110 I am most grateful to my friend 'Alireza Anisi for providing the architectural drawings for this article.

7

Pilgrims and patrons: *ziyāra* under the Samanids and Bavandids

Melanie Michailidis[1]

The practice of *ziyāra* (*ziyārat* in Persian), which entails visiting the mausoleums of religiously significant individuals and circumambulating their cenotaphs, is generally classified as a Shiʿi phenomenon which has characterised the sites of important Shiʿi burials since the interment of Imam ʿAli at Najaf and Imam Husayn at Karbala. The association of Shiʿism with sites of pilgrimage has been so enduring that Shiʿism is generally accepted as a primary explanation for the sudden growth of funerary architecture in the 10th and 11th centuries, in what is commonly viewed as defiance of an earlier ban on lavish funerary displays.[2] My examination of some of the earliest extant funerary monuments in northern Iran and Central Asia shows that this practice was not exclusively Shiʿi during this period. Not only was the boundary between Shiʿi and Sunni practices not rigidly defined in the 10th and 11th centuries, but also the encouragement of *ziyāra* through architectural patronage was primarily linked to the political goals of each of the various dynasties of Iran and Central Asia rather than being determined by their confessional divisions. This analysis calls into question the monolithic categories of Shiʿi and Sunni and also sounds a cautionary note against ascribing solely religious motives to the construction of religious buildings.

The eastern Islamic world in the 10th and 11th centuries was divided between a diverse group of Persianate rulers, both Shiʿi and Sunni, among whom were Persian speakers as well as those who spoke other Iranian languages such as Tabari (also known as Mazanderani). This paper will focus on two of these dynasties, the Samanids and the Bavandids, but will also include a brief discussion of the Zaydis, who serve as an interesting counterpoint even though the remnants of their architectural patronage have not been well documented. The Samanids were one of the largest and most important of the regional powers, ruling over much of Central Asia and north-eastern Iran, whereas the Bavandids and Zaydis controlled relatively small swathes of territory in the eastern and western Alborz mountains of northern Iran respectively. The Bavandids and Zaydis were both Shiʿi, albeit of different sects, whereas the Samanids were Sunni. The Zaydis were descendants of the Prophet, whereas the Bavandids and Samanids both proudly proclaimed descent from the pre-Islamic Sasanian dynasty. For the Zaydis, their religious and political goals were inseparably intertwined; as will be shown below, this was not the case with the Samanids and Bavandids. And for their own unique reasons, the Zaydis and the Samanids both patronised funerary structures which were the focus of *ziyāra*, whereas the Bavandids did not.

Ziyāra under Zaydi patronage

The Zaydi Shiʿas were neither Ithna ʿasharis nor Ismailis; they believed instead that anyone who was a descendant of the Prophet and had both religious learning and sufficient military strength was qualified to rule.[3] They were vigorously suppressed and only managed to establish dynasties in the remotest of areas, such as the mountains of Yemen and the westernmost regions of the Alborz mountains of northern Iran, known as Daylam and Gilan. Here two separate Zaydi groups held sway in the 10th century: the Qasimiyya, based in Gilan, with close ties to their fellow sectarians in Yemen; and the Nasiriyya, based in Daylam. Both carried out successful missionary work amongst the mountain tribesmen of the region, most of whom were still adherents of Zoroastrianism when the Zaydi regimes came to power. This missionary zeal, combined with their ideological and actual military warfare against one another and against neighbouring regimes such as the Bavandids and the Samanids, inevitably meant that their descent from the Prophet and their particular sectarian beliefs played a large role in the construction of their dynastic identity and political legitimacy. Hence it is hardly surprising that the patronage of ʿAlid shrines and the encouragement of *ziyāra* to these shrines was a major priority of the Zaydi rulers.[4]

The first Zaydi regime was established in the ninth century by al-Hasan b. Zayd, an ʿAlid outsider who was invited in by the Daylamite tribesmen and made the Caspian coastal city of Amul his capital. Ibn Isfandiyar, a 13th-century court historian of the Bavandids and the most detailed source on the history of this region, informs us that it was al-Hasan's brother and successor, Muhammad b. Zayd, who rebuilt the shrines of ʿAli at Najaf and Husayn at Karbala, both of which had been destroyed by the Abbasid caliph al-Mutawakkil. Muhammad b. Zayd continued to donate funds annually for the upkeep of the shrines of Imams ʿAli, Hasan and Husayn as well as distributing money to prominent descendants of the Prophet.[5] Najaf and Karbala are located in Iraq, a considerable distance from Amul, and no mention is made of any large-scale architectural patronage within the Zaydi realm at this time; this is a clear indication of the degree to which their ʿAlid descent was fundamental to the construction of Zaydi identity.

Although Muhammad b. Zayd was killed in battle by the Samanids in the year 900, the new Zaydi regimes of the 10th century continued his policies of supporting the most important Shiʿi shrines, but in addition to shrines within their own territory. The founder of the Nasiriyya, who was titled al-Nasir al-Kabir, endowed his own funerary complex at Amul, consisting of a mausoleum, madrasa and library; this complex became a regional focal point of *ziyāra* for the Zaydis.[6] Ibn Isfandiyar also refers to three other tombs of respected ʿAlids built either in conjunction with or in close proximity to madrasas.[7] No mention is made of any other architectural patronage by Zaydi rulers; they focussed exclusively on the construction of ʿAlid funerary complexes designed to encourage the practice of *ziyāra*. One particularly interesting aspect of this patronage is the early date of the complexes: there is textual evidence for the development of madrasas in the eastern Islamic world during this era, and the institution then became much more widespread in the late 11th and 12th centuries under the rule of the Sunni Saljuqs.[8] The building of mausoleums in conjunction with madrasas and other charitable institutions in extensive endowed complexes is a phenomenon that became prevalent throughout the Islamic world in the 14th century.[9] The early date of the Zaydi complexes is explained by their emphasis on funerary architecture for prominent ʿAlids as a site of *ziyāra*, combined with their emphasis on missionary activities, which were closely associated with the early madrasas.

Architectural patronage under the Shiʿi Bavandids

The Bavandids were also Shiʿi rulers and were neighbours and rivals of the Zaydis, ruling over much of the eastern Alborz region known at that time as Tabaristan, but they never engaged in religiously-driven architectural patronage. The extant corpus of Bavandid buildings consists of three royal tomb towers from the 11th century, and there is no literary evidence for the construction of any shrines or, indeed, of any mosques or madrasas. The reason for this disparity is that the Bavandids and the Zaydis had completely different bases for their political legitimacy. Zaydi claims to rule were based upon their descent from the Prophet and their religious learning, and hence they focussed their patronage on shrines for themselves and other ʿAlids, as well as madrasas and libraries. Bavandid legitimacy, however, was based not upon any religious criteria, but upon their claims of Sasanian descent. The dynasty first came to power during the twilight years of the Sasanian era as military governors, or *ispahbads*, a title they clung to tenaciously until their demise in the 14th century. The Bavandids were originally Zoroastrian; Qarin b. Shahriyar converted to Sunni Islam in 841. By the 10th century, they had switched their allegiance to Ithna ʿashari Shiʿism, but the majority of their subjects still remained Zoroastrian.[10] Whereas their Zaydi neighbours had strong sectarian ties to Yemen and a realm which encompassed the easily accessible cities of the Caspian coast, the Bavandids remained confined to their remote mountain strongholds, in a terrain which was virtually impervious to military conquest but well suited to nurturing a very conservative culture resistant to outside influences. For this reason, their funerary architecture took a very different form to that seen in the principal Shiʿi shrines.

Indeed, the major shrines at Najaf, Karbala, Qum, Mashhad, and even Amul have been repeatedly extended and remodelled over the centuries, so that it is very difficult to ascertain their original form. The 10th-century geographer, Ibn Hawqal, described the tomb of ʿAli at Najaf as a *chahārṭāq*, a domed square with an opening on each of the four sides.[11] In the Sasanian period, the *chahārṭāq* form had been used for Zoroastrian fire temples, but by the 10th century it had been adapted as a mausoleum form in the eastern Islamic world; as will be discussed below, the Samanid mausoleum was also a *chahārṭāq*. With its honorific dome, its openness and its lack of axial emphasis, the *chahārṭāq* was well suited for mausoleums intended for the practice of *ziyāra*.[12] Given the need to accommodate pilgrims, it is safe to assume that all of the shrines would have had a similarly open and accessible design, with a cenotaph in the centre of the mausoleum to denote the presence of the body underneath and plenty of space for circumambulation. Literary sources and the shrines themselves also indicate the presence of subsidiary structures from an early date, providing additional services for pilgrims. Although the Bavandid tomb towers are also funerary structures, they are very different from this description: everything about them, from their location, to their siting in the landscape, to their architectural features, was designed to positively discourage entry.

All three of the extant Bavandid mausoleums are baked brick constructions situated in remote areas in the Alborz mountains, with bilingual foundation inscriptions in Arabic and Pahlavi (the official written language of the Sasanians). The earliest tomb tower in this series is the Mil-i Radkan, constructed in 1016–1021 as the tomb of Muhammad b. Vandarin Bavand (fig.1). At 35 metres high, this is the tallest of the three towers, befitting the fact that it was built by its incumbent during his lifetime. The second Bavandid funerary structure is located near the remote and isolated village of Lajim (fig.2). The inscription indicates that this tower was constructed in 1022–1023 for Shahriyar b. ʿAbbas b. Shahriyar by his mother, Chihrazadh; the builder's name, al-Husayn b. ʿAli, is also given. The third tomb tower is close by, on top of a steep hill from which the nearest village, Resget, is just visible in the distance (fig.3). The foundation inscription names the incumbents as Hurmuzdyar and Habusyar, the sons of Masdara. The date of construction is not legible in the foundation inscription, but the elaborate decoration in the bands just under the dome enables the building to be roughly dated to the late 11th or early 12th century.

Numerous features of these buildings render them completely unsuitable for the practice of *ziyāra*. They are located away from settlements, in rough terrain that is extremely difficult to access even today. Both Mil-i Radkan and Resget are a considerable distance from any villages; the modern village of Resget is visible in the distance from the tomb tower, whereas Mil-i Radkan is completely isolated (nor are earlier remains evident in the vicinity of either tower). The Lajim tower is situated at the edge of a village by the same name, but earlier ruins (possibly contemporaneous with the tomb tower or even earlier) are located at the opposite end of the village under land which is currently farmed. The modern village has grown up between the earlier village and the tomb tower; originally there would have been about a kilometre between the two. All three of the towers stand absolutely alone, without any subsidiary structures. There are modern steps leading up the hill to the Mil-i Radkan, indicating that previously access was at least moderately difficult. The Lajim and Resget towers are sited on steep, rocky ground, so that great care must be taken to walk around the buildings without stumbling.

The interiors of these structures are equally forbidding. They all have single, high entrances at least five feet off the ground, without any original staircases. Their interiors are very small and could not fit more than a few people at one time, and consist of single, dark, windowless, undecorated chambers. Finally, there are not any original cenotaphs marking the location of the burials underneath to circumambulate (and indeed, there are no burials underneath).[13] Both the form and function of these structures are very different from the typical Shiʿi shrines patronised by the Zaydi rulers at Amul, a relatively short distance away. Whereas the Zaydi shrines, like the larger Shiʿi complexes

Fig.1
Mil-i Radkan, tomb tower of
Muhammad b. Vandarin Bavand,
1016–1021, Iran

Fig.2
Lajim, tomb tower of Shahriyar
b. ʿAbbas b. Shahriyar, 1022–1023, Iran

Fig.3
Resget, tomb tower of Hurmuzdyar
and Habusyar, the sons of Masdara,
late 11th or early 12th century, Iran

Fig.1

Fig.2

at Najaf and Karbala, would have encouraged *ziyāra*, the Bavandid tomb towers made this nearly impossible. Access is very difficult given the height of the entrances and the lack of stairs, and efforts to gain entry are rewarded with a small, dark space and blank brick walls. And despite the foundation inscriptions ringing the exteriors of the buildings, their location in the landscape is not even conducive to circumambulation on the outside.

The only possible connection between these buildings and the practice of *ziyāra* is the foundation inscription encircling the exterior of the Mil-i Radkan referring to the building as a *mashhad*. *Mashhad* is derived from the verb *sh-h-d*, meaning 'to witness', and is more commonly used for the burial place of a martyr (*shahīd*), or more generally for that of a holy person; in other words, just the type of person who would be the incumbent of a mausoleum designed for *ziyāra*. The inscription over the doorway of Mil-i Radkan, however, uses the mixed Persian and Arabic title '*al-kiyā al-jalīl*' or 'important lord'. This secular terminology, combined with the fact that this Bavandid ruler had the tomb tower constructed for himself, makes it unlikely that he was designating himself as a figure of religious significance with the use of the term *mashhad*. In the Pahlavi inscription, the building is termed a *gunbad* (i.e. dome). This is a term used to refer to Islamic mausoleums by their most prominent architectural feature, and it would be the equivalent of the Arabic word *qubba* rather than *mashhad*. Since the terminology of Islamic funerary architecture is inherently ambiguous as well as changeable over time, there is no reason to believe that the word *mashhad* on this building referred to anything other than a funerary monument, particularly when the Pahlavi inscription is taken into account.[14] In the foundation inscription above the doorway, the building is called a *qaṣr* (i.e. palace) and hence has definite secular overtones.

The foundation inscription on the Lajim tower refers to that structure as a *qabr*, the Arabic term for a place of burial, as well as a *qubba* in Arabic and *gunbad* in Pahlavi. Although this is an equivalent translation, there are grammatical errors in the Arabic inscription indicating a lack of Arabic fluency, which also must be taken into account when analysing the terminology used in these inscriptions.[15] Finally, the

Fig.3

Arabic inscription at Resget calls the building a *qubba* and the Pahlavi translation is too badly damaged to read. There is no assertion of the Bavandids' Shiʿi beliefs in any of the inscriptions.

I have argued elsewhere that the unusual features of these tomb towers, including their inscriptions in Middle Persian, or Pahlavi, their use of the Sasanian calendar, distance from habitation, location on high ground, double domes, single entrances high off the ground, lack of windows, undecorated interior chambers, and the lack of burials, can be explained through Bavandid emulation of their Sasanian predecessors.[16] Emulation of what the Bavandids perceived to be the essential features of royal Sasanian funerary monuments served to emphasise their Sasanian connection. Unlike the Zaydis, the Bavandids were not descendants of the Prophet; however, they did have what every other Persianate dynasty of this era wished to have, namely a believable line of descent from the Sasanians. Their realm was also more culturally conservative than that of the Zaydis, with many of their subjects still espousing Zoroastrianism. The Zaydi Shiʿa had launched a considerable amount of missionary activity in Daylam and Gilan, resulting in the conversion of many of the inhabitants, whereas there is no evidence of missionary activity or inter-communal strife in areas ruled by the Bavandids. Travellers who visited the region remarked on its unique and conservative culture, with many customs pre-dating the arrival of Islam.[17] Unlike the Zaydis, who drew upon their ʿAlid lineage, the Bavandids stressed the Sasanian past and never made their Shiʿism a key element in the construction of their dynastic identity. Although their coinage did bear Shiʿi phrases, this was the only public statement of their confessional beliefs and can be explained by the wider geographic circulation of coinage, which therefore needs to address an external as well as an internal audience.[18] Furthermore, Bavandid coinage also occasionally deferred to Buyid overlordship, which the tomb tower inscriptions, aimed at the Bavandids' internal constituents, did not.[19]

By modelling their tomb towers on their understanding of Sasanian examples, the Bavandids cannot have intended for anyone to have ever entered their funerary monuments. Contemporary literary sources such as the *Shāhnāma* and the *Qābūsnāma* reveal the 11th-century perception of Sasanian royal funerals, with descriptions of royal corpses being embalmed, then wrapped in brocade and placed on a platform inside a mausoleum, with the door being sealed to prevent entry. The typical royal mausoleum was located in a remote spot and was of great height, with a high and inaccessible entrance, and a foundation inscription above the door identifying the incumbent and extolling his greatness. These features correspond perfectly with the Bavandid tomb towers and explain how these unusual structures would have been utilised, by placing the embalmed bodies on platforms rather than the standard Islamic practice of burying the remains beneath the floor. This does not imply that these Caspian dynasts were Zoroastrians or even insincere Muslims; local sources such as Ibn Isfandiyar are clear on the fact that the Bavandid rulers were Muslim following the conversion of Qarin b. Shahriyar in 841, and there are neither other sources nor any other evidence to cast any aspersions on their religious beliefs. This does imply that secular objectives outweighed religious concerns in the formation of a Bavandid dynastic identity and the assertion of their political legitimacy. Visible from a distance due to their prominent locations in the landscape, the tomb towers would have reified the Sasanian connection that the Bavandids always sought to emphasise to their subjects. For the Bavandids, then, this was a

Fig.4

Fig.5

fundamental political goal and much more important than the patronage of shrines, despite their adherence to Ithna ʿashari Shiʿism.

Ziyāra under Samanid patronage

For the Sunni Samanids, on the other hand, encouragement of *ziyāra* was a very important political and religious goal. The construction of shrines was an integral part of the Islamization of Central Asia, and helped both to transform the holy sites of other religions and to create new sites of pilgrimage to draw adherents away from earlier sites. The Central Asian shrines of the Samanid period were not dedicated to ʿAlids, however, but to Companions of the Prophet, mystics, and the Samanids themselves, in the form of a dynastic mausoleum expressly designed to accommodate the practice of *ziyāra* and visually symbolise the connection of the Samanids to their capital, Bukhara.

The Samanid dynasty was founded in the late ninth century by Ismaʿil, the descendant of a noble Central Asian who had converted to Islam in the Umayyad period. Ismaʿil established Bukhara as his capital, and the city flourished and expanded under his rule, as his court became a magnet for scholars and literati as well as traders and craftsmen. The Samanids consciously promoted the use of Persian as a language of literature and government, and it is under their patronage that New Persian came into its own as a literary language. The main pillars of Samanid dynastic identity, then, were a strong adherence to Sunni Islam, the promotion of Persian language and culture, and an attachment to the city of Bukhara. Their encouragement of Persian, however, does not imply a denigration of the Arabic language; the elite of the Samanid court were equally comfortable with either language, and it is the Samanid combination of impeccable Muslim credentials with a bold assertion of Persian culture that was instrumental in catapulting Islam from an Arab religion to a world religion.

One of the earliest and most celebrated extant monuments of Islamic architecture, the Samanid mausoleum is situated in a park in the western part of the city of Bukhara. The building is a domed cube measuring nearly ten metres per side, with slightly battered walls (fig.4). It is offset from the cardinal directions and has an entrance on each side, giving it the open and accessible shape known as *chahārṭāq*, which was also used for the shrine of ʿAli at Najaf, as noted earlier. The Samanid mausoleum is built of baked bricks, which are not only the material of construction but also the primary material of decoration, arranged in such a way as to give a basket-weave appearance to the surface of the building. The interior walls are also deeply textured in a similar pattern, a decorative effect that indicates that the building was meant to be entered. The interior is flooded with light from the four open entrances and from the windows in the squinches under the dome and from the brick lattice which fills the arches in the flat sections of the zone of transition, allowing light to enter from the exterior gallery (fig.5). The cenotaph is offset from the centre, but there is still sufficient space to circumambulate. An inscription over the eastern doorway names the third Samanid ruler, Nasr b. Ahmad b. Ismaʿil (d. 943); however, the Soviet excavators found three bodies interred under the floor, and I have argued elsewhere that the building was constructed by Ismaʿil Samani (d. 907), the founder of the Samanid dynasty, who is buried there with his father.[20] Since the inscription is carved into the wood of the doorframe rather than forming an epigraphic programme integral to the building, it could have been added later, after the death of Nasr, which accounts for the third body.

Ismaʿil was known to patronise architecture in particular, and the Samanid historian Narshakhi tells us that Ismaʿil constructed a *ribāṭ* (fortification) by the Samarqand gate in Bukhara, courts and gardens in a suburban area known as the Juy-i Mulian, a Friday mosque in the Juy-i Mulian area, and a mosque with a courtyard near the citadel of Bukhara. He also enlarged the Friday mosque of Bukhara by one third.[21] None of

Fig.4
Samanid mausoleum, 10th century, Bukhara, Uzbekistan

Fig.5
Interior window grille, Samanid mausoleum, 10th century, Bukhara, Uzbekistan

these constructions have survived, and they were almost certainly built of unbaked brick, the usual building material of Central Asia during this period. Covered with a decorative revetment of stucco, this was a much cheaper option than baked brick, yet still an aesthetically effective one. Even under the 11th-century successors to the Samanids, the Qarakhanids, the Friday mosque of Bukhara was only partially composed of baked brick.[22] The Samanid mausoleum, therefore, was innovative in this respect as well. Baked brick denoted importance, and it was used to an unprecedented degree in this building. But what really makes the Samanid mausoleum exceptional is not just the quality and quantity of the decoration, but the fact that brick imitates and replaces other materials that were cheaper and more readily available. The motifs around the doorways, the window grilles, the roundels in the spandrels of the arches of the zone of transition, and the bands of decoration at the base of the dome are some of the elements that would normally be composed of stucco. Soviet scholars have long noted the resemblance of the brick colonettes of the zone of transition to contemporary wooden columns, citing this as an example of a local tradition. But the local tradition was precisely to use *wooden* columns, as evidenced by the Friday mosque at Khiva, by discoveries in mountainous regions in Tajikistan and by textual references to the use of wood.[23] Both stucco and wood were used in the Samanid mausoleum to a very limited degree: the ribs of the squinches and the colonettes of the exterior arcade are accented with carved stucco, and the entrances of the building have wooden lintels. The relative lack of these materials indicates that the intention was also to luxuriate in the conspicuous use of that expensive and esteemed material, baked brick, as well as to differentiate the building from the prominent constructions of the past. This resulted in the creation of a monument fitting for the Samanid dynasty and for Bukhara, with its new status as a capital and as one of the most illustrious cities in the Islamic world.

Isma'il had entered Bukhara as governor in 874. His main rivals for power were the Bukhar Khodahs, an aristocratic family who had ruled the Bukharan oasis in the pre-Islamic period, when it was a Soghdian city-state. Although they had lost all formal political power in 782, the Bukhar Khodahs still remained wealthy and influential. In order to consolidate his position, Isma'il purchased the suburban estates of the Bukhar Khodahs at Juy-i Mulian, built palaces and gardens, and gave these as *waqf* (endowments) to his own clients. He also expropriated the Bukhara property of the Bukhar Khodahs; this was justified on the basis of one member of the family's conviction for apostasy a century earlier, but Isma'il compensated the grandson with a stipend equal to the income from the estates. Therefore, the most notable Soghdian family in the city did not lose financially, but did lose one of the main bases of their tie to Bukhara. The Soghdian aristocracy did not take kindly to this, and Isma'il ultimately had several of the members of the Bukhar Khodah family imprisoned for some time. He tried to convert their palace at Varakhsha, near Bukhara, into a mosque, but had to back down in the face of popular opposition. Generally, though, he did manage to decrease the standing of the old Soghdian aristocracy, and even his abandonment of the outer defences of Bukhara can be seen at least in part as a populist move against these potential rivals. These walls of the oasis had been started around 775 at the behest of a group of Soghdian nobles; they were not completed until 830. Although the walls were necessary to protect the settled population of the oasis from nomadic incursions, the annual maintenance that was required took an enormous amount of both time and money, both levied from the populace. Hence Isma'il's famous declaration, 'As long as I live, I am the walls of Bukhara', can be seen as a rejection of the *ancien regime* as well as an assertion of his own strength.

This assertion also embodied Isma'il's own identification with his adopted city, and underlines the personal nature of his rule and of the loyalty of Bukharans to him. Roy Mottahedeh has shown how political legitimacy in this period was based upon the establishment of contractual, personal bonds between a ruler and his subjects and the continual calculation of the benefit derived from the relationship.[24] The establishment of a dynastic mausoleum in Bukhara would have visually symbolised these bonds and the links between the dynasty and the city. By choosing

Fig.6

to remain in Bukhara for all eternity, in a mausoleum that was both conspicuously expensive and readily accessible, the Samanids expressed their strong ties to the city, effectively competing with the long-established Soghdian aristocracy, led by the Bukhar Khodahs.

In addition to being attached to their most prominent local family, the Bukharans were also still fond of their local pre-Islamic festivals. Narshakhi relates that the grave of the legendary hero, Afrasiab, was located inside the city by one of the gates, while the tomb of another legendary figure, Siyavush, was next to another gate.[25] The tomb of Siyavush was venerated by the Zoroastrians, who still at this time sacrificed roosters at the site for the Zoroastrian New Year's celebrations, while Bukharans (not specifically Zoroastrians) also held lamentations at the site for the death of Siyavush. Afrasiab, in spite of being ostensibly buried in Bukhara, was associated more with Ramitan, a town in the oasis where the Bukhar Khodahs had previously had their winter residence. Siyavush, however, and specifically his eponymous burial site, was closely connected with Bukhara. And despite being a hero rather than a religious figure, there were definite religious overtones to the sacrificial and mourning ceremonies held in his honour. Hence it is quite likely that the Samanids were also competing with the cult of Siyavush; since mourning at the grave of this legendary figure was a long-standing tradition of Bukhara, the Samanids probably intended for this to be replaced by *ziyāra* to the dynastic mausoleum. As Narshakhi reported, the tomb did indeed become a focus of pilgrimage for Bukharans, and it has remained so to this day.[26] Isma'il was a secular ruler, but has been remembered and revered as a 'just' ruler, from the time of Narshakhi onwards.[27] His construction of a dynastic mausoleum and successful implementation of a tradition of *ziyāra* associated with the structure is therefore an excellent example of the appropriation of a religious practice for secular goals.

In addition to their own dynastic mausoleum, the Samanids patronised the shrines of religiously significant individuals such as Hakim al-Tirmidhi (d. *circa* 898), a Sufi shaykh who was born in the southern city of Tirmidh, in the early 9th century. Al-Tirmidhi left his home town for the Hajj in his late twenties and then studied hadith in Basra. He later returned to Tirmidh, where he preached his own brand of mysticism. He believed in esoteric knowledge, and his thought contained strands of Neoplatonism and Gnosticism, as well as Shi'i themes, while in some ways he also foreshadowed Ash'arism. This type of mysticism, difficult to characterise in terms of religious categories which solidified later, was typical of this formative period.[28] It is quite likely that the original construction of the mausoleum of Hakim al-Tirmidhi was carried out by one of the early Samanids.[29] The family had a strong connection to the city of Tirmidh, which was near the birthplace of their ancestor, Saman, the great-grandfather of Isma'il. Moreover, Isma'il in particular was known for his patronage of the religious classes, regardless of sectarian affiliation: for example, he purchased the village of Barkad and endowed the proceeds, with one third going to the descendants of the Shi'i Imams 'Ali and Ja'far, one third to the poor, and one third to his own descendants.[30] This is an excellent example of the fluidity of categories during this period and the acceptability of Sunni veneration of the family of the Prophet.

The mausoleum of Hakim al-Tirmidhi was appended to a pre-existing structure; an arched opening connects the two, but the newer mausoleum is five feet taller than the original structure (fig.6). Soviet excavations have shown that the older section was originally a Buddhist sanctuary and dates back to the second century; Buddhism was the dominant religion in this region and there have been many finds in and around Tirmidh.[31] This Buddhist shrine was transformed into a small mosque, probably a nine-domed structure, when the mausoleum was constructed in the early 10th century (fig.7). This is a different phenomenon from the intended replacement of the veneration of Siyavush with *ziyāra* to the dynastic mausoleum in Bukhara; in that case, a new structure was built in a different part of the city in the hopes of luring loyalty away from the older site and creating a completely new tradition. The transformation of an ancient Buddhist shrine into the shrine of Hakim al-Tirmidhi, on the other hand, represents

Fig.7

Fig.6
Mausoleum of Hakim al-Tirmidhi, view from the mosque, 10th century and later, Tirmidh (Termez), Uzbekistan

Fig.7
Exterior of the mosque and mausoleum of Hakim al-Tirmidhi

a process seen in many parts of the world when one religion supersedes another, with the identity of holy places evolving while their location remains the same.[32] A shrine intended for *ziyāra* can be a more accessible way of effecting such a transition than a large congregational place of worship, since it involves personal piety on a smaller scale and lends itself more readily to an emphasis on similar practices; the circumambulation of a cenotaph associated with *ziyāra*, for example, is rather analogous to the Buddhist circumambulation of a stupa, which can also be associated with the remains of a holy individual.

The mausoleum of Hakim al-Tirmidhi is a small, domed square, measuring 5.1 × 4.7 metres, which can be entered through a door on its southern side. The dome rests on pendentives rather than squinches, a feature which is unusual in the eastern Islamic world but which can be seen in this region at this time. The pendentives are now covered by stucco *muqarnas* decoration but their structure is visible in archival photos and drawings. The current stucco revetment and design scheme is a restoration of modifications that were made in the late 11th century by a Qarakhanid ruler, Ahmad b. Hizr. The shrine has been a regional focal point of *ziyāra* since its construction, as is evidenced by the continued high level of patronage the site has attracted. Later accretions include two additional mausoleums and a *khānaqāh* (Sufi lodge), as well as the magnificent marble cenotaph from the Timurid period (fig.8). The mausoleum could never have held very many people at one time, but the cenotaph is clearly visible from most parts of the mosque. Indeed, the very fact that the mausoleum was attached to a mosque indicates that the patron intended for the faithful to visit it. And the form of the relatively diminutive nine-domed mosque in particular was often associated with the burial sites of religiously prominent individuals, and hence more readily associated with *ziyāra* rather than with Friday prayer, which would have occurred in a large congregational mosque.[33]

Conclusions

Just as the mystical thought of Hakim al-Tirmidhi defies easy definition according to the rigid categories of Shiʿi and Sunni, which have become so entrenched today, so the practice of *ziyāra* and the patronage of shrines cannot be definitively categorised as Shiʿi in the 10th and 11th centuries. For the Samanids, the construction of their own dynastic

Fig.8

mausoleum as a site for pilgrimage, as well as patronising shrines marking the burial places of religiously significant individuals, formed part of their larger goals of establishing themselves in the city of Bukhara and providing Islamic alternatives to the celebration of older holy sites. Neither the Samanids nor the incumbents of the shrines they sponsored were Shiʿi, and yet the encouragement of *ziyāra* was a part of their policy. The Bavandids, on the other hand, were Shiʿi but never engaged in architectural patronage which would encourage the practice of *ziyāra*. As their Sasanian connections were the key component of their dynastic image and the source of their claims to political legitimacy, it was this historic link they chose to emphasise in their funerary monuments, leading to a form that definitely did not lend itself to *ziyāra*. Both textual and architectural evidence for any other shrines in their realm are lacking. Only the Zaydi rulers of the western Alborz fit the expected model, but it can also be argued that, with their particular brand of Shiʿism, their political and religious goals were one and the same, and those goals were definitely advanced through the construction of shrine complexes. For the rulers of this period, it was their particular political programmes rather than their confessional divisions that determined their architectural patronage, but it is also clear that those confessional divisions were not clear-cut or absolute. In the 10th and 11th centuries, *ziyāra* was not an exclusively Shiʿi practice, and could also be utilised by Sunni rulers to promote Sunni shrines. By taking political as well as religious factors into account, we can gain a much more nuanced view of the existing corpus of buildings from this period and the motivations of the patrons who constructed them.

Fig.8
Mausoleums, shrine of Hakim al-Tirmidhi

1 Editor's note: Melanie Michailidis tragically passed away on 1 February 2013 before this volume was published. Sincere thanks are due to Heghnar Watenpaugh, member of the Melanie Michailidis Legacy Project, for her assistance in ensuring Melanie's contribution is published to the highest standard.

2 See, for example, the seminal article by Oleg Grabar, 'The Earliest Islamic Commemorative Structures', *Ars Orientalis,* 6 (1966), pp.39–40.

3 For secondary sources on the Zaydi regimes of northern Iran, see Wilferd Madelung, 'The Minor Dynasties of Northern Iran', in *The Cambridge History of Iran*, vol.4, *The Period from the Arab Invasion to the Saljuqs*, ed. Richard Frye (Cambridge, 1975), pp.206–212, 219–222; Muhammad Saber Khan, 'The Early History of Zaydî Shî'ism in Daylamân and Gîlân', in Seyyed Hossein Nasr, ed., *Mélanges offerts à Henry Corbin* (Tehran, 1977), pp.257–277.

4 This was also true of their Sunni rivals, such as the Hanbali missionary Abu Ja'far al-Thumi, whose funerary shrine at Rasht was a focus of *ziyāra* into the 20th century. Madelung, 'Minor Dynasties', p.209.

5 Muḥammad b. Ḥasan b. Isfandiyār, *Tārīkh-i Ṭabaristān. An Abridged Translation of the History of Ṭabaristán compiled about A.H. 613 (A.D. 1216) by Muḥammad b. al-Ḥasan b. Isfandiyár, based on the India office MS. compared with two MSS. in the British Museum*, trans. Edward G. Browne (Leiden and London, 1905), p.48.

6 Ibn Isfandiyār, *Tārīkh-i Ṭabaristān*, p.49.

7 Ibid., pp.55, 57–58.

8 See André Godard, 'L'origine de la madrasa, de la mosqueé et du caravansérail à quatre *īwāns*', *Ars Islamica*, 15, 16 (1951), pp.1–9; Robert Hillenbrand, *Islamic Architecture: Form, Function & Meaning* (Edinburgh, 1994), pp.173–180.

9 See Sheila S. Blair, 'Sufi Saints and Shrine Architecture in the Early Fourteenth Century', *Muqarnas*, 7 (1990), pp.35–49; Lisa Golombek, 'The Cult of Saints and Shrine Architecture in the Fourteenth Century', in Dickran Kouymjian, ed., *Near Eastern Numismatics, Iconography, Epigraphy and History: Studies in Honor of George C. Miles* (Beirut, 1974), pp.419–430.

10 Muḥammad b. Aḥmad al-Muqaddasī, *The Best Divisions for Knowledge of the Regions: A Translation of Aḥasan al-taqāsīm fī ma'rifat al-aqālīm. Al-Muqaddasi*, trans. Basil A. Collins (Reading, 1994), pp.320–324; *Ḥudūd Al-'Ālam: The Regions of the World, a Persian Geography, 372 A.H.– 982 A.D.*, trans. Vladimir Minorsky (London, 1937), p.135, also asserts that most of the inhabitants of the Bavandid realm were Zoroastrian; see also Ibn Ḥawqal, *Kitāb Ṣūrat al-arḍ,* ed. Johannes H. Kramers (Leiden, 1967), p.366.

11 Ibn Ḥawqal, *Kitāb Ṣūrat al-arḍ*, p.232.

12 On the architectural symbolism of the dome, see Karl Lehman, 'The Dome of Heaven', *Art Bulletin*, 27, 1 (1945), pp.1–27; Alexander Soper, 'The Dome of Heaven in Asia', *Art Bulletin*, 29 (1947), pp.225–248; Doris Behrens-Abouseif, 'The *Qubba*: An Aristocratic Type of *Zawiya*', *Annales Islamologiques*, 19 (1981), pp.157–189; Oleg Grabar, 'From Dome of Heaven to Pleasure Dome', *Journal of the Society for Architectural Historians*, 49, 1 (1990), pp.15–21.

13 There is currently a cenotaph in the Lajim tower, but this was added when the building acquired a holy association with the 18th-century caretaker and became known as the 'Imamzada 'Abdallah'.

14 For a discussion of this inscription and the etymology of the word *mashhad,* see Sheila S. Blair, *The Monumental Inscriptions from Early Islamic Iran and Transoxiana* (Leiden, 1992), pp.85–87. On the ambiguity of Islamic funerary terminology generally, see Hillenbrand, *Islamic Architecture*, pp.255–260; see also Grabar, 'Commemorative Structures', pp.9–12.

15 See Blair, *Monumental Inscriptions*, pp.88–89.

16 Melanie Michailidis, *Landmarks of the Persian Renaissance: Monumental Funerary Architecture in Iran and Central Asia in the Tenth and Eleventh Centuries* (Ph.D. dissertation, Massachusetts Institute of Technology, Boston, 2007), pp.274–315; Melanie Michailidis, 'In the Footsteps of the Sasanians: Funerary Architecture and Bavandid Legitimacy', in Sussan Babaie and Talinn Grigor, ed., *Persian Kingship and Architecture: Strategies of Power in Iran from the Achaemenids to the Pahlavis* (London, forthcoming 2015).

17 al-Muqaddasī, *Divisions for Knowledge*, p.324.

18 Madelung, 'Minor Dynasties', p.217.

19 Ibid., p.217.

20 Michailidis, *Persian Renaissance*, pp.242–245.

21 Muḥammad b. Ja'far Narshakhī, *Tārīkh-i Bukhārā,* ed. Mudarris Razavi (Tehran, 1351/1972), pp.21, 39–40, 69, 71; Richard Frye, *History of Bukhara* (Cambridge, MA, 1954), pp.15, 27–28, 50, 52.

22 Narshakhī, *Tārīkh-i Bukhārā*, pp.69–70; Frye, *History of Bukhara*, p.51.

23 Narshakhī, *Tārīkh-i Bukhārā*, pp.20, 24, 70–71; Frye, *History of Bukhara*, pp.14–15, 17–18, 50–51.

24 Roy P.Mottahedeh, *Loyalty and Leadership in an Early Islamic Society* (Princeton, 1980).

25 Narshakhī, *Tārīkh-i Bukhārā*, pp.23–24, 32; Frye, *History of Bukhara*, pp.17, 23.

26 Frye, *History of Bukhara*, p.93.

27 Niẓām al-Mulk, *The Book of Government or Rules for Kings: the Siyar al-Muluk, or, Siyasat-nama of Nizam al-Mulk*, trans. Hubert Darke (London, 1960), pp.14–22, 61.

28 Yves Marquet, 'al-Tirmidhī', *EI2*, vol.10, pp.544–546.

29 See Michael E. Masson, *Starii Termez i ego Izucheniye* (Uzbekistan, 1959), inv. no. SD1531/M31, p.70.

30 Narshakhī, *Tārīkh-i Bukhārā*, p.22; Frye, *History of Bukhara*, p.16.

31 V. M. Filimonov, *Obobshchayushchii Otchet po issledovaniyu, analizy arkhitekturi i dekora, datirovke otdel'niikh sooruzhenii i periodov razvitiya arkhitekturnogo kompleksa Khakim al' Termezi v gorode Termez* (Uzbekistan, 1957), Inv. no. SD1599/F53, pp.167–170.

32 An excellent case in point is the Great Mosque of Damascus, where a Phoenician temple was superseded by the Roman Temple of Jupiter, which in turn was superseded by the Byzantine Church of St John the Baptist, and finally by the Umayyad Great Mosque.

33 Geoffrey R. D. King, 'The Nine Bay Domed Mosque in Islam', *Madrider Mitteilungen,* 30 (1989), pp.332–390.

Part 3: Inscriptions on art, architecture and coinage

8

Early Qur'ans 'signed' by the Shiʿi Imams

Sheila R. Canby

In the summer of 1598 Shah ʿAbbas I, the Safavid ruler of Iran, defeated his eastern neighbours, the Uzbeks, who had occupied Khurasan province since 1589. They had ransacked the shrine of Imam Reza (ʿAli al-Rida) at Mashhad, a place of enormous importance to the Safavids as it contains the tomb of the only Shiʿi Imam to be buried in Iran. The damage to the shrine exceeded that of previous raids on the holy site.[1] The Uzbeks stole all the gold from the dome over the Imam's tomb, killed all the shrine attendants and emptied the treasury.[2] They also reportedly defiled the tomb of Shah ʿAbbas's grandfather, Shah Tahmasp.[3] Although the physical renovation of the shrine began a few years after the reconquest of Khurasan, Shah ʿAbbas apparently began giving books to the shrine's library as early as 1599. Some of the early Qur'ans donated to the shrine by Shah ʿAbbas and a few related manuscripts are the subject of this paper.

In the course of identifying objects to include in the British Museum's exhibition, *Shah ʿAbbas: The Remaking of Iran*, I encountered a group of early Qur'ans donated to the shrine of Imam Reza by Shah ʿAbbas containing signatures of several of the Shiʿi Imams. The Qur'ans are datable on the basis of style to the 9th or 10th century, but most of the Imams in question died in the 7th or 8th century, resulting in a conundrum of style and dating versus authorship. Since the authenticity of the manuscripts themselves is not at issue, the question is whether the signatures appear in the Qur'ans as a result of skulduggery or in response to official pressure. The following discussion will consider the Safavid context of these manuscripts.[4] Do they indicate the creation of a market for historically important antiquities or are they examples of the art-historical consciousness that developed in the courts of 15th- and 16th-century Iran?[5]

In his *Calligraphers and Painters*, Qadi Ahmad states that the first thing that God created was the '*qalam* of marvellous writing'.[6] He goes on to ascribe the invention of kufic script to the first Shiʿi Imam, ʿAli, saying, 'Then that writing which, like kohl, cleared the sight of men of understanding with divine revelation and the commands and prohibitions of His Holiness the Prophet – God's prayer on him and his family! – was the *kufi* writing. And there exist tracings by the miraculous *qalams* of His Holiness the Shah, the Refuge of Sanctity (i.e. ʿAli) which enlighten the sight of the soul and brighten the tablets of the heart. None wrote better than that Holiness – God's blessing on him! – and the most excellent *kufi* is that which he has traced – God's peace on him!'[7]

Qadi Ahmad describes ʿAli's treatment of the letter *alif* and notes that he was succeeded in excellent writing by his son, Imam Hasan, the second Imam, who copied the Qur'an while in seclusion from the Umayyad 'usurper' Muʿawiya. Qadi Ahmad then states that, 'One Qur'an in the writing of His Holiness [Imam Hasan] was in the library of the king, ...Sultan-Shah Tahmasp al-Husayni.' Furthermore, in one recension of his text he notes that he had had 'the honour to see that Qur'an'.[8] Was this the same Qur'an that some 30 years after the death of Shah Tahmasp in 1576 was donated by Shah ʿAbbas to the shrine of Imam Reza (fig.1)? Qadi Ahmad also singles out the fourth Imam, Zayn al-ʿAbidin, and the eighth Imam, ʿAli Reza b. Musa b. Jaʿfar b. Muhammad al-Baqir, who is buried at Mashhad, as having carried on the calligraphic tradition. Like the Qur'an copied by Imam Hasan, Qadi Ahmad signals the existence of copies of the Qur'an in the handwriting of these two later Imams.[9]

This Safavid awareness of extant copies of the Qur'an copied by the Shiʿi Imams is echoed in the *History of Shah ʿAbbas* of the chronicler

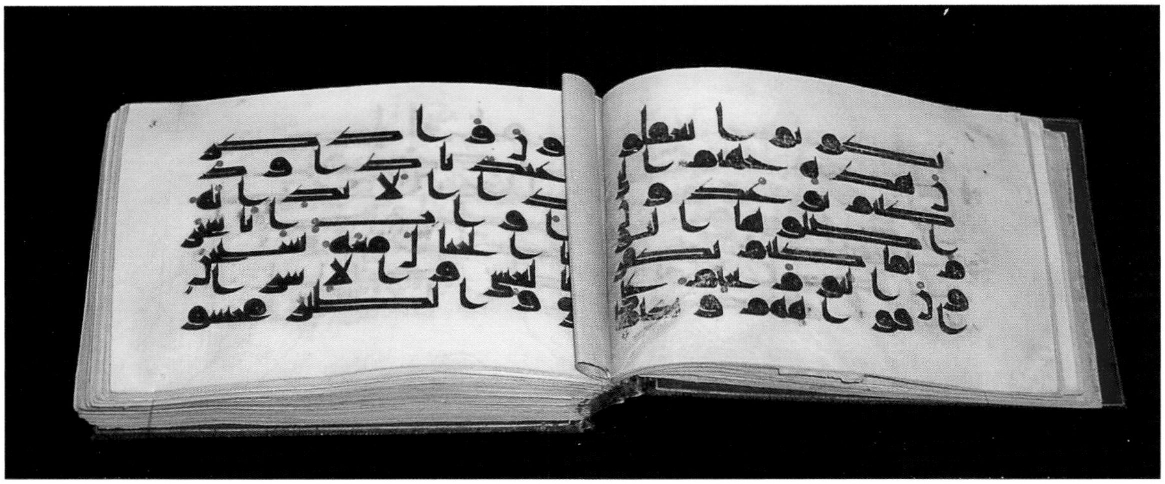

Fig.1

Fig.1
Qur'an section signed by Imam Hasan, start of *juz'* 23 to end of *juz'* 25, dated 41/661–662

Iskandar Beg Munshi. Describing the pillaging of the shrine of Imam Reza at Mashhad in 1589, Iskandar Munshi states, 'The shrine library, which housed a collection of books from all parts of the Islamic world, including precious copies of the Koran in the writing of the immaculate Imams and masters of the calligraphic art such as Yaqut Mosta'semi and the six masters, and other learned works of priceless value, was pillaged; and the Uzbegs sold these masterpieces to one another like so many potsherds'.[10]

Qur'ans in the shrine of Imam Reza, Mashhad

In his catalogue of Qur'ans in the library of the shrine of Imam Reza at Mashhad, the first Qur'an that Gulchin-i Ma'ani lists is an example with 15 lines of kufic script to the page and the 'signature' of Imam 'Ali b. Abi Talib, the first Imam (fig.2). The author dates the manuscript to the third century AH (i.e. tenth century AD) and notes that it is a section starting at the beginning with sura *Hūd* (Q.11) and ending at the end of sura *al-Kahf* (Q.18).[11] On the first folio of the manuscript is a *waqfnāma* (endowment notice) in the hand of Shaykh Baha'i 'Amili, the leading theologian, jurist and polymath at the court of Shah 'Abbas, stating that it was made *waqf* to the shrine of Imam Reza in Jumada I 1008 AH (November-December 1599). The signature is written on the last page of the Qur'an section, on two lines and enclosed with marginal rulings. According to Gulchin-i Ma'ani the manuscript does not have marginal rulings on the other pages. Thus, the person who added the signature of Imam 'Ali highlighted it by adding marginal lines to the page.

Aside from the impossibility of a 9th or 10th-century Qur'an being signed by someone who died in 661, the actual letters themselves are inconsistent with the account given by Qadi Ahmad. He describes 'Ali's writing of the letter *alif* as follows: 'In the blessed writing of the Shah, the Refuge of Sanctity, the tops of the *alifs* are twin-horned and the beauty of these *alifs* is manifested in the highest degree of elegance, grace, and delicacy.'[12] In the manuscript in Mashhad very few of the *alifs* have 'twin horns' and on those that do, the horns are not particularly pronounced.

In the chronology of the Shi'i Imams the next Qur'an to bear a signature is *juz'* 23 to 25 with seven lines to the page and elegant, elongated letters (fig.1). This one is signed by Hasan b. 'Ali, the second Imam who

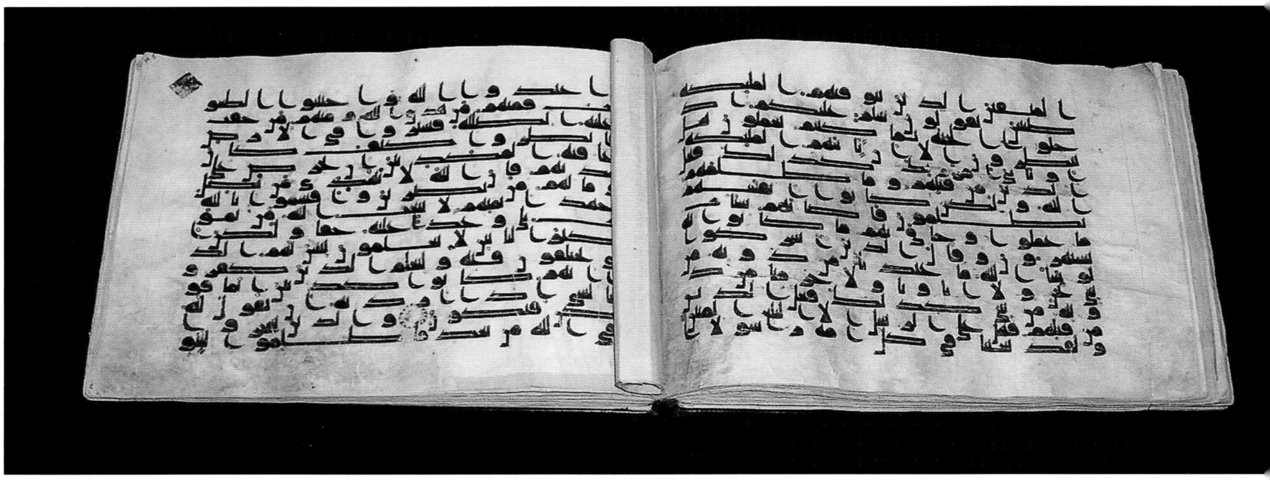

Fig.2

Fig.3

Fig.2
Qur'an section signed by Imam 'Ali, suras 11–18, 3rd/10th century

Fig.3
Qur'an section signed by Imam Husayn, sura 20:72–135

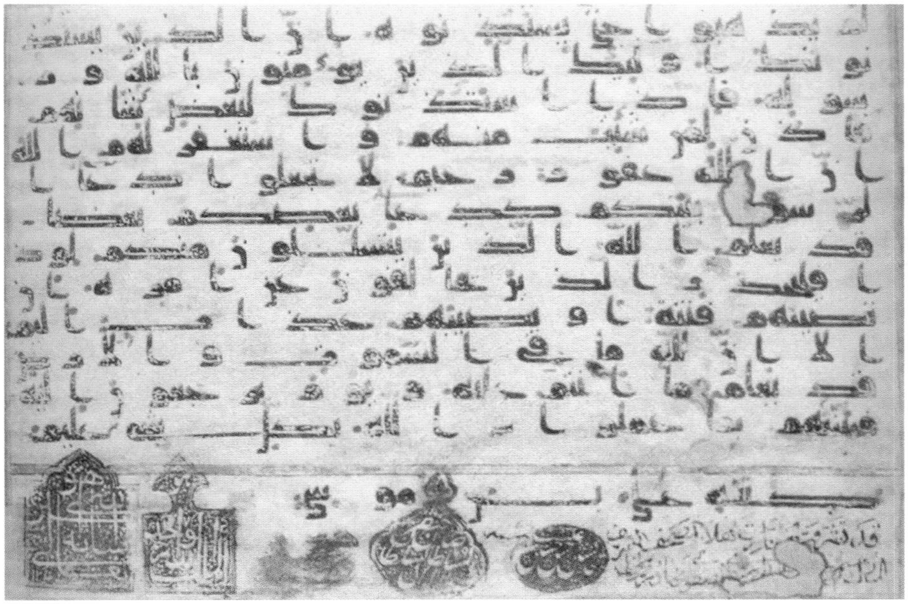

Fig.4

was reputed to have been a skilled calligrapher, known for copying the Qur'an. As with the Qur'an 'signed' by Imam 'Ali, this one contains a *waqfnāma* written by Shaykh Baha'i but no date. The signature of Imam Hasan appears on the last page along with the date 41 AH (661–662). As with the other Qur'ans in this group, the style of the letters indicates a date over two hundred years later than this signature. Estelle Whelan, Sheila Blair and others have noted that there are very few dated early kufic Qur'ans and none that can reliably be placed in the seventh century AD.[13] One famous example bears an endowment notice, dated 262 AH (876) and name of Amajur, Abbasid governor of Damascus.[14] The style of the letters in the Imam Hasan Qur'an closely resembles those in the Amajur volume, especially the joined up letters *lām-wāw* and the initial *alif*s. While this does not allow us to date the Mashhad Qur'an precisely to the 870s, it does preclude a dating to the seventh century.

The Imam Hasan Qur'an in the Mashhad shrine does not contain the name of Shah Tahmasp. Nonetheless, the possibility exists that this manuscript came into the possession of Shah 'Abbas along with the rest of the contents of the Safavid royal library and may be the very Qur'an that Qadi Ahmad claimed to have seen. Although the texts do not state that Shaykh Baha'i made the choice of which manuscripts to donate to the shrine of Imam Reza, his position as a leading theologian at the Safavid court and the fact that he wrote the *waqfnāma*s himself strongly suggest that he advised the Shah on what to include in his *waqf* to the shrine of Imam Reza. Additionally, the *waqfnāma*s are not all dated to the same year. From shortly after Shah 'Abbas's conquest of Khurasan from the Uzbeks in 1598, he began to make gifts to the shrine of Imam Reza and continued to do so for at least a decade.

A Qur'an *juz'* (section) in the shrine of Imam Reza (fig.3) containing a signature of Imam Husayn on the last page, but without a date or the *waqfnāma* of Shah 'Abbas, presumably was not among the gifts chosen by Shaykh Baha'i. It consists of seven lines of text per side. Although the style of the script resembles that of the Imam Hasan Qur'an, it is distinct from another example in a private collection that is signed *'katabahu Ḥusayn b. 'Alī'* (it was penned by Husayn b. 'Ali).[15] The lines of text are closer together on the page in the private collection, and the individual letters differ in the two examples. Where the tail of the *alif* in the Mashhad text swings gracefully to the right, it is less exaggerated and forms a short hook in the other version. Clearly, even if one person added the signature of Imam Husayn to both pages, the pages themselves were copied by different hands, as the stylistic differences in the script indicate.

The shrine of Imam Reza has yet another partial Qur'an with an Imam's signature, this time of Imam Reza himself (fig.4). His signature appears below a double marginal ruling along with a number of seal impressions and notes. The inscription on the right, under the signature,

Fig.4
Qur'an section signed by Imam Reza, suras 24–57

implies that this *muṣḥaf* (codex) was brought on pilgrimage by one of the Safavid shahs, the singular one of the Safavi sultans, the Haydari Safavi Bahadur Khan. The seals, as read by Gulchin-i Maʿani divulge little as they only consist of honorific titles, such as 'The Sultan, Son of the Sultan, Lord of the Conjunctions'. The *waqfnāma*, not on this page, attributes the gift of Muhammad Reza Shah Pahlavi in 1338 Sh./1958–1959. Unlike the Qur'ans with the *waqfnāma* copied by Shaykh Baha'i, the manuscript appears to have no connection to a particular librarian. The absence of dates on the seal impressions and of names of specific individuals confirms the natural doubts about the authenticity of the signature.

With the Qur'an section given by Muhammad Reza Pahlavi to the shrine of Imam Reza, the question arises of whether it has any connection to the Qur'ans given to the shrine in Safavid times. Does the absence of any substantive information in the form of early dates or names in the seals and notations around the signature of Imam Reza, whose name is given as ʿAli b. Musa, increase the likelihood of this Qur'an having been altered before the Qajar or Pahlavi era? Although the manuscript includes a brief statement saying that Muhammad Reza Shah Pahlavi made this Qur'an *waqf* in Bahman 1338 Sh. (January 1960), it also includes a note written by Ayatollah Milani dated Jumada II 1379 AH (December 1959). Ayatollah Milani, a noted cleric from Najaf who moved to Mashhad in 1953, states that the manuscript came from the library of Shaykh ʿAbd al-Husayn al-Amini in Najaf before being acquired by Milani himself. One wonders if the Qur'an had originally been in the library of the shrine of Imam ʿAli at Najaf, one of the holiest of Shiʿi shrines which Shah ʿAbbas visited in 1624 during his conquest of Iraq. Although Iskandar Beg Munshi does not specify any gifts that Shah ʿAbbas presented to the shrine, he does note that the Shah stayed there for ten days and ordered improvements to the complex.[16] After leaving Najaf, Shah ʿAbbas proceeded to the other major Iraqi shrine city, Karbala, where he presented the shrine with gifts of carpets and textiles,[17] so the gift of a Qur'an with the signature of Imam Reza would have been in keeping with the rare objects deemed suitable for presentation to the shrines of the Imams. Presumably Ayatollah Milani made the Qur'an available through sale or gift to the Shah who then donated it to the shrine of Imam Reza. Naturally the Shah would have perceived this as a fitting gift to the shrine, and the signature of Imam Reza in itself would have commended the gift to him. However, it is not clear how he felt about the incomplete Safavid honorifics in the manuscript. Moreover, the *waqfnāma* does not state the reason for the Shah giving the manuscript in 1960. As he had married his third wife, Farah Diba, in 1959, the *waqf* may have had some connection with this event.

Imami Qur'ans in other Iranian collections

A manuscript from the Chihil Sutun Palace in Isfahan is a partial Qur'an of the ninth or tenth century written in kufic script on parchment with seventeen lines to the page (fig.5). At some point in its history the manuscript was rebound and at least one gathering of folios was set upside down. Pasted onto the last folio of the manuscript and written on paper is an attribution in *muḥaqqaq* script to the fourth Shiʿi Imam, Zayn al-ʿAbidin. Although there is no ownership information in the manuscript, it is believed to have belonged to Shah ʿAbbas II who ruled Iran from 1642 to 1666. This may be apocryphal but if it is true, it would indicate that Shah ʿAbbas I did not give all of his old Qur'ans to the shrine of Imam Reza, assuming Shah ʿAbbas II inherited the manuscript. Furthermore, a market may have existed in the mid-17th century for Qur'ans with ascriptions to or signatures of the Shiʿi Imams, particularly those mentioned by Qadi Ahmad as the originators of the Arabic script. If so, forged signatures or attributions in early Qur'ans would have continued to attract important, even royal clients.

Two additional fragmentary kufic Qur'ans with signatures of Shiʿi Imams can be found in Iranian public collections. One, in the National Museum of Iran, has six lines of text and is signed '*katabahu wa dhahhabahu ʿAlī b. Abī Ṭālib*' ('Ali b. Abi Talib wrote and gilded [i.e. illuminated] it).[18] The inscription is of particular interest because it assigns the illumination of the manuscript to Imam ʿAli as well as the text. In his chapter on painters, gilders (illuminators) and other artists responsible for the decoration, rather than copying, of manuscripts, Qadi Ahmad apparently refers to the very Qur'an under discussion here. He states: 'The portraitists of the image (*paykar*) of this wonderful skill trace this art to the marvellously writing *qalam* of the Frontispiece of the Five Members of the 'Companions of the Cloak', i.e. ʿAli, the

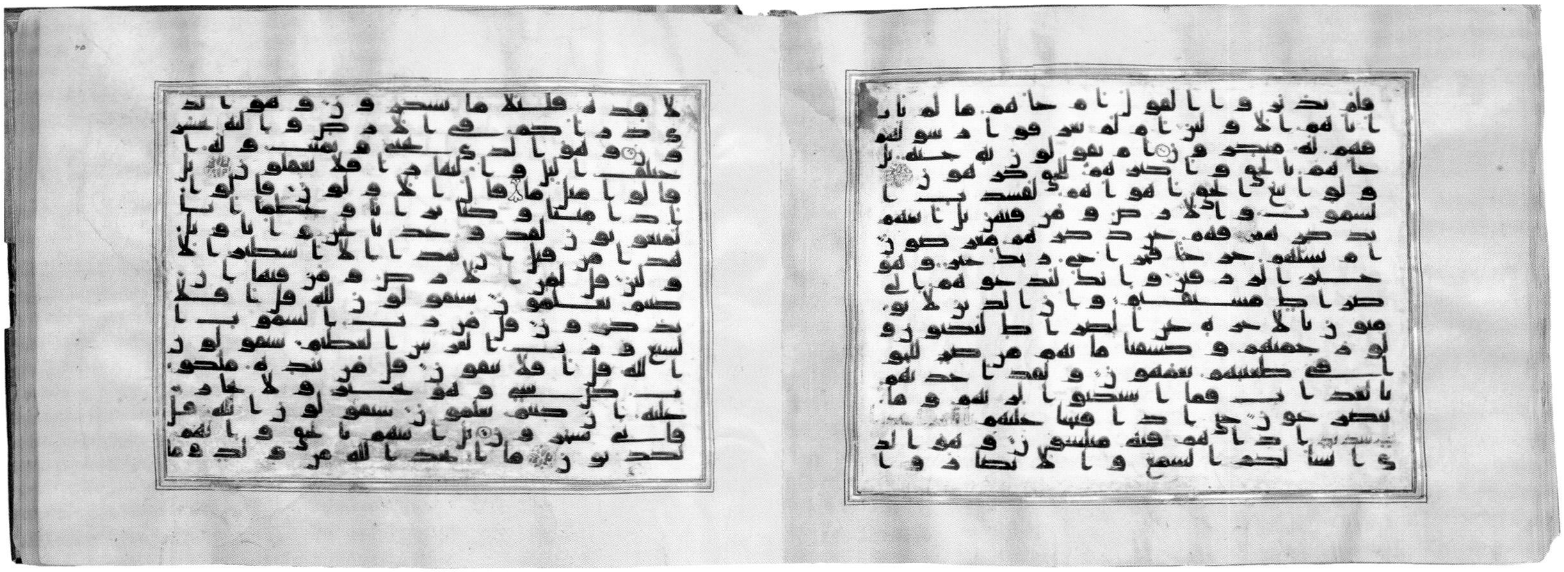

Fig.5

elect, the clement, the heir of Mustafa – on him be God's prayers and peace! – and they cite the fact that among the miracle-working pictures from the *qalam* of that Holiness, which are adorned by his gilding, they have witnessed with their own eyes the signature: "This was written and gilded by ʿAli b. Abi Talib".[19] While Qadi Ahmad has used this example to initiate a discussion of illuminators producing both representational and non-representational forms of illumination, he does not actually suggest that ʿAli was drawing animals or human figures. Equally and earlier, Dust Muhammad, writing in 1544, noted that ʿAli invented the style of illumination known as *islīmī*,[20] one of six ornamental styles mentioned by Qadi Ahmad and thought to be a spiralling vine scroll. By conferring the status of originator of Islamic manuscript illumination on Imam ʿAli, Qadi Ahmad and Dust Muhammad have proclaimed him the patron of all illuminators.

Another Qur'an with the signature of ʿAli b. Abi Talib is housed in the Gulistan Palace Library. According to Sheila Blair, it has 260 folios, six lines to the page, and a colophon in different ink from the text stating it was copied by ʿAli b. Abi Talib.[21] Since the Gulistan Palace was the administrative centre of the Qajar Dynasty (*r.* 1794–1925), the history of its library is closely connected with that of the royal libraries of the late Safavids and the 18th-century rulers of Iran. How long the Imam ʿAli Qur'an had been in the libraries of the shahs of Iran is unknown, but like the Qur'an from the Chihil Sutun, it appears to indicate that the shahs did not donate all their rarest holy books to Shiʿi shrines.

Of course, false signatures of the Imams may have continued to be inserted into kufic Qur'ans in the 19th and 20th centuries, but the historical circumstances of the Safavid period provided the most compelling reasons for the addition of these signatures. The Safavid shahs needed to convince a population that was a mixture of Shiʿi and Sunni of the chain of religious authority throughout the Safavid period. Thus, with these Qur'ans they could demonstrate the unbroken line from God to Muhammad in the form of the Qur'an itself, from ʿAli and the Imams to the Safavid shahs in the form of these early signed kufic Qur'ans, and from the shahs to the shrines and to the pilgrims who visited them through their donations of these particularly holy Qur'ans. By the 19th and 20th centuries the preoccupations of Iran's leaders had changed, being much more focussed on threats and influences from outside Iran than the need to establish and maintain the Shiʿi faith by then firmly rooted in the population.

Qur'ans in other collections

Like the Qur'ans in the Mashhad shrine with Imams' signatures, one in a private collection (fig.6) has been set into paper margins that have a variety of seal impressions and librarians' notes. Two of the seal impressions have legible dates, 1052 AH (1642–1643) and 1213 AH (1798–1799) and one of the librarians' inscriptions contains the numerals 191, which could refer to 1091/1680–1681 or 1191/1777–1778. The Mashhad shrine Qur'ans also contain librarians' notations with dates from the

Fig.5
Qur'an section signed by Imam Zayn al-ʿAbidin, sura 23:68–91 shown above

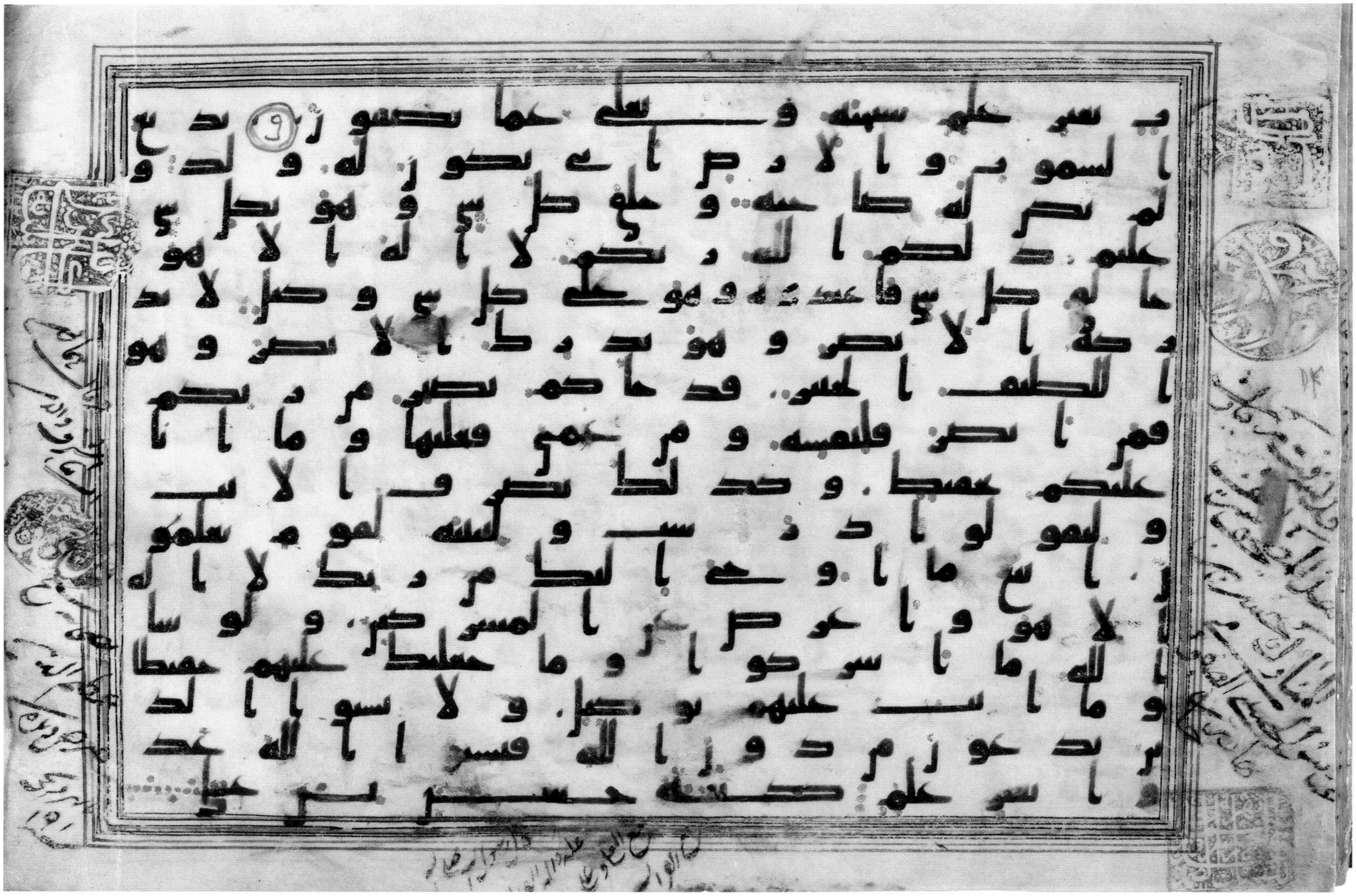

Fig.6

19th century, long after they had been deposited at the shrine. What differentiates the Qur'an in the private collection from those signed by Imams in the shrine is that, instead of being written on the last page of the section, the signature appears in the middle of the *juz'* and in the middle of Q. 6:108, sura *al-An'ām* (the Cattle). This is clearly not canonical as no Muslim would interrupt the text of the Qur'an with his own signature. Whereas a black and white photograph made the folio appear to have a strip added at the bottom, no such addition is evident on the page itself. Rather, the person who inserted Imam Husayn's name must have erased or doctored the words of the verse, '*kadhālika zayyannā li-kuli ummatin*'[22] and replaced them with '*katabahu Ḥusayn b. 'Alī*'. Smudges extend over the marginal rulings, but no trace of the original words remains.

A Qur'an whose present whereabouts are unknown contains the signature of Imam Hasan b. 'Ali and autograph inscriptions of four of the Safavid shahs, Isma'il I (*r.* 1501–1524), Tahmasp (*r.* 1524–1576), 'Abbas I (*r.* 1587–1629), and Sulayman (*r.* 1666–1694).[23] Each of these shahs wrote in the manuscript to record seeing it. While Shah Isma'il, the first

Fig.6
Qur'an section signed by
Imam Husayn,
sura 6:100–108 shown above

Safavid shah, simply states that he saw the manuscript in 917 AH (1511–1512), Shah Tahmasp notes that it was viewed 'through the intermediary of 'Abd al-Hakim' in Rajab 971 (February 1564)'. Likewise, Shah 'Abbas looked at the Qur'an through the intermediary of Allah Verdi Khan in the house of someone whose name is illegible.[24] Allah Verdi Khan, a convert to Islam, was governor of Fars province and a very powerful minister whose tomb was constructed at the shrine of Imam Reza next to that of the Imam. With 14 lines to the page and multiple marginal rulings, this manuscript resembles that with the signature of Imam Husayn b. 'Ali in the private collection mentioned above. As important as the apocryphal signature is, the inscriptions of the Safavid shahs are key to the thesis of this paper as they confer a chain of Safavid approval. Unfortunately, the folio with these inscriptions is not reproduced so the authenticity of the Safavid inscriptions cannot be verified.

In addition to Qur'ans with the signatures of the Shi'i Imams a manuscript in the Haram al-Sharif Library in Jerusalem contains the name of a descendant of Imam Hasan who was not an Imam himself. This beautifully illuminated kufic Qur'an was inscribed by the administrator of endowments of Jerusalem, Gaza, Ramla, Nablus and Safad in 954 AH (1547), named Ahmad b. 'Uthman. According to Khader Salameh, this administrator recorded on a separate page the name of the copyist, 'al-Hasan b. al-Husayn, the son of Fatimah, the daughter of the Prophet Muhammad'.[25] Salameh has noted that the genealogists al-Zubayri and Ibn al-Jawzi state that of the four sons of Imam Husayn the fourth, Imam 'Ali Zayn al-'Abidin, had ten children and the youngest was named Hasan. Salameh suggests this is the person to whom this Qur'an is attributed.[26] Even if this Hasan died in the early eighth century, the manuscript cannot be his work if we accept that it dates from no earlier than the late eighth century.

Style of the Qur'ans

In addition to the implausibility of the Imams' signatures on this group of kufic Qur'ans, the group represents at least two distinct types of early manuscript. While François Déroche, Estelle Whelan and Sheila Blair have codified early Qur'ans by letter forms, page format and systems of verse division, the dating and geographical placement of many of these manuscripts still defy precise clarification.[27] In the case of the Qur'ans with signatures of the Imams, a comparison of two pages from Qur'an sections ascribed to Imam Hasan b. 'Ali (nos 2 and 10 in the appendix) reveals that these are unlikely to be by the same hand. With two exceptions the copyist of the page with seven lines of text has spaced the lines so that the ascending letters neither appear crowded nor do they vary greatly in height. On the page with 14 lines the ascending letters collide with descending letters or vocalisation marks from the line above 20 times, resulting in a crowded appearance to the page. This is particularly evident in line six containing the heading in gold for sura 59 which is squeezed into half a line, giving the impression that it was an afterthought or even the work of a different calligrapher from the one who copied the text.

Although the vowelling system is the same in both examples, letter forms, such as the medial *sīn* or final *yā'* differ. In the Mashhad example the tops of the teeth of the *sīn* descend from right to left while in the other example the teeth are all the same height. In the Mashhad Qur'an the final *yā'* hooks once to the left, whereas in the other example it curves twice so that it resembles an 'S'. These variations not only support the contention that the two Qur'ans in question could not have been copied by the same person but also demonstrate the varying levels of care and skill applied to the production of early kufic Qur'ans. Nonetheless, the fact that these were written in kufic on parchment endowed them with sufficient age and esteem to be considered worthy recipients of the false signatures of the Imams.

Conclusion

Altogether the Qur'ans discussed here fall into three groups: (1) those that had belonged to Shah 'Abbas I and were given to the shrine of Imam Reza at Mashhad in the early 17th century; (2) those that appear to have had the signature or attribution added in the 17th century but which do not belong to the Mashhad shrine; (3) and the one with the signature of Imam Reza which was added either in the 17th century or later with the intention of making it look as if it had belonged to the Safavid shahs. The motivations for acquiring and even ordering the signatures of the Imams to be affixed to the Qur'ans in groups one and two are closely linked to Safavid claims of legitimacy. Already in the

16th century Shah Tahmasp had commissioned Abu'l-Fath al-Husayni to 'revise and correct' the history of Shaykh Safi, the *Ṣafwat al-ṣafā'* in order to declare that Shaykh Safi, the scion of the Safavid dynasty, was descended from Imam ʿAli. Mazzaoui claims that Shah Tahmasp ordered this alteration to the text in an attempt to consolidate his power in Iran.[28] In this context the addition of signatures of the Shiʿi Imams to old Qur'ans makes perfect sense.

By the time of Shah ʿAbbas, the ʿAlid genealogy of the Safavis was proclaimed on buildings such as the Mosque of Shaykh Lutfallah and in the history of his reign by Iskandar Beg Munshi. We will probably never know if Shah ʿAbbas himself suspected that the signatures in the Qur'ans he gave to the shrine in Mashhad might be false. Rather, as Robert McChesney has noted, the gift itself was not just a pious act but also had a strong element of the public relations gesture as well.[29] Considering the purported Uzbek defilement of his grandfather Tahmasp's tomb in the shrine of Imam Reza, Shah ʿAbbas needed to reaffirm the purity of his lineage and his blood kinship with the line of Imam Musa al-Kazim and ultimately his descent from the Prophet Muhammad. Moreover, this fabricated genealogy fitted in with Shah ʿAbbas's intention to normalise the practice of Shiʿism in Safavid Iran and to deemphasise the heterodox activities of some Sufi groups. The gift of 1608 of over one thousand pieces of Chinese porcelain, Persian manuscripts, and other precious items to the shrine of Shaykh Safi at Ardabil demonstrated Shah ʿAbbas's recognition of this shrine as a key symbol of the Safavid dynasty. However, the inscriptions added to the area near the tomb of Shaykh Safi by Shah ʿAbbas stress the shaykh's concocted Shiʿi lineage. Even here, at the Sufi birthplace of the Safavid dynasty, Shiʿism was emphasised in the period of Shah ʿAbbas.

As a group these Qur'ans bear out our perception of the Safavid shahs and perhaps Muhammad Reza Shah Pahlavi as rulers who sought to reaffirm their links with the most revered figures of Shiʿi Islam. Shah ʿAbbas maintained the fiction of Safavid descent from Imam Musa al-Kazim with monumental inscriptions placed prominently in buildings he constructed and renovated. He also apparently accepted the signatures of the Imams on his kufic Qur'ans as authentic. That Muhammad Reza Shah Pahlavi should have followed the Safavid example in giving a Qur'an signed by a Shiʿi Imam to the shrine of Imam Reza demonstrates that such gifts continued to be potent means of projecting royal piety and the special connection between the kings of Iran and the early leaders of the Shiʿi faithful. As for who wrote the false signatures, we may never know. Even if these anonymous people were only seeking commercial gain, once the Qur'ans entered the libraries of kings and shrines, no one was questioning their authenticity. Instead, the Qur'ans enjoyed an afterlife functioning almost as relics of the Shiʿi Imams and providing a direct, physical link to the most significant figures in Shiʿi Islam. In terms of artistic style, the Qur'ans do not represent a distinct Shiʿi idiom, since Qur'ans of the ninth and tenth centuries AD do not reveal differences along sectarian lines. As religious and cultural artefacts, however, their importance, indicated by Muhammad Reza Shah's 1960 gift to the Mashhad shrine, endured and cannot be underestimated.

Appendix: published Qur'ans with Imami signatures

1 Qur'an, 15 lines, signed 'Ali b. Abi Talib, AQRQM (Astan-i Quds Razavi Qur'an Museum), 16.5 × 25 cm., from sura 11 to sura 18, 69 folios, Gulchin-i Ma'ani 1969, no.1

2 Qur'an, 7 lines, signed Hasan b. 'Ali b. Abi Talib, dated 41 AH, AQRQM, 6.5 × 12.5 cm., from start of *juz'* 23 to end of *juz'* 25, Gulchin-i Ma'ani 1969, no.2

3 Qur'an, 7 lines, signed Husayn b. 'Ali, AQRQM, 6.5 × 12 cm., sura 20, verses 72–135, 7 folios, Gulchin-i Ma'ani 1969, no.3

4 Qur'an, 12 lines, signed 'Ali b. Musa al-Reza, AQRQM, 11.3 × 17.6 cm., from sura 24 to sura 57, 16 folios, Gulchin-i Ma'ani 1969, no.5

5 Qur'an, 16 lines, signed Husayn b. 'Ali, Private collection, 16 × 23.3 cm., Canby 2009, no.95

6 Qur'an, 17 lines, signed Zayn al-'Abidin, Chihil Sutun, Canby 2009, no.94

7 Qur'an, 6 lines, signed 'Ali b. Abi Talib wrote and gilded it, National Museum of Iran, 23.5 × 34 cm., 77 folios, Hayward 1976, no.499

8 Qur'an, 6 lines, signed 'Ali b. Abi Talib, Gulistan, 260 folios, Blair 2006, p.127, n.106

9 Qur'an, 7, 9 and 15 lines, signed Hasan b. Husayn b. Fatima bint Muhammad, Haram al-Sharif, 22.6 × 31 cm., sura 56:79–96, 173 folios, Salameh 2001, no.5

10 Qur'an, 14 lines, signed Hasan b. 'Ali, collection unknown at present, 12.2 × 18.7 cm., suras 56:6–59:16, 12 folios, Atil 1985, no.4

11 Qur'an, 6 lines, attributed to Imam Hasan on fol.1a, 20.6 × 28.2 cm., part 2 of a 30-part Qur'an, Khalili collection qur 372, Déroche 1992, no.24

1 Eskandar Beg Monshī, *History of Shah 'Abbas the Great: (Tārīkh-i 'Ālamārā-ye 'Abbāsī)*, tr. Roger M. Savory (Boulder, CO, 1981), vol.1, pp.85, 91; Sheila R. Canby, *Shah 'Abbas: the Remaking of Iran* (London, 2009), p.189. The Uzbeks occupied Mashhad in 932/1524–1525 and 935/1528–1529 and raided the city four times between 1548 and 1570.

2 Monshī, *History*, vol.2, pp.589–591.

3 Ibid., p.703.

4 Early Qur'ans with attributions to the Caliph 'Uthman will not be considered here.

5 David J. Roxburgh, *The Persian Album, 1400–1600, From Dispersal to Collection* (New Haven and London, 2005), pp.309–315.

6 Qāḍī Aḥmad, *Calligraphers and Painters: a Treatise / by Qādī Aḥmad, son of Mīr-Munshī, circa A.H.. 1015/A.D. 1606*, tr. V. Minorsky (Washington, DC, 1959), p.48.

7 Qāḍī Aḥmad, *Calligraphers*, pp.53–54.

8 Ibid., p.55.

9 Ibid., p.55.

10 Monshī, *History*, vol.2, p.590.

11 Ahmad Gulchin-i Ma'ani, *Rāhnamā-yi ganjīnah-'i Qur'ān* (Mashhad, 1969), pp.53–54.

12 Qāḍī Aḥmad, *Calligraphers*, p.54.

13 Estelle Whelan, 'Writing the Word of God: Some Early Qur'an Manuscripts and Their Milieux, Part I', *Ars Orientalis*, 20 (1990), p.124; Sheila S. Blair, *Islamic Calligraphy* (Edinburgh, 2006), p.105; François Déroche, *The Abbasid Tradition: Qur'ans of the 8th to the 10th centuries AD* (Oxford, 1992), p.13.

14 Blair, *Calligraphy*, p.106; François Déroche, 'The Qur'ān of Amāǧūr', *Manuscripts of the Middle East*, 5 (1990–1991), pp.59–66; Alain Fouad George, 'The Geometry of the Qur'ān of Amāǧūr: A Preliminary Study of Proportion in Early Arabic Calligraphy', *Muqarnas*, 20 (2003), pp.1–16.

15 Canby, *Shah 'Abbas*, p.201, no.95.

16 Monshī, *History*, vol.2, p.1227.

17 Ibid., p.1233.

18 Hayward Gallery, *The Arts of Islam* (London 1976), p.316, cat. no.499, inv. no.4289; Blair, *Calligraphy*, p.136, n.63, refers to Mehdi Bahrami, *Rāhnamā-yi ganjīnah-i Qur'ān dar Mūzah-i Īrān-i Bāstān* (Tehran, 1940), no.2, as does Hayward Gallery, *Arts*, but gives a different inventory number, no.4293 and different number of folios, 77 instead of 154. The discrepancy in folio numbers can be explained by a confusion of pages versus folios. Blair, presumably relying on Bahrami, states that the manuscript came from Ardabil. Thus, it would have been amongst the manuscripts that Shah 'Abbas donated to that shrine in 1608, despite the wording of the *waqf* designating his Persian historical and poetic manuscripts to Ardabil and his religious and scientific texts to the Mashhad shrine.

19 Qāḍī Aḥmad, *Calligraphers*, p.174.

20 W. M. Thackston, *A Century of Princes: Sources on Timurid History and Art* (Cambridge, MA, 1989), p.349.

21 Blair, *Calligraphy*, p.127 and n.107.

22 Translation of erased verse: 'Thus unto every nation have We made [their deed] seem fair.'

23 Khader Salameh,*The Qur'an Manuscripts in the Al-Haram al-Sharif Islamic Museum, Jerusalem* (Reading, 2001), p.54.

24 Salameh, *Qur'an Manuscripts*, p.54.

25 Ibid., p.55.

26 Ibid., p.55.

27 Whelan, 'Writing the Word', pp.114–116; Blair, *Calligraphy*, pp.114–115; Déroche, *Abbasid Tradition*, pp.14–17, 34–47.

28 Michel Mazzaoui, *The Origins of the Safavids* (Wiesbaden, 1972), p.47.

29 Robert D. McChesney, 'Waqf and Public Policy: the Waqfs of Shāh 'Abbās, 1011–1023/1602–1614', *Asian and African Studies*, 15 (1981), p.186.

9

Writing about faith: epigraphic evidence for the development of Twelver Shiʿism in Iran

Sheila S. Blair

Twelver Shiʿism had a long, if intermittent, history in Iran before its establishment as a state religion in Safavid times. This essay investigates the epigraphic evidence for its development from the 10th century to the early 16th century, examining the inscriptions on buildings and works of art made for (and sometimes by) Twelver Shiʿa and the relationship of those objects to others of similar form, decoration and style. It looks first at the words inscribed on works of art made for Shiʿi patrons from the Buyid to the early Safavid period to determine what kinds of statements were written down. It then compares these objects to contemporary ones made for other patrons to ascertain whether the differences in words were accompanied by differences in technique, imagery or style. It thus seeks to investigate whether there was any specific Shiʿi visual identity evident in works of art made in Iran up to the period of Safavid rule.

Let us begin with the Buyids, Shiʿi rulers of Iran and Iraq in the 10th century. The Buyids inaugurated ceremonies still practised by Twelver Shiʿa today, such as the lamentations of ʿAshura' and the festival of Ghadir Khumm. The Buyids also built tombs to commemorate the dead, members of both the Prophet's family and their own.[1] Unconventionally, the Buyids also wrapped the bodies interred in these tombs in silk shrouds.[2]

Unfortunately, little art remains from the Buyid period – and many of the complete objects that do survive seem to be fakes – so that it is difficult to assess its sectarianism.[3] One of the large architectural remains in Iran that dates from the Buyid period is the mosque portal in Isfahan known as Jurjir (fig.1). It can be identified as a Buyid congregational mosque on the basis of a brief mention in al-Mafarrukhi's *Kitāb Maḥāsin Iṣfahān* (*circa* 1020) of a new congregational mosque built by al-Sahib b. ʿAbbad (d. 995), vizier to the Buyid rulers of Rayy.[4] The entrance door is surmounted by an inscription band in kufic script with part of Qur'an 3:18 (from sura *Āl-ʿImrān*), that 'God bears witness that there is no god save Him, as do the angels and those who have knowledge. He upholds justice (*qisṭ*). There is no god but Him, the Almighty, the Wise.'

The brief excerpt on the Jurjir portal in Isfahan shows the complexities in explicating a Qur'anic text, particularly from a single example. With its reference to witnessing, the verse evokes the *shahāda*, the first of the five so-called 'pillars' required of all Muslims to signify acceptance of Islam.[5] Witnessing is often a general assertion of Islam, and the text is frequently part of a foundation text. The verse also encapsulates the Qur'anic emphasis on the authority of prophetic duty.[6] Finally, the verse was frequently cited in Muʿtazilite theological works, as the word *qisṭ* supports the Muʿtazilite theology of rationality.[7] In addition to trumpeting Islam and the duties incumbent on Muslims, the use of this verse on the Jurjir portal may therefore reflect the Muʿtazilite leanings of the patron, al-Sahib b. ʿAbbad.

Clearer epigraphic evidence about the development of Twelver Shiʿism survives from the succeeding centuries. Although the main rulers of the area were ardent Sunnis, Twelver Shiʿism flourished in certain locales. The major Shiʿi shrines for Imam Reza (ʿAli al-Rida) at Mashhad and his sister Fatima at Qum were embellished repeatedly. Towns such as Kashan had large communities of Twelver Shiʿa.[8]

Our knowledge about the development of Twelver Shiʿism in Iran during these centuries is enhanced by a new source of information: the inscriptions on lustre tiles, which were produced by Shiʿi potters working in the city of Kashan at least from 1203 to 1339.[9] Oliver Watson's classic study of Persian lustreware documented 132 dated tiles, usually part of larger ensembles, produced in this 140-year span. Most of the potters were Twelver Shiʿa, belonging to families of Husaynid or Hasanid *sayyids*. In some cases we can even trace how the craft was passed down in families: we can document, for example, four generations of the Abu Tahir family of Husaynid *sayyids*.[10] Members of this family often collaborated on large projects with Abu Zayd, the most famous lustre potter who signed at least thirty-one works and belonged to a family of Hasanid *sayyids*.[11]

Fig.1
Portal of the Jurjir mosque, Isfahan, 10th century

Fig.2
Lustre tiles on the cenotaph of Fatima, Qum, 602/1206

Fig.3
Lustre tiles in the shrine of Imam Reza, Mashhad, 612/1215

Fig.1

These Shiʿi potters made large ensembles for Shiʿi shrines. The first major project was the tiles to cover the large box-like cenotaph of Fatima at Qum (fig.2).[12] The sides were clad in stars and octagons, sandwiched between a large foundation inscription signed by Abu Zayd on 2 Rajab 602 (12 February 1206). On the top of the cenotaph is a set of 15 panels signed by the second-generation member of the Abu Tahir family, Muhammad. The colonettes at the corners signed by Muhammad b. Abi Tahir's son ʿAli were probably added a generation later. The lower walls may have also been revetted with lustre tiles, but the present tile work dates from a restoration carried out in AH 950 (1543–1544).

Work at the tomb chamber in the shrine of Imam Reza at Mashhad (fig.3) carried out a decade later by the same pair of potters, Abu Zayd

Fig.2

Fig.3

Fig.4

and Muhammad b. Abi Tahir, was even more ambitious. The walls were revetted with a tall dado comprising a large inscription frieze above five rows of tiles arranged like those around the cenotaph at Qum. Several of the lustre tiles are signed by Abu Zayd and dated AH 612 (1215).[13] The doorway was framed with a tile band containing the foundation inscription with the name of Muhammad b. Abi Tahir and the date 1 Jumada I 612 (28 August 1215).[14] Two large mihrabs were installed in the south wall of the chamber.[15] The one on the left is unsigned, but the large (2.4 m) one on the right contains an invocation on the lintel requesting forgiveness for he who asks forgiveness for Abu Zayd.[16] A third lustre mihrab installed on the opposite wall is signed by Muhammad b. Abi Tahir's son 'Ali and dated a generation later in AH 640 (1242).[17]

These same Shi'i potters working at Kashan also made lustre tiles installed on the interior walls of *imāmzādas*, smaller shrines built to commemorate descendants of Shi'i Imams.[18] These smaller shrines became particularly popular from the 11th century onward, as Shi'i scholars recognised pilgrimage to an *imāmzāda* as a valid form of devotion.[19] The largest surviving ensemble of lustre tiles on such a smaller shrine comes from the Imamzada Yahya at Varamin (fig.4), thought to commemorate the grave of a sixth-generation descendant of Imam Hasan, Yahya b. 'Ali b. 'Abd al-Rahman b. Qasim b. Hasan b. Zayd.[20] The lustre dado for Varamin, part of a surge in activity at the Kashan kilns in the 1260s, comprised large star-and-cross tiles dated in the three months between the months of Dhu'l-Hijja 660 and Safar 661 (October–December 1262).[21] At least 150 examples are known in around two-dozen

Fig.5

Fig.4
Exterior of the Imamzada Yahya, Varamin, 660–661/1262 and later

Fig.5
Mihrab from the Imamzada Yahya, Varamin, 663/1265

Fig.6
Panel with lustre tiles from the cenotaph in the Imamzada Yahya, Varamin, 705/1305

Fig.7
Lustre tiled walls in the mosque of 'Ali, Quhrud, 700/1300

collections. Two and a half years later in Sha'ban 663 (May 1265), 'Ali, the third-generation potter of the Abu Tahir family who had added colonettes to the cenotaph at Qum, made a large mihrab for the shrine at Varamin (fig.5). Composed of more than 60 individual tiles, it measures 3.85 × 2.96 metres and is the largest lustre mihrab known.[22]

A second campaign of decoration was carried out at the Imamzada Yahya forty years later under the patronage of the hereditary governors of Rayy.[23] On 10 Muharram 705 (2 August 1305) 'Ali's son Yusuf, working with another potter from Kashan, 'Ali b. Ahmad b. 'Ali al-Husayni, made a flat panel of four tiles that probably covered the cenotaph (fig.6).[24]

Kashan potters also produced lustre revetments for the walls inside mosques. One of the best documented is that in the Friday mosque (also called the Masjid-i 'Ali) in the village of Quhrud near Kashan (fig.7).[25] In Rabi' I 700 (November 1300) some 205 tiles were installed there. Unlike most tiles from the period, the lustre tiles at Quhrud are six- (rather than eight-) pointed stars, set in patterns alternating with monochrome turquoise hexagons.

These lustre tiles – whether mihrab ensembles, cenotaph covers, or star-and-cross dados – are inscribed with three types of Arabic text: Qur'anic quotations, sayings by the Prophet and his family, and pious invocations.[26] The most common are Qur'anic quotations, and they are particularly revealing since Qur'an commentary was a subject of great popularity with Twelver Shi'a in Iran at this time.[27]

The Qur'anic verses on lustre tiles often include familiar texts, such as the Throne Verse (*Āyat al-kursī*, 2:255) that extols the omnipotence of God. It is used as the large outer border on the top of the Qum cenotaph, several times on the Varamin mihrab,[28] and often around individual lustre tiles. Qur'an 2:286 (from *al-Baqara*), a verse about the common theme of God's forgiveness, is found in the border around the cenotaph at Qum and the mihrab from the Maydan mosque at Kashan.[29] Other short suras, especially the opening one and those from the end of the Qur'an, are ubiquitous, probably because they were poetic and familiar, likely known by heart by the potters and their audiences alike. Practically, they also fit around the edge of an individual tile. The Varamin mihrab, for example, includes suras 1 (*al-Fātiḥa*), 93 (*al-Ḍuḥā*) and 97 (*al-Qadr*) in the narrow frame bands around the colonettes. The mihrab from the Maydan mosque at Kashan has suras 1 and 112 (*al-Ikhlāṣ*). The six-pointed star tiles from the mosque at Quhrud have many of the same texts.

Some Qur'anic citations used on lustre tiles were chosen because they reflect the function of the piece or ensemble. Thus, many mihrabs prominently display Qur'an 17:78 (from *al-Isrā'*), in which the believer is enjoined to perform prayer (*al-ṣalāt*) from the setting of the sun to the darkness of the night as well as the dawn recitation of the Qur'an. This verse is used on the two mihrabs added in AH 612 (1215) along the south wall in the shrine at Mashhad; in big blue *thuluth* letters around

Fig.6

Fig.7

the frame band on the mihrab from the Maydan mosque at Kashan in AH 623 (1226); and on the upper arch on the Varamin mihrab dated AH 663 (1264). It is one of the few Qur'anic verses about prayer that uses the word *al-ṣalāt* not as an object, but as a verbal noun denoting an activity. The verse conveys the verbal force of Qur'anic recitation and highlights not the architecture, but the believers' actions that will take place within it.[30]

Lustre tiles designed for tombs, in contrast, often have verses that were associated with burial. The cenotaph for Fatima's tomb at Qum is a good example. One of the texts encircling the cenotaph is sura 36 (*Yā Sīn*), known as 'the heart of the Qur'an.' Jurists across the Muslim lands commend reciting it as death approaches, for it will bring forgiveness in the hereafter, even a martyr's blissful status.[31] The rectangular frame around the trilobed arch on the top of the cenotaph begins with the opening six verses of sura 67 (*al-Mulk*), which invoke God as the creator of the seven heavens who has power over life and death. According to another tradition, whoever dies after reading texts that glorify God will be rewarded with Paradise, including suras 1, 67, 112, 113 (*al-Falaq*), and 114 (*al-Nās*).[32] The same inscription on the top of the cenotaph includes Qur'an 10:10–12 (from *Yūnus*), a text which mentions the salutation with which inhabitants of heaven greet each other and a well-known expression of gratitude for God's blessings.[33]

Other Qur'anic texts on lustre tiles, particularly those installed in the major Twelver Shi'i shrines at Qum and Mashhad, were chosen for sectarian reasons. Qur'an 5:55–59 (from *al-Mā'ida*), for example, is of prime importance for Shi'a, as Shi'i exegetes take the opening phrase with God's allies (*walīkum*) to refer to the Imamate of 'Ali b. Abi Talib.[34] It is no surprise, therefore, to find this text inscribed in kufic at both Qum (around the top of the cenotaph) and Mashhad (on the left mihrab on the south wall). These verses, by contrast, are not found on the many individual lustre tiles, whose inscriptions seem to carry more generic meanings, thereby making them suitable for installation in a variety of contexts.

The second category of inscriptions found on lustre tiles comprises sayings by the Prophet and his family, a theme that occurs frequently on tiles installed in the major Twelver Shi'i shrines. Some of these sayings are generic. A star tile from the Imamzada 'Ali b. Ja'far at Qum, for

Fig.8

Fig.9

Fig.8
Carved stucco mihrab,
Friday mosque, Isfahan, 710/1310

Fig.9
Cut-work paper calligraphy in the form of a lion by Mir 'Ali Haravi, gold and polychrome pigments on card, mid-16th century, Istanbul University Library, f1426, folio 46b.

example, has a Prophetic hadith about prayer.[35] Other texts are more specifically sectarian, containing sayings related not only by the Prophet's son-in-law ʿAli, but also by other Imams.[36] The mihrab made by Abu Zayd in AH 612 (1215) for the shrine at Mashhad has three such pointed sayings that were chosen specifically for the site.[37] One on the canopy lists the rewards for visiting the tomb. Another on the front of the mihrab specifies further that a visit to Mashhad is equivalent to a thousand visits to the Kaʿba in Mecca. A third inscription around the inner arch relates a tradition of ʿAli about the origin of the tomb following the murder of one of his offspring in Khurasan. Other lustre tiles from the revetment at the shrine also contain Shiʿi traditions related by Imams ʿAli, Hasan and Husayn.[38]

The third category of text found on lustre tiles comprises pious invocations and blessings. The profession of faith is common, often including a third phrase that ʿAli is God's friend (*walī*). He sometimes receives further accolades.[39] The top of the cenotaph for Fatima at Qum was once framed by a large inscription with blessings on the Fourteen Immaculate Ones (Muhammad, Fatima and the Twelve Imams).[40]

The Arabic texts on lustre tiles made in the 13th and early-14th centuries thus show us that Kashan potters could deliberately adapt their texts to specific situations, and a contemporary mihrab confirms how inscriptions on religious architecture were used polemically to fit a Twelver Shiʿi context: the mihrab added to the congregational mosque at Isfahan in the month of Safar 710 (July 1310) (fig.8).[41] Like the lustre mihrabs, this one of carved plaster is covered in writing. A nine-line foundation inscription across the tympanum records that the work took place during the reign of the Ilkhanid sultan Uljaytu under the supervision of ʿAdud b. ʿAli al-Mastari using monies from the vizier Saʿd al-Din Muhammad Savaji.[42] The inscriptions also identify the craftsman responsible, Haydar, whose name is included at the end of the band around the tympanum arch.

In addition to the precise historical text, the other inscriptions on the Isfahan mihrab contain the same three types of text found on contemporary lustre tiles: Qur'anic verses, sayings of the Prophet's family and pious invocations. The inscription on the arch around the tympanum records a tradition about the revelation of the Qur'an 4:59 (*al-Nisā'*), a verse admonishing believers to obey God, His Prophet and those charged with authority among them. The verse is the only one of eleven Qur'anic citations about obedience to God and His Prophet that adds the phrase about 'those having authority among you.' This additional phrase is usually glossed as a reference to those appointed to represent the Prophet's authority in his absence and hence of particular significance to all Shiʿa.[43]

On the Isfahan mihrab, the Qur'anic verse is explicated by a hadith recorded by Jabir b. Zayd al-Jawfi (d. *circa* 720), a famous early traditionist, jurist, and authority on the Qur'an.[44] He is said to have heard the hadith from the Prophet's companion Jabir b. ʿAbdallah, a prolific narrator of hadiths held in exceptionally high rank by Shiʿa.[45] The inscription on the mihrab says that when Jabir heard about the revelation of Qur'an 4:59, he asked the Prophet, 'Who are those charged with authority to whom obedience is due?' The Prophet's answer to Jabir's question, inscribed around the lower frames of the mihrab, says that those to whom obedience is due are my [the Prophet's] successors and then names the Twelve Imams in succession. The inscription is thus a vindication of Twelver Shiʿa legitimacy, and its importance to contemporary viewers is shown by the care given to recording the unimpeachable line of sources (*isnād*) back to the Prophet.

The Shiʿi emphasis on the Isfahan mihrab continues in the large framing band, which contains sayings ascribed to Muhammad and ʿAli. The text opens with a Prophetic hadith saying that God will build a house (*bayt*) in Paradise for anyone who builds a mosque as a nesting place for a partridge. The inscription continues with a saying by ʿAli on a similar theme, relating that whoever frequents a mosque will acquire one of eight blessings. The text thus links Muhammad and ʿAli by both subject and placement.

The fourth inscription on the Isfahan mihrab, set above the lower arch and distinguished by its unusual style of interlaced kufic, contains the third type of text, an invocation. It gives the profession of faith (*shahāda*) in its full form as typically given by Shiʿa.

Looking at the historical context shows why it was so important to emphasise Shiʿism on the Isfahan mihrab. Sultan Uljaytu, baptised a Christian but then successively a Buddhist and an adherent of Sunni Islam (first a Hanafi and then a Shafiʿi), subsequently converted to Twelver Shiʿism. Using numismatic evidence we can trace his conversion to late 1310 (AH 709), when a new type of coin was issued with an obverse containing the expanded Shiʿi profession of faith and blessings on the Twelve Imams.[46] This type was struck in that year at only a few mints in the Ilkhanid heartlands before becoming widespread the following year.

The Isfahan mihrab was part of the state sponsorship of Twelver Shiʿism, and its inscriptions trace the Shiʿi line back to the Prophet. Such justification was needed because the local population did not entirely favour the change. The Moroccan globetrotter Ibn Battuta (d. *circa* 1370s), who travelled through the area several decades later, reported that there was widespread resistance to the conversion and rioting in the major cities including Baghdad, Shiraz and Isfahan.[47] A staunch Sunni from North Africa who was horrified by some of the Shiʿi practices he encountered, Ibn Battuta may have exaggerated the anger and extent of the destruction in Isfahan (he reported that the greater part of the city was in ruins from the fighting between Sunnis and Shiʿa[48]), but his report does indicate that both cajolement and coercion were needed. No wonder, then, that the inscriptions on the mihrab in Isfahan are so polemical.

One final object shows how inscriptions with sectarian content were used on objects of different media in later centuries: an inlaid bronze jug with a dragon handle in the Metropolitan Museum of Art (91.1.607).[49] The jug bears no date on it and can be attributed only on stylistic grounds to the late 15th or early 16th century. What sets the Metropolitan jug apart from the others in the series is the inscription on the moulded collar at the neck.[50] It contains the prayer to ʿAli b. Abi Talib known as the *Nād-i ʿAlī*:

> Call upon ʿAli, the revealer of miracles.
> You will find him a comfort to you in crisis
> Every care and every sorrow will pass
> Through your companionship, O ʿAli, O ʿAli, O ʿAli.

The *Nād-i ʿAlī* prayer became popular in the late 15th and early 16th centuries when it was inscribed on works in several media. It occurs on a signet ring of nephrite, a material found only in Khotan in Central Asia and associated with the Timurid rulers of Khurasan (1370–1506).[51] The prayer was also cut out in the shape of a lion (fig.9). A stunning example of zoomorphic calligraphy, the design shows a splendid leonine figure of gold *thuluth* letters set against a brilliant blue ground decorated with a delicate arabesque scroll punctuated with red, white and green flowers.[52] The design is a rebus, for ʿAli is known as the Lion of God. The designer cleverly signed the work along the back legs of the lion: *qaṭaʿahu ʿAlī kātib* (the calligrapher ʿAli cut it out). This probably refers to Mir ʿAli Haravi (*circa* 1476–1543), the acclaimed noted master of *nastaʿlīq* calligraphy who worked at Herat under the Timurids and Safavids before being taken to Bukhara by the Uzbeks and whose works are incorporated in this album, known as the Shah Mahmud Nishapuri Album after his contemporary whose name appears on the front page.

The *Nād-i ʿAlī* prayer was also inscribed on a handful of gold and silver coins issued by the first ruler of the Safavid dynasty, Shah Ismaʿil (*r.* 1501–1524), but never on later Safavid issues.[53] Its use on the coinage, one of the two signs of sovereignty (the other is the Friday sermon or *khuṭba*), marks the official adoption of Twelver Shiʿism in Iran.

In sum, then, some of the inscriptions on buildings and objects made for (and sometimes by) Twelver Shiʿa in Iran between the 10th and the early 16th centuries were designed to underscore their sectarian intent, whether by the choice of a significant Qurʾanic verse, the use of an ʿAlid tradition, the invocation of the Imams, or the inclusion of a prayer calling upon ʿAli as intercessor. The question arises: by looking at these works of art, would we be able to identify them as specifically Shiʿi? That is, beyond the words, is there something in the technique, form, or decoration that identifies these works of art as specifically Shiʿi?

One reason to pose the question is Oliver Watson's suggestion that the extensive use of lustre tiles in the 13th and 14th centuries reflected not just an increased popularity in architectural tiling, but was exclusively restricted to the decoration of funerary monuments designed for the minority Twelver Shiʿi sect.[54] He hinted, in other words, that lustre tiling did have specifically Shiʿi connotations, especially as the potters themselves were Twelver Shiʿa.

I disagree and think that Watson's suggestion was wrong for several reasons. He was correct in noting that most of the buildings whose lustre tiles have survived are Shiʿi shrines, but his argument for the Shiʿi exclusivity of lustre tiling rests on negative evidence: no Sunni shrines have survived in Iran, so we do not know what type of decoration they might have had. Furthermore, lustre tiles were used elsewhere, most notably on the Ilkhanid palace at Takht-i Sulayman.[55] The texts there were typically verses or adaptations from the *Shāhnāma*, the Persian national epic, and the selections chosen to underscore the Ilkhanids' link to the pre-Islamic rulers of Iran.[56] The different subject matter shows that Kashan potters could therefore adapt their texts to the specific setting.

Furthermore, the examples of the carved plaster mihrab from Isfahan and the inlaid bronze jug from Khurasan confirm how designers and craftsmen could select appropriate texts for specific objects made for a sectarian audience but could make similar objects with other texts for other audiences. A year before he designed the Isfahan mihrab, the same craftsman Haydar had designed the stucco revetment for the shrine complex at Natanz.[57] His signature comes at the end of the band across the edge of the *īwān* (barrel-vaulted hall) on the north side of the courtyard, following Qur'an 9:18 (*al-Tawba*), the most common citation on mosques. The complex honours the grave of a local Suhrawardi shaykh Nur al-Din ʿAbd al-Samad. We know little about the shaykh personally, but descriptions of the traditions and duties of fasting and prayer given by his pupils ʿIzz al-Din Mahmud al-Kashani (d. 1334–1335) and Kamal al-Din ʿAbd al-Razzaq al-Kashani (d. 1335) suggest that they, like their counterpart in the Kubrawiyya order, ʿAla' al-Din Simnani, were Sunnis who adhered to the Shafiʿi school of law but who also held special reverence for ʿAli b. Abi Talib and other members of the Prophet's family. Increased veneration for the Prophet's family, especially among Sufi orders, was a major feature of 14th and 15th-century Iran, and invocations to ʿAli on individual objects and buildings are not necessarily indicative of adherence to Shiʿism.

Furthermore, the style of finely carved plaster found on the Isfahan mihrab, with multiple layers of arabesque decorated with punching and stamping, was also exported to Egypt, where it was readily employed (and enjoyed) by Mamluk patrons.[58] These staunch Sunnis clearly did not see any hidden Shiʿi message in the technique. Similarly, inlaid bronze jugs of virtually identical form and style as the one with the *Nād-i ʿAlī* prayer were made for a variety of patrons, including the Timurid sultan Husayn Bayqara (*r.* 1468–1506).[59] It is thus not the form, materials or decoration that make these objects specifically Shiʿi, but rather the words inscribed on them. We should not be disheartened by this conclusion, but rather turn to the texts as remarkable sources documenting the spread of Shiʿism in Iran up to the Safavid period.

1 Oleg Grabar, 'The Earliest Commemorative Structures', *Ars Orientalis*, 6 (1966), pp.7–46.
2 Sheila S. Blair, Jonathan Bloom and Anne Wardwell, 'Reevaluating the Date of the 'Buyid' Silks', *Ars Orientalis,* 22 (1992), pp.1–42.
3 Sheila S. Blair, 'Būyid Art and Architecture', *EI3*, 4 (2009), p.132; Jonathan Bloom, 'Fact and Fantasy in Būyid Art', *Oriente Moderno,* 23 (2004), pp.387–400.
4 Sheila S. Blair, *Monumental Inscriptions from Early Islamic Iran and Transoxiana* (Leiden, 1992), no.14. His biography is given in Cl. Cahen and Ch. Pellat, 'Ibn ʿAbbād', EI2, vol.3, pp.671–673.
5 Andrew Rippin, 'Witness to Faith', EQ, vol.5, pp.488–491.
6 Matthias Radscheit, 'Witnessing and Testifying', EQ, vol.5, pp.492–506.
7 Richard Bulliet, 'A Muʿtazilite Coin of Maḥmūd of Ghazna', *American Numismatic Society Museum Notes*, 15 (1969), pp.119–129; Sheila S. Blair, 'The Octagonal Pavilion at Natanz: A Reexamination of early Islamic Architecture in Iran', *Muqarnas,* 1 (1983), p.88.
8 For Kashan, see J. Calmard, 'Kāshān', EI2, vol.4, pp.694–695.
9 Oliver Watson, *Persian Lustre Ware* (London, 1985).
10 Oliver Watson, 'Abū Ṭaher', *EIR,* vol.1, Fasc. 4, pp.385–387; Sheila S. Blair 'Abu Tahir', *Grove Art Online*; Watson, *Persian Lustre Ware*, pp.178–179.
11 Sheila Blair, 'A Brief Biography of Abu Zayd', *Muqarnas*, 25 (2008), pp.155–176.
12 Mudarrisi Tabataba'i, *Turbat-i pākān* (Qum, 1976), 1, pp.45–71.
13 Mehdi Bahrami, 'A Master-Potter of Kashan', *Transactions of the Oriental Ceramic Society,* 20 (1944), plates. 18b and 19a-c; ʿAbdallah Ghuchani, *Ashʿār-i farsī-i kāshīhā-yi Takht-i Sulaymān* (Tehran, 1992), figs 16 and 20.
14 Étienne Combe, Jean Sauvaget, and Gaston Wiet, eds. *Répertoire chronologique d'épigraphie arabe* (Cairo, 1931ff), no.3784.
15 Dwight Donaldson, 'Significant Miḥrābs in the Ḥaram at Mashhad,' *Ars Islamica,* 3 (1935), pp.118–127.
16 Bahrami, 'Master-Potter', plates. 20–21 and Watson, *Persian Lustre Ware*, plate 104a–b.
17 Ibid., plate 109.
18 Multiple authors, 'Emāmzāda', *EIR,* vol.8, Fasc. 4, pp.395–412.
19 Hamid Algar, 'Emāmzāda, i. Function and devotional practice', *EIR,* vol.8, Fasc. 4, pp.395–397.

20 Parviz Varjavand, 'Emāmzāda, III. Number, distribution and important examples', *EIR*, vol.8, Fasc. 4, pp.400–412; Donald Wilber, *The Architecture of Islamic Iran: The Il Khānid Period* (Princeton, 1955), no.11.

21 The star tiles have a diameter of 31 cm. Watson, *Persian Lustre Ware*, p.191, no.27 and plate K.

22 Watson, *Persian Lustre Ware*, p.142, says that the largest mihrab is the one made by Yusuf b. ʿAli b. Muhammad b. Abi Tahir in Ramadan 734 (May 1334) for the Imamzada ʿAli b. Jaʿfar at Qum (Iran Bastan Museum, no.3270), which measures 3.28 metres in height, but the one in Honolulu is clearly taller.

23 Sheila Blair, *The Shrine Complex at Natanz, Iran* (Cambridge, MA, 1986), p.11 and n.41.

24 St. Petersburg, Hermitage Museum.

25 Oliver Watson, 'The Masjid-i ʿAlī, Quhrūd: An Architectural and Epigraphic Survey', *Iran*, 13 (1975), pp.59–74.

26 Some of the inscriptions on lustre tiles are neither written in Arabic nor religious, but rather contain Persian verse. Examples can be found in sites ranging from the cenotaph in the shrine of Fatima at Qum and the revetment at Mashhad to the Friday Mosque at Quhrud and the Imamzada Jaʿfar at Damghan (Tabataba'i, *Turbat-i pākān*, I, p.50; Ghuchani, *Ashʿār-i farsī*; Watson, *Persian Lustre Ware*, p.134), though the texts are often not quoted. Such tiles may well have been part of a stockpile.

27 Meir M. Bar-Asher, 'Shīʿism and the Qur'ān', *EQ*, vol.4, pp.593–604.

28 It occurs on the inner frame band and around the smaller colonette on the right.

29 Daniel C. Peterson, 'Forgiveness', *EQ*, vol.2, pp.244–245; Ernst Kühnel, 'Zwei Persische Gebetnischen aus Lüstrierten Fliesen', *Berliner Museen*, 49, (1928), pp.126–131.

30 Sheila S. Blair, 'Written, Spoken, Envisioned: The Many Facets of the Qur'an in Art', in Fahmida Suleman, ed., *Word of God, Art of Man: The Qur'an and its Creative Expressions* (London, 2007), p.279.

31 Juan Eduardo Campo, 'Burial', *EQ*, vol.1, pp.263–265.

32 Campo, 'Burial'.

33 Devin J. Stewart, 'Blessing', *EQ*, vol.1, pp.236–237.

34 Louise Marlow, 'Friends and Friendship', *EQ*, vol.2, pp.273–275.

35 Yedda Godard, 'Pièces datées de céramique de Kāshān à décor lustré', *Āthār-i Īrān*, 2 (1937), fig.146.

36 One of Abu Zayd's star tiles for Mashhad, dated Jumada I 612 (November 1215), even has a text describing God's revelation to Moses in the Old Testament; Ghuchani, *Ashʿār-i farsī*, p.12 and fig.20.

37 Donaldson, 'Significant Miḥrābs', pp.126–127.

38 Ghuchani, *Ashʿār-i farsī*, pp.9–12.

39 Kühnel, 'Zwei Persische Gebetnischen', p.131 and fig.5.

40 Tabataba'i, *Turbat-i pākān*, I, p.47 and n.1 says that it was removed when the cenotaph was refurbished and installed on the walls of the room.

41 Max van Berchem, 'Une inscription du Sultan Mongol Uldjaitu', in *Melanges Hartwig Derenbourg* (Paris, 1909), pp.367–378; Lutfallah Hunarfarr, *Ganjīna-yi āthār-i tārīkhī-yi Iṣfahān* (Isfahan, 1344/1965), pp.115–121.

42 Brief biography in Blair, *Ilkhanid Shrine Complex*, pp.6–7.

43 Khalid Yahya Blankinship, 'Obedience', *EQ*, vol.3, pp.566–569. The verse is not recorded elsewhere in Erica Dodd and Shereen Khairallah, *The Image of the Word* (Beirut, 1981), but its omission may reflect the partisan nature of their material, which is drawn mainly from buildings erected by Sunnis outside of Iran.

44 R. Rubinacci, 'Djābir b. Zayd', *EI2*, vol.2, pp.359–360.

45 M. J. Kister, 'Djābir b. ʿAbd Allāh', *EI2*, vol.12, pp.230–232.

46 Sheila S. Blair, 'The Coins of the later Ilkhanids', *American Numismatic Society Museum Notes*, 27 (1982), pp.211–230 and *Journal of the Economic and Social History of the Orient*, 26 (1983), pp.295–317.

47 *The Travels of Ibn Battuta A.D. 1325–1354*, tr. H. A. R. Gibb (repr., India, 1993), II, pp.302–304.

48 Ibn Baṭṭūṭa, *Travels*, II, pp.294–295.

49 Linda Komaroff, 'Timurid to Safavid Iran: Continuity and Change', *Marsyas*, 20 (1979–80), pp.11–16.

50 The prayer also occurs on the lid of a jug dated AH 889 (1484) (James W. Allan, *Islamic Metalwork: the Nuhad Es-Said Collection* (London, 1982), no.25, but the lid is not contemporary with the jug. I thank Linda Komaroff for this information.

51 Metropolitan Museum of Art 12.224.6; Thomas Lentz and Glenn Lowry, *Timur and the Princely Vision* (Los Angeles, 1989), no.142.

52 Istanbul University Library, F1426, fol.46b; Sheila Blair, *Islamic Calligraphy* (Edinburgh, 2006), pp.449–51 and fig.10.15.

53 Komaroff, 'Timurid to Safavid Iran.'

54 Watson, *Persian Lustre Ware*, pp.153–56.

55 Tomoko Masuya, 'The Ilkhanid phase of Takht-i Sulaimān' (Ph.D. dissertation, New York University, pp.1997) and 'Ilkhanid Courtly Life', in Linda Komaroff and Stefano Carboni, ed., *The Legacy of Genghis Khan* (New Haven, 2002), pp.74–103.

56 Sheila S. Blair and Jonathan Bloom, *The Art and Architecture of Islam 1250–1800* (London, 1994), p.6 and n.5.

57 Blair, *Ilkhanid Shrine Complex*.

58 Blair and Bloom, *Art and Architecture*, p.77 and n.9.

59 Komaroff, 'Timurid to Safavid Iran', p.13 and n.29. The jug is BM no.1962,0718.1, dated Shaʿban AH 903 (1498).

10

The writing on the walls: selections from the Twelver Shiʿi epigraphs of Lucknow's Hussainabad Imambara

Hussein Keshani

'The Imambara looks from the street like a crescent of Id ... Its golden cupola shines like the sun. The pilgrim's heart and eye gather the wealth and the bliss of the two worlds when he looks at it or goes around it as an act of religious sanctity.'[1]

The admiring words in the above passage described the Hussainabad Imambara – or Chhota (Little) Imambara as it is sometimes called – in the north Indian city of Lucknow and were written by the poet and administrator, Mirza Rajab ʿAli Beg Suroor (1786–1849) of Lucknow, who served under the building's patron Muhammad ʿAli Shah (*r.* 1837–1842), the ruler of Awadh (Oudh) (fig.1). Completed in 1837, the monumental *imāmbārā* (lit. 'enclosure of the Imams') and its courtyard were part of the new urban quarter 'Hussainabad' established by Muhammad ʿAli Shah as a place for Twelver Shiʿi communities to assemble and ritually commemorate the martyrdom of Imam Husayn during the month of Muharram. Muhammad ʿAli Shah was not the first ruler of Awadh to build a monumental *imāmbārā*. Asaf al-Dawla (*r.* 1775–1797) commissioned the nearby Bara (Great) Imambara, which was completed in 1791 (fig.2).[2] However, the two buildings are remarkably different. The Hussainabad Imambara with its dome and square plan resembles a tomb, whereas the earlier and much larger Bara Imambara with its rectangular plan and flat roof resembles a palatial residential building. It is not only architectural design that differentiates the two buildings; it is the use of calligraphic epigraphs on the exterior that distinguishes them.

The Bara Imambara has no exterior inscriptions, but the front exterior of the Hussainabad Imambara makes dramatic use of Arabic calligraphy. Altogether there are 55 unique epigraphs, but since many are used more than once, the total number of epigraphs is 117. With so many epigraphs, the facade of the Hussainabad Imambara is like an album filled with creative calligraphic compositions of key Twelver Shiʿi religious phrases and prayers, providing a window into both the calligraphic traditions and Twelver Shiʿi beliefs of 19th-century Lucknow. The Hussainabad Imambara epigraphs have not yet been comprehensively documented and identified, no reading sequence has been proposed, and their significance has not been interpreted.[3] This paper presents a selection of ten epigraphs found on the most visible portion of the building's facade and front entrance; it also proposes

Fig.1

Fig.1
Muhammad ʿAli Shah's Hussainabad or Chhota (Little) Imambara, Lucknow, 1837

Fig.2

a reading sequence and offers an initial contextualisation of the selected epigraphs. The Hussainabad Imambara's surprisingly numerous calligraphic epigraphs, even more so than the structure itself, reference central Twelver Shiʿi doctrines and rituals through the citation of key textual and historical touchstones that underpin Awadhi Twelver Shiʿism. These epigraphs offer a pronounced assertion of the legitimacy of Twelver Shiʿism and can be seen as signs of a maturing tradition increasingly under siege.

In the predominantly Sunni courts of late-Mughal South Asia, believers in Twelver Shiʿism increasingly became a prominent part of courtly life, and in some regional courts like Awadh they became ruling minorities and privileged elites. In the 18th and 19th centuries their numbers in north India swelled due to people fleeing the turmoil in the Iranian plateau in the post-Safavid era. Awadh was located across the Ganges and the Yamuna rivers in the Doab region of the Indo-gangetic plain and was mostly encompassed by the state of Uttar Pradesh, when modern India emerged. It was an affluent, fertile and populous province of the Mughal Empire, but in the early and mid-18th century, some of its inhabitants grew increasingly rebellious and were subdued by the Twelver-Shiʿi Iranian solider-aristocrat, Saʿadat

Fig.2
Asaf al-Dawla's Bara (Great)
Imambara, Lucknow, 1791

Khan Burhan al-Mulk, on behalf of the Mughal emperor. Burhan al-Mulk's success gave rise to a largely Twelver Shiʿa ruling elite and military aristocracy that presided over Awadh's more numerous Sunni Muslims and its Hindu majority. As the power of the late-Mughal imperial court receded, Awadh grew increasingly independent and its principal cities, first Faizabad and then Lucknow, blossomed, rivalling in some eyes the historic Mughal capital Shahjahanabad (Delhi).

In Awadh, the practice of Twelver Shiʿism was initially a family affair, one that was confined to elite households. Congregational Friday prayers performed by Sunni communities were initially uncommon for the Twelver Shiʿa and there were no specially designated Friday mosques for them like there were for the Sunnis.[4] However, Twelver Shiʿi communities became more publicly visible during the month of Muharram. Assemblies (*majālis*) were held in households and private *imāmbārā*s during Muharram, to listen to poetic recountings of the events leading up to the martyrdom of Imam Husayn and deeply mournful songs that lamented his violent death. It was also a time of ritualised self-flagellation (*mātam*) as part of the collective effort to empathise with the suffering of Imam Husayn and his followers and to express pious outrage over his martyrdom. Most visible were the public processions inspired not only by Iraqi and Iranian precedents but by South Asia's processional cultures, in which Shiʿas and other city dwellers paraded through the city with effigies of Husayn's tomb and other symbolic figures and objects (*taʿziya*). As these processions grew more elaborate over time, people installed the effigies in the growing number of neighbourhood *imāmbārā*s and began burying them in special newly-established suburban burial grounds known evocatively as 'Karbalas', a reference to the site where Imam Husayn was martyred and said to have been buried. Muharram rituals had a transformative effect on Awadh's built landscape and city life as a whole, especially during the month of mourning.

The reign of Asaf al-Dawla marked an important turning point in which the visibility of Twelver Shiʿism in the region was heightened through the ruler's architectural commissions. Having moved his headquarters from Faizabad to Lucknow, Asaf al-Dawla enlarged Lucknow's pre-existing Panj Mahal palace complex – one of the city's key focal points – to include a large religious court with two monumental structures, a Friday Mosque for the Twelver Shiʿi communities and an *imāmbārā*. The entire complex, including the Panj Mahal, Great Mosque and *imāmbārā*, was surrounded by fortifications and known collectively as the Machhi Bhawan (lit. fish house). Before Asaf al-Dawla's Imambara complex was built, Lucknow's cityscape was dominated by a Sunni mosque, which was perched atop the city's highest hill, Lakshman Tila and attributed to the Mughal emperor Awrangzib (d. 1707). The deeply symbolic site is widely believed to have been a gift from the Hindu Lord Rama to his brother Lakshmana as mentioned in the religious epic, the *Ramayana*. Asaf al-Dawla's additions to Lucknow can be interpreted as part of an effort to make the presence of Twelver Shiʿism and its importance to Awadh's elite more visible to Lucknow's diverse population through a transformation of the cityscape. For the first time, the city saw monumental architecture erected in service of Twelver Shiʿi ritual practice.

The construction of Asaf al-Dawla's Shiʿi Friday Mosque was spurred in part by local religious and aristocratic elites interested in aligning Awadh's Twelver Shiʿi communities more closely with the practices of the Twelver Shiʿa in Iraq and Iran, as well as with those of north Indian Sunni Muslims at a time when Sunni-Shiʿa polemics were escalating. The *imāmbārā*, apparently Asaf al-Dawla's initiative, provided a monumental ritual space whose very presence and scale asserted that Twelver Shiʿi Muharram rituals were to be accorded the same regard as ritual prayers offered in mosques. Curiously, inscriptions were not significant features of either Asaf al-Dawla's mosque or his *imāmbārā*, leaving their purpose as a place for Shiʿi rituals somewhat ambiguous to the uninitiated.

The example of Asaf al-Dawla's *imāmbārā* and Great Mosque complex loomed large when the urban quarter of Hussainabad was developed a few decades later just a short distance away to the northwest. Like the Bara Imambara complex, the Hussainabad complex had a large forecourt that served as a commercial centre and an adjoining court with peripheral buildings, small tombs and, most significantly, the impressive Hussainabad Imambara, which was lavishly adorned with calligraphy. The patron of the *imāmbārā*, Muhammad ʿAli Shah, also commissioned a monumental Friday Mosque. However, he did not locate it adjacent to the Hussainabad Imambara. Instead, it

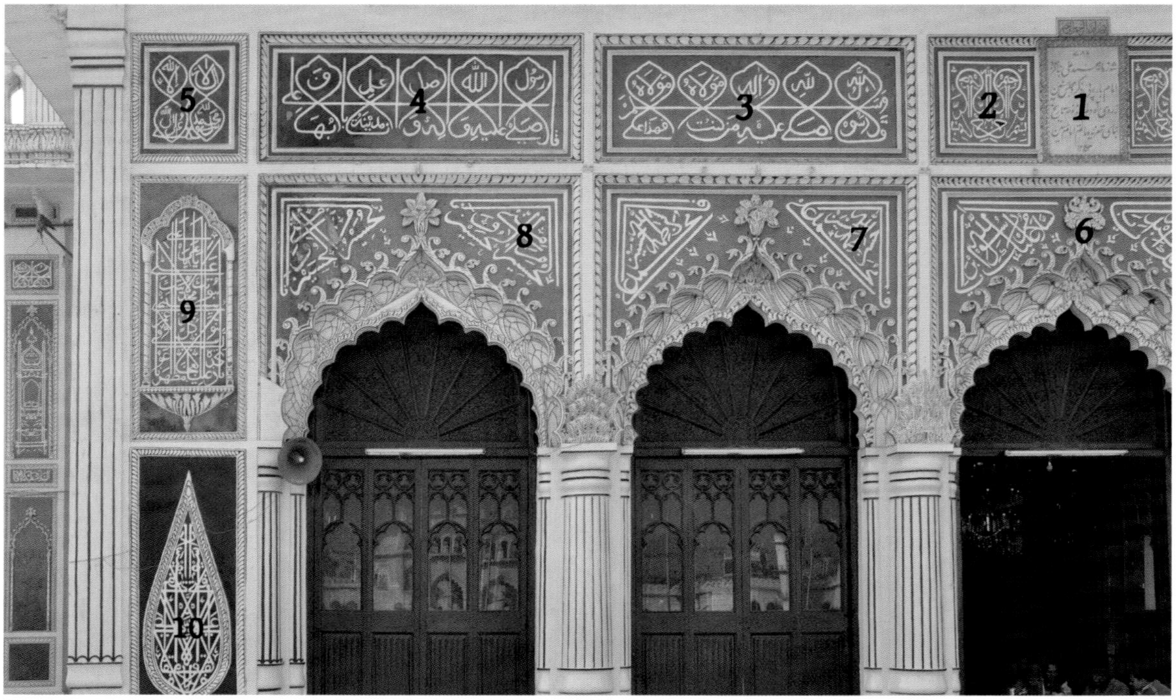

Fig.3

was placed in its own precinct to the west, separating mosque and *imāmbārā* and their respective ritual activities unlike the Bara Imambara complex.

The writing on the walls

The Hussainabad Imambara epigraphs are written mostly in Arabic, though a few are written in Persian, and they are carefully incorporated into the architectural design. Presently, the epigraphs are light coloured texts on a dark background and some are carved in plaster in low relief, while others, which have perhaps deteriorated over time, are painted on the plaster surface. It is not entirely clear whether the epigraphs that are visible today correspond with the building's original epigraphs nor is it certain that the original colour scheme has been preserved.

The building's central arched facade projects forward and the inscriptions are located both on the front and on sides of this projecting architectural feature, which provides the principal way to enter the *imāmbārā*. Given their prominence, these epigraphs are the most important ones to consider first. Looking at the overall arrangement of the epigraphs, the first thing to notice is the importance of symmetry. The epigraphs used on both sides of the central entrance are exactly the same so only one side needs to be deciphered. In total, there are 23 epigraphs on the entry facade but only ten are unique.

Since the sequence in which the epigraphs are read can shape how they can be interpreted as a collective composition, it is important to ask if there is an order in which the ten epigraphs should be read? With respect to content, the epigraphs are best read in rows starting from the centre and the top and ending at the periphery and the bottom (fig.3). The chief reason being that the group of epigraphs at the top and centre use the *basmala* (i.e. *Bismi'llāh al-raḥmān al-raḥīm*) in various forms, not once, but six times. The *basmala* refers to the ubiquitous Arabic phrase that is found at the beginning of almost all of the chapters of the Qur'an and is also customarily used to initiate Islamic ritual. The phrase, which acknowledges Allah's authority and His generous and merciful nature, signals beginnings, which suggest that this is the place where the reading of the epigraphic programme can begin.

Creedal epigraphs – the epigraphs on the top row

The first *basmala* appears over an inserted tablet with Persian text written in *nastaʿlīq* script (fig.4). Foundation tablets like these often specified the building's patron and date of construction. The text

Fig.3
Suggested order to read the entry facade epigraphs based on content. The epigraphs on the other side of the central door are identical

Fig.4
Epigraph 1: The foundation tablet of the Hussainabad Imambara mentioning its patron Muhammad ʿAli and the date of completion 1253/1837

Fig.5
Epigraph 2: Calligraphic rendering of the *basmala*
بسم الله الرحمن الرحيم
(*In the name of Allah, Most Gracious, Most Merciful*)

Table 1
Transcription, transliteration and translation of the Hussainabad Imambara foundation tablet

In the name of Allah, Most Gracious, Most Merciful. 786 The ruler of the age Muhammad ʿAli has established an *imāmbāra* for beautiful *dhikr* and *majlis*. My melancholy heart has composed the sad chronogram, 'This is built for *taʿziya* and *mātam* of Imam Husayn.' 1253 AH (1837 AD)	*Bismi'llāh al-raḥmān al-raḥīm* *786* *Shah zamāna Muḥammad ʿAlī banā faramūd imāmbāra pa'a dhikr wa majlis-e ḥasnayn zaruya ah dilam khwand nawhha tārīkh banā-e taʿziya wa mātam Imām Ḥusayn* *1253*	بسم الله الرحمن الرحيم ٦٨٧ شه زمانه محمّد علي بنا فرمود امامباره پيء ذكر و مجلس حسنين زروى آه دلم خواند نوحّه تاريخ بناى تعزيه و ماتم امام حسين ٣٥٢١

within the tablet's borders begins with another citation of the *basmala* but in the form of the number '786'. Arabic letters have a set of numerical equivalents according to a standardised system known as *abjad*. Phrases could be rendered into numbers whilst important numbers, such as the date of a building's construction or the death of an individual, could be rendered into words – a chronogram. Using the *abjad* system, the letters of the *basmala* add up to 786, providing a shorthand method of invoking the phrase. The rest of the tablet goes on to identify Muhammad ʿAli Shah as the patron, provides the date of construction using the chronogram 'This is built for *taʿziya* and *mātam* (i.e. mourning rituals) of Imam Husayn' as well as the actual numerical date 1253 AH (1837 AD); the text alludes to the building's purpose as a place to install *taʿziya* (Muharram shrines) and attend Muharram gatherings (Table 1).[5]

To the left of the foundation tablet is the second epigraph, which is a calligraphic rendering of the *basmala* and is the same as the epigraph that appears to the right of the tablet (Fig 5). This epigraph not only plays with word placement but it also mirrors the text to create a calligraphic emblem that displays the *basmala* twice.

If the *basmala* epigraphs are the place to begin reading the building's epigraphic programme, then where should the reader look next – down or across? If the reader looks across and reads the top row of epigraphs they will encounter creedal epigraphs that establish the general premises of Twelver Shiʿism. In contrast, the lower row epigraphs are mostly drawn from devotional or prayer rituals; they are prayer epigraphs.

Continuing on the top row to the left of the calligraphic *basmala*, the third epigraph employs a hadith or saying of the Prophet

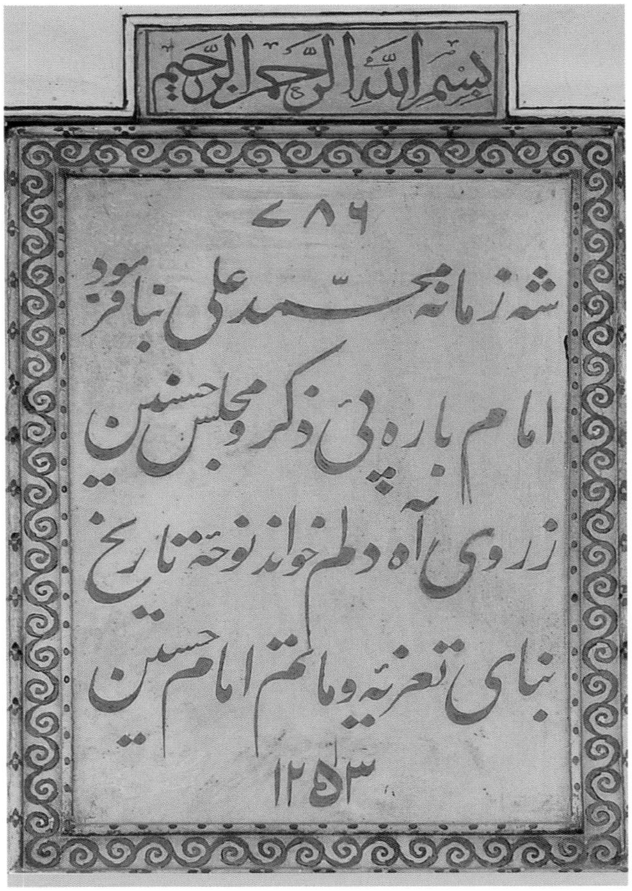

Fig.4

Fig.5

Fig.6

Fig.7

Muhammad that affirms the Twelver Shiʿi conviction that Muhammad designated his cousin and son-in-law, ʿAli b. Abi Talib, as his rightful successor (fig.6).[6] The hadith is a phrase from the Prophet's last sermon said to be delivered at Ghadir Khumm on his way back to Medina from his last pilgrimage to Mecca in 632. In his sermon, Muhammad declared that the one who considers him (i.e. the Prophet) his *mawlā* (protector) should also consider ʿAli as his *mawlā* (i.e. *man kuntu mawlāhu fa-ʿAlī mawlāhu*).[7] For Shiʿi interpreters this declaration made plain Muhammad's public designation of ʿAli as the true leader (*imām*) of the Muslims after the death of their Prophet.[8]

The fourth epigraph to the left is another hadith of the Prophet that is frequently used to assert ʿAli's authority to guide the Muslim community (fig.7).[9] The hadith likens Muhammad to a city of knowledge and ʿAli to its gate (i.e. *Anā madīnatul-ʿilm wa ʿAlīyun bābuhā*) thereby asserting that to follow ʿAli's teachings is the best way to follow Muhammad's teachings.

The fifth and last epigraph to be read on the top row is the Muslim profession of faith (*shahāda*) (fig.8). It proclaims that 'there is no god but God and Muhammad is the messenger of God' (i.e. *Lā ilāha illā llāh Muḥammadan rasūlu llāh*). The epigraph also includes a third phrase, often appended to the *shahāda* by the Shiʿa, namely, "ʿAli is the Friend of God' (*ʿAliyyun waliyyu llāh*).[10] The description of ʿAli as a friend of God also derives from Shiʿi accounts of the Prophet's sermon at Ghadir Khumm and expresses the belief that ʿAli had a superior standing in the world that was affirmed by Muhammad. The Shiʿa profession of faith declared not only the acceptance of the one God, Allah, and that His messenger was Muhammad, but that ʿAli was the sanctioned guide of Islam.[11]

Prayer epigraphs – The epigraphs on the lower row

The central epigraphs on the second row include the sixth epigraph, located above the main entrance. Here, the emphasis shifts from Imam ʿAli to Imam Husayn, reflecting a genealogical progression (fig.9). Unlike the top row of epigraphs, which are composed to fit a rectangle, the sixth one consists of a pair of duplicate epigraphs designed to fit within triangles that fill the spandrels of the archway like the second epigraph. But unlike the second epigraph, the spandrel epigraphs are not executed in intertwined mirror-script. Instead, they are rotated,

Fig.6
Epigraph 3: Calligraphic rendering of the hadith,
قال رسول الله صلى الله عليه وسلم من
كنت مولا فعلى مولا
The Messenger of God said, peace be upon him: ʿAli is the mawlā (protector/master) *of all those who consider me their mawlā*

Fig.7
Epigraph 4: Calligraphic rendering of the hadith
قال رسول الله صلى الله عليه وسلم أنا
مدينة العلم وعلي بابها
The Messenger of God said [peace be upon him]: I am a city of knowledge and ʿAli is its gate

maintaining the right to left direction of the Arabic text, and they can be translated as 'Peace be upon you, O father of the slave of God' (i.e. *Assalamu ʿalaika ya abā ʿabdillāh*). The phrase offers the ubiquitous Islamic salutatory greeting towards none other than Imam Husayn, who is referred to with his honorific name (*kunya*) 'father of the slave of God' (*abā ʿabdillāh*).[12]

More significantly, the phrase is commonly used at the beginning of the supplicatory prayers called the *ziyārāt ʿāshūrā*'.[13] *Ziyārāt* are

Fig.8

collections of devotional phrases, a kind of litany, to be used during pilgrimage or visits to sacred sites, and *ʿāshūrā*' refers to the tenth day of Muharram when Husayn is said to have been killed. For the Twelver Shiʿa of South Asia, a visit to the *imāmbārā* was similar to making pilgrimage to the tomb of Imam Husayn and, as was the case in historical Twelver Shiʿi ritual practice, special *ziyārāt* – the *ziyārāt ʿāshūrā*' – were recited on the tenth day of Muharram.[14] The epigraph then makes reference to *ziyārāt ʿāshūrā*' and the Twelver Shiʿi ritual practices associated with the *imāmbārā*.

Like the sixth epigraph, the seventh and eighth are also designed in triangular formations within the spandrels of an arch to the left. The seventh consists of the names of Allah and the *Ahl al-Bayt*; that is, Muhammad, ʿAli, Fatima, al-Hasan and al-Husayn (fig.10). For all Shiʿa, these select members of the Prophet's family are collectively known in Arabic as the 'People of the Cloak' (*Ahl al-kisā*') or in Persian as the Holy Five (*Panj tan*). The concept of the 'People of the Cloak' originates with a hadith in which Muhammad is said to have affectionately brought these individuals under his cloak and the Qur'anic verse 33:33 (from sura *al-Aḥzāb*) was revealed.[15] Since the verse mentions the 'People of the House' (*Ahl al-bayt*) Shiʿi interpreters maintain the 'People of the Cloak' – ʿAli, Fatima, al-Hasan and al-Husayn together with Muhammad and his lineage – are the 'People of the House' mentioned in the Qur'an and that they have been purified by God, thus endowing them with the spiritual authority to guide Muslims. For the Shiʿa, the names of Muhammad, ʿAli, Fatima, al-Hasan and al-Husayn form a holy quintet, and a coded reference to a key hadith and Qur'anic verse that legitimate their version of Islamic history and doctrine.

The eighth epigraph is an excerpt from a hadith in which Muhammad declares: 'Husayn is from me and I am from Husayn' (i.e. *al-Ḥusayn minnī wa anā min al-Ḥusayn*).[16] The hadith emphasises the dearness with which the Prophet held his grandson and it along with other related hadith are interpreted by the Shiʿa as an affirmation of their belief that the descendants of ʿAli were infallible beings designated by Muhammad to be the leaders of the Muslim community.[17]

The ninth epigraph is the most elaborate of all the epigraphs on the front entry facade and is configured in the shape of a balcony (fig.12). The text is the short version of the famous Shiʿa *Nād-i ʿAlī* prayer ('Call on ʿAli'). One hagiographic account of its origins relates that the Prophet Muhammad and his soldiers were vastly outnumbered when attacking the Jewish inhabitants of Khaybar, 150 kilometers from Medina. The Angel Gabriel came and taught him the *Nād-i ʿAlī* prayer, calling for ʿAli's aid. ʿAli came and was victorious despite the odds, establishing his reputation as an extraordinary hero and warrior.[18] The prayer is commonly used by some Shiʿa Muslims in times of difficulty with the expectation that ʿAli will intervene through his grace.

The tenth and final epigraph continues with the theme of ʿAli as heroic warrior. The epigraph is once again written in mirror script and shaped in the form of a spearhead or cypress tree, the latter being

Fig.8
Epigraph 5: Calligraphic rendering of the Shiʿi *shahāda*,
لا إله إلاّ الله محمد رسول الله علي ولی الله
There is no god but God. Muhammad is the messenger of God. ʿAli is the friend of God

Fig.9

Fig.10

a favourite Persianate literary and decorative motif used to describe strong lofty warriors (fig.13). The text asserts that ʿAli has no equivalent and nor does his famous double-edged sword, *Dhu'l-faqār* (i.e. *lā fatā illā ʿAlī lā sayfa illā Dhu'l-Faqār*). This phrase has often been finely inscribed on swords for apotropaic purposes from the medieval period to the present day throughout the Muslim world. The sword is said to have been obtained by the Prophet as booty from the battle of Badr and was later given to ʿAli as a present.[19] More hagiographical accounts trace the origins of the phrase to a mysterious, possibly divine utterance, which took place during the battle of Uhud where, once again, ʿAli displayed extraordinary heroism against insurmountable odds. There, the sword was presented as a gift from the Angel Gabriel to Muhammad who gave it to ʿAli, who then, according to some traditions, passed it down to his descendants, including Imam Husayn. The sword is, thus, understood not only as a symbol of ʿAli's prowess as a warrior but as the transmitter of religio-political authority from Muhammad.[20]

Although the content of the epigraphs reveals that the top row consists of general creedal statements and the lower row tends to include pious phrases to be used in ritual practice, there is another way to read the epigraphs that emphasise their spatial distribution across the entry facade. Epigraphs relating to Imam ʿAli are relegated to the periphery (the top and the sides) and the more central epigraphs reference Imam Husayn. The central placement of epigraphs referencing Husayn arguably gives them greater emphasis and parallels the centrality of Imam Husayn and his martyrdom in the religious imagination and ritual practices of Awadh's Twelver Shiʿi community.

Calligraphic creativity

The Hussainabad Imambara epigraphs are intriguing not only for their content but for their creative designs. Many are visual puzzles in which the reader must figure out how words are arranged within a composition and designed to fit various shapes and architectural

Fig.9
Epigraph 6: Calligraphic rendering of the phrase,
السلام عليك يا ابا عبد الله
Peace be upon you, O father of the slave of God [Muhammad] [i.e. Imam Husayn]

Fig.10
Epigraph 7: Calligraphic rendering of the names of Allah and the 'People of the Cloak',
الله محمد علی فاطمة حسن حسين
Allah, Muhammad, ʿAli, Fatima, Hasan and Husayn

Fig.11

forms. Texts are composed to fit within the shape of a rectangle (fig.6), triangle (fig.10) and other distinctive shapes (fig.13). Furthermore, both rotational and reflective symmetry are employed. For example the sixth epigraph (fig.9) uses a triangular shaped epigraph to fill an arch spandrel which is rotated 90 degrees to fill the complementary spandrel; the use of rotational symmetry maintains the right to left directionality of the Arabic text. Instead of using rotational symmetry to create two separate epigraphs, the second epigraph (fig.5) uses reflective symmetry to form a single composition; the right to left directionality of the text is reversed in the reflected image requiring part of it to be read backwards.

To achieve these design goals, certain liberties were taken. Letters in one word also belong to other words. Letter and word order varies considerably, sometimes going from top to bottom, bottom to top, or other sequences and letters and words are overlapped, further complicating the task of reading the epigraphs. The creative compositions transform key highly symbolic Arabic phrases into recognisably distinct visual emblems that can be identified at a distance and serve as an additional strategy to emphasise certain texts.

Concluding remarks

The epigraphs of the entry facade of the Hussainabad Imambara are only the first series in an elaborate epigraphic programme spread across the rest of the building's exterior front facades. The other epigraphs await more detailed discussion but they include Qur'anic passages, additional *ziyārāt* excerpts addressed to ʿAli, Fatima, Khadija (the Prophet's first wife) and Jesus, among others. Since the history of the development of Hussainabad and the Hussainabad Imambara as well as the course of Twelver Shiʿism in 19th-century Awadh still requires detailed investigation, the wider significance of the Hussainabad epigraphs remains challenging to interpret.

What is clear thus far is that the construction of the Hussainabad Imambara took place shortly after the British East India Company

Fig.11
Epigraph 8: Calligraphic rendering of the hadith,
الحسين مني و أنا من الحسين
Husayn is from me and I am from Husayn

installed the elderly Muhammad ʿAli Shah as ruler of Awadh, following a period of unrest. The building is a visual assertion of Muslim authority at a time when the British were clearly in control of Awadh. In addition to being a semi-public ritual space, the building may also have been constructed as personal funerary monument for the patron himself, since Muhammad ʿAli Shah was buried there when he died in 1842.[21]

The epigraphic programme of the Hussainabad Imambara knowledgeably invokes key phrases that signal the core concepts of the Twelver Shiʿi tradition. These assured citations reflect how Awadh's Twelver Shiʿi religious discourse was benefitting from increased scholarly exchange with the shrine centres of Iraq, the development of local scholarly expertise and institutions under Muhammad ʿAli Shah, in constrast to Asaf al-Dawla's reign, when there was a considerable lack of available expertise.[22] The epigraphs were also conceived when Lucknow's Twelver Shiʿi religious scholars (*ʿulamāʾ*) increasingly had to articulate and justify Twelver Shiʿi beliefs and practices and compete intellectually with the religious learning of the Sunni *ʿulamāʾ* of Lucknow's historic Firangi Mahal and other influential Sunni religious scholars. Also in need of challenge were the influential and critical attitudes of scholars like Shah Waliullah and his son Shah ʿAbd al-ʿAziz of Delhi, who saw the rise of Twelver Shiʿi regimes in the north and south coupled with the rise of non-Muslim powers such as the British, Sikhs, Jats and Marathas, as signs that Islam in South Asia was in danger of decay and needed to be purified along Sunni lines.[23]

The heightening of Twelver Shiʿi and Sunni sectarianism expressed itself on the ground in Lucknow as latent tensions between Shiʿa and Sunnis erupted during the Muharram processions of the 1820s and 1830s, especially when the Twelver Shiʿa ritually cursed the first three caliphs revered by the Sunnis.[24] Against this backdrop, the Hussainabad Imambara epigraphs appear to be ardent declarations of the validity of Twelver Shiʿi doctrines within the late-Mughal Islamic and British colonial milieu through the presentation of coded phrases that reference central beliefs, key religious personas and common ritual practices. That being said, the Hussainabad Imambara epigraphs deserve further study. The rest of the epigraphs on the front facade still need to be documented and identified. It is not yet clear why the Hussainabad Imambara makes such prolific and public use of epigraphs when the earlier Bara Imambara does not, nor is it clear whether the epigraphs express a distinctly South Asian conception of Twelver Shiʿism. Finally, it remains to be seen how the use of epigraphs at the Hussainabad Imambara compare with other instances of Twelver Shiʿi architectural epigraphy across the history and geography of the Islamic world.

Fig.12

Fig.13

Fig.12
Epigraph 9: Calligraphic rendering of the *Nād-i ʿAlī* prayer,
ناد عليا مظهر العجائب تجده عونا لك فى
النوائب كل هم وغم سينجلى بولايتك يا على
يا على يا على
Call on ʿAli, (he) is able to bring about the extraordinary. You will find him an effective supporter in all calamities. (All) worries and sorrows will soon disappear. O ʿAli! O ʿAli! O ʿAli!

Fig.13
Epigraph 10: Calligraphic rendering of the saying,
لا فتى الا علي لا سيف الا ذوالفقار
There is no hero except ʿAli; there is no sword except [his sword] Dhu'l-Faqār

1 Mirzā Rajab ʿAlī Beg Surūr, '*Fasāna-i ʿIbrat*', in Safi Ahmad, *Two Kings of Awadh: Muhammad Ali Shah and Amjad Ali Shah* (1837–1847), (Aligarh, 1971), p.164.

2 Hussein Keshani, 'Architecture and the Twelver Shiʿi Tradition: The Great Imāmbārā Complex of Lucknow', *Muqarnas*, 23 (2006), pp.219–250. See the essay by Peter J. Chelkowski in this volume.

3 Four of the epigraphs on the building are identified in Ahmad, *Two Kings of Awadh*, pp.165–166.

4 Ibid., p.127; J. R. I. Cole, *Roots of North Indian Shīʿism in Iran and Iraq: Religion and State in Awadh* 1722–1859 (Oxford, 1989), p.127.

5 Ahmad, *Two Kings of Awadh*, p.165. See the essay by Tryna Lyons in this volume.

6 Ibid., p.165.

7 Laura Veccia Vaglieri, 'Ghadīr Khumm', *EI2*, vol.2, pp.993–994.

8 In contrast, Sunni interpreters asserted that the Prophet 'was simply exhorting his hearers to hold his cousin and son-in-law in high esteem and affection.' See Vaglieri, 'Ghadīr Khumm'.

9 Ahmad, *Two Kings of Awadh*, p.165.

10 This tripartite profession of faith is sometimes referred to as the 'Shiʿi *shahāda*' or the 'Shiʿi *adhān*.' See the essay by Luke Treadwell in this volume.

11 Joseph Eliash, 'On the Genesis and Development of the Twelver-Shiʿi Three-tenet Shahadah', *Der Islam*, 47 (1971), pp.265–272.

12 Syed Kazim Hussain, *Ziyarats and Weekday Prayers* (Chicago, 2010), p.25. S. K. Hussain's translation of the *ziyārāt ʿāshūrā*' is based on Arabic texts found in the late-Safavid era text *Bihār al-Anwār* by Muḥammad Bāqir Majlisī (d. 1699) and the 20th-century text *Mafātīḥ al-jinān* by al-Qummī (d. 1940).

13 Hussain, *Ziyarats*, p.25.

14 Khalid Sindawi, 'Visit to the Tomb of Al-Husayn b. ʿAlī in Shiite Poetry: First to Fifth Centuries AH (8th–11th Centuries CE)', *Journal of Arabic Literature*, 37, 2 (January 1, 2006), pp.230–258. Yitzhak Nakash, 'The Visitation of the Shrines of the Imams and the Shiʿi Mujtahids in the Early Twentieth Century', *Studia Islamica*, 81 (1995), p.155; Cole, *Roots of North Indian Shīʿism*, p.117.

15 Farhad Daftary, 'Ahl al-Kisāʾ', *EI3*, 1 (2008), p.83; Wilferd Madelung, *The Succession to Muhammad: A Study of the Early Caliphate* (Cambridge, 1998), pp.14–16; M. Ayoub, 'The Excellences of Imam Husayn in Sunni Hadith Tradition', *al-Serāt*, 12 (1986), pp.60–62.

16 Ayoub, 'The Excellences', p.69.

17 David Pinault, 'Shia Lamentation Rituals and Reinterpretations of the Doctrine of Intercession: Two Cases', *History of Religions*, 38, 3 (February 1999), pp.287–288.

18 Jan Knappert, *Islamic Legends* (Leiden, 1985), pp.224, 263. See also, Muḥammad Bāqir Majlisī *Biḥār al-anwār* (Beirut, 1983), vol.20, pp.72–73.

19 E. Mittwoch, 'Dhu'l-Faḳār', *EI2*, vol.2, p.233. See Zeynep Yürekli's essay in this volume.

20 Francesca Bellino, 'Dhū l-Faqār', *EI3*, 4 (2012), p.77; David Alexander, 'Dhu'l-faqār and the Legacy of the Prophet, *Mīrāth Rasūl Allāh*', *Gladius*, 19 (1999), pp.157–188; John Renard, *Islam and the Heroic Image* (Macon, GA, 1999), pp.206–207. Knappert, *Islamic Legends*, pp.256–257.

21 Ahmad, *Two Kings of Awadh*, p.35.

22 Cole, *Roots of North Indian Shīʿism*, pp.123–148 and 194–220.

23 Ibid., pp.229–244.

24 Ibid., pp.239–241.

11

ʿAlī walī Allāh and other non-Qur'anic references to the *Ahl al-bayt* on Islamic coinage before the Saljuq period

Luke Treadwell

In a recent article I examined the use of non-standard Qur'anic texts on coinage struck by members of the Prophet's family (*Ahl al-bayt*) from the 7th–11th centuries (i.e. in the first four centuries AH).[1] The evidence suggests that rulers who placed these Qur'anic excerpts on their coins used both the explicit text, and in many cases the implicit sense conveyed by the Qur'anic verses surrounding the cited verse, to make a series of claims about the elevated status of the Prophet's family and their right to the leadership of the Muslim community. In some cases, the verses seemed to have formed part of a political manifesto which these rulers publicised in more than one medium, including their coins. The creative use of Qur'anic material by the *Ahl al-bayt* appears to have been largely concentrated in the 8th and 9th centuries (second and third centuries AH).

This essay turns to non-Qur'anic references to ʿAli b. Abi Talib and other short phrases in praise of the *Ahl al-bayt*. Coins bearing these statements first become relatively common in the 10th century (4th century AH). They were issued by rulers who wished to express their love for the Prophet's family or their allegiance to the political aspirations of one or other branch of the Shiʿa. The dynasties involved include the Idrisids (*r.* 788–985) of western North Africa, founded by the uncle of the ʿAlid rebel al-Husayn b. ʿAli, Sahib Fakhkh, who fled to the region of present-day Morocco in 786; the Bavandids of Tabaristan, who claimed descent from a local notable family of Sasanian provenance and ruled until 1349; the Daylami Musafirid/Sallarid/Kangarid dynasty of the South Caucasus/Northern Iranian region who ruled in the 10th to 11th centuries; the Arab ʿUqaylids of the Jazira region in northern Iraq, active in the late 10th to 12th centuries; several dynasties which competed for power in the aftermath of the political decline of the Abbasids in the early 10th century, including the Hamdanids, Buyids, Marwanids, as well as the Ikhshidid governors of Egypt; and finally, the Fatimids, who need no introduction.[2]

The inscriptions can be divided into two categories, those referring specifically to ʿAli (*ʿAlī walī Allāh* [ʿAli is the Friend of God]; *ʿAlī khalīfat Allāh* [ʿAli is the Deputy of God]; *al-Imām ʿAlī; ʿAlī khayr al-nās baʿda al-Nabī kariha man kariha wa raḍiya man raḍiya* (ʿAli is the best of men after the Prophet: he who 'denies' [this statement] is an ungrateful believer and he who 'accepts' it is a grateful believer) and those referring to the members of the *Ahl al-bayt* in the form of the *taṣliya* (*ṣallā Allāh ʿalay-hi wa [ʿala] āli-hi* [May the prayers of God be upon him and his family]). The phrase *ʿAlī walī Allāh* is particularly significant, both because it is the mostly widely used and because it is known to have formed part of the *shahāda* recited by the Shiʿa.[3] It was not just an expression of praise of the Prophet's son-in-law, but a statement with a political meaning for those Shiʿi Muslims who believed that ʿAli had been wrongfully deprived of his right to succeed the Prophet.[4] In the 16th century, *ʿAlī walī Allāh* was adopted by the Safavids as part of their official formulae, and was included in the *adhān* (call to prayer), on documents, coins and building inscriptions, thus becoming emblematic of the state's adherence to Shiʿism.[5]

In the centuries before the Safavids, however, most Shiʿi scholars, while accepting it as a fundamental element of the *shahāda*, expressly prohibited its public expression in the *adhān*, perhaps because they feared that the *ghulāt* (extremist Shiʿi groups) would use the *adhān* to support their claim that ʿAli, the first of the Imams, was endowed with superhuman powers.[6] It may be that the scholars' disapproval of the use of the phrase in public texts included not only its prohibition from the *adhān* but also from other public documents like the coinage. While I have found no textual evidence to support this idea, it may explain why the phrase is only rarely found on coins struck by rulers who believed in the *wilāya* of ʿAli.[7]

Numismatic references to ʿAli b. Abi Talib before 386 AH (996 AD)

ʿAlī khayr al-nās baʿda al-Nabī kariha man kariha wa raḍiya man raḍiya

This was the earliest known numismatic phrase that praises ʿAli.[8] It was used in a small cluster of mints (Baht, Warzīgha and Wazeqqūr) controlled by the descendants of ʿIsa b. Idris b. Idris, the latter being the founder of the dynasty. ʿIsa's descendants, who were vassals of the reigning Idrisid amir, struck coins bearing this phrase between 233–276/847–889, although the published evidence gives little indication of the frequency of striking within this period.[9]

ʿAlī walī Allāh

The rare numismatic occurrence of the phrase is intriguing. It occurred on a single silver coin dated 252/866 (mint uncertain: al-ʿAlīya?) issued by the Idrisid ruler ʿAli II b. ʿUmar, who may have come to power in the year it was issued.[10] This dirham (fig.1) was clearly not part of ʿAli b. ʿUmar's regular issues. The inscription is written in three lines beginning at the bottom of the field and is quite different in style to contemporary Idrisid dirhams. The phrase occurs on no other 9th-century coins.

The next numismatic appearance of the phrase also occurred on the periphery of the Islamic world, on the northern fringes of the Iranian plateau. In 353/964 the phrase is found on the earliest known dirham of Rustam b. Sharwin, the Bavandid ruler of Firīm in Tabaristan. On this coin, like all the dirhams of Rustam and his immediate successors, it occurs directly after the phrase *Muḥammad rasūl Allāh* on the reverse field, suggesting that it formed part of the *shahāda* as pronounced in the Bavandid territories. The phrase is found on the coins of Rustam b. Sharwin (Firīm 353/964, 361/971, 365/975, 367/977),[11] his brother Marzban (Firīm 371/981),[12] his son Shahriyar b. Rustam (Firīm [3]73/983,[13] and Shahriyar b. Dara (*circa* 358–396/968–1005) who overthrew Shahriyar b. Rustam briefly (Firīm 376/986).[14] All these coins bear the titles of the Abbasid caliph and the Bavandids' Buyid overlords. By 387/997, at the latest, the phrase had disappeared from the coins of this dynasty.[15]

The dirham of Rustam b. Sharwin struck in 365/975 is a particularly interesting coin (fig.2). Like the other early Bavandid issues, it was probably struck from dies made by the engraver al-Hasan b. Muhammad, who worked for several Buyid mints.[16] Unlike the other Bavandid dirhams, however, this coin was of the highest quality. The intricate epigraphy and quality of execution suggest that it was intended as a donative, rather than a regular, issue. The appearance of the words *Muḥammad wa ʿAlī* around the outer margins of both sides of the coin may have been an abbreviated reference to the phrase *Muḥammad wa ʿAlī khayr al-bashar/al-nās* (Muhammad and ʿAli are the best of men), which formed part of the Shiʿi *adhān* in the 10th century.[17] This exceptional marginal inscription does not appear to have been used regularly on Bavandid coins, however, and may have been engraved at the whim of the die engraver.[18]

Fig.1

Fig.2

Fig.1
Idrisid dirham, al-ʿAlīya? 252/866, after Eustache, *Dirhems idrisites*

Fig.2
Bavandid dirham of Rustam b. Sharwin, Firīm 365/975: Lundberg collection

ʿ*Alī khalīfat Allāh* (ʿAli is the Deputy of God)

Two sets of coins, from northern Iran and the Caucasus, bore the phrase *ʿAlī khalīfat Allāh*. The first, which consisted of both silver dirhams and gold dinars, was struck in the mint of Jalālābād in 343/954. The type was first published in detail by Samuel Stern, who noted its Ismaili features, including the names of the Imams revered by the Ismailis, the phrase *ʿAlī khalīfat Allāh* on the reverse and the name and title of the issuer, the Musafirid amir, Wahsudan b. Muhammad (b. Musafir), who styled himself *sayf āl Muḥammad* (Sword of the family of Muhammad) on this coin.[19] Further research suggested that the mint-name Jalālābād was an epithet for Wahsudan's capital of Ṭārum, while scrutiny of the coin itself (fig.3) suggests that it, too, was a donative issue. The phrase *ʿAlī khalīfat Allāh* was presumably intended to

Fig.3

remind the coin user not only that ʿAli had held the office of caliph for a few short years, but that he was the true 'deputy of God' in the sense that the Prophet had designated him as his successor as leader of the *umma*.[20] The accompanying Qur'anic text (5:55), on the reverse margin, is the proof-text adduced by the Shiʿa to support the designation of ʿAli as the *walī* of Allah.[21] Its presence indicates that the issuer regarded ʿAli as the holder of both titles, *khalīfat Allāh* and *walī Allāh,* although only the first of these titles is explicitly cited.

While the coins of Jalālābād were certainly issued by a Musafirid ruler, the dynastic origin of the second coin type is not so clear. This is a medallion (fig.4) bearing the *shahāda* on one side with the date and mint (Bardaʿa 373/983), while on the other the figure of a horseman dominates the field with three lines of inscription, from the top: *abū al-hayjā'/ʿAlī khalīfat Allāh/Muḥammad b. al-Sallār.* The piece was traditionally attributed to the Musafirids, on account of the presence of the same phrase as is found on the Jalālābād coin and the name of the founder of the dynasty, Muhammad b. Musafir. But the coin has recently been assigned to the Shirwanshah Muhammad b. Ahmad, principally on the grounds that the city of Bardaʿa was under his control, and not that of the Musafirids, in the year that it was struck.[22] While there is insufficient evidence for certainty, I would incline to the traditional attribution because the date at which the city passed out of Musafirid into Shirwanshahid control is not precisely known and also because it is unlikely that the Shirwanshah Muhammad would have

Fig.4

adopted the title 'Ibn al-Sallar' which was the designation of the founder of the Sallarid dynasty with whom he was at war.[23] The *kunya ʿabu'l-hayjā'* (Father of Victory) presumably refers to the Sallarid founding father, which suggests that this rare figurative medallion may have been issued in the last days of Sallarid control of the city, in order to recall the martial qualities of the eponymous founder of the dynasty.[24]

al-Imām ʿAlī

The ʿUqaylid amirs, rulers of one of the successor states that took over the northern territories of the former Hamdanid dynasty (i.e. Syria and Iraq), were Shiʿa and their coins display a number of different *taṣliya*s

Fig.3
Musafirid dirham of Wahsudan b. Muhammad, Jalālābād 343/854: FINT 92-2-25

Fig.4
Sallarid medallion, Bardaʿa 373/983: after Akopyan and Vardanyan, 'Shirwānshāh'

after the phrase *Muḥammad rasūl Allāh,* including the phrase *ṣallā Allāh ʿalay-hi wa āli-hi* (see following section). On one particular issue, a dirham of Takrīt 396/1005 issued by Rafiʿ b. Husayn, the words *al-Imām ʿAlī* appear below the obverse field.[25]Although the term probably refers to ʿAli b. Abi Talib, there is no explanation why it appears on this issue alone and on no other ʿUqaylid coins. In 394/1003 and 396/1005 the word 'ʿAli' appears above the obverse of dirhams struck in Barqaʿīd, which might also be a reference to the Prophet's son-in-law.[26] If so, it seems that there was a brief fashion for citing his name in these few years, but the trend did not continue.

The numismatic use of the extended *taṣliya 'ṣallā Allāh ʿalay-hi wa (ʿala) āli-hi'* in the 4th–5th/10th–11th centuries

The *taṣliya 'ṣallā Allāh ʿalay-hi wa (ʿalā) āli-hi'* was quite frequently, though intermittently, cited on the coinage of south-eastern Anatolia, northern Syria, Mesopotamia and Egypt in the 10th and early 11th centuries, by rulers of the Hamdanid, Ikhshidid, Marwanid and ʿUqaylid dynasties. To understand the meaning of the phrase in its numismatic context, we should begin by looking at the changes introduced to the standard format of Abbasid coinage by the various amirs who fought for control of Iraq in the dying days of the unitary Abbasid caliphate. In 330/941, Nasir al-Dawla the Hamdanid was awarded the title of *amīr al-umarāʾ* (chief amir) by the caliph al-Muttaqi and in the same year he introduced a short form of the *taṣliya* (*ṣallā Allāh ʿalay-hi*), the so-called *ṣalāt ʿalā al-Nabī*,[27] on the dirhams which he struck in Madīnat al-Salām (i.e Baghdad). Three years later, his rival al-Muzaffar Tuzun, employed his own version of the *taṣliya* (*ṣallā Allāh ʿalay-hi wa sallama* [May the prayers and peace of God be upon him]) on the coins he struck in the same mint.[28] In the following year, 334/945, the Buyid Muʿizz al-Dawla seized control of Baghdad and included the same *taṣliya* as Tuzun on his coins.[29] In the same year, 334/945, the Hamdanid Sayf al-Dawla went one step further and introduced the extended *taṣliya* (*ṣallā Allāh ʿalay-hi wa ʿalā āli-hi*) on the dirhams which he struck in Aleppo (i.e. Ḥalab) and Ḥarrān.[30]

Al-Suli states that Nasir al-Dawla introduced the *taṣliya* (*ṣallā Allāh ʿalay-hi*) below the name of the Prophet on the new high-quality dinars which he struck in the caliphal capital, implying that the phrase was meant to mark out these coins, while Ibn Miskawayh tells us that the Hamdanid ruler aimed to raise the standard of fineness of both dinars and dirhams, but says nothing about the *taṣliya*.[31] Al-Suli gives no details regarding the success or otherwise of the reform and metallurgical analysis has not demonstrated unequivocally that Nasir al-Dawla succeeded in raising the fineness of the precious metal coinage. He certainly marked his new dinars as being of high quality, by placing the Arabic word *ibrīz* (purified) on them (in addition to the *taṣliya*), but studies of his dirhams show no marked increase in their silver content.[32] No source suggests that the use of the *taṣliya* by amirs other than Nasir al-Dawla was associated with an attempt to produce coins of increased fineness. Instead it seems that once the caliph had lost control of his administrative apparatus including his capital mint – and we may assume that none of the coin types mentioned above were commissioned by the caliph – the rival amirs strove to demonstrate their pious credentials in order to counteract the negative publicity they had generated by their disdain for caliphal proprieties.

The extended *taṣliya* first appeared in Aleppo and Ḥarrān in 334/945 and was thereafter only intermittently used on coins struck in some mints under Sayf al-Dawla's control.[33] In the same year the short *taṣliya* was first adopted by the Ikhshidids, rivals of the Hamdanids, in the mints of Damascus (i.e. Dimashq) and Filasṭīn (Palestine), their main Syrian mint. Within two years, the Ikhshidids adopted the extended *taṣliya* in their capital mint of Miṣr, and two years later in Filasṭīn.[34] The other major Ikhshidid mints in Syria (Damascus and Ṭabariyya) were, like Sayf al-Dawla's mints, less consistent, although by 340/951, Ṭabariyya had adopted the extended *taṣliya* for all its dirham issues. Widespread use of the extended *taṣliya* by both dynasties continued until the end of the Ikhshidids and the death of Sayf al-Dawla. In the post-Hamdanid period, the ʿUqaylids and the Marwanids, the two minor dynasties which inherited the northern territories once governed by Sayf al-Dawla, both made use of the different forms of the *taṣliya*.[35]

Given that the *taṣliya* in all its forms, shorter or longer, constitutes an expression of reverence towards the Prophet, the expansion of the numismatic use of the *taṣliya* should be seen as a sign of a competition for recognition of pious status. But what significance should we ascribe to the use of the extended *taṣliya,* with its blessing on the family of the

Prophet? Is it legitimate to regard the latter as the analogue of coins with *ʿAlī walī Allāh,* in other words as a sign of the Shiʿi orientations of the rulers who issued these coin types? In answering this question, it is important to begin by making a clear distinction between philo-ʿAlid sentiment, which might be summarised as an expression of affection for the members of the Prophet's family that could be made by Sunnis as well as sectarian Shiʿa, and declarations of Shiʿi intent, which were made by rulers who believed in the concept that the Imamate, in the sense of the religious and political leadership of the *umma,* was the sole right of Imams who were descended from the Prophet, via his daughter Fatima. Based upon these criteria, it is difficult to decide precisely what Sayf al-Dawla's initial motivation might have been for using the extended *taṣliya.* Sayf al-Dawla was known to favour ʿAlid scholars, and is also said to have commissioned a *mashhad* (Shiʿi commemorative tomb).[36] Moreover, Maqrizi tells us that during his governorship of northern Syria, the *adhān* in Aleppo was changed, by order of an unidentified Hasanid Imam, from the Sunni form to the Shiʿi form.[37] It may be that Sayf al-Dawla commissioned this particular form of the *taṣliya* as a demonstration of his favour towards ʿAlids, and even as a sign of his pro-Shiʿi inclinations.[38] The intermittent appearance of the extended *taṣliya* on his coins does indicate that Sayf al-Dawla himself made no effort to ensure that this form of the *taṣliya* appeared regularly on all this coinage. After its first appearance in his capital Aleppo in 334/945, the Hamdanid ruler appears to have left the decision to include it or not up to the local authorities in charge of the mint. But by the same token, the persistence of the phrase proves that he never prohibited its use. The intermittent use of such inscriptions is just one manifestation of the irregular monetary practices which emerged after the breakdown of caliphal control over coinage production. The survival of the phrase on the coins of the Ikhshidids, as well as the Hamdanid successor dynasties, one Sunni (the Marwanids of Mayyafāriqīn, 373 to mid-5th century/983 to mid-11th century),[39] the other Shiʿi (ʿUqaylid),[40] suggests that it quickly became a standardised numismatic inscription and shed any sectarian associations which it might once have carried.

On the other hand, Ramzi Bikhazi interpreted the use of the extended *taṣliya* by the Sunni Ikhshidids in the mints of Damascus and Filasṭīn in a different way. He floated the idea that the Ikhshidid regent Kafur adopted the phrase in the mid-330s/mid-940s as a public acknowledgement of the Fatimid right to the caliphate. Bikhazi suggested that Kafur came to an accommodation with his powerful western neighbours in order to prevent them from invading Egypt and that the Ikhshidid coinage provides proof of his concession of their rightful claim to the caliphate, in return for which the Fatimids desisted from invasion.[41] Bikhazi points out that while the phrase quickly became a standard feature of the mint of Miṣr, it was used only intermittently in the Syrian mints. He argues that it was a political statement that was fully endorsed by Kafur in his capital mint, but less enthusiastically received by the members of the Ikhshidid family who served as governors in Syria, particularly in Damascus. However the periodic appearance of the phrase on Ikhshidid Syrian dirhams can be better explained by the generally chaotic state of mint organisation in the former Abbasid mints after 334/945, which affected both Hamdanid and Ikhshidid mint practice and is reflected in the Samanid and Buyid cases as well.[42] The Ikhshidid minters simply took over the phrase from the Hamdanid coins which preceded them.[43] Unlike *ʿAlī walī Allāh,* the extended *taṣliya* carried no overt political connotations. On whichever medium it appeared, it spoke to all members of the *Ahl al-bayt,* not just to the Fatimids.[44]

Fatimid use of phrases referring to ʿAli b. Abi Talib

ʿAli's *wilāya* is a theme that is taken up relatively late in the Fatimid coinage record, even though it is reasonable to assume that the Fatimid *shahāda* contained the phrase *ʿAlī walī Allāh* from the very beginning of the Fatimid *daʿwa*: the Ismailis, from whom the Fatimids sprung, revered ʿAli as the first Imam of the heptad which led directly from him to the occulted Imam Muhammad b. Ismaʿil. But were Ismaili scholars against the declaration of ʿAli's *wilāya* in the *adhān,* as were the Ithna ʿashari scholars? One major early Fatimid thinker and law-maker, al-Qadi al-Nuʿman, was certainly aware of the dangers of the deification of the Imams. He devoted a section of the chapter on *wilāya* (he uses the term *walāya*) in his *Daʿāʾim al-Islām* (The Pillars of Islam) to the condemnation of those Shiʿis who ascribed supernatural powers to the Imams and those who deified them.[45] The Fatimids themselves insisted on the public declaration of their faith in the territories which they controlled, through the employment of the Shiʿi form of the *adhān*. But I have not been able to discover whether the Fatimid *adhān* included the phrase *ʿAlī walī Allāh*. In 307/919, we hear of a *muʾadhdhin* in Qayrawan being executed for failing to include the phrase *hayya ilā khayr al-ʿamal* in the *adhān* and one of the first acts of Jawhar, conqueror of Egypt, when entering Miṣr, was to change the *adhān* to the Shiʿi form.[46] This form of the *adhān* remained standard in Egypt throughout the Fatimid period, with brief interludes during al-Hakim's reign when the Sunni version was reinstated between 400–401/1009–1010 and early in the 12th century when a Twelver vizier of the Fatimids made changes to the *adhān* and other rituals of Fatimid worship.[47]

Coinage has proved to be a conservative medium in most cultures in which it has been used, no less so in the Islamic world than others. When assuming power, Muslim dynasts often retained features of the existing coinage of their new realms in order to ensure continuity of use in the markets. The first Fatimid gold coinage closely resembled that of the Aghlabid dynasty, which they deposed, but replaced the names of the Aghlabid amirs with those of the Imams and their titles.[48] The stimulus for more radical change appears to have been the rebellion of the Khariji rebel Abu Yazid Sahib al-Himar, who struck coinage in his own name, bearing a non-standard Qurʾanic verse, as well as the phrases *lā ḥukm illā lillāh/Muḥammad rasūl Allāh khātim al-nabiyyīn* (Muhammad is the Messenger of God, the Seal of the Prophets)/ *al-ʿizza lillāh rabbunā Allāh al-Ḥaqq al-Mubīn* (Glory to God, who is our Lord, the Clear Truth) (dinar of Qayrawān 333/944).[49] The Fatimid caliph al-Mansur (*r.* 334–341/945–952) who came to the throne after the defeat of the rebel, introduced an empty circle between the field inscription and the marginal inscription of his dinars, perhaps taking his cue from the contemporary coinage of Yemen, and created a coin that was quite distinctive in appearance.[50]

Towards the end of his reign, al-Mansur rearranged the inscriptions on both sides of the dinar, placing all the data pertaining to the caliph (name and titles) and the mint (date and place of striking) on one side, and the religious inscriptions (Qurʾanic verses and *shahāda*) on the other (fig.5). But he made no changes to the contents of the inscriptions.[51]

Al-Muʿizz li-Din Allah (*r.* 341–365/952–975), by contrast, made radical changes to the appearance and inscriptional content of his coinage, taking some inspiration, at least in as far as the inscriptions were concerned, from the coinage of the rebel Abu Yazid.[52] He invented the so-called 'bullseye' type along with a programme of inscriptions which highlighted the caliph's role as the reviver of the *sunna* of the Prophet and the promulgator of the concept of *tawḥīd Allāh* (Unity of God) and underlined ʿAli's role as the *waṣī* (legatee) of the Prophet, as well as his role as councillor (*wazīr*) to the Prophet and his son-in-law. Of these the most important was his role as *waṣī,* which highlighted his intimate association with the Prophet as his executor and his crucial role within the Ismaili cosmological system as the interpreter of the Prophetic revelation.[53] The phrase *ʿAlī walī Allāh* does not appear to have been used on any of his coins.[54]

As for al-ʿAziz billah (*r.* 365–386/975–996), he abandoned the concept of ʿAli as the legatee of the Prophet and replaced it with a new phrase, *ʿAlī khayr ṣafwat Allāh* (ʿAli is the best of the chosen ones of God), which appears on the majority of his coins. As with his predecessors, there are a number of smaller, less legible fractional coins, on which the phrase *ʿAlī walī Allāh* has been read. Some of these issues, like those of the faraway mint of Multān, do indeed appear to have carried a reference to ʿAli as *walī Allāh,* but others can probably be discounted as misreadings.[55]

With al-Hakim's accession, *ʿAlī walī Allāh* finally appears as a core element in the numismatic repertoire of the Fatimid state. Al-Hakim's

Fig.5
Fatimid dinar of al-Mansur, al-Manṣurīyya 341/952, Institute of Ismaili Studies

earliest issue, a dinar of 386/996, bears a Qur'anic citation (4:54), which was interpreted by the Ismailis as referring to God's choice of the descendants of ʿAli through whom the Fatimids traced their descent, as the Imams of the community.[56] The phrase *ʿAlī walī Allāh* is inscribed in the field, directly after *Muḥammad rasūl Allāh,* which suggests that the whole phrase represents the *shahāda* then in use by the Fatimids. The phrase remained on all of al-Hakim's later issues (fig.6) and became a standard feature of Fatimid coinage to the end of the dynasty.

Finally, the phrase was also used on a very small series of gold coins issued by a rebel against the Fatimids during al-Hakim's reign, in 402/1011, from the mint of Filasṭīn.[57] These dinars were struck by Abu al-Fatuh al-Rashid Billah, the ʿAlid governor of Mecca who was invited to make his claim to the caliphate in opposition to the Fatimids by an ex-Fatimid vizier, al-Maghribi, and the leaders of a small Palestinian tribal dynasty, the Jarrahids. Al-Rashid billah's coins bore the names of the Twelve Imams, ending with *al-ḥujja,* and the phrase *Muḥammad rasūl Allāh ʿAlī walī Allāh.* They were struck for only one year, before al-Hakim persuaded him to give up his claim to the caliphate and return to the governorship of Mecca.

Conclusions

The numismatic inscriptions discussed above suggest that *ʿAlī walī Allāh* and related phrases pertaining to ʿAli b. Abi Talib were used by Shiʿi rulers, while the extended *taṣliya* indicated non-sectarian philo-ʿAlidism. The use of *ʿAlī walī Allāh* was rare before the last quarter of the 4th/10th century. One reason is that there were not many Shiʿi dynasties at the time that may have wanted to use it. Dynasties that favoured Shiʿis and sponsored Shiʿi culture, like the Buyids, did not necessarily wish to declare themselves as Shiʿi rulers in the public sphere. The Shiʿi prohibition of the use of the phrase in the *adhān* may well have acted as a further restraint on its use on the coins. Statements in praise of ʿAli crop up on the geographical periphery, and sometimes on exceptional (donative) coins, as well as on regular coins. The longest run of such coins was struck by the Bavandid rulers. They put the Shiʿi *shahāda* on their coins, even though these coins bore the titles of both their Buyid overlords and the Abbasid caliph.

ʿAlī walī Allāh became a standard inscription only from the beginning of the reign of the Fatimid ruler al-Hakim (386/996). Could the late appearance of the phrase have been a consequence of the Fatimid caliphs' use of the personal title *ʿAbd Allāh wa walī-hi* (Servant of God and His *walī*)? This title was certainly used as early as the reign of al-Muʿizz, and probably earlier as well: it appeared on the coinage from al-ʿAziz's reign.[58] Did the use of this personal title by the caliphs make them reluctant to proclaim ʿAli as the *walī Allāh* on the coinage on the grounds that titular parity with ʿAli b. Abi Talib might have been misunderstood by their subjects?[59] It is interesting to note that the three caliphs, al-Muʿizz, al-ʿAziz and al-Hakim, each placed a different set of religious formulae on their coins right from the beginning of their individual reigns. This wholesale variation in the formulaic inscriptions between one reign and another is quite exceptional. Once al-Hakim adopted the phrase *ʿAlī walī Allāh* on his coins, however, all Fatimid coinage inscriptions became standardised, with little variation between reigns.[60]

Fig.6
Fatimid dinar of al-Hakim, al-Mahdiyya, 411/1020, British Museum, no.1877,1103.7

1 Luke Treadwell, 'Qur'ānic Inscriptions on the Coins of the ahl al-bayt (2nd–4th century AH)', *Journal of Qur'anic Studies*, 14, 2 (2012), pp.267–291.

2 Summaries of the histories of all these dynasties may be found in the EI2 and in Edmund Bosworth, *The New Islamic Dynasties: A Chronological and Genealogical Manual* (2nd ed., Edinburgh, 2004).

3 According to Radscheit's article the addition of *'Alī walī Allāh* was a commendable, though not indispensable, part of the Shi'i *shahāda*. Matthias Radscheit, 'Witnessing and Testifying', EQ, vol.5, pp.492–506.

4 Paul E. Walker, 'Wilāya: 2. In Shī'ism', EI2, vol.11, pp.208–209. Both *wilāya* and *walāya* are acceptable usages in the sense of the *wilāyat 'Alī*. *Wilāya* will be used in this paper, except in references to primary sources in which the alternative term is used.

5 For the Safavid coin evidence see, Stephen Album, *Iran After the Mongol Invasion, Sylloge of Islamic Coins in the Ashmolean Museum*, vol.9 (Oxford, 2001).

6 This is suggested by Hossein Modaressi in his *Crisis and Consolidation in the Formative Period of Shi'ite Islam* (New York, 1993), chapter 2. For an analysis of the crucial passage in Ibn Bābawayh's (d. *circa* 391/1000) book *Man lā yaḥdaru-hu al-faqīh,* which condemns the practice of citing *'Alī walī Allāh, 'Alī khalīfat Allāh* and *Muḥammad wa ālu-hu khayr al-barīya*, see, Werner Ende, '"Bid'a or sirr al-īmān" – modern Shi'i controversies over the third shahāda in the adhān', in Muhammad Ali Amir-Moezzi, Meir M. Bar Asher and Simon Hopkins, ed., *Le shi'isme imāmite quarante ans après: Hommage à Etan Kohlberg* (Paris, 2009), p.211; and Joseph Eliash, 'On the genesis and development of the Twelver-Shī'ī Three-tenet Shahādah', *Der Islam*, 47 (1971), p.271.

7 As will become apparent in the following sections, the phrase was used only intermittently and sparingly before the mid-Fatimid period. The phrase does not occur at all on Zaydi coinage of the Caspian region, even though the Zaydi Imams made copious use of Qur'anic inscriptions to broadcast their ideas: see Treadwell, 'Qur'ānic Inscriptions', pp.267–291.

8 Daniel Eustache, *Corpus des dirhams idrisites et contemporains* (Rabat, 1971), pp.62–63.

9 Eustache, *Corpus*, Baht (p.186); Warzīgha (pp.237–8); Wazzeqqūr (241–255). This phrase, which was found on the reverse margin, was combined with the reverse field inscription *Muḥammad / khātim al-nabiyyin ṣā / diq*. Eustache surmised that the field inscription, with its pointed reference to Muhammad's role as the Seal of the Prophets, was directed against the neighbouring Berghawata Berbers who proclaimed allegiance to a prophet named Salih.

10 Eustache, *Corpus*, no.437 and pp.63, 276. The editor thanks Vesta Curtis at the British Museum for help with reproducing the images for figs 1, 4 and 6.

11 For dirhams dated 353, 355, 356 and 360 AH see George C. Miles, 'The coinage of the Bāwandids of Ṭabaristān', in C. E. Bosworth, ed., *Iran and Islam: in Memory of the Late Vladimir Minorsky* (Edinburgh, 1971), nos 1–5; for the dirham of 361 AH, see Miles, 'Bāwandids', no.6 and Zeno.ru no.13849; for the dirham of 365, see Miles, 'Bāwandids', no.8 and the Lundberg collection and Zeno.ru no.85925); for the dirham of 366, see Miles, 'Bāwandids', no.9; for the dirham of 367, see Miles, 'Bāwandids', no.10 and Zeno.ru no.13850); for the dirham of 368, see Miles, 'Bāwandids', no.11.

12 Zeno.ru no.70200. Michailidis refers to Marzban as the son of Rustam (Melanie D. Michailidis, *Landmarks of the Persian Renaissance: Monumental Funerary Architecture in Iran and Central Asia in the Tenth and Eleventh Centuries* (Ph.D. dissertation, MIT, Boston, 2007).

13 [3]73/983 (Zeno 13851).

14 Miles, 'Bāwandids', p.451, no.14.

15 The dirham of Firīm? [date missing, but attributable to 380–387/990–997] (Zeno no.63072) lacks the phrase. It bears the names of Shahriyar b. Rustam and his Buyid overlord Fakhr al-Dawla, with the latter's title *shāhānshāh*, which appeared on his coinage from 380–387 AH.

16 Luke Treadwell, *Craftsmen and Coins: Signed Dies in the Iranian World (Third to the Fifth Centuries AH)* (Vienna, 2011), chapters 6 and 7.

17 *Mu/ḥa/mma/d/wa/'A/l/ī* is written thus in isolated letters in the outer margins of the obverse and reverse of the coin. For the reference to the new 'Shi'i' *adhān* (containing the words *Muḥammad wa 'Alī khayr al-bashar*) said to have been introduced at Aleppo in 347/958 by a Hasanid 'Alid, during the reign of the Hamdanid ruler, Sayf al-Dawla, see below.

18 For Buyid dirhams of Qazwin struck from dies which were probably also made by al-Hasan b. Muhammad and bear the phrase *Muḥammad wa 'Alī* in the outer margin, see Treadwell, *Craftsmen*, p.75, n.198.

19 Samuel M. Stern, 'The early Ismā'īlī missionaries in North-West Persia and in Khurāsān and Transoxania', BSOAS, 23, 1 (1960), pp.72–76. Stern's reading of the small isolated letters above Allāh on the reverse field as *'adl* does not appear to be correct: the letters look like *'ayn* or *ghayn/bā'* or *yā'* etc. /*dāl* or *kāf*. Daftary points out that the presence of the seven Imams showed that Wahsudan adhered to the Qarmati form of Ismailism, rather than the Fatimid. Farhad Daftary, *The Ismā'īlīs: Their History and Doctrines* (2nd ed., Cambridge, 2007), p.154.

20 Patricia Crone and Martin Hinds, *God's Caliph* (Cambridge, 1986), p.100, no.18: 'Ali was often depicted as the only Muslim *khalīfa* (full title: *khalīfat Allāh fī arḍi-hi*) in Twelver literature on the Imamate, his predecessors as *khulafā'* being Adam, David and Aaron.

21 Walker, 'Wilāya', pp.208–209.

22 Alexander Akopyan and Aram Vardanyan, 'A donative dirham of the Shirwānshāh Muḥammad b. Aḥmad (AMH 370–381) struck at Barda'a in AH 373 (982/3)', *The Numismatic Chronicle*, 169 (2009), pp.261–267.

23 Wilferd Madelung, 'The minor dynasties of northern Iran', in *The Cambridge History of Iran, vol.4, The Period From the Arab Invasion to the Saljuqs*, ed. R. n.Frye (Cambridge, 1975), p.272, states that Barda'a passed out of Sallarid hands in around 372/982, an indication that the primary sources give no precise date for the transfer of power.

24 The figure of the horseman is slightly too large in relation to the horse itself. He appears to be inclined forwards and brandishing a weapon in front of his face. If this were, indeed, a commemorative medallion, struck to recall the presence of the first Sallarid in both word and image, it would be a unique occurrence in the Islamic numismatic field.

25 Ivar Leimus, *Sylloge of Islamic Coins: Estonian Public Collections* (Tallinn, 2007), no.899.

26 Barqa'īd 394 and 396 (Abu Shibl Ibrahim b. al-Rajih [Rujayh?]): See e.g. FINT 2005–16–164 (394) and Leimus, Sylloge, no.3717 (396). I am grateful to Lutz Ilisch for supplying information about 'Uqaylid coins.

27 See Andrew Rippin, 'Taṣliya', EI2, vol.10, pp.358–359.

28 Nasir al-Dawla coin type 35 (ANS 1975.73.7), Madīnat al-Salām 330 (Bates, Michael L., 'Madinat al-Salām' unpubl. PDF document): Tūzūn dinar and dirhams of 333 in n.Douglas Nicol, *Later 'Abbasid Precious Metal Coinage (from 219 AH), Sylloge of Islamic Coins in the Ashmolean*, vol.4 (Oxford, 2012), nos 1199–1201.

29 Luke Treadwell, *Būyid Coinage: A Die Corpus (322–445 AH)* (Oxford, 2001), p.139.

30 Ramzi J. Bikhazi, 'The struggle for Syria and Mesopotamia (330–58/941–69) as reflected on Ḥamdānid and Ikhshīdid coins', *American Numismatic Society Museum Notes*, 28 (1983), pp.137–186 (see pp.176 and 181 for dirhams of 334 AH).

31 al-Ṣūlī, *Akhbār al-Rāḍī billāh wa al-Muttaqī billāh,* vol.2, tr. Marius Canard (Algiers, 1950), pp.57, 62: Miskawayh, *Kitāb Tajārub al-umam*, vol.2, ed. H. F. Amedroz (Oxford, 1921), p.31.

32 Ramzi J. Bikhazi, 'Ḥamdānid coins of Madīnat al-Salām A.H. 330–331', in *Near Eastern Numismatics, Iconography, Epigraphy and History: Studies in Honor of George C. Miles*, ed. D. Kouymjian (Beirut, 1974), pp.255–278, esp. p.271.

33 The mints include Mayyāfāriqīn, al-Anṭākiyya, al-Maṣṣīṣa, Thaghr al-Shāmiyya and al-Raqqa (Bikhazi 1983 passim.). All these mints used one version or another of the *taṣliya* during Sayf al-Dawla's reign.

34 Jere Bacharach, *Islamic History Through Coins: An Analysis and Catalogue of Tenth-Century Ikhshīdid Coinage* (Cairo, 2006): (Damascus and Filasṭīn 334 AH) pp.132–133; (Miṣr 336) p.123; and (Filasṭīn 338) p.127.

35 See www.zeno.ru for the coinage of both dynasties. The Marwanid coins employed the form *ṣallā Allāh ʿalay-hi wa āli-hi*, while the 'Uqaylid coins used *ṣallā Allāh ʿalay-hi, ṣallā Allāh ʿalay-hi wa sallama and ṣallā Allāh ʿalay-hi wa āli-hi.*

36 Thierry Bianquis, 'Sayf al-Dawla', *EI2*, vol.9, pp.103–110; Marius Canard, 'Ḥamdānids', *EI2*, vol.3, pp.126–131.

37 al-Maqrīzī states that the *adhān* was changed in 347/958 to include the phrases *ḥayya ilā khayr al-ʿamal* and *Muḥammad wa ʿAlī khayr al-bashar* (Aḥmad b. ʿAlī al-Maqrīzī, *al-Mawāʿiẓ wa al-iʿtibār bi-dhikr al-khiṭaṭ wa al-āthār*, vol.2 [Baghdad n.d.], p.271). Whether or not the city was under Sayf al-Dawla's control in 347 – Linder Welin records a dirham of his from Aleppo dated 347 (?) (Ulla S. Linder Welin, 'Sayf al-Dawlah's reign in Syria and Diyārbekr in the light of the numismatic evidence', in Nils L Rasmusson, Lars O. Lagerqvist and Brita Malmer, ed., *Commentationes de nummis saeculorum IX-XI in Suecia repertis*, vol.1 (Stockholm, 1961), no.26) – it is safe to assume that its use was probably approved by Sayf al-Dawla, if only after its introduction.

38 But see Bikhazi 'Struggle', p.155, for a different opinion. Bikhazi claims that Hamdanid rule 'was less Shi'ite in character than that of their fellow Twelvers, the Buwayhids (who, incidentally, did not adopt the 'Alid legend)' and concludes that Sayf al-Dawla employed the *taṣliya* simply as a means of distinguishing his own coins from those issued by his brother, Nasir al-Dawla, which were otherwise identical to his, as 'an occasional assertion of independence within the family'. The Buyid mint of Baghdad maintained the short *taṣliya* on its coinage from 334 AH until the second quarter of the fifth century AH, when the amir Abu Kalijar introduced a new version – *ṣallā Allāh ʿalay-hi wa āli-hi* (Treadwell, *Būyid Coinage*, p.158).

39 The Marwanids used the phrase *ṣallā Allāh ʿalay-hi wa āli-hi* on all the dirhams they struck in Mayyāfāriqīn and al-Jazīra. Mayyāfāriqīn was one of the mints controlled by Sayf al-Dawla which had used the extended *taṣliya* in the mid-4th century AH (see above).

40 The 'Uqaylids struck coins in the former Hamdanid mints of Mayyāfāriqīn, Naṣībīn and Mawṣil.

41 Bikhazi, 'Struggle', pp.163–169.

42 Bikhazi adduces no evidence for Kafur's accommodation with the Fatimids, other than the coinage. On the other hand, al-Maqrīzī states that the Fatimids realised that Kafur was the main obstacle in the way of their ambitions to conquer Egypt. Aḥmad b. ʿAlī al-Maqrīzī, *Iṭṭiʿāẓ al-ḥunafā' bi-akhbār al-a'immah al-Fāṭimīyīn al-khulafā*, vol.1, ed. J. Shayyal (Cairo, 1967), pp.102–103.

43 This is the view expressed in Bacharach, *Islamic History Through Coins*, p.63.

44 See a similar argument made for the non-sectarian nature of the *taṣliya* found on Egyptian tombstone inscriptions in the pre-Fatimid period (*ṣallā Allāh ʿalay-hi wa ʿalā āli-hi al-ṭāhirīn* in Christopher S. Taylor, 'Re-evaluating the Shīʿī role in the development of monumental Islamic funerary architecture: the case of Egypt', *Muqarnas*, 9 (1992), pp.1–10. Taylor's understanding of the meaning of the funerary *taṣliya* suggests that the fashion for offering blessings to the Prophet's family was a feature of funerary ritual as well as state documentation under the Ikhshidids.

45 Ismail K. Poonawala, *The Pillars of Islam: Daʿā'im al-islām of al-Qāḍī al-Nuʿmān*, vol.1 (New Delhi, 2002–2004), pp.59–72.

46 Marius Canard, 'Fāṭimids', *EI2*, vol.2, pp.850–862; al-Maqrīzī, *Khiṭaṭ*, vol.2, p.270.

47 al-Maqrīzī, *Khiṭaṭ*, vol.2, p.271.

48 Sherif Anwar and Jere Bacharach, 'Shiʿism and the early dinars of the Fāṭimid imām-caliph al-Muʿizz li-Dīn Allāh (341–365/952–975): an analytic overview', *al-Masaq*, 22, 3 (2010), pp.259–278.

49 See Samuel M. Stern, 'Abū Yazīd al-Nukkārī', *EI2*, vol.1, pp.163–164; and Anwar and Bacharach, 'Shīʿism and the early dinars'.

50 The Abbasid gold coins of the mint of Baysh adopted the empty margin from 331/942, if not earlier. Stephen Album, *Arabia and East Africa, Sylloge of Islamic Coins in the Ashmolean*, vol.10 (Oxford, 1999), plate 1.

51 Some fractional dinars of al-Manṣūriyya with *ʿAlī walī Allāh* in the bottom line of the reverse field have been attributed to late in Mansur's reign (Stanley Lane-Poole, *Catalogue of Oriental Coins in the Brit*ish Museum, vol.4: The Coinage of Egypt (London, 1879), nos 22 and 23; n.Douglas Nicol, *A Corpus of Fāṭimid Coins* (Trieste, 2006), nos 220 and 223; n.Douglas Nicol, *The Egyptian Dynasties, Sylloge of the Islamic Coins in the Ashmolean*, vol.6 (Oxford, 2007), no.247 where the last line of the reverse [Nicol, Manṣūr, Type C] is misread as *lā sharīka la-hu*). Close scrutiny of their obverse fields reveals the legends *al-Manṣūr/abū ʿAlī al-Imām/ amīr al-mu'minīn*, which is a combination of title and *kunya* used by al-Hakim bi amr Allah (386–411/996–1020). These coins should be reattributed to al-Hakim (Nicol, al-Ḥākim, Type I1), probably to the year 400/1009 (*sana arbaʿa* is visible on Lane-Poole, *Coinage of Egypt*, no.23). I am grateful to Vesta Curtis for providing images of the British Museum coins.

52 Al-Muʿizz adopted the phrase *al-ḥaqq al-mubīn* as well as short tags in praise of God (e.g. *al-qudra lillāh*) from Abu Yazid's coinage.

53 See E. Kohlberg, 'Waṣī', *EI2*, vol.11, pp.161 ff; and Wilferd Madelung, 'Ismāʿīliyya', *EI2*, vol.4, pp.198–206. According to the Ismailis, the *waṣī* was the 'silent' one (*al-ṣāmit*) who succeeded each of the seven *nāṭiq*s, or 'speaking' Prophets who made up the Ismaili heptad, and explained and interpreted the Prophet's revelation. 'Ali was the *waṣī* whose task was to interpret the *tanzīl* of Muhammad.

54 Nicol Type H3 of Muʿizz (see Nicol, *Fāṭimid Coins,* p.40) is said to have been found on quarter dinars of Siqilliyya and al-Manṣūriyya, dated 342–343/953–954. The only legible specimen of this type cited by Nicol is in M. De Luca, *Le Monete con Leggenda Araba della Biblioteca Comunale di Palermo* (Palermo, 1998), no.389. This coin has the words *ʿAlī waṣī al-rasūl* on the outer reverse margin (not *ʿAlī walī*

Allāh) – corrected reading and enlarged image kindly provided by Professor De Luca (personal communication, October 2011). As for Nicol, al-Muʿizz Type F2 (p.39), mint of Fās, dated 348/959, with *ʿAlī walī Allāh* in the inner margin, I have been unable to read the publication of Farrugia de Candia ('Monnaies fatimites du Musée du Bardo: premier supplément', *Revue tunisienne* (1948), pp.105–130) in which the coin is published. But the inscription cited in Nicol, *ʿAlī walī Allāh waṣī-hi*, does not make grammatical sense and may result from a mistaken reading. In any case this was the only known dinar of Fās from the reign of Muʿizz.

55 Nicol, *Fāṭimid Coins*, al-Azīz Type A1c (p.72, with *Muḥammad rasūl Allāh ʿAlī walī Allāh*) is described as a probable 'local imitation' of Miṣr and bears a date (360/970) which precedes al-Aziz's accession by five years. Nicol states that al-Azīz, Type H (p.74) bears the phrase *ʿAlī walī Allāh* in the reverse field, but Brown reads the inscription as *walī ʿahd al-muslimīn* (Helen M. Brown, 'Early silver coinage of the Fāṭimids', *Rivista Italiana de Numismatica e Scienze Affini*, 86 (1984), pp.61–73. As for the Mulṭān mint in al-Aziz's reign, its coins do indeed appear to have borne the inscription *Muḥammad rasūl Allāh ʿAlī walī-hi* (Nicol, Azīz, Type J p.76), as is confirmed by the images in Nicholas M. Lowick, 'Fāṭimid coins of Multān', *Numismatic Digest*, 7 (1983), pp.62–69. But the Mulṭān mint was a long way from Egypt and produced coinage of a unique format: it cannot be considered a part of mainstream Fatimid coinage.

56 See Poonawala, *Pillars*, p.28.

57 S. Shamma, 'Nuqūd al-rāshid billāh khalīfa bilād al-shām', *Yarmouk Numismatics*, 2 (1990), pp.53–63.

58 For al-Muʿizz's use of the title on a *ṭirāz* textile of 355/965, see Ernst Kühnel and Louise Bellinger, *Catalogue of Dated Tiraz Fabrics : Umayyad, Abbasid, Fatimid* (Textile Museum,Washington, DC, 1952), no.73.632. For an earlier example of an ʿAlid ruler who gave himself the title *walī Allāh*, see the dinar of Āmul (311/923), struck by Abu'l-Qasim Jaʿfar, son of the Zaydi Imam al-Hasan b. ʿAli al-Utrush (*Sotheby's Coin Auction*, 20 May 1986, no.508).

59 In light of the condemnation of the tendency to deify the Imams which al-Qāḍī al-Nuʿmān expressed in the *Daʿāʾim al-islām* (Poonawala, *Pillars*, pp.59–72), it seems that the early Fatimids feared the consequences of the inappropriate ascription of divine powers to their Imams no less than the Twelvers.

60 The title *walī Allāh* was used for both caliph and ʿAli from al-Hakim's reign onwards. See for example from *Corpus Inscriptionum Arabicorum: Égypte*, Max van Berchem and Gaston Wiet, ed. (Paris, 1894–1930), no.28 (al-Hakim referred to as *ʿAbd Allāh wa walī-hi* in al-Hakim's mosque in 393/1002); no.39 (Mosque of Nilometer dated 485/1092, has *ʿAbd Allāh wa walī-hi al-Mustanṣir billāh*); no.13 (al-Hafiz is referred to as *ʿAbd Allāh wa walī-hi* on a wooden panel from the mosque of Ahmad [b. Tulun] in 526/1131).

Part 4: Iconographic studies: Shiʿi contexts and beyond

12

Between the past and the future: the *fālnāma* (book of omens) in the 16th and early 17th centuries

Massumeh Farhad

One of the most remarkable illustrated texts from 16th-century Iran is the so-called dispersed Safavid *Fālnāma* (Book of Omens).[1] Completed between the mid-1550s and early 1560s at the court atelier of Shah Tahmasp in Qazvin, its extant 30 monumental paintings are among the most original and boldly conceived compositions of the period (fig.1). They are also the most widely published *fālnāma* folios, but three other large-scale compilations have survived from the later 16th and early 17th centuries.[2] The Topkapı Palace Library houses a bound volume (H. 1702) with 59 illustrations, which are attributable to the 1580s and executed by a number of painters in a hybrid Safavid-Ottoman style (fig.2). A third copy, now in the State University Library in Dresden (E445), also includes pictorial auguries in a distinct Safavid-Ottoman artistic idiom. It was probably assembled at the end of the 16th century or in the early 17th century but incorporates several Safavid compositions from the 1540s. Although damaged, these are the earliest known *fālnāma* paintings. Another copy of the *Fālnāma* in the Topkapı Palace Library (H. 1703) was commissioned by the statesman, Kalender Pasha, sometime between 1614 and 1616 as a gift to the Ottoman sultan Ahmed I (*r.* 1603–1619). Its 35 illustrations, dateable to the third quarter of the 16th century and early 17th century, are largely the work of Ottoman painters, drawing on Safavid models. This is the only *fālnāma* written in Ottoman Turkish with an important preface on its role and function. At least three smaller and later versions, probably done in India, are also known, but no other large-scale copies were created after the early 17th century.[3]

None of the extant volumes share an identical text or cycle of illustrations, but the subject matter and certain formal characteristics lend the compilations an iconographic cohesion. For example, all four monumental copies include depictions of Abrahamic prophets (e.g. Adam, Joseph, Moses and Solomon) (fig.3), and Muslim religious personages, especially the Prophet Muhammad, Imam ʿAli and his descendants. In addition, they incorporate apocalyptic scenes, such as the Day of Judgement, Hell and Heaven, and all but the dispersed Safavid copy incorporate signs of the zodiac. Some of these compositions are unique to the *fālnāmas*, while others are repeated in subsequent texts, such as the *Qiṣaṣ al-Anbiyāʾ* (Stories of the Prophets) or the *Tercüme-i Miftah-i Jifr al-Câmi* (Translation to the Key to the Comprehensive Prognostication), which flourished in the third quarter of the 16th century and early 17th century respectively.[4] As a group, the illustrated *fālnāmas* offer a singular glimpse into shared Safavid and Ottoman religious practices, and their distinct hybrid style expands our understanding of manuscript painting in the latter part of the 16th century. This essay will discuss some of the salient characteristics of

Fig.1

Fig.1
The Prophet Muhammad's Night Journey (miʿrāj), folio from a dispersed *Fālnāma*, Iran, Qazvin, Safavid period, mid-1550s to early 1560s. Arthur M. Sackler Gallery, Washington, DC, S1986.253

Fig.2

Fig.3

the monumental *fālnāmas*, especially their religious inspired imagery, and will offer a possible explanation for their sudden popularity in the latter part of the 16th century in both the Ottoman and Safavid worlds.

The Persian and Ottoman term *fāl*, derived from the Arabic *fa'l*, refers to an omen and augury, used to offer insight into the world of the unknown (*al-ghayb*) and the nature and outcome of events, occurrences and actions of which the seeker is unaware.[5] The *fālnāma* falls within the category of bibliomancy, a text-based form of prognostication, that gained currency with the arrival of Islam in the 7th century.[6] Here, the key to the augury was the written word, more specifically, a letter, which the seeker identified by randomly selecting a text passage. The most popular device for bibliomancy in the Islamic world was the

Fig.2
The Prophet Splitting the Moon, folio from a *fālnāma*, probably Iran, Safavid period, 1580s. Topkapı Palace Museum, Istanbul, H.1702, folio 22b

Fig.3
Angels Bow Before Adam and Eve in Paradise, folio from a *fālnāma*, Iran, Qazvin, Safavid period, mid-1550s to early 1560s. Arthur M. Sackler Gallery, Washington, DC, S1986.254

Qur'an, which intermittently met with strong condemnation by religious scholars.[7] Although it proved impossible to ban the practice, the need to control and regulate the use of the Qur'an for prognostication led, in part, to the creation of '*fālnāmas*' or prognostication manuals. The earliest examples date from the 14th century and were created either independently or as appendages to Qur'ans. The text usually begins with clear instructions on the use of the holy text for divination and prescribes reciting various Qur'anic verses and a set prayer before making a wish and opening the volume randomly. As will be discussed, this method was also adopted for other forms of bibliomancy.

Qur'ans with *fālnāma*s reached a new level of artistic sophistication in Shiraz in the second half of the 16th century at the same time as illustrated *fālnāma*s were compiled elsewhere (fig.4). The rich colours and lavish illumination visually underscore the importance of augury tables and confirm their pervasive acceptance and use, at least in 16th-century Shiraz. As the city was a major supplier of illustrated and unillustrated texts to Ottoman Turkey, Shirazi Qur'ans with *fālnāma*s also enjoyed widespread circulation outside of Iran.[8] The *Dīwān* of the poet Hafiz (d. 1390) and the *Mathnawī* of Rumi (d. 1273) were other texts favoured for divination. According to the *Rāznāma* (Book of Secrets) by Husayn Kefevi (d. 1601), an Ottoman scholar, judge and man of letters, members of the Istanbul *literati* and social elite would gather regularly to consult the works of Hafiz, Jami, Rumi and, of course, the Qur'an to seek guidance on their queries and dilemmas.[9] Kefevi does not mention the use of pictorial *fālnāma*s, but a reference to prognostication manuals with images occurs as early as the 10th century in the work of the Persian poet, Manuchihri (d. 1040), suggesting that they probably existed prior to the 16th century, even if none have survived.[10]

According to Kalender Pasha's introduction to Ahmed I's *Fālnāma*, to consult the text, seekers first had to purify themselves, recite the sura *al-Fātiḥa* (1:1–7) three times, and the sura *al-Ikhlāṣ* once (112:1–4).[11] Only then could they make a *nīyat*, that is, pose a question or a wish, and randomly open the volume, which was identical to the method used for Qur'anic *fālnāma*s. Each opening consists of an image on the right and a folio of text on the left, which together constitutes the augury. The illustration, which appears on the verso or 'b' side, therefore, precedes the text, a reversal of the traditional text-image relationship in Persian and Turkish manuscripts. Instead of an unfolding narrative, intermittently interrupted by illustrations, the images now appear at regular intervals and determine the meaning of the text, which lends them unprecedented importance. Moreover, in order to increase the element of chance, the auguries in each *fālnāma* follow a different order and sequence.

The prognostications fall into three categories, good, bad and middling. Regardless of their particular subject, each one comprises the

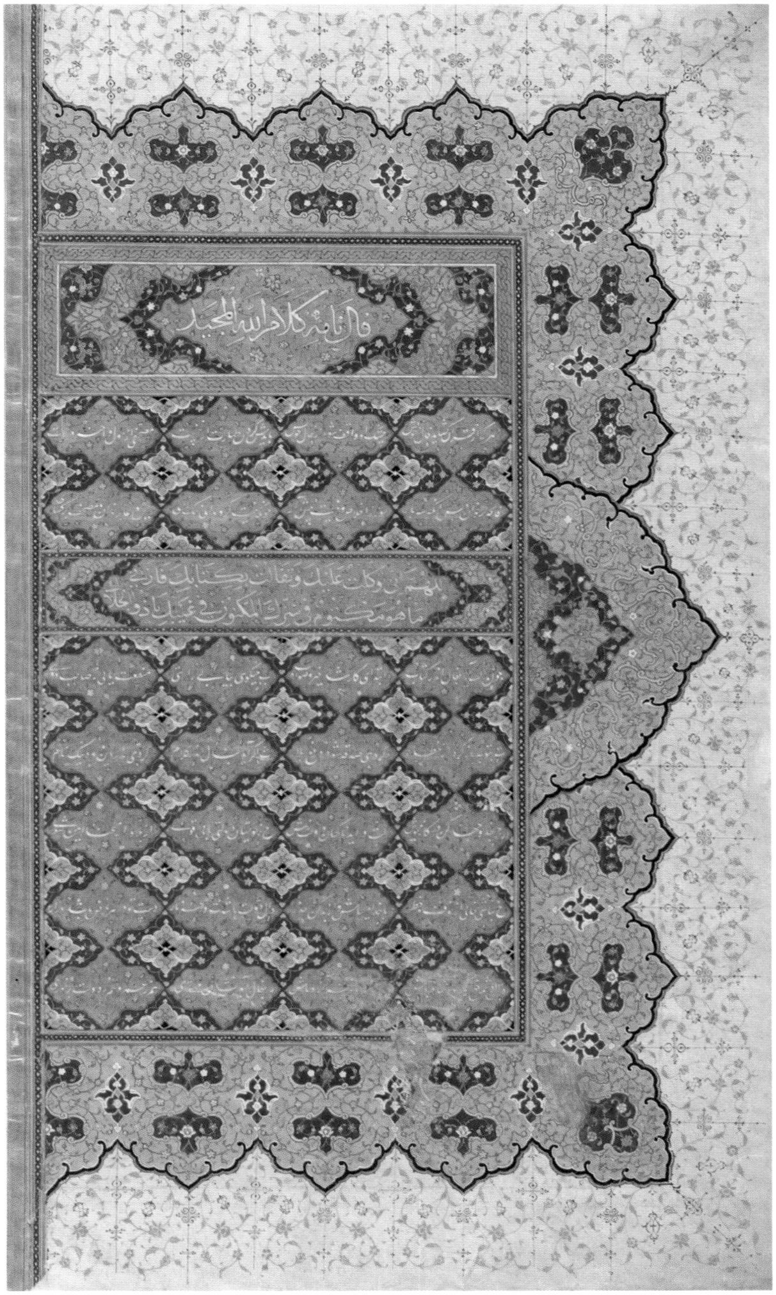

Fig.4

Fig.4
Folio from a Qur'an, Iran, Safavid period, dated 1598. Freer Gallery of Art, Washington, DC, F1932.65, folio 70b

following elements – a reference to the accompanying image, at times called a 'sign' (*nishān*), an identification of the nature of the augury, a series of prognostications, and finally a list of recommendations. The text is a poignant testimony to some of the mundane concerns that shaped daily social, cultural and religious life in 16th- and early 17th-century Safavid Iran and Ottoman Turkey: travel and relocation, feasibility of commercial transactions, starting new businesses or partnerships, petitioning for royal favours, pilgrimage to religious sites, building and restoring mosques, bridges, and other public structures, marriage, news about loved ones and ways to secure the affection and respect of a beloved. The final recommendations are intended to help secure the seekers' wishes. Religious in nature, they advocate daily prayers, performing pilgrimages, giving alms and visiting shrines and tombs. They also prescribe wearing amulets and burning wild rue to ward off evil, two popular religious practices. Only by following these suggestions could seekers hope for salvation and the realisation of their wishes and aspirations.[12] In short, the auguries offer not only insight into the world of the unknown but also encourage and stress the importance of religious and ethical conduct in the known world, which are critical to all Muslims.

The authorship of unillustrated *fālnāma*s has often been attributed to prominent secular and religious figures. These include the Abbasid caliph Harun al-Rashid (*r.* 786–809), the Ghaznavid ruler Sultan Mahmud of Ghazna (*r.* 998–1030), as well as the Prophet Daniel, Imam ʿAli and, most frequently, to the sixth Shiʿi Imam, Jaʿfar al-Sadiq (d. 765), to lend the texts an air of legitimacy and prestige.[13] By extension, the auguries of the pictorial *fālnāma*s have been also associated with Imam Jaʿfar al-Sadiq, but as they include references to Imam Jaʿfar's grandson, Imam Reza (d. 818), and to the Mahdi, the twelfth Imam, there is little evidence to support this attribution. Based on comparative study of the illustrated *fālnāma*s, the written auguries seem to have been largely inspired by popular hagiographic sources, such as the *Qiṣaṣ al-Anbiyā'* (Stories of the Prophets) and the rich oral tradition that was prevalent in the region and would explain the colloquial tone of the texts and its variances.

The most common theme in all extant *fālnāma*s is the lives and deeds of the Prophet Muhammad and his descendants, especially Imam ʿAli and his sons Imam Hasan and Imam Husayn, as well as Imam Reza. First and foremost, the illustrations stress miracles (*muʿjizāt*), underscoring the Prophet and his progeny's divinely inspired status; after all, without God's consent these acts would be considered illicit and magic. Secondly, the miracles also exemplify the ability of the Prophet Muhammad and the Imams to mediate between the tempo-ral and spiritual worlds and convince non-believers of the power and validity of the divine message. According to Islamic traditions, Muhammad himself refused to be associated with any miracles, except for the greatest of all – the divine revelation. Over time, however, scholars and popular storytellers found references in the Qur'an to unusual events in the Prophet's life, which became the basis for elaborate tales and descriptions of extraordinary events.

One of the most celebrated of such miraculous events was the Prophet Muhammad's Night Journey (*miʿrāj*), which is also included in the dispersed Safavid *Fālnāma* as an augury (fig.1). Following the established iconography for this scene, the Prophet is riding on the back of his steed, Buraq, led through the heavens by Gabriel and a host of other angels. A notable exception to normative representations is the crouching, growling lion in the upper left corner to whom the Prophet is extending a ring. The feline is identifiable with Imam ʿAli who is often referred to as the 'Lion of God' (*asadullāh*). ʿAli's role as the rightful heir to Muhammad is corroborated in the accompanying text, which maintains, 'Everything that happened that night, blow-by-blow, Murtaza Mujtaba [i.e. Imam ʿAli] recounted to him [i.e. the Prophet] the next day'. More recently, Raya Shani has offered a more precise interpretation by linking the specific iconography to a Sufi Bektashi lore, indicating the different religious sources that were used for *fālnāma* imagery.[14] Like all auguries centred on the Prophet and his descendants, the accompanying text guarantees happiness and success as long as the seeker prays, 'perpetually for the Prophet and his family'.[15] While the *Prophet Muhammad's Night Journey* is a familiar composition and its iconography is drawn from a large body of classical Arabic and later Persian literature, other illustrations of miracles, such as *The Prophet Splitting the Moon* (fig.2) is based on more popular literary sources and its depiction is unique to the *fālnāma*. *ʿAli Saving the Sea People*, an illustration that appears in three of the four copies, is also particular to the *fālnāma*, but its origin and exact meaning still remain unclear. Here,

Fig.5

Fig.6

the Imam is performing one of his awe-inspiring acts by killing a demon, and the image underlines ʿAli's role as defender of the faith and protector of the innocent, a reccurring theme in the *Book of Omens*.[16]

Imam ʿAli's prowess is also demonstrated in depictions of the historical battle at Khaybar, a Jewish settlement close to Medina (fig.5). Allegedly, when ʿAli lost his shield, he lifted the gate of the fortress off its hinges with his bare hands and used it to protect himself, as is illustrated in the dispersed Safavid *Fālnāma*.[17] The accompanying augury emphasises ʿAli's supernatural strength by focusing on his hand, 'O augury-user, let there be good news to you that the hand (*panja*) of his Khaybar-seizing, Khaybar-opening Majesty, King of Saints, Proof of the Pious...has appeared in your augury.'[18] A quite different composition accompanies the same augury in the Ottoman *Fālnāma*. Instead of an elaborate narrative scene of the conquest of Khaybar, the illustration has been distilled to its most essential element by representing a large stylised hand, flanked by a pair of cypress trees, which stands as a 'sign' for ʿAli's supernatural feat (fig.6). The prognostication is almost identical to that of the dispersed Safavid copy and celebrates the power of ʿAli's hand. It is not surprising that as affirmation of ʿAli's extraordinary strength and his role as defender of the righteous, his legendary

Fig.5
ʿAli and Muhammad at the Gates of Khaybar, folio from the dispersed Safavid *Fālnāma*, Iran, Qazvin, Safavid period, mid-1550s to early 1560s. Trustees of the Chester Beatty Library, Dublin, MS.395

Fig.6
Khaybar: The Conquering Palm of ʿAli, folio from a *fālnāma*, Turkey, Ottoman period, *circa* 1580s. Topkapı Palace Museum, Istanbul, H.1703, folio 33b

double-headed sword, the *Dhu'l-faqār*, appears in several of the *fālnāma* illustrations. Allegedly given to him by the Prophet, it is even the subject of an auspicious augury in the bound Persian copy (H. 1702, fol.31b). In the dispersed Safavid *Fālnāma*, when ʿAli's hand emerges from his own sarcophagus to cleave Murraʿ b. Qays, who had entered his tomb at Najaf, his fingers resemble the double blades of the *Dhu'l-faqār*, affirming once again the sword's symbolic association (fig.7).[19]

Depictions of holy sites, such as the shrine of Imam ʿAli at Najaf or the *qadamgāh*, literally 'stepping place (i.e. footprints)' of Imam Reza near Nishapur, also play an important role in the *fālnāma* auguries. After all, these spaces are not only physical memorials to revered religious figures, but, in the popular imagination, they also represent the nexus where the earthly and the heavenly, the temporal and the spiritual converge. In the dispersed Safavid *Fālnāma*, Imam Reza's footprints, much like ʿAli's hand in the Ottoman copy, have been transformed into an aniconic image or sign, embodying the noble attributes and the miraculous strength of Imam Reza.[20]

The bound Persian *Fālnāma* (H. 1702) also incorporates two paintings of the Mahdi, the hidden Imam of Twelver Shiʿism, who it is believed will return to rule the world before the Day of Judgement.[21] More restrained in style and execution than some of the other illustrations, the first of the two depicts *The Abode of the Imam*, presumably the place from which he went into occultation (fig.8). The second image, the last in the manuscript, portrays an enthroned Mahdi in a landscape, which is closely based on compositions of secular rulers dispensing justice. His face is concealed by a veil, which is inscribed with the title,

Fig.7

Fig.8

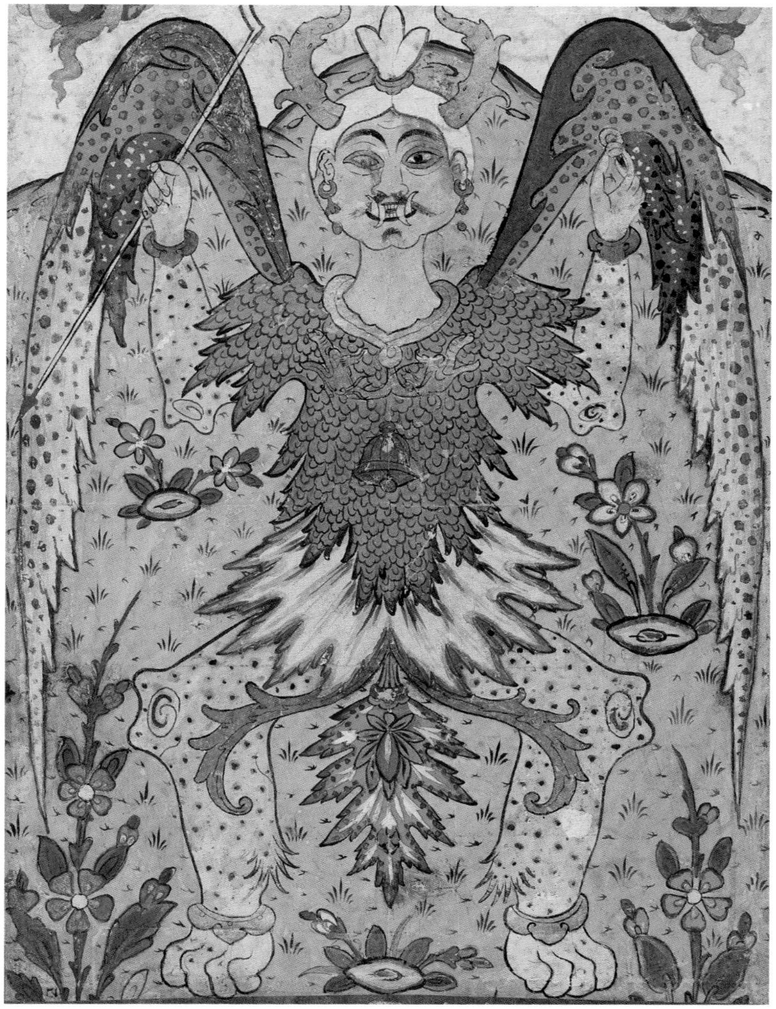

Fig.9

'*Ya Ṣāḥib-i Zamān*' (O Master of Time), and he is gesturing to a man to his left, identifiable as the prophet Idris. In the Persian couplet, the Mahdi is linked to Imam 'Ali, who will be at his side to help mankind. This interpretation differs somewhat from Islamic canonical understanding of the Mahdi's arrival, who is allegedly aided by Jesus and not 'Ali. Finally, scenes of the Apocalypse and its warning signs such as the 'Beast of the Earth' (*Dābbat al-arḍ*) and the 'Anti-Christ' (*al-Dajjāl*), also feature in the illustrated *fālnāma*s. These unusual compositions conjure up, both verbally and visually, the dire consequences of failure to adhere to the principles of Islam (fig.9).[22]

With the preponderance of images portraying the Twelver Shiʿi Imams and emphasis on miraculous acts, sites and symbols, can the *fālnāma* be viewed and understood as a religious text, emphasising Shiʿi hagiography?[23] An appropriate starting point to address this issue is the *Fālnāma* of Ahmed I and its first illustration – *The Poet Saʿdi Dressed as a Monk*. This unusual augury is inspired by a story in Saʿdi's famous work, the *Būstān* (Orchard) about the idol of Sumnat, and condemns idolatry. As Ahmed I was known for his piety, the placement of the image at the beginning of the volume could be interpreted as an affirmation of orthodox Sunni views and a warning against the practice

Fig.7
Murraʿ Being Chased out of 'Ali's Tomb, folio from the dispersed Safavid *Fālnāma*, Iran, Qazvin, Safavid period, mid-1550s to early 1560s. Aga Khan Museum, Toronto, AKM96

Fig.8
Imam Mahdi's Abode, folio from a *fālnāma*, probably Iran, 1570s to 1580s. Topkapı Palace Museum, Istanbul, H.1702, folio 49b

Fig.9
Dābbat al-arḍ (Beast of the Earth), folio from a *fālnāma*, Turkey, Ottoman period, 1580s. Topkapı Palace Museum, Istanbul, H.1703, folio 22b

of prognostication. His *Fālnāma*, however, includes several Shiʿi inspired subjects.[24] As Zeynep Yürekli has pointed out in her essay in this volume, depictions of the *Dhu'l-faqār* and the hand, symbolising the *Ahl al-bayt* (Family of the Prophet), were relatively common in 16th-century and 17th-century Ottoman visual culture. After all, ʿAli was the fourth rightly-guided caliph and much revered as the Prophet's cousin and son-in-law in the Ottoman world. Yürekli convincingly argues that by appropriating these symbols as talismans, the Ottoman Sunnis ensured that the Safavids did not 'monopolise the legacy of the *Ahl al-bayt*'. She further maintains that the hand was often inscribed with the names of the Prophet's immediate family (Fatima, ʿAli, al-Hasan and al-Husayn), which also occur in Ahmed I's *Fālnāma* painting.[25] More curious, however, are the names of the other Twelver Shiʿi Imams, which appear along the fingers and transform the palm into a clear Shiʿi symbol. The verbal interpretation also begins by stating that ʿAli's palm 'has the form of the word Allah. This became in truth a sign of God's hand', thus equating Imam ʿAli with God and further espousing an explicit, and more extreme, Shiʿi point of view. In addition, the Ottoman *Fālnāma* includes auguries depicting other Twelver Imams, such as Imam Reza rescuing the sea creatures (fol.29b) and Imam Husayn, who miraculously discovers water under his prayer rug (fol.14b).

The acceptance and use of illustrated *fālnāma*s with Shiʿi inspired subjects in both the Ottoman and Safavid worlds suggest that at least in the context of divination and popular piety, sectarian differences between the Safavid Shiʿa and the Ottoman Sunnis were less defined and articulated than in the more official political and religious arena. Just as the Qur'an or the *Dīwān* of Hafiz were non-sectarian and open to different readings and interpretations by Muslims of all creeds, the illustrated *fālnāma*s, too, were intended for all who sought solace, advice and guidance.[26] In his preface to Ahmad I's *Fālnāma*, Kalender Pasha justifies the creation of a *fālnāma* by maintaining that 'the history of past nations is a manual for people and it is appropriate to learn a lesson in any and every affair from those who have preceded'. Without making any distinction between 'those who preceded', he then elaborates:

> By means of augury from whichever of those pages is opened, the seeker of the augury can apply to his own situation whatever is written and depicted of the history of the prophets and rulers on that page, make an analogy from those situations with his own desire, and act accordingly.[27]

According to the compiler, therefore, all Muslims should emulate the words and deeds of prophets and sages of the past. In the *fālnāma*, Abrahamic prophets, Shiʿi Imams, and sages have been transformed into symbols of spiritual, human and often supernatural qualities, which serve as the leitmotif for the written and pictorial auguries. The figures have been appropriated as new and potent signs, intended to lead, inspire and warn all seekers on their life journey, whilst also reminding them of their ethical and religious responsibilities, regardless of their status or creed.

In content, format, style and intent, the four monumental *fālnāma*s clearly stand out among other illustrated texts of the period. Except for Kalender Pasha's copy, little is known about the historical and artistic circumstances surrounding their creation and compilation.[28] The unusual compositions, much like the richly illuminated 16th-century Qur'anic divination tables, were characteristic of a period, when both the Safavids and the Ottomans were gripped with millennium fever and expectations.[29] With the approach of the Hijri year 1000, corresponding to 1591–1592, which was believed to herald the end of the known world and usher in temporal renewal, the need to make the right decisions and take the proper course of action seemed of utmost urgency for both rulers and their subjects. The *fālnāma*s offered counsel and guidance by portraying eminent religious and secular individuals, whose words, actions and piety were exemplary at a time of heightened uncertainty with the imminent arrival of the year 1000. The creation of these *fālnāma*s coincided with a moment in time when Kalender Pasha's comment, 'If you wish power and glory increase for you, let your gaze always be upon past events',[30] was relevant for all Sunnis and Shiʿa.

1 This essay is drawn largely from the exhibition catalogue, Massumeh Farhad with Serpil Bağcı, *Falnama: The Book of Omens* (Washington, DC, 2009). I would like to thank my co-author Serpil Bağcı.
2 For a full discussion and bibliography of these four texts, see Farhad with Bağcı, *Falnama*, pp.41–75 and the catalogue entries.
3 For references to these copies, see Farhad with Bağcı, *Falnama*, p.28.
4 See Rachel Milstein, Karin Rührdanz and Barbara Schmitz, *Stories of the Prophets: Illustrated Manuscripts of the Qiṣaṣ al-Anbiyā'* (Costa Mesa, CA, 1999), esp.pp.70–86; and Cornell H. Fleischer, 'Ancient Wisdom and New Sciences', in Farhad with Bağcı, *Falnama*, pp.232–243.
5 Mahmud Omidsalar, 'Divination', *EIR*, vol.7, pp.440–443; T. Fahd, 'Divination', EQ, vol.1, pp.542–545; and Christiane J. Gruber, 'Divination', in *Medieval Islamic Civilisation: An Encyclopedia*, vol.1, ed. Josef W. Meri (New York, 2006), pp.209–211.
6 Gustav Flügel, 'Die Loosbücher der Muhammadaner', *Berichte über die Verhandlungen der Königlisch Säsischen Gesellshaft der Wissenschaften zu Leipzig, Philologish-Historische Klasse*, vols. 12–13 (1860–1861), pp.32–33, 43–44.
7 For examples of Qur'anic auguries, see Farhad with Bağcı, *Falnama*, cat. nos 7 and 8; see also Sergei Tourkin, 'The Use of the Qur'an for Divination in Iran', in *Mélanges de l'Université Saint-Joseph*, 59 (2006), pp.387–394; Christiane Gruber, 'The "Restored" Shīʿī *muṣḥaf* as Divine Guide? The Practice of *fāl-i Qur'ān* in the Ṣafavid Period', *Journal of Qur'anic Studies*, 13/2 (2011), pp.29–55; I am grateful to Christiane Gruber for providing me with an early draft of this article. For the earliest extant independent *fālnāma*, see Muhammad b. Masʿud Tabrizi, *Safineh-ye Tabriz: A Treasury of Persian Literature and Islamic Philosophy, Mysticism, and Science, Facsimile Edition of a Manuscript Compiled and Copied in* 721-31/1321-23 (Tehran, 2003), p.397, reproduced in Gruber, *'fāl-i Qur'ān'*, Fig.2. The earliest known and dated Qur'an with a *fālnāma* is the so-called Gwalior Qur'an, dated 1398–1399 in the Aga Khan Collection. I would like to thank Dr Brac de la Perrière and her team for generously sharing their findings. For illustrations of the Qur'an, see Anthony Welch and Stuart Cary Welch, *Arts of the Islamic Book. The Sadruddin Aga Khan Collection* (Ithaca, 1982), no.42.
8 Gruber, *'fāl-i Qur'ān'*, pp.35–38. For Shirazi manuscripts in the Ottoman world, see Lâle Uluç, *Turkman Governors, Shiraz Artisans, and Ottoman Collectors. Sixteenth-Century Shirazi Manuscripts* (Istanbul, 2006). Although fewer Ottoman Qur'ans with *fālnāma* tables are known, one of the earliest examples is in the Topkapı Palace Library (A5). Dated to 1503, it was copied by the celebrated calligrapher Shaykh Hamdullah for Sultan Bayazid II (*r.* 1481–1412). The *fālnāma* is in Persian verse and written in *nastaʿlīq*, but follows a much simpler format than those created in Iran; see Farhad with Bağcı, *Falnama*, cat. no.9.
9 A copy of the *Rāznāma* in the British Library (Or. 1114) has three paintings that depict Ottoman literati holding books at open-air gatherings. Unfortunately, the illustrations have been defaced. See Charles Rieu, *Catalogue of the Turkish Manuscripts in the British Museum* (London, 1888), p.133; and Norah M. Titley, *Miniatures from Turkish Manuscripts* (London, 1981), p.47, no.37. See also Jan Schmidt, 'Hafiz and other Persian Authors in Ottoman Bibliomancy; the Extraordinary Case of Kefevī Hüsayn Efendi's *Rāznāme* (late sixteenth century)', *Persica*, 21 (2006–2007), pp.63–74.
10 See Manūchihrī, *Dīvān-i Manūchihr-ī Dāmghanī*, ed. Muhammad Dabir Siyaqi (Tehran, 1347 Sh./1968–1969), p.3. Also, cited in Iradj Afshar, 'Fāl-nāma', *EIR*, vol.9, p.175.
11 TKS H. 1703, fols. 5b–6a.
12 See Farhad with Bağcı, *Falnama*, Appendix A.
13 See Henri Massé, 'Fāl-nāma', *EI2*, vol.2, p.761. Afshar, 'Fāl-nāma', pp.175–176; and Gruber, *'fāl-i Qur'ān'*, pp.11–13.
14 'The Lion Image in Safavid Miʿraj Paintings', in *A Survey of Persian Art from Pre-historic Times to the Present*, vol.18, ed. Abbas Daneshvari (Costa Mesa, CA, 2005), pp.265–267; see also Farhad with Bağcı, *Falnama*, cat. no.22.
15 TKS H.1702, fol.22b and E445, fol.14b; see Farhad with Bağcı, *Falnama*, fig.5.5.
16 For other illustrations see, Farhad with Bağcı, *Falnama*, cat. nos 28 and 29.
17 Laura Veccia Vaglieri, 'Khaybar', *EI2*, vol.4, pp.1137–1143; Farhad with Bağcı, *Falnama*, cat. nos 23 and 24.
18 For the full text of these and other auguries, see Farhad with Bağcı, *Falnama*, Appendix A.
19 Other illustrations with the *Dhu'l-faqār* include TKS H.1702, fols 15b, 33b, 44b; TKS H. 1703, fols 19b, 20b, 26b. It is interesting to note that representations of the *Dhu'l-faqār* do not occur in the illustrations of the dispersed Safavid *Fālnāma*. For a discussion of the sword and its meaning in the Ottoman world, see Zeynep Yürekli's essay in this volume. I am grateful to the author for sharing an advanced copy of this essay.
20 The augury of Imam Reza's tomb is also included in TKS H.1702 (fol.43b). The image is more conventional in its iconography and shows a group of worshippers praying around a sarcophagus. See Farhad with Bağcı, *Falnama*, Appendix A.2, p.286.
21 See Farhad with Bağcı, *Falnama*, figs 2.12 and 4.12.
22 The apocalyptic images are repeated in the *Tercüme-i Miftah-i Jifr al-Câmi* (Translation to the Key to the Comprehensive Prognostication); see Farhad with Bağcı, *Falnama*, cat. no.60; and Fleischer, 'Ancient Wisdom', pp.232–243.
23 It is important to remember that these *fālnāmas* also include auguries of Abrahamic prophets as well as prominent sages, but images of Muslim prophets still predominate.
24 See Bağcı, 'The *Falnama* of Ahmed I (TKS H.1703)', in Farhad with Bağcı, *Falnama*, pp.74–75; see also cat. no.36.
25 In her essay, Yürekli refers to the large medallions in Ottoman imperial mosques that are inscribed with the names of al-Hasan and al-Husayn in addition to those of the four rightly-guided caliphs, which she interprets as another Ottoman attempt to lay claim to the family of the Prophet.
26 In her article, Christiane Gruber suggests that there may have been some Qur'ans with an intended Sunni audience and others with a Shiʿi one. See Gruber, *'fāl-i Qur'ān'*, pp.29–55.
27 TKS H.1703, fols. 4b-5a. For a full translation see, Wheeler M. Thackston Jr., in Farhad with Bağcı, *Falnama*, Appendix A.3 (erroneously ascribed to Sergei Tourkin).
28 The dispersed Safavid *Fālnāma* has been attributed to the patronage and workshop of Shah Tahmasp; for a full discussion and bibliography, see Massumeh Farhad, 'The Safavid Dispersed *Falnama*', in Farhad with Bağcı, *Falnama*, pp.43–53.
29 Ahmed I's *Fālnāma* of 1614–1616 was compiled after the arrival of the new millennium but Kalender clearly states that for his volume, he had gathered already existing illustrations, which is also supported by their style (TKS H.1702, fol.5b).
30 TKS H.1703, fol.5a.

13

Exploring *Ahl al-bayt* imagery in Qajar Iran (1785–1925)

Maryam Ekhtiar

In the past few decades the study of figural images in Islamic Art has expanded beyond the realm of iconography and style to include discussions of their social and even performative functions. These new approaches mark a fundamental shift from an artist- and school-centred discourse to one that is practice- and response-centred, emphasising the emotional and spiritual effects and meanings of images in religious and secular contexts.[1] To use David Freedberg's terminology in his seminal study, the 'power' and 'presence' of images are more vividly apparent in portraiture of the Qajar period, particularly in the latter half of Qajar rule, than in any other period in Islamic Iranian history.[2]

This essay will examine the ways in which images of the Prophet Muhammad and his family (*Ahl al-bayt*) were thought to embody sacred and even magical powers beyond themselves in 19th-century Qajar Iran. These images were capable of eliciting emotional responses from a wide range of individuals from different echelons of society. It will also show the evolution of *Ahl al-bayt* imagery into a trope that was modified to accommodate an array of political and religious agendas. This period witnessed the flowering of both royal and religious portraiture rooted in popular culture dating back to the Safavid period.[3]

With the arrival of the Safavids in 1501 and their adoption of Twelver Shiʿism as the state religion of Iran, Shiʿi rituals took on new dimensions reflecting a synthesis of Persian, Sufi and Shiʿi identities. Sufism and devotion to the *Ahl al-bayt*, particularly to Imam ʿAli, was practised by individuals from all levels of society from the ruler and his courtiers to the urban craftsmen. The Prophet and ʿAli were perceived in mystical terms as one body cloaked by the same divine light.[4] The Safavids looked to the Prophet and his family as intercessors through which to attain blessings, spiritual success and salvation. Their belief in the power of divination and prognostication to calm their fears was the subject of the 2009 exhibition, *Falnama: The Book of Omens*, at the Arthur M. Sackler/Freer Galleries in Washington, DC.[5] This exhibition explored the use of the large-scale paintings of the *Fālnāma* as visual devices to predict the future in 16th- and 17th-century Safavid Iran and the Ottoman Empire.

The Qajars inherited this passion for and extensive use of Shiʿi religious images (*shamāʾil*) from the Safavids and their successors. They developed and elevated religious imagery to an art form and popularised it. Like the Safavids, they used Shiʿi rituals to consolidate their power and reinforce their relationship with their subjects. The following verses, inscribed on the border on the back of a lacquered mirror-case made for the Qajar ruler, the young Nasir al-Din Shah (*r.* 1848–1896), encapsulate the beliefs and powerful spiritual messages contained in imagery

Fig.1

Fig.1
Mirror-case depicting the *Ahl al-bayt* and Niʿmatullahi Sufis, Isfahan, *circa* 1860. Lacquered papier-mâché, 27.7 × 21.6 cm. Nasser D. Khalili Collection of Islamic Art, London, UK, LAQ43

of the *Ahl al-bayt* during the second half of the 19th century in Iran (fig.1). Dated to around 1860 and executed by the master lacquer painter of the Qajar period, Muhammad Isma'il Isfahani (d. *circa* 1882), the case depicts portraits of the Prophet Muhammad, Imam 'Ali, Fatima, al-Hasan, al-Husayn and two Sufi devotees of the Ni'matullahi Order. The translation of the Persian inscription reads:

> O you through whom the house of Hashim has become wearers of the crown! O you whose abundant mercy has reached oceans and continents! Your Family and your Book are Noah's ark: without them there would be no recourse on this sea of tumult and turpitude. You have a son-in-law, a daughter and two grandsons, each one of whom is a favourite at the court of the just King. You are one soul with parts appointed to five bodies, one luminous sun shining through five doors, five spirits constant in one nature, five heads emerging from one neck. The Lion of God, 'Ali the Guardian, whom, as it were, the whole Qur'an praises from beginning to end. Fatima-yi Zahra, who cherished flowers, and who, out of love, nurtured in her skirts two blossoms finer than the sun and the moon. Both those two cypresses in faith's garden, without whom the orchard of religion would be bereft of fruit, like the cypress tree.[6]

The shah's devotion to 'Ali was unconditional. Under his rule, Shi'i popular rituals were sponsored and enforced by the state. He considered 'Ali as not just the Prophet's chosen successor, but as a guardian, the embodiment of Divine Truth and mystical insight, and as a model of a just ruler. Jacob Eduard Polak, Nasir al-Din Shah's private physician between 1855 and 1860, lived on the palace grounds and had direct access to court activities and rituals. Polak provided an eyewitness account of the shah's unusual and sometimes excessive attention to images of Imam 'Ali. In his memoirs, the Austrian doctor wrote: 'The shah received several portraits (*shamā'il*) of 'Ali as a gift from India which he kept in a gold enamel-painted box. Whenever he brought them out, the court officials would bow before them and the Shah himself would pray to them. ' He added: 'A few years ago, the Shah founded a circle whose main objective was to venerate these portraits of 'Ali. The rituals performed before these images were quite elaborate and dramatic and in order to legitimise them at court, he invited the state-appointed *'ulamā'* to participate. They, of course, viewed these practices with disgust and attended with great reservation.' Polak concluded: 'If 'Ali was alive to witness such rituals, he would have forbidden them without a doubt.'[7]

Because of their widespread popularity and the extraordinary demand for them, the production and exchange of portraits of the Prophet and the Shi'i Imams became a lucrative trade. They appeared on all manner of objects, from the monumental to the miniature, and were sought after and given as gifts by people from all walks of life. People responded to the *shamā'il* of the Prophet and his family as though they were alive;[8] they prostrated themselves before them, kissed them, carried them around in processions and used them in *ta'ziya* performances.

The view that images were charged with transformative powers and efficacy is also extensively reflected in royal portraiture throughout the Qajar period. Life-sized portraits of the Shah functioned as duplicates for the king himself (fig.2).[9] In the absence of modern means of mass

Fig.2

Fig.2
Portrait of Fath 'Ali Shah Qajar, Iran, *circa* 1820. Oil on canvas, 246 × 125 cm. Sa'dabad Museum, Tehran

communication, such as newspapers, television and the Internet, the state relied on royal portraits as instruments of propaganda to galvanize political support. For this reason, they were produced in large numbers and distributed throughout the empire and sent abroad as diplomatic gifts.

The Prophet stood at the apex of the Shiʿi cosmological pyramid followed by ʿAli, Fatima and their two sons, al-Hasan and al-Husayn, and occasionally other members of the family and close companions. The *miʿrāj* or the Prophet's Night Journey to the heavens is perhaps the most popular narrative featuring his image. Considered the Prophet's most intimate encounter with God, illustrations of the *miʿrāj* from the 14th to 17th centuries are found in a variety of historical, literary and religious texts. They are naturally seen in manuscripts of the *Miʿrājnāma* (Book of Ascension), but are also occasionally inserted into famous literary and divinatory manuscripts, particularly in the prefaces, such as the *Khamsa* (Quintet) of the poet Nizami (d. 1209), the *Būstān* (Orchard) of Saʿdi (d. 1291), Jami's (d. 1492) *Yūsuf and Zulaikhā,* the *Khāvarānnāma* (focussing on the heroic exploits of Imam ʿAli) and the *Fālnāma* (Book of Omens). These images often correspond to references within the text expressing high praise of the Prophet even if the *miʿrāj* itself is not specifically mentioned. For example, both prefaces of the *Būstān* of Saʿdi and Nizami's *Khamsa* enumerate the virtues and attributes of God and the role of the Prophet as the exalted messenger, intercessor and the ultimate embodiment of sanctity and blessing.

Christiane Gruber, among others, has undertaken extensive research in interpreting *miʿrāj* imagery in Islamic art.[10] These studies demonstrate how accounts of the ascension were depicted in fascinating ways and in diverse contexts and how they were adapted to accommodate disparate religious and political concerns throughout the centuries. They also investigate how such imagery was used in a variety of narratives to buttress claims of legitimacy by many groups of Muslims at various junctures in history.[11] The relevance of this imagery to the present study, however, pertains to the introduction and increasing occurrence of the inclusion of ʿAli's portrayal in *miʿrāj* paintings beginning in the Safavid period and continuing throughout the 19th century.

Fig.3

Fig.3
The Prophet's *miʿrāj* depicting ʿAli as a lion, from the dispersed *Fālnāma*, Qazvin, Iran, mid-1550s to early 1560s. Opaque water-colour and gold on paper, 58.9 × 44.9 cm. Arthur M. Sackler Gallery, Washington, DC, S1986.253a

Fig.4
Panel depicting the Prophet's *miʿrāj* and ʿAli as a lion, Iran, early 19th century. Painted and lacquered pasteboard, 29.2 × 43.8 cm. George Walter Vincent Smith Art Museum, Springfield, MA, 67.23.13

Fig.4

From the Safavid period onward, the *miʿrāj* is usually represented in a distinct Shiʿi cast and includes an image of ʿAli, often in the form of a lion. A painting of the *miʿrāj* in a *fālnāma* manuscript in the Arthur M. Sackler Gallery, Washington, shows ʿAli as a lion encountering the Prophet in the heavens (fig.3).[12] Another painting from a *fālnāma* manuscript now in Dresden includes the crouching lion but not the Prophet himself, who is instead represented by a blazing nimbus on the back of his celestial steed, Buraq.[13] The roots of representing ʿAli as a lion in textual and visual accounts of the *miʿrāj* are not entirely clear, although they may have been inspired by one of his many exalted titles, the Lion of God (*asadullāh*). It has been suggested that ʿAli's appearance as a lion in *miʿrāj* narratives signals the auspicious moment at which the Prophet transfers the seal of succession to ʿAli.[14] In the Qajar period, Shiʿi representations of the *miʿrāj* that include ʿAli in the form of a lion occur more often than in previous periods (fig.4).

In a late-Qajar painting of the *miʿrāj*, the Prophet and Buraq, surrounded by cherubim, encounter ʿAli depicted as a roaring lion amidst dense clouds (fig.5). This composition, painted in the thoroughly Europeanising style of the late 19th century, curiously crowns a talismanic chart that includes Qurʾanic verses, prayers (*duʿāʾ*), the Beautiful Names of God (*al-Asmāʾ al-ḥusnā*), astrological dials and talismanic grids and symbols. Here, the association between the *miʿrāj* and the chart suggests that the *miʿrāj* scene was intended to reinforce the talismanic properties of the chart. This juxtaposition provides clues about the possible uses and meanings of such imagery to the beholder. Charts of this kind were likely hung or folded several times and placed in an amulet. Traces of fold marks on similar charts of the period serve as further evidence for their function.[15]

During the Qajar period, particularly during Nasir al-Din Shah's rule, an important trend developed in which images of the Prophet

Fig.5

Fig.5
Talismanic chart featuring a *miʿrāj* scene with the Prophet and ʿAli as a lion, Iran, late 19th century. Ink, opaque water-colour and gold on paper. Formerly Negaristan Museum, Tehran, current location unknown

Fig.6

Fig.7

were either reduced in scale or disappeared entirely from compositions depicting the Shiʿi cosmological pyramid. Instead, ʿAli emerged as the dominating figure. An image of ʿAli holding his bifurcated sword (*Dhu'l-faqār*) shown with al-Hasan and al-Husayn and two other figures atop a talismanic chart of the same period presents similar associations as the example illustrated in figure five (fig.6). This unfinished Shiʿi chart is organised into an architectural framework containing suras from the Qur'an (e.g. 108, *al-Kawthar*), prayers (*duʿā*'s), and several of the *Asmā' al-ḥusnā*. The haloed image of Imams ʿAli, Hasan and Husayn are seen at the centre of a triple arcade with two elderly figures flanking them on both sides. One of them is possibly Hazrat ʿAbbas (the half-brother of Imam Husayn and a chief protagonist in the Karbala tragedy who served as his standard-bearer) and the other remains unidentified.[16] A second unfinished rectangular cartouche containing a double arcade at the bottom of the composition was probably meant to feature further images of prominent Shiʿi figures. Here, the placement of the image of the *Ahl al-bayt* at the top of a talismanic chart endows it with a strong protective and possibly prophylactic element. In both charts discussed here, the fusion of word and image transforms the work into a potent devotional object.

Paintings of ʿAli with his two sons, sometimes accompanied by the Prophet and Fatima or other religious personages, abound in the 18th and particularly the 19th centuries in Iran as attested by the sheer number of surviving examples. During this period, a distinct iconography for images of the *Ahl al-bayt* developed and became standardised in Iran from the 1850s onward (fig.7). Like *miʿrāj* images, depictions of the *Ahl al-bayt* were altered to suit various religious and political agendas throughout the Qajar era.

Two paintings of the subject show disparate interpretations of typical *Ahl al-bayt* iconography. The first example is a painting in the Free Library in Philadelphia showing Imam ʿAli accompanied by Imams Hasan and Husayn, sitting to his right and two figures standing on either side of them (fig.8). Since the identity of the two standing figures is not disclosed, we can only speculate that the one with a

Fig.6
Talismanic chart with Imams ʿAli, Hasan, Husayn and two figures, Iran, late 19th century. Ink, opaque water-colour and gold on paper, 71.5 × 75 cm. Library of Congress, Washington, DC, ACXX

Fig.7
Painting depicting Imams ʿAli, Hasan and Husayn, Iran, late 18th to early 19th century. Oil on canvas, 140 × 94 cm. Saʿdabad Museum, Tehran

Fig.8
Album page with Imams ʿAli, Hasan and Husayn and possibly Bilal and Salman al-Farsi, Iran, 1850s to 1890s. Ink, opaque water-colour and gold on paper, 35.5 × 22.5 cm. Free Library of Philadelphia, Lewis Oriental Collection

Fig.9
Image of Imams ʿAli, Hasan and Husayn with Nur ʿAli Shah and a Sufi, Iran, 1850s to 1890s. Opaque water-colour and gold on paper, 35.9 × 23.8 cm. Harvard Art Museums/Arthur M. Sackler Museum, Alpheus Hyatt Purchasing Fund, Cambridge, MA, 1958.137

darker complexion is the Abyssinian Bilal, one of the earliest converts to Islam and the Prophet's first muezzin, and the bearded figure is Salman al-Farsi, the Prophet's companion who came to be regarded in later traditions as the first Persian convert to Islam. The image is enclosed in an oval medallion framed by several tiers of lobe-shaped designs. The first tier contains the names of the Fourteen Infallibles (i.e. Muhammad, Fatima and the Twelve Shiʿi Imams) inscribed in gold within an alternating blue and red scalloped frame. An inscription in a gold rectangular cartouche at the top centre contains the invocation (*ṣalawāt*): 'O God, bless Muhammad and the family of Muhammad.' This is flanked by two inscriptions in star-shaped medallions that together read: 'And the Prophet, peace be upon him, said: I am the city of knowledge and ʿAli is its gateway.' Two rectangular cartouches on the bottom corners of the composition inscribed in blue on gold contain a rhyming couplet of poetry in the *mulamaʿ* style with one hemistich in Persian and the other in Arabic that read: '[This] portrait has been fashioned to reveal his countenance/There is no hero (*fatā*) except ʿAli and no sword except [his sword] *Dhu'l-faqār*.' The composition is framed with a blue band lettered in gold with a well-known Shiʿi poem which is a versified prayer to the Fourteen Infallibles. These inscriptions, along with the central image, accentuate the intercessory role of the *Ahl al-bayt* and the Shiʿi Imams.

Another standardised image of the *Ahl al-bayt* in the Sackler Museum at Harvard University depicts ʿAli seated with his two sons in the usual way; however, in this type of composition, the Imams are accompanied by Sufi personages from the Niʿmatullahi order (fig.9). A brief history of this Sufi order will help explain the iconography used in such paintings.[17] Originally founded in the 14th century in Mahan, Kirman, the Niʿmatullahi order shifted its base to the Deccan, India, in the 15th century, although the Niʿmatullahis who remained in Iran continued to prosper until the time of Shah ʿAbbas (*r.* 1587–1629). The Niʿmatullahi order was reintroduced into Persia with considerable vigour in the late 18th century and became the most widespread Sufi order in the country. However, the master of the order, Maʿsum ʿAli

Fig.8

Fig.9

Fig.10

Shah (d. 1797) and several of his followers had to confront the hostility of opposing Shiʿi jurists (*mujtahids*) and conservative members of the *ʿulamāʾ*. As a result, Maʿsum ʿAli Shah and his disciples were cruelly persecuted and put to death. Among those killed was the master's principal disciple and companion, Nur ʿAli Shah (d. 1797), a talented and prolific poet and scholar.

As a result of the aggression faced by the order from the jurists, an atmosphere of persecution and an aura of martyrdom permeated the didactic poetry of Nur ʿAli Shah, who openly criticised and antagonised the *ʿulamāʾ* in his writings.[18] Particularly provocative was his assertion that the Sufi master is the true deputy (*nāʾib*) of the Hidden Imam, thus contradicting both Shiʿi and Sufi principles by elevating the master to excessive levels. This explains why Niʿmatullahi representations of the *Ahl al-bayt* almost always include both an image of Nur ʿAli Shah and the Sufi master. Following the death of the chief opposing Shiʿi *mujtahid* in 1801, clashes between the *ʿulamāʾ* and the Niʿmatullahis slowly began to subside, and by the time of the reign of Muhammad Shah Qajar (*r.* 1834–1848), relations between the court and the order were revived and strengthened. Intermittent ties between the Qajar court and the Niʿmatullahis persisted throughout the remainder of the century.[19]

The Harvard painting of the *Ahl al-bayt* is signed by the artist, Muhammad Taqi, and depicts the three seated Imams ʿAli, Hasan and Husayn, flanked by Nur ʿAli Shah holding a *tabarzīn* (ceremonial battle-axe) on the right and an elderly, bearded Sufi master (*pīr*) standing on the other side (fig.9). The surrounding inscriptions include verses by Imam Shafiʿi (d. 820) in praise of the *Ahl al-bayt*. Paintings such as these were being produced as early as the 1860s. Another example is the lacquered mirror-case discussed previously (fig.1). Made in large numbers, probably for the Niʿmatullahi order's many devotees, these paintings present a distinct iconography characteristic of images of the *Ahl al-bayt* during this period.

Several are by Ismaʿil Jalayir (d. 1868–1873), the renowned late-Nasiri court painter and instructor at Tehran's Dar al-Funun (the first modern institution of higher learning in Iran), who was a passionate follower of the Niʿmatullahi order.[20] A painting in grisaille by Jalayir depicts Imam ʿAli seated with his two young sons, flanked by Nur ʿAli Shah and a Sufi *pīr,* as well as two other Niʿmatullahi dervishes, with a host of cherubim in the background and a group of animals including a lion, a lion cub and a hyena in the foreground (fig.10).[21] The reason behind the addition of wild animals in the main composition is unclear but one could perhaps interpret them as symbols of protection against imminent danger. In these types of compositions featuring portraits of the first three Shiʿi Imams together with Nur ʿAli Shah and other members of the Niʿmatullahi order, the message is two-pronged, reflecting a conflation of Shiʿi and Niʿmatullahi concerns. Like the paintings of the Prophet's *miʿrāj*, the two standardised compositions of the *Ahl al-bayt* also embody layers of meaning to fulfil the religious, political and spiritual needs of their followers.

Fig.10
Painting of Imams ʿAli, Hasan and Husayn with Niʿmatullahi order dervishes, signed by Ismaʿil Jalayir, Iran, 1870. Oil on canvas, 86 × 66 cm. Current location unknown. After Sotheby's London, *Arts of the Islamic World*, 1 April 2009, Lot 36

Figs 11a–b
Ceremonial battle-axe (*tabarzīn*) with miniature of Imams ʿAli, Hasan and Husayn, Iran, late 19th century. Engraved and damascened steel with painted miniature, 86.5 × 24.4 cm. After Antoni Romauld Chodynski, *Museum w Malborku Orez Perski*, pp.353–355

As a final example of the use of *Ahl al-bayt* imagery in Qajar art, we shift from the painted canvas to metalwork. A steel ceremonial battle-axe (*tabarzīn*), similar to the one depicted in the two paintings discussed above (figs 9–10), from the collection of the National Museum of Poland in Krakow, bears a small painted image of ʿAli seated with his sons, Imams Hasan and Husayn, enclosed within a teardrop-shaped finial (figs 11a–b).[22] This object, with inscriptions and gilded decoration, was likely a symbolic accoutrement of a dervish, possibly of the Niʿmatullahi order, rather than a deadly weapon. In paintings of the period, Sufi figures are often depicted holding accessories like the *tabarzīn*, the *kashkūl* (alms bowl) and the *mantasha* (cudgel). The curved edge of the blade is decorated with gold damascened vegetal scrolls and its straight edge bears a lobed cartouche on either side inscribed with the following Persian verse in *nastaʿlīq* script:

> This axe landed at the centre of Yalan's head[23]
> Like the crest of a fighting cockerel.
> This axe descended on the champion's head – like a fighting cockerel's crest

Here, the curved blade of the axe is likened to a fighting cockerel's crest, descending upon the middle of Yalan's head, splitting it in half. The reference to Yalan, champion of the Turanian army who fought – and lost – against the Iranians in the *Shāhnāma*, would be obvious to the reader. These words may have been intended to empower the owner of the *tabarzīn* by warning the enemy of his ill fate should it come his way. This example illustrates the way in which text and image work together to invest an object with powers beyond itself – the power to intimidate an enemy and protect the owner. Nur ʿAli Shah is often portrayed in paintings of the Nasiri era with a battle-axe, implying the lurking presence of physical danger and the need for protection in the face of adversity. The inclusion of the *tabarzīn* as a symbol of martyrdom and security in these compositions can be explained by the historical context during which time members of the Niʿmatullahi order were constantly persecuted and Nur ʿAli Shah, the young disciple himself, was killed by so-called orthodox forces.

The paintings and objects examined in this essay present the *Ahl al-bayt* as a pervasive trope that, along with the accompanying poetic and textual references, invest objects with the potency to protect and empower their owners. They served as vehicles of intercession with the Divine in times of hardship, fear and threat and as symbols of hope and solace for people from all walks of life. The multi-layered nature of these Shiʿi devotional objects also helps us navigate the intricate political and, at times, uneasy relationship between the Sufis and the court and religious establishment and facilitates an understanding of the possible meanings they held for Shiʿi believers during this period.

Fig.11a

Fig.11b

1 David Morgan, *The Sacred Gaze: Religious Visual Culture in Theory and Practice* (Berkeley, CA, 2005) p.32; Layla S. Diba, 'Images of Power and the Power of Images: Intention and Response in Early Qajar Painting (1785–1834)', in Layla Diba and Maryam Ekhtiar, eds., *Royal Persian Painting: The Qajar Epoch 1798–1924* (London, 1998), pp.30–49; and Moshe Barasch, *Icon: Studies in the History of an Idea* (New York, 1992).

2 David Freedberg, *The Power of Images: Studies in the History and Theory of Response* (Chicago, 1989).

3 Diba, 'Images of Power', pp.30–49.

4 Kathryn Babayan, *Mystics, Monarchs and Messiahs: Cultural Landscapes of Early Modern Iran* (Cambridge, MA, 2002), p.161.

5 Kathryn Babayan, 'The Cosmological Order of Things in Early Modern Iran', in Massumeh Farhad with Serpil Bagçi, *Falnama: Book of Omens* (London, 2010), pp.246–255. See also Massumeh Farhad's essay in this volume.

6 This mirror-case is in the Nasser D. Khalili Collection in London (inv. no. LAQ43). I am indebted to Manijeh Bayani for her reading and translation of the Persian inscriptions. See Manijeh Bayani's translation in, B.W. Robinson and Tim Stanley, *Lacquer of the Islamic Lands*, Nasser D. Khalili Collection of Islamic Art, vol.22, Part Two (Oxford, 1997), pp.72–73. The mirror-case is discussed in detail in an article with the Prophet Muhammad as the focus of the discussion in, Maryam Ekhtiar, 'Infused with Shiʿism: Images of the Prophet Muhammad in Qajar Iran', in Avinoam Shalem and Christiane Gruber, ed., *The Image of the Prophet Between Ideal and Ideology. A Scholarly Investigation* (Berlin and Boston, 2014), pp.87–102.

7 Translated from Jacob Eduard Polak, *Persien: Das Land und Seine Bewohner* (1865, repr., Hildesheim, NY, 1976), pp.322–323.

8 Diba, 'Images of Power', pp.30–49.

9 Ibid., pp.41–45.

10 Christiane Gruber and Frederick Colby, eds., *The the Islamic Mirʿāj Tales* (Bloomington, IN, 2010).

11 Gruber and Colby, *The Prophet's Ascension*, p.2.

12 This painting is also discussed in the essay by Massumeh Farhad in this volume. For discussions of the significance of the lion in Shiʿi religious imagery see also, Thierry Zarcone, 'The Lion of ʿAli in Anatolia: History, Symbolism and Iconology'; and Fahmida Suleman, 'The Iconography of ʿAli as the Lion of God in Shiʿi Art and Material Culture', in Pedram Khosronejad, ed., *The Art and Material Culture of Iranian Shiʿism: Iconography and Religious Devotion in Shiʿi Islam* (London, 2012), pp.104–122, 215–233.

13 Farhad with Bagçi, *Falnama*, p.118.

14 Ibid., p.335.

15 These include pieces from the Aga Khan Museum Collection (ex-Sadruddin Aga Khan Collection) and the Tareq Rajab Museum in Kuwait. See the Library of Congress website entry written by Christiane Gruber: http://memory.loc.gov/cgi-bin/query/h?intldl/ascsbib:@field(DOCID+@lit(ascs000258)).

16 Since the figures are not identified, we can only speculate. See, Maria Vittoria Fontana, *L'Iconografia dell'Ahl al-Bayt: Immagini di Arte Persiana dal XII al XIX Secolo* (Naples, 1994), pp.47–55 and figs. 51–61.

17 For a more detailed account see Hamid Algar, 'Niʿmat-Allāhiyya', *EI2*, vol.8, pp.44–48.

18 Julian Baldick, *Mystical Islam: An Introduction to Sufism* (New York, 1989), pp.139–140.

19 Ibid., pp.139–140; see also, Kathryn Spellman, *Religion and Nation: Iranian Local and Transnational Networks in Britain* (New York, 2004), pp.109–110.

20 B. W. Robinson, 'Art in Iran, x., Qajar 2. Painting', *EIR*, vol.2, pp.637–640.

21 Grisaille is a term for painting executed entirely in monochrome or near-monochrome, usually in shades of grey. The painting was reproduced in a 2009 Sotheby's auction catalogue. See, Sotheby's London, *Arts of the Islamic World*, 1 April 2009, Lot 36.

22 Antoni Romauld Chodynski, *Museum w Malborku Orez Perski i Indoperski XVI-XIX Wieku ze zbiorow Polskich, Katalog Wystawy pod redakcja, Antoniego Romualda Chodynskiego, Museum Zamkowe w Malboroku* (Malbork, 2000), pp.353–355.

23 Yalan was the champion of the Turanian army in the *Shāhnāma*. The Turanians were the arch-enemies of the Iranians and a constant force to be contended with in the epic.

14

Shiʿism and contemporary Iranian art

Venetia Porter

Ready to Order: Takhti by Khosrow Hassanzadeh (b. 1963), one of Iran's leading contemporary artists, is a powerful example of how symbols of Shiʿism continue to have resonance in the work of a significant number of Iranian artists today (fig.1).[1] This essay analyses Hassanzadeh's piece by exploring what role Shiʿi elements play within its overall concept and design and, more broadly, within the larger body of work of the artist himself. It also examines how Shiʿi themes are played out in the works of some of Hassanzadeh's contemporaries and places *Ready to Order: Takhti* within the context of the artistic production of Iranians of the previous generation for whom Shiʿi symbols also formed key elements of their creative vocabulary.

Hassanzadeh began his *Ready to Order* series in 2006. His intention was to commemorate icons – people whose life, music or actions have affected him or others profoundly. Apart from his homage to Takhti, the famous Iranian wrestler, Hassanzadeh's other subjects thus far have included the Indian nationalist leader, Mahatma Gandhi (d. 1948), the much-loved Iranian singer and star, Googoosh (b. 1950), the popular Iranian singer, Javad Yasari (b. 1954), the celebrated Egyptian singer, Umm Kulthum (d. 1975), and the renowned Lebanese singer and actress, Fairuz (b. 1935). He places photographic representations of the figures in a box over one metre high, surrounding them with symbolic objects, and frames them with gently flashing lights.

Ghulamreza Takhti (b. 1930), the subject of the work under discussion, was a *jahān pahlavān* (world wrestler or athlete) who won several Olympic medals for wrestling, but he died tragically at the age of 37 in 1968. Idolised in his lifetime, his death in questionable circumstances was profoundly mourned by both Iranians and the international wrestling community. It was not simply his physical prowess but his personality, kindness and generosity that are remembered. In particular it was his actions following the 1962 earthquake of Buin Zahra in Qazvin province, when he and his friends brought blankets and food to the people of the city, that are still recalled. Another often repeated story was how in the 1962 fight with his fiercest competitor, the world famous Russian wrestler, Aleksandr Medved, Takhti avoided touching his opponent's injured leg. Thus, for Iranians and for Hassanzadeh personally, Takhti epitomises the chivalrous qualities known as *javānmardī*.[2]

Takhti and another body of work based on *pahlavāns* (his *Ya Ali Madad* series) were produced by Hassanzadeh in 2003 following a dark period in which he created not only the *Ashura* series (2000) of works (fig.2), but also the *Prostitutes* series (2002), which was based on real events of the serial murder of prostitutes in Iran's holy city of Mashhad.[3] He realised then that he needed to find a 'lighter side' to his work. What he loved about the *pahlavān* was that, 'They were men who belonged

Fig.1

Fig.1
Takhti, from the *Ready to Order* series, Khosrow Hassanzadeh.
Mixed media, Iran, 2007, height: 1.5m.
British Museum, 2008,6032.1

to an age of generosity and civility, who at the peak of their authority and power taught us the lessons of humility. These are men who always bowed before heroes such as Imam ʿAli, who always supported the weak and unprotected.'[4]

When talking about Imam ʿAli, Takhti himself had said: 'I learnt from Imam ʿAli that one has to stand up to any injustice...and to rely on God when entering the platform (*maidān*).'[5] Takhti's world was the *zūrkhāna* (traditional gymnasium, lit. 'house of strength'), an institution which came into being during the Safavid period (*r.* 1501–1722), but which embodied the wrestling traditions of ancient Iran and actions of the pre-Islamic heroes: Rustam, the great hero of the *Shāhnāma*, is considered the first *jahān pahlavān*.[6] Another key figure in the evolution of the *zūrkhāna* was the 13th-century Sufi mystic and wrestling champion, Purya-yi Vali (d. 1322).[7] It was under the Safavids that the ancient traditions of the *pahlavān* culture with its ideals of not only physical aptitude and strength but notions of chivalry combined with the symbols of Twelver Shiʿism. Here, the reverence for Imam ʿAli took central place and in the context of the *zūrkhāna* the Imam was also regarded as a *jahān pahlavān*. Key elements of the routines practised in the *zūrkhāna* were modelled on ʿAli's courageous actions, notably the lifting of the large wooden door-shaped shields (*sang*) in an echo of the event in which, during the famous battle to capture the stronghold of Khaybar (7/628), ʿAli ripped open the door of the fortress and used it as a shield.[8] The interiors of traditional *zūrkhāna*s are generally covered with images of Imam ʿAli as well as famous Iranian *pahlavān*s and religious leaders as captured by Iranian artist Mehraneh Atashi (b. 1980) (fig.3).[9] They also often include illustrations from the *Shāhnāma* featuring the epic tales of Rustam.

In Hassanzadeh's *Takhti*, the wrestler stands proud, his Olympic medals on his bare chest, wearing the traditional embroidered trousers (*tonbān*) of the *pahlavān*.[10] On his upper arm is a *bāzūband*, an arm bracelet worn by *pahlavān*s as far back as Rustam. According to the *Shāhnāma*, Rustam gave the mother of his unborn child a *bāzūband* with an amulet: 'Take this,' said Rustam to Tahmineh 'and if you

Fig.2

Fig.3

Fig.2
Ashura, Khosrow Hassanzadeh. Silkscreen and acrylic on paper, Iran, 2000, 250 × 107 cm. Collection of the artist

Fig.3
Bodiless I, from the *Zourkhaneh Project* series, Mehraneh Atashi. Digital C-print, Iran, 2004, 112.5 × 76.5 cm. British Museum, 2009,6035.1

should bear a daughter, braid her hair about it as an omen of good fortune; but if the heavens give you a son, have him wear it on his upper arm, as a sign of who his father is.'[11] When their son Sohrab grew up, Tahmineh gave him the *bāzūband* before he set off to find his father. Unknowingly, the two heroes confronted each other in battle and Sohrab was killed by his father. It was Sohrab's *bāzūband* that revealed to Rustam the tragic fate of his actions, a scene from the *Shāhnāma* that is frequently illustrated (fig.4). Sohrab's *bāzūband* probably included some kind of precious stone, which clearly had amuletic properties as suggested in the story; in the post-Safavid tradition the wrestlers' *bāzūband* was likely to have contained amulets inscribed with religious texts.[12] Indeed Takhti's own *bāzūband*, housed in the Astan-i Quds Razavi Museum attached to Imam Reza's ('Ali al-Rida) shrine at Mashhad, has an amulet engraved with an invocation to the Twelve Imams. Similarly, a wrestler's *bāzūband* in the British Museum has 15 carnelian and chalcedony amulets inscribed with verses from the Qur'an that are fastened to a leather band (fig.5).

Within Hassanzadeh's 'box', nothing is randomly placed; each object is intended to convey a particular meaning and it is as though all the main elements of popular Iranian imagery and culture are combined in this one object: the peacock feathers, grapes and pomegranates as symbols of abundance and good fortune; a scene from a relief at ancient Persepolis dating back to the 5th century BC of a hero-king slaying a lion; Imam 'Ali's forked sword, *Dhu'l-faqār*, at the base of the box; the hand of 'Abbas to the right pierced with the names of the *Ahl al-bayt* (Muhammad, Fatima, 'Ali, al-Hasan and al-Husayn); a photographic impression of Imam 'Ali; a familiar style of modern poster image used for portraits of Imam 'Ali's family (e.g. Hazrat 'Abbas, Imam Hasan and Imam Husayn);[13] and invocations to Imam 'Ali and the Twelve Imams. But it is not only these objects which contain Shi'i allusions but the form of the box itself which is a deliberate echo of a *ḥijla*.

The *ḥijla* was traditionally an elaborately decorated bridal chamber prepared by the families of the bride and groom. Although it continued to be used in parts of Iran for this purpose, the institutionalisation of

Fig.4

Fig.5

Fig.4
Rustam and the dying Sohrab (note Sohrab's *bāzūband*). Painting by Mu'in Musavvir from a *Shāhnāma* of Ferdowsi. Ink, opaque water-colour and gold on paper, Isfahan, Iran, 1059/1649, 35.4 × 20.9 cm. British Museum, 1922,0711,0.2

Fig.5
Wrestler's *bāzūband* (arm-band) with amulets inscribed with Qur'anic verses, including 'help from God and a speedy victory' (61:13). Leather, chalcedony and carnelian, Iran, 1850–1900. British Museum, 2008,6040.1

Shiʿism under the Safavids brought greater emphasis to the use of overt Shiʿi symbols commemorating the martyrdom of Imam Husayn.[14] As a result, the emblem of the *ḥijla* grew to be associated with the tragic story of the betrothal of Imam Husayn's daughter, Zubayda, to his nephew, Qasim b. al-Hasan, just before the young hero was to die along with Imam Husayn and other Shiʿi martyrs at the battle of Karbala. European travellers from the 16th century onwards remarked on seeing the Muharram rituals in which this scene was re-enacted in different parts of Iran, and the 'Bridegroom of Karbala' continues to be represented in dramatizations of the story amongst the Shiʿa of India and Iran.[15]

In contemporary Iran, *ḥijla*s were erected when an unmarried young man died unexpectedly and *ḥijla*s were frequently put up to commemorate the lives of the *basīj* (youth militia) during the Iran-Iraq war (1980–1988). This association between the deaths of the *basīj* during the Iran-Iraq war armed with their keys to Paradise and the commemoration of Shiʿi martyrs at Karbala is one that continues to be perpetuated in Iran. The conflation is seen on walls and posters[16] and it also appears in art; a notable example are the embroidered felts by Bita Ghezelayagh (b. 1966) with their series of metal keys attached to the fabric and the accompanying text, 'martyrdom is the key to Paradise' (fig.6). In studying the complexity of the allusions in Hassanzadeh's *Takhti*, it comes as no surprise to learn that before he became a painter he fought in the Iran-Iraq war. His early paintings from the late 1980s act like diaries and his series, *War* (1998), are dark works that caused him as much pain in creating them as they do to the viewer studying them, and stand as his memory of this period.[17]

It is striking how that profound sense of belonging and that passion for Iran in all its facets has taken such an extraordinary range of artistic forms and how Shiʿi themes constantly recur. The *ḥijla*, for example, is recreated by Monir Shahroudy Farmanfarmaian (b. 1924) in her characteristic idiom of mirror and mosaic (fig.7).[18] While the artist Sadegh Tirafkan (d. 2013) produced a series of golden *ḥijla*s in which he remembered those lost to him and, by adding strips of cloth to the structure, he evoked the tradition of placing pieces of fabric on a shrine for remembrance (fig.8). Tirafkan explained the significance of this series, entitled *Always in Our Thoughts*, installed at the 2011 exhibition, *Gifts of the Sultan*:

Fig.6

Fig.7

Fig.6
Embroidered shepherd's cloak (*namad*) with 1,001 metal keys sewn in rows, from the *Felt Memories* series, Bita Ghezelayagh. Felt, silk and metal, Iran, 2008, 102 × 116 cm. British Museum, 2009,6029.1

Fig.7
Hejla, The Eight, made of mirror mosaic and reverse glass painting, Monir Shahroudy Farmanfarmaian. Mirror, metal, plaster and mixed media, Iran, 2005, 220 × 80 × 80 cm. Collection of the artist

Fig.8

Fig.9

With *Hijla*, I wanted to present a gift from the living to the deceased in their honour, but to also celebrate life. The word actually means marriage, and traditionally it is an image of a deceased man, but I wanted to break the taboos and use pictures of living people and also women and include mirrors, so that the viewer can share in the celebration.[19]

Artists such as Sadegh Tirafkan, Khosrow Hassanzadeh, Monir Shahroudy Farmanfarmaian and Bita Ghezelayagh are not the only ones to refer to aspects of Shiʿism in their work.[20] Parastou Forouhar (b. 1962) in her work, *The Funeral* (2003), wraps office chairs with fabrics covered with images of the Shiʿi shrines and texts relating to the Karbala story produced every year to mark 'Ashura' (fig.9). This is in deliberate reference to her annual commemoration of the assassination of her parents in 1998.[21] Thus, as with Sadegh Tirafkan's use of the *ḥijla*, the rituals of the Karbala paradigm are used to express a personal tragedy.[22]

The use of Shiʿi iconography is an integral feature of the work of artists of a previous generation in Iran, who have sometimes been grouped together under the term *Saqqākhāneh* (Persian, 'drinking fountain').[23] It was during the late 1950s that the renowned painters and sculptors, Charles-Hossein Zenderoudi (b. 1937) and Parviz Tanavoli (b. 1937) became fascinated by folk art, popular printed posters, talismans and other objects in which were contained imagery and texts relating to the martyrdom of Imam Husayn and that could be found in the bazaars of south Tehran which they loved to frequent. As Hamid Keshmirshekan explains, 'They were searching for local Iranian raw material to be used and developed in their works. The simplicity of forms, repeated motifs, and bright colours attracted them.'[24] What they were to create has been called 'spiritual pop art'.[25] According to Tanavoli, it is Zenderoudi's first works, drawings inspired by some of the objects they first encountered, that can be considered the first examples of *Saqqākhāneh*. Such works were given a high profile at the Third Tehran Biennale of 1962 and it was here that the scholar and literary critic, Karim Emami (d. 2005), first used the term *Saqqākhāneh*, and later explained that it came to him upon seeing the works of Zenderoudi as they 'reminded [him] of Shiʿi shrines and assemblies. The atmosphere of the paintings was religious and a reminder of Muharram mourning, of candles reflected in shiny brass bowls, of chants of 'Ya Hossein' and 'Blessed be the Prophet'. The impression was not as lofty, grand or spacious as some of the distinguished Iranian mosques, but as familiar and intimate as that of the (traditional) *Saqqākhāneh*.'[26]

A work that is a clear precursor of *Saqqākhāneh* is Zenderoudi's '*Who is this Hossein that the World is Crazy About*?' This remarkable work, made from designs cut into lino blocks of different sizes stamped

Fig.8
Hijla: Always In Our Thoughts, Sadegh Tirafkan. Metal wire, cloth, glass, digital prints, Canada, 2010, height 210.03 × diameter 56.04 cm, each. Los Angeles County Museum of Art, CA, M.2012.120a-d

Fig.9
The Funeral, Parastou Forouhar. Office chairs covered in printed textiles, Germany and Iran, 2003. Collection of the artist

onto linen, tells the story of the martyrdom of Imam Husayn. It is a deliberate echo of coffee-house paintings (*pardah*) used as backdrops for the telling of the Karbala story (*ta'ziya*). Zenderoudi's textile was first shown at the Reza 'Abbasi Hall in 1960, two years prior to the Third Tehran Biennale, and presaged what was to come.[27] The work exists in the form of panels of linen cloth, one of which is in the British Museum (fig.10), and the other was published by Fereshteh Daftari, but its whereabouts are now unclear.[28] The difference between the two textiles is that the individual elements have been stamped onto different parts of the cloth. Otherwise they are identical. That Zenderoudi also stamped the same lino blocks onto paper is clear from the two examples in the Grey Art Collection in New York.[29] Other works by Zenderoudi were inspired by talismanic shirts that he saw in the Iran Bastan Museum of Tehran covered with magic squares and numbers and by the early 1960s as Daftari describes, 'Zenderoudi had established a fully developed syntax brewing a private mythology out of religion, superstition, augury, numerology, divination and coded signs.'[30]

The idea of *Saqqākhāneh*, spawned works by numerous artists and there began to be an increasing trend in the use of calligraphy; it was this that Tanavoli reacted against in his *Heech* ('nothing' or 'nothingness') series. According to Shiva Balaghi, 'What had once been a creative appropriation of traditional Persian cultural paradigms had now become sublimated by artists painting script onto canvases in an attempt to garner their share of the growing art market…Tanavoli decided to limit himself to a single word: *heech*'.[31] The bronze example illustrated here has the *heech* climbing out of a cage-like structure that evokes the actual water fountain of the *Saqqākhāneh* itself (fig.11).

It is debatable whether *Saqqākhāneh* was a movement in the sense that groups of artists were deliberately working together to make art. Some artists in fact resented being lumped together in this way.[32] One such is Siah Armajani (b. 1939), an Iranian-born American sculptor, who like Zenderoudi and Tanavoli derived much of his early inspiration from Iranian religious, folk and poetry traditions clearly visible in his *Persian* series made between 1958 and 1962, but he did not consider himself part of any group. In these early works he covered strips of cloth with verses of poetry, seal impressions, religious allusions and invocations to Imam 'Ali and Imam Husayn (fig.12).[33]

Fig.10

Fig.11

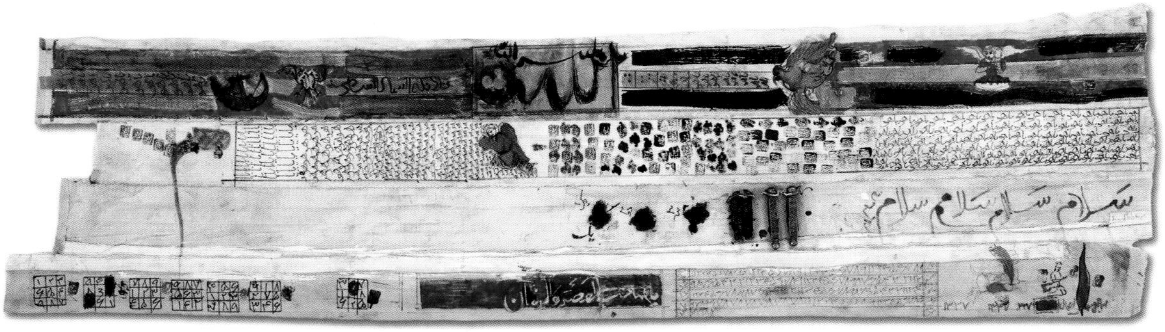

Fig.12

Whether or not *Saqqākhāneh* can be described as a group or a movement, it is clear that Shiʿism and its iconography – along with other aspects of Iranian cultural traditions such as the stories of the *Shāhnāma* – have continued to provide a powerful source of inspiration among successive generations of Iranian artists. Among some artists this gives their work a very specific character. If one is seeking to define what this character is, relevant in this context is Daftari's analysis of Zenderoudi's work, *K+L+32+H+4: Mon Père et Moi*, which she describes as 'Islamic in appearance'.[34] This interesting comment invites us to question the nature of the relationship between what is traditionally referred to as 'Islamic art' and contemporary art, a topic most recently discussed by Sussan Babaie. She argues that Iranian artists have been perhaps the most successful in negotiating this relationship because 'art related to contemporary Iran is deeply rooted in a locally understood history of Persian art...[and that] those relationships are forged with self-awareness of an idea of Iran and its history or histories'.[35] Hassanzadeh and the artists whose works have been considered in this essay are clearly utterly comfortable with the role that Iranian religious and cultural history plays in their oeuvre: they are imbued with it and see no boundaries between past and present, it is simply the artistic language that they use and which does not need to be defined. *Takhti* is an entirely contemporary work, reminiscent of the works of the British painter Peter Blake, but which tells a thoroughly Iranian story.[36]

1 I am extremely grateful to Fahmida Suleman for all her work on the conference and this volume and for her encouragement, and to Sussan Babaie and Hamid Keshmirshekan for reading this article and for their very useful comments.

2 *Takhti* was on display at the British Museum in 2009 in an exhibition entitled, *Takhti: A Modern Iranian Hero.* During the course of the exhibition in London and its subsequent tour to the Whitworth Art Gallery Manchester and the Hatton Museum Newcastle (2010) it was remarkable how familiar and beloved Takhti was to Iranians from across the generations.

3 Mirjam Shatanawi, *Tehran Studio Works: The Art of Khosrow Hassanzadeh* (London, 2007), pp.64–80; 96–106.

4 Ibid., p.30.

5 Venetia Porter, 'Takhti: A Modern Iranian Hero', *British Museum Magazine*, 62 (Winter 2008), p.31. Takhti's words were kindly translated by Dr Vesta Curtis.

6 John Chardin was the earliest Westerner to provide an eyewitness description of the *zūrkhāna* during his travels through Safavid Iran in the 1670s. See Houchang E. Chehabi, 'Zur-Khāna', EIR Online.

7 Lloyd Ridgeon, 'The Zūrkhāna Between Tradition and Change', *Iran*, 45 (2007), pp.245, 248.

8 Laura Veccia Vaglieri, 'Khaybar', EI2, vol.4, p.1140.

Fig.10
Who is this Hossein the world is crazy about? Charles-Hossein Zenderoudi. Linocut print on linen, Iran, 1958–1959, 228.52 × 148.5 cm. British Museum, 2011,6034.1

Fig.11
Heech in a Cage, Parviz Tanavoli. Bronze, Iran, 2005, 118 × 49 × 42 cm. British Museum, 2006,0206.1

Fig.12
Meem 1958, Siah Armajani. Ink, sealing-wax and paint on linen, Iran, 1958, 138.8 × 37.5 cm. British Museum, 2007,6031.1

9 Venetia Porter, 'Behind the Image', in Marta Weiss, *Light from the Middle East: New Photography* (London, 2012), p.125. See online http://www.vam.ac.uk/users/node/18035.

10 He won silver medals at Helsinki in 1951 and 1952 and gold in Melbourne in 1956.

11 Abu'l-Qāsim Ferdowsī, *Shāhnāmeh: The Persian Book of Kings*, tr. Dick Davis (London, 2006), pp.189, 209. Davis translates the Persian word used to refer to the arm bracelet or armband as a 'clasp'; however, another translation is 'onyx', which also makes sense in terms of the bracelet's amuletic properties. See http://www.iranchamber.com/literature/shahnameh/08rostam_sohrab.php.

12 See for example Barbara Brend and Charles Melville, ed., *Epic of the Persian Kings: The Art of Ferdowsi's Shahnameh* (London, 2010), p.198. For examples of these types of amulets see V. Porter, *Arabic and Persian Seals and Amulets in the British Museum* (London, 2013), pp.143ff.

13 James W. Allan, *The Art and Architecture of Twelver Shiʿism* (London, 2012), p.115; Peter J. Chelkowski and Hamid Dabashi, *Staging a Revolution: the Art of Persuasion in the Islamic Republic of Iran* (London, 2000), p.47.

14 Jean Calmard, 'Ḥejla', EIR, vol.12, 2, pp.143–144. See also Jean Calmard, 'Shiʿi Rituals and Power. II. The Consolidation of Safavid Shiʿism: Folklore and Popular Religion', in Charles Melville, ed., *Safavid Persia: The History and Politics of an Islamic Society* (London, 1996), pp.139–190. For the first appearance of specifically Shiʿi texts on objects such as the *Nād-i ʿAlī* prayer, see Allan, *Twelver Shiʿism*, pp.99ff; and Sussan Babaie, 'Epigraphy. IV. Safavid and Later Inscriptions', in EIR, vol.8, 5, pp.498–504.

15 The story of the betrothal is not regarded by Shiʿi *ʿulamā'* as having any basis in fact. Calmard, 'Ḥejla', pp.143–144. For the re-enactment of this story in an all-female setting in Iran, see the essay by Ingvild Flaskerud in this volume.

16 The *basīj* were young men who volunteered to fight during the Iran-Iraq war. The link between the events of the Iraq war and the Karbala paradigm are discussed in Chelkowski and Dabashi, *Staging a Revolution*, pp.135 ff.; 272 ff.; and p.288, fig.18.7.

17 Venetia Porter, *Word into Art: Artists of the Modern Middle East* (London, 2006), pp.102–103; Shatanawi, *Tehran Studio*, pp.38ff., 53–61.

18 Hans Ulrich Obrist and Karen Marta, ed., *Monir Shahroudy Farmanfarmaian: Cosmic Geometry* (Dubai, 2011). See the essay by Yasser Tabbaa in this volume on the tradition of mirror mosaic in Shiʿi architecture.

19 This was an installation at the Los Angeles County Museum of Arts' exhibition, *Gifts of the Sultan: The Arts of Giving at the Islamic Courts* (5 June 2011–5 September 2011) and shown again at the Museum of Islamic Art in Doha (2012). http://lacma.wordpress.com/2011/08/08/artist-interpretations-in-gifts-of-the-sultan-qa-with-sadegh-tirafkan/

20 Sussan Babaie, 'Voices of Authority, locating the "Modern" in "Islamic" Arts', *Getty Research Journal*, 3 (2011), pp.133–149, esp. p.137.

21 Lutz Becker's introductory essay in Rose Issa, ed., *Parastou Forouhar: Art, Life and Death in Iran* (London, 2010), pp.16–17 and plates 34–39.

22 Similarly, see the essay by Nacim Pak-Shiraz in this volume on the play upon the Karbala story as personal tragedy, conveyed through the works of contemporary Iranian filmmakers.

23 The word in Persian refers to votive fountains installed all over Iran. They have a particular association with the martyrdom of Imam Husayn as one element in the tragedy was that the Imam and his companions were denied water to drink during the battle. Hamid Keshmirshekan, 'Saqqā-Khāna II. School of Art', EIR Online. For an analysis of *Saqqākhāneh* and the key artists connected to it see Shiva Balaghi, 'Iranian Visual Arts in the "Century of Machinery, Speed and the Atom": Rethinking Modernity', in Shiva Balaghi and Lynn Gumpert, eds., *Picturing Iran: Art, Society and Revolution* (London, 2003), pp.73ff; Fereshteh Daftari, 'Redefining Modernism', in Fereshteh Daftari and Layla S. Diba, *Iran Modern* (New York, 2013), pp.29 ff.; and Hamid Keshmirshekan, *Contemporary Iranian Art: New Perspectives* (London, 2013) pp.94ff.

24 Keshmirshekan, *Contemporary Iranian Art*, p.94.

25 See the relevant section in Rose Issa, Ruyin Pakbuz and Daryush Shayeganet, *Iranian Contemporary Art* (London, 2001).

26 Keshmirshekan, *Contemporary Iranian Art*, pp.95–96.

27 Ibid., p.95. During the Qajar period, paintings detailing the different episodes of the Karbala story started to be produced on large canvases (*pardah* paintings). The coffee houses became the places where story telling took place, these included the *Shāhnāma* as well as the Karbala story, and hence their name, 'coffee-house paintings'. These were commissioned from artists, and one of the best known was Muhammad Modabber. See Chelkowski and Dabashi, *Staging a Revolution*, pp.54–65.

28 For an analysis of the different scenes identified by Ladan Akbarnia see British Museum Collections Online, http://www.britishmuseum.org/research/collection_online/collection_object_details.aspx?objectId=3421951&partId=1&searchText=Zenderoudi&page=1; Dafari 'Redefining Modernism', pp.30–31; Fereshteh Daftari, 'Another Modernisn: An Iranian Perspective', in Balaghi and Gumpert, *Picturing Iran*, pp.68–69. Zenderoudi studied the linocut technique in Marcus Grigorian's studio.

29 *A View of Islam*, 1961, woodcut on silver foil, 49.5 × 45.4 cm (G1975.39), and *A View of Islam*, n.d., woodcut on paper, 59.7 × 36.8 cm (G1975.40), both at Grey Art Gallery, New York University Art Collection, Gift of Abby Weed Grey. http://www.nyu.edu/greyart/collection/iranian%20art/i-zenderoudiwebpages/pictures/1g197537z.html

30 Daftari, 'Another Modernism', p.72.

31 Shiva Balaghi, 'The Nothingness of Hope', in B. Sherrill, ed., *Works of Parviz Tanavoli: 3 Heech* (Tehran, 2011), p.11.

32 According to Hamid Keshmirshekan 'The name was initially applied to the works of artists, both in painting and sculpture, that used existing elements of votive Shiʿi art in their modern work. It gradually came to be applied to various forms of modern Iranian painting and sculpture that used traditional decorative elements.' However, some of the artists were later unhappy about the inclusion of their names as members of the movement. See his, 'Neo-Traditionalism and Modern Iranian Painting: The Saqqa-khaneh School in the 1960s', *Iranian Studies*, 38, 4 (December 2005), pp.607–630.

33 Venetia Porter, 'Meem 1958', in Venetia Porter and Mariam Rosser-Owen, ed., *Metalwork and Material Culture in the Islamic World: Art, Craft and Text, Essays Presented to James W. Allan* (London, 2012), pp.461–467; Venetia Porter 'The Persian Period', in Ziba Ardalan, ed., *Siah Armajani: An Ingenious World* (London, 2013), pp.17–25; Daftari 'Redefining Modernism' p.39.

34 Daftari, 'Another Modernism', p.72; Daftari, 'Redefining Modernism', p.32.

35 Babaie, 'Voices of Authority', p.141.

36 See for example Peter Blake, *An Alphabet by Peter Blake* (London, 2008). His work uses collage made from vintage prints and cards and depicts cultural icons such as Marilyn Monroe or Elvis Presley.

15

Dhu'l-faqār and the Ottomans

Zeynep Yürekli

The sword known as *Dhu'l-faqār* was transformed into a celebrated commemorative object as a result of the legends that grew around it. Abbasid sources state that the Prophet Muhammad gave it to ʿAli b. Abi Talib during the Battle of Uhud (3/625), while Shiʿi tradition reports that Imam Husayn fought with it at the battle of Karbala (60/680). Its presence is recorded in the Abbasid palace in Baghdad, whence Ismaili supporters managed to take it to Fatimid Cairo.[1] The sword then seems to have disappeared, leaving behind a plethora of legendary accounts.

While the shape of the original *Dhu'l-faqār* (literally meaning 'with notches') is not known, it came to be represented with a two-pointed blade in the medieval period.[2] That is how it appears in the hand of ʿAli b. Abi Talib in early 14th-century Ilkhanid illustrated manuscripts.[3] Among other scenes, it figures in key events in Shiʿi history. A painting in one manuscript of al-Biruni's *al-Āthār al-bāqiya* (The Vestiges of the Past), for example, illustrates the famous episode during the Farewell Pilgrimage in which Prophet Muhammad stopped at a place called Ghadir Khumm, between Mecca and Medina. There he designated as his successor his cousin and son-in-law, ʿAli, who is shown girt with the double-pointed *Dhu'l-faqār*.[4]

This particular shape of sword remains an attribute of ʿAli till today. For example, in the 1976 film, *Muhammad, the Messenger of God* (released as *The Message* in the USA), the presence of ʿAli, who like the Prophet never appears in person, is indicated by the tip of a two-pointed blade entering the frame. No further clue was required to suggest his presence to modern Muslim cinemagoers. During the centuries that elapsed between the Ilkhanid manuscripts and the film, painters continually depicted ʿAli holding a sword of this shape and the object became inextricably connected to him. Over the course of time, the bifurcated sword depicted on its own also came to represent ʿAli.

Although few motifs have such clear associations with Islam, the exact meaning of the motif depends on the context. For the Twelver Shiʿa, the *Dhu'l-faqār* belongs to the Imams, and will reappear in the hand of the Mahdi. Thus as a signifier of Muslim leadership handed down from Muhammad to ʿAli and then to his son al-Husayn and the later Imams, the motif has served to express allegiance to the *Ahl al-bayt*. However, its significance has not been restricted to the Shiʿa. As a signifier of invincibility, it served as an amulet, especially on the battlefield, and was adopted as an emblem by groups devoted to *ghazā'* (war for the faith) also by those who did not consider themselves Shiʿi. In fact, in the 16th century, the Sunni Ottomans seem to have used it more frequently on ceremonial objects than their Shiʿi rivals, the Safavids.

Dhu'l-faqār as an Ottoman emblem and amulet

The image of the *Dhu'l-faqār* seems to have entered the Ottoman world primarily as an element of the folklore of *ghazā'*. The earliest Ottoman references to it come from this milieu. Konstantin Mihailović, a Serbian warrior who fell captive to the Ottomans in 1455 and fought with the Ottoman Janissaries until 1463, records what he heard from them about the sword:

> The heathens hold ʿAli to be a prophet like Mohammed. For the heathens greatly praise ʿAli because he was a mighty and brave man, and had a sword called *dilfficary* of such wondrous keenness and also hardness, so say the heathens, that whatever ʿAli struck with his sword *dilfficary*, whether iron or steel, was hewn like a spider-web. Some heathens say that his wife Fatima was some kind of sorceress, that she placed such hardness and keenness upon the sword.[5]

In the late 15th century, the imperial policies of Mehmed II (*r.* 1444–1446, 1451–1481) began to threaten the ideology of *ghazā'*. This led those who were eager to preserve and protect the *ghāzī* ideals to record the oral traditions of the frontier warriors in writing. ʿAli figures prominently in these accounts. The *Ṣalṭūḳ-nāme* (Book of Saltuk), which is based on legends compiled from oral sources in the Balkans in the 1470s for the Ottoman prince Cem, portrays the medieval protagonist, Saru Saltuk, riding ʿAli's horse and using his sword.[6] This motif is repeated in the late 15th-century versified biography of an Ottoman raider commander, Mikhal-oghlu ʿAli, based in the Balkans; he, too, rides his revered namesake's horse and uses the *Dhu'l-faqār* against the Christians.[7]

In the reign of Mehmed's son Bayezid II (*r.* 1481–1512), historical accounts written about the first two centuries of the Ottoman dynasty purposely presented the early Ottomans as frontier warriors for the faith (i.e. *ghāzīs*). Bayezid thus sought to bolster the links between his dynasty and the culture of *ghazā'*, which had been weakened by his father.[8] At the same time, he looked for ways of preventing his Shiʿi subjects from sympathising with the growing Safavid threat from the east. It is in this context that we should place the replica of ʿAli's bifurcated sword made for Bayezid.[9] In addition to the Qur'anic 'Throne Verse' (*Āyat al-Kursī*, 2:255) and the sultan's name, the sword is inscribed with the names of the four Righteous Caliphs (the *Rāshidūn*), including the three who preceded ʿAli and were rejected by the Shiʿa. Bayezid's *Dhu'l-faqār* thus projected a patently Sunni image at a time when the Safavid ruler Shah Ismaʿil I (d. 1524) was exploiting the Shiʿi-millenarian connotations of the same sword in his poems, claiming: 'Muhammad's miracle and the Shah's *Dhu'l-faqār* / Are in my hand as signs. Here I come.'[10]

Bayezid's son Selim I (*r.* 1512–20) adopted a harsh policy towards the Safavids in the east and towards Shiʿi groups within his empire. He waged open war against Shah Ismaʿil, defeating him at Chaldiran in 1514. That victory was followed by another military campaign in 1517, which brought an end to Mamluk rule and resulted in the Ottoman annexation of Egypt and Syria. The banner used by Selim during his campaigns demonstrates that his anti-Shiʿi policy did not prevent him from using the *Dhu'l-faqār* motif (fig.1). The enormous banner, mounted on a pole with a pinnacle inscribed with the sultan's name, measures approximately four by two and a half metres.[11] Embroidered with gold thread on a red silk background, the banner features the bifurcated sword with a rounded pommel in the shape of a crescent encircling a star, and two dragons' heads emerging from the hilt. The two blades of the sword are inscribed with Qur'anic verses reiterating the notion of holy war (*al-Fatḥ*, 48:1–4):

> (1) We have given you a manifest conquest, (2) so that Allah may forgive you for your past sins and those to come, complete His favour upon you, and guide you on a right path. (3) Allah grants you a powerful victory/help. (4) It is He who sent down tranquillity into the hearts of believers so that they might add faith unto their faith. [The rest of the verse was omitted on the banner probably for lack of space: 'To Allah belong the soldiers of the heavens and the earth, and Allah is the Knower, the Wise.']

The inscribed band at the hoist end repeats the first three verses several times. The sword is flanked by a row of three inscribed crescents on each side. The two crescents closest to the hoist end, flanking the pommel, encircle the invocation 'O Muhammad' and contain the Qur'anic verse (*al-Ṣaff*, 61: 13): 'A victory/help there is from Allah, and a conquest is near, so give good tidings to the believers!' The inscriptions of these

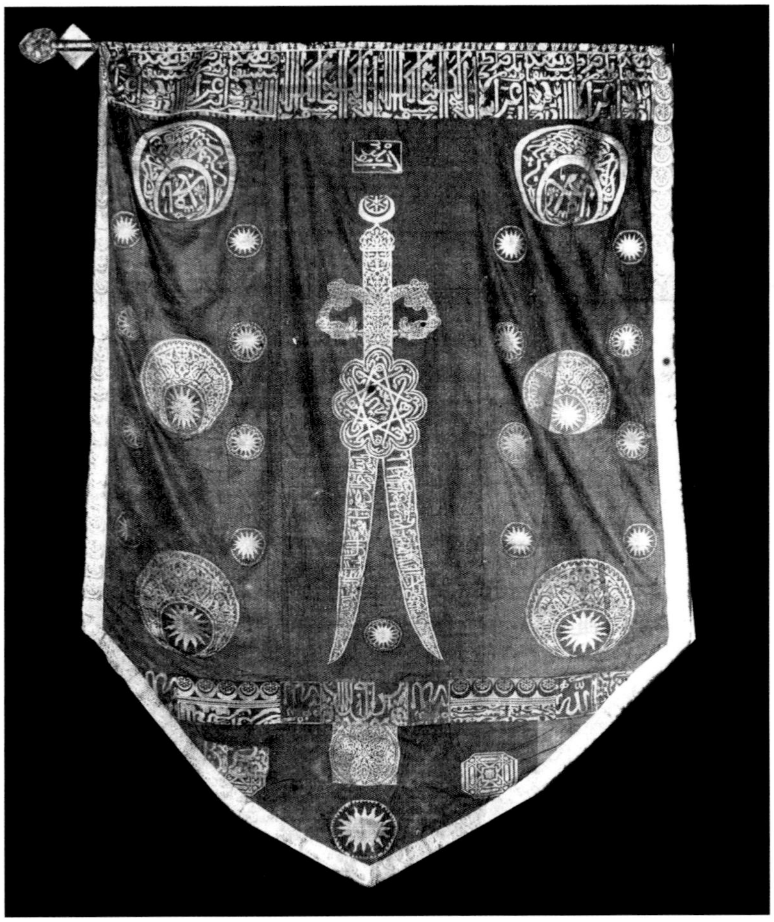

Fig.1

each other. The other four crescents contain mirror-image inscriptions of the *shahāda*: 'There is no god but Allah. Muhammad is the Messenger of Allah'.

After Selim's defeat of the Mamluks, memorabilia from the time of the Prophet Muhammad and the first caliphs that were kept in the Mamluk palace in Cairo were transferred to the imperial palace (now the Topkapı Palace) in Istanbul. The *Dhu'l-faqār* was allegedly one of them, but none of the swords currently in the Topkapı Palace collection that have been ascribed to Muhammad and the first caliphs can be reliably identified as such.[12]

The image of the two-pointed *Dhu'l-faqār* then appears on the banner of the infamous red-bearded pirate known in the multilingual milieu of 16th-century Mediterranean seafarers variously as Barba Rossa, Barba Roja, Barbe Rousse and Barbaros (d. 1546). He was appointed admiral (*ḳapudān-ı deryā*) by the Ottoman sultan Süleyman (*r.* 1520–1566) in 1533 and charged with the reorganisation and expansion of the fleet with the aim of turning the Ottomans into the dominant power in the Mediterranean. The admiral's banner bears the image of the *Dhu'l-faqār* at its centre, and an inscribed band at the hoist end with an invocation of the Prophet's name and Qur'an 61:13, as on Selim's flag (fig.2).

This banner is decorated with two more motifs to which Muslims around the Mediterranean attributed protective powers. One is the Seal of Solomon, the six-pointed star positioned between the two tips of the *Dhu'l-faqār*. The other, depicted on one side of the sword's hilt, is the Hand of Fatima, known in the Ottoman world as *Pençe-i āl-i ʿabā'* (the Palm of the Family of the Mantle) from the Persian *Panj āl-e ʿabā'* (the Five Members of the Family of the Mantle), referring to Muhammad, ʿAli, Fatima, al-Hasan and al-Husayn. Perhaps because the coupling of the Hand of Fatima with the *Dhu'l-faqār* might easily be taken to imply Shiʿi affiliation – and the Ottomans certainly wished to avoid such an implication – they are surrounded by the names of the first four caliphs, as on the replica of the *Dhu'l-faqār* made for Bayezid II. In the view of Sunni Ottoman scholars, the Safavid practice of cursing the first three caliphs in public rituals (established by Ismaʿil I) was a blasphemy that justified a call to holy war against the Safavids. Barba Rossa's tenure as admiral (1533–1546) witnessed an escalation of tensions between the two sides, which would only be eased by the peace treaty of 1555, by the terms of which the Safavid ruler Shah Tahmasp was compelled to proscribe the cursing of the caliphs in his territory. The coupling of the names of the four caliphs with iconographic references to the *Ahl al-bayt* (the Hand of Fatima and the *Dhu'l-faqār*) parallels the position of Ottoman religious policy-makers, who supported Sunni orthodoxy whilst remaining determinedly resolved not to allow the Safavids to monopolise the legacy of the *Ahl al-bayt*.

The same attitude may have informed the practice of decorating the interior of imperial mosques with large medallions bearing the names of al-Hasan and al-Husayn in addition to those of the *Rāshidūn* caliphs. These two names seem to have been included for the first time in the inscriptional programme of the Süleymaniye (1550–1558) and became standard features in later mosques built by the chief imperial architect Sinan.[13] The medallions in Sinan's mosques are similar in form to the roundels that contain the names of the *Rāshidūn* caliphs in gold letters on Barba Rossa's flag.

The banner of Barba Rossa, which today is housed in the Maritime Museum in Istanbul, used to be in the admiral's tomb next to the museum. A photograph from 1913 and a painting by the Turkish artist

Fig.2

Fig.1
Banner of Selim I, Topkapı Palace Museum, Istanbul, no.1/824

Fig.2
Banner of Barbaros Hayreddin Pasha, Maritime Museum, Istanbul, no.2964

Fig.3

Feyhaman Duran (1886–1970) show the interior of the tomb chamber with the banner. Commissioned by Barba Rossa himself from the architect Sinan and located close to the imperial dockyards, the tomb became a ceremonial site after his death. A paragraph added at the end of an undated manuscript containing the memoirs of Barba Rossa mentions that it was an established custom for newly-appointed admirals to hold a celebratory feast at Barba Rossa's tomb when they assumed their new post.[14] The text does not mention the banner inside the tomb, but the design of Barba Rossa's personal device was adopted by several later Ottoman admirals. Some of the Ottoman naval banners that were captured in battle during the late 16th and early 17th centuries depict the *Dhu'l-faqār* and bear similar inscriptions.[15] The 17th-century author Nadiri, when describing the fleet of admiral Güzelce ʿAli Pasha (d. 1621), notes that the flags flown on his ships bore the image of the *Dhu'l-faqār*, even though the double-page painting that accompanies the text does not reveal the decoration of the banners.[16]

The image of the *Dhu'l-faqār* seems to have become increasingly common on Ottoman military flags in the 17th century. This phenomenon is often explained as a consequence of the association of the Janissary corps with the Bektashi Order of dervishes, whose Shiʿi inclinations are well known. There are, however, reasons to question this assumption. For one thing, the motif appears not only on Janissary flags but also on naval banners. Another point to note is that none of the depictions of the *Dhu'l-faqār* that arise from a Bektashi context is earlier than the middle of the 18th century. Moreover, though a mythical association between Ottoman soldiers and the Bektashis – based on

Fig.3
Janissary insignia including the *Dhu'l-faqār* after L F Marsigli's *Stato militare dell'Imperio Ottomano* (1732)

Fig.4
Janissaries depicted in an album commissioned by Bartholomäus von Pezzen, *circa* 1586-1591. MS Vienna, Austrian National Library, Codex Vindobonensis 8626, plate 10

Fig.5
Delis depicted in an album commissioned by Bartholomäus von Pezzen, *circa* 1586-1591. MS Vienna, Austrian National Library, Codex Vindobonensis 8626, plate 20

anachronistic claims that the Janissary corps was established by Hacı Bektaş – was posited in some sources from the late 15th century onwards, it was contested in others.[17]

The *Dhu'l-faqār* was, in fact, just one of many Janissary insignia, the wide variety of which is demonstrated in the drawings of Count Luigi Ferdinando Marsigli from the early 18th century (fig.3).[18] An album commissioned by Bartholomäus von Pezzen, Austrian ambassador to Constantinople from 1586 to 1591, shows the Jannisaries carrying similar insignia on their processions, including not only the *Dhu'l-faqār* but also the Hand of Fatima, animals, tents and ships (fig.4).[19] Furthermore, it is not only the Janissaries who carry the *Dhu'l-faqār* motif there, but also the *deli*s, front-line warriors who were the Ottoman counterparts of the Norse *berzerks* (fig.5).

Besides being a symbol of holy war, the *Dhu'l-faqār* was put on amulets to protect soldiers from disaster, as related by Konstantin Mihailović:

> Now the heathens have small books by the name of *hama hely* [*ḥamā'il*, i.e. 'carried things' or amulets] and keep them as a sacred thing, just as we have the Holy Scripture. And they always carry them with them under the arm, and especially at war. And on them the sword *dilfficari* is painted from below; and they say that it is very helpful to them in wars.[20]

The protective powers ascribed to the *Dhu'l-faqār* are also evident in an inscribed undershirt made for sultan Murad III in order to ward off evil and protect him from his enemies (fig.6). A *Dhu'l-faqār* motif is embroidered in the middle of the shirt, standing on its hilt and pointing upwards, with the two tips of the blade framing the neckline. On both sides of the blade are written invocations to 'Ali and the well-known saying attributed to the Prophet Muhammad: 'There is no hero but 'Ali. There is no sword but *Dhu'l-faqār*'. According to a note

Fig.4

Fig.5

Fig.6

attached to the undershirt, Murad's mother Nurbanu gave it to him as a present when he came to visit her in the palace on the last day of Muharram 990 (24 February 1582).[21] In trying to understand the meaning of the *Dhu'l-faqār* motif on the sultan's undershirt, should we really be looking any further than a mother's concern for her son's health? She must have been worried about her overworked son who had recently found himself in charge of an empire that was in the midst of a grave economic crisis approaching the point of bankruptcy, and would soon necessitate a dramatic debasement of silver coinage.[22] Murad's times seemed laden with uncertainty; it is understandable that his notoriously protective mother resorted to protective amulets such as the sword of ʿAli.

If the sultan wore the *Dhu'l-faqār* to protect himself, it should not come as a surprise that the rest of the Ottoman military class did too, especially given the association of the symbol with the war for the faith. An image of the *Dhu'l-faqār* also appears in a Persian 'Book of Omens' (*Fālnāma*), which was produced in the late 16th century and must have entered the Ottoman treasury at some point before the early 18th century.[23] The lengthy interpretation accompanying the image, telling the augury seeker that his/her wish will be realised beyond doubt, highlights the downright auspicious connotations of the *Dhu'l-faqār* in the socially prevailing realm of established beliefs that many of us now tend to dismiss as superstition.

Dhu'l-faqār on a pasha's *dhahabiyya*

Banners depicting the *Dhu'l-faqār* appear in a different context in the *Veḳāyiʿ-i ʿAlī Paşa* (The Incidents of ʿAli Pasha), the early 17th-century illustrated account of the governorship of Yavuz ʿAli Pasha (d. 1604) in

Fig.6
Undershirt of Murad III, Topkapı Palace Museum, Istanbul, no.13/1135

Fig.7
Kelami, *Veḳāyiʿ-i ʿAlī Paşa* (The Incidents of ʿAli Pasha), *circa* 1603-1604. MS Istanbul, Süleymaniye Library, Halet Efendi 612, folios 26b and 14a, bound as 24b–25a

Fig.7

Egypt from 1601 to 1603, written by the poet and scribe Kelami.[24] The illustrated manuscript was produced around the time Yavuz ʿAli Pasha was appointed grand vizier in 1603.[25] It has one double-page and six single-page paintings executed in the contemporary style of the Ottoman court atelier. Four out of the first 26 folios were misplaced when the manuscript was bound or rebound.[26] All of the paintings are within the first 56 folios of the 149-folio manuscript (folios 5b, 7b-8a [bound as 9b-10a], 14a [25a], 15b [6b], 26b [24b], 32a, 56b), and illustrate the narrative portion of the work, which turns into an anthology of poems from folio 61b. Empty frames facing three of the paintings (folios 6a [8a], 13b [26b], 16a [7a]) and the use of different paper for illustrated folios suggests a lapse between the writing and illustration of the text. This complicated codicology may be explained with Yavuz ʿAli Pasha's promotion during the manuscript's production. Though the project started while he was still in Cairo and the text may have been written there, the paintings were probably added in Istanbul during his 14 months as grand vizier. The manuscript seems to have been left incomplete after his death in 1604.

The *Dhu'l-faqār* figures prominently in the fifth painting (folio 26b [24b]) (fig.7), which shows Yavuz ʿAli Pasha aboard a vessel that resembles a small galleon. He sits under a canopy at the stern accompanied by a group of men in turbans, while another group of men stand playing music in the bows. The surrounding text on the five pages that precede the painting (folios 24a [22a]-28a) tells us about a festival that Yavuz ʿAli Pasha organised on the occasion of the flooding of the river Nile, following a long Cairene tradition dating back to Fatimid times. The festivities included night-time performances by singers, musicians and various artists, for which the city was lit with torches. And for that particular occasion, Yavuz ʿAli Pasha had a *dhahabiyya* (sailing vessel) gilded and adorned for a night ride on the Nile. The governor and his distinguished guests sailed along the Nile all night, eating confectionery, listening to music and watching the city, which was alive with the lights of torches lit for the festivities along the banks. In the painting, which is a depiction of this excursion, the *dhahabiyya* appears, in imitation of the galleons of the Ottoman fleet, adorned with a huge banner hanging from its mast. The banner bears the image of the *Dhu'l-faqār* embroidered in gold. The same motif adorns the standards at the four corners of the canopy. Yavuz ʿAli Pasha came from the Malkoch-oghlu family, which produced generations of illustrious raider commanders committed to the concept of *ghazā'*. The enormous golden *Dhu'l-faqār* flying above his vessel may have served to advertise his familial identity, even though contemporary Ottoman sources hint at his aversion to warfare.[27]

When the manuscript was bound, almost certainly after the patron's death, or rebound later, this painting was coupled with another painting (folio 14a [25a]), which actually illustrates an earlier part of the text. It depicts Yavuz ʿAli Pasha seated in front of his tent near Alexandria, en route to his new post in Cairo, overseeing the execution of a criminal. Sixteen men in turbans and cloaks stand next to him. With their hands clasped respectfully on their bellies, they look sternly towards the beheaded man who lies in their midst. Curiously, the executioner who severed the head from the body is nowhere to be seen. This execution scene bears striking similarities to a series of paintings in the *Siyer-i Nebī* (Life of the Prophet) produced by the imperial atelier in 1594–1595 under the supervision of Naqqash Hasan Pasha. They show ʿAli b. Abi Talib wielding the *Dhu'l-faqār* to slay his enemies and, in one instance, a dragon, highlighting the sword's potency as an instrument of good versus evil, and of justice and vengeance against opponents of the new Muslim community. In one painting he is shown beheading ʿAtaba, a Qurayshi opponent of the Muslims (fig.8).[28] The artist, who clearly perceived the early *umma* in Ottoman imperial terms, depicted the Prophet Muhammad seated on a throne accompanied on one side by religious scholars, or officers, in turbans and cloaks, and on his other side, by an army led by ʿAli with the *Dhu'l-faqār* in hand, advancing towards the enemy. The anonymous artist who made the paintings of the *Veḳāyiʿ-i ʿAlī Paşa* may have worked with Naqqash Hasan Pasha on the *Siyer-i*

Fig.8

Fig.8
ʿAtaba slain by ʿAli b. Abi Talib at the Battle of Badr, from a 17th- or early 18th-century copy of Darir, *Siyer-i Nebī*, vol.4, based on an original from *circa* 1594–1595 that is now in a private collection. MS Istanbul, Turkish and Islamic Art Museum, T.1974, folio 253b

Nebī project, which was completed in 1595.[29] Images designed for this massive sultanic commission may have inspired the execution scene in the grand vizier's manuscript. Yet, the concept of warfare that is so prominent in the *Siyer-i Nebī* is entirely missing from the *Veḳāyiʿ-i ʿAlī Paşa*. No army is in sight in any of the paintings. In the execution scene, the pasha's entourage consists solely of civilian officers in turbans and cloaks. Even the sword that cut off the head of the condemned man is absent from the picture.

Thanks to an arguably very cunning binder, the legendary sword that beheads the enemy commander in the *Siyer-i Nebī* painting appears in the *Veḳāyiʿ-i ʿAlī Paşa* on the facing page, but in a very different context: it adorns the vessel of the pasha entertaining his guests at night. Earlier in the text Kelami compares Yavuz ʿAli Pasha's virtues to those of his revered namesake, ʿAli b. Abi Talib.[30] The adornment of the vessel with ʿAli's sword may be a visual pun. Perhaps this inspired a further pun during the binding process, achieved by rearranging the folios so that the *Dhu'l-faqār* in one scene points towards the executed man in the other scene – one which was modelled after an image of ʿAli b. Abi Talib to start with. When seen together, the two paintings encapsulate the public persona of ʿAli Pasha, whose governorship, Kelami says, brought unprecedented prosperity to Egypt as well as justice and order, raising the profile of the Ottoman sultan in the region.[31] The *Dhu'l-faqār* motifs that adorn the pasha's *dhahabiyya* thus assume a meaning that the artist does not seem to have intended, given that the original context of the folio does not have any reference to the concept of justice or the memory of ʿAli b. Abi Talib.

Conclusions

The evidence I have presented here would suggest that the Ottomans succeeded in stripping the *Dhu'l-faqār* of its Shiʿi connotations within their realm. Under the Ottomans, the *Dhu'l-faqār* motif was employed as a protective charm and military emblem by warriors on land and sea. It also transcended its military connotations and became a symbol of justice and governance, as we have seen from the illustration of an excursion enjoyed by the Ottoman governor of Egypt.

However, though the Ottoman establishment conceived of the *Dhu'l-faqār* as a non-sectarian motif, its Shiʿi connotations continued to be recognised by some marginal groups, such as the itinerant dervishes known as Abdals. Writing in 1522, Vahidi describes the Abdals, one of eight groups of dervishes whom he considers deviants from the true religion, as itinerant holy fools who went about barefoot and half naked, wearing only a felt garment secured with a wooden belt.[32] Both ʿAli's name and the outline of his sword *Dhu'l-faqār* were incised or tattooed on their chests. They carried on one shoulder a hatchet associated with Abu Muslim, the leader of the Abbasid revolt in Khurasan who was later adopted as a Shiʿi hero and whose legend was cultivated in militant millenarian movements in Iran and Anatolia, including the early Safavid state.[33] In Vahidi's view, these amulets and charms signalled that the Abdals were 'the enemies of Imam ʿAli's enemies', since they considered him their guide and cherished his descendants, the Ithna ʿashari Imams.

Paradoxical though it may appear, it was the orthodox Sunni stance of the Ottoman state that compelled the Ottomans to display the symbols of the Prophet's family in public, in order to prevent the Safavids (and their sympathisers in the Ottoman lands) from laying sole claim to the 'love of the *Ahl al-bayt*', a widespread and politically potent element of Islamic heritage. As deepening hostilities led to ever more frequent conflicts with the Safavids, the Ottomans tried to associate themselves more closely with the *Ahl al-bayt*. They did this by means of ceremonial veneration of the Prophetic memorabilia transferred from Cairo to Istanbul after Selim's defeat of the Mamluks in 1517; and the public display of symbols like the *Dhu'l-faqār*. Any supposed Shiʿi associations that such practices may have generated were refuted by juxtaposing them with invocations of the *Rāshidūn* caliphs. Just as imperial mosques were decorated with medallions inscribed with the names of Allah, Muhammad, Abu Bakr, ʿUmar, ʿUthman and ʿAli as well as those of al-Hasan and al-Husayn, so too, the memorabilia stored in the imperial palace included those of the first three caliphs as well as ʿAli, Fatima and al-Husayn. The mosque medallions were matched by the roundels inscribed with the names of the *Rāshidūn* caliphs, which surrounded the image of the *Dhu'l-faqār* on flags and banners. In this way, the Ottomans managed to neutralise the Shiʿi connotations of the 'love of the *Ahl al-bayt*' and prise the *Dhu'l-faqār* symbol from the hands of their Safavid enemies.

1 For the early history of the sword, see David Alexander, 'Dhu'l-Faqār and the Legacy of the Prophet: Mīrāth Rasūl Allāh', *Gladius*, 19 (1999), pp.157–187, 157–163. For the *Dhu'l-faqār* motif under the Ottomans, see Jane Hathaway, *A Tale of Two Factions: Myth, Memory, and Identity in Ottoman Egypt and Yemen* (Albany, 2003), pp.167–180.

2 E. Mittwoch, 'Dhū'l-Faḳār', EI2, vol.2, p.230.

3 al-Bal'amī, *Tārīkh al-Rusul wa al-Mulūk*, MS Washington DC, Freer Gallery of Art, F. 1957, undated, *circa* 1300; al-Bīrūnī, *al-Āthār al-bāqiya*, MS Edinburgh University Library, Arab 161, dated 1307–1308; Rashīd al-Dīn Faḍl Allāh, *Jāmiʿ al-tawārīkh*, MS Topkapı Palace Museum Library, H. 1653, dated 1314. See Serpil Bağcı, ''Alī in Manuscript Painting', in A. Y. Ocak, ed., *From History to Theology: 'Ali in Islamic Beliefs* (Ankara, 2005), pp.229–263, pp.236–240 and figs 2–4; Teresa Fitzherbert, *Balʿami's Tabari. An Illustrated Manuscript of Balʿami's tarjuma-yi tarikh-i Tabari in the Freer Gallery of Art, Washington (F57.16, 47.19 and 30.21)*, (Ph.D. thesis, University of Edinburgh, 2001); Priscilla Soucek, 'The Life of the Prophet: Illustrated Versions', in Soucek, ed., *Content and Context of Visual Arts in the Islamic World* (University Park, PA, 1988), pp.193–218, 195–198; Priscilla Soucek, 'An Illustrated Manuscript of al-Bīrunī's Chronology of Ancient Nations', in P. J. Chelkowski, ed., *The Scholar and the Saint: Studies in Commemoration of Abu'l-Rayhan al-Biruni and Jalal al-Din Rumi* (New York, 1975), pp.103–168; Robert Hillenbrand, 'Images of Muhammad in al-Biruni's Chronology of Ancient Nations', in R. Hillenbrand, ed., *Persian Painting from the Mongols to the Qajars: Studies in Honour of Basil W. Robinson* (London, 2000), pp.129–146.

4 MS Edinburgh University Library, Arab 161, fol.162a; Soucek, 'An Illustrated Manuscript', pp.154–155, fig.25; Hillenbrand, 'Images of Muhammad', pp.134–135, 141, fig.13.

5 Konstantin Mihailović, *Memoirs of a Janissary*, tr. Benjamin Stolz, ed. Svat Soucek (Ann Arbor, 1975), pp.6–7.

6 Ebü'l-Hayr-ı Rūmī, *Ṣaltuk-nāme*, ed. Şükrü H. Akalın (3 vols, Ankara, 1987–1990), vol.1, pp.5, 8.

7 Agah Sırrı Levend, *Ġazavāt-nāmeler ve Mihaloğlu Ali Bey'in Ġazavāt-nāmesi* (Ankara, 2000), pp.278, 300.

8 Cemal Kafadar, *Between Two Worlds: The Construction of the Ottoman State* (Berkeley, 1995), p.97.

9 Topkapı Palace Museum, no.1/384.

10 Vladimir F. Minorsky, 'The Poetry of Shāh Ismāʿīl I', BSOAS, 10, 4 (1942), pp.1006a–1053a, 1036a; *Il Canzoniere di Šāh Ismāʿīl Ḫaṭā'ī*, ed. Tourkhan Gandjei (Napoli, 1959), p.109.

11 Topkapı Palace Museum, no.1/824; Fevzi Kurtoğlu, *Türk Bayrağı ve Ay Yıldız* (Ankara, 1938), pp.76–78.

12 Alexander, 'Dhu'l-faqār and the Legacy of the Prophet', pp.178–182; Tahsin Öz, *Hırka-i Saadet Dairesi ve Emanat-ı Mukaddese* (Istanbul, 1953), pp.36–46, figs 17–35.

13 Gülru Necipoğlu, *The Age of Sinan: Architectural Culture in the Ottoman Empire* (London, 2005), pp.202, 219.

14 Murādī, *Ġazavāt-ı Ḫayreddīn Paşa (MS 2639 Universitätsbibliothek Istanbul): Kommentierte Edition mit Deutscher Zusammenfassung*, ed. Mustafa Yıldız (Aachen, 1993), p.245.

15 These banners include the admiralty banner of Müezzinzade 'Ali Pasha (d. 1571), which according to the records of the Maritime Museum in Istanbul, was captured by the Christian fleet in the battle of Lepanto in 1571 and donated to the museum by Pope Paul VI in 1946; see Rasim Ünlü, *Deniz Tarihimizde İz Bırakanlar, Türbe ve Mezarları*, 3 vols (Istanbul, 2007), vol.1, p.222. For an Ottoman flag captured by the Knights of St Stephen, see Alessandro Martinelli, 'Bandiere turche a Pisa', *Vexilla Italica*, 31, 2, n.58 (2004), pp.38–43, figs 2 and 6.

16 Nādirī, *Şehnāme-i Sulṭān 'Oṣmān Ḫān*, MS Istanbul, Topkapı Palace Library, H.1124, folios 28b-29a.

17 The late-15th-century historian, 'Aşıkpaşazade, refutes the claims that the Janissary corps was connected to the Bektashis: 'Aşıkpaşazade, *Tevārīḫ-i Āl-i 'Oṣmān* (Istanbul, 1332/1913–1914), p.205; 'Aşıkpaşazade, *Die altosmanische Chronik des 'Āşıkpaşazāde auf Grund mehrerer neuentdeckter Handschriften*, ed. Friedrich Giese (Leipzig, 1929), p.201.

18 Luigi Ferdinando Marsigli, *Stato militare dell'Imperio Ottomanno, incremento e decremento del medesimo* (The Hague and Amsterdam, 1732), vol.2, plates 20–21; Zdzislaw Zygulski, *Ottoman Art in the Service of the Empire* (New York, 1992), pp.29–32.

19 Austrian National Library, Codex Vindobonensis 8626; Alberto Arbasino, ed., *I Turchi. Codex Vindobonensis* 8626 (Parma, 1971).

20 Mihailović, *Memoirs*, pp.8–9.

21 Topkapı Palace Museum, no.13/1135; Hülya Tezcan, *Topkapı Sarayındaki Şifalı Gömlekler* (Istanbul, 2006), p.71.

22 Cemal Kafadar, 'Les troubles monétaires de la fin du xvie siécle et la prise de conscience ottomane du déclin', *Annales: Economies, societes, civilizations*, 11 (1991), pp.381–400; Şevket Pamuk, *A Monetary History of the Ottoman Empire* (Cambridge, 2000), pp.131–138.

23 Massumeh Farhad with Serpil Bağcı, *Falnama: Book of Omens* (London, 2009), p.280; MS Istanbul, Topkapı Palace Library, H. 1702, folios 31b–32a.

24 MS Istanbul, Süleymaniye Library, Halet Efendi 612; Soner Demirsoy, *Kelâmî-i Rûmî: Vekāyiʿ-i Ali Paşa [Yavuz Ali Paşa'nin Mısır Valiliği (1601–1603)]* (Istanbul, 2012).

25 Tülün Değirmenci, *Resmedilen Siyaset:* II. *Osman Devri (1618–1622) Resimli Elyazmalarında Değişen İktidar Sembolleri*, Ph.D. thesis, Hacettepe University, Ankara, 2007, pp.55–60; Emine Fetvacı, 'Enriched Narratives and Empowered Images in Seventeenth-Century Ottoman Manuscripts', *Ars Orientalis*, 40 (2010), pp.245–266, 248–252.

26 The original folio order has been reconstructed in Demirsoy's edition; see n.24 above.

27 Değirmenci, *Resmedilen Siyaset*, pp.57–59.

28 The painting, detached from the fourth volume of the work which is currently in the Chester Beatty Library in Dublin, is now in a private collection (Newport, Rhode Island, John Slocum Collection); see Zeren Tanındı, *Siyer-i Nebî: İslam Tasvir Sanatında Hz. Muhammed'in Hayatı* (Istanbul, 1984), p.34. The painting reproduced here is from a later copy of the same volume; MS Istanbul, Turkish and Islamic Art Museum (TIEM), T.1974, fol.253b; Tanındı, *Siyer-i Nebî*, plate 56.

29 Serpil Bağcı et al, *Osmanlı Resim Sanatı* (Ankara, 2006), p.209.

30 MS Istanbul, Süleymaniye Library, Halet Efendi 612, fol.10b [12b].

31 Ibid., fols 20b-21a [18b-19a], 24a [22a].

32 *Vāhidī's Menāḳıb-ı Ḫvoca-i Cihān ve Netīce-i Cān: Critical Edition and Analysis*, ed. Ahmet T. Karamustafa (Cambridge, MA, 1993), pp.7–8, 126–128 (fols 41a–43a).

33 Irène Melikoff, *Abū Muslim: le 'Porte-Hache' du Khorassan dans la tradition épique turco-iranienne* (Paris, 1962).

16

The Hand of Fatima: in search of its origins and significance

Fahmida Suleman

If you walk along the markets and jewellery quarters in any part of the Muslim world today, you will come across representations of an open hand. Some are meant to be worn as jewellery, others used as hangings (whether for the car or house), doorknockers or woven into cloth – especially on traditional bridal garments, where the motif is combined with other images such as fish and eyes (figs 1–2).[1] The open hand also appears stamped on paper talismans or engraved on hard-stone amulets that often include verses from the Qur'an, magic squares, and the names of God (*al-asmā' al-ḥusnā*) or those of holy Muslim personages.[2]

Fig.1

Muslims and Jews share a common belief in the talismanic significance of the motif and refer to it as the '*khamsa*' (five). This has acquired a number of patently Muslim religious associations over time and its nomenclature has expanded to include '*Yad Fāṭima*' or Hand of Fatima, referring to the Prophet Muhammad's daughter. Within a specifically Shiʿi context it is often called the '*Panj-i ʿAbbās*' or Hand of ʿAbbas, relating to a famous hero at the Battle of Karbala (680 AD).[3] Moreover, the *khamsa* is also identified with the five select members of the Prophet's household, his *Ahl al-bayt* or *Ahl al-kisā'* (People of the Prophet's mantle).[4] This essay examines the origins, evolution and multivalent meanings of the *khamsa* within both Sunni and Shiʿi Muslim contexts, including its association with the figure of Fatima as an expression of female piety and spirituality.

Earliest sources for the *khamsa*

The iconography of the open hand pre-dates the advent of Islam by millennia and was a universally recognised sign of divine power, protection and blessing among many ancient Near Eastern religions, as well as in Hinduism, Buddhism and among all three Abrahamic faiths.[5] In addition, the motif appears as a symbol of divine protection specifically against the 'evil eye' or 'eye of envy', a notion that has no universal distribution but was limited to Europe, North Africa, the Middle East and the Indian Subcontinent.[6] The wearing of amulets in the form of an open hand as protection against the evil eye, which arises from the human emotions of jealousy and envy, extended to the contexts of marriage and 'female reproductive experiences' such as protection during conception, pregnancy, childbirth and lactation, as well as in the domestic sphere comprising the nurture and care of children, preparation of food and protection against disease and illness. The use of such amulets often featured in societies whose livelihoods depended on the fertility of crops and herds.[7]

Fig.1
Bride wearing *khamsa*s and other charms on her headdress, Moknine, Tunisia, 1920s-1930s, photographed by G. Duchemin

Fig.2

In the ancient Near East and North Africa, the open hand was also identified with female goddesses, such as Ishtar, the supreme Mesopotamian goddess of love, fertility and war,[8] and with Tanit, the chief Punic goddess whose cult flourished in North Africa and across the Western Mediterranean.[9] Long after the fall of Carthage (146 BC), Tanit continued to be venerated in North Africa under the Latin name *Juno Caelestis* (i.e. the Roman goddess Juno). According to Rivka Gonen's study on the origins of the *khamsa* in North Africa, she and other scholars maintain that the *khamsa* developed from the iconography of the ancient cult of Tanit around the fifth–fourth centuries BC. This iconography comprised the so-called 'sign of Tanit', which was a stylised depiction of a female figure (a circular head over a triangular body with lines indicating arms and hands) that was sometimes juxtaposed with a detached and open, amuletic right hand (fig.3).[10] Gonen asserts that despite the continuous wave of foreign conquerors into North Africa, including the Romans, Byzantines and, from the seventh century onwards, the Muslims, the cult of Tanit and the iconography of her 'hand of protection' survived as a result of the persistent devotion and beliefs of the indigenous Berber populations of North Africa.[11]

'Five in your eye'

The early 20th-century publications by Edward Westermarck and Edmond Doutté remain the standard works on the use and meaning of the *khamsa* in North Africa.[12] Both scholars devote substantial sections on the belief in the evil eye and the amulets and gestures used to combat the effects of another person's malevolent intentions. As Westermarck discovered during his ethnographic research in Morocco in the late 19th to early 20th centuries:

> So firmly is the evil eye believed in, that if some accident happens at a wedding or any other feast where a person reputed to have an evil eye is present, it is attributed to him and he may have to pay damages; and if such a person looks at another's animal and it shortly afterwards dies, he is likewise held responsible for the loss.[13]

One of the many charms against the evil eye, especially within the North African context but also in the Middle East, is the use of the hand gesture of stretching out the fingers of the right hand towards the person who is suspected of having the evil eye. This gesture was often accompanied by the utterance, *Khamsa fī 'ainik!*, meaning 'Five in your eye!'[14] Other permutations of the formula containing the number five

Fig.2
Doorknockers in the form of female right hands, Sidi Bou Said, Tunisia, 2012

Fig.3

Fig.4

were equally effective, such as, *khamsa wa khamīsa* (five and little five); *'addat yeddek* (the number of your hand); or *khamsa wa khamīs* (five and Thursday), the latter phrase referring to the fifth day of the week as this was considered a propitious day for undertaking voyages, transactions and ceremonies.[15]

Thus, the number five possessed a magical value in connection with the fingers of the hand as a defence against the evil eye, and this is obviously why the amulet of the open hand came to be called a '*khamsa*' (fig.4). The question remains as to when it was ascribed the alternate name of the Hand of Fatima? According to Doutté and J. Herber the term is not an indigenous North African concept, but a European invention.[16] Neither scholar elucidates further on the matter, but perhaps they were relying on the earlier publication by Eugène Lefébure (1907) who laid the blame squarely on French colonialists for making up the term.[17] Interestingly, Westermarck does not even mention the phrase Hand of Fatima in his studies and therefore neither confirms nor denies this theory. The figure of Fatima al-Zahra' (her given epithet as 'the Radiant One') is undoubtedly revered in North African society, as Westermarck's findings repeatedly confirm. For example, in his chapter on the prevalence of *baraka* – 'a mysterious wonder-working force which is looked upon as a blessing from God' – in Moroccan society, he explains:

> There is much baraka in Fāṭimah, the name of the Prophet's daughter, and also in the names derived from it, such as Fáṭma, Fṭôma, Făṭṭôm, Fṭêṭem, Ṭâma, Ṭôma, Ṭâmů, and Ṭṭām.[18]

Consequently, married women specifically named Fatima were called upon to assist in elaborate healing rituals in that society.[19] Is it so far-fetched to conjecture that an indigenous Muslim society was responsible for the original assimilation and identification of the *khamsa* as the Hand of Fatima?

Ernest A. Wallis Budge, writing around the same time as Doutté and Herber, had no issue in accepting the phrase Hand of Fatima as indigenous to Arab society. He said,

> Among the Arabs figures and drawings of the right hand of the lady Fâṭimah, i.e. the 'Weaver,' [sic] were held to be powerful amulets... She is called 'Al-Zahra,' the 'bright blooming' (a name for Venus),

Fig.3
Funerary stele fragment of the Punic goddess Tanit including a hand, Carthage, 4th–2nd century BC, British Museum, no.1927,0922.1

Fig.4
Silver *khamsa* pendant with enamelling, Morocco, 19th century, 13 cm × 8 cm, British Museum, no.2014,6009.1

and 'Al-Batûl' i.e. 'clean maid' or 'Virgin,' even after motherhood. Muḥammad held her to be one of the four perfect women, the other being his wife, Khadîjah, Asia, the wife of Pharaoh, and the Virgin Mary. According to commentators the hand of Fâṭimah represents the whole religion of Islâm and its fundamental duties [i.e. Five Pillars of Islam]...Her hand too symbolized the family of Muḥammad, the thumb represented the Prophet himself, the first finger Fâṭimah, the second finger 'Alî her husband, the third and fourth fingers her sons Ḥasan and Ḥusain.[20]

Similarly, Jean-Henri Probst-Biraben, writing in the early 1930s, does not refute the use of the term Hand of Fatima as an indigenous phrase, but instead, provides a local legend for its origin:

Le terme de main de Fatma vient d'une légende. Fatima fille du prophète Mohammed aurait trempé sa main dans le sang pendant une bataille et l'aurait apposée sur un étendard, disant aux Musulmans: 'que ce soit votre emblème'. Le signe est autrement ancien et universel.[21]

Later scholarly attempts have been made to trace the origins of the term Hand of Fatima within a North African Muslim context, in particular during the reign of the Fatimid Shi'i caliphs of North Africa and Egypt.

The Fatimid connection

According to Rivka Gonen, the continuity of the belief and prevalence of the *khamsa* in North Africa was not only due to the endurance of the pre-Islamic beliefs of the indigenous Berbers, but also to the influence and beliefs of the Shi'i Ismaili caliphs who overthrew the last Aghlabid amir seated in Raqqada, Tunisia, in 909 with the help of their Kutama Berber supporters.[22] She argues that in most Shi'i contexts the image of the hand symbolised the omnipotent hand of Allah (*yadullāh*); thus, the new Shi'i rulers of Tunisia would have easily adopted the *khamsa* motif within their religious iconography.[23] Hence for Gonen, the ubiquitous and downward facing *khamsa* amulet in North Africa fuses together three important elements: the stylised body of the goddess Tanit; the symbol of the goddess' detached hand; and the 'hand of God' from Shi'i iconography. She concludes:

In further support of this [theory], it is significant that the feminine aspect of the goddess Tanit has been preserved in the name by which the *hamsa* is also known, i.e., 'the hand of Fatima,' she being the daughter and only direct descendant of [the Prophet] Muhammad, as well as the mother of [Imam] Husayn, through whom the Shi'ites claim their doctrine of Divine Right.[24]

Although Gonen's theory of the pre-Islamic origins of the *khamsa* derived from the cult of Tanit seems plausible, her proposition that the Fatimid Shi'a adopted and perpetuated the symbol in North Africa remains unfounded. There are three main problems with Gonen's argument. The first issue is her mistaken assumption that the hand in most Shi'i contexts is predominantly a symbol of 'the hand of God'. Secondly, she presumes that since the Fatimids were Shi'a they also understood the significance of the motif in this way.[25] However, there is no material or literary evidence attesting to the use of the *khamsa* motif in Fatimid material culture neither in North Africa nor during the dynasty's rule in Egypt (*r.* 969–1171).

The third problem is her reliance on the 1954 article published by Richard Ettinghausen on the origins of the *khamsa* imagery painted on lustre ceramics from late 13th to early 14th-century Muslim Spain. Examining the *khamsa* motifs on the so-called 'Alhambra vases' that measure over a metre high and have large, wing-shaped handles (see fig.7), Ettinghausen proposed that this iconography migrated with the Fatimids from North Africa to Egypt once they established their new capital city of al-Qahira (Cairo) in 969. He further argued that the amulet was subsequently transferred to Muslim Spain by an influx of

Fig.5

Egyptian lustre potters who gradually set up their workshops in al-Andalus, especially after the fall of the Fatimids in 1171.[26] His only material evidence for this hypothesis is a lustre bowl from the Detroit Institute of Arts with an enigmatic depiction of a large *khamsa* placed between two seated figures, which he believed was made in Fatimid Cairo in the 12th century (fig.5).[27] A tempting argument indeed; the Fatimids, a Shiʿi dynasty that traced its lineage to Fatima, the daughter of the Prophet, cultivated the Hand of Fatima as a talismanic symbol from an existing indigenous North African tradition and transferred the motif to Egypt and beyond. Unfortunately, subsequent investigations of the Detroit lustre bowl have revealed that it is not Fatimid Egyptian in origin at all, but dates to 13th-century Spain.[28]

Did the Fatimids have any connection with the Hand of Fatima? Interestingly, the great Fatimid jurist, al-Qadi al-Nuʿman (d. 974), includes a saying of the Prophet Muhammad in his *Pillars of Islam* that recognises the existence and power of the evil eye and accepts the use of certain talismans and amulets: '[The Messenger of God] said: Charms [or amulets] should not be used except in three cases – venomous bites (*ḥuma*), the evil eye (*ʿayn*), and blood which does not cease flowing.'[29] The Prophet is also said to have forbidden the use of amulets except those with Qur'anic inscriptions or the names of God.[30] Clearly, amulets and charms were used in the Fatimid period – as in other periods – but there is no literary or material evidence to demonstrate that these were in the shape of a hand or referred to as the Hand of Fatima.[31]

Muslim Spain and North Africa

The 13th-century Spanish origin of the Detroit lustre bowl is particularly pertinent to our study of the origins of the *khamsa*. Nearly eight centuries of Muslim rule in al-Andalus came to an end in 1492 when the Castilian Christians ousted the last ruler of the Nasrid dynasty from his court at Granada.[32] Around the time this bowl was produced, the Almohads (Ar. *al-Muwaḥḥidūn*), a Muslim dynasty of Berber origin, ruled over North Africa and parts of Spain (*r.* 1123–1276) whilst the Nasrids (Ar. *Banū Naṣr* or *Banu'l-Aḥmar*) governed the kingdom of Granada in southern Spain (*r.* 1232–1492).[33] Berber influence in Muslim Spain, however, began as early as the eighth century, when small numbers

Fig.6

originating in the mountainous regions of Morocco began settling in al-Andalus following the establishment of the Umayyad Dynasty of Spain (*r.* 711–1031). Subsequently, waves of North African immigrants settled in al-Andalus from the end of the tenth century, following the Umayyads' large-scale recruitment of Berber mercenaries from central and eastern Maghreb.[34] The settlement of peoples and exchange of cultures between Spain and North Africa continued to flow during the reign of the Berber Zirid dynasty, a branch of which ruled southern Spain from its seat at Granada for almost eighty years (*r.* 1013–1090) and another branch ruled *Ifrīqiya* (i.e. the eastern Maghreb) from its capital at Kairouan for significantly longer (*r.* 972–1148), until the last emir lost his kingdom to the Normans of Sicily.[35]

Given the persistence of the hand motif in early Berber culture, one may assume that the transfer and adoption of the *khamsa* motif from North Africa to Spain, and the beliefs attached to it, was a gradual process with the influx of Berber populations from eastern and central Maghreb and dating from at least the tenth century. Although it remains uncertain at what stage the iconography of a popular personal amulet was adopted by official court culture in al-Andalus, the available material evidence seems to point to the Nasrid period. Not only does the *khamsa* appear on the high status Alhambra lustre vessels discussed by Ettinghausen, but the symbol of an open right hand with palm facing up is also carefully carved in marble on the archway of the entrance to the Alhambra palace complex, the Bab al-Shariʿa (Gate of Justice/Puerta de la Justicia), which is dated to 1348 (fig.6).[36]

Fig.5
Lustre bowl with a large khamsa and seated figures. Spain, 13th century d.23.5 cm. Detroit Institute of Arts, no.26.181.

Fig.6
Marble carving over the Gate of Justice, Alhambra, Granada

This principal gate along the Alhambra's southern walled enclosure would have been a fitting location for a *khamsa* of protection.

This prophylactic belief in the *khamsa* is also apparent from the depictions of the motif on the lustre vases. A good example is the Alhambra vase housed at the State Hermitage Museum in St Petersburg, which includes an open right-handed *khamsa* on each winged-handle (fig.7). One of the *khamsa*s includes white circles that most likely represent a pair of eyes and the other has a teardrop shaped motif that may also signify an eye. The inclusion of an eye within the palm of the open hand was thought to increase the efficacy of the amulet to repel or divert the eye of envy.[37] Secondly, the smallest fingers of the *khamsa*s end with a hooked shaped nodule, which Ettinghausen and others have remarked give an overall impression that the hand itself is a stylised rendering of the word 'Allah' in Arabic and further contributes to the symbol's protective power (fig.8).[38] Thirdly, and more obviously, the lustre vases are inscribed with the Arabic words *ghibṭa* (felicity) and *'āfiya* (good health). Significantly, although the root of the word *ghibṭa* (GH-B-Ṭ) encompasses the meaning 'to envy' or 'make someone envious', the word *ghibṭa* itself also means 'to wish or desire for the happiness of another without envy'.[39] Thus, it is reasonable to surmise that within a Nasrid courtly context, these motifs also served as symbols of good fortune, prosperity and protection.

The belief in the talismanic hand in Muslim Spain seems to have pervaded not only the courtly sphere but also popular urban contexts as attested from its appearance on silver jewellery and less costly examples of glazed ceramics from the 13th and 14th centuries.[40] The scholar collector W. L. Hildburgh, cites a Spanish work of the early 15th century which mentions the pinning of small open-hand amulets on the shoulders of the clothing of children to ward off the evil eye, and these are referred to as '*gumças*' (i.e. *khamsas*).[41] There is also evidence for its acceptance as a talisman not only for Muslims and Jews, but also Christians, if one takes into account the exquisite gold pendants from Nasrid Spain that are shaped as *khamsa*s and once formed part of a necklace with a central circular pendant, now housed at the Metropolitan Museum of Art in New York (fig.9). They are exquisitely formed and decorated from gold filigree, granulation and enamelling and were undoubtedly made for an affluent Christian woman because of the inscription on the circular pendant:

AVE MARIA GRACIA PLEN[A] (HAIL MARY FULL OF GRACE).[42]

Hildburgh was the first to identify these pendants as *khamsa*s in 1955; although his suggestion has been challenged by Juan Zozaya of the Museo Arqueologico Nacional (Madrid), who argues that they are lotus blossoms, not *khamsa*s.[43] An important element of the design that Hildburgh noted (though Zozaya failed to mention) are the small enamelled crosses set within eye-shaped lozenges that decorate the *khamsa* pendants in groups of five (fig.10). The combination of crosses and the number five as another form of the *khamsa* charm against the evil eye is well documented by Westermarck who remarked that 'the [number] five is commonly represented in the form of a cross'.[44] The circular pendant is also replete with enamelled elements with small crosses, set in combinations of five.

Although the last Muslim ruler of Granada was expelled in 1492, the use of the *khamsa* amulet persisted in Spain and led to an official decree issued in 1526 to ban them all together. Presided over by the Holy Roman Emperor Charles V (d. 1558), this Grand Council of

Fig.7, 8

Figs 7–8
Alhambra vase, Nasrid Spain, 14th century, H.117 cm, State Hermitage Museum, no.F317

Figs 9–10
Elements of a necklace with *khamsa* pendants. Gold filigree, granulation and cloisonné enamel. Granada, Spain, late 15th–16th century, 8.4 cm × 5.2 cm (each *khamsa*), Metropolitan Museum of Art, no.17.190.161a-j

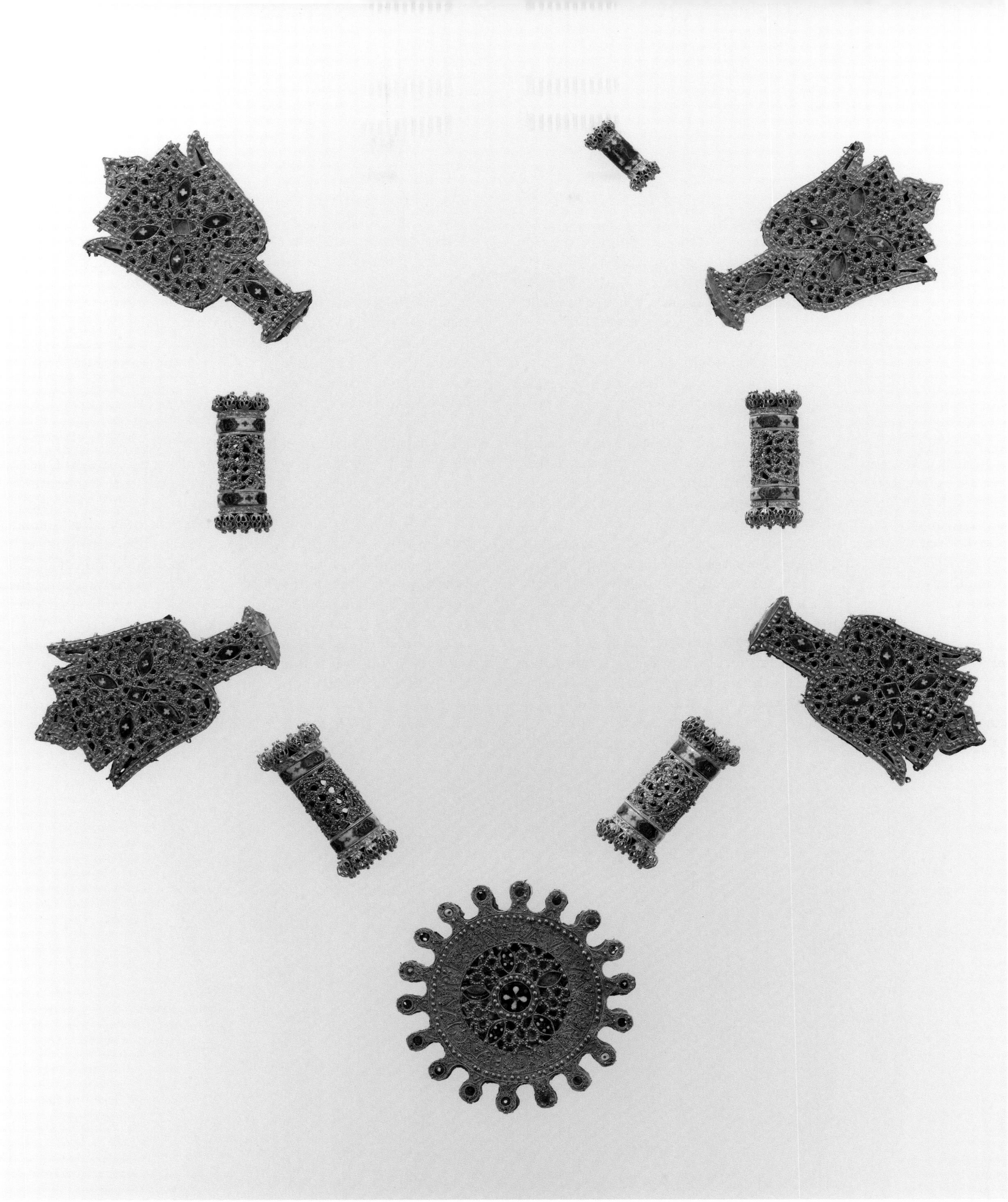

Figs 9–10

archbishops, bishops and councillors was organised for the purpose of instituting reforms for the Muslims who had recently converted to Christianity. These so-called 'Moriscos' and their children were officially banned from using *khamsa*s in any way and silversmiths were also prohibited from making *khamsa*s or crescent moons. Instead, the Moriscos were ordered to wear and use crosses where they had been previously accustomed to using such emblems.[45]

Fatima: *Sayyidat al-nisāʾ* (Queen of all Women)

While the widespread use of the *khamsa* in Spain probably came to an abrupt end after Charles v's interdiction of 1526, the amulet may have already spread to other parts of the Middle East, not only by Muslims themselves, but most likely by Sephardic Jews, many of whom were jewellers making the *khamsa*s, who were also expelled from Spain along with Muslims in 1492.[46] According to Shalom Sabar:

> The *khamsa* and the belief in the power of the number five prevailed among the Sephardim who settled in predominantly Islamic regions, such as Turkey, Syria, Palestine, Morocco, Tunisia, and Algeria. It was likewise extremely popular among the Jews in certain other Islamic lands, including Iran, Afghanistan, Bukhara, Iraq, and Kurdistan, where the Jews shared these beliefs with the local populace.[47]

Both Jews and Muslims living in these Islamic lands produced and wore jewellery, including the *khamsa*, intended for sympathetic magic, protection from the dangers of the evil eye (Heb. *ʿayin ha-raʿ*; Ar. *al-ʿayn*; Per. *bad chasm*), and to enhance fertility (fig.11).[48] What remains unclear is when the *khamsa* came to be associated with the historical figure of Fatima al-Zahraʾ (d. 632), the youngest daughter of the Prophet Muhammad and his first wife, Khadija. We may never know precisely when and in what context this occurred.

What we do know is that there existed a long-standing pan-Islamic piety towards Fatima as the role model *par excellence* of a devoted daughter, wife and mother who dedicated herself to justice and service for the happiness and security of others. Fatima's life and legend resonated with Muslim women across the globe who sought – and continue to seek – protection, intercession and support from her for themselves and for those dearest to them. Furthermore, the magical associations

Fig.11

Fig.12

with the number five, represented by the fingers of one hand, were also aligned with the reverence for the five holy members of the Prophet's Household (i.e. the *Ahl al-bayt*): Muhammad, Fatima, 'Ali, al-Hasan and al-Husayn, and it is within this broad cultural and theological environment that the transference of the *khamsa* to the Hand of Fatima took place.[49]

Several scholars have attempted with varying degrees of success to separate the historical from the legendary life of Fatima by examining a range of Sunni and Shi'i primary sources dating between the ninth and nineteenth centuries. However, as Denise L. Soufi cautions, 'one must question the idea that the historical figure of Fāṭima can be elicited from traditions already colored by partisan views [i.e. both Sunni and Shi'i viewpoints]'.[50] Nevertheless, for our purpose, it is important that we also try to ascertain some aspects of the historical and legendary Fatima in order to grasp why she has been accorded her special status by Muslims – Sunni and Shi'i alike – and how her portrayal ultimately connected her to a potent personal amulet.

Fatima was born around five years prior to the Prophet's mission and was the youngest of four sisters, Zaynab, Ruqayya and Umm Kulthum, and the only daughter to have outlived her parents and bear numerous offspring.[51] Following the Hijra (the nascent Muslim community's emigration to Medina) in 622, the sources report that the Prophet refused marriage proposals for Fatima from his two close companions, Abu Bakr and 'Umar (later the first and second caliphs, respectively), and said that he was waiting for the moment fixed by destiny. 'Ali b. Abi Talib (d. 661), the Prophet's cousin and closest companion, was reluctant to put forward his marriage proposal because of his poverty. Hence, the Prophet advised his cousin how best to raise the money for the bridal gift and was instrumental in the betrothal of his daughter to 'Ali. The sources disagree about Fatima's reaction. Some say she remained silent, which the Prophet interpreted as her consent, while according to others she protested against the arrangement until her father explained the merits of her bridegroom as a learned and wise member of the family and the first male to embrace Islam.[52] Both Sunni and Shi'i sources agree that Fatima held a special closeness to her father. For example, on her wedding night, the Prophet pre-warned the bridal pair that he would be stopping by for a visit to perform a special rite. Upon his arrival, he asked for a jar of water and after washing his hands he sprinkled the chests, shoulders and forearms of the couple and invoked God's blessings on them (fig.12).[53]

Another example that illustrates this closeness between father and daughter and exemplifies Fatima's elevated status in the nascent Muslim community is an episode in which 'Ali and Fatima had a serious dispute and the Prophet intervened on the side of his daughter. When someone from the Banu Hisham tribe proposed that 'Ali take the daughter of Abu Jahl as his second wife, Fatima was furious and took the matter to her father. Although details of the accounts differ, the gist is that the Prophet protested from the pulpit against 'Ali, as 'one who dared to propose sheltering the daughter of the Apostle of God and the daughter of the enemy of God under one roof' (the enemy of God being Abu Jahl – a Meccan leader who showed a great deal of hostility to Muslims during his lifetime).[54] The Prophet also made the following pronouncement about his daughter: 'She is indeed a part of me, and whoever offends or angers her, offends or angers me'. Sunni sources also record the Prophet saying, 'If 'Ali wishes to marry another, then he must first divorce Fatima'.[55] Needless to say, 'Ali broke off the engagement.

Some authors have deduced from this episode that monogamy was one of the privileges bestowed only upon the daughter of the Prophet.[56] As a result, 'Ali only took another wife after Fatima's death. Fatima and 'Ali had two sons, born a year apart, al-Hasan (who became the second Shi'i Imam) and al-Husayn (the third Imam and martyr of Karbala). Fatima also had two daughters, both reputed to have intrepidly confronted Umayyad authority and named after their maternal aunts, Umm Kulthum and Zaynab. Although both daughters are revered in Shi'i sources, they were not granted the privilege of being part of the holy pentad.[57]

In addition to the historical importance of her husband and sons, Muslims revere Fatima as the Prophet's beloved daughter and as the source of transmission of a number of Prophetic sayings (hadith).[58] Furthermore, Fatima is not simply portrayed as a submissive female figure in the sources. Following the Prophet's death, Fatima openly disputed the caliphate of Abu Bakr and had fierce public altercations with him and his supporter 'Umar over 'Ali's right to the caliphate and on her own right to inherit land that once belonged to her father.[59]

Fig.11
Gilded filigree *khamsa* with turquoise, 19th century, Palestine, 2.7 × 2 cm, British Museum, AS1966,01.440

Fig.12
The Prophet Muhammad holding the hands of Fatima and Imam 'Ali, Tehran, about 1850. Ink, opaque watercolour and gold on paper, 46.4 × 28.1 cm, Aga Khan Museum, AKM116

According to most sources, Fatima subsequently shunned Abu Bakr and instructed ʿAli that the caliph was not allowed to attend her burial.[60] She died in her late twenties, only a few months after the Prophet, and was buried secretly and at night according to her wishes. Some sources also attest that ʿAli and the rest of the Banu Hashim gave their oath of allegiance to the caliph Abu Bakr only after Fatima's death in order to reconcile the rift within the Muslim community.[61]

From about the tenth century onwards, Shiʿi writers promulgated stories and accounts about Fatima that elevated her status to legendary and even cosmic significance. Although not an Imam herself, she was considered infallible (*maʿṣūm*) and one who possessed the power of intercession (*shafāʿa*) – eschatological privileges of the same order as those attributed to the Prophet and the Imams.[62] She is believed to have the role of *Sayyidat al-Nisāʾ* (Queen of all Women), which will be fully manifested on the Day of Judgement when she acts as an intercessor for those who loved her and her family.[63] According to one version recorded by Bess A. Donaldson (d. 1974) during her missionary work in Iran from 1910–1940:

> [On the Day of Resurrection] Fatima tells the women that all those who have wept for her son Ḥusain, and have kept their tears, will have great merit and will go to heaven, then the women take hold of the fringe of her garment…and away they will go like a flash of lightning across the bridge of Ṣiráṭ, 'which is narrower than a hair and sharper than a razor's blade.' The bad will drop off and fall into hell, but the good will be able to hold on and will be carried across safely. Muhammad will perform the same service for the men…[64]

Shiʿi sources attribute several miracles to her including the details of her conception. For example, Fatima's origin was from an apple in heaven that the Prophet Muhammad had eaten on his miraculous night journey (*miʿrāj*), which then became the 'water of his loins'. This fruit had been previously touched by the sweat and plume from Angel Gabriel's wing and for this reason the Prophet always said Fatima was a celestial being in human form, and emitted the perfume of Paradise.[65] In her exhaustive study of the portrayal of Fatima in early Muslim sources, Denise Soufi concludes that because Fatima is venerated by medieval Muslims as the manifestation of the feminine ideal, an infallible member of the *Ahl al-bayt* and as the feminine counterpart to the Imams, she is ultimately,

> [F]urther out of reach as a role model for Muslim women than the Imams are for Muslim men…[Hence] it is not the life and person that inspired her veneration; rather, it is her function: she is the only one of the Prophet's children to leave a continuing line of descendants.[66]

Here, I would tend to disagree with Soufi on one important matter; Fatima may be venerated for her function as the progenitor of succeeding Imams after Imam ʿAli, and as a member of the Prophet's *Ahl al-bayt*, but, as we all recognise, Islamic history and the institutionally prescribed beliefs and rituals of Muslim believers of all sects have always been formulated and written down from a predominantly male perspective. Hence, if we want to understand the true meaning of Fatima's role in Muslim piety, we must read the official sources in tandem with ethnographic accounts of her position in female ritual and practice. In this way, the stories recorded about Fatima's daily trials, the injustices inflicted upon her following the Prophet's death and her life of poverty make her a very real and accessible role model for many Muslim women.

Fatima's special role in female piety and ritual

There are several episodes from Fatima's life that attest to the domestic hardship she faced as daughter of the Prophet and wife of ʿAli. A few are notable as they mention her hands. She is described as 'passing on what her father taught her in the midst of an over-busy life; with blistered hands from grinding corn, pacifying the children with one hand while keeping the grindstone turning with the other' and that the Prophet was accustomed to visiting his daughter at home and kissing her hands.[67] On one occasion, during the early years of her marriage, Fatima approached her father for domestic help to ease her burden at home. The Prophet denied her a housemaid, but gave her a prayer to recite instead:

> The *tasbīḥ* [litany/prayer] of Fāṭima, as reported to us on the authority of ʿAlī is as follows: One of the foreign kings sent slaves to the Messenger of God. So I told Fāṭima to ask for a servant from him…The Messenger of God told her, 'O Fāṭima, I shall give you

> something better than that…After every prayer declare God's greatness [i.e. to utter *Allāhu akbar* (God is great)] thirty-three times; and praise Him [i.e. to say *al-ḥamdu lillāh* (Praise be to God)] thirty-three times; and extol Him [i.e. to say *subḥāna 'llāh* (Glory be to God)] thirty-three times. Thereafter end [your orisons] by saying *lā ilāha illa 'llāh* (there is no deity other than Allah). This will be [for the utterer] better than the world and what it contains, and better than what you (O Fāṭima) desire!'…[Henceforth, Fatima] made this *tasbīḥ* a fixed practice for herself after every prayer, and thus the orison was named after her.[68]

The custom of reciting the *tasbīḥ* of Fatima is practised today by both Shiʿi and Sunni Muslims around the world, often for the purpose of alleviating personal difficulties. Therefore, by reciting Fatima's litany, the believer is relying on the power of the prayer that was given to her in order to reap similar benefits. It is also believed that the recitation of Fatima's litany following the mandatory prayer results in God's forgiveness of one's sins, and thus she indirectly plays the role of intercessor.[69] The *Ṭibb al-a'imma*, a manual of Islamic medicine compiled in the ninth century and attributed to the early Shiʿi Imams, also prescribes the recitation of Fatima's *tasbīḥ*, together with specific potent Qur'anic verses, for the treatment of the weakness of the body, and cites the authority of Imam Jaʿfar al-Sadiq (d. 765).[70] In another passage, Imam Jaʿfar recommends the recitation of direct appeals for help from Allah, the Prophet, Imam ʿAli and Fatima for treatment against the evil eye (*al-naẓar wa al-ʿayn*), ailments of the belly and migraine:

> Al-Ṣādiq, peace be upon him, said: When you have performed the obligatory prayer, stretch out your hands together to the heavens and say humbly and submissively: 'I take refuge in Your Sublimity, Your Power, Your Magnificence, and Your Sovereignty, from what I suffer. O my Succour, O Allah, O my succour, O Messenger of Allah, O my succour, O Amīr al-Mu'minīn, O my succour, O Fāṭima, daughter of the Messenger of Allah, help me.' Then pass your right hand over your head (*al-hāma*) and say: 'O He in Whose trust is what is in the heavens and what is in the earth calm what is in me by Your Strength and Your Power; bless Muḥammad and his family and calm what is in me.'[71]

The connection made between the intercession of Fatima and members of the *Ahl al-bayt* for treatment against the evil eye and one's physical ailments is thus a long-standing Shiʿi tradition that can be traced back to at least the ninth century, if not earlier. There are, in addition, many rituals that are performed exclusively by women, often transcending the Sunni – Shiʿi divide, in which Fatima alone acts as a direct intercessor for believers. We have already mentioned Westermarck's account of the healing rituals in early 20th-century Moroccan society that required the assistance of married women called Fatima to perform the rite effectively. Similarly, Louis Massignon refers to childbirth rituals practised by some Qizilbash Turkmen tribes during which the midwife touches the expectant mother with an instrument and recites: 'This is not my hand, it is the hand of Fatima'.[72] Noor Kassamali's more recent research on the role of Fatima in healing, birthing and votive rituals amongst immigrant Muslims in Boston, United States, reveals a number of exclusively female practices conducted by women from Iran, Pakistan, India, Tanzania, Somalia and Uzbekistan, which invoke the assistance of Fatima.[73] Notably, some of these rituals take place without the knowledge of male members of the household.

A final example of a ritual practice from contemporary Iran underscores the point that the historical and legendary figure of Fatima remains undeniably accessible to Muslim women who rely on her example and intercession to subvert their customarily subservient social positions within a male-dominant religious and cultural hierarchy.[74] The ritual, known as the *sofreh-e nazri* (a ceremonial votive meal in honour of a holy person) usually forbids male participation and is therefore a feminised religious rite for Iranian women.[75] There are many types of *sofreh*s, each honouring an important Shiʿi figure (male or female), who in turn will grant the hostess her desired wish, or offer her hope and comfort during her time of crisis or need. Even guests of *sofreh*s can make a vow to host another votive meal in honour of the same saint should their prayers be answered.[76]

There is indeed a votive meal entitled *sofreh-ye Fāṭima al-Zahrā'*, which usually serves the purpose of attaining peace of mind, being able to repay debts, regain health from sickness and find the means to make a religious pilgrimage.[77] According to Faegheh Shirazi's study of this *sofreh*, the hostess must make her intentions plain from the start

Fig.13

by stating, 'Oh Fatima, I seek your help in fulfilling [statement of desire].' An interesting detail about this votive meal is that it is arranged over three consecutive Thursdays. On the first two occasions, the hostess measures around half a kilo of flour in a green cloth sack and hangs it above her doorway so that she can pass under it and gain *baraka* (divine blessing) from it. She repeats this on the third Thursday and uses a portion of the flour to cook a dish known as *kāchi* for the guests. *Kāchi* is a kind of semi-sweet halva made of flour, butter, sugar, rose water, saffron and turmeric, and is customarily prepared for pregnant women or new mothers.[78] Once cooked, the *kāchi* is poured in a bowl and covered with a clean, white cloth and placed in a room together with other items including sweets, bread, fresh herbs and fruit, sweet drinks and a large melon. After the guests arrive around noon, the sermon of the *Panj tan*, or five holy ones (i.e. the *Ahl al-bayt*) is recited and then the *kāchi* is revealed to the guests. Significantly, at this point, guests may have visions of the handprint of Fatima – symbolising the *Panj tan* (fig.13). Everyone must taste the *kāchi* in order to reap the benefits of the *baraka* and then the remaining food is consumed. Men and boys are forbidden from tasting this food.[79]

A more simplified votive offering to Fatima is called the *ḥalva-e Fāṭima al-Zahrā'*, in which a woman cooks a sweet halva dessert and distributes it to other women. If her wish is fulfilled, she vows to prepare the same halva at least once a year to express her gratitude and honour her intercessor.[80] Shirazi cites a number of other *sofreh*s to venerate and appeal to different members of the Prophet's family. Although they are not directly in honour of Fatima, some of them require the participation of girls and women named Fatima to increase the efficacy of the ritual.[81] As Shirazi eloquently concludes, the *sofreh* is an important part of Iranian women's spirituality, offering them comfort, community and an opportunity to participate in their religion in a way that is open to them, since most leadership roles are not.[82]

Conclusions

The belief and use of the *khamsa* amulet originates from an ancient North African context and its well-established meanings were supplemented with Islamic notions and principles, producing a multivalent symbol. The *khamsa* in Muslim contexts is first and foremost an amulet against the evil eye and a symbol of divine providence and power. For some it also signifies the holy pentad of the Prophet's household (*Ahl al-bayt*, *Āl-i ʿabā'*, or *Panj tan*), and the Five Pillars of Islam. For some women, it also represents the Hand of Fatima, a symbol of protection, personal support and feminine spirituality.[83]

The historical accounts and narratives about Fatima may have played an insignificant role in the development of official Muslim

Fig.13
Silver *khamsa* pendant with incised decoration, Morocco, 19th century, 6.5 cm × 3.5 cm, British Museum, 2014,6009.2

canon and religious practice. Nevertheless, because they were propagated through popular oral or hagiographic literature, they had a profound impact on the development of popular piety towards the figure of Fatima, especially among female Muslim adherents. This intense belief in Fatima's ability to act as an intercessor and guardian, particularly for women – both in this world and the next – would have facilitated the smooth adaptation of the talismanic *khamsa* as the Hand of Fatima. In this respect, Fatima's role has often been compared to that of the Virgin Mary, a fascinating discussion that is beyond the scope of this essay.[84] Another important expression of Shi'i ritual that we have not touched upon is Fatima's veneration and pervasive presence as part of the *ta'ziya* plays and *rowzeh khānī* recitations during the annual Muharram commemorations when key episodes of her personal suffering are retold alongside the narration of the tragic events at Karbala.[85] In Hyderabad, Deccan, a large decorated standard called *Bībī ka 'alam* (i.e. Fatima's standard), made of gold with pouches full of diamonds suspended as earrings, is carried on a caparisoned elephant as part of the climax of the all-male 'Ashura' processions.[86] It is said to house a fragment of the wooden plank on which her corpse lay whilst 'Ali performed Fatima's final ablutions before burial, signifying her spiritual presence and the continuation of her memory in the hearts of men and women alike.

1 I wish to express my deepest thanks to my colleague at the BM, St John Simpson, for his comments and suggestions on an earlier draft of this essay. For good examples see Khalid El Gharib, *Le Main au Maroc/The Hand in Morocco* (Paris and Casablanca, 2012); D. Champault and A. R. Verbrugge, *La main: Ses figurations au Maghreb et au Levant (Catalogues du Musée de l'Homme)* (Paris, 1965); and Rudolf Kriss and Hubert Kriss-Heinrich, *Volksglaube im Bereich des Islam: Amulette, Zauberformeln, und Beschwörungen* (Wiesbaden, 1962).

2 Francis Maddison and Emilie Savage-Smith, *Science, Tools & Magic. Part One: Body and Spirit, Mapping the Universe. Nasser D. Khalili Collection of Islamic Art, vol.12* (London, 1997), pp.140–141.

3 For the 'Hand of 'Abbas' see Bess Allen Donaldson, *The Wild Rue: A Study of Muhammadan Magic and Folklore in Iran* (London, 1938), p.208.

4 For an explanation of the hadith of the Prophet's Mantle, see the introduction to this volume.

5 E. A. Wallis Budge, *Amulets and Superstitions* (Oxford, 1930), pp.467–471; Frederick Mathewson Denny, 'Hands', *Encyclopedia of Religion*, vol.6, Lindsay Jones, ed., (2nd ed., Farmington Hills, MI, 2005), pp.3769–3771; J. A. MacCulloch, 'Hand', *Encyclopaedia of Religion and Ethics*, vol.6, James Hastings, ed., (Edinburgh, 1913), pp.492–499; Richard Ettinghausen, 'Notes on the Lusterware of Spain', *Ars Orientalis*, 1 (1954), pp.149–150.

6 Belief in the 'evil eye' is altogether absent in East Asia, Siberia, Western and Southern Africa, most of Aboriginal America and all of Oceania. See Rivka Gonen, 'The Open Hand: On the North African *Hamsa* and Its Sources', *The Israel Museum Journal*, 12 (1994), p.47. In early Mesopotamia, amulets in the shape of an open hand or clenched fist date from the 4th–3rd millennium BC onwards. James Hall, *Illustrated Dictionary of Symbols in Eastern and Western Art* (London, 1994), p.125.

7 Diane Apostolos-Cappadona, 'Discerning the Hand-of-Fatima: An Iconological Investigation of the Role of Gender in Religious Art', in Amira El-Azhary Sonbol, ed., *Beyond the Exotic: Women's Histories in Islamic Societies* (Syracuse, NY, 2005), pp.354–356; Alan Dundes, ed., *The Evil Eye: A Casebook* (New York, 1981); Siegfried Seligmann, *Der Böse Blick und Verwandtes. Ein Beitrag zur Geschichte des Aberglaubens aller Zeiten und Völker* (Berlin, 1910); Frederick Thomas Elworthy, *The Evil Eye* (London, 1895).

8 For Ishtar see, Diane Apostolos-Cappadona,

'Hand-of-Ishtar', *Encyclopedia of Women in Religious Art* (London, 1996).

9 Carole Mendleson, *Catalogue of Punic Stelae in the British Museum* (London, 2003).

10 Gonen also discusses how the Canaanite/Phoenician cult of Tanit was transferred to North Africa following the settlement of the Phoenicians (i.e. Punes, as the Romans called them) along the western Mediterranean beginning in the ninth century BC. Gonen, 'Open Hand', pp.50ff. See also, Champault and Verbrugge, *La main*, pp.30–31; and Edward Westermarck, *Pagan Survivals in Mohammedan Civilization* (Amsterdam, 1973), p.34.

11 For her argument and sources see, Gonen, 'Open Hand', p.51.

12 Edmond Doutté, *Magie & Religion dans L'Afrique du Nord* (Algeria, 1908), esp. pp.317ff; Edward Westermarck conducted his research in Morocco between 1898–1926 and published a number of articles and books on the topic including, 'The Magic Origin of Moorish Designs', *Journal of the Anthropological Institute of Great Britain and Ireland*, 34 (1904), pp.211–222; and *Ritual and Belief in Morocco* (2 vols., London, 1926), esp. vol.1, pp.414ff. Also relevant is the 1927 article by J. Herber, 'La Main de Fathma', *Hespéris*, 7 (1927), pp.209–219.

13 Westermarck, *Ritual and Belief*, vol.1, p.414.

14 Ibid., p.445. Sometimes uttered, '*Khamsa 'alà 'ainek!*' – 'Five on your eye!' The hand gesture is used in Pakistan, although it is accompanied by a curse (*la'nat*) in Urdu.

15 Doutté, *Magie & Religion*, p.327; Westermarck, *Ritual and Belief*, vol.1, p.447; Westermarck, 'Magic Origins', p.213; 'Khamsa', *EI2*, vol.4, p. 1009.

16 Herber, 'Main de Fathma', p.209, n.1; Doutté, *Magie & Religion*, p.326. It appears that later scholars accept this as fact. See Pessah Shinar, 'Magic and Symbolism in North-African Jewellery and Personal Adornment', in Na'ama Brosh, ed., *Jewellery and Goldsmithing in the Islamic World* (Jerusalem, 1987), p.133.

17 Eugène Lefébure, 'Le main de Fatma', *Bulletin de la Société de géographie d'Alger et de l'Afrique du Nord*, 12 (1907), p.412. In fact, he claimed that French colonialists called it many names including Hand of Fatima, Hand of 'Aisha' and Hand of Mary.

18 Westermarck, *Ritual and Belief*, vol.1, pp.35 and 140.

19 Ibid., p.330.

20 Budge, *Amulets and Superstitions*, p.469.

21 My translation: "The term hand of Fatima comes from a legend. Fatima daughter of the Prophet Muhammad, having dipped her hand in blood during a battle, applied it onto a banner and proclaimed to the Muslims 'that is your emblem'. Otherwise the sign is old and universal." Probst-Biraben's main aim in this article was to refute Herber's 1927 article in which he argued that the Hand of Fatima is a phallic symbol. J. H. Probst-Biraben, 'La main de Fatma et ses antécédents symboliques', *Revue Anthropologique*, 43 (1933), p.370, n.1.

22 Gonen, 'Open Hand', pp.51–53.

23 Ibid., pp.53–55.

24 Ibid., p.55.

25 Gonen cites Ettinghausen's article, 'Lusterware of Spain', but misunderstands the symbolism of the hand for the Shi'a as elaborated by him. Ettinghausen maintains that the hand is a multivalent symbol in Shi'i contexts, comprising the 'hand of 'Ali' (in Iraq, Iran and Syria) and 'the hand of 'Abbas' (in Iran). He also goes on to say that the hand may also possess apotropaic qualities for many Muslims because of the Qur'anic concept of 'the divine hand as the fountainhead of power and bounty' combined with the magical character of the number five. See his, 'Lusterware of Spain', pp.150–151.

26 Ettinghausen,'Lusterware of Spain', pp.133–156. For the Alhambra vase with a *khamsa* see, Jerrilynn D. Dodds, *Al-Andalus: The Art of Islamic Spain* (New York, 1992), pp.356–357.

27 Ettinghausen, 'Lusterware of Spain', pp.153–154.

28 For the history of the dynasty see, M. Shatzmiller, 'al-Muwaḥḥidūn', *EI2*, vol.7, pp.801–807.

29 al-Qāḍī al-Nu'mān, *The Pillars of Islam. Da'ā'im al-Islām of al-Qāḍī al-Nu'mān. Vol. 2: Mu'āmalāt: Laws Pertaining to Human Intercourse* (New Delhi, 2004), A. A. A. Fyzee, trans., revised and annotated by I. K. Poonawala, p.124.

30 Ibid., pp.124–125.

31 See the section on amuletic jewellery in S. D. Goitein, *A Mediterranean Society: The Jewish Communities of the Arab World as Portrayed in the Documents of the Cairo Geniza. Volume IV: Daily Life* (Berkeley, CA, 1983), pp.218–219. See also Goitein's suggestion that one piece of jewellery referred to in the Geniza as a '*mukhammas*' may represent the *khamsa*, though he cautiously added: 'we must wait for actual finds from the Fatimid period for confirmation'. Ibid, p.215.

32 Muslim rule over the Iberian Peninsula began in 711 with the Umayyad caliphate of al-Andalus (*r.* 711–1031). What constituted 'al-Andalus' gradually shifted over time with the protracted disintegration of Islamic Spain until, at last, it came to refer solely to the kingdom of Granada. See E. Lévi-Provençal, et al., 'al-Andalus', *EL2*, vol.1, pp.486–503.

33 Although Shatzmiller explains that Almohad authority was never completely established in Spain and their defeat at Las Navas de Tolosa (1212) loosened their hold on Spanish towns and rural areas, and marked the beginning of their decline. M. Shatzmiller, 'al-Muwaḥḥidūn', *EL2*, vol.7, esp. pp.802. See also, J. D. Latham, et al., 'Naṣrids', *EL2*, vol.7, pp.1020–1029.

34 Lévi-Provençal, 'al-Andalus: Population of al-Andalus', p.490.

35 Amin Tibi, 'Zīrids', *EL2*, vol.11, pp.513–516.

36 Built during the reign of the Nasrid ruler Yusuf I (*r.* 1333–1354). For a plan of the site and precise location of the Gate of Justice see Sheila Blair and Jonathan Bloom, *The Art and Architecture of Islam* 1250–1800 (New Haven, CT, 1995), pp.124–125.

37 Shinar, 'Magic and Symbolism', pp.133, 135; Champault and Verbrugge, *La main*, pp.36–37.

38 Ettinghausen, 'Lusterware of Spain', p.153.

39 See '*ghibṭa*' in J. G. Hava, *Al-Farā'id Arabic-English Dictionary* (Fifth ed., Beirut, 1982).

40 See the silver bracelet from the Almohad period illustrated in, *El Tresor d'època Almohade* 1203–1229 (Mallorca, 1991), p.25, cat. no.7; For ceramics see, W. L. Hildburgh, 'Image of the Human Hand as Amulets in Spain', *Journal of the Warburg and Courtauld Institutes*, 1955 (18), p.73; and Anna McSweeney, *The Green and the Brown: A Study of Paterna Ceramics in Mudéjar Spain*. Ph.D. Thesis, University of London, School of Oriental and African Studies, 2012.

41 Hildburgh, 'Image of the Human Hand', p.74. He cites the 15th-century *Tratado de el aojo ó de fascinación*.

42 Inv. no. 17.190.161. Dodds, *Al-Andalus*, pp.302–303.

43 Hildburgh, 'Image of the Human Hand', p.74. Hildburgh's identification was disputed by Zozaya in Dodds, *Al-Andalus*, pp.302–303.

44 Westermarck, *Ritual and Belief*, vol.1, pp.450–452; Westermarck, 'Magic Origin', pp.213–214. The inclusion of crosses on a Christian piece of amuletic jewellery would have, of course, also served as a symbol of the crucifixion.

45 Hildburgh, 'Image of the Human Hand', p.77; Apostolos-Cappadona, 'Discerning the Hand-of-Fatima', p.357. Apostolos-Cappadona claims that at this time they were 'known as the Hand-of-Fatima', but I was unable to locate this in the original text. See Francisco Bermúdez de

Pedraza, *Antiguedad y Excelencias de Granada* (Madrid, 1608), Book 1, Chapter x, pp.17ff. I wish to thank Maria de Montserrat Rodriguez-Marquez for her assistance in translating relevant passages from this work.

46 Some Jewish jewellers may have chosen to convert to Catholicism (the 'Conversos') like the former-Muslim Moriscos. Ester Muchawsky-Schnapper, 'Jewelry Smithing', *Encyclopedia of Jews in the Islamic World* (Leiden, 2010), vol.3, p.22–25; Shinar, 'Magic and Symbolism', p.134. Although Muchawsky-Schnapper suggests that Jewish goldsmiths in Morocco are believed to be descendants of Spanish exiles, it is more likely that there were Jewish goldsmiths in North Africa long before 1492.

47 Shalom Sabar, 'Khamsa', *Encyclopedia of Jews in the Islamic World* (Leiden, 2010), vol.3, p.144.

48 Shalom Sabar, 'Amulets', *Encyclopedia of Jews in the Islamic World* (Leiden, 2010), vol.1, p.202.

49 See the discussion in the introduction of this volume on who constituted the *Ahl al-bayt*.

50 Denise L. Soufi, *The Image of Fāṭima in Classical Muslim Thought*. Unpublished Ph.D. dissertation (Princeton, NJ, 1997), p.30. Other important studies with key bibliographies include: Laura Veccia Vaglieri, 'Fāṭima', *EI2*, vol.2, pp.841–850; Mohammad 'Ali Amir-Moezzi and Jean Calmard, 'Fāṭema. I and II.', *EIR*, vol.9, pp.400–404; and Bärbel Beinhauer-Köhler, *Fatima bint Muhammad Metamorphosen einer frühislamischen Frauengestalt* (Wiesbaden, 2002). I wish to thank Jeanette C. Fincke for her assistance in translating relevant sections discussing the Hand of Fatima amulet from the latter work.

51 Vaglieri, 'Fāṭima', pp.841–842.

52 Ibid., p.842; Soufi, *Image of Fāṭima*, pp.33–38.

53 Vaglieri, 'Fāṭima', pp.842–843.

54 Ibid., pp.842–843; Soufi, *Image of Fāṭima*, p.51–56; Amir-Moezzi, 'Fāṭema', p.400.

55 Vaglieri, 'Fāṭima', p.843; Soufi, *Image of Fāṭima*, pp.54, 65–66.

56 Vaglieri, 'Fāṭima', p.843; Soufi, *Image of Fāṭima*, p.54.

57 See the discussion in the introduction on the 'People of the Prophet's Mantle'.

58 Soufi, *Image of Fāṭima*, pp.69–74.

59 Vaglieri, 'Fāṭima', p.844; For the different accounts of these events see Soufi, *Image of Fāṭima*, pp.82–116.

60 Vaglieri, 'Fāṭima', pp.844–845; Soufi, *Image of Fāṭima*, p.123; p.

61 Muḥammad b. Jarīr al-Ṭabarī, *The History of al-Ṭabarī (Ta'rīkh al-rusul wa'l-mulūk). Volume IX: The Last Years of the Prophet*. Ismail K. Poonawala, trans., (New York, 1990), pp.196–198.

62 For details see Vaglieri, 'Fāṭima', pp.845–848; Soufi, *Image of Fāṭima*, pp.153ff.; Amir-Moezzi, 'Fāṭema', pp.400–402.

63 Soufi, *Image of Fāṭima*, pp.180–190.

64 Donaldson, *Wild Rue*, p.77.

65 Vaglieri, 'Fāṭima', p.847; Amir-Moezzi, 'Fāṭema', p.400.

66 Soufi, *Image of Fāṭima*, pp.iv, 2, 204–207.

67 Charis Waddy, *Women in Muslim History* (London, 1980), p.50; Soufi, *Image of Fāṭima*, pp.58, 68–69.

68 al-Qāḍī al-Nu'mān, *The Pillars of Islam. Da'ā'im al-Islām of al-Qāḍī al-Nu'mān. Vol. 1: Acts of Devotion and Religious Observances* (New Delhi, 2002), A. A. A. Fyzee, trans., revised and annotated by I. K. Poonawala, pp.210–211; Soufi, *Image of Fāṭima*, pp.57–58.

69 Ibid., pp.210–211. According to other Companions of the Prophet, he taught Fatima several supplications in addition to her *tasbīḥ*, including one that would always be answered. Soufi, *Image of Fāṭima*, p.73.

70 Islamic *Medical Wisdom: The Ṭibb al-a'imma*, Batool Ispahany, trans., and Andrew J. Newman, ed., (London, 1991), pp.76–77.

71 Ibid., pp.90–91.

72 Louis Massignon, 'La notion du voeu et la dévotion musulmane à Fāṭima', in *Studi orientalistici in onore di Giorgio Levi Della Vida*, vol.2 (Rome, 1956), p.112.

73 Noor Kassamali, 'Healing Rituals and the Role of Fatima', in Susan Sered, ed., *Religious Healing in Boston: Body, Spirit, Community* (Cambridge, MA, 2004), pp.43–45. Some of the participants also call upon the assistance of other key figures including Eve, Khadija, Hagar, Mary, and other female members of the Prophet's family. On the importance of Fatima for Chinese Muslim women see Elisabeth Allès, 'China: Fāṭima Day', *Encyclopedia of Women and Islamic Cultures*, vol.5, Suad Joseph, ed., (Leiden, 2006), pp.357–358.

74 I am paraphrasing Noor Kassamali, 'Healing Rituals', p.45.

75 Faegheh Shirazi, 'The Sofreh: Comfort and Community among Women in Iran', *Iranian Studies*, 38/2 (2005), pp.295–296. All of my references to this ritual are taken from Shirazi's article.

76 Ibid., p.295.

77 Ibid., p.305.

78 Ibid., p.298, n.18.

79 For the full details of this sofreh see Shirazi, 'The Sofreh', pp.305–306.

80 Ibid., pp.306–307.

81 Shirazi, 'The Sofreh', pp.299–302.

82 Ibid., p.309.

83 For a discussion on the Hand of Fatima within a broader context of women's ritual and religion see Apostolos-Cappadona, 'Discerning the Hand-of-Fatima', pp.357–359.

84 On this topic see Jane Dammen McAuliffe, 'Chosen of All Women: Mary and Fāṭima in Qur'ānic Exegesis', *Islamochristiana*, 7 (1981), pp.19–28; and Susan Sered, 'Rachel, Mary, and Fatima', *Cultural Anthropology*, 6/2 (1991), pp.131–146.

85 Soufi, *Image of Fāṭima*, pp.127–149.

86 Calmard, 'Fāṭema', p.403.

Part 5: Ritual expressions

17

Lasting elegy: Shiʿi art and architecture

Peter J. Chelkowski

Introduction

Shiʿi art and architecture is primarily devoted to popular beliefs and rituals. It is remarkable to note the breadth, depth and richness of these expressions. From painting and graphic design to the performing arts and architecture, Shiʿi artistic achievements are notable for their range and for their powerful ability to impact not only religious, but also social and political attitudes. This essay provides a broad survey of the breadth and richness of Ithna ʿashari Shiʿi artistic and ritual expressions. It begins with an exploration of the differences between Indian and Iranian ritual observances and moves to a comparison of Shiʿi monumental architecture in the two regions. These comprise *ʿāshūrkhāna*s and *imāmbārā*s of the subcontinent, with specific focus on the Great Imambara at Lucknow, and the *takiya*s and *Ḥusayniyya*s of Iran, with brief mention of the monumental Takiyeh Dowlat in Iran. The essay then shifts to a discussion on the observances held in these types of buildings, including the ritual of *rowzeh-khānī* and *taʿziya* Passion play performances. This leads to an investigation of later Shiʿi traditions in Iran that continued to memorialise the death of Imam Husayn, including *pardah* paintings, the *Saqqākhāneh* School of art and the rise of graphic design in Iran. Finally, the essay turns briefly to Muharram observances outside Iran and India in order to underscore the diversity among Shiʿi communities by highlighting the *Hosay* rituals in Trinidad.

From the early years of the 16th century, when Twelver Shiʿism became the state religion, Iran has been a powerhouse of Shiʿi rituals. During the last four centuries, many of these rituals have been exported from Iran to other places. It is enough to mention here the recent impact of the Iranian *taʿziya* on the 'Ashura' Passion play performance in southern Lebanon.[1] The most fertile ground for absorbing Shiʿi rituals has been the Indian subcontinent, but observances related to Imam Husayn have spread as far as the Caribbean basin. Factors such as distance, culture and climate have impacted the ways in which Shiʿa worldwide variously observe these rituals and create artworks to accompany and facilitate them.

Indian Muharram-related observances differ significantly from their Iranian counterparts and distance must be ascribed as one of the major reasons for this disparity. The proximity of Karbala to Iran has always allowed Iranians not only to go on pilgrimage (*ziyāra*) to Imam Husayn's tomb, but even to carry their dead to the cemetery there. However, for Indian Shiʿa, Karbala has always been a distant place, far away and difficult to reach. In order to bridge that distance, the Indians built their own 'Karbalas'. Soil from Karbala was brought to the designated locality in India and sprinkled on the earth, thus creating a local Shiʿi cemetery. Once these cemeteries were established, Indian Shiʿa also wanted local versions of Imam Husayn's tomb to venerate. Indian artists and artisans built, and continue each year to construct, creative interpretations of the tomb in great numbers. These structures, called *taʿziya*, are built with bamboo, coloured paper, tinsel, paper-mâché, and, in more recent times, plastic and polystyrene, and have no resemblance to the original tomb of Husayn. In Iran, the term *taʿziya* means 'the Passion play of Imam Husayn'. In India, a *taʿziya* is an artistic conception of the tomb of Imam Husayn. Indian *taʿziya*s are displayed during the months of Muharram and Safar and are also carried in procession.

*ʿĀshūrkhāna*s and *imāmbārā*s of the Subcontinent and the Great Imambara at Lucknow

Differences between Indian and Iranian ritual observances may also be ascribed to disparity in ethno-religious composition. Ninety per cent of the Iranian population is Twelver Shiʿi. The population of India, however, is a kaleidoscope of ethnic and religious identities. The Shiʿa of India are a tiny minority compared to Hindus and Sunnis. A further factor in ritual performance is climate. While Iran's weather is dry and temperate, India's is typically hot, humid and plagued by the uncertainties of monsoon. Therefore, in India, permanent Shi'i ritual-oriented buildings, called *'āshūrkhānas* and *imāmbārās*, have been necessary from the 17th century onwards. These structures have served as the location for various stationary rituals, the departure and arrival point for processions, and as the repository for symbolic objects used in different ceremonies, including *ta'ziyas* (replica tombs), *'alams* (standards) and *zarīḥs* (replica caged tombs of metal). They predate by almost two centuries those permanent edifices in Iran devoted to Twelver Shi'i rituals. The notion that the origin of the buildings devoted to these rituals is to be found in Iran, as some western and Indian scholars assert, is erroneous. *'Āshūrkhānas* in southern India and *imāmbārās* in northern India can be traced to the end of the 16th century, whereas the Iranian equivalents, denoted *Ḥusayniyyas* or *takiyas*, were not introduced until the second half of the 18th century.[2]

'Āshūrkhāna means 'the house of *'Ashura*" (the tenth of Muharram, the day of Imam Husayn's martyrdom). The *'āshūrkhānas* were the architectural forerunners of the *imāmbārās* and were first built in the Deccan – an important centre of Shi'ism in south-central India that attracted many Persians – to house the *'alams*. *'Āshūrkhānas* also served as loci for mourning rituals. The Badshahi 'Ashurkhana built in 1596 in Hyderabad, Deccan's capital, is thought to be the oldest *'āshūrkhāna*. It is nearly 200 years older than the Asafi Imambara at Lucknow. The nawab Asaf al-Dawla (*r.* 1775–1797) erected magnificent monuments in Lucknow both to assert his complete independence from Delhi and to leave to posterity an irrefutable testament of his splendour. Among all of his architectural achievements, the Asafi Imambara is the most magnificent (fig.1). The *imāmbārās* in Awadh were much larger and grander than their southern counterparts in Hyderabad and functioned primarily as places of devotion to the martyrs of Karbala, as well as display centres for *ta'ziyas* and permanent houses for *zarīḥs*. Lucknow became the centre of Shi'ism in northern India thanks in part to the multitude of *imāmbārās*, both public and private, which were established there.

With the exception of the Takiyeh Dowlat in Tehran, Persian Muharram-related structures never achieved the same size or architectural grandeur as their counterparts in Awadh. As the official royal Muharram theatre built by the Qajar ruler, Nasr al-Din Shah (*r.* 1848–1896) in the 1870s, the Takiyeh Dowlat (i.e. State Takiyeh) attracted a great number of foreign visitors who praised it for its lavish decor. Despite its exterior and interior magnificence, however, the Takiyeh Dowlat was poorly constructed and was razed after the Second World War.

Decentralisation of power in Mughal India at the beginning of the 18th century coincided with a shift in the emperor's religious affinities from Sunni Islam towards a tolerance of Twelver Shi'ism. Bahadur Shah I (*r.* 1707–1712), who succeeded the emperor Aurangzeb in 1707, was sympathetic to the Twelver Shi'a. This made it possible for a Persian from Khurasan, Mir Muhammad Amin Nishapuri (d. 1739),

Fig.1

Fig.1
A view southwest over the Asafi Imambara, also known as the Bara Imambara. December 1864 to early 1865. Photo by Samuel Bourne, Alkazi Collection of Photography

to establish himself at the royal court in Delhi. With his gifts for administration and diplomacy, Nishapuri was soon noticed: he was given the title of Saʿadat Khan Burhan al-Mulk and made governor of Agra. A few years later he was rewarded in an even more splendid fashion by being appointed the nawab (vicegerent) of Awadh; eventually establishing an independent hereditary governorship, and later, a kingship, which would both endure for 134 years.

Nishapuri's family claimed that their ancestors originally came from Najaf and were brought to Nishapur by the first Safavid ruler, Shah Ismaʿil (*r.* 1501–1524), to spread Twelver Shiʿism in Persia. Although the Nishapuris' primary desire was to spread their religious faith, they were also committed to promoting and celebrating Persian culture in their homes. A parallel may be drawn between the nawabi house of Awadh and the later Qajar dynasty (*r.* 1796–1925) in Persia: Shiʿi rituals and popular beliefs were central to the activities of both. However, the Muharram observances in Awadh – and elsewhere on the Indian subcontinent – also included the participation of Sunnis and Hindus.[3]

Imāmbārās may be public or private fabrications, and often they are simply a room, or even just a small shrine on the wall, in a private house. In every instance, however, they are places of honour reserved to house the *taʿziya*. The prominence, size and decoration of the *imāmbārā* may reflect more than mere religious devotion. As J. R. I. Cole notes, 'the imambarahs made statements not only of piety, but also of wealth, power and status'.[4]

The Bara Imambara in Lucknow ('Great Imambara' or the Asafi Imambara) was built at a time when its counterpart institution in Iran, the *takiya*, was still in its earliest stages.[5] Although the architect of the Bara Imambara is believed to have been Persian, there are no similar structures predating it in Iran. The *imāmbārā* at Lucknow is the grandest and most extensive structure related to the rituals devoted to the martyrdom of Imam Husayn. Rosie Llewellyn-Jones remarked:

> These portable shrines (*taʿziya*), representing the graves of Husain and Hasan, are often extremely elaborate and are housed for a year in imambaras before they are taken through the streets to be ceremoniously buried. The *taʿziya*s are invested with an immense feeling of sacredness and the fact that they must be housed in a suitable solemn and grand building led to the development of the imambaras which reached its ultimate expression in Lucknow and especially in the Great Imambara built by Asaf-ud-daula in 1784, which, at one time, contained the largest vaulted hall in the world.[6]

The construction of the Asafi Imambara adjoining t he royal palace of Machhi Bhawan in Lucknow took place during the years between 1784–1791. The project reflected a mixture of religious and political motives on the part of nawab Asaf-al-Dawla. He had moved the capital of Awadh from Faizabad to Lucknow in 1775, and was a prolific builder, especially of *imāmbārās*.[7] The immense size of the complex and the architectural, topographical and structural obstacles that had to be overcome in order to unite the palace with the Twelver Shiʿi mosque and *imāmbārā* sent an unmistakable signal of the nawab's power to the local population, as well as to the government in Delhi.

It was not only the locals and fellow countrymen who were impressed by the scale of the Asafi Imambara. Europeans contemplated its splendour in admiration and astonishment. William Knighton (d. 1900), member of the royal household of the nawab Nasiruddin of Awadh (d. 1842), described its architectural layout:

> The royal Emanbarra stands near the 'Constantinople gate' of Lucknow [the Rumi Darwaza] – a gate built on the model of that which gave to the court of the sultan the title of 'the Sublime Porte'. Both structures, the gate and the Emanbarra, are elegant and harmonize well with each other. Two square courts extend in front of the building of the Emanbarra, beautifully decorated with rich tessellated pavements. The inner of these courts is raised several feet above the level of the outer. The Emanbarra belongs to that style of architecture aptly called by Bishop Heber 'the oriental Gothic'.[8]

Many European tourists found the complex so incredible as to summon up fantastical and mythical associations. The author and traveller, Emma Roberts (d. 1840), wrote in 1837:

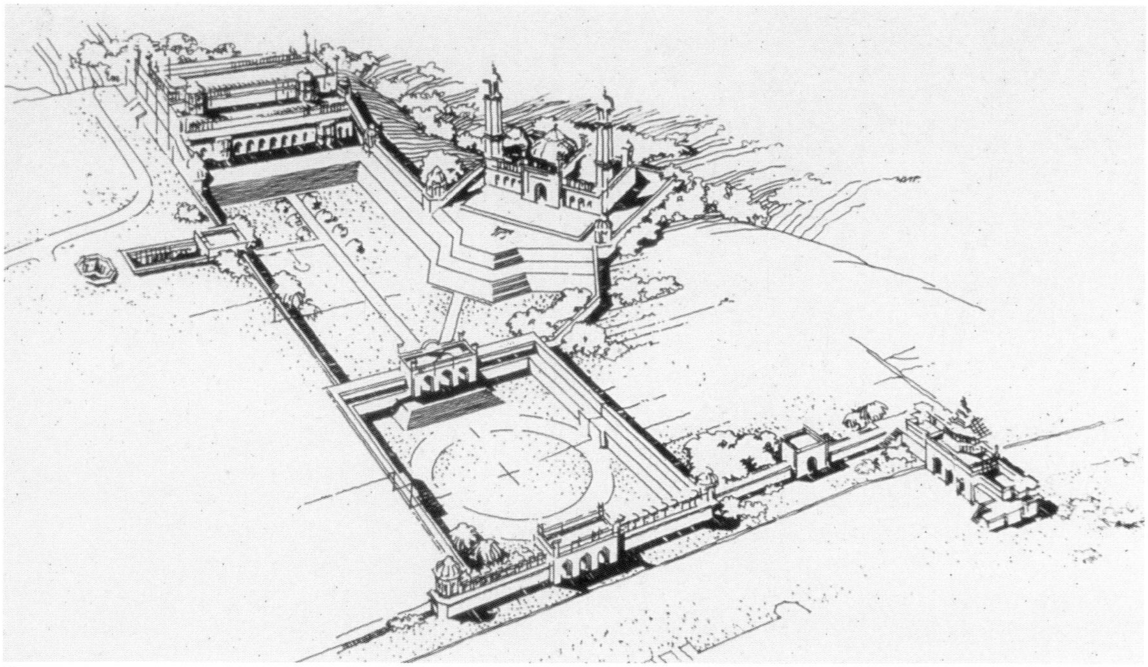

Fig.2

> Without entering further into dry descriptive details, it may be sufficient to say, that in no place in India can there be a more vivid realization of visions conjured up by a perusal of the splendid fictions of the *Arabian Nights*. Those who have visited the Kremlin have pronounced that far-famed edifice to be inferior to the Imambara.[9]

And in 1803, the British peer and politician, George Annesley (d. 1844), the 9th Viscount Valentia, reflected:

> The Rumi Derwazah was built after, [it] was supposed, one of the gates of Constantinople, though it is of that light, elegant, but fantastic architecture which has some little resemblance to the Gothic and Morisco, but none to the Grecian. The Imaumbarah, the mosque attached to it, and the gateways that lead to it, are beautiful specimens of this architecture. From the brilliant white of the composition, and the minute delicacy of the workmanship, an enthusiast might suppose that Genii had been the artificers.[10]

The Machhi Bhawan Palace site was razed to the ground by the British after the Indian Rebellion of 1857. The present day *imāmbārā* complex consists of the *imāmbārā* itself, approached through three successive courtyards, the ceremonial Rumi Gate, the Asafi Mosque, and the Baoli, which served as a royal residence during the hottest months of the year (fig.2). The principal axis of the *imāmbārā* runs north-south while a secondary axis runs east-west. The secondary axis once contained a forecourt, which today is a road open to traffic. The elaborately decorated Rumi Gate occupies the western end of this court and a similarly designed gate once stood at the eastern end. The British demolished the eastern gateway when they destroyed the palace. Both gates were equidistant from the first gate on the north–south axis, which is today the main gate to the *imāmbārā* complex. The entire area between the Rumi and eastern gates was enclosed by a wall, thus securing the first courtyard. Opposite the main gateway there was a facsimile or *jawāb* gate with foliated arches built to provide symmetry with the first courtyard but providing no access to any space.

A second rectangular courtyard measuring approximately 230 × 300 feet is flanked on its southern side by a flight of 19 stairs leading to the interior gate. Of all the many elegant portals in the *imāmbārā* complex, the triple-arched interior gate is considered the most graceful and well designed because of the superb focal point it provides when viewed from the third courtyard. The third courtyard is nine feet higher than

Fig.2
Birds-eye view of the Asafi Imambara complex

the second: the two were originally connected by an inclined dirt path leading to the interior gate. The path was used to lead animals taking part in ritual processions into the third courtyard. Today, animals are only allowed in the first and second courtyards.

Fronting the *imāmbārā* itself is the third and main courtyard. In length, it is one and a half times the size of the second courtyard and in appearance it substantially differs from its original incarnation. Where once the entrance to the mosque on the western side of the courtyard was through an inconspicuous door in a wall, today the approach is via a magnificent sweep of steps. The British considered the wall a security threat (since it could provide cover for potential attackers) and tore it down. As it spreads south, the third courtyard opens up and becomes wider. Gazing from the interior gate, one has a 'telescopic' view, which creates the impression that the width of the courtyard at the north is equal to the width at its southern end. In addition, the north–south axis running from the *imāmbārā* building to the main gate is angled so that the northern facade of the *imāmbārā* does not receive direct sunlight and thus enjoys a kind of natural air-conditioning (fig.3).

Topographic considerations imposed limitations on the layout of the *imāmbārā* complex. Additionally, the mosque was built on its own axis so that it would face southwest towards Mecca. Its placement constituted a break in the symmetry beloved of Indian, and, in particular, of Muslim Indian architects. Yet despite this lack of perfect balance, the complex achieves an impressive harmony. Situated on the top of a hill sloping northward to the River Gomti and westward towards a gorge, the *imāmbārā* rests upon a brick platform (fig.4). The two main courtyards were formed by cutting into the hillside, the eastern portion of which became a decorative retaining wall with 88 arches on two levels (the Machhi Bhawan Palace was more than ten feet above the third

Fig.3

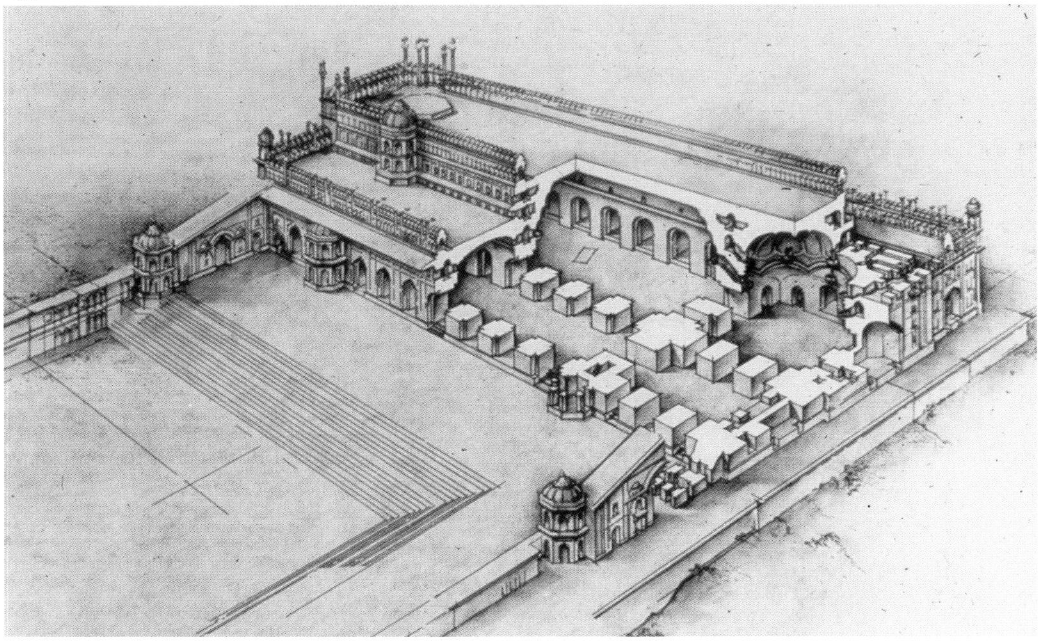

Fig.4

Fig.3
The northern facade of the Asafi Imambara under restoration, 1870s. Alkazi Collection of Photography

Fig.4
Cutaway drawing showing the interior of the Asafi Imambara

Fig.5

courtyard). Also on the eastern side of the third court, is a small gate that leads to the nawabi Baoli or stepped well. The Baoli was dug sufficiently deep to be level with the River Gomti, which winds north of the *imāmbārā* from the northwest to the southeast.

A flight of 18 stairs at the end of the third courtyard leads to the terrace of the *imāmbārā*, which measures 71 × 260 feet. The progression of elevated courtyards and steps leading to the *imāmbārā* creates a sense of anticipation as well as veneration. The faithful coming to pray at the *imāmbārā* feel as if they are making a symbolic pilgrimage to the real tomb of Imam Husayn in Karbala; a fitting sentiment since the word '*imāmbārā*' means 'dwelling place of the Imam'.

During the period in which the *imāmbārā* was built, the masons of Lucknow were highly skilled. Since marble and sandstone were not available in the area, such expert masonry work was all the more valued (fig.5). The *imāmbārā* was built of brick covered with plaster applied in such a way that it resembled marble. Small, hard lakhori bricks were used with mortar to lend elasticity to the walls.[11] The stucco was long lasting and retained an extraordinary lustre. John Pemble noted:

> The Lucknow stucco, made from the calcareous deposits of ancient lake beds, gave an effect of great chasteness when not covered with surface distemper, and its toughness was fully attested in 1858, when the plastered walls of [a] building called Sikandarbagh proved indestructible by a nine-pound cannon shot and yielded to the British eighteen-pounders only after more than an hour's bombardment.[12]

The interior of the *imāmbārā* also shone brilliantly with the patina of the local stucco. Using recovered lime or shells from dried-up lakes, the local masons were able to produce a surface that was more dazzling than the marble tombs of the Mughals. The radiance of the stucco combined with a magnificent array of chandeliers and an abundance of mirrors created an atmosphere of unforgettable splendour. In fact, the lighting made an even greater impression on visitors than did the architecture. Llewellyn-Jones remarked:

> But the most striking feature (for Europeans at any rate) is the absolute profusion inside the imambara of chandeliers of all shapes and sizes and the huge stands for lamps and candles, often five feet or more in height, and made from highly decorated china, coloured glass, and metals. The effect when all the chandeliers and stands are lit is dazzling, especially in the cool and dark halls of the imambara.[13]

Fig.5
The south side of the Asafi Imambara, 1890s. Photo by G. W. Lawrie & Co., Alkazi Collection of Photography

The *imāmbārā* is divided into nine chambers, with the middle hall measuring 163 × 53 feet. This space, popularly known as the 'Persian' Hall, was believed to be the largest vaulted hall in the world at the time of its completion in 1791. At the point where the vaulting of the roof begins at 49.5 feet, there is an enclosed gallery running around the perimeter of the hall. There, women of the royal court could watch the ritual proceedings unseen behind stone balustrades. On the north and south sides of the Persian Hall, there are galleries of the same length but only half the width of the central chamber. The southern gallery is elevated three feet above the middle hall in order to better display the cenotaphs that at one time lay between the foliated arches. This type of arch is used as a motif throughout the complex. The nine large and four small arches on the northern facade of the *imāmbārā* are in this style, as are the arches that connect the nine interior chambers to one another. The Rumi Gate also adheres to this design.

The Persian Hall is adjoined by the 'Chinese' Hall on the east and by the 'Indian' Hall on the west. Both of these flanking chambers are built on a square floor plan opening to an octagonal space surmounted by a dome. These domes are visible only from the interior of the *imāmbārā* and, save for their graceful curves, the two chambers – measuring 53 feet at their length, height and apex respectively – would be perfect cubes. A series of intricate squinches, or corbels, supports the ceiling. The roof is buttressed by a labyrinth of small-arched corridors which run along the length and width of the *imāmbārā*. This maze of arches rises from the ground to four levels above and is considered to be the crowning architectural achievement in Lucknow. Although the building has stood for more than 200 years, no evidence of structural damage or instability has ever been noted. This is surely a testament to the ingenuity and supreme artistic sensibility of the architect.

The central hall contains the tomb of the nawab Asaf al-Dawla. Viscount Valentia described the tomb in his memoir:

> The Imaumbarah is certainly the most beautiful building I have seen in India; it was erected by the late Nawaub, for the double purpose of celebrating this festival [Muharram], and of serving as a burial place for himself. It consists of three very long and finely proportioned apartments, running parallel to each other: in the middle is his tomb, level with the ground. The centre is earth covered with a scanty herbage, and surrounded with a broad margin of white marble, in which sentences from the Koran are inlayed in black. At one end lies the sword, turban, etc. which he had on when he died. Over it is a rich canopy supported by four pillars, covered with a cloth of gold, now in decay. Unfortunately, it was necessary to place his tomb diagonally, that he might lie in a proper Mahomedan position respecting Mecca; and, consequently, instead of an ornament, it is an unsightly object.[14]

Valentia was not the only one to find the position of the nawab's tomb incongruous with the overall level of architectural consideration and forethought displayed throughout the complex. Some observers have speculated that the *imāmbārā* was never meant to be the nawab's final resting place based on the tomb's seeming misplacement. As discussed above, however, the tomb is unaligned with the axis of the building as a result of the topography of the site. It was impossible to orient the entire complex towards Mecca because of the already-constructed Macchi Bhawan Palace. Therefore, only those elements mandated by Islamic law to face Mecca – the mosque and the tomb of the founder – were aligned in that direction.

The nawab's interment in the *imāmbārā* is considered to be a perquisite granted to him as the founder of the complex. Thanks to his splendid act of devotion in building the *imāmbārā*, he is entitled to receive vicarious merit through the prayers offered by pilgrims to Imam Husayn. It is Imam Husayn, after all, who is the focal point of the entire site. In addition to commemoration of the Imam, there were also at one time 14 cenotaphs of pure silver on display representing the 'Fourteen Infallibles': Prophet Muhammad, Hazrat Fatima and the Twelve Imams.

The Takiyeh Dowlat in Iran

The magnificence of the Great Imambara at Lucknow made the Muharram rituals attractive to all levels of the Shiʿi population. As was mentioned above, in its scope and size as a Shiʿi edifice, Lucknow's Imambara can only be compared to the Takiyeh Dowlat in Iran. The Takiyeh Dowlat was the crowning example of the structure known as a

Ḥusayniyya or *takiya* (fig.6). From the tenth century onwards, temporary *Ḥusayniyya*s, usually simple black tents, were erected by pious Shiʿa during the months of Muharram and Safar to serve as places to observe the rituals devoted to the Passion and death of Imam Husayn. When Shiʿism became the state religion of Iran in the 16th century, participation in these rituals swelled. The rituals were performed in mosque yards, in courtyards attached to private residences, and in public squares and on village commons. In most cases, an awning was erected to protect participants from the elements. But until the late 18th century, there were no permanent structures specially built for Shiʿi mourning rituals.

Under the Qajars, the construction of permanent *Ḥusayniyya*s flourished. In many towns in the northern provinces of Iran the number of *Ḥusayniyya*s or *takiya*s equalled the number of mosques. Nonetheless, no truly characteristic form of *Ḥusayniyya* architecture developed; even Nasr al-Din Shah's great Takiyeh Dowlat is believed by many to be modelled on the Royal Albert Hall in London. Like the nawab in Lucknow, Nasr al-Din Shah undoubtedly had a mixture of social, religious, and political motives in mind when he embarked on his monumental project. Visitors to the Takiyeh Dowlat were just as awed as those travellers who had viewed the Asafi Imambara. The American envoy to the court of Nasr al-Din Shah, Samuel Greene Wheeler Benjamin (d. 1914) observed:

> I was invited to attend on the fifth day of the Taʿziyeh. We arrived at the Takiyeh [Dowlat] toward noon. On alighting from the carriage I was surprised to see an immense circular building as large as the amphitheater of Verona, solidly constructed of brick...On looking over the vast arena a sight met my gaze which was indeed extraordinary. The interior of the building is nearly two hundred feet in diameter and some eighty feet high. A domed frame of timbers, firmly spliced and braced with iron, springs from the walls, giving support to the awning that protects the interior from the sunlight and rain. From the centre of the dome a large chandelier was suspended, furnished with four electric burners – a recent innovation. A more oriental form of illuminating the building was seen in the prodigious number of lustres and candlesticks, all of glass and protected from the air by glass shades open on the top and variously coloured; they were concentrated against the wall in immense glittering clusters. Estimating from those attached on one box, I judged that there were upwards of five thousand candles in these lustres...In the centre of the arena was a circular stage of masonry, raised three feet and approached by two stairways. On one side of the building a pulpit of white marble was attached to the wall...But I soon discovered that all the architectural details of this remarkable building were secondary to the extraordinary spectacle offered by the assembled multitude.[15]

The roof of the Takiyeh Dowlat remained unfinished and the exact reason for this has proved a particularly fertile point of debate among scholars. Was it due to a construction error or was the Shah's ambitious architectural scheme simply beyond the technological capabilities of Iranian builders of the period? There is a third possibility that should be considered. The majority of *Ḥusayniyya*s or *takiya*s, including the Takiyeh Dowlat, are covered with the canvas of a tent during performances. This canvas is not only a practical device to keep the elements at bay (if necessary); it is a direct reference to the tents of Imam Husayn's encampment, the *khaimagāh* (from the Arabic *khaima*, 'tent'), at Karbala. In the Shiʿi conception of time and space in relation to the suffering and death of Imam Husayn, what happened in the year 680 at Karbala takes places concurrently wherever and whenever rituals are observed. Therefore, an awning resembling a tent helps to recreate the atmosphere of the Imam's encampment and makes the tragic events that took place there seem even more immediate.

The rituals of *rowzeh-khānī* and *taʿziya*

The stationary rituals of *rowzeh-khānī* and *taʿziya* are both performed in *Ḥusayniyya*s or *takiya*s. The *rowzeh-khānī* (i.e. *rawḍa khānī*, lit. 'recitation from *The Garden* [*of Martyrs*]') is a dramatic narration in words, songs and through body language of the suffering of Imam Husayn and other Shiʿi martyrs. Its name is derived from a Persian work composed by Husayn Waʿiz al-Kashifi (d. 1504–1505) entitled *Rawḍat al-Shuhadāʾ* (The Garden of Martyrs). The *rowzeh-khān* or man in charge of the performance, can stir up intense emotional responses from his audience by his cries, weeping and rhythmic chest beating. The set up for a *rowzeh-khānī* is not elaborate.

Fig.6

Fig.7

The arrangements typically consist of a *minbar* (a wooden elevation of seven steps) on which the *rowzeh-khān* sits, black flags and banners covered in calligraphy, and audience seating on carpets. Modern *rowzeh-khānīs* may also incorporate microphones and speakers as well as separate seating in chairs for men and women. Whether the performance is traditional or more modern, refreshments are always served to the audience by the children of the patrons.

Taʿziya, the Passion play theatre, is one of the most artistic creations of the Shiʿa of Iran. The *taʿziya* as a dramatic theatrical form is a product or result of the 18th-century fusion of ambulatory and stationary rituals. This is theatre-in-the-round (fig.7). The main performance space is a stark, uncurtained, raised platform in the centre of the *takiya* or any other covered or uncovered (roofed or roofless) locality. Surrounding the stage is a circular strip usually covered with sand. This is used for equestrian and foot battles. It is also used to indicate journeys and the passage of time. For example, when an actor jumps off the stage, then circumambulates it, and finally jumps back on, it signifies that he has travelled and then arrived at his destination. Stage décor for the *taʿziya* is non-existent as the desolate, bleak stage is meant to represent the desert of Karbala. Most of the props are symbolic; for example, a basin of water signifies the Euphrates River. The protagonists are dressed predominantly in green (the colour of Paradise and the family of the Prophet). The antagonists are dressed in red, which represents blood and cruelty. The protagonists sing their parts and the antagonists recite theirs. This is a music drama.

The *taʿziya* performance expands from the central stage to the audience, engulfing them. In this fashion, the spectators are drawn into the action and become participants in the ritual. Male actors playing women have veiled faces and are dressed in baggy black garments covering them from head to toe. The actors hold their scripts in their hands. This is to indicate that they are only role-carriers and not the personages they portray. However, due to the influence of movies and television, this tradition is quickly dying out. Another tradition that is dying out is the presence of the director in the middle of the action; in the past, it was usual for him to regulate the movement of the actors, musicians and even the audience.

The core of the *taʿziya* repertory is the plays devoted to the Karbala tragedy and the events surrounding it. The massacre at Karbala is divided into many individual plays performed on separate days. With the exception of the day of ʿAshura' on the 10th of Muharram, when *The Martyrdom of Imam Husayn* is always performed, any *taʿziya* may be

Fig.6
Takiyeh Dowlat and surrounding buildings in Tehran. After Feuvrier, *Trois ans à la cour de Perse*, 1906

Fig.7
Takiyeh Dowlat after Kemal al-Mulk's paintings

Fig.8

given on any day. A traditional schedule of *ta'ziyas* might have *The Martyrdom of Muslim b. 'Aqil*, portraying the cruel murder of the loyal cousin and emissary of Imam Husayn, on the first day of Muharram. The following day would be devoted to the *ta'ziya* depicting the martyrdom of Muslim's two little sons who accompanied him to Kufa. On the 6th of Muharram, *The Martyrdom of Hurr* would be performed. General Hurr switched sides and left the camp of the Umayyad enemy forces to ally himself with Imam Husayn, with the certain knowledge that he would pay for his action with his life at Karbala. *The Martyrdom of Qasim the Bridegroom* is performed on the next day.[16] Qasim was the nephew of Husayn, the son of his brother, Imam Hasan. It was the wish of the deceased Imam Hasan that his son would marry Husayn's daughter, Fatima. In order to honour his brother's wish, and knowing that the next day all the male members of his family will die, Husayn hosts a wedding celebration in the encampment at Karbala; however, before the marriage can be consummated, Qasim is called to the field of battle and is killed. The wedding celebration becomes a funeral observance. The performance of these dramatic events has a great impact on the audience.

The next *ta'ziya* could be *The Martyrdom of 'Ali Akbar*, the eldest son of Imam Husayn. Usually this is followed by *The Martyrdom of the Imam's Standard-bearer, 'Abbas*. On the 'Ashura' day, *The Martyrdom of Imam Husayn* is performed. This *ta'ziya* does not end the cycle, however, as there are still plays to be performed that are devoted to the plight of the women and the Imam's only surviving son. In fact, Shi'i audiences are so enthusiastic for *ta'ziya* that productions are staged year-round. No matter what *ta'ziya* is performed, it always contains a reference to the tragedy at Karbala. Nobody knows how many *ta'ziyas* have been written. The Cerulli Collection at the Vatican Library holds 1055 *ta'ziya* manuscripts, which roughly represent 200 story plots.

Pardah paintings and the *Saqqākhāneh* School

The dramatic events of the *ta'*ziya were not only confined to the stage; they were also depicted by artists on canvas. Attempts to visualise the Karbala tragedy had been made since the late-Safavid period (*r.* 1501–1722). In particular, the tradition of narrative painting known as *shamā'il* or *pardah* had served as a means of promoting religious and secular aims. *Pardah* (lit. 'curtain') painting, popularly known as 'coffee-house painting' (since Iranian coffee houses once served as artists' ateliers and lodgings) is accompanied by a performance in the form of storytelling, which describes the action depicted on the canvas. Religious *pardah* are devoted to the Karbala tragedy (fig.8).

Staging a *ta'ziya* required substantial expenditure and organisation. Smaller rural villages usually did not have the resources to mount such a spectacle. By combining the traditional storytelling ritual of the *rowzeh-khān* with some of the visual drama of the *ta'ziya*, *pardah* paintings allowed even the tiniest and most remote hamlets to 'witness' the events at Karbala. The itinerant narrator who accompanied the *pardah* from place to place used a pointer to highlight the part of the painting that corresponded to whichever portion of the story he was then relating. Like the *rowzeh-khān* he employed theatrical gestures and changes in voice modulation to immerse his audience in the drama to the fullest extent.

Fig.8
Pardah painting with a scene from the Battle of Karbala, exhibited at the Shiraz Art Festival in 1976

Fig.9
A poster inspired by a photograph that was later transformed into a postage stamp issued for the birthday of Hazrat Fatima. The inscription on the green banner reads 'O Zahra!'

Narrative *pardah* paintings eventually began to be used as wall hangings in *Ḥusayniyya*s and *takiya*s. The Takiyeh Dowlat itself was decorated with splendid examples of this type of art. In time, such paintings were also found on the walls of private residences. The tradition of *pardah* painting lasted until the late 1960s. Concurrently with the demise of coffee house painting, there emerged a new group of Iranian painters who had trained both at home and abroad, known as the *Saqqākhāneh* School. A *saqqākhāna* is a small water receptacle set into a tiled niche found in an alley or the streets of the old quarter of an Iranian town. This small shrine is always dedicated to Hazrat ʿAbbas, Imam Husayn's standard bearer, and is adorned with images depicting the tragic events at Karbala. The painters of the *Saqqākhāneh* School, though modern in their technique and outlook, used the symbolism of Karbala and its related rituals in their work.[17]

Concurrent with the *Saqqākhāneh* School's activity during the 1960s, a flourishing of the graphic arts also occurred. Commercial, cultural and political objectives were communicated via graphic images that were intelligible to all Iranian citizens, regardless of their background or education. Though many of the leading Iranian graphic artists had trained in the West, they drew on popular Shiʿi Muslim beliefs and rituals when producing images for mass consumption.

Fig.9

The leaders of the 1978–1979 Islamic Revolution continued the practice of using Shiʿi symbols and motifs in graphic images. Indeed, they consciously drew on the Karbala paradigm to promote the revolution in a range of different media including posters, graffiti and murals. In these various media, the events of Karbala were appropriated and the roles of its key participants reassigned. Thus, Imam Husayn and his enemy, the Umayyad Caliph Yazid, were replaced by a victorious Ayatollah Khomeini and a vanquished Shah of Iran. Khomeini's image, as well as his words, were ubiquitous throughout the revolutionary period and during the subsequent eight-year-long bloody war with Iraq. His success was in a large measure attributable to the way in which he was able to mobilise the populace by using popular Shiʿi rituals and beliefs, as well as to the way in which he exploited Western mass communication techniques to wage the revolution.

After the Shah was deposed, the arts in Iran underwent a time of renewal and every type of art flourished, from socialist realism and the Beaux Arts to indigenous Persian traditions. Although many artists of the revolution incorporated elements of the *pardah* technique in their work, untraditional forms of imagery were also employed. Scrawled graffiti would be captured in a photograph, which itself would become the basis for a poster. Eventually, the poster image might be transmuted onto a postage stamp or even used on currency (fig.9). In this way, an unknown street artist might find that his creation had been selected by the authorities to adorn a banknote. Among all these media, posters were particularly effective in stimulating war preparedness and readiness for sacrifice.

At every level of society and in every moment of daily life, Iranians were confronted with visual reminders of the revolutionary struggle and triumph, which were masterfully and inextricably woven with the core symbols of the Shiʿi faith. This was particularly true during the 'Imposed War' with Iraq. Any blank surface that could serve as a canvas was considered fair game. Murals, posters and graffiti adorned the high walls that stood between traditional Iranian dwellings and the street. Where there were no walls, billboards sprang up. Demonstrators carried images and banners in processions and at weekly rallies. The authorities launched an all-out propaganda campaign for total control, organising their own army of graphic artists to mobilise the general public and to immobilise potential rivals and opponents.

Muharram observances in Trinidad: *Hosay* rituals

Muharram rituals were used in Iran to mobilise the masses in a demonstration of solidarity and national identity. Shiʿi symbols and art were utilised in a political and cultural context, which, nevertheless, retained grounding in religious beliefs. Halfway around the world, in Trinidad, the Muharram procession was also employed as a means to express identity and shared cultural observances: in the celebration of pan-Indian national unity known as *Hosay* (the name is derived from Husayn, which is often spelled, 'Hosayin'). However, in Trinidad and other countries in the Caribbean basin, the *Hosay* rituals took place outside of a strictly Shiʿi framework.

The *Hosay* rituals in Trinidad have their origins in the second half of the 19th century when thousands of Indians were brought as indentured labourers to work on the British-owned sugar cane plantations in the Caribbean islands. Barakat Ahmad explains,

> More than 140,000 Indian labourers migrated to Trinidad between 1845 and 1917. A vast majority of these Indians came from the district of United Provinces (now Uttar Pradesh) and Bihar. It was estimated that in 1891, 13.44% of these Indians were Muslims. This represented the original pattern. According to the 1901 census in India, 85% of the population in U.P. was Hindu and 14% was Muslim.[18]

By the time of the Indians' arrival in the Caribbean, the customary observances of Carnival had been infused with African and Creole traditions and had become the main annual Creole celebration. In order to assert their own identity in an equally exuberant festival, the Indians introduced the Muharram processions. In India, both Hindus and Sunnis had participated in Muharram rituals, but it is nonetheless remarkable that *Hosay* rituals developed into a demonstration of Indian unity. Especially when one considers that the percentage of Shiʿi Muslims among the Indian migrants was incredibly small.

The main preparation of *Hosay* observances is the construction of the *taʿziya*, which in Trinidad and other Caribbean countries is called *tadjah*. Traditionally, this construction activity took place on the plantations and there was fierce competition between neighbouring estates to produce the most impressive *tadjah*. An atmosphere of great secrecy prevailed as the work proceeded over a period of 40 days in a shack called an *imāmbārā*; a place restricted to men, and only those men who actively worked on the *tadjah*. Because the Indian labourers had limited time off, the *tadjah* display and procession lasted only for 24 hours and the main *Hosay* rituals took place during the night on the eve of ʿAshura' (fig.10). On the following day, the *tadjah*s were immersed in the ocean and gradually disappeared into the watery depths of the sea. Because *tadjah*s are summarily destroyed at the close of the ʿAshura' day, we can only rely on anecdotes and photographs for descriptions of 19th-century versions. Modern *tadjah*s differ from their forebears in height (contemporary *tadjah*s are shorter), colour and materials used for construction. Modern *tadjah*s are also usually wheeled as opposed to being carried.

Trinidad is the only place in the Caribbean where *Hosay* is still observed annually in the lunar month of Muharram. There are two centres of *Hosay* observances in Trinidad: St James in the north, near Port of Spain (the capital city), and the Cedros District in the south-west. In the north, the *tadjah* camps, also known as yards or *imāmbārā*s, are predominantly organised by Muslims. In contrast, the camps in the south are principally run by Hindus and Christians,

Fig.10

since there are few Muslims living there. Additionally, two of the camps in the north construct crescent-shaped half moons: one red, representing Imam Husayn, and the other green, representing Imam Hasan. They measure six feet in diameter and are studded with daggers. Camps in the south do not build moons.

The mourning aspect of the Muharram rituals as observed in Iran and India is muted in Trinidad; there is no self-mortification. Furthermore, it is generally only the core group of those who build and carry the *tadjah*s and half-moons who view the proceedings as a religious observance. *Hosay* is a sincere and vibrant celebration of Imam Husayn's life that reaches its peak on Big *Hosay* Night, the eve of 'Ashura'. A crowd of thousands sways in time to the music as the *tadjah* procession passes by. The procession includes a small group of *tadjah* and moon builders turned performers and accompanying drummers. The dazzling display of proud *tadjah*s and spectacular moons is a memorable sight that draws all who see it into the festivities. Although there is an element of Carnival found in *Hosay*, the bystanders express a definite sense of respect for the observances.

In the south, on the 'Ashura' day, towards six o'clock in the evening, the *tadjah*s are moved to the beach, a short prayer is recited, and a farewell eulogy is sung. As the sun sinks gradually on the horizon, a brace of strong men carry the *tadjah*s into the ocean and set them gently on the water. As night falls, the *tadjah*s are claimed by the sea and slowly slip beneath the waves. The following year, the rite is observed anew. This type of *ta'ziya* or *tadjah* is indeed what Shakeel Hussain refers to as, 'ephemeral architecture'.[19] Once built, it is displayed and carried in procession. At the end of the journey, the *ta'ziya* is either buried in a local Karbala or submerged in the nearest lake, river or sea.

Shi'a throughout the world and across the centuries have used an array of materials and media to create art and architecture devoted to Imam Husayn, the Prince of Martyrs. The itinerant *pardah* painter in a remote village in Iran shares a connection with the architect of the Great Imambara at Lucknow or the member of a *tadjah* camp in Trinidad. All are artists who have used their talents to express a lasting elegy to Imam Husayn and his sacrifice. Although political and cultural considerations may sometimes be intertwined with these expressions, they are, nevertheless, primarily manifestations of Shi'i piety and reverence.

Fig.10
A pair of *tadjah*s representing the shrine of Imam Husayn in procession on the eve of 'Ashura' in southern Trinidad, 1991

1 Sabrina Mervin, 'Shiite Theater in South Lebanon: Some Notes on the Karbala Drama and the Sabaya', in Peter J. Chelkowski, ed., *Eternal Performance: Ta'ziyeh and Other Shiite Rituals* (London and Calcutta, 2010), pp.322–333.
2 However, prior to this period, temporary *Ḥusayniyya*s and *takiya*s did exist in Iran.
3 Sadiq Naqvi, *Qutb Shahi 'Ashur Khanas of Hyderabad City* (Hyderabad, 1982), p.5.
4 Juan R. I. Cole, *Roots of North Indian Shī'ism in Iran and Iraq: Religion and State in Awadh, 1722–1859* (Berkeley, CA, 1988), p.103.
5 See the essay by Hussein Keshani in this volume for a discussion on the nearby Hussainabad Imambara, also known as the Chhota (Little) Imambara, in Lucknow.
6 Rosie Llewellyn-Jones, *A Fatal Friendship: The Nawabs, the British and the City of Lucknow* (New Delhi and Oxford, 1985), p.203.
7 Banmali Tandan, *Architecture of Lucknow and Its Dependencies, 1722–1856* (New Delhi, 2001), p.30.
8 William Knighton, *The Private Life of an Eastern King*, new edition, (London, 1855, rev. ed. 1921), p.91.
9 Emma Roberts, *Scenes and Characteristics of Hindostan, with Sketches of Anglo-Indian Society* (London, 1835, 2nd ed., 1837), p.349.
10 George Annesley, *Voyages and Travels to India, Ceylon, the Red Sea, Abyssinia and Egypt in the years 1802, 1803, 1804, 1805, and 1806* (London, 1809), p.156.
11 The bricks measure 0.75 × 3.94 × 5.91 inches.
12 John Pemble, *The Raj, the Indian Mutiny, and the Kingdom of Oudh*, 1801–1859 (Hassocks, 1977), p.13.
13 Llewellyn-Jones, *Fatal Friendship*, p.203.
14 Annesley, *Travels to India*, p.157.
15 Samuel Greene Wheeler Benjamin, *Persia and the Persians* (London, 1887), pp.382–388.
16 See the essay by Ingvild Flaskerud in this volume.
17 See the essay by Venetia Porter in this volume.
18 Barakat Ahmad, High Commissioner of India in Trinidad, a diplomat and scholar, in a letter to Peter J. Chelkowski, 1976.
19 Shakeel Hussain, 'Ritual Architecture and Urbanity', a poster designed for the exhibition at GSFA Gallery, University of Pennsylvania, Philadelphia, September 1997.

18

ʿArūze Qāsem – a theatrical event in Shiʿi female commemorative rituals

Ingvild Flaskerud

Introduction

The legend of the wedding (*ʿarūsī*) and subsequent martyrdom of Imam Husayn's juvenile nephew, Qasim b. al-Hasan, during the battle at Karbala in 680, remains a popular theme in Shiʿi rituals of commemoration. The event is enacted and commemorated in the Twelver Shiʿi religious theatrical tradition, known as *taʿziya* (condolence) in Persian and as *tamthīliyya* (play) *or shabah* (similar, resembling) in Arabic, which developed in Iran in the mid-18th century, and since then spread to other parts of the Shiʿi world. This tradition of theatre has not developed a canonised script. Nevertheless, the episode enacting the fate of Qasim typically includes scenes of lamentation preceding Qasim's wedding to his cousin Fatima, followed by the celebration of the marriage, which eventually transforms into mourning. In *taʿziya* all parts are typically played by male amateur actors who are often trained in the tradition since childhood.[1] Less known or researched is the *taʿziya* played by and for women.[2] Even lesser known is the theatrical performance of *ʿArūze Qāsem* (i.e. *ʿArūsī Qāsim*, lit. 'the wedding of Qasim') enacted by women as part of their commemoration rituals in Muharram, which otherwise include a lecture, prayers, the recitation of stories about the battle at Karbala (*rowzeh*), elegies (*nawḥa*), and rites of flagellation (*sīneh*).

In this essay, I present a synthesised description of six performances staged in three different locations (a living room, a private courtyard, and a public ceremonial hall) in Shiraz, southwest Iran, between 2000 and 2002. Devoid of any recorded history, such performances have no written script, libretto or performance manual. The repeated presentation of a certain repertoire of roles, props, costumes and texts do, however, indicate that *ʿArūze Qāsem* has become an established theatrical model in this local environment. More research is needed to establish whether the practice is common elsewhere. This analysis of *ʿArūze Qāsem* as a theatrical model and ritual strategy draws on Willmar Sauter's concept of a 'theatrical event' which gives importance to the interaction between actors and spectators during a given time in a specific place; the cultural context of the performance; and the sensory experiences of a theatrical situation.[3] The essay, thus, explores the following questions: What characterises *ʿArūze Qāsem* as a theatrical event? How does the theatrical event serve rituals of commemoration? Why is *ʿArūze Qāsem* popular among women?

Performing *ʿArūze Qāsem*

In this local environment of Shiraz, commemorative ceremonies are organised every day by and for women during the first ten days of Muharram.[4] *ʿArūze Qāsem* is typically performed on the eighth of Muharram, towards the end of a two-hour-long ceremony.[5] After a series of rites commemorating the martyrs at the battle of Karbala, the theatrical performance of *ʿArūze Qāsem* begins when a procession of women (between ten to twenty persons) appears in the ceremonial room (fig.1). If the space allows, they walk through the crowd of ritual participant-spectators seated on the floor or standing in the room. If not, they position themselves near the main prop, a model of a nuptial chamber called the *ḥijla*, placed in a visible location in the room.[6] Dressed in black chadors, the procession of women cover their faces for this occasion. They carry trays (*khunche*) on their heads, laden with burning candles, fruits, sweets, henna and burning wild rue (*esfand*).[7] The women represent the female relatives of Fatima, the bride, identified in the legend as the daughter of Imam Husayn (i.e. Zubayda, also known as Fatima al-Kubra), bringing gifts to her new home. On the appearance of the procession, the ritual participant-spectators respond with ululation (*helhela* or *kel zadan*), a conventional cultural expression of joy. Whilst the procession tours the room, many ritual participant-spectators touch the trays. Simultaneously, the ritual leader (*maddāḥ*) who stands near the pulpit (*minbar*), invites ritual participant-spectators

Fig.1

to join her in praising God, the Prophet Muhammad and his descendants, a liturgical prayer known as *ṣalawāt*.[8]

At this point, two young actors representing Qasim and Fatima are led into the room accompanied by two mature women. Qasim and Fatima are dressed in bright green robes that cover their bodies completely. Qasim wears a green turban with pieces of fabrics concealing his face and Fatima wears a green veil covering her head and face. The two women accompanying them act as Fatima's relatives but in the unrehearsed, though conventional, theatrical event they also provide the actors with instructions on what to do. Qasim and Fatima are made to stop by the *ḥijla*, if this has been prepared. If not, they are made to stop by the *minbar*. They stop in front of a prayer rug laid out on the floor. They remain silent as they walk up to the prayer rug, while the *maddāḥ* performs the *rowzeh* of Qasim, a short and emotional narration of the fate of Qasim and Fatima at Karbala typically performed at Shiʿa commemorative rituals.[9] The narrative combines a hagiographic description of the wedding in the midst of the battle with an imagined conversation between Qasim and Imam Husayn and commentaries by Qasim and Fatima:

> Qasim was eager to get permission [to fight at Karbala] and Imam Husayn finally agreed to let him go. Imam Husayn came and took Qasim by his hand and said: I want to fulfil your father's (i.e. Imam Hasan's) will before you go to battle. Then Imam Husayn read the *āya khuṭba ʿaqd* (i.e. the sura from the Qurʾan performed at the wedding) and put Qasim's hand in the hand of Fatima. At that moment there was the sound of the drum of war. Qasim made two *rakaʿāt* of prayers (customarily performed on the wedding night) and said: This is my farewell prayer. Fatima said: My courageous cousin, our hands will be red by the henna of your blood. This is not the real custom of a wedding party. Where is my *rupūsh* (face veil, i.e. a black cloth used to cover the face when in mourning)? She asked God to help Qasim. The prayer was finished and Qasim said his last farewell. He said: I want to make a trip to the other world. Please forgive me.

The content of the *rowzeh* provides a background to the plot as well as offering a synopsis of its development. In addition, while Qasim and Fatima stand by the prayer rug, senior ritual participant-spectators often take the microphone from the *maddāḥ* and present popular elegiac poetry (*nawḥa*) in a sad melody, thus continuing the *maddāḥ*'s narration but elaborating its tragic aspects. For example:

> Stranger who cut your head (i.e. Qasim's head was cleaved)
> O ʿAbd Allah, peace be upon you (i.e. greeting Imam Husayn)
> Dear darling of Fatima, peace be upon you (i.e. reference to Husayn)
> The martyrs of Karbala, peace be upon you

Fig.1
At the start of *ʿArūze Qāsem* a procession of women representing the family of Fatima carry trays (*khunche*) bearing wedding gifts, Shiraz, Iran, 2002

Don't cry, followers of Husayn in this happiness
I am preparing the wedding party
Umm Layla don't cry (i.e. mother of ʿAli Akbar b. al-Husayn)
The body of the ransom of Husayn is full of blood (ʿAli Akbar)
And in the world is the cry of Imam Husayn
A bloom was killed and a flower in the garden of Imam Husayn, Qasim.
Injustice took the life of Husayn, *va veila, va veila*! (i.e. O alas! O alas!)

The content of this elegy connects the wedding celebration to the battle at Karbala and its tragic outcome. The elegies make many ritual participant-spectators cry and ritual leaders may continue to appeal to their empathy by elaborating on the destined yet devastating wedding-martyrdom theme:

Did you see anyone like Husayn, to witness his children killed in front of him one by one? What should I do to make Qasim return from his trip (to the world of the dead)? I put on henna for the happiness of Qasim. Take off the wedding clothes, he wants to go to battle, and call the bride so she can come and see him.

The response is a mixture of joyful ululation as well as of weeping and lament. Senior participant-spectators may also take the microphone from the *maddāḥ* and verbally impersonate Qasim and his aunt Zaynab (sister of Imam Husayn):

Qasim says: 'I want to go to Karbala. Bring me my bride I want to see her. My God, I am ashamed in front of her because I shall die.' Zaynab says: 'What kind of happiness is this, that I cannot prepare the happiness ceremony for you? I don't like this kind of situation for you. No bridegroom has decorated his hand with blood instead of henna.' Qasim says, 'It is not a custom for a wedding party, but I would like to give my life to Imam Husayn, and I am in a hurry. Give me my sword, I want to go to battle!'

In this elegy, Qasim's intentions are made clear; he willingly joins the battle knowing he will be killed. In the voice of his aunt Zaynab, the elegy expresses frustration as tragedy is anticipated. At some point during the performance of the elegies and imagined conversations, Qasim and Fatima are usually made to sit down next to each other on two chairs (fig.2). At this point, the *maddāḥ* typically engages the ritual participant-spectators in singing a cheerful song (*surūd*), and sweets are thrown at the couple, imitating the custom at an actual wedding party.

Fig.2

Maddāḥ: Tonight is the night of happiness of the young,
Tonight is the night of the *ḥanā-bandān*[10]
Qasim will be the bridegroom, say congratulations
Tonight, wearing nice clothes
Tonight, making the *ḥijla* of happiness

Fig.2
Young actors playing Qasim (left) and Fatima (right) sit surrounded by spectators-turned-actors

Fig.3
Qasim and Fatima embrace for their last farewell, surrounded by weeping spectator-participants

Fig.4
Fatima covered in black cloth is guided by a ritual assistant away from her new bridegroom Qasim

Fig.5
Qasim performs his last prayer in front of the nuptial chamber (*ḥijla*) before being martyred at the battle of Karbala

Answer: Qasim will be the bridegroom, say congratulations
Maddāḥ: Tonight is the wedding of Qasim
Qasim will be bridegroom, say congratulations
Answer: Qasim will be the bridegroom, say congratulations

While people sing, the joyful ululation continues and people clap their hands, although not in a very joyful manner. Then Qasim and Fatima are made to embrace and those standing around them sometimes weep. A black piece of fabric is placed over Fatima's head (fig.3). This marks the end of the wedding celebration and the beginning of the mourning. The actor embodying Fatima is told to hit her head with her hands, a kinaesthetic expression of mourning in the Iranian funerary tradition. Fatima is then led out of the room while the *maddāḥ* engages the ritual performer-spectators in singing responsorial elegies accompanied by flagellation, another expression of mourning (fig.4).

Maddāḥ: O, alas! (*va veila*!) This wedding party, shall I call it sadness or happiness?
O, alas! Qasim, the new bridegroom, congratulations to the king of Karbala
Answer: O, alas! This wedding party, shall I call it sadness or happiness?
Maddāḥ: Your aunt gives her life to you, where is your sweet, where is your henna?
For how long shall I say, my son, my son?
For how long shall I say, my son, my son?
For how long shall I beat my head and say, my son, my son?
Answer: O, alas! (*va veila*! repeated several times)

The woman enacting Qasim performs the prayer, is then covered by a black cloth symbolising his death, and led out of the room (fig.5). The procession of women carrying trays also leaves the room. This marks the end of the theatrical performance but the commemorative ritual continues. Ritual participants continue to sing *nawḥa*s lamenting the fate of Qasim.

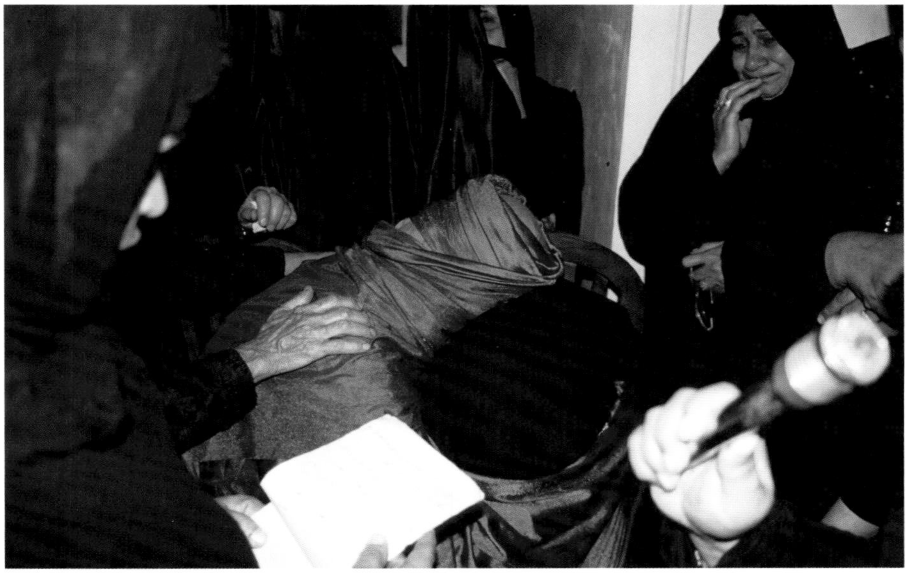

Figs. 3, 4

Fig.5

Maddāḥ: O, alas (*va veila*), for the happiness of this bridegroom
A hundred O, alas, for the happiness of this bridegroom
Dear aunt, where is your sweet, where is your henna (Qasim speaking to Zaynab)
Answer: O, alas, for the happiness of this bridegroom
Maddāḥ: Sister come and see my face (Husayn speaking to Zaynab)
Answer: Hundred O, alas, for the happiness of this bridegroom
Maddāḥ: When you go to Medina (tell them about the martyrs)
Answer: O, alas, for the happiness of this bridegroom

The ritual participants also sing *nawḥa*s elaborating on how lonely Imam Husayn and his sons felt at Karbala, the injustice they suffered, the beheading of Imam Husayn, and the disrespect shown to Zaynab. The elegies are accompanied by self-flagellation in the form of standing while beating the chest (*sineh sarpay*) accumulating with slapping the cheek (*lat*) and whilst exclaiming: 'My martyred bridegroom!' 'His face is washed by his blood!' and 'You are my bright moon!' (fig.6). The rite is closed by an elegy lamenting Imam Husayn, in which the women repeatedly shout 'O Husayn!' Whilst proclaiming their exclamations in loud voices, many participants slap their faces and toss their heads (and their hair if their headscarves have come off). This represents the climax and the mourning rite turns into a prayer for petition, *duʿā'*, addressing Imam Husayn:

Cure our patients, give our hands, help our youths, help Qur'an and Islam, don't take us to your self (let us die) until you have forgiven us. O Husayn! Husayn! Husayn! Husayn! Husayn!

Following the ritual, fruit and sweets from the trays are distributed to the participants to spread God's grace (*baraka*) among them.

Dramatic characters, actors, audience and modes of representation

The performance of *ʿArūze Qāsem* follows a conventional dramatic composition. Conventions allow ritual leaders, assistants and participant-spectators to engage in a familiar theatrical event. The performance is not rehearsed in a structured manner but is known to those involved through prior experience and, in some cases, through the immediate guidance of ritual assistants-turned-directors (*zākirs*). The ritual leader functions as the main 'director' adjusting acting and recital to the competence of actors and the duration according to the time available in the ritual programme. The communication and interaction between actors and spectators is characterised by reciprocal influence, not uncommon to theatre performance. More particular to *ʿArūze Qāsem* is the spectators' and actors' transitions in and out of their roles, constantly changing their status between spectators and actors. In fact, the theatrical performance relies on spectators becoming actors. In addition, the acting of some roles is shared between several actors and spectators-turned-actors, combining their skills in the representation of a character.

The only identified dramatic characters in *ʿArūze Qāsem* are Qasim and Fatima. The actors communicate through movement and sound, but also through immobility and silence.[11] Visually, Qasim and Fatima are portrayed by two girls or young women. The symbolic nature of the performance emphasises the characters' semiotic bodies and the representation of their status as either bride and bridegroom or as soon-to-be martyr and widow. Both characters are presented dressed in green garments and face veils. These are established iconographic markers known from the *taʿziya* tradition and religious paintings to signify their status as holy protagonists at the battle of Karbala.[12] The veil, moreover, is a way to deal with the phenomenal body when women play men's roles. In addition, props such as black textiles are used to signify their changing status from bride to widow and from bridegroom to martyr. The semiotic body allows spectators to easily recognise the characters, recollect their fate and evoke responses such as ululation. The actors, moreover, do not act out emotions but express them symbolically. While being guided, the actors perform culturally embedded gestures such as embracing to signify their separation, prayer to signify Qasim's preparation for death, and the slapping of cheeks to signify Fatima's grief. Consequently, the actors' portrayals as the main protagonists do not require any special training or skills.

The two young women embodying Qasim and Fatima remain silent during the performance. Instead, the ritual leader and lay participant-spectators impersonate their voices. Imaginary conversations between Qasim and his uncle, Imam Husayn, and remarks made by Qasim

Fig.6
Participants perform commemorative rites, such as beating their chests, after the performance

and Fatima expressing their attitudes, intentions and emotions, are voiced by the *maddāḥ* through the literary genres of *rowzeh* and *nawḥa*, with which the listeners are already familiar. Other methods applied by ritual leaders and senior lay-participants to give voice to Qasim's and Fatima's emotions include modulation of tone of voice and the interjection of speechless assertions such as lamentation and weeping. The expressions might be perceived as sensory embodiments of the characters and are deeply moving to those who hear them, some of whom burst out crying and moaning.[13]

Sauter points out that it is difficult to research the sensory level of theatrical communication.[14] Drawing on Benjamin's notion of 'aura', we speak about the actors' radiation but are short of proper terminology to describe the exhibitory actions and the spectators' response. In the case of *ʿArūze Qāsem*, I suggest it is useful to speak about the presentness and aura of the dramatic characters, rather than the actors' presentness and aura.[15] It is not the actors but the dramatic characters who motivate lamentation, wailing and self-flagellation from participant-spectators. Here, however, the dramatic character is a very complex entity. The character's social role and status are enacted through a semiotic body guided by ritual assistants-turned-directors, and the emotions, attitudes and intentions of the main characters are vocally expressed by skilled senior ritual leaders as well as spectators-turned-actors.

The theatrical communication in *ʿArūze Qāsem* is, additionally, facilitated by the objectification of the dramatic characters. The dress, including the face veil, and the symbolic gestures enhance the objectification of the two actors embodying Qasim and Fatima to the extent that they function as props. The appearance of props may carry strong performative feature.[16] In *ʿArūze Qāsem,* Qasim and Fatima are acted upon by ritual leader-directors as well as ritual spectators-turned-actors, who are deeply moved and take it upon themselves to voice the protagonists' sentiments, as well as expressing their own personal joy, grief and sorrow.

A second group of characters are Fatima's unidentified face-veiled female relatives bringing trays with wedding gifts. The characters are enacted by women from the lay public. Through the use of dress and props their mode of representation conveys mixed sentiments. The trays bearing candles and gifts (*khunche*) signify a wedding celebration but the black chadors in which they are dressed, convey a sinister sensation, reminding the spectators that the joyful celebration will be followed by Qasim's imminent self-sacrifice. Similarly, mixed cheerful and sad sentiments permeate the response from the participant-spectators. A third group of characters comprises the guests of the wedding party and mourners in the subsequent funeral, enacted by spectators-turned-actors. The spectators arrive dressed in black chadors, the common attire when participating in a mourning ceremony in this local community. As the theatrical performance takes place amid the crowd of spectators, it is sometimes difficult to identify who among them participates in the space of acting and who remains in the space of ritual performance. In effect, the spaces are blurred and fluid.

ʿArūze Qāsem also includes characters that are never seen and represent events that take place 'off stage'. Imam Husayn and his sister Zaynab, for example, are addressed through the presentation of *rowzeh* and *nawḥa* and 'heard' through ritual leaders' and singers' impersonations of their voices. Their presence, thus, has to be imagined by the listeners. While the theatrical performance enacts the wedding of Qasim and Fatima and the commemoration of Qasim's death, the event of his death is symbolically represented by placing a black cloth over Qasim. In contrast, *taʿziya* performances give great attention to the battles fought by the protagonists at Karbala and the circumstances surrounding their death (fig.7).

The relationship between the audience and the performer in *taʿziya* is unique.[17] The actors in the drama express their sorrow and grief through the verbal text of the performance. As a response, the audience provides explicit, forceful and sometimes violent expressions of grief and mourning. The audience thus completes a portion of the dramatic action. While both actors and spectators in *ʿArūze Qāsem* contribute to its theatrical performance in a similar manner, the distinction between

Fig.6

actors and spectators is less clear-cut. It is sometimes difficult to identify who is an actor and who is a spectator. Furthermore, as the spectators become actors they bring to their performance emotions they have developed as spectators. There is, thus, an ongoing interaction of performers and audiences in which both are simulta-neously producers and products of the performance, a process Erika Fischer-Lichte calls an autopoiesis.[18] According to Fischer-Lichte, the process is characterised by the collapsing of the binaries of spectator and actor. In *ʿArūze Qāsem* there is, however, not a collapse of spectator and actor. Instead, the theatrical performance is characterised by a doubling or incomplete presence in which theatrical and ritual frames are continuously negotiated and actors and spectators constantly change their status. Nevertheless, they still remain ritual participants.

Theatrical and ritual frames negotiated

To be effective, Richard Schechner argues, theatre must maintain its double or incomplete presence, as a 'here and now' performance of 'there and then' events.[19] The gap between 'here and now' and 'there and then', allows the audience to contemplate action and to entertain alternatives. Theatricality is thus a 'doubling' to something that is not theatre. The 'here and now' performance of *ʿArūze Qāsem* comprises the whole constellation of events, from the time the spectators arrive until they leave, and thus includes the commemorative ritual, whereas the 'there and then' event is the enactment of the wedding of Qasim and Fatima, and Qasim's subsequent martyrdom and Fatima's widowhood. Rituals, Schechner suggests, may carry participants across boundaries, transforming them into different persons, whereas the function of aesthetic drama is to provide a place for, and a means of, transformation.[20] Because of its particular doubling, connected to ritual commemoration, the enactment of *ʿArūze Qāsem* functions as a site for spiritual transgression in which actors and spectators may communicate with divine and saintly personages and express alliance, support and devotion, whilst asking for intercession and redemption. The communication with the spiritual realm is carried out through the principle of *tashabbuh* 'imitation'. Within a theatrical frame, *tashabbuh* refers to 'appearing to be the same as someone else', for example, to imitate and impersonate the martyrs at Karbala.[21] Within a ritual

Fig.7

frame, *tashabbuh* refers to 'making resemblance', that is, to weep for Husayn and other Shiʿi martyrs and to cause other people to imitate the weeping.[22] Here, lamentation is considered a meritorious act through which participants position themselves to request salvation for the souls of dead family members, to ask for their own eternal salvation on the Day of Judgement, as well as to receive help in this life through the mediation of saintly personages. From the perspective of meriting imitation, the theatrical performance therefore includes a category of spectators and agents not yet mentioned: God and saintly Shiʿi personages. Within the larger ritual frame they are perceived as agents who will, hopefully, bestow benediction upon humans.

The perceived divine presence gives orientation and energy to the actors' performance of *ʿArūze Qāsem* and the participant-spectators' attention. During the performance, there is an increased intensity in the actors' kinaesthetic behaviour and vocal expressions which are emulated in the participant-spectators' theatrical and ritualised behaviour. The intensified performance causes actors and participant-spectators to undergo an emotional transformation exhibiting passionate expressions of grief. Within the theatrical frame, such passionate expressions communicate the emotions of the protagonists at Karbala. Within a ritual frame, they are the ritual participants' expressions of sympathy and alliance with those protagonists, as well as an outlet for personal grief. The atmosphere created during the acting enhances this transformation and the communicative effect of the performance.

Fig.7
A *taʿziya* scene with male actors in which ʿAli Akbar (son of Imam Husayn), dressed in green and white, fights the enemy at the battle of Karbala. Masjed Nadir al-Mulk, Shiraz, 1999

Fig.8
Women prepare the props called *khunche*, trays laden with votive gifts, the day before the *ʿArūze Qāsem* is performed. Shiraz, 2002

The atmosphere that frames the theatrical performance situates the time and place of the event. To create a sad atmosphere, the walls of the ceremonial room are often decorated with black wall hangings (*parcham*) or draped in black fabrics, called *siāh pūshī*, 'clothed in black', or *taʿziya*, 'condolence'.[23] There are no scenographical representations alluding to the plains of Karbala. Instead the prop of the model 'bridal chamber', the *ḥijla Qāsem*, defines the time and space of the wedding of Qasim during the battle at Karbala. The props, both the *ḥijla* and the *khunche* (trays), clearly represent the duality of the theatrical event. As props, they belong to the enactment of the 'then and there' of the theatrical performance, but as votive gifts they express the 'here and now'. By the time *ʿArūze Qāsem* is introduced, there is a general atmosphere of quiet lamentation and anticipation. In rites preceding *ʿArūze Qāsem*, ritual leaders prepare the audience for the theatrical performance. For example, ritual participants perform supplications to improve the welfare of named members of the local community. They also listen to lectures by the ritual leaders, to the *rowzeh* of the protagonists at Karbala, and participate in the performance of elegiac poetry.

The first part of the commemorative ritual thus provides the background information needed to properly understand the story, to know the protagonists and the basic conflict as well as the setting. The twofold purpose of the theatrical performance in the ritual, that is to remember God and important Shiʿi personages and to secure their benediction, was expressed by one of the ritual leaders with the following words: 'We take out the *ḥijla Qāsem* in memory of the martyrs of Karbala. It is also in memory of the young people who lost their youth. It is like *taʿziya*.' The expression *taʿziya* here refers to 'condolences'. Her comment served to create a mental orientation in the spectators and to generate certain expectations.

ʿArūze Qāsem as devotional culture and strategy

The theatrical performance of *ʿArūze Qāsem* as ritual has developed strategies that maximise the meriting effect of participation. The fluctuating transition between actor and spectator status allows as many people as possible to receive religious merit, *savāb* (Arabic *thawāb*), by taking up roles. However, it is important that actors and spectators-turned-actors always retain their status as ritual participants. It is, after all, their status as ritual participants that defines their activities as devotional practices. Thus, while the theatrical performance is characterised by a doubling in which actors and spectators continuously change, there is a collapse between theatrical and ritual agents. For example, when the procession of wedding guests carrying trays on their heads arrives, the spectators become actors by imitating the (imagined) ululation of Fatima's family members. At the same time, they retain their status as ritual participants, since the act of imitation is meriting. Moreover, while acting as wedding guests, they simultaneously perform a devotional act when they attempt to touch the trays loaded with ex-votos to benefit from their blessing.

To understand the role of *ʿArūze Qāsem* in devotional culture and as devotional strategy, it is necessary to also look at what takes place before and after the theatrical performance. While there is no rehearsal of actors and dramaturgy, a considerable time is spent preparing the main props, that is, the nuptial chamber (*ḥijla*) and the trays with gifts (*khunche*). The preparation usually takes place on the evening of the seventh of Muharram, the day before *ʿArūze Qāsem* is performed. The preparations are typically carried out by female friends and relatives of the host of the ritual-theatrical event (fig.8). By doing so, they perform 'religious works' which function as forms of prayers with meriting and redemptive potential. The preparations are accompanied by recitation of *ziyārāt ʿāshūrāʾ*, *rowzeh* and *nawḥa*, which frame the practical work within a spiritual setting and underline its devotional and redemptive quality.

The end of the theatrical performance is marked by the exit of Fatima, Qasim and the procession of women with the trays (*khunche*) from the room. When the ritual is concluded, props such as the *ḥijla* and food on the *khunche* are turned into religious objects. Many participants linger on to drink tea, smoke the water pipe and talk with

Fig.8

friends and relatives. At this point the sweets and fruit of the *khunche* are distributed amongst those present. The practice illustrates well the fluidity and complexity of the props. Props are made out of votive gifts, presented as thanks giving to God and saintly Shiʿi personages in return for their intercession and benediction. As return-gifts they are treated as *tabbaruk*, things that will spread good fortune. Such objects are often much sought after and are typically distributed among the ritual participants when the ritual is over. The *ḥijla* is also made from votive gifts. The *ḥijla* is typically made of a wooden frame, decorated with layers of fabrics in bright colours and covered in fairy lights. After the ritual, many women approach it seeking mediation from God and saintly Shiʿi personages. Their requests are accompanied by different gestures that may draw the benefactor's attention to a supplicant and bind her to the benefactor. Strategies include kissing the *ḥijla*, touching it with her hands and then wiping the face, or making knots in the textiles that partly cover the entrance of the *ḥijla*. It is believed that when the knots are untied, the wishes will be fulfilled.[24]

Why is *ʿArūze Qāsem* popular among women?

In Iran, male and female parts in the *taʿziya* are played by men to a gender-mixed audience. Actors and musicians must be skilful and undergo extensive training. In the theatrical event of *ʿArūze Qāsem* all roles are enacted by women to an all-female audience. It is thus an opportunity for women to organise, stage and direct a performance, and to act and sing. In terms of cost, space and competence, the theatrical performance of *ʿArūze Qāsem* is suitably met by women's resources. The performance involves low economic costs. Props are made from donated gifts and the organisation and acting is conducted by volunteers. Only ritual leaders receive a small economic compensation. The performance can be adjusted to the space available, whether large ceremonial halls or domestic spaces that are made public for the occasion. Special performative skills are required only from ritual leaders and assistants-turned-directors who are familiar with the performative convention and commonly recited texts. Their professional competence is combined with the cultural competence of the other participants. Actors and spectators-turned-actors draw on conventional wedding and mourning traditions. Props and acting patterns imitate Iranian matrimonial traditions and Shiʿa mourning rites. Such borrowings of cultural customs into theatre can also be observed in *taʿziya*.

Sadeq Humayuni suggests that the presence of cultural customs help to bind the *taʿziya* deeply into the lives, consciousness and emotions of people.[25] The narrow and specific focus on the wedding of Qasim and Fatima in *ʿArūze Qāsem* may be motivated by the economic constrains felt by many lay participants and organisers. But it may also represent a preferred angle to, and interpretation of, the battle of Karbala, from women's perspectives. It is particularly appealing to women because it is one of the few 'domestic' issues dealt with during the battle at arbala. Indeed, in their own social lives, female ritual performers are deeply involved in matrimonial and funerary rites.

Concluding remarks

The theatrical performance of *ʿArūze Qāsem* is designed to serve rituals of commemoration during Muharram. Performed by a combination of skilled and unskilled actors it allows lay participants of the rituals to use the sphere of theatrical performance in order to communicate with the divine and saintly personages and position themselves as supplicants. The strategies employed are characterised by the actors' and spectators' fluctuating transitions in and out of roles, constantly changing their status as actors and spectators. In fact, the theatrical performance relies on spectators becoming actors. In addition, the portrayal of some roles is shared between several actors and spectators-turned-actors, combining the skills of several actors in the representation of a character. Sensory expressions and experiences function as bridges between theatrical and ritual frames and contribute to the development of both. The rites preceding *ʿArūze Qāsem* set the atmosphere for the theatrical performance, whereas the sentiments shaped by the theatrical performance are essential to a successful ritual performance. The theatrical presentation is created by and for women to meet their resources in terms of competence and funding to tend to their spiritual needs.

1 For comprehensive studies on Twelver Shiʿi religious theatre through history and in different cultural settings see: William O. Beeman, *Iranian Performance Traditions* (Costa Mesa, CA, 2011); Peter J. Chelkowski, ed., *Taʿziyeh: Ritual and Drama in Iran* (New York, 1979); Peter J. Chelkowski, ed., *The Drama Review* 49, 4 (2005), Special Issue: *Taʿziyeh*; and Peter J. Chelkowski, ed., *Eternal Performance: Taʿziyeh and Other Shiite Rituals* (London, New York and Calcutta, 2010). For descriptions of performances and librettos dealing with the fate of Qasim see: Lewis Pelly, *The Miracle Play of Hasan and Husain*, vol.2 (London, 1879, repr., Farnborough, 1970), pp.1–17; Sadeq Humayuni, 'An Analysis of a *Taʿziyeh* of Qasim', in Chelkowski, ed., *Taʿziyeh, Ritual and Drama*, pp.12–23; and Jean and Jacqueline Calmard, 'Muharram Ceremonies Observed in Teheran by Ilya Nicolaevich Berezin (1843)' in Chelkowski, ed., *Eternal Performance*, pp.53–73. Qasim is represented rather differently in the context of Muharram rituals in South Asia, see Karen G. Ruffle in *Gender, Sainthood, and Everyday Practice in South Asian Shiʿism* (Chapel Hill, NC, 2011). In rituals in Hyderabad, Qasim is symbolically represented by a standard (*ʿalam*). The *ʿalam* is brought from its ritual location, the *ʿāshūrkhāna*, and carried around in a street procession before returning it to the *ʿāshūrkhāna*. In the process, the *ʿalam* is clad in different textiles signifying the transformation in Qasim's status as bridegroom, when departing the *ʿāshūrkhāna*, into the martyred warrior upon the return.

2 Berezin's description from 1843 offers an early account of women performing *taʿziya* in private settings in Iran during the Qajar era. See Calmard, 'Muharram Ceremonies', p.57. Negar Mottahedeh draws on Persian sources to describe women rehearsing, performing and watching *taʿziya* in women-only settings during the reign of the Qajar shahs, 'Karbala Drag Kings and Queens' in Chelkowski, ed., *Eternal Performance*, pp.160–164. In present-day Lebanon women do, however, act the female parts in public performances, see Sabrina Mervin 'Shiite Theater in South Lebanon: Some Notes on The Karbala Drama and the Sabaya', in Chelkowski, ed., *Eternal Performance*, pp.322–333.

3 Willmar Sauter, *Eventness: A Concept of the Theatrical Event* (2nd ed., Stockholm, 2008), pp.9–12. I wish to express my gratitude to Professor Anita Hammer at the University of Oslo for her valuable suggestions on an earlier draft of this paper.

4 Ingvild Flaskerud, 'Shiʿa-Muslim Women as Ritual Performers in Iran', in Ingvar Mæhle and Inger Marie Okkenhaug, ed., *Women and Religion in the Middle East and the Mediterranean* (Oslo, 2004); Ingvild Flaskerud, 'Oh, my heart is sad. It is Moharram, the Month of Zaynab. Aesthetics and Women's Mourning Ceremonies in Shiraz', in Kamran Scot Aghaie, ed., *The Women of Karbala. The Gender Dynamics of Ritual Performances and Symbolic Discourses of Modern Shiʿi Islam* (Austin, 2005); Ingvild Flaskerud, *Standard-Bearers of Hussein: Women Commemorating Karbala* (35 min. DVD film, 2003).

5 Sometimes a performance is staged on the evening of the seventh of Muharram after the host and her friends have completed preparing the props for *ʿArūze Qāsem* to be performed on the following day.

6 For the composition and use of the *ḥijla* in Shiʿi rituals see, Jean Calmard, 'Ḥejla', *EIR*, vol.7, 2, pp.143–144.

7 Known in Persian as *esfand dāna* (Latin, *Peganum harmala*). The pungent smoke produced by the burning seeds is believed to chase away the evil eye and is a well-known custom.

8 *Allāhumma ṣalli ʿala Muḥammad wa āl-e Muḥammad,* 'O Allah send thy blessings on Muhammad and his family.'

9 *Rowzeh* (i.e. *rawḍa-khānī,* lit. 'recitation from *The Garden [of Martyrs]*') is a genre of Shiʿa lamentation literature which narrates the sufferings of the Imams in general and of the battle at Karbala in particular. It is commonly performed at various types of commemoration rituals.

10 The *ḥanā-bandān*, or rituals of henna (Pers. *ḥanā*, Ar. *ḥennāʾ*) are practised as part of marriage customs in many Middle Eastern communities. In Iran, the ceremony is performed one or two days before the wedding celebration and the bride and the bridegroom decorate each other's palms with henna.

11 Sauter, *Eventness*, p.76.

12 Peter Chelkowski, 'Popular Shiʿi Mourning Rituals', *al-Serāt*, 12 (1986), pp.209–229; Peter Chelkowski, 'Narrative Painting and Painting Recitation in Qajar Iran', in *Muqarnas*, 6 (1989), pp.98–111; Ingvild Flaskerud, *Visualizing Belief and Piety in Iranian Shiism* (London and New York, 2010).

13 Erika Fischer-Lichte, *The Transformative Power of Performance: A New Aesthetics*, tr. Saskya Iris Jain (London and New York, 2008), p.125.

14 Fischer-Lichte, *Transformative Power*, pp.58–59.

15 For a discussion of the actor's aura see Fischer-Lichte, *Transformative Power*, pp.93–95.

16 Sauter, *Eventness*, p.64.

17 William O. Beeman and Mohammad B. Ghaffari, 'Acting Styles and Actor Training in *Taʿziyeh*', in Peter J. Chelkowski, ed., *The Drama Review*, 49, 4 (2005), p.26.

18 Fischer-Lichte, *Transformative Power*, pp.7–8.

19 Richard Schechner, *Performance Theory* (London and New York, 1988), p.169.

20 Ibid., p.171.

21 Ibid., p.105.

22 Mayel Baktash, '*Taʿziyeh* and its Philosophy', in Chelkowski, ed., *Taʿziyeh: Ritual and Drama*, pp.101–102.

23 Flaskerud, *Visualizing Belief*, p.200.

24 Anne Betteridge, *Ziarat: Pilgrimage to the Shrines of Shiraz*, (Ph.D. dissertation, University of Chicago, 1985), p.220 and p.222; Flaskerud, *Visualizing Belief*, p.187

25 Humayuni, 'Analysis', p.19.

19

Cinema as a cultural reservoir for the Shiʿi performing art of *taʿziya*

Nacim Pak-Shiraz

The religious practices of Muharram have historically played an important role within the socio-political milieu of Iran, influencing vast areas of cultural expressions including more recently that of cinema. This essay will explore the ways in which film provides a new medium of expression for one of the oldest Shiʿi narratives, the story of Imam Husayn. I will begin by looking very briefly at the eventful history of the Muharram practices in Iran and then examine two works of the notable Iranian theatre and film director, Bahram Beyzaie (b. 1938), in order to illustrate how he uses the medium of film to reinterpret and reintroduce these older traditions to his audience.[1]

Taʿziya is a re-enactment of the events that led to the death of Husayn b. ʿAli the grandson of the Prophet and the third Shiʿi Imam. In 680, Husayn finally accepted the calls of the Kufans who had long invited him to rise up against the Umayyad usurpers of the caliphate. However, he was soon stopped in his tracks by the 4,000-strong army of Yazid, the Umayyad caliph. Accompanied only by members of his family and close companions, Husayn realised that the Kufans had betrayed their oath of allegiance to him and would not come to his aid. He refused to submit to Yazid and was forced to camp in Karbala. Denied access to water and parched from thirst, Husayn and his companions were attacked on ʿAshura', the tenth day of the month of Muharram. By afternoon, Husayn and his men, including children, were brutally slain. The battle of Karbala also provided the 'prototype for the only indigenous dramatic form in the world of Islam'.[2]

The events of Karbala have been commemorated extensively in Iran particularly with the advent of the Safavids in 1501 and the establishment of Shiʿi Islam as the official religion of the state.[3] The practice of *rowzeh-khānī* (i.e. *rawḍa khānī*), participation in the delivery of sermons about the tragedy of Karbala, also comes to the fore around this time.[4] Mourning processions during the ten days of Muharram, complete with standards, horses and drums, also become significant at this time. Even though theatrical elements were present in these rituals, the re-enactment itself of the events of Karbala, which is properly referred to as *taʿziya* or Passion play, are not found until the Zand period in the 18th century.[5]

Despite its religious motifs, *taʿziya* did not at first meet with the approval of all the *ʿulamā'* (religious scholars). They objected to it on various theological grounds that condemned representation, music, and women's participation in performances and demonstrations.[6] In the case of *taʿziya*, it provided a new space for women's public appearance and participation since they were allowed to watch the play (fig.1).[7] Most importantly, however, its great popularity became a threat to *rowzeh-khānī*, a ceremony that was customarily organised by the *ʿulamā'*, and from which they earned an income.[8] *Taʿziya*, nevertheless, reached its peak under Qajar patronage, a period referred to as the golden age of *taʿziya*. Moreover, the emerging new social class of merchants and politicians also supported *taʿziya*. In his travels to Europe, Nasir al-Din Shah Qajar (*r.* 1848–1896) had developed a taste for European theatre venues. He wanted a playhouse similar in architectural style to that of the Royal Albert Hall in London. Subsequently in 1869, he ordered the building of the magnificent Takiyeh Dowlat in Tehran, located on the south-eastern side of the Golestan Palace. But even before it was completed, there were protests from the religious strata about the types of performances it might hold. Nasir al-Din Shah, ultimately designed the Takiyeh Dowlat for *taʿziya* performances.[9]

By the beginning of the 20th century, the last two Qajar monarchs were increasingly becoming westernised and *taʿziya* gradually came to lose its royal patronage.[10] Many years later, Takiyeh Dowlat fell by the wayside under Reza Shah Pahlavi's modernisation project, which included the ban on *taʿziya* performances. After the demolishment of Takiyeh Dowlat, *taʿziya* was pushed out of the bigger cities and into the suburbs and villages, where performers went in the hope of finding new audiences.[11]

Fig.1

More recently, within the Islamic Republic, the practices of Muharram have once again caused contention amongst some of the religious strata. One of them is Hujjatul-Islam Mehdi Daneshmand, an Iranian cleric and author of a number of books on religion. He is a frequent public speaker and delivers sermons in different parts of Iran. Daneshmand is highly entertaining, with a great talent for doing impressions and, unusually for a cleric, has no qualms about swearing during his speeches. The reach of his sermons now extends beyond the mosques and other public sessions, thanks to the virtual world of the Internet and particularly YouTube. Some of his clips on YouTube have received hundreds of thousands of hits. Given the fact that the clips are in Persian and not subtitled, one can safely assume that most of his virtual audience is also Iranian. Not all of these audiences, however, can be classified as enthusiastic viewers, as some of the obscenities left in the comments section testify. My main interest in Daneshmand's speeches, however, revolves around his references to the commemorative practices of Muharram.

Daneshmand is critical of many aspects of these practices. He particularly takes issue with the *maddāḥ*s (eulogists). Like the *rowzeh-khān* who leads the *rowzeh-khānī* sermons, *maddāḥ*s lead the narration of the stories of the Prophet, Imams and saints in public and private ritual settings. *Maddāḥ*s are not necessarily educated in madrasas and many draw their material from a broad spectrum of literature, including their own compositions. Daneshmand criticises the ways in which many of the current *maddāḥ*s praise the Shiʿi Imams and the family of the Prophet. He holds that such 'ignorant and uneducated' *maddāḥ*s are responsible for providing Sunni Muslims with the ammunition to condemn Shiʿi rituals and practices. The Internet, he states, is rife with Sunni sites that are anti-Shiʿa and they use extracts from these *maddāḥ*s to prove that Shiʿas are heretics. His own selective extracts from the *maddāḥ*s provide him with the perfect foil for condemning those religious ceremonies that are held independently of the *ʿulamā'*. He characterises such *maddāḥ*s as not only uneducated, uninformed and bereft of any religious knowledge, but also, and more dangerously, their ignorance offers the enemies of Shiʿism an excuse to revile it. The audiences of these *maddāḥ*s are not spared either. They are held equally responsible for attending these sessions and keeping quiet during such disgrace, which brings untold shame upon the religion. He states:

> A bunch of uneducated good-for-nothings get together and chant 'Husayn, Husayn!'...You beating your chest for three hours, how many sermons of Imam Husayn have you studied? How many books have you studied on Imam Husayn?
>
> ...I was in one of the provinces and I actually disrupted the session.

Fig.1
A man playing the role of Fatima in a *taʿziya* performance. Traditionally, women are not allowed to act in *taʿziya* so male actors play the female roles

The *maddāḥ* there was singing: 'Hasan [Husayn's elder brother and preceding Imam] has one dot [a reference to the dots in the Arabic/ Persian script], Husayn has three dots, Fatima [Husayn's mother, he Prophet's daughter] has one dot, Zaynab [Husayn's sister] has five dots, Wah! Wah!...' I said, 'Shut it, and why are you [the audience] wailing?'...CDs of these sessions are made and then put on the Internet and the Sunnis come and show it around and say: 'See! This is the share of the Shiʿas' [i.e. their contribution to Islam]...What is this you [the *maddāḥs*] are saying? Don't you have brains?...Didn't Zaynab have sermons? Didn't she have speeches?...What kind of a *rowzeh* is this that you are feeding people in the name of religion?

In another speech, he further criticises mourning sessions set up independently of the *'ulamā'*, which result in heretical and blasphemous talk. Religion, Daneshmand implies, should remain within the domain of the clergy whose prerogative it is to authorise religious rituals and practices. It is certainly not for the *maddāḥ*s to bring in music as an accompaniment to their singing. For Daneshmand, the entire practice, whether it is the lyrics, the *maddāḥ*s themselves or the audience clapping their hands together, is problematic. It should be noted, however, that the very fact that the Ministry of Culture and Islamic Guidance broadcasts *nawḥa*s (elegies) with music, if not necessarily the exact ones that Daneshmand points to, on national radio and television, gives them some degree of legitimacy, if not outright endorsement. At the very least, it points to the plurality of practice sanctioned by the state even as it attempts to strike a delicate balance between filling in a gap 'demanded' by the laity, and being cognizant of the concerns of more conservative elements within the state who fear the erosion of their power and influence. As we shall see below, Daneshmand is conscious of this perceived sanction and addresses it, here, squarely:

A few *maddāḥ*s, who have studied under only God knows which master, string together some rubbish so that they can supposedly attract the youth to them...

When not even one *'ālim* [singular of *'ulamā'*] is present [in organising and guiding] your gathering, it is no surprise that the result is this kind of catastrophe.

Daneshmand then goes on to provide an example of lyrics he had heard a *maddāḥ* sing:

'I who hold on to the love of Husayn, am only the dog of Husayn.'
For God's sake, what kind of a lyric is this?...They say '*lā ilāha illa Ḥusayn*' [There is no God but Husayn]...They've no clue what they're saying. This is blasphemy!...
Tapes of this group of uncouth *maddāḥ*s, who have distanced themselves from the *'ulamā'*, are being distributed in Zahidan [a province bordering Pakistan], in the Arab countries, in Saudi Arabia. This has closed the mouths of [i.e. silenced] the [Shiʿi] *'ulamā'*. They [the anti-Shiʿi Sunnis] say you are heretics! You consider Fatima and Husayn as God!!!...The reputation of religion is not in the hands of these few *maddāḥ*s.
They sing their *maddāḥi*s with the keyboard, with the santoor [a traditional string instrument].
You've taken the bloody music into the pulpit, into the mihrab (prayer niche) and into *rowzeh* as well!!!
The Ministry of [Culture and] Islamic Guidance that has spent millions and trillions of tomans on *daf* and *tonbak* [both traditional percussion instruments]. What does it want from the mihrab and religion? Leave Husayn alone...leave religion alone...leave the keyboard for the television and radio, and the Ministry of Culture and Islamic Guidance. Wherever there are *tonbak*s, all the cameras are ready and present, but they don't want to have anything to do with a session of such grandeur [pointing to his own session]...
I have to say that religion has a master...Husayn's head did not go on top of the spear so that I and you could get together now in his sessions and clap our hands and whistle, play the santoor, take the santoor inside the mihrab. Whoever has heard of *maddāḥi* played with a flute?

Fig.2

Fig.3

They justify that the Islamic Republic of Iran Broadcasting shows it [these *maddāḥis*]; the Islamic Republic of Iran Broadcasting shows a lot of things, like the struggle of the fittest in the jungle, should you imitate?...The Islamic Republic of Iran Broadcasting is not a source of emulation (*marjaʿ-e taqlīd*), the radio is not a source of emulation, they cannot be the source of emulation, they cannot show jurisprudence.

Many Shiʿi practices such as pilgrimage to the shrines of the Imams and saints, and visual representations of the Imams and the prophets, have been condemned by mainstream Sunnis.[12] Shiʿas, however, have not necessarily shied away from rituals that may be perceived as 'un-Islamic' by the Sunnis. Daneshmand's concerns about the above-mentioned 'malpractices' do not appear to stem solely from anxiety about believers losing salvation, but also the disrepute that they can bring to Shiʿism. This constant awareness of the 'Other's' perception and condemnation of 'Self' appears to precipitate attempts to comply and reconcile with what is acceptable to that 'normative' view, and, in turn, to shape local practices. One could even question if Sunni normativity is replacing Shiʿi sensibilities. It is, therefore, pertinent to ask if the recent banning (in Muharram 2007) of certain practices, some of which had been observed for centuries in Iran is a reaction to anti-Shiʿa propaganda or a political discourse used to strategically condemn rival factions.

The official bans in 2007 included public displays of the images of the Imams, the use of *ʿalams* (standards) during the mourning processions and playing of instruments as part of the commemorative ceremonies (fig.2). It is, however, debatable whether as individuals, the Shiʿas themselves will remove pictures of the Imams from their homes, shops or cafes. But for now, another video clip on YouTube very tellingly streams a *maddāḥ* beating his chest and singing passionately in a very crowded mourning session: 'They can say whatever they want, I am the dog of Husayn!' and the congregants beat their chests and repeat this refrain after him. Interestingly, a fragment of a Safavid silk and gold carpet dating from 1600–1625, displayed at the British Museum's 2009 exhibition, *Shah ʿAbbas: The Remaking of Iran*, bears a *waqf* inscription referring to the Shah as 'the dog of this shrine'. Indeed, the exhibition catalogue cites additional references where Shah ʿAbbas is referred to as 'the dog of ʿAli b. Abi Talib' or 'the dog of the shrine'.[13] One can, therefore, safely assume that the phrase 'dog of Husayn' has been in currency for a long time within the Shiʿi Iranian vocabulary and is not a recent innovation as Daneshmand asserts. The issue raised above is obviously far more complex and requires further research that

Fig.2
Musicians playing for a *taʿziya* and *naqqālī* (storytelling) performances. The music cues the passage of time, heightens the merriment, drama and suspense and sets the scene for battles

Fig.3
A lively battle scene between Imam ʿAli (in green) and Qanbar before the latter's conversion to Islam

lies outside the scope of this essay. However, it is clear that the current commemorative events of Muharram are not just about Imam Husayn and his message. What is interesting is that the Muharram commemorations have themselves turned into a battle for retaining authority over defining what these commemorations do and do not entail. It is the official versus the popular discourse on Imam Husayn, a battle that is not so easily won on either side (fig.3).

As for Iranian cinema, a few Iranian filmmakers have engaged with *taʿziya* in their films. In the face of these pressures on Muharram rituals, through their reinterpretation of this older form of performing art, they have – even if inadvertently – reintroduced *taʿziya* to their audiences. One can, therefore, argue that despite the destruction of the Takiyeh Dowlat theatre, the symbol of *taʿziya*'s glorious period, the cinema screens revived some of the recognition and significance that *taʿziya* once enjoyed. Here, I would like to outline a few such examples in the works of Bahram Beyzaie, the Iranian filmmaker and scholar of Iranian performing arts.

Bahram Beyzaie was born in Tehran in 1938. He is a distinguished playwright, screenwriter, film and theatre director, film editor and renowned scholar of Iranian performing arts.[14] He left his studies at the University of Tehran incomplete, and began his own independent research on Iranian theatre, epic literature (including Ferdowsi's *Shāhnāma* or Book of Kings), as well as the traditional plays of *taʿziya*. His research also encompassed the study of pre-Islamic Persian history and Persian painting. Later, he extended his studies to Eastern art and spent a decade writing about it, as well as Iranian theatre and cinema.

Beyzaie has consistently maintained that his passion is to understand ordinary people and their cultural and historical roots, and that this has driven his work and research. Beyzaie's 1984 screenplay, *Rūz-e Waqīʿa* or *The Day of the Incident*, recounts one of the most important Shiʿi narratives, the story of Karbala. *Rūz-e Waqīʿa* was not just an attempt to put *taʿziya* on screen or document a dying tradition. Rather, Beyzaie successfully brings the two elements of film and *taʿziya* together, employing both the Western-secular medium of filmmaking and the Iranian religious tradition of the retelling of the martyrdom of Imam Husayn and his companions. Even though it is based on the historical incident of Karbala, it makes no claims to be a historical film. Instead, like *taʿziya,* it encompasses larger Islamic historical and mythological elements as well as those that are specifically Iranian in its narrative. Despite Beyzaie's numerous attempts to make the film himself, he failed to obtain the necessary government permits. As a result, in 1994, the film was given to Shahram Asadi to direct. Beyzaie's solid script, however, did much to turn it into one of the best narratives on the events of Karbala, a narrative that is remarkably influenced by the elements of *taʿziya* (fig.4).

During Nasir al-Din Shah's reign (*r.* 1848–1896), when *taʿziya* reached its peak in terms of its artistic and entertainment values, it was divided into two parts: the *pīsh waqīʿa* or 'before the incident' and the *waqīʿa* or the 'incident' itself. The *pīsh waqīʿa* usually consisted of lighter performances and varied from love stories to satire. It was usually an opportunity to criticise those in positions of power,[15] or enact stories with titles such as 'The Queen of Sheba's meeting with Solomon' and 'Fatima's attendance at a Quraysh wedding', for example. This was then followed by the *waqīʿa,* which was three times as long and focused on the tragedy at Karbala.[16] Thus, the *taʿziya* performance would make people laugh and cry at the same time. It was both a joyous and sad occasion.

The title of the film, *Rūz-e Waqīʿa*, can be read as paying homage to these earlier forms of *taʿziya*. The film draws from both the *pīsh waqīʿa* and *waqīʿa* portions of the *taʿziya* performance by starting with a love story. Interestingly, the wedding scenes comprise roughly one third of the entire film (27 out of 95 minutes). More importantly, the wedding dances and music with which the film begins are in sharp contrast to the current more sombre forms of commemorating Muharram in modern-day Iran under the Islamic Republic. Like *taʿziya*, the film is not just about the martyrdom of Imam Husayn, but includes the lighter story of the protagonists' love. Similarly, like *pīsh waqīʿa* in

Fig.4

Fig.5

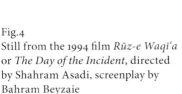

Fig.6

taʿziya, which provided the space to criticise the feudal landlords, the first part of the film provides an opportunity to criticise those who use their privileged social status to inflict injustice on the dispossessed.

The film's narrative also emphasises the Shiʿi obligation of upholding Imam Husayn's message. Thus, Beyzaie's script is not simply a retelling of the events of Karbala on screen. In fact, very little is dedicated to the events of Karbala itself. Instead, he emphasises the impact of Imam Husayn's martyrdom in the lives of the Shiʿa and in the formation of their religious identity. The *taʿziya* motifs are, however, restricted in *The Day of the Incident*. The overall dramatic aspects of the film would have certainly looked different had Beyzaie directed the film himself. This is clearly borne out in Beyzaie's later film, *Mosāferān* or *The Travellers*, made in 1992, which provided him the opportunity to both write and direct a film that employed a variety of *taʿziya* motifs, even though it was a story set in modern times that did not focus on the martyrdom of Imam Husayn (fig.5).

One of the most striking elements of *taʿziya* is the complete lack of suspense in the story and performance. Both the spectators and the actors know the tragic ending. They know that Imam Husayn and his companions will be killed and his family taken captive. It is, therefore, moot to keep this a secret to retain the story's suspense. Similarly, at the beginning of *The Travellers,* Mahtab, the female protagonist, faces the camera and tells the audience that she and her family are on their way to Tehran to attend her sister's wedding. She then goes on to confess that none of them will make it and that they will all die, thus giving away the ending of the story right at the start of the film. Moreover, like the performance of *taʿziya* and unlike the commonly used shot/reverse camera angle, Mahtab faces the audience and speaks to them directly.[17] The dramatic acting in the film is also a departure from the preferred realist or neo-realist styles in filmmaking. Instead, the acting of the various actors is a tribute to the different traditional performing arts of Iran including *pardah-khānī* (storytelling using a large painting) (fig.6), *naqqālī* (traditional form of public storytelling) (fig.7), and *taʿziya*. The constant circular movements of the camera throughout the film simulate the *taʿziya* arena, which is traditionally a round stage with spectators gathered around it.

The method Beyzaie used in depicting the tragic deaths in *The Travellers* can be paralleled to the conventions of staging deaths in traditional *taʿziya* performances. For example, in *taʿziya*, an injured actor departs the stage on horseback, usually followed by a few men. Soon after, the horse returns on stage without its rider and with its body pierced by numerous bloodied arrows. The return of the horse without its rider is an old metaphor in Persian literature used to indicate the rider's death. In *taʿziya*, the actual moment of Imam Husayn's martyrdom is also hidden from the spectators' eyes even though it occurs on stage. Traditionally, ten people from the opposing army surround the Imam, gradually tightening the circle around him. Suddenly, they throw themselves upon him and freeze in this position. Then the actor who

Fig.4
Still from the 1994 film *Rūz-e Waqīʿa* or *The Day of the Incident*, directed by Shahram Asadi, screenplay by Bahram Beyzaie

Fig.5
Still from the 1992 film *Mosāferān* or *The Travellers* showing the bride's reflection in the mirror that Mahtab carries to her ancestral home. Written and directed by Bahram Beyzaie

Fig.6
The traditional storytelling art of *pardah-khānī*, using a large painting on a portable screen or curtain (i.e. *pardah*). The main image depicts Imam ʿAli cleaving his enemy in half with his famous sword, *Dhu'l-faqār*

plays the role of the murderer of Imam Husayn, Shimr, who was the commander of the enemy's army, weeps loudly and invites the audience to also cry (since he is a Shiʿi believer in real life), before storming into the middle of the circle to behead the Imam. At this moment, because the Imam cannot be seen even though he is on stage, pigeons are released into the sky. They symbolise both the ascendance of the Imam's soul into the heavens and the messengers who carry the news of the Imam's death.[18]

In homage to this tradition, the exact moment of the tragic deaths of the family in *The Travellers* is also hidden from the audience. The viewer is aware from very early on in the film that the family will not make it to the wedding in Tehran. Numerous warning signals throughout the film are a constant reminder of the unpleasant incident that is about to take place. The car's navigation through the dangerous, twisting mountainous roads seem to close in on them, the dark ominous tunnel they pass through, the musical cues that constantly change from merry beats to suspenseful tones and, finally, the tanker that approaches the camera threatening a crash but that calmly steers back onto the road, all suggest the imminence of the incident. The fire and smoke in the next sequence and the traffic lieutenant reporting on the incident all combine to inform the viewer that the fatal accident has indeed occurred. No gory details are shown, nor is there an emphasis on the bodies. Indeed, there is only one quick shot of a draped corpse. Instead, the tragedy is depicted through the body of the smashed car with broken and bloodstained windows, just like the horse pierced with arrows on the *taʿziya* stage returns without its rider.

One of the sequences in the film that best alludes to the *taʿziya* stage is the mourning ceremony held in the family's home. The camera constantly makes circular movements on the guests, suggesting a round stage in the centre of the room. This then becomes the centre stage for various family members, just like the *taʿziya* actors, to make their speeches.

In the *taʿziya* tradition, one of the techniques of distancing the actors from the characters they play is by referring to them as 'readers' (*khāns*) of a particular role or character. Put simply, the actors play the roles of one of the 'good guys' (*maẓlūm-khāns*, i.e. the oppressed) or one of the 'bad guys' (*mukhālif-khāns*, i.e. the oppressors), and usually remain confined to these types of roles for life (fig.8). Hence, the *mukhālif-khān* who plays the role of the murderer of the Imam is called *Shimr-khān* and, as mentioned above, because he is a Shiʿa in real life, he also cries when he kills Imam Husayn and recites elegies to that effect, reminding the audience that what they see is just a performance (fig.9). Beyzaie also uses this theatrical form of *taʿziya* in the film. Indeed, the family of the deceased can be compared to the *maẓlūm-khāns* (the readers of the oppressed, i.e. the Shiʿa) and the truck driver and his assistant who caused the death of the family to the *mukhālif-khāns* (the readers of the opposing army) in *taʿziya*. The truck driver and his assistant attend the mourning ceremony to pay their respects and beg for forgiveness. They vociferate how, despite their desperate efforts to avoid the accident, the truck had slid on the slippery road and crashed into the taxi. The loud, crude and rough voices of the driver and his assistant and their frequent use of slang and colloquial terms is very similar to that used by the *mukhālif-khāns* in *taʿziya*.

Taʿziya also provides a cathartic release for its spectators, and is similarly experienced in this way by the family of the deceased in *The Travellers*, who not only grieve the loss of their loved ones, but also lament their old inner pains. The mourning ceremony in the film, just like the one on the *taʿziya* stage, allows the open, permissible and acceptable expression of these strong emotions. The family openly grieve their painful loss and misfortune just as the spectators of a *taʿziya* performance are allowed to openly grieve not only Imam Husayn's fate, but also their own misfortunes.

Fig.7
The famous *naqqāl* (storyteller), Ostad Torabi, performing *naqqālī* (storytelling) of the *Shāhnāma*

Fig.7

Figs. 8, 9

The Travellers, thus, employs many of the established *ta'ziya* forms of story narration. The elements of lack of suspense, veiled moments of death, impact and reaction of the bereaved, the circular movements of the camera, the delivery of the dialogue and the cathartic nature of the mourning rituals are all comparable to *ta'ziya*. Beyzaie employs all of these features of *ta'ziya* to narrate a modern tragedy. *The Travellers* also allows Beyzaie, who laments the loss of older Iranian forms of performing arts, to employ the medium of film to reintroduce and reinterpret these older traditions to his audience. Both films, *The Day of the Incident* and *The Travellers,* are particularly important in the face of the evolving traditions of Muharram ceremonies discussed above. They act as a reservoir of a tradition within a context where there is a growing concern about the 'Other's' perception of 'Islamic' practices, which include the omission of some of these older traditions.

It is within this evolving context of the Shi'i religious tradition in Iran that *ta'ziya*, which originated from much older pre-Islamic forms of performance, has survived its many centuries of eventful history. It has been condemned by some *'ulamā'* as un-Islamic and endorsed by some others, *ta'ziya* flourished under royal patronage but was banned and ignored for being 'backward' during the rule of subsequent monarchs. The tradition has moved from the greatest performance halls in cities to remote rural plateaus. Thus, the lifeblood of *ta'ziya* has historically been held largely in the hands of the religious and ruling authorities and more recently continues to cause concern amongst them for the reputation of religion.

Films provide *ta'ziya* with a new space that is controlled by the artist rather than those in positions of political power. A filmmaker such as Beyzaie employs many of *ta'ziya*'s established modes and motifs, both in terms of its form and content when writing and directing his film. In Beyzaie's reinterpretation, *Ta'ziya* is employed to narrate one of the most powerful Shi'i-Iranian narratives. *Ta'ziya* informs the narrative structure of *The Day of the Incident,* and its motifs are applied to narrate a modern-day tragedy in *The Travellers*. In this way, Beyzaie not only revives the old performing art but also demonstrates it relevance to the modern Iranian imagination. Like *ta'ziya,* his films encompass the historical, mythological, national and the religious as they all relate to Iranian society and culture.

Fig.8 (left)
Young *maẓlūm-khān*s as Hasan and Husayn. Actors performing these roles, particularly as members of the Prophet's family, usually wear the colour green

Fig.9 (above)
A *mukhālif-khān* playing the warrior, Malik al-Ashtar, prior to his conversion to Islam. Although Malik al-Ashtar then became a loyal companion of Imam 'Ali, this actor will have to play the role of another *mukhālif-khān* ('bad guy') in subsequent performances, as according to *ta'ziya* rules he cannot shift to the role of a *maẓlūm-khān*

1 For a broader discussion on this topic see Nacim Pak-Shiraz, *Shi'i Islam in Iranian Cinema: Religion and Spirituality in Film* (London, 2011).

2 Peter J. Chelkowski, 'Popular Entertainment, Media and Social Change in Twentieth Century Iran', in *The Cambridge History of Iran, vol.7, From Nadir Shah to the Islamic Republic*, ed. Peter Avery, et al. (Cambridge, 1991), p.771.

3 The first recorded public commemoration of Muharram has been traced to the 10th-century Persian Shi'i Buyid ruler, Mu'izz al-Dawla, who enforced it in Baghdad in 963. See Edward G. Browne, *A Literary History of Persia* (Cambridge, 1956), p.31.

4 *Rowzeh-khānī* (i.e. *rawḍa khānī*, lit. 'recitation from *The Garden [of Martyrs]*') is a genre of Shi'i lamentation literature which narrates the sufferings of the Imams in general and of the battle of Karbala in particular.

5 Bahram Beyzaie, *Namāyesh dar Iran* (Tehran, 2001), p.117.

6 Sadeq Homayuni, *Ta'ziyeh dar Iran* (Shiraz, 2001), p.61.

7 Traditionally, women are not allowed to act in the drama and male actors play the female roles. The exceptions that I am aware of were the productions by theatre students at Talar-e-Shahr (City Theatre) in Tehran, which I attended in 2006. One was particularly interesting, in which women played both male and female roles. For a discussion of Muharram commemorations for and by women, see the essay by Ingvild Flaskerud in this volume.

8 There were obviously exceptions such as Mirza Abu'l-Qasim (d. 1815), known as Fazil-i Qumi, a prominent religious authority during the reign of Fath 'Ali Shah Qajar, who supported *ta'ziya*. In a religious fatwa he expressed that not only religious plays were lawful and not prohibited, but that they were among the greatest of religious works. See Vanessa Martin, *The Qajar Pact: Bargaining, Protest and the State in Nineteenth-Century Persia* (London, 2005), p.105.

9 Homayuni, *Ta'ziyeh*, pp.82–83.

10 Beyzaie, *Namāyesh*, p.143.

11 It is important to note that the decline of theatre was not limited to Iran, but extended throughout the world. According to Chelkowski, this worldwide crisis in theatre was the result of the 'advancement of film and television in the post-World War II period, together with a decline of religious ritual'. See Peter J. Chelkowski, *Ta'ziyeh: Ritual and Drama in Iran* (New York, 1979), p.10.

12 This is not to say that these practices did not exist amongst Sunnis. For example, there are numerous historical manuscripts from the Ottoman period that include depictions of the prophets and Shi'i Imams.

13 Sheila R. Canby, *Shah 'Abbas: The Remaking of Iran* (London, 2009), p.245.

14 See his own website, *http://www.bahrambeyzaie.com.*

15 It has been argued that this tradition was derived from older forms of performance art (i.e. *Kūseh-bar neshīn* and *Mīr-e Nowrūzī*) in which people had the opportunity to criticise their landlords or those under whom they were generally suffering. See Willem M. Floor, *The History of Theater in Iran* (London, 2005), esp. p.18.

16 Beyzaie, *Namāyesh*, pp.132–133.

17 Some Western productions have used similar modes such as the BBC drama series of Anthony Trollope's, *He Knew He Was Right,* broadcast in April-May 2004. In this drama, some actors would look at the camera and speak about their innermost feelings and thoughts as well as the course of action they were about to take. However, they did not give away the whole story and maintained its suspense for the viewers.

18 Beyzaie, *Namāyesh*, pp.140–141.

20

Some historic *ta'ziya*s of Multan

Tryna Lyons

The early centuries of Islamic expansion set in motion soon after the Prophet's death, saw geographers dividing South Asia into two parts: nearby Sind, and the more distant and inaccessible Hind. The land that the Arabs called Sind, corresponding roughly with the Pakistan of our day, was dominated by the inland port cities of Multan and al-Ror (now *Rohṛī*). This region, a staging ground for caravans and river trade, was from the beginning the refuge of dissidents fleeing conflicts on the Arabian Peninsula. In addition to religious and political exiles, emissaries from Bahrain and Yemen brought the teachings of various schismatic groups, including Twelver Shi'as and Qarmatis. Ismaili missionaries (*dā'īs*) arrived slightly later, in the tenth century, from their Fatimid strongholds in North Africa and Egypt. Their doctrines were well received in Multan, and the city even had Ismaili governors for a few decades before Mahmud Ghaznavi drove them out in the early 11th century.[1]

The Ghaznavid victory was far from absolute, since various Shi'i sects continued to survive underground in Multan and its environs. Like a thread that sometimes disappeared from view but never snapped, the transmission of teachings and discipleship persisted for centuries. A key factor enabling such resilience was the uniquely Shi'i institution of *taqiyya*, or religious dissimulation in times of danger. Far from being perceived as a fault, camouflaging one's true beliefs has been recommended since at least the eighth century, when the followers of Imam Ja'far al-Sadiq suffered Abbasid persecution. The practice has played out in interesting ways in Multan, where memories of suppression and concealment linger.

Many of the medieval saints for whom Multan is renowned were either Ismailis with Sufi colouration or Ismailis dissembling as Sufis (mystics). In other cases, the followers of Ismaili preachers gradually merged with one of the Sufi orders.[2] In the discussion of Muharram artistic practices that follows we should keep in mind that the divisions among Sunnis, Ithna 'asharis and Ismailis are difficult to establish in Multan, and may even be irrelevant. For, as one scholar has pointed out, there is not much to distinguish a Shi'a who poses as a Sunni from a Sunni whose heart is touched by the Karbala tragedy.[3] I believe that the unique flavour of Multan's Muharram commemoration, in which both sectarian groups participate, owes as much to its history in an Arabo-Persian frontier state and extended association with the esoteric orders as it does to the examples of Awadh and the Deccan. The long record of Shi'i penetration made feasible a later influx of Twelvers from Safavid-influenced centres of the Subcontinent, leading to an elaboration of the Muharram rite.

The focus of this essay is the *ta'ziya*s, or Muharram shrines, of Multan.[4] The spectacular objects used and venerated in today's Indo-Pakistani Muharram solemnities have usually been assumed to be indigenous innovations. I shall present evidence linking them to processional models described by early European visitors to Iran. Extensive interviews with participants in Multan and other nearby centres provide a fresh interpretation of the *ta'ziya*'s meaning. Far from being an emblem of defeat, for many viewers it represents the martyr's heavenly reward. The inner and outer structures of these architectural artefacts are imbued with symbolic significance in ways that might not be apparent to the casual observer. The *ta'ziya*s are crucial to the performance and experience of Muharram.

The wooden *ta'ziya*

The *ta'ziya* of South Asia is commonly described as a model tomb, carried in procession for various rituals that unfold during the first ten days of the month of Muharram.[5] In most parts of the subcontinent, it is an ephemeral object made of bamboo, paper, mica, metallic foil and similar lightweight materials. There is another funerary artefact of more valuable composition called the *zarīḥ*. Often constructed of repoussé metal over a wooden core, this kind of tomb replica may be paraded but, unlike the *taʿziya*, is not disposed of on ʿAshuraʾ (the tenth day of Muharram).[6] In regions where decorative wood carving was important, such as Kashmir and Punjab (the present-day location of Multan), a kind of hybrid object was produced, called a *taʿziya* but broken down into pieces for storage at the conclusion of the Muharram observances. These models of *deyār* (*Cedrus deodara*, a type of cedar) were frequently embellished with floral and calligraphic paintings, both on their wooden surfaces and on mica or glass insets, and boasted elegant stucco domes inlaid with mirror work.[7]

Just as the ornate cut-paper patterns of fine ephemeral *taʿziya*s show- case the cobbler's art, so the wooden shrines display the best collaborative efforts of *tarkhān* (woodworker) and *kamāngar* (bow-maker; decorative painter). That these ritually significant objects also serve as a kind of advertisement for artisanal excellence does not seem a contradiction to hereditary craftsmen.[8] For example, in the Punjabi town of Chiniot, known throughout Pakistan for its furniture production and grand *taʿziya*s, woodworkers may debate the technical and aesthetic merits and deficiencies of particular shrines for hours. Their discussions focus on issues such as structural integrity, balance and proportion, but also on the innate capacity of a given *taʿziya* to trigger sorrowful affect and even to work miracles. The carpenters of Chiniot (and of Multan, with a single exception) are all Sunnis, yet they are deeply invested in both sacred and secular aspects of production. However, rising sectarian divisions in recent years have made some Sunni artisans pull back from *taʿziya* production and repair.

The master and his pupil

Every Pakistani child has viewed television footage or newspaper photographs of Multan's best-known *taʿziya*s, the Ustad (from the Arabic *ustādh*, 'master') and Shagird (Persian *shāgird*, 'pupil' or 'novice') (fig.1). The history of these two imposing structures (both are about 25 feet in height) is not entirely clear. Legends about an apprentice carpenter, who assisted his master in building one shrine during the day, whilst secretly replicating it at another location at night, are charming but improbable. We can state with some assurance, however, that Ustad is the older construction. According to the present custodian

Fig.1

of the shrine, who belongs to the Sunni silk-spinner (*paṭolī*) artisan group, the *taʿziya* was commissioned by his ancestor Muhammad Muhyi ud-din. By counting back generations, we arrive at a mid-19th-century birthdate for Muhyi ud-din, which fits with the date 1895 scrawled on the earliest photograph of the Ustad *taʿziya* (fig.2).[9]

A comparison of the 19th-century photograph with the present-day object being carried through city streets indicates significant revisions. These modifications in the *taʿziya*'s basic structure should not surprise us, since Ustad has gone out on ʿAshura' every year for more than a century. A *taʿziya*'s journey to the cemetery and back is fraught with danger. Not only must the heavy wooden structure be shouldered through turbulent crowds (the bearers sprint a short distance then take a breather, resting the shrine on four stools before hoisting it again), but it faces the ever-present threat of malicious destruction. While some may view the procession as a pilgrimage to Karbala, for many participants it is more like a battle. Occasionally, *taʿziya*s are smashed or burned, in which case they are said to be *shahīd*s (martyrs) who must be buried. At other times, the shrines become 'partial martyrs', capable of repair. Because the object is in some sense personified as a victim of the Karbala debacle, a *taʿziya*'s dome (representing its head) is the particular target of ill-wishers. This vulnerability may explain the successive changes to Ustad's superstructure revealed in a series of old photographs.[10]

In the 1895 photograph, Ustad displays typical crowning elements familiar from depictions in Company Style Muharram paintings.[11] The lobed dome, set on an eight-sided transitional element, is topped by a double canopy on slender poles. Later versions of Ustad, however, tend to corroborate local lore claiming that an artisan from Chiniot reconstructed the shrine. It reproduces the format of a typical Chinioti *taʿziya* in which a screened portion (the *pālkī*, or palanquin) replaces the dome, and the single canopy is fully integrated within the design of the superstructure. Although we cannot be certain of the woodworker who made either the original Ustad or its present instantiation, we are on secure ground in crediting premier Chinioti craftsman, Ilahi Bakhsh Pirjhah (*circa* 1880–1960), with authorship of the existing Shagird *taʿziya*. The earlier structure had been burned during Muharram disturbances in 1943, and the master craftsman was summoned from Chiniot in the following year to prepare a new shrine.[12]

Fig.2

Fig.1
The Ustad *taʿziya* leading the ʿAshura' procession with the Shagird *taʿziya* following behind, Multan, 10 Muharram (9 February 2006)

Fig.2
The Ustad *taʿziya* in 1895, Pir Qazi Jalal Darbar, Kupri Patoliyan, Pak Gate, Multan. Collection of Khalifah Altaf Husayn, Multan

The Gardezi family of Multan

The Master and Novice *taʿziya*s signify Multani Muharram to contemporary Pakistan's wider Muslim community, but they are not the city's oldest processional shrines nor are they situated at what might be termed its spiritual core, an amalgam of Sufi and Shiʿi mysticism that characterises the town's religious identity. To approach that distinctively hybrid nucleus we must enter historic Bohar Gate and visit the tomb of Shah Muhammad Yusuf Gardez. This saint from Gardez (near Ghazni, now in Afghanistan) was said to have arrived here on the back of a lion in 1088, at a time when the recurring conflict between the Ismailis and Ghaznavis had nearly depopulated Multan. Although family members living around the saint's tomb are today deeply Ithna ʿashari Shiʿi, the past identity of the lineage may have been more fluid. Evidence of this ambiguity appears in a 1540 succession dispute that pitted Sunni and Shiʿi branches against each other. When the case was decided in favour of the Shiʿas, the Sunni Gardezis shifted to Kashmir whilst those who remained, reverted to dissimulation of belief.[13]

Certainty about the sectarian identity of Shah Gardez himself is impossible at this remove. Nevertheless, local tradition places his descendants at the heart of Multan's *ʿazādārī* (the practice of mourning for Karbala's martyrs) since at least the mid-18th century. When the city fell under Afghan Durrani authority in 1752, the clan was forced to 'break' its *taqiyya* and flee Multan for a time. Shiʿas claim that Sikh rule (1818–1849) brought periods of tolerance alternating with harsh suppression. The leitmotif of concealment followed by exposure surely explains why the heirs of Shah Gardez have never taken their own *taʿziyas* out on the streets. Indeed, Muharram rituals within the shrine precincts still retain an air of secrecy. On the night of the ninth of Muharram, long-time retainers bring a freshly made seven-foot paper *taʿziya* and set it up within the compound. It remains there the entire night, but is crushed and buried at the time of the first prayer on the morning of the tenth.

These Muharram rites carried out under cover of darkness are said to have been instituted by high-born Mughal captives given in servitude to the *makhdūm* (hereditary successor of a saint and keeper of his tomb) soon after the Indian Rebellion of 1857. According to senior family member Khurshid ʿAbbas Gardezi (b. 1931), the British rewarded their supporters in Multan with enslaved relatives of the defeated Emperor in recompense for help during the uprising. Perhaps these Shiʿi Mughals brought a tradition of paper *taʿziya*s to Multan (where they are otherwise little used); the annually renewed structure may constitute the earliest Gardezi *taʿziya*. Mirza Zamir al-Hasan Beg, a descendant of the original group of prisoners, closely supervises the preparation of the model and the observances associated with it. A smaller paper *taʿziya* is also sent to the ladies of the Mirza family for their private devotional meetings. A popular belief that Indian *taʿziyadārī* (the use of shrines as a focus of veneration) was initiated by the Mughal progenitor Timur (Tamerlane) may have originated with 19th-century Shiʿas like the Mirzas of Multan. To this day, pious individuals sometimes fashion replicas of the martyrs' tombs from *khāk-e shifā* (the pure dust of Karbala, supposed to have spiritual and medicinal benefits) in imitation of Timur's supposed first *taʿziya* (fig.3).[14]

Two 19th-century Gardezi shrines

The impermanent paper *taʿziya* aside, a pair of venerable wooden shrines is preserved at Gardezi establishments. The older of the two artefacts was commissioned by Jahan Shah Gardezi in the early 1870s (fig.4), following a pilgrimage he made to Karbala, and is kept at the village of Taliwala (part of the family's extensive landholdings, located about 18 miles north of Multan). The *zarīḥ* now in the Gardezi *imāmbārā* (the hall where Muharram rituals and meetings are conducted) was fashioned a few years later, perhaps at the request of Husayn ʿAli Shah Gardezi (again, conventionally, after a visit to Karbala). It is unusual in bearing a number of painted inscriptions, including a date of 1295/1878 along with the name of *mistrī* (artisan) Meher ʿAli of Bohar Gate. We may assume that this neighbourhood carpenter made the *zarīḥ*, which was kept in an underground room before the 1883 construction of the *imāmbārā*. Because it is moved about within the tomb complex every year, the structure is subject to some wear and tear. Each woodworker and painter called to repair the piece over the years has proudly recorded his name and the date of his service on the Gardezi *zarīḥ*.[15]

In comparison with the much-restored model shrine in Multan, the Taliwala artefact retains more of its original ornament and colour, giving

Fig.3
Shahid Hasan Gardezi (1953–2008) with tomb models (*ziyārat*) of Karbala earth, made by his mother, Sayyida Nasrin Zahra

Fig.4
Taliwala *taʿziya*, dated early 1870s, village Taliwala, Multan district

us a better sense of the harmonious interplay of woodcraft, modelled stucco, inlay and decorative painting that make up a fine old *ta'ziya*. In Figure 4, we see a villager holding up the canopy; a glance at the old Ustad in Figure 1 clues us that this element must also originally have been supported on tall posts. Furthermore, the disjuncture between the middle and upper storeys confirms what elders suggest: a storey is missing. The *takht* (base) has also been lost. The *ta'ziya*, now a mere 12.25 feet, would originally have risen to about 18 feet. Even though it has never gone out in procession, and is only assembled and moved the short distance from its storage room to a courtyard at Muharram, the years have taken their toll on the shrine. Still, the intricately pieced *jālīs* (screens), fitted together without glue, and the bits of blown-glass mirror that cling to the stucco dome with its canopy, and to the small entry roofs, hint at the Taliwala *ta'ziya*'s glamour in its heyday.[16]

Patterns of patronage and the Kaurey Shah *ta'ziya*

Kaurey Shah was a 19th-century holy man who founded an *imāmbārā* just outside of Multan's Delhi Gate. At about the same time as the two wooden shrines we have just discussed were being constructed, a *ta'ziya* was made for his Delhi Gate establishment. Its history illuminates patronage patterns in Multan, for the Kaurey Shah processional shrine was financed by Hamid Shah Gardezi the Elder (d. 1901), builder of the Gardezi *imāmbārā*. Although the family clung to traditions of covert worship, they liberally sponsored Sunni and Shi'i groups wishing to keep or parade *ta'ziyas*. Indeed, when the Sunni Shagird *ta'ziya* was burned in 1943, the Gardezis underwrote its replacement by Chinioti craftsman Ilahi Bakhsh Pirjhah. The master, along with his team of artisans, constructed the new shrine within the Shah Gardez compound and accompanied it when it was carried with great fanfare to

Fig.3

Fig.4

its home at Khuniburj on the eighth of Muharram in 1944. Further investigations will be necessary to determine whether Gardezi support for Sunni establishments was a politically inspired response to later 19th-century communal developments in the Punjab, or represented a longer-standing tradition.[17]

The remarkable Kaurey Shah *ta'ziya* (fig.5) last went out on procession in 1968. After that, it was declared *za'īf* (retired; Arabic *ḍa'īf*, 'feeble', 'old'). Kept disassembled in the storeroom of the *imāmbārā*, it retains great sanctity and receives vows every year in the form of bits of cloth tied to its frame. Each represents a prayer for help and a pledge to give something in return when the request is granted. These days a shiny new *ta'ziya* takes to the streets during Muharram, but old-timers declare that it is no match for the original Kaurey Shah, which, with its canopy (not visible here), measured about 11 feet in height. Secreted inside the structure is an unusual wooden model of a *sabīl*, or public water fountain, featuring domed pavilions and even a miniature well mechanism with moving parts (fig.6). The *sabīl* symbolises Imam Husayn's half-brother 'Abbas, the 'water carrier', whose heroic attempt to reach the Euphrates River and bring back water for the thirsting children of his family is commemorated on the eighth of Muharram. We may surmise that the fountain hidden in the shrine means this *ta'ziya* was initially dedicated to 'Abbas.[18]

Hidden meanings

Over the years, when examining stationary and processional shrines, and interviewing those who make or own them, I have learned that inside most structures is a hidden object, like the water fountain concealed in Kaurey Shah. This secret article is usually a tiny model *tābūt* (coffin), but sometimes there is a little chair, a turban, or a Qur'an positioned on its stand. Once, in the village of Rajo'a, I had to get down on my hands and knees to view a miniature replica of a three-storey shrine, complete with cusped arches and a grille, cached underneath the *zarīḥ*. Usually the object can be spied behind a screen, but it is not always visible. There is heated debate, too, about whether the item should be deposited within the base or up at the top, in the 'palanquin'. Traditional Multani *ta'ziya* builder Ghulam Hur, a Shi'a, terms this object a *mazār mubārak* (blessed shrine/grave), and insists that it must

Figs. 5

Figs. 6

Fig.5
Kaurey Shah *ta'ziya*, dated *circa* 1870s, Imambara Pir Sayyid Kaurey Shah Wala, Thalah Sadat, outside Delhi Gate, Multan

Fig.6
The *sabīl* of the Kaurey Shah *ta'ziya*

be part of the shrine's substructure. He and other Shiʿas with whom I have spoken maintain that, while the object is not required in Sunni shrines, it is indispensable for Shiʿi *taʿziyas*.[19]

The historian of South Asia will be struck by an obvious similarity to the relics that vivify Buddhist monuments. Certainly, the covert placing of the *tābūt* or other item at a ritually determined moment, and its removal before the *taʿziya* is buried, immersed or disassembled, suggests an enlivening role (and, of course, Islam overlaps chronologically with Buddhism in this region). However, I resist a facile conclusion of influence from Buddhist practice, just as I remain unconvinced by easy comparisons between the ten days of Muharram and the ten-day Ramlila festival celebrating the victory of the Hindu deity Ram. Colonial observers, perhaps influenced by the polemical writings of the 18th-century cleric Shah Waliullah, posited Hindu 'infection' of rituals they supposed were more chaste or sober in the Shiʿi heartlands of Iran and Iraq. We should be careful about following this interpretive path without a solid understanding of how Muharram was formerly commemorated in regions to the west of India.[20] At least in the case of the hidden objects, a better approach may be to examine ideas about secrecy in traditions that prized esoteric readings of the Qur'an and stressed the immanence in this world of the hidden Imam. As one scholar has pointed out, *taqiyya* is only partly about hiding one's beliefs in case of danger; even more important may be keeping occult teachings safe from outsiders.[21]

Sakhi Laʿl Shah and Multan's *taʿziya* processions

We have seen that a Karbala pilgrimage often precedes and validates the decision to construct a model shrine. The activities of a *malang* (an ecstatic religious mendicant in the Persian tradition) are frequently used to explain how a customary procession began. Thus the semi-legendary personage Gamey Shah was said to have carried a small *taʿziya* through the streets of early 19th-century Lahore, initiating the great Muharram parades of that city.[22] A renunciant named Shadi Malang fulfilled the same role in Chiniot. A surprising number of informants agree that Sakhi Laʿl Shah was the first to shoulder a *taʿziya* through Multan's neighbourhoods.[23] We should bear in mind that the *making* of shrines as a focus of veneration is not the same as *parading* them; sacred objects like these were surely in private use long before anybody dared to display them publicly. Laʿl Shah, a man of Chakwal district associated with the lineage of the Nurpur Shahan saint Barri Latif, probably arrived in Multan some time in the second half of the 19th century. Although his partisans claim that he travelled extensively around the subcontinent, founding 46 *imāmbārās* in places as far away as Pune and Tonk and converting the Talpur royal family of Khairpur to the Shiʿi faith, the only accomplishment we can be certain of is his establishment of the *imāmbārā* that bears his name in Multan's Qadirabad quarter.[24]

Laʿl Shah is not one of Multan's early saints, yet he looms large due to his association with its initial *taʿziya* processions. The handsome old wooden shrine taken out by his descendants, said to be a replacement for the original model carried by the *malang* as he wandered across India promoting *ʿazādārī*, is seen in a photograph that may date to the 1930s (fig.7). Like all Muharram activities undertaken in the public sphere, when the Laʿl Shah *taʿziya* exits its *imāmbārā* it is governed by Section 30 of the 1861 Police Act. Licences, renewed every year, specify the time and date, the route taken by the assembly and what objects or animals are permitted. When examining meticulously prepared memoranda used to brief officers for crowd duty, I discovered notes about pre-Partition altercations as well as indications of newer flash-points. Precedence and protocol are scrupulously observed; for example, Ustad always comes first in its procession, followed after a 30-foot interval by Shagird. The rationale for these 19th-century directives, with their precise management of the city's crossing and converging crowds of marchers, was never questioned by Muharram participants with whom I spoke.[25]

Multan surprises us with its tradition of women's processions. One female assembly accompanies the ʿAbdullahwala *taʿziya* of Haram Gate, the ancestral quarter of the city's *kanjarīs* (courtesans), while

Fig.7

Fig.7
Procession of the Sakhi Laʿl Shah *taʿziya*, Multan, *circa* 1930s. Collection of Makhdum Sayyid ʿAbbas Raza Mahdi, Multan

another escorts La'l Shah's shrine all the way to his simple grave near the tomb of the 13th or 14th-century Ismaili Shah Shams Sabzavari. There the *ta'ziya* (which has recently been painted white) is placed on the saint's grave before being dismantled and returned in pieces to the *imāmbārā* (fig.8). The theme of female participation appears again in the 'dowry *ta'ziya*' of Sayyida Rasul Zahra, La'l Shah's daughter, who in the early-20th century wedded the *makhdūm* presiding at a village about 50 miles north of Multan. When she travelled to her new home at the village of Pir 'Inayat Shah, the processional shrine that her father had prepared followed her up the Chenab River in a country boat. Every year on the tenth of Muharram it is reverently borne throughout the village to the cemetery where the saint's daughter and other dignitaries are buried (fig.9).

Considering the wooden *ta'ziya*

I mentioned earlier the usual definition of the *ta'ziya* as a tomb replica, seen both as a stand-in for martyrs whose bodies were dismembered and dishonoured at Karbala and as a kind of belated reparation (in what Schubel, following Victor Turner, terms the 'subjunctive mood') to those who did not receive proper burial.[26] We have noted that a pilgrimage to distant Shi'i holy sites may prompt the returned traveller to commission a *ta'ziya*, supposedly a facsimile of sepulchral landmarks he saw there. Yet an obvious objection arises: the structures we have seen bear no resemblance to Near Eastern mausolea or, indeed, to tombs on the subcontinent. Why, then, do the ruined, battle-scarred wooden shrines of historic *imāmbārās* like Haveli Alif Shah and Mozang in Lahore, and the 19th-century artefacts we have seen in Multan, carry such gravitas and inspire such deep emotion among Muharram participants? It has been my privilege to hear stories, recounted with all the urgency of direct experience, in which these shrines facilitated otherworldly encounters. Often the narratives touch on themes of forgetting and recollection that lie at the heart of Sufi teaching and of the Karbala paradigm.[27]

In fact, for many who take part in Muharram, and for most wooden *ta'ziya* builders, these objects do not represent tombs. The tomb is an earthly repository for a corpse while the *ta'ziya*, they claim, approximates a heavenly palace like those in which living Imams dwell. Of

Fig.8

Fig.8
La'l Shah *ta'ziya* being dismantled on the grave of Sakhi La'l Shah at the Shah Shams Karbala in Multan, 10 Muharram 2008. Pieces removed from the structure are seen to the right

Figs. 9, 10

course, several passages in the Qur'an promise the faithful celestial palaces or mansions (notably Q.9:72). More pertinently, however, the 12th-century *Maqtal al-Ḥusayn* of al-Khwarizmi asserts that on the night of the Ascension (*miʿrāj*) the Prophet Muhammad saw two palaces, each made of a single pearl, and was told that they had been prepared for the arrival in paradise of his grandsons Hasan and Husayn.[28] A comparison of the multi-storeyed wooden shrines of Multan, with their *jharokhās* (bow windows) and pierced screens, to Rajput and imperial dwellings of the 15th to 19th centuries confirms their palatial vocabulary. Only the crowning dome alludes to tomb architecture. Artisans explained to me that glass window insets were prepared with paint, varnish and sheets of mica to create an opalescent effect when a tray of burning oil lamps was placed inside the shrine. Observers report an impression of living presence inside the many-windowed edifices, and of the mystic light (the *nūr Muḥammadī*) that belongs to the Prophet's descendants.[29]

Multan in the Shiʿi world

A city as old and multi-layered as Multan might be expected to harbour a secret or two. In touching upon its history with the esoteric orders and later romance with full-blown Shiʿi display (thus earning it the appellation of 'the second Lucknow'), I have wished to give the reader a sense of the town's complex religious and artistic milieu. Unfortunately, space does not permit consideration of the *taʿziya* belonging to the Gilani family, of the handsome Dirkhanawala (fig.10) and Kamangranwala processional shrines, or of the *taʿziyadārī* traditions of the *shamsī*s (who claim to have been converted by the mediaeval Ismaili missionary Shah Shams Sabzavari).[30] Another fascinating aspect of *taʿziya* production that I can only mention in passing is the role played by Sikhs in pre-Partition Punjab. While Sikh rule surely brought some oppressive measures, it is also true that many of the finest shrine builders were Sikh carpenters. Members of the community also took part in the 'summer Muharram' ritual, keyed to the Hindu calendar, said to commemorate the readiness of their martial forebears to defend Imam Husayn at Karbala.[31]

In concluding this overview of the Muharram shrines of Multan, I would like to redirect the reader's attention to the long-term ties

Fig.9
Dowry *taʿziya* of Sayyida Rasul Zahra at Pir ʿInayat Shah village, District Jhang. *Makhdūm* ʿAbbas Raza Mahdi of Multan kneels on the far right

Fig.10
Carpenter Muhammad Naʿim embellishes the Dirkhanawala *taʿziya* at Bohar Gate, Multan, before assembling it for Muharram

between greater Sind and the Near East. I suggest that, when we evaluate these religious artefacts and their uses, we turn our gaze for a moment from captivating subcontinental examples and try to verify what earlier practice may have been in the Shiʿi homelands. Consider the following eyewitness report of an 1808 Muharram procession in Tehran, submitted by a French ambassador: 'There appeared two great mosques of gilt wood, carried by more than 300 men. Both were encrusted with mirrors and crowned with small minarets; from their galleries children intoned sacred hymns [my translation].' Except for the real children perched in the models, one might be reading a description of a Multani *taʿziya*. An even earlier and more enigmatic account by the adventurer Jean-Baptiste Chardin, who visited Isfahan in 1674, describes a splendid parade put on by Indian Muslims residing there. Five elephants bearing towers headed the assembly, while the rear was brought up by oxen pulling two large structures, which Chardin suggests were meant to replicate the mosques of Mecca and Medina.[32]

There is much to ponder in these passages. Did the foreign observers correctly identify the structures as mosques, or might they have represented twin monuments to Hasan and Husayn? Do any architectural models of this kind survive in Iran? The edifices the visitors describe are surely not the *nakhl*, or bier, carried in Persian processions today. And what of the Indian residents of 17th-century Isfahan, who were sufficiently wealthy and established to put on what the European traveller described as the most beautiful of all the parades he viewed? These are questions we may wish to ask as we take measure of Shiʿi processional art in Multan and its neighbouring cities.

1 Sorting out Multan's Qarmati and Ismaili rulers is not easy. While space does not permit naming all the scholars who have written on this historical period in Multan, I would draw the reader's attention to the fourth chapter of Derryl N. Maclean's *Religion and Society in Arab Sind* (Leiden, 1989), pp.126–153.

2 See Saiyid Athar Abbas Rizvi, *A Socio-Intellectual History of the Isnā ʿAsharī Shīʿīs in India* (New Delhi, 1986), vol.1, pp.143–146. Farhad Daftary addresses the complexities of Sufi-Shiʿi identities in medieval times in *The Ismāʿīlīs: Their History and Doctrines* (Cambridge, 1990), pp.451–454; while Vernon J. Schubel points out the historically muted distinctions among Ismailis, Twelvers and Sufis in Sind and Punjab in his *Religious Performance in Contemporary Islam* (Columbia, NJ, 1993), p.8.

3 Keith G. Hjortshoj, 'Kerbala in Context: A Study of Muharram in Lucknow, India' (Ph.D. dissertation, Cornell University, 1977), p.35.

4 I am indebted to the helpful people of Multan – artisans, scholars and Muharram enthusiasts. In particular, I must mention the Gardezi family, Sayyid ʿAbbas Raza Mahdi, ʿAbdul Rehman Naqash and Muhammad Baqir Naqash, and Dr Ghulam Shams-ur-Rehman. Qamar Jalil and Dr David Pinault offered valuable suggestions; Dr Stephen Markel and Dr Charlotte Lacaze assisted in locating publications. My research was partly supported by the American Institute of Pakistan Studies. Dr Munis Faruqui contributed a careful reading of my essay, although any errors are solely my own.

5 In Iran the word has a different (although related) meaning, referring to a kind of passion play; see Peter Chelkowski, 'Shia Muslim Processional Performances', in Peter Chelkowski, ed., *The Drama Review*, 29, 3 (1985), pp.18–30.

6 *Zarīḥ* is a term used for the characteristic silver grille installed around Iranian cenotaphs. It is also the word for tomb replicas processed by Bahraini Shiʿas. Ali Naqi Naqvi plausibly suggests that the *taʿziya* represents the tomb edifice while the *zarīḥ* symbolises the cenotaph or grave; see his *Azadari: A Historical Review of Institution of Azadari for Imam Husain* (Karachi, 1974), part 1, pp.129–130. In Multani practice the terms become nearly interchangeable.

7 Sayyid Shahid ʿAli Shah and Shahid Naqvi describe a comparable wooden shrine from Awadh (the '52-stick *taʿziya*') in *ʿAzādārī: tahzībī, adabī, shaqāfatī va muʿāsharatī manẓar nāme men* (Lahore, 2002), pp.76 and 300.

8 The practice was taken to an extreme in Lucknow, where fanciful constructs like the sugar-candy *ta'ziya* of the sweet-makers probably represented early 20th-century attempts by hereditary caste/guild constituencies to gain political recognition.

9 Conversation in 2006 with Khalifah Altaf Husayn of Astanah Ustadwala, Multan; see also Ajmal Mahar ibn Akbar, *Multān ke qadīm imāmbāṛe aur majālis-e 'aza kī rivāyat* (Multan, 2004), p.90.

10 Recall that Imam Husayn was beheaded. Despite scholarly attempts to link Muharram violence in India with British interference, earlier incidents of such conflict appear regularly in visitors' reports; see, for example, Jean de Thévenot, *Les voyages de m. de Thévenot aux Indes orientales* (3rd ed., Amsterdam, 1727), vol.5, pp.320–321, for a vivid eye-witness account of a 1666 Shi'a-Sunni fray in Hyderabad. C. A. Bayly considers early communalism in 'The Pre-History of "Communalism"? Religious Conflict in India, 1700–1860', *Modern Asian Studies*, 19, 2 (1985), pp.177–203.

11 For example, the 1807 work by Sevak Ram of Patna; see Mildred Archer, *Company Paintings* (London, 1992), no.49.

12 Ilahi Bakhsh Pirjhah made his name with three celebrated *ta'ziyas:* Shadi Malang of Chiniot (*circa* 1934–1936); the *zarīḥ* at Rajo'a (1940); and the 1944 Multan Shagird. It should be noted that senior Chinioti informants claim that their town's earliest *ta'ziya*s also sported lobed domes rather than the streamlined *pālkī/chhatrī* design of more recent times.

13 The case turned on the differences between Sunni and Shi'i law for female inheritance; Ibn Akbar, *Multān ke qadīm imāmbāṛe*, p.52. The traditional date of Shah Gardez's arrival may be too early.

14 Conversations with Mirza Zamir Beg and the learned Khurshid 'Abbas Gardezi, whose library includes an 1861–1869 Persian manuscript history of Multan by his ancestor. An alternate narrative has the Mughals arriving as mercenaries a century earlier, during Afghan rule.

15 Before the *imāmbārā* was built, the *zarīḥ* was hidden underground at *vaḍḍa ghar* (Punjabi for 'big house'), supposed to be the original dwelling of the saint from Gardez.

16 Although no inscription confirms it, villagers recall hearing that the shrine was fashioned by a Multani master. See John L. Kipling, 'Punjab Wood-Carving', *The Journal of Indian Art*, 1, 14 (1886), pp.101–104; and M. F. O'Dwyer, *A Monograph on Wood Manufactures in the Punjab* (Lahore, 1889) for accounts of *tarkhān* and *kamāngar* craftsmanship in late 19th-century Punjab.

17 On communal politics in the region, see N. Gerald Barrier, 'The Punjab Government and Communal Politics, 1870–1908', *The Journal of Asian Studies*, 27, 3 (1968), pp.523–539. To this day, every Sunni or Shi'i group participating in Multan's Muharram rituals expects a contribution (*chanda*) from the Gardezi family.

18 I spoke in 2006 with Khadim Sayyid Hamid al-Hasan of the Kaurey Shah *imāmbārā*; see also Ibn Akbar, *Multān ke qadīm imāmbāṛe*, p.87.

19 The miniature chair may be related to the veneration of the throne of 'Ali; see John Hollister, *The Shi'a of India* (London, 1953), pp.197–198.

20 For example, effigies of 'Umar stuffed with firecrackers and set ablaze in South Asia need not mimic the festive destruction of Ravan's likenesses, since the *'Umar-koshān* rite was well known in Iran. The Italian adventurer Gemelli-Careri observed it in 1664; see Jamshid Malekpour, *The Islamic Drama* (London, 2004), p.34. Emma Roberts offers a typical disapproving response to Indian Shi'i practice in *Scenes and Characteristics of Hindostan with Sketches of Anglo-Indian Society* (London, 1835), vol.1, p.179.

21 Mohammad Ali Amir-Moezzi, *The Divine Guide in Early Shi'ism* (Albany, 1994), p.231, n.680.

22 Gamey Shah (sometimes written Game Shah) was the epithet of Baba Syed Ghulam 'Ali Shah, a fakir said to have been active in Lahore during the Ranjit Singh period.

23 Rarely does a majority of informants agree on anything, making the consensus noteworthy.

24 Common sense helps in separating the probable from the patently hagiographic in the written records on La'l Shah; see Shah and Naqvi, *'Azādārī*, pp.272–273 and 293; Ibn Akbar, *Multān ke qadīm imāmbāṛe*, pp.60–61; Nur Ahmad Khan Faridi, *Tārīkh-e Multān* (Multan, 1971), vol.1, pp.609–610.

25 Records at Multan's Thana Sadar Police Line list 244 licensed Muharram processions, as well as 206 that take place without a license (most of the so-called 'traditional' processions, for which there is no license, occur in outlying areas). There are five main routes for parades in the urban centre.

26 Schubel analyses Muharram using Turner's theories about performance, in which sacred history can be revised through ritual (the 'subjunctive' or 'what-if' mood); Schubel, *Religious Performance*, p.99.

27 Michael M. J. Fischer first used the term 'Karbala paradigm' in his discussion of Shi'i thought patterns in Iran. See his, *Iran: From Religious Dispute to Revolution* (Cambridge, MA, 1980), pp.13–27.

28 Cited in Mahmoud Ayoub, *Redemptive Suffering in Islam* (The Hague, 1978), pp.78–79.

29 According to the renowned 18th-century Qadiri Pir, Shaykh 'Abd ur-Razzaq Bansavi, the spirits of the Imams visited the *ta'ziyas*; Rizvi, *A Socio-Intellectual History*, p.307. Descendants of 19th-century North Indian emigrants to Trinidad say that the shrines shake on the night of eighth Muharram, when the spirits enter them; Frank J. Korom, *Hosay Trinidad* (Philadelphia, 2003), p.177. Other examples of this widespread belief abound.

30 See E. H. Aitken, *Gazetteer of the Province of Sind* (Karachi, 1907), p.162, for the split in the Khoja community over the use of *ta'ziyas*. Many (but not all) Multani *shamsī*s keep *ta'ziya*s (including those living at Jahaz Mahal and Suraj Myani).

31 This pre-1947 custom may be compared to Ladakh's *Yaum-e Asad* ('Day of the Lion') wonderfully evoked by David Pinault in his *Horse of Karbala* (New York, 2001), chapter 9 passim.

32 J. M. Tancoigne, *Lettres sur la Perse et la Turquie d'Asie* (Paris, 1819), vol.2, p.7; Jean-Baptiste Chardin, *Voyages de monsieur le chevalier Chardin, en Perse, et autres lieux de l'Orient* (Amsterdam, 1711), vol.9, pp.286–287. In this context, two structures in an early 20th-century photograph of a procession at Tehran are of interest; see Moojan Momen, *An Introduction to Shi'i Islam* (New Haven, CT, 1985), Fig.44.

21

Chirogh rawshan: Shiʿi ceremonial practised by the Ismaili communities of Xinjiang China

Amier Saidula

Introduction

In Xinjiang, China, where Sunni communities comprise the majority, the Shiʿa account for a tiny fraction of over ten million Muslims of Central Asian stock. Because of this numerical insignificance, very little is known about them outside their close-knit community. In fact, except for a small Twelver Shiʿa group in Yarkand (Shache) County, who number around seven thousand, the Nizari Ismailis form the bulk of the Shiʿa in Xinjiang. Although the Twelver Shiʿa community from Yarkand commemorate ʿAshura' during the first ten days of Muharram, along with most Shiʿa communities worldwide, this essay will focus on the ritual of the *Chirogh rawshan*, a unique religious ceremony of the Nizari Ismaili community in Xinjiang, in order to consider the internal diversity and richness of Shiʿi ceremonial traditions (fig.1).

The Shiʿa Imami Nizari Ismaili communities, scattered over 25 countries from Afghanistan to Zanzibar, all pledge their allegiance to a living Imam whose genealogy traces back to Imam ʿAli and Hazrat Fatima and their descendants through Imam Husayn. However, both ethnically and culturally the Ismailis represent a vast spectrum of diversity. Evolving around an Imam-centric doctrine, the spirituality expressed in each culture also bears the mark of its respective historical and cultural experience. With the spread of Islam, geographic regions where various forms of belief systems coexisted, intermingled and evolved side-by-side over time, older traditions and rituals persisted after adapting to changing religious contexts. This was a synchronic process that contributed to the formation of context-specific diversity within seemingly similar religious communities. One can describe it as a subtle merger that evolves through the encounter of disparate traditions and belief systems, which are then established and perpetuated through continued practice. The *Chirogh rawshan* (Persian *Chirāgh-e-rowshan*, literally 'luminous lamp') is a ceremony performed by Ismailis living in the mountainous regions of Pakistan, Central Asia and China today, although the ritual itself has a much older historical footprint.[1] As Richard Frye asserts, in ancient Central Asia 'older beliefs and practices are frequently accepted, modified, or at least tolerated.'[2] Hence, borrowing a contemporary expression, continuity is deftly embedded within change and erstwhile traditions have marched hand-in-hand with the dynamic world around them.

The Central Asian Ismaili religious tradition is also known as the Nasiri tradition, as it is named after Nasir Khusraw (d. 1088), the

Figs. 1, 2

11th-century Persian poet, philosopher, traveller and Ismaili preacher who was instrumental in establishing Ismailism in this region. *Chirogh rawshan*, as a distinctive religious rite among the Ismailis of the broader Pamir region,[3] is associated with the Nasiri tradition, and the *Chirāghnāma*, a Persian religious text containing Qur'anic verses that are recited during the ritual, is also attributed to Nasir Khusraw (fig.2). Traditionally, there are two forms of the *Chirogh rawshan* ceremony: one is performed as part of funerary ritual and known as *Daʿwat-i-fanā* (invited gathering for death). The other is referred to as *Daʿwat-i-baqā'* (invited gathering for continued prosperity), and is performed during one's lifetime as a sign of gratitude to Allah for an important family event, and at the discretion of the individual. At present, the *Daʿwat-i-baqā'* is practised in parts of Hunza, Gilgit, Afghan Badakhshan, and the Yarkand and Poskam regions of Xinjiang China, but not in Tajikistan or the Tashkurgan district of Xinjiang China (see map). This short ethnographic description of the *Chirogh rawshan* focuses on the *Daʿwat-i-fanā* ceremony of the Nizari Ismaili community in Tashkurgan, China, where the tradition continued for centuries in virtual isolation. It is based on my field research conducted in Tashkurgan between February and May 2004.[4]

Islam has a long history in China. The earliest Muslims arrived by sea during the second half of the seventh century and established themselves as a permanent component of the Chinese socio-cultural landscape.[5] As a result of centuries of interaction with Confucianism, a unique Islamic culture with distinctive Chinese characteristics has flourished in the heartland of China.[6] A few well-preserved historic Islamic monuments in the cities of interior China with strong Chinese architectural influence are the visual representations of a harmonious amalgamation of Islamic and Chinese cultures.[7] In 713, a group of Muslims travelled by land eastward across the Taklamakan Desert en route to interior China. This appears to be the earliest record of the presence of Muslims in what is now known as the region of Xinjiang, in northwest China.[8]

Historically, the land beyond the western end of the Great Wall of China was referred to as the 'Western region' *(Xiyu)* in classical Chinese literature, an unspecified geographical designation that may have included the current territory of Xinjiang and beyond. Xinjiang, a traditional Muslim homeland and a major exit to the west via Central Asia, is a vast, landlocked, resource rich, mainly desert provincial administrative region that accounts for one sixth of China territorially (i.e. about the size of Iran). Located at the heart of the Eurasian landmass, Xinjiang was part of a major junction of the ancient world and witnessed constant human traffic over the centuries; successive waves of nomads roamed through the regions as did seasonal migrants and powerful conquerors.[9] Over millennia, Indo-Iranian tribes, Tibetan warriors, Turco-Mongol hordes, Russian adventurers and Chinese and Muslim pilgrims, emissaries, travellers, and conquerors have all been a part of its history.[10] In antiquity, Xinjiang was associated with the renowned Silk Road, the major commercial artery of its time. As a result, almost every influential religion of the Old World travelled along this ancient highway and left its mark on the soil. The decaying remnants of ancient places of worship, half buried in the middle of sand dunes, stand defiantly as a reminder of Xinjiang's rich cultural legacy. The plethora of local cultural heritage and isomorphic anthropological diversity, even within seemingly one ethnic group, is a living memory of its dynamic past. Most of its 'indigenous' inhabitants, including the Ismaili Tajiks, share a common ethno-linguistic and socio-cultural heritage with the people of Central Asia.

The modern territory of Xinjiang, consisting of the agriculturalist south and the steppe north, bisected by the Tian Shan mountain range, was united under the Mongol Yuan dynasty for the first time in the 13th century. By then, most of the eastern Iranian speaking natives of the Tarim Basin were absorbed into the Altaic speaking settlers, who inherited the local culture whilst giving them their language.[11] Xinjiang 'had slipped from China's grip during both the Han (*r.* 202 BC–220 AD) and Tang (*r.* 618–907) dynasties, and the Ming Dynasty had never seriously attempted its conquest.[12] During the Qing dynasty (*r.* 1644–1911), once again, the region broke free from China's control and established a short-lived independent Muslim state under Yaʿqub Beg (*r.* 1866–1877). Eventually, with the reconquest of the land by the Manchu Qing Dynasty in the second half of the 19th century, this swathe of land became a formal province of imperial China. This is where its present name of Xinjiang, meaning 'the new domain' or 'new frontier', has its origins.[13]

Fig.1
A *Chirogh rawshan* ceremony in progress with the recitation of the *Chirāghnāma*. Yarkand, Xinjiang, August 2006

Fig.2
The recitation of the *Chirāghnāma*, a Persian text believed to have been written and compiled by Nasir Khusraw. Yarkand, Xinjiang, August 2006

The Muslims may have travelled across this terrain as early as around the eighth century, but it took several more centuries for Islam to become the dominant religion of the land.[14] Starting from the early tenth century, Sultan Satuq Bughra Khan (d. 955), the Qarakhanid ruler, was believed to be the first local ruler to convert to Islam.[15] The local Islamic culture, with a strong Middle Eastern and Central Asian imprint, expressed through distinctive forms of art, architecture, customs, dress, literary and dietary traditions, suggest a different historical experience from China proper.

The Ismailis in China

The Ismailis represent a distinct ethnic, racial, linguistic and religious minority in contemporary China, who are referred to locally by their ethnic name as 'Tajiks'. The Tajiks in Xinjiang claim direct descent from the Indo-European speaking east-Iranian stock of antiquity. Streams of classical Chinese literature, historical sources and modern archaeological discoveries were evoked in support of this claim.[16] For example, according to the *Tangshu* (Book of Tang), the Tang Dynasty's official court history, the residents of Sariqol, Shule (Kashgar) and the western part of the Tarim Basin were Indo-Iranian peoples known [in Chinese] as the '*Sairen*' (or the *Sakas*), who have deep blue or brown eyes and high, straight nose bridges. They have fair or brown hair and speak a Sogdian dialect (*Sute yu*, an ancient eastern Iranian language).[17] Similar accounts pertaining to the ethno-linguistic and racial attributes of the ancient inhabitants of modern Xinjiang recur in many ancient Chinese official and individual documents.

Strictly speaking, the 'Tajiks' in Xinjiang are different from the Persian-speaking Tajiks of Central Asia. In Xinjiang, they speak the eastern Iranian languages of Sariqoli and Wakhi and are racially classified as the only Caucasian Mediterranean race in China.[18] Linguistically, Sariqoli belongs to the Shughno-Rushani family of the Pamiri dialects, whilst Wakhi is identical with the Wakhi language spoken in the Ishkashim district of Badakhshan, the Wakhan Valley of Afghanistan and the Gujal district of the Northern Areas of Pakistan. Persian, once a *lingua franca* in broader Central Asia, is almost a foreign language, but still widely used in religious ceremonies among the Ismailis in Xinjiang. Furthermore, while the majority of the Persian-speaking Tajiks outside China adhere to Sunni Islam, the Tajiks in Xinjiang follow the Shi'a Ismaili tradition. Nevertheless, such differences do not deter the Tajiks in Xinjiang from considering themselves as a part of greater Iranian civilisation and legitimate heirs to the riches of Iranian cultural heritage.[19]

The Ismailis were one of the earliest Islamized communities from that part of the world, who accepted Islam as early as the late 10th century.[20] However, traditions relating to the spread of the Ismaili *da'wa* (mission) in the region remain elusive. A recent publication, based on ethnographic data collected during the mid-20th century by a group of Chinese scholars, concludes that the Tajik community was converted from Sunni Islam to Ismailism during the late 16th and early 17th centuries by a Persian preacher.[21] A more widely accepted tradition relates that Ismailism began to spread across the high Pamir Mountains and into the eastern region when Ismaili missionaries gained the support of a ruler of the Samanid Dynasty, Nasr b. Ahmad Samani (*r.* 914–943).[22] The continued spread and success of Ismailism is traditionally associated with the aforementioned Nasir Khusraw, who took refuge in Tajik Badakhshan and spent a good part of his life there. His success in spreading Ismaili teachings was enabled by the local ruler of Badakhshan, 'Ali b. Asad, who himself was an Ismaili.[23] Clearly, apart from a few anecdotal stories, our knowledge about the community's religious history remains insufficient.

Chirogh rawshan

The term *Chirogh rawshan* is adopted from the Persian, literally meaning 'luminous lamp'. It is a quintessential Central Asian Ismaili tradition deeply rooted in the cultural and religious consciousness of the community. As a cardinal component of funerary ritual, it constitutes an inalienable aspect of local religious custom. The ritual is performed on the evening of the burial, and is exclusively observed by the Ismailis in the mountainous heartland of the region, including those in western China. Its survival during the tumultuous periods of modern Chinese history is a corollary of its significance, fortitude and endurance. As the nuances of the local languages were mentioned, the ritual is known as *Tsraw Pathid* in Sariqoli and *Chirogh Pitsvik* in Wakhi, and habitually referred to as *Tsraw* or *Chirogh* in their shortened forms within local

Fig.3
The local *Khalīfa* (third from right) offers prayers for the deceased before the gathering sets off for the cemetery. Daftor village, Xinjiang, September 2011

Fig.4
The shrouded body is carried by foot to the cemetery. Daftor village, Xinjiang, September 2011

contexts. Accordingly, we will also use the shortened form *Chirogh* from time to time hereafter.

As a fundamental religious tradition amongst the Ismailis of Xinjiang, the *Chirogh rawshan* ceremony is performed in the bereaved family's home on the night of the burial, which is usually on the third day after the death. To all intents and purposes, this life cycle ritual constitutes an integral part of a set of essential religious funerary services, which are carried out in the following order. Prayers (called *ghusli meyit*) are recited during the ritual cleansing and shrouding of the body (*tāwur ȭod*,[24] pronounced 'tawur thod'). Before the body is moved from the home, the youngest male descendant of the departed takes seven spoons of clean water from a spring and sprinkles it over the body for the last time. This is called the ritual of final water (*marām xats*). This is followed by the seeing off prayer (*mŭrȭā namāz*), which is recited before transporting the body to the graveyard (fig.3). Another

4

prayer is recited at the cemetery (*tabārak*), after the burial. Finally, the *Chirogh rawshan* ceremony takes place at the home of the deceased, on the evening of the entombment. Since the rituals are interconnected, it is best to contextualise the *Chirogh* within the funeral rite as a whole.

Unlike some other Muslim communities, Ismailis in Xinjiang do not bury their dead immediately in order to allow sufficient time for relatives to travel from afar to attend the ceremony, and it also gives the bereaved family enough time to arrange the logistics. Hence, the body is kept in the family home over two nights. On the day of the burial, whilst the bulk of the congregation accompanies the body to the cemetery, a few members stay behind and are given the task of cleaning the house and arranging the space for the extensive funeral feast that follows the burial (fig.4). Traditionally, the household selects a respected individual to organise, oversee and facilitate the funeral procedures and arrangements, designated as the *wakīl* (literally, 'representative'). In order to serve the funeral feast in an organised and orderly manner, the *wakīl* divides the congregation into small groups. Usually, people from the same village are grouped together and seated according to seniority from right to left in the seating area around the house.

It seems certain that the traditional homes in Tashkurgan, comprising a huge single living space supported by five wooden columns, representing the five members of the *Ahl al-bayt* (i.e. Prophet Muhammad, Imam ʿAli, Fatima, al-Hasan and al-Husayn), must have been designed with such ceremonial events in mind.[25] Inside the house, surrounding the *puygoh*, the open space in the middle, the room is divided into separate living areas with raised earthen platforms, called *nāx̱* (pronounced 'nokh'), which are covered with colourful carpets or felt, and made comfortable with rows of cotton-stuffed handmade mattresses and cushions, called *kurpa*. In a typical Pamiri house, the *nāx̱* area is divided into three sections. The *nāx̱* to the right of the entrance is called *nāx̱ kol* or *raj sar* (the leading side of the *nāx̱*), which is reserved for female guests. That section is separated from the other two *nāx̱*s by a small earthen platform and a mud furnace known as the *katsur*. Next to the furnace is the second *nāx̱*, a privileged space that is reserved for the *Pīr*s and the *Khalīfa*s, who are the religious leaders and elders of the community. The hierarchical order of the *nāx̱*s continues counterclockwise, so that the *nāx̱* immediately to the left of the entrance is

Fig.5

Fig.6

called *post nāא̱* (the last *nāא̱*), which is reserved for the youngest members of the family where they are seated and served food.

After the burial, the congregation heads back to the house to partake in the *patfar* (or *petfer*), the funeral repast, before dispersing in a timely fashion to allow others to participate. Outside the home, numerous young boys hold pots of water and towels waiting for the groups of guests to arrive. As the congregation (*jamaʿat*) arrives gradually, the boys pour water for guests to wash their hands before entering the house. The funeral meal (usually a rice pilaf) is cooked from vegetable oil, carrot, onion, rice and meat, and is served in groups of four or five. The senior member of each group cuts the cooked meat into small pieces and takes the first bite from the meal. During the funeral, making sure that social etiquette is observed and the propriety of the tradition is fulfilled is the responsibility of the appointed *wakīl*, who ensures that all the essential rules are followed.

A noteworthy detail during the ceremony is the special attention and respect shown to all the womenfolk when the funeral meal is served. This is one of several social occasions when female family and guests are treated with exceptional courtesy (fig.5). As noted, when the assembly returns from the cemetery (unlike in some other Ismaili contexts, females in Xinjiang are permitted to attend the cemetery for the burial itself), they are provided with water to wash their hands before entering the house, and that special service begins with the female guests. They are also the first to be ushered into the house and once inside, they are seated at the *nāא̱ kol* or *raj sar*, which is the most prestigious place in the home. Furthermore, the funeral meal is also served from the female quarter of the house.

As the final component of the funeral rite, the *Chirogh rawshan* ceremony commences after sunset; however, preparation for the *Chirogh* starts immediately after the body is removed from the house for burial. As soon as the cleansed and shrouded body leaves the family home on its last journey, and after the farewell prayer in front of the household, the bulk of the congregation takes the body to the cemetery for burial. Then a *pīr* or a *khalīfa*, the religious clerks, gathers together with those individuals left behind, and offers a prayer known as *futa-i pesh takbīr* (supplication in preparation for *takbīr*), in the very spot where the body was kept for two nights (fig.6).[26] The ritual is called *ched ḥalol chāig* or *khūn ḥalol khak* (purifying the home), signifying the purification of the house (i.e. making it *ḥalāl*, or lawful again; some refer to the prayer as *davāzdah Imām futa* [prayer for the Twelve Imams]).[27] A house is considered polluted or *ḥarām*, after someone dies in it, hence purifying the house spiritually is an essential religious imperative. Before the body is removed and the aforementioned prayer is performed, everything inside the family household is also regarded as impure and not fit for use. Therefore, friends and neighbours bring over the essential cooking utensils and ingredients from their homes to prepare the funeral meal (*patfar* or *petfer*).

Following the house cleansing prayer, a respected male from the community is put in charge of the *Chirogh rawshan* ceremony designated as the *Khudam* (pronounced, 'Khodam'; from *khādim*, 'serv-

Fig.5
Female mourners participating in the funerary rituals. Daftor village, Xinjiang, September 2011

Fig.6
Following the removal of the body from the house, a *Pīr* (seated in the corner) recites prayers for the soul of the deceased and other prayers that ritually cleanse the home. Daftor village, Xinjiang, September 2011

Fig.7
The appointed *Khudam* holds the sacrificial lamb (*tsraw kalo*), representing the soul of the departed, at the centre of the house. Daftor village, Xinjiang, September 2011

ant') who oversees, organises and assists the *Khalīfa* (leader of the community) during the *Chirogh rawshan* ceremony. Historically, the *Khudam* was appointed by a head *Pīr* and each village had one designated *Khudam*. However, nowadays, anyone with an upright moral character can be selected as the *Khudam* for a funeral, and the position is no longer fixed. A *Khudam* is different from the *Wakīl*; the latter is responsible for the funeral service during the day and the former is in charge of the *Chirogh rawshan* ritual at night. Any individual with good organisational skills can be put in charge of the funeral during the day, but a *Khudam* must be someone perceived as having a good character, and who is both pious and well respected in the local community. Both positions are given to male members of the community.

As the funeral participants gather in the house where the body was kept over two nights, the youngest son or daughter (or a close relative) of the deceased leads a sacrificial lamb inside the home (a goat is forbidden as it is perceived as the incarnation of Satan) and passes it to the *Khudam* (fig.7). He, in turn, brings the animal into the centre of the *puygoh* (the open space in the centre of the home), and turns its head towards the *qibla* (i.e. the direction of Mecca). The sheep's face is anointed and washed with water as a symbolic ablution, and it is fed some half-pounded barley and salt. Then, the *Pīr* and members of the household and close relatives of the dead surround the animal and raise their hands for a prayer to Allah (*futa*). The sacrificial lamb is called *tsraw kalo* (lamb or animal for the *Chirogh rawshan*) and symbolises the soul of the departed on its final journey. Because of the emblematic importance attached to it, the lamb acquires sacred status, and must be slaughtered inside the house.

Fig.7

The sacrificial process requires precision and utmost caution, as it is important to avoid spilling the animal's blood on the ground, which would result in the defilement of the sacred animal's purity. After the short *futa*, which lasts only a few minutes, the *Khudam* slits the throat of the lamb and drains its blood in a clean bucket in front of the *katsur* (the mud furnace). In order to keep the meat clean and pure, it is suspended from a tree or a shaft once it is skinned. Moreover, it is also a prerequisite to cook every edible part of the sacrificial animal, which literally means everything apart from the wool, including its internal organs (i.e. stomach, liver, intestines and kidneys), and the entire head and feet, so that the animal reaches its final destination in one piece. There are strict rules for disposing the waste as well. For instance, the blood, bones and other inedible parts of the sheep, and the water used for washing the kitchen utensils during the ceremony, must be buried in a clean location away from the road or residential areas. This is to keep them free from pollution and from the reach of wandering dogs or other sources of possible contamination.

A special dish, called *budʒ* (pronounced 'buj') is prepared from the meat of the sacrificial lamb cooked with barley or wheat grain. This dish is separate from the meal (*patfar*), which is served after the house cleansing ritual to funeral guests. While the funeral meal is being served, the *Khudam* prepares the *Chirogh* meat following strict methods of chopping the meat; no bones should be broken randomly and joints must be severed properly. The internal organs must be washed thoroughly, ideally in water from a clean spring, and the hair from the head and feet should be singed off and washed properly as well. As soon as the last guest leaves the house after partaking in the *patfar*, the *Khudam* places a huge wok over the fire and starts cooking the *Chirogh* meal (*budʒ*) (fig.8).

At dusk, close relatives, friends and neighbours gradually gravitate towards the home of the bereaved family to attend the *Chirogh rawshan* ceremony, as a final phase of the funeral rite. Unlike the earlier parts of the funerary ritual, when everyone is welcomed to attend, the *Chirogh rawshan* is an exclusive event open to Ismailis only, and people from both genders may attend after making the proper ablutions. Close relatives and friends of the deceased are all expected to attend the ritual, if conditions allow.

A *Khalīfa* usually presides over the ritual. After making his ablutions, the *Khalīfa* assumes his place, cross-legged, at the head of the main *nāẋ*, with a platform made of cushions in front of him, where he places the religious text – the *Chirāghnāma*. The others also sit according to seniority starting from the left side of the *Khalīfa* along the edge of the *nāẋ* in a circle. Women are seated separately on the other side of the house and listen quietly whilst the menfolk join the *Khalīfa* in reciting the incantations and repeating the *ṣalawāt* invocation: 'O God, bless Muhammad and the family of Muhammad'. While the participants take their seats, the *Khudam* mixes the food and repeats the following prayer: '*Har sāʿat-u har zamān bismi'llāh, barakati-faiz bismi'llāh, sāḥibi zamān, bismi'llāh al-raḥmān al-raḥīm*' (Every hour, every moment is in the name of God, the Lord of the Age [i.e. the Ismaili Imam] is the abundant blessing, in the name of God, the Most Beneficent the Most Merciful).

Then he brings a bundle of cotton in a tray, from which the wick for the *Chirogh* is prepared, and a knife and some grain in an enamelled bowl. The *Khalīfa* prays, then blows on the knife. Holding the tray over his head, the *Khudam* takes one step towards the *Khalīfa* and says, '*Allāh humma ṣalli ʿalā saidinā*' (O Allah, Bless our Master) and stands there whilst the crowd recites the complete invocation in unison: '*Allāh humma ṣalli ʿalā saidinā Muḥammad wa-āle Muḥammad, paighambari khudo, ṣalawāt bar Muḥammad dasti ʿAlī*' (O Allah, Bless our Master Muhammad and the family of Muhammad, the Messenger of God, *ṣalwāt*s upon Muhammad and [the supporter of] ʿAli's hand). Then the *Khudam* takes another step and completes the invocation he began: '*Muḥammad wa-āle Muḥammad, paighambari khudo, ṣalawāt bar Muḥammad dasti ʿAlī*' (fig.9).

The crowd repeats the *ṣalawāt* again. Then the *Khudam* touches his forehead with the tray, a sign of humble submission, before placing it to the right of the *Khalīfa*, and he sits down next to the *Khalīfa*. The *Khalīfa* accepts the tray with his right hand and says '*Bi'smillāh*' (In the Name of God) and opens his text to begin reading the *davāzdah Imām futa* (prayer for the Twelve Imams), while both of them start to braid the cotton into a wick to the thickness of a finger (figs 10–11). At the end of each verse, the *Khalīfa* raises his voice and instructs, '*ṣalawāt bar Muḥammad!*' ([Recite the] *ṣalawāt* upon Muhammad!), and the crowd repeats the invocation: 'O Allah, Bless our Master Muhammad and the

Fig.8
The *Khudam* prepares and cooks the meat for the *Chirogh rawshan* meal (*budʒ*). Daftor village, Xinjiang, September 2011

Fig.9
The *Khudam* holds a plate of flour with a bundle of cotton for the *Khalīfa* to bless and use to make the wick. Daftor village, Xinjiang, September 2011

Fig.10
The *Khalīfa* braids the cotton into a wick whilst reading prayers and pious invocations aloud. Daftor village, Xinjiang, September 2011

Figs. 8, 9, 10

family of Muhammad, the Messenger of God, *ṣalawāt*s upon Muhammad and [the supporter of] 'Ali's hand.' The process, usually lasting for about half an hour, continues until the wick is ready. When the wick is complete, the *Khudam* pours the liquidised fat of the sacrificial sheep into the tray over the wick while the *Khalīfa* keeps reciting the prayer (*futa*).

Then the *Khalīfa* lights the wick and starts to read the verses of the *Qandīlnāma* (literally, 'Epistle of the Candle/Lantern') from the *Chirāghnāma* text in a melodic tone (fig.12). After each verse, the crowd repeats the *ṣalawāt* for the entire duration of the process (fig.13). Long after midnight, the recitation reaches its climax and everyone stands up and raises their hands for the final *futa* before the *budʒ* is served. The last prayer is a remembrance of the Ismaili Imams, from Imam 'Ali until the 48th Ismaili Imam, Mawlana Sultan Mahomed Shah Aga Khan III (d. 1957).[28] It is also a prayer for the soul of the departed and a supplication for the betterment of the living. When the prayer ends, the congregation is excused for a short break to stretch their limbs after hours of sitting, before the *Chirogh rawshan* meal is served.

As with the *patfar*, the guests, apart from the immediate family members of the deceased, partake in the *budʒ*. No food should be left uneaten, and the bones and leftovers must be disposed of accordingly. With that, the *Khalīfa* offers a final *futa* for the soul of the departed and for the wellbeing of the living, before calling an end to the ritual. Upon the *Khalīfa*'s closing remarks, the guests stand up and offer a few final consoling words to the bereaved before dispersing into the night.

As a final formality, the *Khalīfa* receives a gift as gratitude for the services he rendered during the entire ritual. Traditionally, the gift includes a piece of silk cloth, enough for a shirt or more, and the best part of the meat from the lamb slaughtered for the *Chirogh rawshan* ceremony. These days, some prefer to offer cash, and well-to-do families may present an expensive carpet or an animal, such as a horse, yak or an ox. The *Khalīfa* accepts the gift with gratitude and offers another *futa*. The *Khudam*, as the main administrator and organiser of the *Chirogh*, also receives a gift for his service. Traditionally, he receives the wool and the neck of the sacrificial animal, together with some bread and meat from the funeral feast. Nowadays, the gift can be in the form of an expensive garment, a nice carpet or even a live sheep, depending on the material wellbeing of the family.

Fig.11
The *Khudam* firmly holds the other end of the braided wick for the *chirogh* (lamp). Daftor village, Xinjiang, September 2011

Fig.12
The *Khalīfa* lights the *chirogh*. Daftor village, Xinjiang, September 2011

Fig.13
Once the *chirogh* is lit, the *Khalīfa* commences the recitations from the *Chirāghnāma*. Daftor village, Xinjiang, September 2011

Figs. 11, 12, 13

The community to a greater extent is integrated through the principles of reciprocity and mutual obligation created by social events such as births, marriages and funerals and offer a helping hand in time of need, in order to alleviate the occasional burden of individual households. Funerals are important social occasions and even the most modest funeral would expect hundreds of participants. Inevitably, serving food to a huge crowd of hundreds at once requires more people and other resources, including spaces of accommodation. Friends and relatives who have travelled from afar for the occasion are expected to spend the night with the bereaved family. Depending on the number of individuals spending the night, some of the out-of-town guests may be accommodated by neighbours, extended family or friends of the bereaved, who are obliged to provide accommodation and food for extra guests when required; a custom known as *qushṏod* (pronounced 'qush thod').

Apart from making their homes available, neighbours, friends and extended family play a crucial role during the entire process, including assisting with house cleaning, preparing and serving the funeral feast, and attending and helping with the *Chirogh rawshan* ceremony. Moreover, traditions prohibit immediate family members of the deceased from partaking in the special *patfar* and *budʒ* feasts. Therefore, neighbours and extended family feed the bereaved family on the day of the funeral, preparing a separate meal for them after the other guests have left. Furthermore, during the first week of the mourning period, the bereaved household also avoids cooking at home; therefore, the onus is on their neighbours and friends to cater for them during this special period.[29]

Conclusion

The Nizari Ismailis from the northwestern frontier of China maintained a near hermetic existence for centuries, due to both geographic and political constraints. However, traditions like the *Chirogh rawshan* ceremony enabled the society to maintain its unity and sense of identity, and preserved their religious culture in the face of adversity, particularly during periods of political uncertainty. The essence of the *Chirogh rawshan* ceremony is the adoration of Allah, the veneration of His Prophet and the Ismaili Imams, and the performance of supplicatory prayers for Allah's grace upon the soul of the departed and for the well-being of the living. With its rich religious literature, the ritual guides the believer to contemplate the meaning and purpose of life in the physical world and in the life hereafter. While conveying the teachings of the Ismaili Imams, it also played a salient role in the spread of the Ismaili message, when the *daʿwa* (mission) was initiated in the region.

The spatial and temporal distances and the cultural peculiarities that separated those living on the periphery from those in the heartland of religious 'orthodoxy' enabled a creative domestication of such religious practices and principles in isolation. The periphery-core dialogue, in cultural terms, has been subtle and complex. The characteristic cultural diversity of this region over the ages meant a mélange of spiritual practices intermingled or coexisted, each within its realm of influence, but they always found inroads into new religious systems that supplanted them. Like many living traditions whose origins are not easy to trace, we may find it difficult to piece together a holistic picture about the *Chirogh rawshan* ceremony from threads long buried under the dusts of time. Nevertheless, from the ways the ritual is performed today and the importance attached to it locally, we may not be too far off to suggest that it is one of the most successful living traditions in the region with a long history behind it. As Richard Frye rightly observed, 'Beliefs are difficult to reconstruct without written "holy" texts, but practices, including rites and rituals, are more observable.'[30] As a result, ethnographic observations enabled us to examine this living religious ritual, with longstanding spiritual and cultural significance.

In the absence of standardised religious education and organised congregations in contemporary China, traditions like the *Chirogh rawshan* ceremony are able to pass on the light of spiritual heritage and assure their continuity. Although the secular definition of the term 'ethnicity' intentionally avoids listing religion as an important identity marker, in daily existence, religion has never ceased from being invoked in self-representation in the local context. In other words, it has become almost impossible to understand ethnic identity without incorporating cultural symbols with religious derivation. In this sense, the *Chirogh rawshan* is more than a mere religious ritual; it is an inalienable part of a cultural fabric that defines the community with a distinctive cultural inheritance.

1 Farhad Daftary, *The Ismāʿīlīs: Their History and Doctrines* (2nd ed., New York, 2007), p.494. See also, Wladimir Ivanow, 'Sufism and Ismailism. Chiragh-nama', *Revue Iranienne d'Anthropologie*, 3 (1959), pp.13–17.

2 Richard N. Frye, *The Heritage of Central Asia: From Antiquity to the Turkish Expansion* (Princeton, NJ, 1996), p.41.

3 By the broader Pamir region, I mean the mountainous heartland of Central Asia, which is divided between Afghanistan, Pakistan, China and Tajikistan, and where the Ismaili communities account for the majority of the local population.

4 I would like to sincerely thank The Institute of Ismaili Studies for providing generous funding towards my extended fieldwork on which this paper is based. I am also grateful to the Ismaili community in Tashkurgan County, China, for assisting me to observe, record and document *Chirogh rawshan* ceremonies in three different localities during my field research. The images from actual *Chirogh rawshan* ceremonies that accompany this essay were taken during subsequent field visits in 2006 and 2011.

5 Feng Jinyuan, *Zhongguo Yisilanjiao* (Islam in China), (Ningxia, 1991), pp.1–5. There are at least ten different accounts on the history of the arrival of Islam in China spanning over seven centuries, from the 7th to the 14th centuries.

6 Ding Jun Zhu, *Yisilan wen hua san lun* (Essays on Islamic Culture), (Lanzhou, 2006), pp.168–190. See also, Muriel Atkin, 'Religious, National, and Other Identities in Central Asia', in Jo-Ann Gross, ed., *Muslims in Central Asia: Expressions of Identity and Change* (Durham, NC, 1992), pp.46–72.

7 These include the *Huajuesi* (Great Mosque) in the Tang capital Chang'an (present Xi'an) and the Huaishensi/Guangtasi Mosque (Remembering the Sage/Light Tower mosque) in Guangzhou (Canton), along with a tomb of a holy man in Quanzhou (Madinat al-Zaytun), which are all dated to within the first millennium AD.

8 Zamir Saʿdullohzoda, et al., 2002. *Ottura Asiadiki Islam Mazhapliri* (Islamic Sects in Central Asia), (Urumqi, 2002), p.39.

9 James A. Millward, *Eurasian Crossroads: A History of Xinjiang* (London, 2007), pp.1–38.

10 Li Sheng, et al., *Zhongguo Xinjiang, Lishi yu Xianzhuang* (The Past and Present of Xinjiang, China), (Urumqi, 2006), pp.2–5; Hodong Kim, *Holy War in China: The Muslim Rebellion and State in Chinese Central Asia,* 1864–1877 (Stanford, CA, 2004), p.1.

11 Frye, *Heritage of Central Asia*, p.231.

12 Kim, *Holy War in China*, p.xiv.

13 Interestingly, official Chinese history textbooks claim that Xinjiang was a part of China since 60 BC. See Li Sheng, *Zhongguo Xinjiang,* pp.10–11; and Shrin Qorban, et al., *Zhongguo Tajikliri* (Tajiks of China), (Urumqi, 1994), p.232.

14 Chen Hui Sheng, ed., *Xinjiang Yisilan jiao shi* (History of Islam in Xinjiang), (Urumqi, 2006) p.79; Ren Jiyu, ed., *Yisilan jiao shi* (History of Islam), (Beijing, 1990), p.433.

15 Mullah Musa Sayrami, *Tarihi Hamidi* (1911, repr. Beijing, 2007), p.108; Saʿdullohzoda, *Ottura Asiadiki*, pp.38–39; and, Millward, *Eurasian Crossroads*, p.78.

16 See the studies in Shrin Qorban, et al., *Zhong guo Tajike shi liao hui bian* (A Collection of Historical Sources Concerning the Tajiks of China), (Xinjiang, 2003).

17 Qorban, *Zhong guo Tajike*, p.4.

18 The languages are named after the places from where they first originated.

19 Atikem Zamiri, et al., *Tajik Adibiyati Tarihi* (History of Tajik literature), (Urumqi, 2005), esp. pp.143–179.

20 Li Dezhu, *Tajike shehui lishi diaocha* (An Examination of Tajik Social History), (Beijing, 2007), pp.74–76; Amier Saidula, 'The Nizari Ismailis of China in Modern Times', in Farhad Daftary, ed., *A Modern History of the Ismailis: Continuity and Change in a Muslim Community* (London, 2011), pp.77–92.

21 Dezhu, *Tajike shehui*, p.74. This account of the alleged Persian preacher, and the timing of his activities, remains ambiguous. A similarly confusing account also appears in Qorban's ethnographic study of the Tajiks in China. See Qorban, *Zhong guo Tajike*, pp.410–412.

22 Hakim Elnazarov and Sultonbek Aksakolov, 'The Nizari Ismailis of Central Asia in Modern Times', in Farhad Daftary, ed., *A Modern History of the Ismailis: Continuity and Change in a Muslim Community* (London, 2011), pp.45–75.

23 Saidula, 'Nizari Ismailis of China', pp.77–92.

24 This and other phrases that follow are Latin phonetic transliterations of words in the Sariqoli language, which is an unwritten language.

25 Abusaid Shokhumorov, *Pamir strana ariev* (Pamir, Land of Arians), (Dushanbe, 1997), pp.116–152.

26 This is a reference to the *takbīrat al-iḥrām*, the *takbīr* with which the ritual prayer (*ṣalāt*) begins, and which puts the worshipper into a temporary state of a special relationship with God.

27 None of my informants knew for certain why there is a prayer for the Twelve Imams (*davāzdah Imām futa*) in an Ismaili ceremony. However, a *Khalīfa* from Tashkurgan suggested the most plausible explanation. He believed that the incorporation of this prayer has to do with the centuries of *taqiyya* (religious dissimulation) practised by various Nizari Ismaili communities living in Syria, Persia, Central Asia and South Asia during the post-Mongol period. This Shiʿi principle of precautionary dissimulation of one's true religious beliefs and identity was necessary for these communities to safeguard themselves from rampant persecution in hostile environments. Thus, between the 13th to early 16th centuries, Ismaili communities across Persia, Afghanistan and Central Asia assumed different religious identities, including Sunnism, Ithna ʿashari Shiʿism and Sufism, adopting new practices and external guises (See Daftary, *The Ismāʿīlīs*, pp.4–5, 410–413, 435–439). Thus, it is within these complex historical circumstances that the prayer to the Twelve Imams may have entered the *Chirogh* ceremony and remains a part of it to this day.

28 The current Imam is the 49th Ismaili Imam, Shah Karim al-Hussaini Aga Khan IV, who is referred to implicitly as *Ṣāḥib al-Zamān* (Lord/Master of the Age) in the ritual.

29 The mourning period could last up to a year.

30 Frye, *Heritage of Central Asia*, p.67.

22

Building and performing Shiʿi Islam in Sufi Senegal: a photo essay

Mara A. Leichtman

Islamic reformist movements have been developing in West Africa for over a century, gaining their greatest popularity in the 1980s. As with similar processes throughout the Muslim world, there is a tendency to return to earlier religious traditions in search of an authentic Islam perceived as a solution to the failures attributed to Western influence and modern innovation (*bidʿa*) in Islamic practice. It is this desire for 'true' knowledge about Islam in a return to scriptural sources that drove some Senegalese Muslims to read various religious and legal books, visit Islamic scholars and clerics seeking the truth about their religion, and learn about other ways of being Muslim. Unlike other reformist movements, Shiʿism, one of the more recent religious traditions adopted by African Muslims, is constructed and performed in Senegal in dialogue with – not opposition to – Sufi Islam. Some Senegalese Shiʿa are attracted to Shiʿi Islam's intellectual tradition and gain followers through contrasting Sunni and Shiʿi jurisprudence. For others, the performance of Shiʿi rituals in ways that complement Sufi traditions is key to convincing other Senegalese to join their growing community.

Shiʿi Islam was brought to Senegal through the migration of people and ideas, with both Lebanese and Iranian influences. Competition is emerging over who will shape this new movement: Lebanon, Iran, or indigenous African Shiʿi leaders. Tension between Arab and Iranian schools of Shiʿi thought results from opposing political views: Iranians defend Khomeini's *velāyat-e faqīh,* which gave religious judges the divine right to rule. On the other hand, Lebanese Shiʿa do not support this view, nor do they approve of the propagation of the ideals behind the Iranian Revolution. Despite the efforts of the Iranian embassy and a prominent Lebanese shaykh, many Senegalese came to Shiʿism on their own. Typically, leaders of Senegal's small but growing Shiʿi community are fluent in Arabic and many have a university education from the Middle East.

Fig.1

This essay will illustrate manifestations of Shiʿi Islamic material culture in Senegal, focusing on the building of mosques, schools and NGOs; the embodiment of Shiʿi authority through dress and libraries; and the presentation of religious holidays. Shiʿa have begun to introduce themselves into the geographies and economies of religious ceremonies in Senegal, of which they had not previously been a part, by explicitly bringing into conversation and ritualisation ideological and theological comparisons of select aspects of Sufi and Shiʿi Islam. Arguments are not only debated, but are disseminated through media coverage, the publication of books, and the invitation of speakers to address these topics on television and radio shows. Through the medium of photography and other images, this essay aims to illustrate the distinct *Sénégalité* of these religious demonstrations.

Senegal today is more than 90 per cent Sunni Muslim, dominated by a tradition of Sufi orders founded by shaykhs (religious clerics who have become saints), whose descendants continue to lead each order having inherited the spiritual power or *baraka* of the founder. Referred to as marabouts (Arabic *murābiṭ*) in Senegal, these shaykhs teach and guide the *talibé* (Arabic *ṭālib*), their students, who study in Islamic schools called *daara* (Arabic *madrasa*), where they learn the Qur'an by rote memorisation (fig.1). The ultimate social, political and economic power perceived to be granted to these marabouts, and their occasional abuses of this power, led some Muslim reformists, both Sunni and Shiʿi, to contest the hierarchies of Sufi orders in Senegal.

Lebanese migrants first arrived in West Africa as the result of a colonial fluke. As early as the 1880s, and especially during the 1920s, emigrants left Lebanon because of economic and political hardship for

Fig.2

Fig.3

Marseilles, France, the transportation hub of the time. They planned to continue on to the United States or South America, where there had been previous Lebanese immigration, but their ships docked at Dakar. French colonialists convinced the Lebanese to stay in West Africa to work as intermediaries in the peanut trade between the French in the cities and Senegalese peasants in the rural areas. Religion, in particular Shiʿi Islam, had not been featured in the Lebanese process of settling and forming a new identity in Senegal until the arrival in 1969 of ʿAbdul Munʿam al-Zayn, a shaykh from Lebanon who trained in Najaf, Iraq. There was no formal Shiʿi religious representation in Senegal until the founding of the Lebanese Islamic Institute in Dakar in 1978. Shaykh al-Zayn opened *Collège al-Zahraa*, a primary and secondary Islamic school, in 1979 (fig.2). Note the depiction of both Lebanese and Senegalese flags on the school's sign, symbolic of the Lebanese community's loyalties to both nation-states.

The Lebanese school teaches Islamic Studies and Arabic alongside the standard Senegalese curriculum. Classes are a mix of students of Lebanese, Senegalese and mixed heritage (fig.3). Girls are required to wear the head-cover (*ḥijāb*) inside the school, but classes are coeducational with gender segregation only in that girls share desks with other girls. A photograph of Shaykh al-Zayn is displayed at the back of the classroom.

Fig.1
Qur'anic school in Kaolack, Senegal, 2007

Fig.2
The sign for *Collège al-Zahraa*, depicting both Lebanese and Senegalese flags, 2013

Fig.3
Students learning at the coeducational *Collège al-Zahraa*, 2003

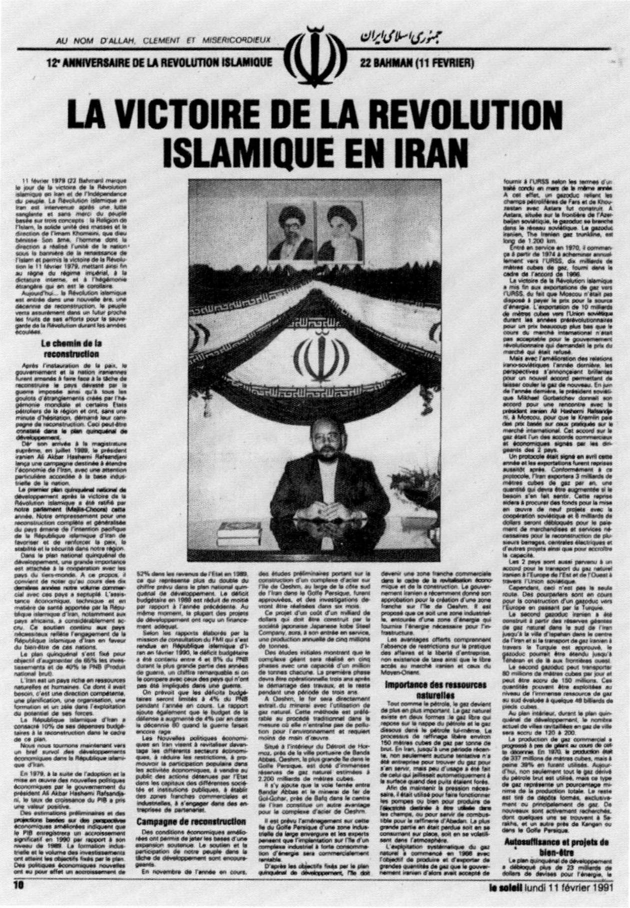

Fig.4

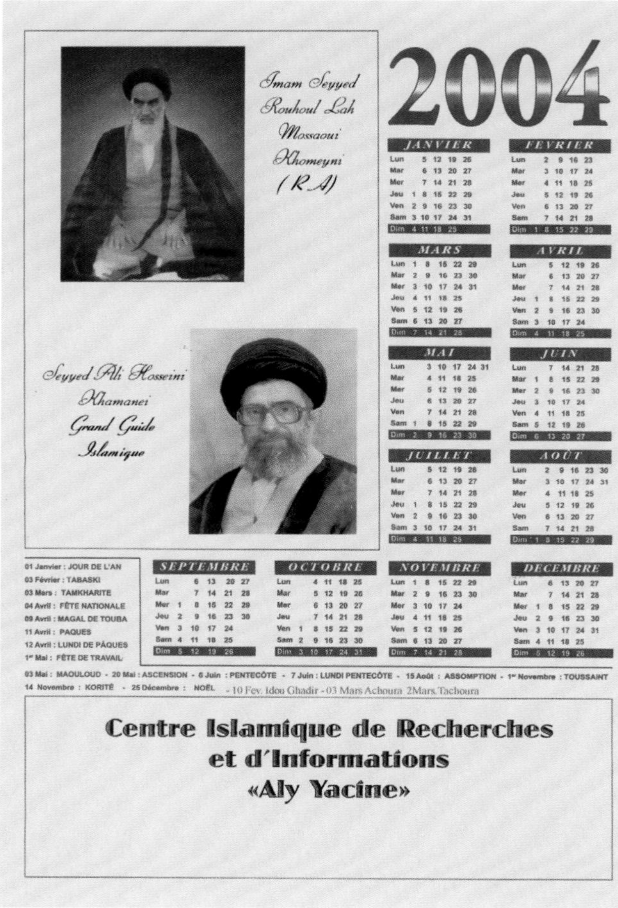

Fig.5

In contrast, in 2002 an Iranian shaykh built a traditional all-male Shiʿi school in Dakar, *Hawza al-Rasūl al-Akram*, where Senegalese shaykhs trained in Shiʿi theology in Iran or Lebanon educate a young generation of boys from Arabic texts.

The Iranian embassy has played a subtle role in encouraging Shiʿi Islam in Dakar. Iran has a history of economic cooperation with Senegal from the time of Reza Shah Pahlavi, but Senegalese President Abdou Diouf closed the embassy in 1984 for spreading Islamic propaganda. The Iranian embassy reopened in the early 1990s and was at first careful to stress only its economic activities in Senegal. However, certain embassy events continued to promote Shiʿi Islam, such as this article published in Senegal's national newspaper, *Le Soleil*, discussing the 'Victory of the Islamic Revolution in Iran' (fig.4). Furthermore, Iranians hold an annual reception for prominent Lebanese and Senegalese Muslims on the anniversary of the Iranian Revolution and finance Senegalese intellectuals to attend Islamic conferences in Tehran.

Bilateral relations between Senegal and Iran have intensified under the two countries' presidents Wade (2000–2012) and Ahmadinejad (2005–2013). Senegalese President Abdoulaye Wade visited Iran multiple times in 2003, 2006, 2008 and 2009, and met with the Supreme Leader of the Islamic Republic, Ayatollah Sayyid ʿAli Khamenei. President Mahmoud Ahmadinejad's attendance at the 2008 'Organisation of the Islamic Conference' (OIC) in Dakar was highly publicised, as was his follow-up visit in 2009, which obtained President Wade's support of Iran's controversial nuclear program. However, Senegal broke diplomatic ties with Iran in February 2011 following suspicions that Iran sold weapons

Fig.4
Senegal's national newspaper, *Le Soleil*, discussing the 'Victory of the Islamic Revolution in Iran'

Fig.5
Calendar published by the *Aly Yacine* Shiʿi Centre with images of the ayatollahs Khomeini and Khamenei

to rebels in the Casamance region that were used against Senegalese soldiers in southern Senegal's struggle for secession. Two years later, Senegalese President Macky Sall reestablished diplomatic ties with Iran on 6 February 2013 when he met President Ahmadinejad at the 'Organisation for Islamic Cooperation' (OIC's new name) conference in Cairo. It remains to be seen how current Iranian President Rouhani will prioritise relations with Africa.

This calendar publicises the Senegalese Shiʿi Islamic Centre called *Aly Yacîne* with images of Iranian Ayatollahs Khomeini and Khamenei (fig.5). It is customary in Senegal at the start of each New Year for businesses to advertise their services by distributing calendars among their clientele, often with images of Sufi marabouts. Some Senegalese have adapted this practice to promote Shiʿi Islam. Note that both Christian feasts (e.g. Easter, Christmas) and pan-Muslim holidays (e.g. the *Mawlid* or birthday of the Prophet) are highlighted, as well as national holidays in Senegal. Shiʿi-specific holy days are emphasised on the calendar in red.

Al-Hajj Ibrahim Derwiche, a prominent Lebanese industrialist, built a large Shiʿi mosque in his name next to the *Collège al-Zahraa* and Dakar's main intercity bus station (figs 6–7). The mosque is headed by a Senegalese shaykh and is the only Senegalese Shiʿi institution in a central location. It attracts over 2,000 (predominantly Sufi) Muslims during Friday prayer. Sermons (*khuṭbas*) are orated in the Wolof language, with the Shiʿi *adhān* (call to prayer), which includes references to Imam ʿAli along with the Prophet Muhammad. The shaykh of the mosque teaches religious classes where Shiʿi students study Jaʿfari *fiqh* (the Shiʿi school of Islamic jurisprudence) on one side of the mosque, and Sunnis study Maliki *fiqh* (the Sunni school of law followed in North and West Africa) in the opposite corner. Such discursive strategies demonstrate how Shiʿi Islam in Senegal is not intended to be a complete break with Sufi Islam; its authenticity is envisioned in the ability to integrate Sufi Muslims into its institutions without requiring any formal transformation of their religious beliefs or practices, merely the exposure, at times unknowingly, to other Islamic traditions.

Shiʿi books in the library of the *Aly Yacîne Centre Islamique de Recherche et d'Information* (in a suburb of Dakar) are in Arabic and French and come from Iran and Lebanon, along with a few books published in Dakar by Shaykh al-Zayn (fig.8). Literacy is increasing

Fig.6

Fig.7

Fig.6
The interior of the Derwiche mosque, with high ceilings and a tiled and painted stucco mihrab, 2013

Fig.7
The Derwiche mosque's impressive dome decorated with carved and painted stucco, 2013

in Senegal, in French as well as Arabic. At the same time, reformist Islamic publicity is disseminating to more remote areas, some specifically targeting the African communities – such as the books in French in this library written by Ayatollah Musavi Lari of Qum. Inherent in Islamic education is the authority bestowed on those who are knowledgeable, and with the spread of religious knowledge through books, media and the Internet comes a broadening of the scope of religious authority and the resulting conflict with the old political communities. Religious scholars who were once revered for their guidance are losing their monopoly over religion with a growing number of educated Muslims turning directly to the texts, which they interpret themselves. Senegalese converts to Shiʿi Islam use their literacy in the Arabic language and their individually acquired libraries of Islamic legal books to bypass the authority of Sufi marabouts.

Madrasa Imām al-Bāqir is an Arabic-French school that was founded in a Dakar suburb in 1992 (fig.9). The shaykh who directs the school (pictured here with his son) studied in Iran and does not renounce Sufi Islam, but builds on the notion of *njebbel*, the vow of obedience to a marabout, in serving both as a *muqaddam* (Sunni representative) for Khalif Général Mansour Sy (the head of one of the Tijani orders in Senegal, d. 2012) as well as a *wakīl* (Shiʿi representative) for Ayatollah Khamenei. His knowledge of Islamic Studies enables him to go beyond the obligation within the Tijani order that *talibé* do not follow any other doctrines. Photos in the director's office of the mosque of Medina and the Kaʿba at Mecca are meant to counter stereotypes prevalent among Sunni Senegalese that Shiʿa do not use minarets in mosques for the call to prayer or perform the Hajj. The shaykh remarked that Senegalese generally form opinions based on images, therefore showing them other images enables them to accept differences. New forms of religious authority in Senegal are about acquiring Islamic knowledge as well as learning how to apply this knowledge in culturally appropriate ways in order to command respect from others.

Shiʿi schools are located outside of city centres in Dakar's remote suburbs (such as the Benne Barak school, pictured in these photos) or hidden in agricultural fields in the southern Casamance region of Senegal (figs 10–11). *Taqiyya*, or religious dissimulation, is permitted when persecution is imminent. Senegal is not a country where people are oppressed, therefore, Senegalese Shiʿa claim, they do not need to employ *taqiyya*. However, some of them are not open about being Shiʿa and do, indeed, practise dissimulation. For example, when praying in Sunni mosques, many Senegalese Shiʿa pray in the Sunni manner (arms crossed, not open, and without the *turba* or clay tablet often from the holy city of Karbala) to avoid lengthy explanations to people who are unlearned, who may not have open minds, and who may think that the Shiʿa are mistaken in their practise of Islam. Built in the outskirts of villages, or deep inside the residential maze of suburbs, the almost invisibility of Shiʿi schools and institutes is another form of *taqiyya*. Hard to find, and therefore difficult to be targeted by opponents of Shiʿi Islam, institutions exclusively cater to those who are open to learning from them, Shiʿi and Sunni Muslim alike. Senegalese use of dissimulation to move adeptly between the Sunni and Shiʿi worlds gives them additional flexibility to convince other Senegalese that Shiʿi Islam is the true path.

The *Aly Yacîne Centre* has expanded to become an 'Association for Sustainable Human Development', with plans to apply for non-governmental organisation (NGO) status for its work with the environment, drugs, malaria, AIDS and famine relief. This includes a *Fatima Zahra Association*, a women's development organisation that functions as a *tontine*, a Senegalese rotating credit association; it encourages women to work, for example, in selling powdered soap or vegetables in small quantities (fig.12). The association also provides free medical consultations for those in the neighbourhood and envisions itself as working to eradicate poverty. *Aly Yacîne*'s founder said that being merely an Islamic organisation no longer suffices without also providing services to the people (fig.13).

Mozdahir International, an institution in Dakar founded by a Senegalese Shiʿa of Mauritanian origin, works in religious education as well as health and agro-pastoral development. It runs agricultural projects in Kolda, a town in the Casamance, with the goal of teaching workers how to farm banana plantations and share the profits, in the hope of keeping young farmers rooted in Senegal and helping to prevent illegal immigration, a growing problem in West Africa. Like *Aly Yacîne*, *Mozdahir International* promotes Shiʿi Islam, and the teachings of the Prophet Muhammad, such as 'work in this world as if you will live forever, and for the next world as if you will die tomorrow,' to carry out development activities in the name of religion (fig.14). One village in the south of

Fig.8
The library of the *Aly Yacîne Centre Islamique de Recherche et d'Information*, 2003

Fig.9
The shaykh who directs the *Madrasa Imām al-Bāqir*, with his son, 2003

Fig.10
A teacher at the remotely located Benne Barak School, 2003

Fig.11
Students at the Benne Barak School, 2003

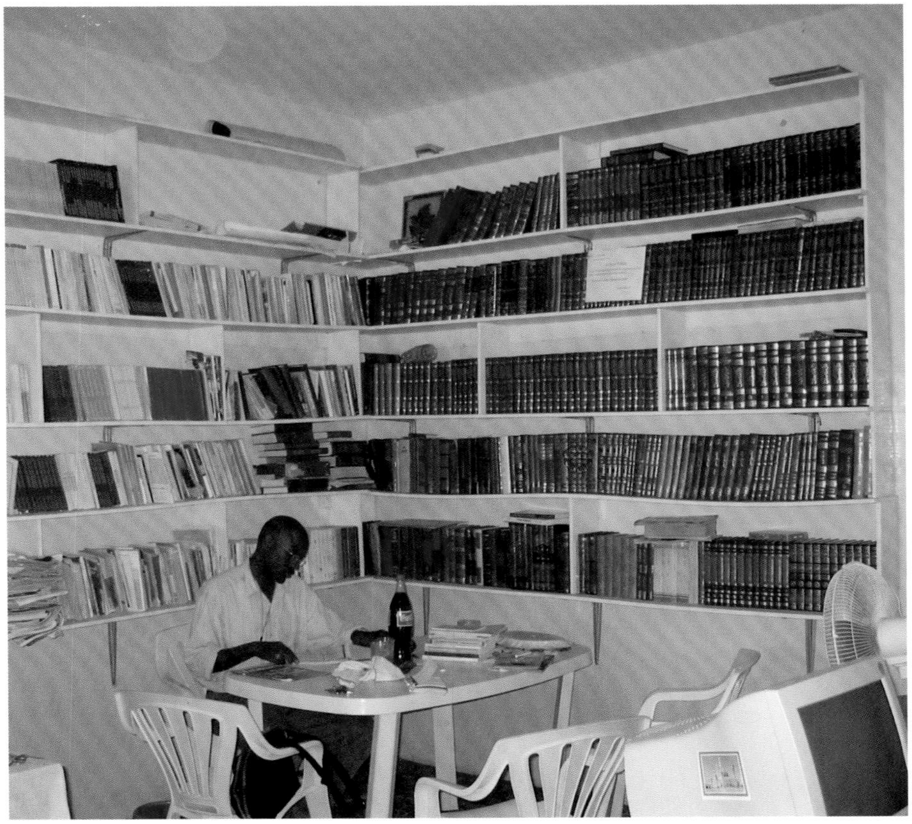

Fig.8

Fig.9

Fig.10

Fig.11

Fig.12

Fig.13

Senegal where the NGO carries out its work was even renamed 'Najaf', after the holy Iraqi Shiʿi city.

'Ashura', the tenth day of the Islamic month of Muharram during which the martyrdom of Imam Husayn, his family and army is commemorated, is often taken as an essential cultural paradigm for Shiʿi Islam. In the past decade, Senegalese converts to Shiʿi Islam have begun to commemorate 'Ashura' in their own way. The Shiʿi practice of self-flagellation has been most controversial in Western media coverage as well as hotly disputed by Shiʿi Muslim clerics. Senegalese Shiʿa insist that such 'Arab' or 'Iranian' practices are not essential to Shiʿi Islam, stressing in contrast their Senegalese or African Shiʿi identity. For example, during 'Ashura' Shiʿa in Dakar organise public debates in a mixture of Wolof, Arabic and French languages, which also appeal to Senegalese Sunni Muslim audiences (fig.15). The 'Ashura' conference depicted in these images was held outside *Collège al-Zahraa*, but the style of the event followed that of Senegal's Sufi orders: a tent was set up on the street with a cassette playing, amplified by a loudspeaker, announcing the event (fig.16). If one listened closely these were not the usual Sufi litanies chanted during religious events in Senegal, but mournful lyrics in Arabic lamenting the tragic events that took place at the battle of Karbala. This drew the attention of passersby, as did the black banners hanging from the tent and covering the speakers' table, with images of the battle scene and verses written in colourful Arabic letters proclaiming the martyrdom of Imam Husayn and his family. The conference, attended by 200 school children and a few dozen adults, was led by Senegalese converts to Shiʿi Islam dressed in Senegalese *boubou*s or Iranian- and Lebanese-style robes and turbans (fig.17). It featured the appearance of the Iranian ambassador and a speech by Lebanese Shaykh al-Zayn. Instead of the sombre black dress of other Shiʿi women, Dakar's Shiʿi conferences are populated with African women wearing their finest fashion – *boubou*s of pure white or bright cheerful colours.

Fig.12
The author seated with members of the *Fatima Zahra Association* who participate in a rotating savings and credit scheme (*tontine*), 2007

Fig.13
Aly Yacîne's founder pictured with children in the library, 2007

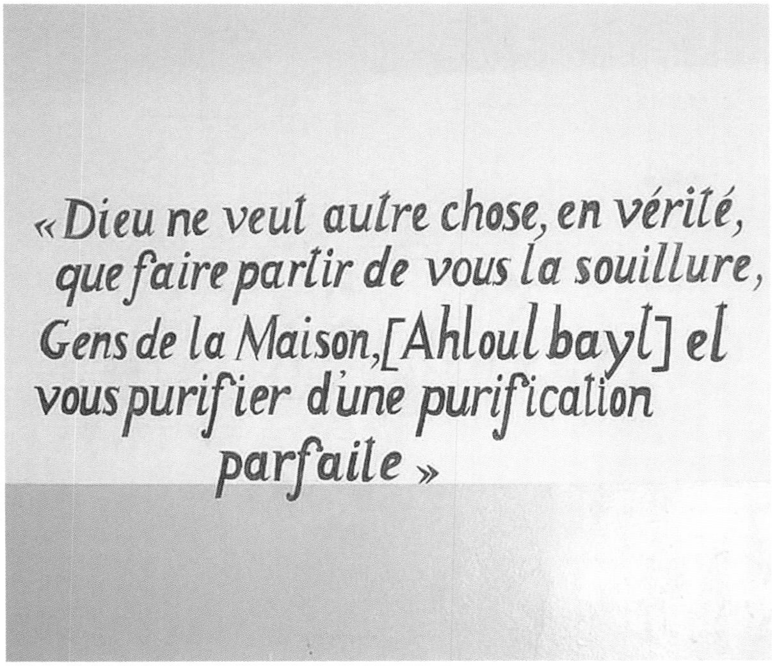
« Dieu ne veut autre chose, en vérité,
que faire partir de vous la souillure,
Gens de la Maison, [Ahloul bayt] et
vous purifier d'une purification
parfaite »

Fig.14

Fig.15

Fig.16

'Ashura' is a date that divides many Senegalese Sunnis and Shi'a as it is a day of celebration for some Muslims, marking the festival of Tamxarit (or Tamkharit), while for others it is a day of profound mourning and sadness. Conferences, television and radio appearances, and written publicity, such as the booklet illustrated here (fig.18), aim to educate Senegalese about the history of the battle of Karbala and play up the closeness that African Sufis also feel towards the Family of the Prophet (*Ahl al-bayt*). Shi'a additionally address the origins of the Senegalese holiday Tamxarit, whose carnival-like festivities conflict with the sombre remembrance of the tragic events at Karbala.

Tamxarit is a joyful occasion, a sort of Muslim Halloween where girls dress as boys and boys as girls, and children go door to door to receive gifts to the rhythm of drums. Senegalese Sufi Muslims chant nocturnal evocations on the night of the ninth of Muharram, and fast during the day of 'Ashura' followed by a feast of couscous with beef. Tamxarit is thought to be a syncretism between Islamic rituals and

Fig.14
Key Qur'anic verses and hadiths central to Shi'ism, such as Qur'an 33:33, are translated into French and painted on the walls of *Mozdahir International*, 2009

Fig.16
The 2008 'Ashura' conference in Dakar held outdoors under a tent, appealed to a wider audience by following the style of events usually held by Sufi orders in Senegal, 2008

Fig.15
In contrast to 'Ashura' rituals held in Iran or South Asia, the occasion is commemorated through an academic conference, with Muharram banners and songs of lamentation playing in the background, 2008

Fig.17

Tout ce que nous possédons vient de Achoura
Imam Khomeyni (ra)
Association pour le Développement Humain Durable " Ali Yacine" (as)
LA VRAIE SIGNIFICATION DE TAMXARIT OU ACHOURA
Considéré par les uns comme Fête et les autres comme Deuil
JANVIER 2008

Fig.18

pre-Islamic popular practices linked to the Lebou ethnic group's offerings to pagan divinities. Others trace the origin of Tamxarit to the time of the Umayyads when it is believed that Yazid, the son of the caliph Mu'awiya, promoted a glorification of this day in celebration of his victory over Imam Husayn and his companions. A flyer created for the 2008–2009 Muharram season advertised: 'Be with Husayn or be against Husayn and the Family of the Prophet'. Such provocative statements are meant to encourage Senegalese Sufis to rethink their celebration of Tamxarit and the meaning of the day of 'Ashura'.

Although the leaders of Shi'i organisations in Senegal are men, institutions are starting to involve more Muslim women. *Mozdahir International* organised an event to commemorate the opening of a new Shi'i Islamic complex (*Al-Hassanayni Centre*) in the Dakar suburb of Guediawaye around the birthday of Fatima, the daughter of the Prophet, which also corresponded with International Muslim Women's Day and the Senegalese celebration of Mother's Day. Although the focus of the event was a religious conference, organisers referred to this event as a *gamou*, the Wolof term for a large celebration commemorating the birthdays of the Prophet Muhammad or one of the Tijani Sufi shaykhs. At the head table leading the conference were the male leaders of the organisation, joined by a teacher from Mauritania and two members of the *Mozdahir* delegation from France of Congolese origin. Several hundred attendees included mostly Senegalese students in addition to members of Mauritanian origin. A few male Iranians representing the Embassy and Iranian Cultural Centre were also present for the beginning of the ceremony. The evening celebration took place underneath a large tent and was broadcast nationally by one of the Senegalese television stations.

As part of the conference, a group of female students sang a song in Arabic in praise of Fatima, and were dressed in t-shirts over their *boubou*s advertising the new *Al-Hassanayni Centre* (fig.19). A (male) speaker addressed the women in the audience informing them that this day was their day and their celebration. He announced that Fatima had organised the first protest against injustice after the death of her father, the Prophet Muhammad. He expressed that there is no difference between man and woman in terms of responsibility and that the

Fig.17
The 'Ashura' conference was led by Senegalese converts to Shi'i Islam dressed in both traditional *boubous* and Iranian- and Lebanese-style robes and turbans, 2008

Fig.18
This booklet discussing 'Ashura' and Tamxarit plays up the closeness that both Shi'a and African Sufis feel towards the *Ahl al-bayt*

Fig.19

relationship between men and women is not one of authority and superiority but is a complementary relationship. The speaker recounted a conversation between Fatima and her father when he told her she is the matron of women and an exemplar for women to follow, distinguishing her from the other important women in the Qur'an. He also expressed that the director of *Mozdahir* (who was not present at this event) was very proud of the efforts of its female members.

Conclusions

Orthopraxy is a fundamental aspect of Islam. In Senegal, Shiʿi discourse is articulated through material culture – distinct from other Shiʿi contexts in that it specifically caters to a Sufi Muslim audience. The Lebanese shaykh, and later Iranian officials, first built Shiʿi mosques and schools in Dakar. Senegalese Shiʿa expanded the religious movement by reaching out to Sunni Muslims using formats similar to those of the Sufi orders: tents and loudspeakers, Wolof proverbs and Qur'anic verses, Shiʿi religious gatherings labelled (Tijani) *gamous*. As a minority community, Senegalese Shiʿa aim to teach others in order to gain more followers and to avoid conflict, and doing so necessitates forms of disseminating new religious ideas in a manner that does not highlight fundamental differences. Senegalese converts to Shiʿism believe that there is a religious conscience in the Senegalese people favourable to Shiʿi Islam, which shares many attributes of Sufi Islam. African Sufis, like Shiʿa, practice *tawassul*, the act of supplicating to God through the Prophet, an Imam or Sufi saint. Sufis and Shiʿa both practice *ziyāra*, visits to shrines. They both respect the family of the Prophet and have the notion of *sharīf*s, those who can claim their genealogical descent directly from the family of the Prophet.

Efforts concentrate on uniting as *Senegalese* Muslims by way of events that orchestrate a new Shiʿi Islamic message through local Sufi Islamic practices. From initial hesitation to publicly professing a new Shiʿi identity (sometimes using *taqiyya*), Shiʿi authority has become established in Senegal by the wearing of robes and turbans typical of Middle Eastern Shiʿi clerics and creating libraries of Islamic books in Arabic and French from Iran and Lebanon. Calendars replace Sufi marabouts with Iranian Ayatollahs, Shiʿi schools teach both Maliki and Jaʿfari *fiqh*, and one Senegalese shaykh serves simultaneously as Sufi *muqaddam* and Shiʿi *wakīl*. 'Ashura' commemorations decorated with Shiʿi banners depicting the battle of Karbala merge with lectures clarifying the origins of Tamxarit. Islamic material culture in Senegal thereby blurs the presumed distinction between 'Sufis' and 'reformists', where neither group forms a homogenous movement.

Fig.19
Female students dressed in t-shirts over their *boubous* advertising the new *Al-Hassanayni Centre* sing Arabic songs in praise of Fatima at the *Mozdahir International* event, 2009

Imam ʿAli receives the *bayʿa* (oath of allegiance) from the Kufans, from a *Maktel-i Āl-i Resūl* of Lami'i Çelebi. Turkey, late 16th–early 17th century, British Library, Or.7238, folio 9v

Acknowledgements

I wish to thank all the speakers who participated in the 2009 conference at the British Museum and made it such a memorable event, including two inspirational individuals who are sadly no longer with us and to whom this volume is dedicated: Oleg Grabar (1929–2011) and Melanie Michailidis (1966–2013). I also wish to convey my sincere gratitude to all the contributors for their hard work, commitment and patience throughout this project. In addition, I want to extend my deepest appreciation to the following individuals for their guidance, encouragement and support: Sheila Canby, Robert Gleave, Andrew Newman, Sheila Blair, John Curtis, Vesta Curtis, Oliver Leaman, Alnoor Merchant, Azim Nanji, Naz Jiwa and all the volunteers who assisted me at the conference. For their invaluable editorial expertise I wish to acknowledge Omar Ali-de-Unzaga, Hasan Al-Khoee, Thallein Antun, Nadia Holmes, Isabel Miller, St John Simpson and Heghnar Watenpaugh. My special thanks are for Patricia Salazar, editor at The Institute of Ismaili Studies, who oversaw the book to final publication. I am deeply indebted to Zahra Kazani and Professor Wilferd Madelung for their assistance and advice on the Shiʿi genealogical chart, and to Russell Harris for the wonderful maps. The book is beautifully designed and produced thanks to the painstaking efforts of Lorna Raby, Misha Anikst and their team at Azimuth Editions. This project would not have been possible without the institutional support and academic collaboration between The Institute of Ismaili Studies under the guiding hand of Farhad Daftary, Co-Director and Head of Academic Research and Publications, and the British Museum, under the Directorship of Neil MacGregor and with the support of Jonathan Tubb, Keeper of the Middle East Department. Finally, words fail me in expressing my gratitude for the support from my family, especially from Aly and Khadija.

Note on transliteration and abbreviations

In order to make this book accessible to both specialist and general readers, the Arabic, Turkish, Persian, Sariqoli, Wakhi, Urdu and Wolof transliterations in the main text and the notes are limited to italicised words, including titles of books. However, diacritics are included for names of medieval authors in bibliographic references in the notes and in the select bibliography at the end of the book for ease of reference. The letters *ʿayn* and *hamza* are generally retained throughout, but frequently-used foreign words or those having a recognised English form are anglicised and not italicised. Diacritical marks for place names have been omitted throughout except for Chapter 11, where place names are also mint names. The basic system of transliteration adopted is that of the second edition of *The Encyclopaedia of Islam*, which is Arabic based, with minor modifications: *d̲j̲*, *k̲h̲*, *d̲h̲*, *s̲h̲* and *ḳ*, are replaced with *j*, *kh*, *dh*, *sh* and *q* respectively. Whilst we attempted consistency throughout, we also respected individual authors' requests if they preferred more Persianised or Turkish spellings for specific terms in their chapters. A glossary of significant terms and concepts is provided at the end of the book.

The following abbreviations have been used: b. for 'ibn' (son of); AD (*Anno Domini*, for common era dates); AH (*Anno Hegirae*, for Hijri calendar dates); Sh. (Shamsi, for Persian solar calendar dates); (*r.*) for regnal dates of individuals and dynasties; *EI*, *EI2* and *EI3* for the first, second and third editions of the Encyclopaedia of Islam respectively; *EQ* for the *Encyclopaedia of the Qur'an*; *EIR* for *Encyclopaedia Iranica*; and *EIS* for *Encyclopaedia Islamica*.

FS

Glossary

Term	**Definition**
Ahl al-bayt	Lit. the people of the house; members of the household of the Prophet, in the broadest sense comprising all of the Banu Hashim clan; understood by the Shiʿa as including especially, Muhammad, Fatima, ʿAli, al-Hasan, al-Husayn and their progeny. Also referred to as *Āl Muḥammad/Āl al-Nabī* (Muhammad's family/the Prophet's family).
Ahl al-kisāʾ; (Turk. and Per. *Āl-i ʿabāʾ)*	Lit. the people of the cloak; the holy pentad identified in the *ḥadīth al-kisāʾ* (q.v.) as the Prophet, Fatima, ʿAli, al-Hasan and al-Husayn. In the Indo-Iranian context also referred to as *Panj tan* or *Panj tan pāk* (five pure bodies) and in Turkish and Persian contexts as *Āl-i ʿabāʾ* (Family of the mantle/cloak).
Ahl al-sunna wa'l-jamāʿa	Lit. the people of the tradition/example and the community; a collective term for Muslim adherents who eventually coalesced into the Sunni branch of Islam, which today makes up 85–90 per cent of the *umma*. Their characteristic feature is the recognition of the sayings (*ḥadīth*) and example (*sunna*) of the Prophet as codes of conduct and, together with the Qur'an, as the basis of Islamic law. See also hadith.
ʿalam	Lit. signpost, flag; in Indo-Persian Shiʿi contexts a highly decorated religious standard or device made of steel fretwork inlaid with gold and affixed to the top of a wooden shaft; usually in the shape of a teardrop, hand or circle, *ʿalam*s are often inscribed with the names of the *Ahl al-bayt* (q.v.), including those of the Twelve Imams (q.v.), and pious phrases; carried during public ʿAshuraʾ (q.v.) processions.
ʿAli b. Abi Talib (d. 40/661)	Cousin of the Prophet Muhammad and husband of his daughter Fatima; among the first to embrace Islam and fourth caliph; first Shiʿi Imam. See also ʿAlid and Shiʿa.
ʿAlid(s)	Descendant(s) of ʿAli b. Abi Talib (q.v.) and Fatima through their sons, al-Hasan and al-Husayn; they can also be more specifically referred to as Hasanids/*sharīf*s (q.v.v.) or Husaynids/*sayyid*s (q.v.v.).
ʿArūze Qāsem (Per. *ʿarūsī Qāsim*)	Lit. the wedding of Qasim; part of the taʿziya (q.v.) repertoire of Passion plays devoted to the Karbala tragedy and performed during the first nine days of Muharram. The play centres on the story of the marriage and subsequent martyrdom of Qasim b. al-Hasan, the nephew of Imam Husayn. Special female-only performances are also organised and enacted by women in Iran as part of their ritual commemorations. See also *ḥijla*.
ʿAshuraʾ (Ar. ʿĀshūrāʾ)	Derived from *ʿashara* (Ar. ten) and referring to the tenth day of the Muslim month of Muharram (q.v.), the day of Imam Husayn's martyrdom at Karbala (q.v.) in 60/680. A voluntary fast day for Muslims and a

Term	Definition
	day of mourning and ritual commemorations particularly sacred to Shiʿi communities around the world.
ʿāshūrkhāna	Lit. the house of ʿAshura' (q.v.); permanent Shiʿi ritual-oriented buildings, which serve as locations for collective mourning rituals e.g. taʿziya (q.v.) and *rowzeh-khānī* (q.v.), the departure and arrival point for processions, and as the repository for ceremonial objects including taʿziyas (replica tombs), *ʿalams* (q.v.) and *zarīḥ*s (q.v.). They can be traced back to the end of the 16th century in the Deccan, south-central India; forerunners of the *imāmbārā*s (q.v.) in northern India. See also *Ḥusayniyya* and *takiya*.
ʿatabāt; (Per. *ʿatabāt-i ʿāliya*; *ʿatabāt-i muqaddasa*)	Lit. thresholds; also qualified as lofty (*ʿāliya*) or sacred (*muqaddasa*) thresholds and referring to the Shiʿi shrine cities of Iraq (Najaf, Karbala (q.v.), Kazimayn (q.v.) and Samarra) and Iran (Mashhad); loci of the tombs of seven of the Imams as well as a number of secondary shrines and places of visitation. Also referred to in Arabic and Persian as *maqām*, *mashhad*, *marqad* and *mazār*.
baraka	Blessing(s); beneficent force of divine origin.
basmala	Qur'anic formula: *Bismi'llāh al-raḥmān al-raḥīm*, 'In the name of God, the Merciful, the Compassionate'. Muslims say the *basmala* before important acts to seek God's blessing.
bāṭin	The inner, hidden or esoteric meaning behind the literal wording of the Qur'an and the *sharīʿa* (Islamic law), as distinct from the *ẓāhir* (q.v.). Shiʿi Imams can interpret the *bāṭin* meanings of sacred texts using their *ʿilm* (divine knowledge), which was first transferred from the Prophet to ʿAli and then to successive Imams through *naṣṣ* (q.v.).
Bavandids (Per. *Āl-i Bāvand*)	An Iranian dynasty that ruled in Tabaristan (Mazandaran) for over 700 years (*r.* 45–750/665–1349) and claimed Sasanian descent. By the tenth century the dynasty had switched its allegiance from Sunni (q.v.) Islam to Ithna ʿashari Shiʿism.
dharīḥ (Per. *zarīḥ*)	In architecture, a silver or steel caged enclosure that surrounds a Shiʿi shrine's cenotaph. See also *ziyāra*.
Dhu'l-Faqār; (Per. *Zolfaqār*)	Lit. possessing notches or grooves; the Prophet's legendary sword, obtained as booty in the battle of Badr and later given to ʿAli (q.v.). It is related that within this context Muhammad uttered the phrase: *lā fatā illā ʿAlī, lā sayfa illā Dhu'l-faqār* (There is no hero except ʿAli and no [mighty] sword except the *Dhu'l-faqār*).

Term	Definition
fālnāma	Lit. book of divination. In the Muslim world (especially in Iranian and Turkish contexts), *fālnāma*s are consulted in order to foresee the future or, at least, the signs or circumstances that are auspicious for some decision. One of the most authoritative *fālnāma*s is attributed to the sixth Shiʿi Imam Jaʿfar al-Sadiq (d. 765).
Fatimids (Ar. *Fāṭimiyyūn*)	Ismaʿili Shiʿi dynasty of Imam-caliphs (*r.* 297–567/909–1171), claiming descent from ʿAli and Fatima and named after the latter; ruled from North Africa and later in Egypt. See also ʿAlid.
Fourteen Immaculate Ones; Fourteen Infallibles (Ar. *maʿṣūmūn*)	In Twelver Shiʿism they comprise Muhammad, Fatima and the Twelve Imams. See also *ʿiṣma*.
Ghadir Khumm	Name of a pool between Mecca and Medina. On 18 Dhu'l-Hijja 10/16 March 632 on the way back to Medina following his final pilgrimage to Mecca, the Prophet stopped at Ghadir Khumm to deliver a sermon which, as understood by the Shiʿa, included an implicit appointment of ʿAli to the succession of the leadership of the community in the following words: 'He of whom I am the *mawlā* (the patron/master), of him ʿAli is also the *mawlā* (*man kuntu mawlāhu fa-ʿAlī mawlāhu*).'
ghayba	Lit. absence; period of occultation of someone who has been withdrawn by God from human eyes and whose life may be miraculously prolonged until his return. A number of Shiʿi groups have recognised the *ghayba* of a particular Imam (q.v.), with the implication that no further Imam was to succeed him and he was to return before the Day of Resurrection as the Mahdi (q.v.). The twelfth Ithna ʿashari Imam has remained in *ghayba* since 260/874.
hadith (Ar. *ḥadīth*)	Lit. report; sometimes translated as Tradition, relating to actions or sayings of the Prophet and his Companions, or the corpus of such reports. For the Shiʿa it also refers to the sayings and deeds of their Imams (q.v.).
ḥadīth al-thaqalayn	Lit. hadith of the two weighty things; a report in which the Prophet said at his final sermon that upon his death he would leave behind two sources of guidance for the Muslim *umma*, the Qur'an (*kitāb Allāh*) and his progeny (*Ahl al-bayt*). The group that coalesced into the Sunni (q.v.) branch of Islam interpreted the term *Ahl al-bayt* as the entire community of Muslim believers. In contrast, the group that eventually formed the Shiʿa interpreted *Ahl al-bayt* as a successor from amongst the Prophet's family.
Hajj	The annual pilgrimage to Mecca and other sacred localities in the last month of the Muslim calendar, Dhu'l-Hijja; required of every Muslim at least once in his or her lifetime if possible.

Term	Definition
Hamdanids	Two Twelver Shiʿi dynasties of Taghlibi Arab descent that ruled from Iraq (Mosul) and Syria (Aleppo) in the fourth/tenth century.
Hasanid(s)	See ʿAlid and *sharīf*.
ḥijla	Nuptial or bridal chamber; developed as Shiʿi religious iconography derived from the tragic story of Qasim and Fatima's wedding, *ʿArūze Qāsem* (q.v.) at their encampment in Karbala. In contemporary Iran, a symbolic *ḥijla* structure was erected when an unmarried young man died unexpectedly and *ḥijla*s were frequently put up to commemorate the lives of young soldiers during the Iran–Iraq war (1980–1988).
Husaynid(s)	See ʿAlid and *sayyid*.
Ḥusayniyya	Similar to the earlier *ʿāshūrkhāna*s (q.v.) and *imāmbārā*s (q.v.) in southern and northern India respectively, *Ḥusayniyya*s (also called *takiya*s) are permanent Shiʿi ritual-oriented buildings, which serve as loci for collective mourning rituals (e.g. taʿziya (q.v.) and *rowzeh-khānī* (q.v.)), the departure and arrival point for processions, and as the repository for ʿAshuraʾ related ceremonial objects.
ʿId al-Ghadīr	Shiʿi celebration of the event that took place at Ghadir Khumm (q.v.).
Imam	Lit. leader; used in Sunni contexts to refer to a leader of a group of Muslims in prayer; in reference to a founder of a *madhhab* (school of law); a great scholar of religious sciences; or a political leader. Used by the Shiʿa to refer to persons recognised by them as legitimate heads of the Muslim community after the Prophet. Among various branches of the Shiʿa, the Shiʿi Imams are recognised as descendants of the *Ahl al-bayt* (q.v.).
Imāma	The Imamate; institution or office of the Imam (q.v.).
imāmbārā (Urdu *imāmbāṛā*)	Lit. enclosure of the Imams; similar to the earlier established *ʿāshūrkhāna*s (q.v.) of the Deccan, the *imāmbārā*(s) of northern India functioned primarily as places of devotion to the martyrs of Karbala, as well as display centres for taʿziyas (replica tombs) and permanent houses for *zarīḥ*s (q.v.). See also *Ḥusayniyya*s and *takiya*s.
imāmzāda(s)	A Persian word used to designate both the descendant of a Shiʿi Imam and the shrine of such a person. The *imāmzāda*s are thus all ʿAlids but not all ʿAlids are accorded the title of *imāmzāda*. In common usage it is given to the sons and grandsons of the Imams, but excludes those who themselves became Imams, and also to those of their descendants

Term	Definition
	distinguished by special sanctity or by suffering martyrdom. It is not normally accorded to the female descendants of the Imams.
ʿiṣma	Inerrancy, infallibility; a quality attributed to the prophets and in Shiʿi Islam, especially to Imams. One who is endowed with *ʿiṣma* is called *maʿṣūm*.
Ismailis (Ar. *Ismāʿīliyya/Ismāʿīlī*)	A branch of the Shiʿa that traced the Imamate through Imam Jaʿfar al-Sadiq's eldest son Ismaʿil, after whom it is named. Several sub-divisions developed over time (i.e. the Tayyibis and their subdivisions and the Nizaris).
Ithna ʿasharis (Ar. *Ithnā ʿashariyya*)	A branch of the Shiʿa that believes in twelve Imams (*ithnā ʿashar* meaning 'twelve' in Arabic) beginning with ʿAli and ending with Muhammad al-Mahdi (q.v.).
Karbala	A place in Iraq (60 miles SSW of Baghdad); the site of the battle in 680 between the armies of the Umayyad caliph Yazid and al-Husayn b. ʿAli b. Abi Talib, grandson of the Prophet and Shiʿi Imam, in which the latter was killed and his body was buried there. A major pilgrimage site for Shiʿa Muslims and also known as *mashhad al-Ḥusayn*.
Kazimayn/Kazimiyya; Kadhimayn/ Kadhimiya (Ar. Kāẓimayn/Kāẓimiyya)	A town in Iraq located in what is now a northern neighbourhood of Baghdad; one of three most celebrated Shiʿi places of pilgrimage in Iraq, located to the south of Samarra and north of Karbala and Najaf. Kazimayn means 'the two Kazims' and refers to the two ʿAlid Imams buried there, Musa b. Jaʿfar al-Sadiq, nicknamed al-Kazim (d. 183/799) and his grandson, Muhammad al-Jawad (d. 220/835), the seventh and ninth Imams of the Twelver Shiʿa (q.v.) respectively.
Mahdi (Ar. *mahdī*)	Lit. the rightly-guided one; the expected one. The name applied to the restorer of true religion and justice who, according to a widely held Muslim belief, will appear and rule before the end of the world. A messianic figure who, in Muslim tradition, is expected to appear and usher in a new order. Within Shiʿi Islam, over the course of history, the Ithna ʿasharis (q.v.) came to acknowledge their twelfth Imam as their hidden Mahdi whilst the majority of the early Ismailis recognised their seventh Imam, Muhammad b. Ismaʿil; the Zaydis (q.v.) did not generally recognise any of their Imams as the Mahdi.
maʿṣūm	One who possesses *ʿiṣma* (q.v.).

Term	Definition
Muharram	The first month of the Muslim year; considered one of four sacred months. Some Muslims fast on the ninth and/or tenth day of Muharram and ritual commemorations amongst the Shiʿa are held during the first ten days of the month. The tenth day ('Ashura', q.v.) is the anniversary of Karbala (60/680) and therefore a great day of mourning particularly, but not exclusively, for the Shiʿa.
Nād-i ʿAlī prayer	Lit. 'Call upon ʿAli'; A Shiʿi prayer in Arabic that can be traced back to Safavid (q.v.) times: *Nād-i ʿAliyyan maẓhar al-ʿajāʾib tajiduhu ʿawnan laka fī al-nawāʾib. Kullu hammin wa ghammin sa-yanjalī bi-wilāyatika yā ʿAlī* ('Call upon ʿAli, manifestation of wonders; you will find him a helper in all adversity. Every care and sorrow shall surely be removed through your saintly protection, O ʿAli'). During the Safavid and Qajar (q.v.) eras, protective tunics for soldiers known as *pīrāhan-i Nād-i ʿAlī* (vestments of the *Nād-i ʿAlī*) were inscribed with this prayer.
naṣṣ	Explicit designation of a successor by his predecessor, particularly relating to the Shiʿi view of succession to the Imamate, whereby each Imam (q.v.), under divine guidance, designates his successor.
nawḥa (Per. *nowḥeh*)	Elegy, lament; from the Arabic *nāḥa* 'to wail, weep, lament, mourn'. In Persian literature, a genre of poetry focusing on the Karbala tragedy, which is sung on occasions involving breast-beating (*sīneh*) or self-flagellation. The *rowzeh-khānī* (q.v.) ritual ends with the congregational singing of *nawḥas*.
pardah; *pardah-khānī*	Lit. curtain; a narrative painting. Sometimes referred to as coffeehouse (*qahwa-khāna*) paintings since Iranian coffee houses once served as artists' ateliers and lodgings. The tradition of *pardah* or *shamāʾil* (q.v.) narrative paintings served as a means of promoting religious and secular aims. Usually accompanied by a performance in the form of storytelling (*pardah khānī*), which describes the action depicted on the canvas. Religious *pardah* are devoted to the Karbala tragedy. See *pardah-khān*.
pardah-khān	A person who narrates a story using a *pardah* (q.v.) painting.
Qajars (Per. *Qājār*)	A Turkmen dynasty that ruled Persia for a century and a half (*r.* 1193–1344/1779–1925). Followers of Ithna ʿashari (q.v.) Shiʿism who, unlike the Safavids (q.v.), did not claim ʿAlid ancestry. Under Qajar rule, religious imagery, *shamāʾil* (q.v.), featuring portraits of the *Ahl al-bayt* (q.v.) were elevated to an art form and greatly popularised.
rowzeh-khān (Ar. *rawḍa khān*)	One who leads the recitation of the *rowzeh-khānī* (q.v.). In the past, the *rowzeh-khān* recited chapters from Kashifi's book; today, the original

Term	Definition
	text has been almost abandoned as each reciter uses his own creative skills to narrate the Karbala story. A successful *rowzeh-khān* is able to heighten the emotional state of the audience so that participants can identify with the suffering of Imam Husayn and other Shiʿi martyrs.
rowzeh-khānī (Ar. *rawḍa khānī*)	Lit. the garden recitation; a Shiʿi Persian mourning ritual commemorating the suffering and martyrdom of Imam Husayn and other Shiʿi martyrs. The name of this public lamentation is derived from the title of a literary masterpiece called *Rawḍat al-shuhadā'* (The Garden of the Martyrs). Written in Persian but under an Arabic title, the *Rawḍa* was composed by Husayn Waʿiz Kashifi in 908/1502–1503 soon after Ithna ʿashari Shiʿism was established as the state religion of Persia under the Safavid (q.v.) dynasty.
Safavids (Ar. *Ṣafawiyya*)	Dynasty of Kurdish origin that ruled Persia as sovereigns (shahs) from 907–1135/1501–1722, as puppet monarchs from 1142–1148/1729–1736, and thereafter, existed as pretenders to the throne up to 1186/1773. The first ruler, Shah Ismaʿil I (*r.* 907–930/1501–1524) declared Ithna ʿashari Shiʿism as the official religion of the new state.
ṣalawāt	The invocation of God's blessing and peace upon the Prophet Muhammad; also referred to as *taṣliya*. In Shiʿi contexts the *ṣalawāt* extends to the Prophet and his family (i.e. the *Ahl al-bayt*) with the following formula: *Allāhumma ṣalli ʿalā Muḥammadin wa āl-i Muḥammadin* (O Allah bestow your blessings on Muhammad and the family of Muhammad).
Saqqākhāneh	A term coined by the Iranian art critic Karim Emami in 1962 to refer to a contemporary art movement in Iran. Initially applied to modern painting and sculpture that used elements of votive Shiʿi art, it gradually came to be applied more widely to art works that used traditional decorative elements.
sayyid	Meaning 'lord'. To be a *sayyid* meant having a claim to some type of Hashimid descent (from the family or Banu Hashim clan of the Prophet) or ʿAlid (q.v.) descent. More narrowly Ḥusaynid descent.
shafāʿa	Intercession, mediation; used in an eschatological sense to refer to the Prophet, and in Shiʿi Islam also to the Imams (and in Sufism to Sufi masters), as intercessors on behalf of believers on the Day of Judgement. Also referred to as *tawassul*.
shahāda	Muslim profession of faith in the belief in one unique deity, namely Allah, and in Muhammad as His final messenger. The extended Shiʿi *shahāda* attests to the oneness of God, the apostleship of Muhammad,

Term	Definition
	and thirdly the guardianship of ʿAli: *lā ilāha illā Allāh, Muḥammad rasūl Allāh, ʿAlī walī Allāh.*
shamā'il	Lit. good qualities; character. In Persian Shiʿi contexts the term refers to the tradition of narrative paintings (see *pardah*) and also religious images, particularly portraits of the Prophet and the *Ahl al-bayt* (q.v.). See Qajars.
sharīf	Meaning 'noble, exalted or eminent'. To be a *sharīf* meant having a claim to some type of Hashimid descent (from the family or Banu Hashim clan of the Prophet) or ʿAlid (q.v.) descent. More narrowly Ḥasanid descent.
Shiʿa (noun); Shiʿi (adj.)	Derived from *shīʿat ʿAlī* (i.e. the party or partisans of ʿAli), as a collective name for several Muslim religious communities that regard ʿAli b. Abi Talib (q.v.) and his descendants as the true heirs of the Prophet and as legitimate heads (Imams) of the Muslims. Today comprising 10–15 per cent of the Muslim *umma.*
shīʿat ʿAlī	See Shiʿa.
Sunni	See *Ahl al-sunna wa'l-jamāʿa.*
sura (Ar. *ṣūra*, pl. *ṣuwar*)	Chapter of the Qur'an; there are 114 in total. A sura is made up of several verses or *āyāt.*
takiya	See *Ḥusayniyya.*
taqiyya (Per. *kitmān*)	Precautionary dissimulation of one's true religious beliefs, especially in times of danger; used historically particularly by Ithna ʿasharis, Ismailis and Nusayris (ʿAlawi Shiʿis).
tawassul	See *shafāʿa.*
tawḥīd	The Islamic doctrine denoting the oneness of God, His absolute existence, and that He has no equal.
taʿziya	From the Arabic *ʿazza* (to mourn or console); In Iran *taʿziya* denotes a theatrical production of a Shiʿi Passion play focusing on the martyrs of Karbala (q.v.). The term can also refer to any ritual devoted to the suffering of Imam Husayn. In South Asia and Trinidad, *taʿziya* represents a replica or model tomb of Imam Husayn, carried on procession during the first ten days of Muharram (q.v.).
Twelver Shiʿism	See Ithna ʿasharis.

Term	Definition
walāya	Devotion; in Shiʿi usage *walāya* denotes the loyalty, devotion and support that is due to the Imam from his followers because of his *wilāya* (q.v.) or authority. *Walāya* is regarded as one of the main principles of Islam for the Shiʿa.
walāʾ	See *walāya*.
walī	Friend; possessor of authority. In the tri-partite Shiʿi *shahāda* (q.v.), ʿAli is invoked as *walī Allah* (guardian [of the *umma*] and friend of God).
wilāya	Authority; for the Shiʿa, *wilāya* applies to the position of ʿAli b. Abi Talib as the single, explicitly designated heir and successor to the Prophet in whom all responsibility for the guidance of the Muslims was subsequently vested. See *walāya*.
ẓāhir	The outward, literal, or exoteric meaning of sacred texts, notably the Qurʿan and Islamic law, as distinct from the *bāṭin* (q.v.).
zarīḥ	See *dharīḥ*.
Zaydis (Ar. *Zaydiyya*)	A branch of the Shiʿa arising out of the abortive revolt of Zayd b. ʿAli b. al-Husayn in Kufa, Iraq, in 122/740. They ruled as two rival schools and communities from the Caspian region in northern Iran. A Zaydi Imamate was also established in Yemen in 284/897. In political terms they espoused a militant stance against Sunni rule, which was seen as a religious duty. They believed that anyone who was a descendant of the Prophet and had both religious learning and sufficient military strength was entitled to rule.
ziyāra (Per. *ziyārat*)	Pious visitation, pilgrimage to a holy place, tomb or shrine. In Shiʿi Islam the term usually refers to a pilgrimage to the shrines of Imams or burial places of other members of the *Ahl al-bayt* (q.v.).
ziyārat ʿāshūrāʾ	Special supplicatory prayers recited during visits (*ziyāra*) to the shrines of Twelver Imams or during pilgrimages to *ʿāshūrkhānas* (q.v.) and *imāmbārās* (q.v.) on the tenth day of Muharram (q.v.).

Contributors

James W. Allan is Emeritus Professor of Islamic Art at Oxford University and former Keeper of Eastern Art at the Ashmolean Museum.

Sheila S. Blair is the Norma Jean Calderwood University Professor of Islamic and Asian Art at Boston College and holds the Hamad bin Khalifa Endowed Chair in Islamic Art at Virginia Commonwealth University.

Jonathan M. Bloom is the Norma Jean Calderwood University Professor of Islamic and Asian Art at Boston College and holds the Hamad bin Khalifa Endowed Chair in Islamic Art at Virginia Commonwealth University.

Sheila R. Canby is Patti Cadby Birch Curator in Charge of the Department of Islamic Art at the Metropolitan Museum of Art.

Peter J. Chelkowski is Professor of Middle Eastern and Islamic Studies at New York University.

Maryam Ekhtiar is Associate Curator in the Department of Islamic Art at the Metropolitan Museum of Art.

Massumeh Farhad is Chief Curator and Curator of Islamic Art at the Freer Gallery of Art and the Arthur M. Sackler Gallery, Smithsonian.

Ingvild Flaskerud is a Post Doctoral Fellow at the Faculty of Theology, University of Oslo.

Oleg Grabar (1929–2011) was the first Aga Khan Professor of Islamic Art and Architecture at Harvard University and Professor Emeritus at the Institute for Advanced Study in the School of Historical Studies at Princeton University.

Robert Hillenbrand is Professor Emeritus of Islamic Art at Edinburgh University and currently Professor of Art History at St Andrews University.

Shainool Jiwa is Head of Constituency Studies at The Institute of Ismaili Studies and a member of the Board of Governors for Edinburgh Napier University.

Hussein Keshani is Associate Professor of Art History and Visual Culture at the University of British Columbia.

Mara A. Leichtman is Assistant Professor of Anthropology and Muslim Studies at Michigan State University.

Tryna Lyons is a Seattle-based art historian who has written on a broad range of South Asian topics.

Melanie Michailidis (1966–2013) held the Korff Post-Doctoral Fellowship in Islamic Art at Washington University and the Saint Louis Art Museum.

Nacim Pak-Shiraz is Lecturer in Persian and Film Studies and Head of Persian Studies at Edinburgh University.

Venetia Porter is Curator of the Islamic and Modern and Contemporary Middle Eastern Art Collections at the British Museum.

Amier Saidula is a Research Associate in the Central Asian Studies Unit within the Department of Academic Research and Publications at The Institute of Ismaili Studies.

Fahmida Suleman is Phyllis Bishop Curator for the Modern Middle East at the British Museum.

Yasser Tabbaa holds the Dorothy K. Hohenberg Chair of Excellence in Art History at the University of Memphis.

Luke Treadwell is University Lecturer in Islamic Numismatics and Curator of Islamic Coins in the Heberden Coin Room, Ashmolean Museum.

Zeynep Yürekli is Associate Professor of Islamic Art and Architecture at the University of Oxford.

Photo credits

Cover photo
Fahmida Suleman
Frontispiece
Jour des malédictions, from al-Bīrūnī's *Āthār al-bāqiya*, Cairo, *c.*1560, ms. Arabe 1489, f.86 © BnF

Part 1 Introduction
Chapter 1 Suleman & Jiwa
figs 1–6, 8–9 © Trustees of the British Museum; fig.7 chart by Fahmida Suleman/Azimuth Editions; fig.10 © Aga Khan Museum, akm678
Chapter 2 Grabar
figs 1, 3–7 © Museum of Islamic Art, Cairo; fig.2 © Sheila S. Blair; fig.8 © Oleg Grabar

Part 2 Pilgrimage and patronage
Chapter 3 Allan
figs 1, 10 after Matrakçi Nasuh, *Beyan-ı menazil-i sefer-i Irakeyn-i Sultan Süleyman Han. Nasuhü's-Silahi (Matrakçı); tıpkı basımı yayına haz,* ed., H. G. Yurdaydın (Ankara, 1976), pl.62b and 64b; fig.2 Art Directors & TRIP/Alamy; fig.3 © Salma Samar Damluji; figs 4–5 Chadirji collection, czgh 1/65; fig.6 © Freer Gallery of Art, Smithsonian Institution; fig.7 © James W. Allan; fig.8 after Mehmet Aga-Oglu, *Ṣafawid Rugs and Textiles: The Collection of the Shrine of Imām ʿAlī at al-Najaf* (New York, 1941), pl.xviii; fig.9 after Suʿad Mahir, *Mashhad al-Imām ʿAlī fī al-Najaf wa-mā bihi min al-hadāyā wa'l-tuḥaf* (Cairo, 1969), pl.84
Chapter 4 Tabbaa
figs 1–3, 5–11 © Yasser Tabbaa; fig.4 after Arnold Nöldeke, *Das Heiligtum al-Husains zu Kerbela* (Berlin, 1909), courtesy of James W. Allan
Chapter 5 Bloom
figs 1–7 © Jonathan M. Bloom
Chapter 6 Hillenbrand
figs 1–2, 5, 7 © Alireza Anisi; figs 3, 6, 8–9 © Robert Hillenbrand; fig.4 © Friedrich Sarre
Chapter 7 Michailidis
figs 1–8 © Melanie Michailidis

Part 3 Inscriptions on art, architecture and coinage
Chapter 8 Canby
figs 1–4 © Astan Quds Library, Museums and Documents Organization; fig.5 © Trustees of the British Museum/Ebrahim Khadem Bayat; fig.6 courtesy of the owner
Chapter 9 Blair
figs 1, 4–6, 8 © Sheila S. Blair; fig.2 after Mudarrisi Tabataba'i, *Turbat-i pākān* (Qum, 1976), pl. 6; fig.3 after Bijan Saadat, *The Holy Shrine of Imam Reza* (Shiraz, 1976), pl. 34; fig.7 © Oliver Watson; fig.9 after Sheila S. Blair, *Islamic Calligraphy* (Edinburgh, 2006), p. 450
Chapter 10 Keshani
figs 1–13 © Hussein Keshani
Chapter 11 Treadwell
fig.1 after Daniel Eustache, *Corpus des dirhams idrisites et contemporains* (Rabat, 1971), plate xxix, no. 437; fig.2 © Lundberg collection; fig.3 fint 92-2-25; fig.4 after Alexander Akopyan and Aram Vardanyan, 'A donative dirham of the Shirwānshāh Muḥammad b. Aḥmad (ah 370–81) struck at Bardaʿa in ah 373 (982/3)', *The Numismatic Chronicle,* 169 (2009), pp. 261–267; fig.5 © The Institute of Ismaili Studies; fig.6 © Trustees of the British Museum

Part 4 Iconographic studies: Shiʿi contexts and beyond
Chapter 12 Farhad
figs 1, 3 © Arthur M. Sackler Gallery, Washington, dc, s1986.253/254. Purchase – Smithsonian Unrestricted Trust Fund, Smithsonian Collections Acquisition Program and Dr. Arthur M. Sackler; figs 2, 6, 8–9 © Topkapı Palace Museum; fig.4 © Freer Gallery of Art, Smithsonian Institution; fig.5 © Trustees of the Chester Beatty Library; fig.7 © Aga Khan Museum, akm96
Chapter 13 Ekhtiar
fig.1 © Nasser D. Khalili Collection of Islamic Art (Khalili Family Trust); figs 2, 7 © Saʿdabad Museum, Tehran; fig.3 © Arthur M. Sackler Gallery, Washington, dc, s1986.253. Purchase – Smithsonian Unrestricted Trust Fund, Smithsonian Collections Acquisition Program and Dr. Arthur M. Sackler; fig.4 © George Walter Vincent Smith Art Museum; fig.5 unknown; fig.6 © Library of Congress; fig.8 © Free Library of Philadelphia, Lewis Oriental Collection; fig.9 © Harvard Art Museums/ Arthur M. Sackler Museum; fig.10 after Sotheby's London, *Arts of the Islamic World,* 1 April 2009, lot 36; figs 11a–b after Antoni Romauld Chodynski, *Museum w Malborku Orez Perski I Indoperski Wieku ze zbiorow Polskich, Katalog Wystawy pod redakcja, Antoniego Romualda Chodynskiego, Museum Zamkowe w Malboroku* (Malbork, 2000), pp. 353–355
Chapter 14 Porter
fig.1 © Trustees of the British Museum/Khosrow Hassanzadeh; fig.2 © Khosrow Hassanzadeh; fig.3 © Trustees of the British Museum/ Mehraneh Atashi; figs 4–5 © Trustees of the British Museum; fig.6 © Trustees of the British Museum/Bita Ghezelayagh; fig.7 © Rose Issa Projects/Monir Shahroudy Farmanfarmaian; fig.8 © Los Angeles County Museum of Art/ The Estate of Sadegh Tirafkan; fig.9 © Rose Issa Projects/Parastou Forouhar; fig.10 © Trustees of the British Museum/Charles-Hossein Zenderoudi; fig.11 © Trustees of the British Museum/Parvis Tanavoli; fig.12 © Trustees of the British Museum/Siah Armajani
Chapter 15 Yürekli
fig.1 after Fevzi Kurtoğlu, Türk Bayrağı ve Ay Yıldız (Ankara, 1938); fig.2 © Istanbul Maritime Museum (İstanbul Deniz Müzesi Komutanlığı); fig.3 after Luigi Ferdinando Marsigli, *Stato militare dell'Imperio Ottomano* (The Hague and Amsterdam, 1732), vol.2, pl. 21; figs 4–5 by permission of the Austrian National Library (Österreichische Nationalbibliothek), after Alberto Arbasino, ed., *I Turchi. Codex Vindobonensis* (Parma, 1971); fig.6 by permission of the Topkapı Palace Museum, after Hülya Tezcan, Topkapı Sarayındaki Şifalı Gömlekler (Istanbul, 2006); fig.7 by permission of the Süleymaniye Library; fig.8 by permission of the Turkish and Islamic Art Museum (*Türk ve İslam Eserleri Müzesi*), after Zeren Tanındı, *Siyer-i Nebî: İslam Tasvir Sanatında Hz. Muhammed'in Hayatı* (Istanbul, 1984), pl.56
Chapter 16 Suleman
fig.1 © Musée de l'Homme/G. Duchemin; fig.2 © Fahmida Suleman; figs 3–4, 11, 13 © Trustees of the British Museum; fig.5 © 2014, Detroit Institute of Arts; fig.6 © John and Sonya Schermann; figs 7–8 © State Hermitage Museum/ photo by Vladimir Terebenin, Leonard Kheifets, Yuri Molodkovets; figs 9–10 © Metropolitan Museum of Art/Art Resource/Scala, Florence; fig.12 © Aga Khan Museum, AKM116

Part 5 Ritual expressions

Chapter 17 Chelkowski

figs 1, 3, 5 © Alkazi Collection of Photography; figs 2, 4, 7, 9 © Peter J. Chelkowski; fig.6 after Docteur Feuvrier, *Trois ans à la cour de Perse* (Paris, 1906); fig.8 © William Shpall; fig.10 © Peter Anthony Chelkowski

Chapter 18 Flaskerud

figs 1–8 © Ingvild Flaskerud

Chapter 19 Pak-Shiraz

figs 1–3, 6–8 © Pejman Pak; fig.4 © Shahram Asadi; fig.5 © Bahram Beyzaie

Chapter 20 Lyons

figs 1, 3–6, 8–10 © Tryna Lyons; fig.2 collection of Khalifah Altaf Husayn; fig.7 collection of *makhdūm* Sayyid ʿAbbas Raza Mahdi, Qadirabad, Multan

Chapter 21 Saidula

figs 1–13 © Amier Saidula

Chapter 22 Leichtman

figs 1–3, 6–17, 19 © Mara A. Leichtman; figs 4–5, 18 collection of Mara A. Leichtman

Final image, p. 252 © The British Library Board. Or.7238, folio 9v

Select bibliography

EIR *Encyclopaedia Iranica,* ed. E. Yarshater. London and New York, 1982–
EI2 *The Encyclopaedia of Islam*, new edition, ed. H. A. R. Gibb et al. Leiden, 1960–2004
EI3 *The Encyclopaedia of Islam*, third edition
EIS *Encyclopaedia Islamica,* ed. W. Madelung and F. Daftary. Leiden, 2008–
EQ *Encyclopaedia of the Qur'ān*, ed. Jane Dammen McAuliffe. Leiden, 2002–

Afshar, Iradj. '*Fāl-nāma*', EIR, vol.9, pp.172–176.
Aghaie, Kamran S. *The Martyrs of Karbala: Shi'i Symbols and Rituals in Modern Iran.* Seattle, WA and London, 2004.
——, ed. *The Women of Karbala: Ritual Performance and Symbolic Discourses in Modern Shi'i Islam.* Austin, TX, 2005.
Ahmad, Safi. *Two Kings of Awadh: Muhammad Ali Shah and Amjad Ali Shah, 1837–1847.* Aligarh, 1971.
Alexander, David. 'Dhu'l-Faqār and the Legacy of the Prophet: *Mīrāth Rasūl Allāh*', *Gladius*, 19 (1999), pp.157–188.
Algar, Hamid. 'Emāmzāda, i. Function and Devotional Practice', EIR, vol.8, pp.395–397.
—— 'Ni'mat-Allāhiyya', EI2, vol.8, pp.44–48.
'Alī b. Abi Ṭālib. *Nahj al-balāgha (Peak of Eloquence): Sermons, Letters and Sayings of Imam 'Alī ibn Abī Ṭālib*, tr. Sayed Ali Raza. Tehran, 1980.
Allan, James W. *The Art and Architecture of Twelver Shi'ism: Iraq, Iran and the Indian Sub-continent.* London, 2012.
Amir-Moezzi, Mohammad 'Ali, et al., ed. *Le shi'isme imāmite quarante ans après: Hommage à Etan Kohlberg.* Paris, 2009.
Amir-Moezzi, Mohammad 'Ali. *The Divine Guide in Early Shi'ism: The Sources of Esotericism in Islam,* tr. D. Streight. Albany, NY, 1994.
—— *The Spirituality of Shi'i Islam: Beliefs and Practices.* London, 2011.
Anwar, Sherif and Jere Bacharach. 'Shi'ism and the Early Dinars of the Fāṭimid Imām-Caliph al-Mu'izz li-Dīn Allāh (341–365/952–975): An Analytic Overview', *al-Masaq,* 22 (2010), pp.259–278.
Asani, Ali S. A. 'Family of the Prophet', EQ, vol.2, p.177.
Ayoub, Mahmoud. *Redemptive Suffering in Islam: A Study of the Devotional Aspects of 'Ashura' in Twelver Shi'ism.* The Hague, 1978.
—— 'The Excellences of Imām Ḥusayn in Sunnī Ḥadīth Tradition', *Al-Serāt*, 12 (1986), pp.58–70.
—— "ĀŠŪRĀ', EIR, vol.2, pp.874–876.
Babaie, Sussan. 'Epigraphy. IV. Safavid and Later Inscriptions', EIR, vol.8, pp.498–504.
Babayan, Kathryn. *Mystics, Monarchs and Messiahs: Cultural Landscapes of Early Modern Iran.* Cambridge, MA, 2002.
Bağcı, Serpil. 'From Texts to Pictures: 'Alī in Manuscript Painting', in A. Y. Ocak, ed., *From History to Theology: 'Ali in Islamic Beliefs.* Ankara, 2005, pp.229–263.
Baker, Patricia L. *Islam and the Religious Arts.* London and New York, 2004.
Baktash, Mayel. '*Ta'ziyeh* and its Philosophy', in Peter J. Chelkowski, ed., *Ta'ziyeh: Ritual and Drama in Iran.* New York, 1979, pp.101–102.
Bal'amī, Muḥammad b. Muḥammad. *Tārīkh al-rusul wa al-mulūk*, MS Washington DC, Freer Gallery of Art, F57.16, 47.19 and 30.21, Iraq or Jazira, *circa* 1300.
Bar-Asher, Meir M. 'Shī'ism and the Qur'ān', EQ, vol.4, pp.593–604.
—— *Scripture and Exegesis in Early Imami Shiism.* Leiden, 1999.
Beeman, William O. and Mohammad B. Ghaffari. 'Acting Styles and Actor Training in *Ta'ziyeh*', in Peter J. Chelkowski, ed., *The Drama Review*, 49 (2005), pp.48–60.
Beeman, William O. *Iranian Performance Traditions.* Costa Mesa, CA, 2011.
Behrens-Abouseif, Doris. 'The Facade of the Aqmar Mosque in the Context of Fatimid Ceremonial', *Muqarnas*, 9 (1992), pp.29–38.
Beinhauer-Köhler, Bärbel. *Fatima bint Muhammad Metamorphosen einer frühislamischen Frauengestalt.* Wiesbaden, 2002.
Bellino, Francesca. 'Dhū l-Faqār', EI3, vol.2012–4, pp.77–79.
Bergeret, Jean and Ludvik Kalus. 'Analyse de décors épigraphiques et floraux à Qazwin au début du VI/XII siècle', *Revue des Études Islamiques*, 45 (1977), pp.89–130.
Betteridge, Anne. *Ziarat: Pilgrimage to the Shrines of Shiraz.* Ph.D dissertation, University of Chicago, 1985.
Bierman, Irene A. *Writing Signs: The Fatimid Public Text.* Berkeley, CA, 1998.
al-Bīrūnī, Abū Raiḥān. *al-Āthār al-bāqiya,* MS Edinburgh University Library, Arab 161, Iran or Iraq, 1307–1308.
Blair, Sheila S. *The Monumental Inscriptions from Early Islamic Iran and Transoxiana.* Leiden, 1992.
—— *Islamic Calligraphy.* Edinburgh, 2006.
—— 'A Brief Biography of Abu Zayd', *Muqarnas*, 25 (2008), pp.155–176.
—— 'Būyid Art and Architecture', EI3, vol.2009–4, pp.132–138.
Bloom, Jonathan M. 'Fact and Fantasy in Būyid Art', *Oriente Moderno,* 23 (2004), pp.387–400.
—— *Arts of the City Victorious: Islamic Art and Architecture in Fatimid North Africa and Egypt.* New Haven, CT and London, 2007.
Bosworth, Edmund. *The New Islamic Dynasties: A Chronological and Genealogical Manual.* 2nd ed., Edinburgh, 2004.
Browne, Edward G. *A Literary History of Persia.* London, 1908; repr., Cambridge, 1956.
Busse, Heribert. *Chalif und Grosskönig. Die Bujiden in Irak. Politik, Religion, Kultur und Wissenschaft, 945–1055.* Beirut, 1969.
Calmard, Jean and Jacqueline Calmard. 'Muharram Ceremonies Observed in Teheran by Ilya Nicolaevich Berezin (1843)', in Peter J. Chelkowski, ed., *Eternal Performance: Ta'ziyeh and Other Shiite Rituals.* London, New York and Calcutta, 2010, pp.53–72.
Calmard, Jean and Mohammad 'Ali Amir-Moezzi. 'Fāṭema. I and II.', EIR, vol.9, pp.400–404.
Calmard, Jean. 'Le chiisme imamite en Iran à l'époque seldjoukide, d'après le *Kitāb al-Naqḍ*', *Le Monde Iranien et l'Islam*, 1 (1971), pp.43–67.
—— 'Shi'i Rituals and Power. II. The Consolidation of Safavid Shi'ism: Folklore and Popular Religion', in Charles Melville, ed., *Safavid Persia: The History and Politics of an Islamic Society.* London, 1996, pp.139–190.
—— 'Ḳum', EI2, vol.5, pp.369–372.
—— 'Ḥejla', EIR, vol.12, pp.143–144.
Calzoni, Irène. 'Shiite Mausoleums in Syria with Particular Reference to Sayyida Zaynab Mausoleum', in Biancamaria Scarcia Amoretti, ed., *La Shi'a nell'impero Ottomano. Roma 15 April 1991.* Rome, 1993, pp.193–201.
Canard, Marius. 'Fāṭimids', EI2, vol.2, pp.850–862.
Canby, Sheila R. *Shah 'Abbas: The Remaking of Iran.* London, 2009.

Chardin, Jean. *Voyages de monsieur le chevalier Chardin, en Perse, et autres lieux de l'Orient.* Amsterdam, 1711, 3 vols.

Chelkowski, Peter J. and Hamid Dabashi. *Staging a Revolution: The Art of Persuasion in the Islamic Republic of Iran.* London, 2000.

Chelkowski, Peter J. *Ta'ziyeh: Ritual and Drama in Iran.* New York, NY, 1979.

——, ed. *Eternal Performance: Ta'ziyeh and Other Shiite Rituals.* London, New York and Calcutta, 2010.

—— 'Popular Shi'i Mourning Rituals', *Al-Serāt*, 12 (1986), pp.209–226.

—— 'Narrative Painting and Painting Recitation in Qajar Iran', *Muqarnas*, 6 (1989), pp.98–111.

——, ed. *The Drama Review*, 49 (2005), Special Issue: *Ta'ziyeh.*

Cole, J. R. I. *Roots of North Indian Shī'ism in Iran and Iraq: Religion and State in Awadh 1722–1859.* Berkeley, CA, 1988 and Oxford, 1989.

Cortese, Delia and Simonetta Calderini. *Women and the Fatimids in the World of Islam.* Edinburgh, 2006.

Daftary, Farhad. *The Ismā'īlīs: Their History and Doctrines.* 2nd ed., Cambridge and New York, 2007.

—— 'al-Ṭayyibiyya', *EI2*, vol.10, pp.403–404.

—— *A History of Shi'i Islam.* London, 2013.

al-Ḍarīr, Muṣṭafā b. Yūsuf. *Siyer-i Nebī*, MS Istanbul, Topkapı Palace Museum, H. 1221–1223 (vols. 1–2, 6); MS New York Public Library (vol.3); MS Dublin, Chester Beatty Library, MS T 419 (vol.4), Istanbul, 1594–1595.

Diba, Layla and Maryam Ekhtiar, ed. *Royal Persian Painting: The Qajar Epoch 1798–1924.* London, 1998.

Dieulafoy, Jane. *Le Tour du Monde. La Perse, la Chaldée et la Susiane 1881–1882.* Paris, 1887.

Eaton, R. M. 'Ḳuṭb Shāhī', *EI2*, vol.5, pp.549–550.

Ekhtiar, Maryam. 'Infused with Shi'ism: Images of the Prophet Muhammad in Qajar Iran', in Avinoam Shalem and Christiane Gruber, ed., *The Image of the Prophet Between Ideal and Ideology. A Scholarly Investigation.* Berlin and Boston, 2014, pp.87–102.

Elnazarov, Hakim and Sultonbek Aksakolov. 'The Nizari Ismailis of Central Asia in Modern Times', in Farhad Daftary, ed., *A Modern History of the Ismailis: Continuity and Change in a Muslim Community.* London, 2011, pp.45–75.

Eskandar Beg Monshī. *History of Shah 'Abbas the Great: (Tārīkh-i 'Ālamārā-ye 'Abbāsī)*, tr. Roger M. Savory. Boulder, CO, 1981, 2 vols.

Far, Mahnaz Shayesteh. *Shî'ah Artistic Elements in the Tîmûrid and the Early Safavid Periods: Book Illustrations and Inscriptions.* London, 1999.

Farhad, Massumeh and Serpil Bağcı. *Falnama: Book of Omens.* London and Washington, DC, 2009.

Fischer, Michael M. J. *Iran: From Religious Dispute to Revolution.* Cambridge, MA, 1980.

Fitzherbert, Teresa. *Bal'ami's Tabari. An Illustrated Manuscript of Bal'ami's tarjuma-yi tarikh-i Tabari in the Freer Gallery of Art, Washington (F57.16, 47.19 and 30.21).* Ph.D thesis, University of Edinburgh, 2001.

Flaskerud, Ingvild. *Standard-Bearers of Hussein: Women Commemorating Karbala.* 35 min. DVD film, 2003.

—— 'Shi'a-Muslim Women as Ritual Performers in Iran', in Ingvar Mæhle and Inger Marie Okkenhaug, ed., *Women and Religion in the Middle East and the Mediterranean.* Oslo, 2004, pp.115–134.

—— 'Oh, My Heart is Sad. It is Moharram, the Month of Zaynab. Aesthetics and Women's Mourning Ceremonies in Shiraz', in Kamran Scot Aghaie, ed., *The Women of Karbala. The Gender Dynamics of Ritual Performances and Symbolic Discourses of Modern Shi'i Islam.* Austin, TX, 2005, pp.65–92.

—— *Visualizing Belief and Piety in Iranian Shiism.* London and New York, 2010.

Floor, Willem M. *The History of Theater in Iran.* London, 2005.

Fontana, Maria Vittoria. *L'Iconografia dell'Ahl al-Bayt: Immagini di Arte Persiana dal XII al XX Secolo.* Naples, 1994, pp.47–55 and figs 51–61.

Gholami, Yadollah, Matthew Melvin-Koushki, et al. ''Alī b. Abī Ṭālib', *EIS*, vol.3, pp.477–583.

Gleave, Robert M. ''Alī b. Abī Ṭālib', *EI3*, vol.2008–2, pp.62–71.

Goldziher, I., C. van Arendonk and A. S. Tritton. 'Ahl al-Bayt', *EI2*, vol.1, pp.257–258.

Golombek, Lisa. 'The Cult of Saints and Shrine Architecture in the Fourteenth Century', in Dickran K. Kouymjian, ed., *Near Eastern Numismatics, Iconography, Epigraphy and History. Studies in Honor of George C. Miles.* Beirut, 1974, pp.419–430.

Grabar, Oleg. 'The Earliest Commemorative Structures, Notes and Documents', *Ars Orientalis*, 6 (1966), pp.7–46.

—— *Constructing the Study of Islamic Art.* Aldershot, 2005–2006, 4 vols.

Gruber, Christiane. 'The "Restored" Shī'ī *muṣḥaf* as Divine Guide? The Practice of *fāl-i Qur'ān* in the Ṣafavid Period', *Journal of Qur'anic Studies*, 13 (2011), pp.29–55.

Gruber, Christiane and Frederick Colby, ed. *The Prophet's Ascension: Cross-Cultural Encounters with the Islamic Mi'rāj Tales.* Bloomington, IN, 2010.

Halm, Heinz. *Shi'ism*, tr. J. Watson and M. Hill. Edinburgh, 2001.

Hillenbrand, Robert. 'Images of Muhammad in al-Biruni's Chronology of Ancient Nations', in R. Hillenbrand, ed., *Persian Painting from the Mongols to the Qajars: Studies in Honour of Basil W. Robinson.* London, 2000, pp.129–146.

Hillenbrand, Robert. 'The Tomb of Shah Isma'il, Ardabil', in Sheila R. Canby, ed., *Safavid Art and Architecture.* London, 2002, pp.3–8.

Hjortshoj, Keith G. *Kerbala in Context: A Study of Muharram in Lucknow, India.* Ph.D thesis, Cornell University, 1977.

Hodgson, M. G. S. 'Dja'far al-Ṣādiḳ', *EI2*, vol.2, pp.374–375.

Hollister, John N. *The Shi'a of India.* London, 1953.

Homayuni, Sadeq. *Ta'ziyeh dar Iran.* Shiraz, 2001.

al-Ḥusaynī, Qāḍī Aḥmad Ibrāhīm b. Mīr Munshī. *Calligraphers and Painters: a Treatise / by Qāḍī Aḥmad, son of Mīr-Munshī, circa A.H. 1015/A.D. 1606*, tr. V. Minorsky. Washington, DC, 1959.

Hussain, Syed Kazim. *Ziyarats and Weekday Prayers.* Chicago, 2010.

Hutton, Deborah S. ''Ādil Shāhīs', *EI3*, vol.2010–2, pp.23–25.

Ibn Akbar, Ajmal Mahar. *Multān ke qadīm imāmbāṛe aur majālis-e 'aza kī rivāyat.* Multan, 2004.

Ibn Ḥawqal, Abu'l-Qāsim b. 'Alī al-Naṣībī. *Kitāb Ṣūrat al-arḍ*, ed. Johannes H. Kramers. Leiden, 1938, 2 vols.

Ibn al-Haytham, Abū 'Alī al-Ḥasan b. al-Ḥasan. *The Advent of the Fatimids: A Contemporary Shi'i Witness. An Edition and English Translation of Ibn al-Haytham's Kitāb al-Munāẓarāt*, ed. and tr. Wilferd Madelung and Paul E. Walker. London, 2000.

Ispahany, Batool, tr. *Islamic Medical Wisdom: The Ṭibb al-a'imma*, ed. Andrew J. Newman. London, 1991.

Izzi Dien, Mawil Y. and Paul E. Walker. 'Wilāya', *EI2*, vol.11, pp.208–209.

Keshani, Hussein. 'Architecture and the Twelver Shi'i Tradition: The Great Imāmbārā Complex of Lucknow', *Muqarnas*, 23 (2006), pp.219–250.

Keshmirshekan, Hamid. 'Neo-Traditionalism and Modern Iranian Painting: The Saqqa-khaneh School in the 1960s', *Iranian Studies*, 38, 4 (2005), pp.607–630.

—— *Contemporary Iranian Art: New Perspectives.* London, 2013.

Khan, Muhammad Saber. 'The Early History of Zaydî Shî'ism in Daylamân and Gîlân', in Seyyed Hossein Nasr, ed., *Mélanges offerts à Henry Corbin.* Tehran, 1977, pp.257–277.

Khosronejad, Pedram, ed. *The Art and Material Culture of Iranian Shiʿism: Iconography and Religious Devotion in Shiʿi Islam*. London, 2012.
Knighton, William. *The Private Life of an Eastern King*. London, 1855; rev. ed., 1921.
Kohlberg, Etan. *Belief and Law in Imāmī Shīʿism*. Aldershot and Burlington, VT, 1991.
——, ed. *Shiʿism*. Aldershot and Burlington, VT, 2003.
—— 'Muḥammad b. ʿAlī Zayn al-ʿĀbidīn, Abū Djaʿfar, called al-Bāḳir', *EI2*, vol.7, pp.397–400.
—— 'Mūsā al-Kāẓim', *EI2*, vol.7, pp.645–648.
—— 'Waṣī', *EI2*, vol.11, pp.161–162.
—— 'Zayn al-ʿĀbidīn', *EI2*, vol.11, pp.481–483.
Korom, Frank J. *Hosay Trinidad*. Philadelphia, 2003.
Lalani, Arzina. *Early Shīʿī Thought: the Teachings of Imam Muḥammad al-Bāqir*. London, 2004.
—— 'Shīʿa', *EQ*, vol.4, p.592.
Lambton, Ann K. S. 'Qum: the Evolution of a Medieval City', *Journal of the Royal Asiatic Society of Great Britain and Ireland*, 2 (1990), pp.322–339.
Leichtman, Mara A. '(Still) Exporting the Islamic Revolution: Senegal's Relationship with Iran', *Shia Affairs Journal*, 1 (2008), pp.79–105.
—— 'The Authentication of a Discursive Islam: Shiʿa Alternatives to Sufi Orders', in Mamadou Diouf and Mara A. Leichtman, ed., *New Perspectives on Islam in Senegal: Conversion, Migration, Wealth, Power, and Femininity*. New York, NY, 2009, pp.111–138.
—— 'Revolution, Modernity and (Trans)National Shiʿi Islam: Rethinking Religious Conversion in Senegal', *Journal of Religion in Africa*, 39/3 (2009), pp.319–351.
—— 'Migration, War, and the Making of a Transnational Lebanese Shiʿi Community in Senegal', *International Journal of Middle East Studies*, 42/2 (2010), pp.269–290.
—— 'The Africanization of Ashura in Senegal', in Lloyd Ridgeon, ed., *Shiʿi Islam and Identity: Religion, Politics and Change in the Global Muslim Community*. London, 2012, pp.144–169.
Maclean, Derryl N. *Religion and Society in Arab Sind*. Leiden, 1989.
Madelung, Wilferd. *The Succession to Muhammad: A Study of the Early Caliphate*. Cambridge, 1998.
—— 'Imāma', *EI2*, vol.3, pp.1163–1165.
—— 'Ismāʿīliyya', *EI2*, vol.4, pp.198–206.
—— 'al-Mahdī', *EI2*, vol.5, pp.1231–1238.
—— 'Shīʿa', *EI2*, vol.9, pp.420–424.
—— 'Zaydiyya', *EI2*, vol.11, pp.477–481.
Majlisī, Mullā Muḥammad Bāqir. *Biḥār al-anwār*. Beirut, 1983, 104 vols.
Malekpour, Jamshid. *The Islamic Drama*. London, 2004.
al-Maqrīzī, Taqī al-Dīn Aḥmad b. ʿAlī. *al-Mawāʿiẓ wa'l-iʿtibār fī dhikr al-khiṭaṭ wa'l-āthār*, ed. Ayman Fu'ad Sayyid. London, 2002–2004, 5 vols.
—— *Ittiʿāẓ al-ḥunafā' bi-akhbār al-a'immah al-Fāṭimīyīn al-khulafā*, ed. J. Shayyal and Muhammad H. M. Ahmad. Cairo, 1967–1973, 3 vols.
Martin, Vanessa. *The Qajar Pact: Bargaining, Protest and the State in Nineteenth-Century Persia*. London, 2005.
Massi Dakake, Maria. *The Charismatic Community: Shiʿite Identity in Early Islam*. Albany, NY, 2007.
Mavani, Hamid. *Religious Authority and Political Thought in Twelver Shiʿism: From Ali to Post-Khomeini*. London, 2013.
Mazzaoui, Michel. *The Origins of the Safavids*. Wiesbaden, 1972.
McAuliffe, Jane Dammen. 'Chosen of All Women: Mary and Fāṭima in Qur'ānic Exegesis', *Islamochristiana*, 7 (1981), pp.19–28.
Meri, Josef W. *The Cult of Saints Among Muslims and Jews in Medieval Syria*. Oxford, 2002.
Mervin, Sabrina. 'Sayyida Zaynab: banlieue de Damas ou nouvelle ville sainte chiite?', *Cahiers d'Etudes sur la Méditerranée Orientale et le monde Turco-Iranien*, 22 (1996), pp.149–162.
Mervin, Sabrina. 'Shiite Theater in South Lebanon: Some Notes on the Karbala Drama and the Sabaya', in Peter J. Chelkowski, ed., *Eternal Performance: Taʿziyeh and Other Shiite Rituals*. London and Calcutta, 2010, pp.322–333.
Michailidis, Melanie. *Landmarks of the Persian Renaissance: Monumental Funerary Architecture in Iran and Central Asia in the Tenth and Eleventh Centuries*. Ph.D dissertation, Massachusetts Institute of Technology, Boston, 2007.
Miskawayh, Abū ʿAlī Aḥmad b. Muḥammad. *Kitāb Tajārib al-umam*, vol.2, ed. Henry Frederick Amedroz and David Samuel Margoliouth. Baghdad, 1921, 1914–1919, 4 vols.
Mittwoch, E. 'Dhu 'l-Faḳār', *EI2*, vol.2, p.230.
Modaressi, Hossein. *Crisis and Consolidation in the Formative Period of Shiʿite Islam*. New York, 1993.
Momen, Moojan. *An Introduction to Shiʿi Islam*. New Haven, CT, 1985.
Morton, Alexander H. 'The Ardabīl Shrine in the Reign of Shāh Ṭahmāsp I', *Iran*, 12 (1974), pp.31–64.
Mottahedeh, Roy P. *Loyalty and Leadership in an Early Islamic Society*. Princeton, NJ, 1980.
Mullā Ṣadrā Shīrāzī. *On the Hermeneutics of the Light Verse in the Qur'ān — Tafsīr āyat al-nūr*, ed. Latimah-Parvin Peerwani. London, 2004.
al-Muqaddasī, Muḥammad b. Aḥmad Shams al-Dīn. *The Best Divisions for Knowledge of the Regions: A Translation of Aḥasan al-taqāsīm fī maʿrifat al-aqālīm. Al-Muqaddasi*, tr. Basil A. Collins. Reading, 1994.
Mustawfī al-Qazwīnī, Ḥamdallāh. *The Geographical Part of the Nuzhat-al-Qulūb Composed by Ḥamd-allāh Mustawfī of Qazwīn in 740 (1340)*, tr. Guy Le Strange. Leiden and London, 1919.
Nakash, Yitzhak. 'The Visitation of the Shrines of the Imams and the Shiʿi Mujtahids in the Early Twentieth Century', *Studia Islamica*, 81 (1995), pp.153–164.
Nanji, Azim. 'Towards a Hermeneutics of Qur'ānic and Other Narratives in Ismaʿili Thought', in R. C. Martin, ed., *Approaches to Islam in Religious Studies*. Tucson, AZ, 1985, pp.164–173.
Nanji, Azim and Farhad Daftary. 'What is Shiʿa Islam?' in Vincent J. Cornell, ed., *Voices of Islam*, Volume 1: *Voices of Tradition*. Santa Barbara, CA, 2006, pp.217–244.
Naqvi, Ali Naqi. *Azadari: A Historical Review of Institution of Azadari for Imam Husain*. Karachi, 1974.
Naqvi, Sadiq. *Qutb Shahi ʿAshur Khanas of Hyderabad City*. Hyderabad, 1982.
—— *The ʿĀshūr khānas of Hyderābād City*. Hyderabad, 2006.
Nāṣir-i Khusraw, Ḥakīm Abū Muʿīn. *Knowledge and Liberation: A Treatise on Philosophical Theology. A New Edition and English Translation of Gushāyish wa Rahāyish of Nāṣir-i Khusraw*, ed. and tr. Faquir M. Hunzai. London, 1998.
Newid, Mehr Ali. *Der schiitische Islam in Bildern. Rituale und Heilige*. Munich, 2006.
Newman, Andrew J. *The Formative Period of Twelver Shīʿism: Ḥadīth as a Discourse Between Qum and Baghdad*. Richmond, Surrey, 2000.
al-Nuʿmān b. Muḥammad, al-Qāḍī Abū Ḥanīfa. *The Pillars of Islam. Daʿā'im al-Islām of al-Qāḍī al-Nuʿmān*. Vol.1: *Acts of Devotion and Religious Observances*, tr. A. A. A. Fyzee, rev. and annotated by I. K. Poonawala. New Delhi, 2002–2004, 2 vols.
—— *The Pillars of Islam. Daʿā'im al-Islām of al-Qāḍī al-Nuʿmān*. Vol. 2: *Muʿāmalāt: Laws Pertaining to Human Intercourse*, tr. A. A. A. Fyzee, rev. and annotated by I. K. Poonawala. New Delhi, 2004.
Pak-Shiraz, Nacim. *Shiʿi Islam in Iranian Cinema: Religion and Spirituality in Film*. London and New York, 2011.
Pelly, Lewis. *The Miracle Play of Hasan and Husain*, vol.2. London, 1879; repr., Farnborough, 1970.
Pemble, John. *The Raj, the Indian Mutiny, and the Kingdom of Oudh, 1801–1859*. Hassocks, 1977.
Pinault, David. 'Shia Lamentation Rituals and Reinterpretations of the Doctrine of

Intercession: Two Cases', *History of Religions*, 38/3 (1999), pp.287–288.
—— *Horse of Karbala: Muslim Devotional Life in India*. New York, 2001.
al-Qummī, Shaykh 'Abbās b. Muḥammad. *Mafātīḥ al-jinān: wa yalīhi kitāb al-bāqīyāt al-ṣāliḥāt*. Beirut, 2011.
Rabbat, Nasser. 'Al-Azhar Mosque: An Architectural Chronicle of Cairo's History', *Muqarnas*, 13 (1996), pp.45–67.
Rashīd al-Dīn Ṭabīb Faḍl Allāh. *Jāmiʿ al-tawārīkh*, MS Topkapı Palace Museum Library, H. 1653, 1314.
—— *Jamiʿu't-tawarikh — Compendium of Chronicles: A History of the Mongols*, tr. Wheeler M. Thackston. Cambridge, MA, 1998.
Ridgeon, Lloyd. 'The Zūrkhāna Between Tradition and Change', *Iran*, 45 (2007), pp.243-265.
Rizvi, Saiyid Athar 'Abbas. *A Socio-Intellectual History of the Isnā 'Asharī Shīʿīs in India*. New Delhi, 1986, 2 vols.
Rizwi, Kishwar, *The Safavid Dynastic Shrine. Architecture, Religion and Power in Early Modern Iran*. London and New York, 2010.
Robinson, B. W. 'Art in Iran, x. Qajar 2. Painting', EIR, vol.2, pp.637–640.
Ruffle, Karen G. *Gender, Sainthood, and Everyday Practice in South Asian Shiʿism*. Chapel Hill, NC, 2011.
Saidula, Amier. 'The Nizari Ismailis of China in Modern Times', in Farhad Daftary, ed., *A Modern History of the Ismailis: Continuity and Change in a Muslim Community*. London, 2011, pp.77–92.
Sanders, Paula A. *Ritual, Politics, and the City in Fatimid Cairo*. Albany, NY, 1994.
Sayyid, Ayman Fu'ad. *La Capitale de l'Égypte jusqu'à l'époque Fatimide: al-Qāhira et al-Fusṭāṭ, essai de reconstitution topographique*. Beirut, 1998.
Schubel, Vernon J. *Religion and Performance in Contemporary Islam*. Columbia, SC, 1993.
Seipel, Wilfried, ed. *Schätze der Kalifen: Islamische Kunst zur Fatimidenzeit*. Vienna, 1998.
Shah-Kazemi, Reza. *Justice and Remembrance: Introducing the Spirituality of Imam 'Ali*. London, 2005.
Shalem, Avinoam and Christiane Gruber, ed. *The Image of the Prophet Between Ideal and Ideology: A Scholarly Investigation*. Berlin and Boston, 2014.
Shani, Raya. *A Monumental Manifestation of the Shīʿite Faith in late Twelfth-Century Iran: The Case of the Gunbad-i 'Alawyān, Hamadān*. Oxford, 1996.
Sharon, M. 'People of the House', EQ, vol.4, pp.49–53.
—— '*Ahl al-Bayt* — People of the House', *Jerusalem Studies in Arabic and Islam*, 8 (1986), pp.169–184.
Sindawi, Khalid. 'Visit to the Tomb of Al-Husayn b. 'Alī in Shiite Poetry: First to Fifth Centuries AH (8th–11th Centuries CE)', *Journal of Arabic Literature*, 37, 2 (2006), pp.230–258.
—— 'The Shiite Turn in Syria', *Current Trends in Islamist Ideology*, 8 (2009), pp.82–107.
—— 'The Zaynabiyya *Hawza* in Damascus and its Role in Shiʿi Religious Instruction', *Middle Eastern Studies*, 45/6 (2009), pp.859–879.
Soucek, Priscilla. 'An Illustrated Manuscript of al-Bīrunī's Chronology of Ancient Nations', in P.J. Chelkowski, ed., *The Scholar and the Saint: Studies in Commemoration of Abu'l-Rayhan al-Biruni and Jalal al-Din Rumi*. New York, 1975, pp.103–168.
—— 'The Life of the Prophet: Illustrated Versions', in P.Soucek, ed., *Content and Context of Visual Arts in the Islamic World*. University Park, PA, 1988, pp.193–218.
Soufi, Denise L. *The Image of Fāṭima in Classical Muslim Thought*. Ph.D dissertation. Princeton, NJ, 1997.
Spellman, Kathryn, *Religion and Nation: Iranian Local and Transnational Networks in Britain*. New York, 2004, pp.109–110.
Stern, Samuel M. 'The Early Ismāʿīlī Missionaries in North-West Persia and in Khurāsān and Transoxania', *Bulletin of the School of Oriental and African Studies*, 23, 1 (1960), pp.72–76.
Suleman, Fahmida. 'The Iconography of 'Ali as the Lion of God in Shiʿi Art and Material Culture', in Pedram Khosronejad, ed., *The Art and Material Culture of Iranian Shiʿism: Iconography and Religious Devotion in Shiʿi Islam*. London, 2012, pp.215–232.
al-Ṭabarī, Abū Jaʿfar Muḥammad b. Jarīr. *The History of al-Ṭabarī (Ta'rīkh al-rusul wa'l-mulūk)*. Volume 9: *The Last Years of the Prophet*, tr. Ismail K. Poonawala. New York, 1990.
Tabbaa, Yasser. 'Invented Pieties: The Revival and Rebuilding of Shiʿite Shrines in Contemporary Syria', in Linda Komaroff, ed., *Artibus Asiae* (special issue, *Festschrift for Priscilla Soucek*), 66 (2006), pp.142–171.
—— *The Transformation of Islamic Art During the Sunni Revival*. London, 2001.
Tanındı, Zeren. *Siyer-i Nebî: İslam Tasvir Sanatında Hz. Muhammed'in Hayatı*. Istanbul, 1984.
Taylor, Christopher S. 'Re-evaluating the Shīʿī Role in the Development of Monumental Islamic Funerary Architecture: the Case of Egypt', *Muqarnas*, 9 (1992), pp.1–10.
—— *In the Vicinity of the Righteous: Ziyāra and the Veneration of Muslim Saints in Late Medieval Egypt*. Leiden, 1999.
Tourkin, Sergei. 'The Use of the Qur'an for Divination in Iran', in *Mélanges de l'Université Saint-Joseph*, 59 (2006), pp.387–394.
Treadwell, Luke. 'Qur'ānic Inscriptions on the Coins of the *ahl al-bayt* (2nd–4th century AH)', *Journal of Qur'anic Studies*, 14/2 (2012), pp.267–291.
Vaglieri, Laura Veccia, ''Alī b. Abī Ṭālib', EI2, vol.1, pp.381–386.
—— 'Fāṭima', EI2, vol.2, pp.841–850.
—— 'Ghadīr Khumm', EI2, vol.2, pp.993–994.
—— '(al-)Ḥasan b. 'Alī b. Abī Ṭālib', EI2, vol.3, pp.240–243.
—— '(al-)Ḥusayn b. 'Alī b. Abī Ṭālib', EI2, vol.3, pp.607–616.
—— 'Khaybar', EI2, vol.4, pp.1137–1143.
Varjavand, Parviz. 'Emāmzāda, iii. Number, Distribution and Important Examples', EIR, vol.8, pp.400–412.
Walker, Paul E. *Ḥamīd al-Dīn al-Kirmānī: Ismaili Thought in the Age of al-Ḥākim*. London, 1999.
—— *Exploring an Islamic Empire: Fatimid History and its Sources*. London and New York, 2002.
—— *Fatimid History and Ismaili Doctrine*. Farnham, 2008.
—— 'Wilāya: 2. In Shīʿism', EI2, vol.11, pp.208–209.
Watson, Oliver. 'Abū Ṭaher', EIR, vol.1, pp.385–387.
Williams, Caroline. 'The Cult of 'Alid Saints in the Fatimid Monuments of Cairo. Part I: The Mosque of al-Aqmar', *Muqarnas*, 1 (1983), pp. 37–52.
Williams, Caroline. 'The Cult of 'Alid Saints in the Fatimid Monuments of Cairo. Part II: The Mausolea', *Muqarnas*, 3 (1985), pp.48–49.
Yann, Richard. *Shiʿite Islam: Polity, Ideology, and Creed*, tr. Antonia Nevill. Oxford, 1995.
Zarcone, Thierry. 'The Lion of 'Ali in Anatolia: History, Symbolism and Iconology', in Pedram Khosronejad, ed., *The Art and Material Culture of Iranian Shiʿism: Iconography and Religious Devotion in Shiʿi Islam*. London, 2012, pp.104–122.
Zayn al-'Ābidīn, 'Alī b. al-Ḥusayn b. 'Alī b. Abī Ṭālib. *The Psalms of Islam: al-Ṣaḥīfat al-kāmilat al-Sajjādiyya*, tr. William C. Chittick. London, 1988.

Index